WRITING IN RED

MODERNIST LATITUDES

MODERNIST LATITUDES

Jessica Berman and Paul Saint-Amour, Editors

Modernist Latitudes aims to capture the energy and ferment of modernist studies by continuing to open up the range of forms, locations, temporalities, and theoretical approaches encompassed by the field. The series celebrates the growing latitude ("scope for freedom of action or thought") that this broadening affords scholars of modernism, whether they are investigating little-known works or revisiting canonical ones. Modernist Latitudes will pay particular attention to the texts and contexts of those latitudes (Africa, Latin America, Australia, Asia, southern Europe, and even the rural United States) that have long been misrecognized as ancillary to the canonical modernisms of the global North.

Cate I. Reilly, *Psychic Empire: Literary Modernism and the Clinical State*

Adam McKible, *Creating Jim Crow America: George Horace Lorimer, the Saturday Evening Post, and the War Against Black Modernity*

Hannah Freed-Thall, *Modernism at the Beach: Queer Ecologies and the Coastal Commons*

Daniel Ryan Morse, *Radio Empire: The BBC's Eastern Service and the Emergence of the Global Anglophone Novel*

Jill Richards, *The Fury Archives: Female Citizenship, Human Rights, and the International Avant-Gardes*

Claire Seiler, *Midcentury Suspension: Literature and Feeling in the Wake of World War II*

Ben Conisbee Baer, *Indigenous Vanguards: Education, National Liberation, and the Limits of Modernism*

Aarthi Vadde, *Chimeras of Form: Modernist Internationalism Beyond Europe, 1914–2014*

Eric Bulson, *Little Magazine, World Form*

Eric Hayot and Rebecca L. Walkowitz, eds., *A New Vocabulary for Global Modernism*

Christopher Reed, *Bachelor Japanists: Japanese Aesthetics and Western Masculinities, 2016*

Celia Marshik, *At the Mercy of Their Clothes: Modernism, the Middlebrow, and British Garment Culture*

Donal Harris, *On Company Time: American Modernism in the Big Magazines*

For a complete list of books in this series, see the CUP website.

Writing in Red

LITERATURE AND REVOLUTION ACROSS TURKEY AND
THE SOVIET UNION

Nergis Ertürk

Columbia University Press
New York

Columbia University Press
Publishers Since 1893
New York   Chichester, West Sussex
cup.columbia.edu
Copyright © 2024 Columbia University Press
All rights reserved

Library of Congress Cataloging-in-Publication Data
Names: Ertürk, Nergis, author.
Title: Writing in red : literature and revolution across Turkey and the Soviet Union / Nergis Erturk.
Description: New York : Columbia University Press, [2024] | Series: Modernist latitudes | Includes bibliographical references and index.
Identifiers: LCCN 2023043171 (print) | LCCN 2023043172 (ebook) | ISBN 9780231214841 (hardback) | ISBN 9780231214858 (trade paperback) | ISBN 9780231560498 (ebook)
Subjects: LCSH: Turkish literature—Soviet influences. | Turkish literature—History and criticism. | Socialism in literature.
Classification: LCC PL210.S628 E78 2024 (print) | LCC PL210.S628 (ebook)
LC record available at https://lccn.loc.gov/2023043171
LC ebook record available at https://lccn.loc.gov/2023043172

Cover design: Julia Kushnirsky
Cover painting: Abidin Dino, *Uzun Yürüyüş* (The long march), 1955, oil on canvas, 100x50cm, private collection, Istanbul

Canımız Murat'a,
so that you know their story.

"They traveled far,
obliterating rivers and hills,
and when they looked back
where they began was gone! . . ."

"Çok gittiler,
dere tepe yok ettiler,
bir de dönüp baktılar ki
görünmüyor kalkılan yer! . . ."
—NÂZIM HIKMET, *SEVDALI BULUT*

CONTENTS

A NOTE ON TRANSLATION, TRANSLITERATION, AND USAGE   ix

ACKNOWLEDGMENTS   xi

Introduction. Revolutionary Entanglements Across Turkey and the Soviet Union: An Overview   1

Part I. Genres of Entangled Revolutions

Chapter One
The Turkish War of Independence in Literature and Film: Limits of Marxist-Leninist Nationalism and Legacies for the Postcolonial Era   37

Chapter Two
Vâlâ Nureddin's Comic Materialism and the Sexual Revolution   76

Part II. Marxian Form in the Periphery: Modernist Socialist Realisms

Chapter Three
The Prostitute Cevriye as Positive Hero: Suat Derviş and the Ethics of the Socialist-Realist Novel   113

Chapter Four
Abidin Dino's Peasant Theater and the Soviet *Faktura*:
Estranging Socialist Realism   153

Chapter Five
In the Shadow of Lenin: Nâzım Hikmet's Prose Poetics of Seriality
and the Time of (Post)communism   192

Conclusion
In the Anteroom of History   219

NOTES   223

BIBLIOGRAPHY   293

INDEX   327

A NOTE ON TRANSLATION, TRANSLITERATION, AND USAGE

Unless otherwise noted, throughout this book all translations are my own. Titles are given in English and Turkish or Russian at first mention, thereafter in English. Unless I cite a published English translation, titles in the notes are in the original Turkish or Russian only. Transliteration of Russian follows the Library of Congress system. For ease in reading, with Russian authors widely known in the Anglophone world, I have used the most familiar English form (for example, "Gorky" rather than "Gor'kii"). In transliterating names, titles, and other words in Ottoman Turkish, I have followed the modern Turkish orthography of the Turkish Language Association (Türk Dil Kurumu). Where titles and quotations are drawn from existing transliterations, the orthographic conventions of those transliterations, as cited, are retained.

For Anglophone readers unfamiliar with Turkish, the following is a pronunciation guide for the extended Latin character set used for writing and typesetting modern Turkish:

c, C = pronounced *j*, as in "Jane"
ç, Ç = pronounced *ch*, as in "child"
ğ = a "soft" *g* (in Turkish, "yumuşak g"), which lengthens the vowel preceding it, is not pronounced at all when it appears between two vowels, and never appears at the beginning of a word

A NOTE ON TRANSLATION, TRANSLITERATION, AND USAGE

ı, I = pronounced like the second *e* in "legend" in U.S. English pronunciation
i, İ = pronounced sometimes like the *i* in "bit," sometimes like the *ee* in "meet"
ö, Ö = pronounced ö, as in the German *können*
ü, Ü = pronounced ü, as in the German *über*
ş, Ş = pronounced *sh*, as in "she"
A circumflex mark (^) is used to indicate long vowels in Arabic and Persian loanwords.

In 1934, the Surname Law was passed, requiring all Turkish citizens to adopt Western-style family names. It was at this time that Nâzım Hikmet became Nâzım Hikmet Ran, Nizamettin Nazif became Nizamettin Nazif Tepedelenlioğlu, and so on. Throughout, these adopted surnames are enclosed in parentheses. Following scholarly convention in Turkish studies, I refer to Nâzım Hikmet, Nizamettin Nazif, and Vâlâ Nureddin using their first names. Bibliographic information for these authors is listed under an entry for the author's first name. Cross-references appear in the bibliography for other names used for publication.

ACKNOWLEDGMENTS

While researching Azeri modernism with the support of a 2014–2015 American Council Learned Societies Charles A. Ryskamp Research Fellowship, my encounter with Azeri publications of Nâzım Hikmet's poetry set me on the path to this book. Its completion was supported by a Social Science Research Council Postdoctoral Fellowship for Transregional Research on Inter-Asian Contexts and Connections, which sponsored my study of Russian beginning in 2012 at Columbia University. I thank my Penn State colleague Michael Naydan for allowing me to audit his course in Russian translation afterward. Work on this book was also supported by a membership in the School of Historical Studies at the Institute for Advanced Study in Princeton, with funding provided by the Herodotus Fund, an endowed fund of the institute; a Penn State Humanities Institute faculty fellowship; and sabbatical leave granted by the Penn State College of the Liberal Arts.

In the Department of Comparative Literature at Penn State, Bob Edwards and Charlotte Eubanks helped me secure the funding and writing time I required for this project. Penn State Libraries' efficient and resourceful Interlibrary Loan Office helped me obtain copies of primary sources from around the world. Attendees of my graduate seminar Global Cold War in the autumn of 2022 helped me to reread and rethink some of the book's materials and arguments.

ACKNOWLEDGMENTS

Tom Mullaney, Miyako Inoue, the late Robert Bird, Donald E. Pease, Menglu Gao, Rossen Djagalov, Kaan Kurt, and Paul A. Bové offered me opportunities to present my work to audiences at Stanford University, the University of Chicago, Dartmouth University, Northwestern University, New York University, Samsun University, and the University of Pittsburgh. I am grateful to Nancy Condee, Stathis Gourgouris, R. A. Judy, Don Pease, Anita Starosta, Casey Williams, the late David Golumbia, and my other colleagues in the editorial collective of the journal *boundary 2* for their remarks and questions on such occasions. The members of the Cultures of World Socialism Working Group convened by Samuel Hodgkin, Monica Popescu, Sven Spieker, and Christine Ho have inspired me with their work on global socialist cultures. I am especially grateful to Rossen Djagalov and Sam Hodgkin for intellectual comradeship. The support of Rosalind C. Morris, whose work provides a model for me, has been essential.

Over the years, Erden Akbulut of TÜSTAV has patiently addressed many email queries regarding the cultural history of Turkish communism. Özge Serin, Seval Şahin, Serdar Soydan, Tuncay Birkan, and Merve Şen have been valuable interlocutors about the lives and works of this book's protagonists. I thank Duncan Gullick Lien for his reliable assistance with the final logistics of preparing the manuscript for publication, creating the map used in chapter 1, and preparing all the other illustrations. Kate Antanovich located copies of archival materials pertaining to Suat Derviş in the Russian archives and assisted me with translation of Russian-language sources when time was short.

Dr. Nazan Ölçer, director of Sabancı University Sakıp Sabancı Museum (SSM), and the SSM archivist İrem Biçer generously addressed all my queries regarding Abidin Dino. My art historian friend Suzan Yalman, with whom I have traveled so many stages on life's way, gave me her unwavering support. I am deeply grateful to the owner of the painting *Uzun Yürüyüş* (The long march), by Abidin Dino, for permission to reproduce the painting on the book's cover. Deeply moved by this painting about the 1934–1935 retreat of the Chinese communists from pursuing Nationalist forces, Nâzım Hikmet composed a poem after it in 1958, appropriating the Long March as a metaphor for the travails of Turkish communists: "You and me, Dino, / we're among them / us too, Dino, us too / we saw the light blue."

Portions of chapter 2 appeared in modified form as "Vâlâ Nureddin's Comic Materialism and the Sexual Revolution: Writing Across Turkey and the Soviet Union," *Comparative Literature* 73, no. 3 (2021): 299–319, published by Duke University Press.

Portions of chapter 5 appeared in modified form as "Nâzım Hikmet and the Prose of Communism," *boundary 2* 47, no. 2 (2020): 153–80, published by Duke University Press.

At Columbia University Press, I thank Philip Leventhal for his support of this project and Monique Laban for the patience with which she answered all of my queries. I also would like to thank Michael Haskell and Annie Barva for their meticulous work through various stages of the editorial process. The Modernist Latitude series, edited by Jessica Berman and Paul Saint-Amour, will be a good home. I am grateful to two anonymous reviewers for the press for the professionalism of their remarks on an earlier draft. I have made extensive use of their suggestions.

I thank my mother, Feza Ertürk; my late father, Nejat Ertürk; my partner, Brian Lennon; and my family and friends in Turkey and the United States for their support. This book is dedicated to my son, Murat, whose ten years have witnessed the Gezi Park protests, the ISIL attack on Atatürk Airport, a global pandemic, attempted coups d'état in both Turkey and the United States, and the acceleration of environmental, political, and social instability by the tangible effects of climate change. The book tells the story of people who tried to leave a better world to the world's children. It is a story to pass on.

WRITING IN RED

Introduction

REVOLUTIONARY ENTANGLEMENTS ACROSS TURKEY AND THE SOVIET UNION

An Overview

> The ship with a hundred masts,
> Where is the port it sails for?
>
> —NÂZIM HIKMET, *LIFE'S GOOD, BROTHER*

In October 1922, five representatives in Ankara of the banned People's Communist Party of Turkey (Türkiye Halk İştirakiyun Fırkası, THIF) split into two groups for a clandestine journey to İnebolu by the Black Sea, one group traveling on foot and the other in a pickup truck. Denied permission to leave war-torn Anatolia, the Turkish communists, disguised as Russian sailors "with the oil dirt [on their faces] covering racial differences [*rassovykh razlichii*]," sailed from İnebolu to Sevastopol in a Russian submarine, and from there they traveled by train (and in new disguises) to Moscow, where the Fourth Congress of the Communist International was to take place.[1] They included the party secretary Salih Hacıoğlu, who would immigrate permanently to the Soviet Union in 1928 and die in a Stalinist labor camp in 1954, and the Young Communist representative, novelist, and journalist Nizamettin Nazif, whose work is discussed in chapter 1. They were preceded by the poets Nâzım Hikmet and Vâlâ Nureddin, both at the time nineteen years old, who had made their way from Istanbul through Anatolia to Batumi from January to September 1921 and enrolled at the Communist University of the Toilers of the East (Kommunisticheskii universitet trudiashchikhsia Vostoka, KUTV) in the summer of 1922. They would be followed by the newspaper editor Reşat Fuat Baraner and the schoolteacher Zeki Baştımar, who crossed the Black Sea by boat to study at KUTV and to work in its administration, and by the playwright Abidin Dino and the journalist and novelist Suat Derviş, who visited the Soviet Union through official channels during the 1930s. These figures, who later held leading positions in the Turkish Communist Party (Türkiye Komünist Partisi, TKP), would contribute to the emergence of a rich transnational revolutionary literary archive. Despite the repeated arrests and imprisonment these writers would face for possessing copies of manuscripts, books, waxed paper, movable type, or typewriters under the repressive Kemalist regime, they composed remarkable original work of their own as well as translating both Russian classics and Soviet literature into Turkish and editing prominent literary journals such as *New Literature* (*Yeni Edebiyat*).

Bringing together a wide range of writings, including erotic comedy, historical fiction and screenplays, and modernist socialist-realist novels and plays, *Writing in Red* works through this scattered literary archive shaped by the history of Turkish and Soviet state relations of "cultural diplomacy," Comintern policies, and waves of arrests, detentions, and repressive crackdowns aimed at the TKP during the first half of the twentieth century. It shows that these works belong as much to modern Turkish literature as to a transnational Soviet republic of letters and a global archive of "world revolution." Reading the Soviet scenarist Natan Zarkhi together with Nizamettin Nazif, V. I. Lenin with Nâzım Hikmet, the Soviet writers Mikhail Zoshchenko and Iosif Kallinikov with Vâlâ Nureddin, Maksim Gorky with Derviş, and the film director Sergei Yutkevich with the playwright Dino, *Writing in Red* argues that a study of Turkish communist translation and exchange deepens our understanding of the Moscow-centered transnational literary space produced in the aftermath of the Bolshevik Revolution, or what scholars in Slavic studies have called the "Soviet republic of letters."[2] Rejecting the universality ascribed to Soviet Russian literary forms in both transnational modernist studies and contemporary Soviet studies, the book points to another comparative methodology that accounts for the "dual birth" of the universal and the particular in the languages of West Asia. Refusing to subordinate this neglected literary archive to the authority of Western and Russian writings representing Marxian aesthetics, and rejecting defeatist evasions of its legacy, I suggest that in devising a universalizable politics of revolutionary time, sexual ethics, subaltern "aesthetic education," and humanist ontology,

3
REVOLUTIONARY ENTANGLEMENTS

Turkish communist and formerly communist writers recorded a prehistory of contemporary dissent.

THE "GLOBAL MOMENT" OF 1920: *KOMÜNİZM* AND *BOLŞEVİZM*, THE TALE OF TWO FLOATING SIGNIFIERS IN TURKISH

Since 1928, the center of Istanbul's Taksim Square, the site of so many bloody May 1 demonstrations and of the Gezi Park protests in 2013, has been occupied by the Republic Monument (Cumhuriyet Anıtı). Thirty-six feet high, forged in bronze by the Italian sculptor Pietro Canonica, and narrating the establishment of republican Turkey, the monument has served as a landmark for generations of both Turkish locals and tourists, now deliberately overshadowed by an enormous mosque and imagined to represent a "New Turkey" (Yeni Türkiye). Among the prominent Turkish generals and statesmen depicted standing behind Mustafa Kemal on the monument's southern side, which faces the cosmopolitan İstiklal Avenue, a knowledgeable observer might identify Semen Ivanonich Aralov, the Bolshevik ambassador in Ankara in 1922 and 1923, wearing his Lenin cap.[3]

Despite the specific, identifiable historical circumstances that bound Turkey and Russia to each other in the aftermath of the First World War, literary scholarship has generally neglected what the historian Adeeb Khalid calls the "entanglements" of the Anatolian and Bolshevik Revolutions, an essential context for the transnational and exilic life and work of the Turkish writers and other figures identified in this book.[4] First and foremost, I use the phrase "entangled revolutions" to describe the diplomatic and military alliances of Bolshevik Russia with Kemalist Turkey during the Allied occupation of Istanbul and the partition of the Ottoman territories in the aftermath of the First World War. Defying the Ottoman sultan's pro-British policy, active Unionist underground organizations in Istanbul, Thrace, and Anatolia mobilized a Turkish national resistance movement that eventually included army officers, members of the westernized intelligentsia, and local Muslim and other religious leaders. Appealing to the recognition of the sovereignty of "the Turkish portion of the Ottoman Empire" articulated in Woodrow Wilson's Fourteen Points, the nationalists claimed the territory extending from Western Thrace to Batumi as indivisible territory of a sovereign Muslim majority. Under Mustafa Kemal's leadership, they moved the seat of Parliament from Istanbul to Ankara in April 1920, forming the de facto ruling government of Turkey.[5] For Turkish nationalists disenchanted by the encroaching "West," the "Eastern Ideal" (Şark Mefkuresi) embodied in Bolshevik Russia represented a bulwark against Western imperialism.[6] It is in this sense that the Bolshevik Revolution can be considered foundational to the emergence of modern Turkey.[7]

It is fair to say that scholarship in postcolonial studies has neglected the transnational significance of the Turkish War of Independence (Kurtuluş Savaşı), fought on multiple fronts against French-, Italian-, and British-supported Greek armies from 1919 through 1922. The Bolshevik government's financial, ideological, and military support of the nationalist resistance led by Mustafa Kemal was indispensable, and it deserves to be seen as an important contribution to the formation of the Turkish Republic out of the Ottoman imperial core in 1923.[8] In turn, in its ambition to impede Western encroachment in Transcaucasia, Bolshevik cooperation with Turkish national forces shaped the development of Soviet anti-imperialist policy in the Muslim "East" (Vostok). Described by German Comintern representatives as "Russia in Ankara [*Russland in Angora*]," the first Bolshevik foreign mission, established in 1920, became a point of contact for visitors, including prominent Turkish nationalists, Russian visitors, and illegal communists.[9] As the historian Samuel J. Hirst has emphasized, "cooperation between Moscow and Ankara" would come to play a "formative role in the development of Soviet relations with postcolonial states" in the subsequent decades.[10]

Located at the site of so many bloody May 1 demonstrations, the Republic Monument bears witness to the fact that "gifts" from Soviet Russia were not limited to weapons, ammunition, and gold: they also included the loanwords *Bolşevik* (Bolshevik) and *komünist* (communist), which circulated as floating signifiers in Turkish. This brings me to the second sense in which I understand the deep entanglement of these two social revolutions, an entanglement that cannot be described adequately using only the vocabulary of state diplomacy and foreign relations. Manifesting as an event of open communication and translation, the entangled revolutions also represent the necessary and unpredictable *force* of Bolshevik revolutionary language circulating beyond its own context as an effect of translational activities and print technologies.[11] Though official Turkish historiography has refused to acknowledge the many entanglements of the Anatolian Revolution with the Bolshevik Revolution, for a brief period in the spring and summer of 1920 the loanwords *Bolşevizm* and *komünizm* not only served as names for apparently external events and situations but also acquired a range of associations, including those registering the promise of the "Anatolian Revolution" (Anadolu İhtilali) itself.[12]

According to the anthropologist Claude Lévi-Strauss, a floating signifier is "somewhat like [an] algebraic symbol," "represent[ing] an indeterminate value of signification, in itself devoid of meaning and thus susceptible of receiving any meaning at all." He offers as examples the Polynesian word *mana*, the French terms *machin* and *truc*, and the American slang *oomph*, used to "qualify an unknown object, or one whose function is unclear, or whose effectiveness amazes us." As a kind of "simple form" or "symbol in its pure state," a floating signifier is simultaneously empty and full as it carries multiple and sometimes contradictory meanings.[13] Following Lévi-Strauss, the anthropologist James Siegel observes that "without definite reference, the floating signifier takes on the import of all signification before the latter registers as distinctions." Embodying the power to signify, this "signifier-surfeit" has a cohesive, socially integrating function insofar as its incomplete symbolization is accepted and affirmed by the social as "incipiently symbolic."[14] Arriving unexpectedly from the outside, as "gifts" along with the other Bolshevik "gifts" of weapons and gold, the loanwords *Bolşevizm* and *komünizm* became imbricated with the events of the Turkish War of Independence, its outcome at this time still indeterminate. Analogous to their circulation as floating signifiers in revolutionary Russia, they signified at once excessively and indeterminately. As such, they opened a remarkably diverse space of translation across Anatolia, with a shifting range of both Islamic and anti-imperialist associations among numerous self-identified communist groups formed both within and outside the bounds of the newly established Grand National Assembly (Büyük Millet Meclisi).

I begin with an account of this linguistic and translational history first and foremost because it provides context for the exilic itineraries of the Turkish figures examined in this book. In a well-known passage in his fictional autobiography, *Life's Good, Brother* (*Yaşamak Güzel Şeydir Kardeşim*, 1964), Nâzım describes his travel to Soviet Russia as a continuous journey from Anatolia's outer edge to its innermost depth: "Not books or word-of-mouth propaganda or my social condition brought me where I am. Anatolia brought me where I am. The Anatolia I had seen only on the surface, from the edge."[15] Refusing to represent the border between Anatolia and Russia as a divide, Nâzım imagined it as a Möbius strip whose outer and inner edges form a single plane. In this respect, the literary and exilic itineraries of Turkish communist and formerly communist writers should be distinguished from those of their contemporaries in the larger world whom they would meet in Moscow, including the Iranian poet Abdolqasem Lahouti, the Palestinian writer Najati Sidqi, and the Chinese poet Xiao San.[16] Although domestic communist activity was violently suppressed by Mustafa Kemal in 1921, the brief period of unprecedented translation of communism across West Asia represented a time of both origination and impossible future to come for the Turkish figures examined in this book. As *Writing in Red* shows, the year 1920 and its promise of true social revolution, despite its foreclosure, furnished the epistemic condition of Turkish communist literary production across three key moments explored in this book, including the late 1920s, the 1940s, and the 1960s.

My account of the year 1920 and (counter)revolution in Anatolia also aims to contribute something to a deeper understanding of the history of world communism and the literary international. Witnessing "a contagion" of protests, general strikes, and socialist uprisings across the Western world from Hungary through Italy to Germany, the year 1919 is considered an important "global moment" in the history of world communism, which includes other watershed moments, such as 1936, 1956, and 1968.[17] Refusing to represent the first wave of "anti-imperialist contestation" across Asia as a mere continuation (or substory) of European "revolutions and counterrevolutions," recent scholarship in literary studies has recognized the year 1920 as another crucial global moment in the history of world communism.[18] In other work that addresses the language politics of the First Congress of the Peoples of the East, convened in Baku in September 1920, I have reclaimed the history of this first mass meeting of representatives of western European, U.S., and Russian Communist Parties with communist and nonparty delegates from central Eurasia, suggesting that it provides us with another genealogy for the discipline of comparative literature.[19] In *Eurasia Without Borders* (2021), Katerina Clark has recently approached the Baku Congress as a foundational event for the constitution of a Eurasian literary international stretching from Turkey to China.[20] Supplementing these globalizing accounts of the year 1920 and its literary legacies, *Writing in Red* argues that no account of this "origin" moment is complete without a study of the history of the Turkish War of Independence and the other developments in and across Anatolia that helped shape the Baku Congress and were in return shaped by it. In shifting attention from the activities of Comintern Orientologists such as Mikhail Pavlovich to the diverse and various writings of Anatolian communists and Bolsheviks, this book argues that (Eastern) translation is not just an afterlife of Russian Marxist-Leninist texts but more a constitutive force that impelled them from the start. Adapting a metaphor from the work of the Lebanese socialist Waddah Charara, one might say that what was at stake in the "global moment" of 1920 was not the subsumption of the (Turkish) particular under a new communist universal but rather the "dual birth" of the universal and the particular in the entanglement of the Anatolian and Bolshevik Revolutions.[21]

In this section, I provide a description of the Anatolian communist groups in which some of the protagonists of this book were directly involved, though it is important to recognize that both Istanbul and Baku were also important sites of Turkish communist activity and translation during the period.[22] The historian George S. Harris describes the Istanbul group as "Istanbul sophisticates" (because of their intellectual roots in the French Clarté movement) and the Baku group as "Kremlin loyalists." The latter, which convened a conference in Baku to unify Turkish communists immediately after the First Congress of the Peoples of East, is often celebrated as the foundational TKP in official histories of the party. The so-called Anatolian primitives, meanwhile, are distinguished by Harris from these other factions by their "traditionalist," "less intellectual approach."[23] In refusing to establish a hierarchy among these groups, we can suggest that the origin of Turkish communism is represented by this multiplicity of foundational activity distributed across a vast geography. Far from being inferior, the little-known writings of the "Anatolian primitives" represent substantial contributions to the theory and practice of Muslim communism familiar to us from the writings of the Tatar Bolshevik Mirsaid Sultan-Galiev.[24]

The first organization to mention in this context is the Green Army Association (Yeşil Ordu Cemiyeti), established in May 1920 in Ankara by a group of deputies advocating Islamic Bolshevism. Despite its name, the Green Army Association had no military resources until Ethem the Circassian, leader of a powerful irregular unit in Eskişehir, joined it in July 1920. According to its code of regulations, the Green Army aimed "to benefit from and support the movement of Socialism [*Sosyalizm*]" because "Islam and the Muhammedan law had mandated and advocated a thousand and three hundred years ago the principle [of bringing an end to the misery of the poor and the excessive squandering of the rich] through compulsory almsgiving and sacrificial offering."[25] Understanding socialism as a form of gift economy, the association sought to domesticate Bolshevism by transvaluing Islamic practices of almsgiving as socialist in character.[26] In a speech delivered to the National Assembly on July 8, 1920, Sheik Servet Efendi, a leading member of the Green Army Association, reminded his audience that the prophet Muhammad had "refused proprietorship despite receiving millions of liras." Presenting a radical program for the redistribution of wealth, he described Bolshevism as "a step taken toward the truths of Islam."[27]

Disbanded by Mustafa Kemal in the fall of 1920, the Green Army Association was succeeded by the Populist Group (Halk Zümresi) within the Ankara Assembly. The journalist Yunus Nadi, who was one of its leading figures, would publish a series of articles on Bolshevism in his influential Ankara daily *New Day in Anatolia (Anadolu'da Yeni Gün)* in 1920, including "A Short History of Russian Bolshevism and Its Organization" ("Rus Bolşevikliği Tarihçesi ve Teşkilatı"), "Declaration of the Third International" ("Üçüncü Enternasyonalin Beyannamesi"), and "Constitution of the Russian Soviet Republic" ("Rus Sovyet Cumhuriyeti Kanun-i Esasisi").[28] In an editorial titled "New Life" ("Yeni Hayat"), published on September 16, 1920, Yunus Nadi described Bolshevik Russia as "the leader of all East that has or is about to revolt against the imperialist West." Influenced by publications about the First Congress of the Peoples of the East convened in Baku in September 1920,[29] Nadi imagined Bolshevism a global politics of anti-imperialism:

> The greatest kind of revolution rules over material and spiritual forces and powers of humans in the way that unknown and unexpected cyclones rule

over them. The world has now joined in and is caught in such a cyclone. And now this is such a cyclone that among the many great deeds it has accomplished is the birth it gave to our Grand National Assembly. We do not know if we were aware of it at the time. But we now understand that whereas the force that united the Turkish nation against imperialism's unprecedented vile attacks was in appearance a very natural sentiment of self-preservation and insurrection, it was in reality a wave of the worldwide revolution [*cihanşümul bir inkılabın*] embracing and encompassing the whole world.[30]

In Nadi's prose, the word *Bolshevik* stood for anti-imperialist world revolution. In comparing the foundation of the Ankara Assembly under occupation to an "unknown, unexpected cyclone," Nadi described the revolution as a sublime event overwhelming the cognitive faculties of representation. If the global moment of 1920 was profoundly self-estranging, Nadi overcame this self-fragmentation by symbolizing it as "world revolution" after the fact. In his editorial, the signifiers *Bolshevik* and *world revolution* served both to fix and to transcode a traumatic historical situation whose outcome was still deeply uncertain.[31]

"The General Regulation of the Communist Party of Turkey" ("Türkiye Komünist Partisi Umumî Nizamnamesi"), distributed in Anatolia in June 1920, also described the "global moment" of 1920 as a moment of *cihan inkılabı*, or "world revolution." Signed by the Central Committee of the Turkish Communist Party (Türkiye Komünist Partisi Merkez-i Umumîsi) founded in Eskişehir and Ankara by the Russian Muslim émigrés Şerif Manatov and Zinetullah Nuşirevan and the Turkish major Salih Hacıoğlu, the regulation announced that "a communist, that is, Bolshevik party [*Komünist, yani Bolşevik partisi*] was formed in Turkey to institute socialism [*sosyalizmi*] and to bring out in Turkey the world revolution, which will secure affluence and happiness for all humanity."[32] (Historical scholarship refers to this TKP group as the "clandestine" or "hafî TKP" to distinguish it from the two other TKPs established during this period, Mustafa Kemal's "official TKP" and the Baku TKP.) Members of the clandestine TKP would eventually merge with former members of the Green Army Association and the Populist Group in December 1920, but they initially were opposed to domesticating Bolshevism via Islam. Their party program transposed the order of things in Turkey according to the Russian

Soviet model, calling for the adoption of the Soviet system in administration, the elimination of private property, and the abolition of money. In a declaration issued on July 14, 1920, the clandestine TKP emphasized its difference from Mustafa Kemal's "nationalist" and "democratic bourgeois [*demokratik burjuva*]" government, describing the latter as a group of "old Unionists who appear in a new guise and yet are no different from members of the Istanbul government in their relation to the people."[33]

Rejecting the spell of Bolshevism and communism in Anatolia, Mustafa Kemal would intervene in this space of free translation in October 1920 by authorizing the foundation of the Official Communist Party of Turkey (Resmi Türkiye Komünist Fırkası) under the leadership of his associate Hakkı Behiç and by outlawing all communist activity outside this party's domain. Historians of the Turkish Left emphasize that Mustafa Kemal's view of Bolshevism remained generally consistent, affirming an external alliance with the Bolsheviks beginning in the spring of 1919 but rejecting the Bolshevik model for domestic affairs. As Mustafa Kemal put it in a closed session of the National Assembly on May 29, 1920, "We, the Executive Council, are talking about forming an alliance with Bolshevik Russia [*bolşeviklik Rusyasiyle*], but we are not talking about becoming Bolshevik."[34] In another closed session on January 22, 1921, he defended the establishment of an official communist party, reasoning that violent repression of proliferating "Komünistlik" or "Komünizm" organizations would endanger the relationship with Russia. The official TKP was thus directed to "resist ideas with ideas" and to "elucidate the impossibility of accepting communism for our country, nation, and the exigencies of our religion."[35] In an editorial titled "Currents" ("Cereyanlar") published in *National Sovereignty* (*Hakimiyet-i Milliye*) on October 9, 1920, Mustafa Kemal made a case for the official TKP in this way:

> Sometimes merchandise [*meta*] is produced in another country to which great value is attributed either because it is extraordinarily good or because it is highly distinguished for some reason. Then you see some charlatans appear in public, stuffing their pockets with false things and imitations wrapped in a deceptive label; they stand on street corners or in passageways, yelling in a high voice and talking people around so that they recruit special touts and gather passersby.... Thus, in recent times we've seen the emergence of charlatans who do this in this country. "Communism!

Communism," they yell and talk people around in a thousand ways, claiming they are the only ones holding the remedy of peace and salvation called communism, the purest and most exquisite medicine, which can treat seventy-two different afflictions! ... The thing to do for us in this state is simple: because it is very difficult to prevent this behavior ..., our first duty is to call for the attention and care of those who might be deceived by them and to explain to everyone as far as possible the method of separating pure from impure, fake medicine.[36]

Kemal's comparison of communism to counterfeited merchandise suggests that he understood all too well how *communism* and *Bolshevism* circulated as floating signifiers in Turkish. In "Currents" as well as in other editorials of the period, Kemal imagined a "law" segregating the Anatolian and Bolshevik Revolutions as revolutions of different genres, a law whose effect was to stabilize the signifiers *Bolşevik* and *komünist*. Distinguishing between "Russian Bolshevism" and "Turkish communism," he noted that Soviet Russia and Turkey advanced toward identical communist goals despite differences in historical circumstances and revolutionary tactics.[37] Whereas Russian Bolshevism entailed the establishment of "a harsh and absolute dictatorship of the proletariat," the communism to be realized in Turkey was "a swift maturation" entailing a victorious war against European capitalism.[38] Placing emphasis on the intense internal class antagonism between peasants and landowners in Russia, Kemal argued that capitalism had entered Turkey from the outside, enslaving both the wealthy and the poor, who were now united in fighting it.

Over the next few months, a contained sense of communism understood as "the sovereignty of a popular majority" would be mobilized in the Ankara Assembly, though it would end with the liquidation of the official TKP in January 1921.[39] For Mustafa Kemal and his supporters, *komünist* and *Bolşevik* would no longer describe the domestic order of things. One ought not underestimate the influence of Kemal's *National Sovereignty* editorials in shattering the promise of these floating signifiers in Turkish. Despite the apparent embrace of communism, the passage from "Currents" is especially telling. Though the editorial concluded by suggesting that communism is a "path taken by the whole world,"[40] it encoded the word *komünizm* as fundamentally *unheimlich*. Emphasizing the uncontrollable simulation and proliferation of communist speech in Turkish translation, Kemal, the master linguist who eight years later would implement one of the most ambitious language reforms in history, mobilized the indeterminate, surplus signifying power of this loanword against that simulation and proliferation of communist speech. At the closed session of the Assembly on January 22, 1921, he remarked that he had purposefully used the loanword *komünizm* in the title of the official TKP rather than translating it as *iştirakiyun* or *ortaklık* and that the purpose of this refusal to translate was to reveal the word's "true" essence.[41] Open to forgery and counterfeit, communist speech is imagined here as fundamentally inauthentic and suspect, holding the performative power to bewitch the public as a "fake remedy." The "fake" communism delineated by Kemal's official TKP thus paved the way for the conclusive negation of this floating signifier in the Assembly debates of January 1921.

When Ethem the Circassian, the former Green Army member, rebelled against the Ankara government in December 1920, he represented the greatest internal challenge to Mustafa Kemal's leadership. At the same time, hostility to the TKP among conservative members of the Ankara Assembly was on the rise. Facing armed uprising in western Anatolia and this conservative opposition in the Assembly, Mustafa Kemal decided to suppress all communist party organizations both official and clandestine.[42] The THIF, which had been formed in Ankara in December 1920 by clandestine TKP members with members of the liquidated Green Army Association and the Populist Group, was suspended. Also in January 1921, fifteen founding members of the Communist Party of Turkey (Türkiye Komünist Fırkası), established in Baku by Turkish émigrés and prisoners of war in Soviet Russia, were murdered on the Black Sea. The Baku communists, who had arrived in eastern Anatolia in December 1920 to aid the national resistance movement, were forced aboard a Russia-bound boat in Trabzon and then attacked in the open sea.[43] (Because the Baku group is considered the foundational TKP in official party histories, this trauma is of great symbolic significance. The victims were commemorated in a book published in Moscow in 1923 by Şerif Manatov, Zinetullah Nuşirevan, Nâzım Hikmet, and Vâlâ Nureddin.[44])

In a *National Sovereignty* article titled "From Right to Left" ("Sağdan Sola Doğru") dated March 8, 1921, the editor Hüseyin Ragıp suggested that although Turkey would follow the leftward drift of global politics, "the imagination of a Bolshevik or a communist administration for Turkey is only a laughable naiveness."⁴⁵ Though Mustafa Kemal and his supporters rejected the conservative opposition's request to break all diplomatic relations with "deceitful" Russia, they did embrace their colleagues' anticommunism. During the Assembly debates of 1921, the words *komünist* and *Bolşevik* were repurposed as equivalents for *serseri*, or "vagabond," used to describe "foolish" persons of "worthless descent."⁴⁶ The use of *komünist* as a kind of curse (*küfür*), suggesting an uncanny state of familial, national, and religious rootlessness and hence of social death, would intensify and persist into the following decades.⁴⁷

To understand the complete historical arc of these borrowings in Turkish, it is necessary to clarify the concept of *küfür*, "curse," which is a borrowing from Arabic. Just as the English term *curse* carries at least two meanings—the religious meaning of "speak[ing] impiously against . . . the deity, fate, destiny, etc." and the related secular meaning of "swear[ing] profanely in anger or irritation"—the Turkish *küfür* has two meanings.⁴⁸ Derived from the Arabic root *k-f-r*, meaning "to cover, to hide . . . the truth," *kufr* is used in the Quran with a range of meanings, including "denial of God," "rejection of God's signs and other attributes," and "ingratitude in the face of God's favors."⁴⁹ In addition to its religious meaning of "unbelief" in Turkish, *küfür* can be used in everyday speech to denote swearing profanely. Insofar as Turkish communists embody the radical negation of national and religious values, they stand as the greatest danger to "Turkishness" and Islam, represented in the Turkish language by the circulation of this signifier as a swear word. Tekin Erer, an important ideologue of Turkish anticommunism, describes this usage: "Among Turkish people, if it becomes necessary to curse someone, first animal names are uttered. Then if the unsatisfied party would like to use a stronger word, he calls his opponent 'Komünist!' In order to avoid being crushed under this very heavy insult, the other party curses back: 'You're a communist!' 'Your father is a communist!' or 'Communist son of a communist!' How many fights, woundings, and killings happened in Anatolia because of this."⁵⁰

One ought to distinguish the anticommunist negation of a Turkish *Bolşevik* and *komünist* from the dialectical negation of an external enemy, embodied by the British, French, and Greek armies during the War of Independence. What made a Turkish communist more terrifying than a recognizable external enemy, "who offers the possibility of being conquered," is the former's nondialectical otherness, which evades assimilation.[51] As the Tokat deputy Mustafa Bey put it in a closed session of the Ankara Assembly on January 22, 1921: "The problem is inside us [*iş bizim içimizde*]."[52] Or as the Burdur representative İsmail Suphi wrote in a letter to Mustafa Kemal on January 10, 1921: "Even if every place was stopped up by seductive propaganda and gold, [the Bolsheviks] would enter through the smallest hole.... The West openly walks against us and cannot enter inside us, while it is characteristic of the East to rot us from inside."[53] Spreading through the social body without taking a traceable path, the communist other is profoundly uncanny because they represent the internal disintegration of socially recognizable religious and national identity.

Whereas the indeterminate, excess signifying power of *komünist* in its early circulation in Anatolia was affirmed as "incipiently symbolic" and thus socially binding, its recoding as a curse associated it with deathlike negativity. For the anticommunist, the Turkish communist embodied an excess negative force and refusal to reflect the familiar world and was the cause of radical self-estrangement amid the breakdown of a national symbolic order. *Komünist* is a strange performative because to name a communist is not to dispel this uncanniness but to amplify it. In this respect, the act of naming a communist recalls the phenomenon of "naming the witch" examined in anthropological scholarship. It can be distinguished from other forms of "excitable" or "injurious" speech that derive their force from the "encoded memory" of a historical trauma.[54] To modify Erer's remark, one might say that *komünist* is at once the emptiest and the most violent of all Turkish insults: whereas calling someone an "animal" assigns that person to a low yet recognizable place in the hierarchical chain of being, to name someone a "communist" is to fail to fix and control an unpredictable excess of negativity that marks the limit of the social. In spite of or perhaps because of this inefficacy, *komünist* was one of the most powerful insults in the Turkish language and was often accompanied by extreme physical violence.

Mustafa Kemal did not invent a Turkish discourse of anticommunism dating back to 1919. The Allied forces in Istanbul, the Ottoman sultanate, and conservative members of the Ankara Assembly had already shaped this discourse in different ways. Mustafa Kemal's pursuit of an external political and military alliance with Bolshevik Russia distinguished him from conservative members of the Ankara Assembly, who wanted to sever all diplomatic relations with Russia. Recognizing that the diversity of Turkish communist activity made it possible for the Anatolian Revolution to become a true social revolution, Kemal deliberately foreclosed on it. The goal of the anticommunist purge of 1921 was not merely to prevent Soviet encroachment into internal affairs but more immediately to expel the internal difference of the Anatolian Revolution itself.

Historians of modern Turkey aptly describe the year 1920 as one of the most obscure and most interesting periods in modern Turkish history.[55] To supplement universalizing accounts of the Bolshevik Revolution that fail to address its "dual birth" in West Asia, I have described at some length the brief but unprecedented period of Marxist-Leninist translation across the latter area. Not at all an "insignificant geography," war-torn Anatolia shaped in crucial ways the consolidation of an anti-imperialist literary space across Eurasia.[56] In my account, I also provide context for the exilic itineraries of the Turkish figures examined in this book. Receiving their first lessons in Marxism and communism from Turkish Spartacists and other local communists during their travels in Anatolia, Nâzım and his companion, Vâlâ, enrolled at KUTV in 1922, taking courses in mathematics, physics, chemistry, world history, and geography as well as a core curriculum in "political economy, historical materialism, the history of the Russian Bolshevik Communist Party," and "the history of the East."[57] As chapter 1 will show, Nizamettin, who traveled from Istanbul to Ankara to support the national resistance, was radicalized by his encounter with Anatolian Bolshevism in the spring and summer of 1920, traveling to Soviet Russia in a submarine under arrangements made by the Comintern and the Bolshevik foreign mission in Ankara in 1922. Though Baraner, Derviş, and Dino were not in Anatolia at this time, in the following decades each of them would acknowledge the foreclosed promise of the entangled revolutions as an epistemic condition of their work. It is in this sense that *Writing in Red* argues that the entangled revolutions and the "global moment" of 1920 cast a long shadow over the twentieth century.

During the Turkish War of Independence, complex alliances formed among Turkish, Kurdish, Circassian, and Laz Muslim leaders and religious dignitaries in rural Anatolia and the group of urban secular military officials, intellectuals, former Ottoman bureaucrats, and representatives who had fled from occupied Istanbul to Ankara.[58] Though the ideologues of the Kemalist regime would deny the existence of a class society in

Turkey, the republic established in 1923 aimed to protect the interests of the ruling elite in the state bureaucracy, urban and provincial businessmen, and landowners in Anatolia. (Most of these businessmen and landowners had acquired their wealth during the dispossession of Ottoman Armenians, Greeks, and Jews, the forced migrations, and the ethnic genocides of the late imperial era.)[59] Following the murder of the Baku communists in January 1921 and the suppression of the Ankara communists in 1922, the Istanbul communists led by the French-educated Şefik Hüsnü (Deymer) emerged as the TKP's new core.[60]

The principal determinants structuring the political field did not change for Turkish communists during the republican period: despite the official alliance with the Soviet Union, the Kemalist state continued its violent foreclosure of Turkish communism into the years of the Second World War.[61] Turkish communism was further enclosed during the 1930s by the emergence of an official discourse on New Russia (Yeni Rusya) legitimizing the Kemalist state's strong economic, diplomatic, and cultural relations with the Soviet Union.[62] Modifying Mustafa Kemal's "law of genre" of revolutions, this official discourse not only miscoded the floating signifier *revolution* (*ihtilâl* or *inkılâb* used interchangeably) as state modernization but also promised that Kemalism could simulate the "Russian revolution"—that is, assimilate its modernization techniques without losing its national originality. Ultimately, Turkish republican communism would be overshadowed and outmaneuvered by the ersatz political double represented by the Kemalist appropriation of economic statism and ideological populism during the 1930s.[63]

So far I have described the positive and negative boundaries of the political field in which the protagonists of this book operated during the early republican period. A dynamic with far-reaching political reverberations, the entanglement of the Anatolian and Bolshevik Revolutions also had significant literary consequences both within and beyond the region. I explore these consequences in the following section.

ON THE CONCRETE UNIVERSALITY OF TURKISH LITERARY PRODUCTION

Two main pathways of literary exchange opened between Turkey and the Soviet Union in response to the short-lived yet formative critical moment of 1920.⁶⁴ Mediated by the leading organ of Soviet cultural diplomacy, the All-Union Society for Cultural Relations with Foreign Countries (Vsesoiuznoe obshchestvo kul'turnoi sviazi s zagranitsei, VOKS) and local actors in Turkey, the first pathway represents the official exchange developing during the 1920s and 1930s amid Turkey's violent suppression of communism. Following the adoption of "socialism in one country" as state policy in the mid-1920s, the Soviet Union developed a complex system of "cultural diplomacy."⁶⁵ Hosting influential Turkish writers, playwrights, and musicians invited to visit the Soviet Union, VOKS also distributed books, propaganda materials, and films in Turkey.⁶⁶

Whereas significant literary exchange in the mid-1920s was limited to the adaptation of Russian theatrical classics by Muhsin Ertuğrul, a foundational figure in Turkish theater and cinema, it would intensify and expand during the 1930s as economic and diplomatic ties between the two countries grew stronger. Although the Kemalist ruling elite implemented a radical program of westernization, including the replacement of the Perso-Arabic script with the Latin alphabet, they followed closely the success of Soviet modernization in embodying an extra-European path to modernity.⁶⁷ The period 1932–1938 saw a marked increase in translation of Russian classics and Soviet novels by Anton Chekhov, Ivan Turgenev, Fyodor Dostoevsky, Maksim Gorky, and Mikhail Sholokhov, among others, though most were retranslations of French translations, not direct translations from the Russian.⁶⁸ The delegations for reciprocal diplomatic visits in 1929–1930 and 1932–1933 included artists and journalists. The director Sergei I. Yutkevich, who filmed the Soviet delegation's 1933 participation in the public celebration of the tenth anniversary of Turkey's foundation, made the documentary *Ankara—the Heart of Turkey* (*Ankara—Serdtse Turtsii*), showcasing "New Turkey" and celebrating its non-European path to modernity.⁶⁹ Despite their anticommunism, prominent Kemalist ideologues, including Falih Rıfkı and Yakup Kadri, who attended the Soviet Writers' Congress in 1934, drew on the work of Soviet writers and philologists in their attempt to develop a new secular national art and literature whose goal was to span the gap separating the modernized elite from "the people."

This first pathway of exchange crossing Turkish–Soviet borders during the interwar period was formed by official state channels. A second pathway, established by the translational and other literary activities of the prominent Turkish communist and formerly communist writers studied in this book, diverged meaningfully from the first, even if the two were not entirely without intersection. Shaped by the Bolshevik foreign mission in Ankara (what two German Comintern representatives described as "Russland in Angora"), the diverse variety of Bolshevik and communist movements in Anatolia, and the opportunities for geographic travel provided by the TKP and the Comintern's Eastern Bureau, the illegal border crossers who studied at KUTV and who later held leading positions in the TKP, including Nâzım, Vâlâ, Nizamettin, Baraner, and Baştımar, would carry a practice of communist translation into the republican period, extending it into the domain of literature. Facing repression by the authoritarian single-party regime dominated by the Republican People's Party (Cumhuriyet Halk Partisi) and, like their Soviet counterparts, "identify[ing] with the printed word and with literature in particular,"[70] they translated both classics and lesser-known works of Russian and Soviet literature into Turkish directly from Russian originals (instead of from French translations, as was the practice in Turkey up to that point) and published original work of their own. Given the scope of influence of the single-party regime at a time of nation building with limited resources, it was inevitable that the literary itineraries of Nâzım, Vâlâ, and others examined in this book would converge with the programs and institutions of official literary culture at certain pressure points. At the same time, refusing to be limited or bound by the official discourse on "New Russia," work by Turkish communist and formerly communist writers presents us with an alternative heterogeneous literary archive of the entanglements of the Anatolian and Bolshevik Revolutions in its attempt to open Kemalist nation building to its foreclosed promises, social and otherwise.

Consisting of two parts, titled "Genres of Entangled Revolutions" and "Marxian Form in the Periphery: Modernist Socialist Realisms," *Writing in Red* emphasizes three key moments of intensified communist literary translation and production prompted by the border crossing of the travelers examined in this book. Whereas part I primarily (though not exclusively) focuses on the first moment of intensified literary activity during the late 1920s and early 1930s, shaped by the itineraries of Nizamettin, Nâzım, and Vâlâ, part II addresses the second moment of intensified communist exchange during the late 1930s and 1940s, prompted by the return of Derviş, Dino, and their TKP colleagues to Istanbul on the eve of the

Second World War. During the 1950s, Nâzım, Derviş, and Dino escaped from Turkey to France and the Soviet Union, participating actively in transnational socialist literary networks and shaping from a distance a third moment of intensified socialist translation and exchange in Turkey that emerged in the 1960s. Each chapter also addresses the 1960s as an endpoint insofar as these writers emerged as participants in Soviet, Turkish, and Afro-Asian literary alliances of the Cold War era.

In important ways, Nâzım's return from the Soviet Union to Turkey in 1928 and his work for the journal *Illustrated Monthly* (*Resimli Ay*) shaped the first moment of intensified communist literary production during the interwar years. It is widely recognized that *Illustrated Monthly* functioned as a literary school both for Nâzım's closest collaborators (Vâlâ, Nizamettin, and Derviş) and for other influential young writers of the period, including the leftist critic Sadri Ertem and the poet Nail Vahdeti, who became a TKP member under Nâzım's influence and a student of KUTV in 1934.[71] Personifying his nineteenth year as "my firstborn, first teacher, first comrade" in the poem "My Nineteenth Year" ("19 Yaşım," 1930), Nâzım, who imagined his new self or "double" born in the entanglement of the Bolshevik and Anatolian Revolutions, singlehandedly initiated and sustained the poetic vernacularization of communism in Turkey.[72] Transformed by his encounter with Russian futurism and documentary cinema, Nâzım would renovate Turkish poetics by introducing free verse, typographic experimentation, and a new domain of urban proletarian and Marxist-internationalist literary themes. His articles in the *Illustrated Monthly* provided early models of Marxist literary criticism relating the history of Ottoman Turkish poetic and prose forms to the agrarian mode of production. His published reviews of works by young leftist poets and short story writers, including İlhami Bekir and Sabahattin Ali, would educate several generations of Turkish writers about the aesthetic principles of new "modern-realist" (or "realist-modern") prose and poetry.[73]

Unlike Nâzım, who enjoyed global acclaim, the other illegal border crossers I discuss in part I, including Nizamettin and Vâlâ, are barely mentioned in literary anthologies and textbooks today, despite the wide influence of their work during the early republican era. Indeed, my focus in part I will be the neglected writings of Nizamettin and Vâlâ, who returned to Turkey several years before Nâzım, setting in motion the first moment of intensified translation and literary activity. A descendent of

Tepedelenli Ali Pasha (1744–1833), who had served as the Ottoman governor of the northern mainland of Greece, Nizamettin would part ways with the TKP in 1925, but he would go on to compose the serialized bestseller *Dark Davud* (*Kara Davud*) between 1927 and 1928, initiating the popularization of historical fiction. Representing a neglected literary record of Nizamettin's involvement with the suppressed THIF from 1920 and 1922, *Kara Davud* offered a Marxist historical-allegorical representation of the Anatolian Revolution. In the late 1920s and early 1930s, a time when literary translation from Russian was confined largely to stage adaptations of Russian classics, Vâlâ introduced Turkish readers to little-known contemporary Soviet writers through his serialized translation and literary adaptation of Mikhail Zoshchenko's short stories and Soviet erotic fiction. Vâlâ, who would leave the TKP in 1926, can be said to have interrupted the official discourse on Turkish and Soviet convergence, imagining in his translations and adaptations a mirror held up to the failed promise of Kemalist modernization, especially in the domain of women's emancipation. Although the literary international of the interwar years is examined primarily through the lens of the proletarian novel or the international avant-garde, part I of this book shows that forms of revolutionary writing during this period included such neglected genres as historical fiction and erotic comedy.

Chapter 1 begins by exploring historical fiction and film about the Turkish War of Independence as a crucial neglected legacy of the entangled revolutions. Imagined as an early example of anti-imperialist "Eastern" national liberation and Leninist self-determination, the Turkish War of Independence became a crucial theme for both Turkish writers such as Nizamettin Nazif and Nâzım Hikmet as well as Soviet filmmakers such as Yutkevich and Zarkhi. Through a close reading of Nizamettin's *Kara Davud* and Nâzım's *Epic of National Liberation Movement* (*Milli Kurtuluş Hareketi Destanı*, 1939–1941) in relation to the work of these Soviet filmmakers as well as to Mustafa Kemal's foundational *Great Speech* (*Nutuk*) of 1927, I argue that Nizamettin and Nâzım challenged Kemalist elitist and Soviet Orientalist representation in describing the revolutionary agency of Anatolian peoples. Tracing the promises, contradictions, and legacies of these writers and their diverse itineraries, I suggest that their work productively expanded the purview of Soviet "Eastern" film and literature, introducing a new set of critical questions about the articulation of nationalism with Marxism-Leninism.

In reading Vâlâ's neglected erotic historical comedy *Baltacı and Catherine* (*Baltacı ile Katerina*, 1928), unique among his writings in its direct and explicit imagination and specification of an entangled revolution, chapter 2 suggests, by way of specific attention to this work's comedic elements, that Vâlâ imagined the collapse of both Russian and Ottoman imperial sovereignty in terms of sexual revolution. Although the anticommunist defamation of Turkish communists as "immoral" and "hypersexual" deterred many Turkish communist writers from engaging with matters of family and sexuality, Vâlâ, who left the TKP in 1926, was notable in his articulation of a "left morality" in *Baltacı and Catherine* and two other serialized adaptations of Soviet erotic novels in the 1920s.

If early writings by Nâzım, Vâlâ, and Nizamettin represent the first important moment of Marxist-Leninist literary translation across West Asia, writings by Baraner, Baştımar, Derviş, and Dino (as well as Nâzım's prison writings) represent its second crucial moment, shaped by the long shadow of the entangled revolutions and the political conjuncture of the Second World War. The Comintern's order for "decentralization [*desantralizasyon*]" or "separation [*separat*]" in 1937 dealt a major blow to the TKP and had a lasting impact on the generation of Turkish communists who came of age during the Second World War.[74] Countering its previous directives aimed at party radicalization, the Comintern ordered Turkish communists to liquidate the party ranks and to infiltrate Kemalist political, social, and cultural organizations so as to better support the fight against fascism. A complex development amid the shifting political climate of the 1940s, the consolidation of an antifascist front represented a break with the official Turkish–Soviet convergence of the previous decade. Under the leadership of İsmet İnönü, who became president after Mustafa Kemal's death in 1938, the Turkish government maintained a position of neutrality, signing declarations of friendship with Britain and France in 1939 and a nonaggression pact with Germany in 1941. The German invasion of the Soviet Union found support among conservative elements of the Turkish government and armed forces, who called for Turkey to join the war on the German side.⁷⁵ In this repressive climate, Nâzım was tried in 1938 on fabricated charges of inciting the army and the navy to rebellion and began serving a sentence of twelve years.

While Nâzım composed his magnum opus, *Human Landscapes from My Country* (*Memleketimden İnsan Manzaraları*), in prison, his comrades organized a short-lived but effective literary front in the much larger prison that Turkey became under martial law beginning in 1940. Unlike Nâzım, Vâlâ, and Nizamettin, all literary figures first and foremost, Baraner and Baştımar, who served successive terms as heads of the TKP, became literary actors only after the liquidation of the TKP by the Comintern in 1937. A distant cousin of Mustafa Kemal from Ottoman Salonica, Baraner was radicalized during his studies as a chemical engineer in Germany during the late 1920s, subsequently working as an administrator in KUTV's Turkish section in 1934 and in the Comintern from 1936 to 1937. A graduate of the Teacher's School in Trabzon on the Black Sea, Baştımar studied at KUTV between 1926 and 1929, returning to Moscow in 1934 to enroll in KUTV's graduate program.⁷⁶ During the period of decentralization from 1937 until the party's revival in 1942, Baraner and Baştımar returned from Moscow to Turkey, and the TKP made literature a key aesthetic front in the battle against Turkish anticommunism. In their respective roles as head and member of the TKP Central Committee, Baraner and Baştımar collaborated closely with their literary colleagues (Derviş, Dino, and others), introducing key concepts of Soviet socialist realism and Marxist aesthetics to a Turkish readership in the influential bimonthly literary newspaper *New Literature*, a project that lasted from October 1940 through the newspaper's closure in November 1941. Baştımar also took a position in the Prime Ministry's Supervisory Council Library (Başvekalet Murakabe Heyeti Kütüphanesi) in Ankara in 1937, translating such classics as Anton Chekhov's *The Mask* and, in collaboration with Nâzım (still in prison), Leo Tolstoy's *War and Peace*.⁷⁷

The originality of Turkish literary production in this second moment of intensified communist exchange cannot be grasped without an engagement with the work of *New Literature* contributors Derviş and Dino as well as with Nâzım's prison writings. Whereas scholarship on the Soviet literary international has tended to write off the Second World War period as a moment of contraction and retrenchment, *Writing in Red* argues that the 1940s witnessed some of the richest experimentation with Marxian form and socialist-realist aesthetics in the Turkish corner of the Soviet republic of letters.

Examining in detail the contributions of Suat Derviş, one of the most important communist women writers, chapter 3 explores the creative reimagination of the socialist-realist novel in Turkey. Born into a prominent Ottoman family, Derviş was a childhood friend of Nâzım and was married to Nizamettin between 1934 and 1938 and to Baraner from 1940 until his death in 1968. Working as a writer and journalist in Berlin beginning in the late 1920s, she came to socialism both by way of her experiences in Weimar Germany and through her involvement with the *Illustrated Monthly* literary collective.[78] Traveling to the Soviet Union as a journalist in 1937 and again in 1939, she republished her serialized travel essays as a book titled *Why Am I a Friend of the Soviet Union?* (*Niçin Sovyetler Birliğinin Dostuyum?*) in 1944.[79] Reflecting a different itinerary from that of her male collaborators, Derviş composed brilliant socialist-realist novels that thematized her clandestine participation in the TKP underground during the 1940s. Substituting the figure of the prostitute for the originary maternal "positive hero" of Maksim Gorky's *The Mother* (*Mat'*, 1906), her exemplary novel *Phosphorescent Cevriye* (*Fosforlu Cevriye*, 1948) depicts the transformation of an illiterate, urban subaltern sex worker (who aborts her child) into a revolutionary actor. Examining the language politics of this novel as well as its erotic subplot, I argue that *Phosphorescent Cevriye* should be read as an innovative modernist-feminist rewriting of the socialist-realist "master plot" and as a crucial contribution to Marxist feminism in its imagination of a new communist ethics of the act.

Chapter 4 explores the legacies of the 1940s, focusing on the literary and cinematic contributions of the playwright and artist Abidin Dino, who joined the TKP in 1939. Born into a prominent Ottoman family from Albania, Dino, who spent the First World War years in Europe, met Nâzım, Vâlâ, and Nizamettin in Istanbul during the late 1920s and early 1930s, when he produced the illustrations for Nâzım's poetry collections. After working as a set designer (*khudozhnik*) under the patronage of Sergei Yutkevich between 1934 and 1937, he would make a distinct contribution of his own in his plays and visual art about the Turkish rural subaltern, often inspired by his collaboration with Yutkevich. Thoroughly neglected in existing scholarship on the literary international, Dino's work provides an important counterpoint to the work of his influential Soviet and Chinese contemporaries (including Mao, who called for a transformative pedagogic art and literature guided by and produced for the peasant masses).[80] Exiled from Istanbul to southern Anatolia between 1942 and 1945, Dino composed *Baldy* (*Kel*) and *The Inheritors* (*Verese*), two village plays drawing on his set design work at Lenfilm. Both works thematized peasant *faktura* (including "textures and materials of set design but also its objects," as Emma Widdis has suggested)[81] but refused to reproduce the "tactile Orientalism" of Soviet Easterns, instead focusing on the dispossessed peasantry's purposeful destruction of some objects, such as commoditized animals, coins, and discarded goods, and their defamiliarizing use of other objects, such as women's shoes and animal skins. He mobilized the modernist estrangement (*ostranenie*) of theatrical objects and the dialogic form of the peasant theater to educate his rural spectators about the conditions of their exploitation. In exploring the equivalency of Yutkevich's studio school with vernacular theater and expanding the translatability of Marxism by turning to a common language of objects, Dino devised a singular strain of formalist socialist realism.

This book concludes with a study of Nâzım's signature contribution to socialist-realist aesthetics and Marxian form. Diverging from the thought of his influential contemporary Georg Lukács, Nâzım called for a new direction in Marxist aesthetics that would break with the novelistic representation of "types," emphasizing in its place the representation of a collective, interlinked revolutionary subject of the twentieth century. Borrowing from Lenin the concept of serial writing that established the principles of both Nâzım's party activism and his poetics from the late 1920s through the 1960s, Nâzım developed what I call a new "prose poetics of seriality." Focusing on his epic novel in verse, *Human Landscapes from My Country*, and on his final autobiographical novel, *Life's Good, Brother*, chapter 5 argues that Nâzım's work represents a distinctive genealogy in Marxist aesthetics.

"Sitting still all this time, these guys have become rusty. Let's see what Reşat [Fuat Baraner] will do. This business does not resemble anything like publishing a literary magazine with Suat [Derviş] Khanim in Babıali."[82] These dismissive remarks made by the young communist Halil in the late Vedat Türkali's recent novel *Trust* (*Güven*, 2015) represent the final judgment of successive generations on the fate of republican communism bound by literature. Critics of the TKP on both the right and the left sought to break the spell of literature on the party. Whereas those on the right objected to the TKP's use of literature as a "mask" to propagate banned communist ideas, for critics on the left the party's confinement to the "superfluous" domain of literature hindered its ability to mobilize large masses and to contribute something original to Marxism-Leninism.[83]

Others have suggested that the TKP's limited activism during the 1930s and 1940s had a negative impact on the quality of its literary production. *Sources of Socialist Realism* (*Toplumcu Gerçekçiliğin Kaynakları*, 1986), for example, by the prominent literary critic Ahmet Oktay, is an influential comparative account of early republican Turkish literature and its relations with Soviet literatures.[84] Composed at least two decades before the recent transnational turn in Turkish literary criticism, Oktay's study was in many ways ahead of its time in its examination of modern Turkish literature beyond the conventional East–West paradigm. In limiting the scope of his study to socially committed literatures, however, Oktay can be said to have overlooked the thematic, formal, and modal heterogeneity of Turkish communist and formerly communist literature and to have relied on the conventional critical opposition of originality to belatedness that has long haunted Turkish literary criticism.[85] Ascribing a universality to the Russian socialist-realist novel and treating it as a measure of Turkish literary production, Oktay argued that modern Turkish literature produced authentic socialist realism only beginning in the 1950s. For Oktay, the "total dependence of Turkish socialist movement on the Soviet center," the writers' "inadequate" knowledge of canonical works of Marxism-Leninism, and "the absorption of Turkish leftist discourse by the official ideology" (specifically populism and peasantism) contributed to what he considered to be the belatedness and barrenness of the Turkish literary field from the mid-1920s through the 1940s.[86]

Challenging the derivative status assigned to Turkish communist and formerly communist literary production, *Writing in Red* argues that revolutionary entanglements between Kemalist Turkey and Soviet Russia produced an as yet understudied but extraordinarily rich literary archive that cannot be subordinated to the authority of the political discourses of Marxism and communism. As a whole, the works analyzed in this book represent the indeterminate and unpredictable variety of communication and translation that the *force* of the entangled Bolshevik and Anatolian Revolutions sparked across Eurasia. Considering the scope of the repression aimed at the TKP and the internal divisions, purges, and defections it produced, the works examined here cannot be described as a unified party literature.[87] Nor can they be described as an instantiation of what Steven S. Lee and Amelia Glaser have recently called the "Comintern aesthetics." This umbrella term aims "to remap world literature and culture from the perspective of world communism," though it has limited use in the Turkish case, for the Comintern would liquidate the TKP in 1937.[88] Including a wide range of neglected genres such as historical fiction and erotic comedy, the literary archive of the entangled revolutions cannot be examined through the lens of a singular genre or movement (modernist avant-garde or socialist realism).

Writing in Red argues that the works examined in this book, shaped by the experience of "magic pilgrimage" and occupying the foreclosed limit of Turkish national imaginary, embody the concrete universality of literary production across the Soviet republic of letters.[89] Works by Turkish communist and formerly communist writers do not represent national-particular examples of universal socialist form on the stage of Soviet literary international, nor are they derivative copies of Russian literary originality. Resisting or simply turning away from the singularity of each work, such "bourgeois" conceptions of literary production abstract from Soviet Russian texts a universalized or universalizable form or content and understand any given product of Turkish translation or adaptation as the reproduction of such essence. As such, these conceptions recapitulate the governing capitalist logic of the commodity form, which establishes the relation between the universal and the particular as a hierarchical relationship of essential identity.[90]

Against the chrono-logic of belatedness and the onto-logic of sameness in comparative methodology, it is useful to turn to Slavoj Žižek's dialectical conceptualization of the relation between the universal and the particular. "The difference," Žižek observes of this relation, "is not on the side of particular content (as the traditional *differentia specifica*), but on the side of the Universal."[91] Mobilizing this conceptualization in a Soviet context, we might understand the Bolshevik discourse on the "East" as marking the inherent internal difference of Marxist-Leninist universalism and the condition of possibility of its external global translation. The Bolshevik

Revolution, harboring self-excess in its universal address, necessarily spilled onto or was spilled into Turkey as one place among many, opening the literary cultures of Soviet Russia to translation, transformation, and further proliferation.[92] This dialectical image has a reverse implication of equal importance: the "deviant" production of Turkish literary space, distinguished as it is by the unique contemporaneity of its entangled revolutionary temporality, is not a mere appendage of the literary geography of the Soviet Union. Refusing the status of the exception (or pure particularity) within the Soviet republic of letters, the works by Nâzım, Vâlâ, and their comrades that I discuss here *claim* the universal in their concrete thematization of revolution. Registering the unfulfilled universal promise of the global moment of 1920 in their singularity across different periods, they displace the critical imagination of (pure) revolution from its home in the Soviet Russian literature of the period.

LITERARY ARCHAEOLOGY BETWEEN MIDDLE EASTERN AND SLAVIC AREA STUDIES, ACROSS DIVISIONS OF COMPARATIVE LITERATURE

"We are all post-Soviet"; "we are to understand this situation as our own," remarked Susan Buck-Morss in a 2008 essay, emphasizing the post-Soviet as "the universal historical condition" of early twenty-first-century scholarship and politics.[93] After the collapse of the Soviet Union and the opening of Soviet archives, a new wave of comparative scholarship emerged in both the United States and Turkey, challenging the way research boundaries had traditionally been drawn in Cold War area studies. Borrowing, broadly speaking, from the methodology of *histoire croisée*, studies by Adeeb Khalid, Michael A. Reynolds, James H. Meyer, Mustafa Tuna, and Lâle Can, among others, have offered valuable accounts of the transimperial cultural dynamics linking the Russian and Ottoman Empires during the nineteenth century.[94] A 2013 special dossier of the journal *Comparative Studies of South Asia, Africa, and the Middle East* titled "USSR South: Postcolonial Worlds in the Soviet Imaginary" extended the focus of this new transregional scholarship into the twentieth century, tracing "the ideals and realities of Soviet connections immediately southward, to Turkey, Iran, and Afghanistan" as well as to "the more distant South Asia and Africa."[95] Work by a new generation of historians, including Hirst's scholarship on

Turkish and Soviet diplomatic and cultural relations during the 1920s and 1930s and Meyer's new research on Turkish students at KUTV, represent new directions in Russian and Eurasian history.

In Turkey during the Cold War, the collection, anthologization, and publication of archival materials pertaining to the history of the Turkish Left were undertaken by a diverse group of individuals, including academic historians (Mete Tunçay and Erik Jan Zürcher), current and former members of the TKP (Kerim Sadi, Aclan Sayılgan, Kemal Sülker, and Rasih Nuri İleri), and anticommunist ideologues (Fethi Tevetoğlu and İlhan Darendelioğlu) working with limited institutional support (or with support from anticommunist foundations).[96] This process became more systematized with the establishment of the Social History Research Foundation of Turkey (Türkiye Sosyal Tarih Araştırma Vakfı, TÜSTAV) by the General Board of Directors of the United Communist Party of Turkey (Türkiye Birleşik Komünist Partisi) in 1992. TÜSTAV would become an important research center for the collection, preservation, digitization, transliteration, and translation of previously inaccessible archival materials. Through its collaboration with the International Institute of Social History in Amsterdam, which holds the Nâzım and Vâlâ papers, TÜSTAV microfilmed the TKP materials in the Comintern archive in the Russian State Archive of Social-Political History (Rossiiskii gosudarstvennyi arkhiv sotsial'no-politicheskoi istorii),[97] a project that supported the new historiographic scholarship of Emel Akal, Erden Akbulut, Hamit Erdem, Tunçay, and others on the Turkish War of Independence and early republican communism.

Writing in Red aims to supplement this new body of historiographic scholarship by examining what is simultaneously most "freely" available and most neglected in this archive. On the one hand, I say "freely" available because in contrast with the hidden and suppressed records of the TKP and the Comintern, all the literary works examined in this book appeared at least once in the public domain, albeit in censored (or self-censored) forms. They are the most neglected elements of this archive, on the other hand, because as fiction they are viewed as having limited use-value for the methodologies of social scientists and historians seeking either "theory" or empirical data in the archive.[98] In the case of *Life's Good, Brother*, because all the Turkish editions published in Turkey since 1967 have undergone significant alteration, the work cannot be studied without consulting Nâzım's typeset manuscript and the first and only uncensored Turkish book edition published in Sofia in 1964, along with the party writings recently published by TÜSTAV. A novel by Derviş, *Love Novels* (*Liubovnye romany*), has thus far appeared only in Russian translation, and before my own article published in the Turkish journal *Birikim* in 2021, this novel had never been closely studied in Turkish literary criticism.[99] (Because the original Turkish manuscript has never been located, İthaki Publishing House has recently commissioned a Turkish retranslation of *Liubovnye romany* based on the 1969 Russian translation by Radii Fish.) The encoded socialist-realist plot in Derviş's *Phosphorescent Cevriye*, meanwhile, can be adequately "deciphered" only by consulting relevant memoirs and court documents from the 1940s published by TÜSTAV. (One might add here that *Phosphorescent Cevriye* underwent another level of "secondary revision" in its popular film adaptations in 1959, 1969, and 1989, which effaced the novel's gendered social critique.)

Printed by the Adana Türksözü publishing house, Dino's play *Baldy* (1944) was confiscated by the police shortly after its publication and not republished until 1996. Nizamettin's *Kara Davud*, meanwhile, first published in Ottoman Turkish script, represents another example of loss as the "catastrophic success" of the alphabet reform in 1928 and Nizamettin's rejection of his communist past encouraged historical amnesia about this novel's conditions of emergence in the Ankara communist movement.[100] In working through this scattered literary archive, subject as it is to effacement, loss, (self-)censorship, secondary revision, disavowal, and dispersion, *Writing in Red* simultaneously draws on and aims to supplement the new historiographic scholarship by Hirst, Akal, Erbulut, and others. If our present historical moment permits reconnecting these literary works to the transnational context from which they were often severed, it also represents an opportunity to reject the ancillary status of literary texts in much area studies scholarship. Literature as a license to fiction recorded and questioned in its own ways the fundamentals of the Kemalist and Soviet epistemes, and *Writing in Red* argues that the literary limits of the archive that is its subject cannot be abstracted away.

As such, the book supplements the work of the critics Anna Krakus and Cristina Vatulescu, who have called for a new mode of engagement with communist archives. Drawing on their search for the Michel Foucault files in the secret archives of the Eastern Bloc, Krakus and Vatulescu have convincingly argued that the study of communist state archives cannot be limited merely to "the said" or to "truth effects" but must also address gaps, rumors, "silences, stutters, interruptions, and redactions" that structure what they call the "archives of the sayable, the unsayable, and the unsaid."[101] Expanding their work and adapting it to anticommunist contexts, we might describe communist literature itself as another "limit of enunciability" and archive of "the said-otherwise," affirming "literary archaeology" as another method of reading "along the archival grain."[102] In the Turkish case, as *Writing in Red* demonstrates, the practice of literary archaeology requires attentiveness not only to the said otherwise, the unsaid, the sayable, and the unsayable in Russian, Turkish, and other languages but also to the complexity of material encodements imagined by revolutionaries. In activating a plurilingual, historically grounded, theoretically informed close reading practice, the censored and encoded literary works examined in this book productively interrupt our "postcritical" present, which abdicates the responsibility to read.

If one goal of the book is to establish the importance of modern Turkish literature to area studies scholarship, its other goal is to open new directions in Turkish, Slavic, and comparative literary studies. Thus far, the archival revolution that emerged in the aftermath of the Cold War has had little discernible effect on Turkish literary criticism. Responding to the complex dynamics of Turkish modernization, on one hand, and to the repressive circumstances of Cold War anticommunism, on the other, scholars in Turkish studies have focused on the discursive transformation of modern Turkish literature in relation to European literary and linguistic practices.[103] Displacing the Europocentrism that shaped the field, however, recent scholarship by Jale Parla, Hülya Adak, Laurent Mignon, Fatih Altuğ, Mehmet Fatih Uslu, and Ceyhun Arslan, among others, has begun to explore the emergence of modern Turkish literature in relation to Armenian, Greek, Kurdish, Judeo-Spanish, and Arabic languages and literatures.[104] Although this new "postnational," "post-Kemalist" scholarship represents an important transnational turn in the field, none of it deals comprehensively with Turkish and Soviet literary relations.[105]

Challenging theories of world literature that have failed to respond to the post-Soviet epistemic condition, a new body of scholarship in Slavic studies has productively intervened into contemporary critical debates in two crucial ways. One approach has focused on the Soviet imagination of world literature (*vsemirnaia literatura*) by examining domestic Soviet translational practices and institutions, while another expands the literary geography of revolution by looking beyond the Soviet Union.[106] Recent scholarship by Rossen Djagalov, Katerina Clark, Steven Lee, and Amelia Glaser, among others, has explored the consolidation of a Eurasian literary international or a Soviet republic of letters extending from Europe to China during the Comintern years of 1919 and 1943. Although this work has expanded our understanding of "Comintern aesthetics" considerably, it meets its limit wherever it subordinates the contributions by Eastern "intermediaries" to the history of the Comintern. In contrast, treating the Comintern as only one of many determinants shaping communist and formerly communist literary production across Eurasia, *Writing in Red* aims to shift some of the parameters of this new scholarship in Slavic and comparative literary studies.

Throughout this book, I employ the concept of a "Soviet republic of letters," occasionally in a way that makes it equivalent to the term *literary international*.[107] My account reveals that the mediators of this common literary culture were not only such institutions as the International Union of Revolutionary Writers (commonly referred to by its Russian acronym MORP, for Mezhdunarodnoe ob"edinenie revoliutsionnykh pisatelei), the Writers' Association for the Defense of Culture, or other official actors such as VOKS or the Turkish state. Offering a bottom-up instead of a top-down account of a transnational Soviet republic of letters, *Writing in Red* imagines the latter as a liminal literary space or boundary space formed by writers on the run who responded to the diverse aesthetic and political demands of institutions that straddled the Turkish and Soviet border, including the TKP, the Comintern, Soviet domestic and international literary institutions, and the Kemalist government. Where scholarship in Slavic studies treats the translative and adaptive writings of Eastern intermediaries as local particularity,[108] this book takes Eastern writers' points of view as its vantage points, describing their imagination of revolution as a (singular) universal at the limit of life, the socius, the symbolic order, and the Kemalist and Soviet epistemes. The chapters that follow this introduction argue that in the work of Vâlâ this limit is imagined specifically as radical sexual deterritorialization, in the work of Derviş as a communist ethics of the act, in the work of Dino as an encounter with the absolute subjectivity of the dispossessed rural subaltern, and in the work of Nâzım as the endless seriality of communist eventfulness. *Writing in Red* argues that a comprehensive history of the literary international requires an account of this other imagination of the universal in the periphery.

MARXIAN FORM IN THE PERIPHERY AND ON THE EAST-WEST DIVIDE

In exploring neglected questions of Marxian form in the 1940s, *Writing in Red* also aims to suggest new directions for transnational modernist studies and the study of peripheral realisms. In its emphasis on questions of institutional history and literary circulation, recent scholarship on Soviet world literature has encouraged a shift of attention away from questions of poetics and aesthetic form.[109] Resisting this tendency and setting aside the canonical referentiality of the works of Lukács, Bertolt Brecht, Theodor Adorno, and Mikhail Bakhtin, *Writing in Red* describes the writings of Dino, Derviş, and Nâzım as another "origin" of Marxist aesthetics.

Moving from generically diverse representations of the entangled revolutions to socialist-realist novels, the book's division into two parts echoes a conventional narrative in Soviet literary historiography that imagines a coalescence of the literary diversity of the 1920s in the totalizing unity of the 1930s and 1940s. In its structure, *Writing in Red* suggests that by the late 1930s the consolidation of what Hans Günther has called the "strong canon" of Soviet socialist realism had decisive effects beyond Soviet borders—though this impact by no means suggests a freezing of literary creativity in Turkey.[110] Derviş's "dialectical image" of the positive hero, Dino's formalist aesthetic of estrangement, and Nâzım's prose poetics of seriality suggest that despite these authors' unequivocal commitment to realism, their socialist-realist writing also invested in modernist transgression. Neither escape from dogmatic socialist realism nor (as Boris Groys has argued, in the Soviet case)[111] a coalescence of socialist realism with modernism, the modernist deviations of Turkish communist writers should be understood in the context of the concrete struggles in which they were embedded. As *Writing in Red* shows, Turkish communist writers pursued a distinct project of "aesthetic education," which should be distinguished from other educational projects of the period, including Auerbachian philological humanism and the Village Institutes (Köy Enstitüleri) in Turkey.[112] For Nâzım, Derviş, and Dino, the translation of

Marxist-Leninist concepts into (subaltern) orality required the interweaving of formalist-modernist and socialist-realist aesthetic sensibilities. Refusing to mobilize modernism and realism as abstract categories of literary periodization or as unmediated reflective categories of combined and uneven development, *Writing in Red* argues that the history of twentieth-century peripheral realisms and modernisms must take into consideration the literary and linguistic mediation of these terms in specific historical contexts.[113] In this respect, it serves as a useful corrective to recent scholarship that treats modernism and realism as purely ideological terms of the Cold War's aesthetic front and thus effaces the agency and concrete struggles of non-European writers.

Though Robert J. C. Young's pioneering book *Postcolonialism* (2001) has emphasized the significance of the dissolution of so-called traditional empires in the aftermath of the First World War, scholarship in postcolonial studies has, generally speaking, neglected "the explosion of 1914 and its severe consequences" across Eurasia.[114] The recent North–South realignment in postcolonial studies has further reinforced the field's deep-rooted Anglo- and Franco-centrism. Focusing primarily on the Afro-Asian Writers' Bureau, new scholarship by Djagalov, Lydia Liu, and Monica Popescu has productively displaced the field's East–West divide in their examination of literary and cinematic encounters between Soviet and Third World writers during the Cold War era.[115] In tracing the early exilic itineraries of Turkish writers, some of whom would go on to be involved with the Afro-Asian writers' movement, *Writing in Red* aims to offer a historiographic prequel to this new scholarship focused on the Cold War. For the writers described here whose work was initially repressed, then republished in the 1960s, or in some cases published for the first time in the 1960s, that decade represented not a new beginning as much as a foreclosed future in the past.

The long history of the "dual revolution" offered in this book shows that the history of Soviet anti-imperialism, including the "Soviet invention of postcolonial studies," cannot be understood without addressing its entanglements with Turkey.[116] Emerging from the Ottoman imperial core as one of the earliest independent "Eastern" states (along with Iran, Afghanistan, Thailand, and China in Asia as well as Abyssinia and Liberia in Africa) in the shadow of the First Congress of the Peoples of the East in 1920, republican Turkey would follow its own Kemalist program of self-colonization and racial universalism that differed from the postcolonial humanisms embraced by such leading thinkers as W. E. B. Du Bois, Mahatma Gandhi, and Frantz Fanon. The multiple historical temporalities of twentieth-century Turkey justify its description as a postimperial state, a formerly occupied semicolony, and an oppressive nation-state with respect to its Kurdish citizens, all at the same time. *Writing in Red* argues that despite and with these crucial differences, a study of the unfulfilled promise of the entangled Anatolian and Bolshevik Revolutions may serve as a useful historical and geographic link across postcolonial studies' internal divisions. Embodying a neglected history of decolonization after the Second World War, the literatures of the entangled revolutions imagine another political sovereignty, sexual order, aesthetic education, and revolutionary temporality both in Turkey and beyond the Soviet republic of letters.

PART I
Genres of Entangled Revolutions

Chapter One

THE TURKISH WAR OF INDEPENDENCE IN LITERATURE AND FILM

Limits of Marxist-Leninist Nationalism and Legacies for the Postcolonial Era

Scholarship in comparative literary studies has emphasized the "travel" of the Soviet avant-garde as an important mode of literary exchange during the interwar period. Although this book recognizes the importance of this development, it is focused on another, less emphasized dynamic of transnational literary culture: the production of historical fiction and film about the Turkish War of Independence. The main focus of this chapter is the work of Turkish communist and formerly communist writers, but it is important to remember that Soviet writers and filmmakers thematized the history of the entangled Anatolian and Bolshevik Revolutions by using conventions of the Soviet "Eastern" genre developed during the 1920s. Challenging the representation of an exotically timeless Orient in the Western novel, Soviet Eastern films aimed to represent an authentic, historically dynamic "East for the East" in their depiction of Soviet Muslim borderlands and the "foreign East" beyond.[1]

In December 1932, with Turkish and Soviet official exchange at its peak, the screenwriter Natan A. Zarkhi (1900–1935) arrived in Turkey for a month's worth of preliminary research for an Eastern film about the Turkish War of Independence to be produced in collaboration with Sergei I. Yutkevich (1904–1985). In a press conference held shortly after his arrival, Zarkhi went out of his way to distinguish himself from European Orientalists, including Pierre Loti and Claude Farrère, who had "perceived and represented Turkey as a land of fairy tales, a décor."² Remarking on the close spiritual bond between Turks and Russians, he emphasized his commitment to produce an authentic film about the revolutionary war of the Turkish people. Accompanied by the prominent Turkish writer Reşat Nuri, he enumerated sites in Istanbul and western Anatolian towns and battlefield locations where he intended to interview villagers. (Reportedly, during one such interview with an elderly peasant in Bursa, Zarkhi was so impressed by the man's "amazing simplicity of expression and deep foundation of knowledge and culture" that he asked Reşat Nuri to stop translating. Zarkhi reportedly said: "Even if you did not translate, I could almost understand him and follow the events.")³

Little trace of this experience of intimacy and immediacy can be found in the screenplay Zarkhi wrote with Yutkevich, however, which indulged in constrained and indeed stereotypical representation of Anatolian peasants. Titled "The Man Who Did Not Kill" ("Chelovek, kotoryi ne ubil" or, in Turkish, "Katletmiyen Adam"), it might best be described as an ironic rewriting of *L'homme qui assassina*, Farrère's colonial novel of 1906–1907 set in Constantinople.⁴ Narrating the adventures of a Turcophile French colonel of noble birth, Farrère's novel describes the colonel's murder of the British director of the Ottoman Public Debt Administration in revenge for the economic exploitation of the Ottomans. Articulating a conservative critique of European imperialism and finance capital from the perspective of a displaced (and both aging and feminized) French nobleman, Farrère's novel represents the destructive effects of European imperialism on the colonial class itself.

Purporting to reject "the exoticism, salacity, and cruelty of lifestyles, worldviews, characters, and relationships" in Farrère's novel, Zarkhi and Yutkevich saw themselves as portraying "an unfamiliar, little known Orient [*Vostok*] that is authentic [*podlinnyi*] and not mythologized."⁵ Divided into fifteen episodes, "The Man Who Did Not Kill" spanned the period from the outbreak of the First World War through the Allied occupation of Izmir and Istanbul to the Turkish War of Independence, concluding with an epilogue about the tenth-anniversary celebration in 1933 of the foundation of the Turkish Republic.⁶ Grafting the genre conventions of European colonial novel onto those of a Soviet Eastern in contravention of Zarkhi and Yutkevich's own stated goals, the screenplay traced the transformation of the "superwesternized" young Turkish protagonist Khikmet from a hapless, naive supporter of Ottoman westernization into an anti-imperialist nationalist. In the opening scenes, set on the eve of the First World War, Khikmet is portrayed as a Turkish national in European clothing, blinded by his love for the daughter of the Russian ambassador and ashamed of his poor Anatolian peasant family.

Conscripted to fight in Syria in Mustafa Kemal's own unit during the war, Khikmet witnesses the occupation of Smyrna in 1919, gradually "awakening" to the struggle for national independence. With the help of Broveri, a European friend from the prewar years, he procures arms from Bolshevik Russia for the national resistance (though not without realizing that Broveri's real goal is to transfer the weapons to the Greeks instead). Surviving Broveri's attempt to murder him, Khikmet forges an alliance with the Russian Bolshevik worker Mikhail Bul'gin, operating in Baku, who provides rifles seized from Europeans in the Caucasus. With Bul'gin's reappearance in the epilogue, now a consulting engineer for the tenth-anniversary celebration, the screenplay suggests that Turkish national self-determination and republican modernization would not have been possible without the support of Soviet Russia. In this respect, "The Man Who Did Not Kill" might be described as what Michael G. Smith has called a "historical-revolutionary" film, a type of Soviet Eastern depicting the achievement of revolutionary consciousness by the "backward nationalities of the East" under the guidance of Russian Bolshevik mentors.[7]

Though "The Man Who Did Not Kill" was initially approved for production, it was never filmed, mainly because of the Turkish side's reservations about the "excessive 'revolutionism' of its plot."[8] This failed outcome is in many ways unsurprising: Mustafa Kemal, who would rather forget the early history of Bolshevik financial, diplomatic, and military aid, had already established the official account of the Turkish War of Independence in his thirty-six-hour *Great Speech* (*Nutuk*), delivered from October 15 to October 20 in 1927 and later translated into Russian under the title *The Path of New Turkey* (*Put' novoi Turtsii, 1919–1927*).[9] Representing himself as the embodiment of the national will, Mustafa Kemal barely mentioned the history of Anatolian communisms or the early alliance with Bolshevik Russia. Drawing inspiration from the epilogue of "The Man Who Did Not Kill," Yutkevich and Leo O. Arnshtam filmed the Soviet delegation's visit to Turkey in October 1933 for the tenth-anniversary celebration of the Turkish Republic, receiving approval to make the documentary *Ankara—the Heart of Turkey* (*Ankara—Serdtse Turtsii* or, in Turkish, *Türkiye'nin Kalbi Ankara*) in collaboration with Turkish musicians, actors, and statesman.[10] Celebrating a Kemalist order of national appearances, *Ankara* contrasted images of the Turkish countryside including donkeys, camels, and sheep (representing "old Turkey") with images of the new schools, hospitals, factories, and museums built in Ankara during the early republican era.

Contemporary critics regard the successful collaborative production of *Ankara* as a turning point in the history of Turkish and Soviet official convergence. I begin this chapter with the unfinished project of "The Man Who Did Not Kill" because it is an important artistic record of Soviet discourse on the Turkish War of Independence dating to the 1920s. Building on V. I. Lenin's prewar analysis of Ottoman Turkey, Iran, and China as "semicolonies," in the aftermath of the First World War Lenin and other Bolshevik representatives would extend the concept of "the oppressed nation" (*ugnetennaia natsiia*) to partitioned Turkey.[11] In the words of the diplomat Semen Aralov, who lived in Ankara from January 1922 to April 1923, the War of Independence was carried to victory by Soviet support and as such could be located in "a ring of Leninist national politics [of self-determination] that opposed colonial enslavement and fought for the liberation of peoples from the yoke of imperialist oppression."[12] The Fourth Congress of the Communist International in 1922 would salute the workers and peasants of Turkey for "having provided to the entire subjugated East and to all colonial countries the living example of a revolutionary independence movement."[13] In an article titled "The Turkish Victory," published on October 17, 1922, the influential Indian Marxist M. N. Roy remarked: "That not only entire Asia Minor, but a part of Thrace also, will be Turkish, [and] that an Oriental nation has vindicated its ability to challenge successfully the right of European Imperialism to condemn it to perpetual slavery, are in themselves a great inspiration to all the subject peoples."[14] While prominent Comintern representatives and Soviet historians, including "B. Ferdi" (an alias used by the TKP leader Şefik Hüsnü), Ilan Butayev, and Mikhail Godes, would recognize by the mid-1920s that Turkey would follow a capitalist path, in the newly established journals of Marxist-Leninist Oriental studies (Vostokovedenie) the "national revolution" in Turkey was abstracted as a comparative model for the discussion of developments in Persia and China.[15] Although "The Man Who Did not Kill" borrowed elements from Soviet Easterns about the domestic East, it diverged from them insofar as it registered this comparative discourse on Turkey, which imagined the War of Independence as a watershed in the fight against European imperialism across the "foreign East" (*zarubezhnyi Vostok*).[16]

In emphasizing the value of Zarkhi's screenplay in relation to a Soviet discourse on Kemalism, I do not mean to suggest that Marxist-Leninist Orientology was capable of providing an accurate account of the epistemic and historical conditions of Ottoman imperial sovereignty and of the mobilization for war in Anatolia. Rather, I argue that this body of work, despite and against its very real constraints, which include crude historical schematism and plain old Orientalist bias, presents us with a neglected dynamic in Soviet anti-imperialist discourse. Challenging both the Anglocentrism and the Francocentrism of scholarship in postcolonial studies, Rossen Djagalov has valuably examined the continuities of Soviet with Third World literary engagements of the interwar and post–Second World War periods. In Djagalov's account, the leftist proletarian novels and antifascist writings of interwar Asian and Latin American writers who entered the Soviet republic of letters via KUTV and MORP made a real contribution to a literary international. "Sacrificed to the realpolitik of the Popular Front . . . and the primacy of the European theatre in the run-up to the Second World War," the (post)colonial world would "fade from the geopolitical and literary engagements of the Soviet state" between the mid-1930s and the mid-1950s, reemerging as a priority after the Bandung Conference and "inaugurating the second phase of the Soviet–Third World engagements, their Cold War peak (mid-1950s to the 1980s)."[17]

This chapter aims to amplify this groundbreaking scholarship by emphasizing the significance of Turkey as a missing link in the literary historiography of the Soviet republic of letters. During the late 1920s and 1930s, with Soviet anti-imperialism apparently sacrificed for a politics of the Popular Front, writers and filmmakers across the Turkish and Soviet border engaged the history of Turkish "national liberation," generating a precedent for the Marxist-Leninist national literatures of the post–Second World War era. The literary and artistic contributions responding to the Turkish War of Independence included not only the official engagements represented by Zarkhi and Yutkevich but also unofficial ones embodied by Nizamettin Nazif and Nâzım Hikmet, which are the main focus in this chapter.

As I suggested in the introduction, the late 1920s and early 1930s represent the first moment of intensified communist literary exchange and translation in Turkey. In contrast with the second moment of the 1940s, this earlier moment was marked by intersections between official and unofficial channels of exchange. Scholars have conventionally understood Nâzım's involvement with the *Illustrated Monthly* (*Resimli Ay*) magazine in 1929 as a key moment in the dissemination of a Marxist-Leninist avant-garde. This chapter directs our attention to an earlier moment of popularization of historical fiction by the formerly communist Nizamettin Nazif. Despite leaving the TKP in 1925, Nizamettin and Vâlâ Nureddin (discussed in the next chapter) left important literary records of the entangled Anatolian and Bolshevik Revolutions.

In the first section of this chapter, a close reading of Nizamettin's serialized novel *Kara Davud* (1927–1930), I argue that this neglected novel is the earliest Marxist-Leninist literary representation of the Anatolian Revolution as overthrowing an "Asiatic despot." Nizamettin's novel is rarely studied in the context of its author's involvement with the Ankara communist movement during the War of Independence. In a period in which both Soviet and Kemalist so-called Easterns depicted an Anatolia locked in an undifferentiated primitive state of nature, *Kara Davud* recorded the ethnoreligious and regional diversity of subaltern populations across Anatolia, refusing to calcify their difference as something uncanny (*unheimlich*).

Subsequently, turning to Nâzım's *Epic of National Liberation Movement* (*Milli Kurtuluş Hareketi Destanı*), composed in the Istanbul Sultanahmet, Çankırı, and Bursa prisons between 1939 and 1941, I suggest that Turkish communist writers refused to set aside anti-imperialist national liberation during the Second World War years. Like *Kara Davud*, Nâzım's *Epic of National Liberation Movement* intervened into both elitist Kemalist historiography and Soviet Orientology in his representation of the collective revolutionary agency of the Anatolian peoples, while encountering its limit in its refusal to engage with the "social" grammars of Islam across Anatolia. Tracing the promises and contradictions of the literary representation of the War of Independence across these different periods, I argue that work by Turkish communist and formerly communist writers represents an important temporal, literary, and discursive link between the interwar and postcolonial histories of Soviet and Third World engagements.[18]

Nizamettin and Nâzım seem to have haunted the official pathways of Turkish and Soviet exchange embodied by Zarkhi and Yutkevich. Khikmet, the protagonist of "The Man Who Did Not Kill," bears a name that may be an allusion to Nâzım and perhaps also to another influential Turkish communist, Hikmet Kıvılcımlı. In an essay describing the filming of *Ankara*, Yutkevich remarked that images of the Golden Horne and the Sultanahmet House of Detention were intended as references to "the great poet and our friend Nazım Khikmet, who was incarcerated there in those years."[19] Nizamettin, a less well-known former communist as well as journalist, novelist, and screenwriter, was mentioned in Zarkhi's interview for the journal *Kino* in January 1933, following his return from Turkey. Discussing the Turkish film *A Nation Awakens* (*Bir Millet Uyanıyor*, 1932), a celebration of national independence directed by the influential Turkish playwright and film director Muhsin Ertuğrul, who had worked in Ukraine, Zarkhi suggested that Nizamettin was the author of the "weak" and disorganized screenplay.[20] Zarkhi seemed to know little about Nizamettin's communist past and earlier writings shaped by his experience of "Russia in Ankara." A comparative reading of Nizamettin's and Nâzım's transversal literary itineraries, I suggest, not only supplies a deeper understanding of an earlier moment of communist translation and exchange but also introduces new critical questions about the articulation of secular nationalism with Marxism-Leninism that have implications for the postcolonial literatures of the Cold War era.

NIZAMETTIN NAZIF'S HISTORICAL FICTION: CRITIQUE OF FETISHISM OF THE DESPOT

Born in 1901 into an elite Ottoman family, Nizamettin was a descendant of Tepedelenli Ali Pasha (1744?–1822), the Ottoman governor of the northern mainland of Greece.[21] Raised in the Ottoman Balkan cities of Kavala, Drama, and Salonica, he first met Nâzım at the Heybeliada Navy War Academy in Istanbul, where the two studied together. Forced to give up his naval career because of poor health, he became a journalist during the First World War. When Istanbul was occupied by Allied troops, Nizamettin traveled to Ankara to join the national resistance, working at the editorial office of *National Sovereignty* (*Hakimiyet-i Milliye*), the Ankara government's official newspaper.

Radicalized by the red tide of the summer of 1920 in Anatolia, he became a writer for the "Islamic Bolshevik [İslami Bolşevik] newspaper" *New World* (*Yeni Dünya*). Founded in Eskişehir in August 1920 by members of the Green Army, *New World* was published under the patronage of Ethem the Circassian, the powerful leader of an irregular militia unit that suppressed armed resistance to the Ankara government organized by the sultan's supporters. Moved to Ankara in the fall of 1920, the newspaper briefly became the publication organ of Mustafa Kemal's official Communist Party, though not all of its editorial staff remained loyal to Kemal. When Ethem the Circassian rebelled against the Ankara government in December 1920, Nizamettin printed a declaration using the *New World* publishing house, calling on railroad workers to strike and impede the mobilization of government troops. He triggered a diplomatic crisis between Turkey and Soviet Russia when he took refuge in the Soviet embassy in Ankara,[22] and the Soviet representative Y. Y. Upmal, accused by Mustafa Kemal of supporting Turkish communists, was forced to vacate his post.[23] Tried in May 1921 with other members of the People's Communist Party of Turkey (Türkiye Halk İştirakiyun Fırkası, THIF) and sentenced to eight years in prison in Diyarbakır, Nizamettin traveled to southeastern Turkey on foot with guards who verbally abused and beat him.[24] Nizamettin's forced march, an experience that shaped his composition of *Kara Davud*, brought him into contact with the Kurdish and Alevi populations of southeastern Anatolia.

Eager to improve relations with Soviet Russia, the Ankara government in September 1921 released Nizamettin and other members of the THIF under a special amnesty. Nizamettin joined the reassembled THIF in Ankara in the spring of 1922, writing for its weekly paper, *New Life* (*Yeni Hayat*).[25] In a declaration addressed to the Turkish National Assembly in April 1922, the party reiterated its unequivocal support for the national forces fighting imperialist armies. Emphasizing the sacrifices of Turkish peasants, it asked the Ankara government to plan postindependence measures in taxation, land distribution, and administration to benefit them.[26] Identifying itself as a Marxist newspaper in its inaugural editorial, *New Life* described the war in Anatolia as a result of the antagonism of "productive forces [*kuva-yı istihsâliye*]" and "relations of production [*münasebât-ı istihsâliye*]." Extending Lenin's analysis, the editorial collective argued that the overdevelopment of productive forces in Europe and America had produced crisis in the West, which drove the occupation and colonization of the East. "National revolutions in the East," as they put it, were a "necessary result" of this development and should be understood as "a judgment of history [tarihin bir hükmüdür]."[27]

Along with editorializing about current events, *New Life* printed poems by Nâzım Hikmet from Moscow and serialized translations of excerpts from foundational Marxist-Leninist works, including Aleksandra Kollontai's "Prostitution and Ways of Fighting It," Friedrich Engels's *The Principles of Communism*, and Nikolai Bukharin's and E. A. Preobrazhensky's *The ABC of Communism*. Ali Nâzım (Resmor), a former member of the Green Army Association and former representative of Tokat in the Ankara Assembly, emerged as an influential leader in the THIF, attempting to establish an alliance between THIF and Populist Group members in the Assembly. Addressing a broad readership, his essays in *New Life* provided an epistemic translation of key concepts of communism into Anatolian Islam. For example, in an essay examining the different uses of the term *Hak* (right; God) in Turkish, Ali Nâzım sought to explain the party's fight for economic justice by recourse to Islamic genealogy.[28] Nizamettin, meanwhile, who was identified as "editor" (*başmuharrir*) of the twentieth issue, criticized in his essays the Romantic elite representation of Anatolia as a mythical land with "heavenlike forests," "green meadows," and "jade pastures."[29] Admitting that he had only recently awoken from such a dream, he described Anatolia as a land of deep poverty and oppression, which "poisons and kills all pleasure and aesthetic sensations."[30] In another essay composed on the eve of the abolition of the sultanate in November 1922, he celebrated the demise of this "bloodsucking" institution, which had received forceful "blows [*darbeleme*]" from the people "every day for three years."[31] These essays in *New Life* should be understood as important precursors to *Kara Davud*, articulating a Marxian critique of the Ottoman sultan Mehmed II through a mapping of Anatolian terrain.

Nizamettin served as translator for the German and French Comintern representatives who attended the second session of the THIF's first secret congress, convened in the Soviet embassy in August 1922. According to the German attendees Leonid and Friedrich, the party members considered the peasant majority "enslaved [*befangen*] by the religious ideas of Islam and by patriarchal mores" as the principal force to be mobilized in

Turkey and agreed to begin their work with peasants, artisans, and the proletariat only after the victory of Kemalist forces over imperialism.[32] Following the decisive victory of the Kemalists over the Greeks, the Ankara government closed the THIF in the fall of 1922, an event marking the end of Ankara-based communist activism, given that the TKP would be led by the Istanbul cadre throughout the republican period. When news of the crackdown reached the Fourth Congress of the Third Communist International, convened in Moscow in November 1922 to articulate a united front against imperialism and recommend strategies and tactics for the communist parties in the East, the congress denounced the Ankara government's actions while reiterating support for national liberation movements as a necessary first stage of revolution in the East.[33] Nizamettin, who had traveled via Sevastopol to Moscow in a Russian submarine in October 1922, escaped the wave of arrests. After attending the Congress of the Young Communist International in December 1922, he briefly enrolled at KUTV, returning to Turkey in the spring of 1923 and attempting to form a communist group in Izmir the following year.[34] Arrested during the crackdown in the spring of 1925, Nizamettin left the TKP after his release in August and worked as a journalist and novelist until his death in 1970.[35]

Because this history is mostly absent from the small body of scholarship on Nizamettin's life and work, I have assembled his itinerary from a variety of sources. I suggest that *Kara Davud*, his understudied first novel, is a unique literary record of the Ankara communist movement that maintained close ties with "Russia in Ankara" in the early 1920s. Nizamettin himself fostered amnesia about the historical origins of this novel by obscuring his communist period in his later work.[36] In an article in 1965, for example, he described the communist parties of the early 1920s as mere "political instruments [*vasıtalar*], which were a necessity of the general structure of the War of Independence in Anatolia."[37] The development of historical fiction as a genre in Turkey, which occurred under the strong influence of the political Right, doubtless also encouraged the neglect of this novel in Turkish literary criticism. Flourishing at the turn of the twentieth century through the translation of influential works by Léon Cahun and other European Orientalist Turcologists, historical fiction had become the preferred genre of Turkish anticommunist writers, including Abdullah

Ziya (Kozanoğlu) and Nihal Atsız, who imagined the "genesis" of ancient Turks in central Asia.³⁸ In rejecting this paradigm and its capture by the political right, the novels by Nizamettin and Vâlâ examined in this chapter and the next provide us with a genealogy of greater complexity.

Where Marxist-Leninist thought had shaped Nizamettin's representation of Ottoman history in *Kara Davud*, the swashbuckling series *Les Pardaillan* by the French anarchist Michel Zévaco was one model of its literary form.³⁹ This popular series, which narrated the heroic adventures of the knight-errant Pardaillan in sixteenth-century Europe, was first serialized in France in 1902, was translated into Ottoman Turkish during the 1910s, and enjoys a devoted readership in Turkey to this day. Describing his childhood fascination with Pardaillan, whom he called "my master," Jean-Paul Sartre observed that Zévaco's "republican cloak-and-dagger" novels set in the early modern era "predicted . . . the French revolution," representing the defiance of the people against "wicked" monarchs. "Firmly planted on my spindly legs," Sartre wrote, "I slapped Henry III and Louis XIII dozens of times in imitation of [Pardaillan]."⁴⁰

Serialized in the prominent daily *Time* (*Vakit*) from August 1927 to August 1928 and accompanied by black-and-white illustrations possibly produced by the young caricature artist Abidin Dino, *Kara Davud* transposed the world of the Ottoman fifteenth century into the representational schema of European historical romance, blending it with elements of Turkish epic storytelling, modern ethnographic writing, and Marxist-Leninist Easterns.⁴¹ After its publication as a two-volume book printed in Ottoman Turkish script in 1928, a third volume appeared in 1930 printed in the Latin alphabet.⁴² This multivolume bestseller, approximately a thousand book pages in total, included several quite controversial pages depicting the rebel protagonist Kara Davud slapping the Ottoman sultan, Mehmed II, at an audience including other statesmen.⁴³ Deemed both offensive and unrealistic, this episode sparked public outrage, spurring the *Vakit* editorial board to issue an apology emphasizing the novel's fictional character.⁴⁴ Defending the novel against its critics, the influential poet and critic Ahmet Haşim praised it as "baloney literature [*palavra edebiyatı*]" that he had read from cover to cover in a single night.⁴⁵ In a review of the abridged edition published in the Latin alphabet in 1929 by Resimli Ay Publishing, meanwhile, Nâzım rejected this characterization, describing *Kara Davud* as a "roman à thèse," with profound implications for the republican historical present.[46]

Spanning the three years from 1450 to the Ottoman conquest of Constantinople in 1453, *Kara Davud* narrates the adventures of the eponymous fictional rebel and his companion, Kara Duman (Dark Smoke), who travel from the territory of the Byzantine Empire to the Turco-Muslim principalities in central and southeastern Anatolia. Drawing its narrative momentum from the theme of border relations (what Franco Moretti calls "the on/off switch of the historical novel"[47]), *Kara Davud* describes a moment when Anatolia was divided among various Turco-Muslim principalities, with pockets of Byzantine and Pontic Greek rule on the Marmara and Black Sea coasts.[48] Strong Turco-Muslim principalities—including the Karamanids in central Anatolia, the Isfendiyarids in the North, and the Dulkadirids in Maraş in the Southeast—maintained their autonomy by forging alliances both with and against the Ottomans in western Anatolia. In fact, the novel suggests that Mehmed II's alliance with other Turco-Muslim rulers was indispensable to the conquest of Constantinople as "the definitive establishment of the Ottoman Empire."[49] One might suggest that in describing the development of these marital and military alliances, Nizamettin's novel thematizes the consolidation of the Ottoman state as what Gilles Deleuze and Félix Guattari, via the work of Marx, call a "despotic state machine." As Deleuze and Guattari have it, the despotic state overcodes the primitive territorial machine, subordinating the old system of extended filiations and lateral alliances to a new hierarchical order. The new imperial bureaucratic state thus legitimizes itself by linking the people to the despot (and to the clan's deity via the despot) in direct filiation.[50]

Though Davud's birth mother and father are descendants of the ruling families of the neighboring Koçhisar and Isfendiyarid principalities, respectively, Davud is unaware of his "noble" origin because his maternal clan were destroyed by the paternal Isfendiyarids shortly after his birth. Raised by an adoptive father who was chieftain of a small underground clan in western Anatolia, Davud is an undefeated warrior who refuses to submit to any Muslim or Christian rule. He forges an alliance with benevolent Turco-Muslim rulers, including the Karamanid Ibrahim and the

Dulkadir Kılıç Arslan. In a world of unstable border relations, a warrior of unknown origin can claim equality with other sovereigns only after entering into a death struggle with them, then sparing their lives. Having defeated the Ottoman ruler in a sword fight,[51] Kara Davud then assists him in the conquest of Constantinople, his strong antipathy notwithstanding. It is in this way that Kara Davud becomes the first Turkish soldier to enter the city as the siege becomes a victory.

Kara Davud grafts the motifs of Turko-Muslim epic storytelling, such as the secret underground palace where Davud is raised, onto those of swashbuckling historical romance, turning history "into a series of moral lessons for the present."[52] Idealizing the benevolent Davud, "who possesses nothing, nothing," the novel ridicules and negates the cruel sultan Mehmed II as an Oriental despot. Whereas the itinerant Davud, who "wanders in mountains and sleeps in forests," takes on "the duty of helping the poor and victims of injustice," the Ottoman sultan is an arbitrary ruler who tortures his subjects for minor offenses and orders the gratuitous pillaging of Constantinople upon its surrender.[53] The first printed edition included a re-creation of the Italian painter Gentile Bellini's well-known portrait of the Ottoman sultan in 1480, portraying Mehmed II with a comically exaggerated malevolent expression.[54] It is no surprise, then, that critics have suggested that Nizamettin's novel reproduced an official republican discourse of rupture with the Ottoman past.[55] Although we can recognize this ideological congruence with official Kemalist historiography, it must also be understood that Nizamettin's critique of the Ottoman past drew on Marx's imagination of the Asiatic ruler in precapitalist social formations.

In the novel's most controversial episode, mentioned earlier, when the sultan pardons Kara Davud for his past defiance given his indispensable help during the siege, Davud refuses to submit to Mehmed II's authority. In the presence of military leadership and other Turco-Muslim rulers, he slaps the sultan and says to him:

> Chance, which rules humans, has granted you and your army a victory won by my sword.... You found glory! You gained honor! Tomorrow and throughout all history, the world will talk about a young and new *conqueror*! A young and new *conqueror* will be the sovereign with honor, glory, and dignity on this earth tomorrow and throughout all life. Beware of the

man who threw at your feet the keys of this charmed heaven! Just as this man can pardon lives, he can bring into existence countries, glories, honors, crowns, and histories, and grant and give these graciously as if they don't have any value; know this, oh young Shah of Shahs, Kara Davud, who is the son of Akbulut, can set on fire if he wills, burn and kill like volcanoes, kill like Azraels.[56]

Davud's speech points to the gap separating historical reality from its representations, emphasizing the contributions of ordinary soldiers and peasants. Where Sultan Mehmed II had made himself the embodiment of victory in the conquest of Constantinople, taking the name "Fatih" (meaning "conqueror"), *Kara Davud* suggests that this representation conceals historical reality, criticizing the sultan's fetishism as a cause and precondition of collective social achievement. In the passage quoted, Davud is portrayed as a single central agent of conquest. However, in a revised and abridged edition published in 1966, Nizamettin modified this passage with the pluralization "men like Davud," who "grant [the sultan] a victory" and "can take back with the handles of their swords, what they've granted with the tips of their swords."[57] Although the narrative development of the original does register the agency of a plurality of actors, the explicit emphasis added later is a better key to the novel's argument.

Kara Davud suggests that this fetishistic inversion of agency is located in the representation of collective accomplishments, including the construction of the Rumeli fortress and of a road of greased logs for transporting ships by land during preparation for the siege. Praising the "Anatolian workers" who worked like "an army of ants [*karınca sürüsü*]" in constructing the fortress, Nizamettin describes the manual labor of transporting timber from İzmit and Ereğli, ferrying provisions from nearby villages, providing security, and erecting the fortress walls. The despotic sultan personally supervises the construction and orders the execution of "lazy ones" who fail to meet daily work quotas.[58] This critical representation of Mehmed II echoes the image of the Asiatic despot, whom Marx described as a "comprehensive unity standing above all the littler communities [*die* 'zusammenfassende Einheit,' *die über allen diesen kleinen Gemeinwesen steht*]." "The communal conditions of real appropriation through labor, *aqueducts*, very important among the Asiatic peoples; means of communication etc. then," Marx wrote, "appear as the work of the higher unity [*erscheinen dann als Werk der höhren Einheit*]—of the despotic regime hovering over the little communes."⁵⁹

Marx argued that the organizational form of Asiatic society produced alienation through the despot's symbolic integration of the social organization of production, apart from and above the community as a transcendent body and the cause and precondition of collective social achievement. To the community, their cooperation appears to be "a plan drawn up" by the despot, secured by "his authority, as the powerful will of a being outside them, who subject[ed] their activity to his purpose."⁶⁰ Kara Davud's slap, then, can be understood as demystifying the appropriation of the peasants' productive power, representing them as permanent debtors in its fetishistic inversion of agency. Davud's battle cry "Vur ha! Vur ha! Vur bre ha!" (Strike ah! Strike ah! Strike oh ah!), which he shouts at his enemies, is reproduced as the epigraph of each volume of the novel. It should be read as demanding the end of the violence of imperial representation, which transforms the "free gift" of surplus labor, expended for the exaltation of communal unity, as debt service to the despot.

It is true that despite the energy of its critique of the "fetishism" of the despot,⁶¹ in the end *Kara Davud* fails to imagine any fundamentally different form of social organization. The central event of the novel's conclusion is the alliance formed by Davud with the Karamanid ruler Ibrahim and the Dulkadir ruler Kılıç Arslan, who coordinate Davud's escape from the imperial palace after his imprisonment. Davud briefly sojourns on Lesbos in the Aegean Sea, where the people of the island make him their leader. Later, he joins Duman to restore Kılıç Arslan to power after the latter was overthrown by his brother. Duman subsequently becomes Kılıç Arslan's vizier and marries into the ruling family of the Alevi Muslim principality of Poyrazoğlu in the Southeast.

In an insightful review of the abridged edition printed by Resimli Ay in 1929 in the Latin alphabet (which contained a dedication to "the great poet and my genius friend Nâzım Hikmet"), Nâzım Hikmet suggested that *Kara Davud* portrayed the Turkish peasants' uprising against the "feudal social order [*derebeylik içtimai nizamı*]" of the Ottoman state. In his criticism of the novel's conclusion, Nâzım remarked that Davud was the hero mainly of the upwardly mobile "middle peasant," "an enemy of feudal lords but not an enemy of accumulating riches, ruling, or commanding."⁶² Indeed, the conclusion of *Kara Davud* must be read as substituting rule by a cadre of benevolent patriarchs for rule by the sultan. To the extent that the novel's loose narrative structure gives privilege to Davud's perspective in some chapters and moves him to the background in others, making Duman and Kılıç Arslan lead characters instead, the image constructed is, at best, one of shared governance. In different ways, both Marx and Nâzım observed that such a democratic reorganization does not necessarily produce a nonalienating social order. As Marx put it, "The communality can ... appear within the clan system more in a situation where the unity is represented [*repräsentirt*] in a chief of the clan-family, or as the relation of the patriarchs among one another. Depending on that, a more despotic or a more democratic form of this community system."[63] Insofar as the cadre of patriarchs becomes the apparent cause of objective collective accomplishments, a more democratic community does not necessarily also break cleanly from expropriatory imperialism. We can say that in its conclusion the novel fails to imagine a truly *structural* transformation that would make the social body a guarantee of immanent justice.

Shaped by Marxian Orientalism, *Kara Davud* fails to reflect the truth of the Ottoman order of things. Despite and perhaps because of its limits, this novel should be read as an important literary record of the Ankara communist movement. *Kara Davud* aimed to transform its primary addressee, the peasant of Anatolia, by reflecting back an image of that addressee's productive power and revolutionary agency, and it accomplished this in a historical-allegorical representation of the entangled Anatolian and Bolshevik Revolutions. During a period in which Turkish communist literature was addressed primarily to the urban Turkish worker, *Kara Davud* faced the exploitative relations of production in the rural countryside. (The novel's second volume, for example, concludes with an episode in which the peasants of the Poyrazoğlu principality hang the ruling family's son and housekeeper, who have stolen their produce and animals.)[64] While the Istanbul-based TKP, following the Comintern directive, concentrated its organizational efforts among Turkish factory and railroad workers, *Kara Davud* made itself a ghostly token of the lost heterogeneity of early Turkish communism and a reminder of a path not taken, one that might have suited the eliminated Ankara THIF. However ineffective and limited the THIF was during its eight months of life in 1922, we can say that the Ankara "primitives," faced with the Comintern's unrealistic dream of world revolution in Anatolia and with the paternalism of Soviet representatives whose prime concern was to placate Mustafa Kemal, understood the urgency of translating communism to the peasant majority.[65]

In his review, Nâzım had little to say about the novel's representation of Anatolian space, which lends *Kara Davud* its other function as a kind of travelogue. Davud was born in Kastamonu, in the North, was raised in an underground palace in Santur Kaya, near Kütahya, and has traveled the entire area of the newly established Turkish state, from Manisa through Konya to Arguvan and from Constantinople and Edirne to Silifke. Describing the "spatial component" of historical novels "as striking as their temporal one," Franco Moretti observes that "the crossing of an [internal] border is usually also the decisive event of the narrative structure," exerting a determining effect on "stylistic choices." Whereas in the European historical fiction that Moretti discusses proximity to a border is registered by the intensified use of metaphorical language, in *Kara Davud* "space acts upon style," splitting narrative discourse and temporality by including a large number of ethnographic footnotes.[66]

Occasionally referring to himself in the third person (as "the author [*râkım-ul hurûf*]"), Nizamettin's narrator exits the fifteenth-century world of the novel in these notes branching from the main text. Speaking as an implied author, he provides ethnographic information about geographic and social localities, linguistic phenomena, and other regional aspects of culture presumably unfamiliar to his urban (that is, Istanbulite) reader. For example, accompanying a statement of the importance of the Tomb of Abdulvahap Gazi for the "servants of Ali [*Ali kulları*]"—that is, "the Alevis and Shiites"—in southeastern Anatolia, we find the following note: "The author traveled in this area inch by inch, and most importantly, lived among Arguvan Alevis for a long period. The Tomb of Abdulvahap Gazi was the most important pilgrimage site in this area up until two years ago" ("two years ago" refers to the law shuttering dervish lodges and blocking access to tombs in 1925).[67]

In another note, the word *kasr* is provided with an ethnolinguistic definition. "In Kurdish villages, the small houses wherein the tribe leader and his stewards reside are called 'kasr.'" Yet another note (eliminated in the 1966 edition) explains that the Dirican tribe's chosen name "means 'tall ones' in Kurdish" and lauds members of this "brave" nomadic tribe (*aşiret*) for their "wealth and generosity."[68] Moretti may have argued that historical novels "represent internal unevenness" precisely "to *abolish* it," but *Kara*

Davud is clearly an exception, better described as *archiving* the subaltern differences encountered in Anatolia.[69] Although *Kara Davud* pays tribute to workers and warriors imagined as "Turkish," nothing in its narrative structure reflects such discourse. While Davud and Duman engage both "Qizilbash"[70] cavalry soldiers and Kurdish brigands in combat, they rely on other Kurdish and Alevi groups for support, including the Dirican tribe and the Poyrazoğlu clan, and Davud marries the Alevi daughter of the latter's headman, subsequently settling in Arguvan.[71] Whereas Sultan Mehmed II in this novel embodies an assimilationist Turco-Sunni Muslim sovereignty enacted in the burning of Greek ("Rum") villages and the construction of the Rumeli fortress on the foundation of the Aya Mihailos Church, Davud stands for a coexistence in which ethnoreligious difference goes uncoded as uncanny or exotic.

Shaped by Nizamettin's exile in Diyarbakir in 1921 after the first wave of THIF arrests and by his clandestine journey from Ankara to Moscow via İnebolu in 1922, *Kara Davud* should also be read alongside Nizamettin's *New Life* articles on the topic of Anatolia in 1922. In "How Does Anatolia Live?" ("Anadolu Nasıl Yaşıyor?"), published in June of that year, he described Kastamonu as "a village with homes made of cow dung," consisting of "four ruined roofs, two skinny orphans, and a young woman whose rotten, dirty body blossoms with syphilis scars." Aesthetic encounters with sublime nature in Bolu, Erciyes, the Ararat mountains, and Arguvan are followed by an account of the exploitation of peasants by tribe leaders.[72] After the publication of this article, Nizamettin was arrested and held briefly when the minister of internal affairs of the Ankara government decided that the essay would lower morale among peasant soldiers.[73] Whereas the raw descriptions of poverty in the *New Life* essays risked further marginalizing the land and its people, the split narrator of *Kara Davud* imagined "Anatolia" as a lived place with distinct languages, life practices, belief systems, and a social order. Though in the end the novel takes only a small step toward a truly ethical representation of Anatolia, we also ought to recognize its distance from Soviet and Kemalist Easterns, which traded in "typical scenes, settings, and characters" drawn from Orientalist stereotypes.[74] (One might recall here that the timeless, primitive representation of "old" Anatolia in Yutkevich's film *Ankara* stands out as a remarkable convergence of Kemalist and Soviet Orientalisms and thus serves as a useful contrast to *Kara Davud*.)

THE TURKISH WAR OF INDEPENDENCE

FIGURE 1.1. Map of locations mentioned in the novel *Kara Davud*. *Source*: Created by Duncan Gullick Lien using data from the geoBoundaries Global Database of Political Administrative Boundaries (https://data.humdata.org/dataset/geoboundaries-admin-boundaries-for-turkey). It is licensed under a Creative Commons Open Database License, and the map may be used under a CC Attribution-Share Alike 4.0 license.

As *Kara Davud* maps out the villages, towns, and landmarks that Davud visits, including Konya, Sultan Han, Niğde, Kayseri, Deliktaş, Hasan Badrik, Hınzır Mountain, Darende, Kangal, Hasançelebi, the Tohma River, Muşar Kalesi, İzollu, Tahir, and Eymir, the unifying designation "Anatolia" invoked by both Kemalists and communists loses its anchor, becoming a pluralized space whose character is an obstacle to retrospective representations of the War of Independence as a national revolution. The limited pluralism of the Ankara government during the war, which extended to any Muslim community, including Kurdish, Circassian, and Laz peoples within the *misak-ı milli*, or national pact, would yield to ethnic Turkish nationalism during the early republican period, "constituting the people as a fictively ethnic unity."[75] Challenging this Kemalist politics of assimilation developing alongside major Kurdish uprisings in the eastern provinces, *Kara Davud* imagines a federalist common formed by the heterogeneous populations within Turkey, and the state form it supports implicitly is decentralized and regionalist.

The novel might be described as a palimpsest in that Nizamettin's self-censorship of his communist past fostered a general amnesia about its roots in the revolutionary entanglements of Turkey and Bolshevik Russia. The Kemalist "despotic overcoding" of the political field during the late 1920s and early 1930s made illegible Nizamettin's Marxian critique of the fetishism of the despot.[76] *Kara Davud*'s representation of Anatolian subalternity was also obfuscated by the author's preface to the 1928 edition, which celebrated "the bravery and nobleness" of the Turkish nation.[77] The publication of revised editions in the Latin alphabet elided critical study of this novel still further by drawing readers of modern Turkish away from the original text. The complexity of this history of effacements and rewritings requires that we reconnect *Kara Davud* to the revolutionary context from which it was severed and reclaim it as a literary record of the entangled Anatolian and Bolshevik Revolutions.

A NATION AWAKENS: FROM MARXISM TO KEMALISM

In becoming a bestseller during the early republican era, *Kara Davud* would popularize historical fiction in Turkey, though contemporaneous examples of the genre by Abdullah Ziya, İskender Fahrettin, and M. Turhan Tan did not follow its Marxist-Leninist representation of political sovereignty. Providing one of the earliest examples of the "historical-revolutionary" subgenre, Nizamettin's *Kara Davud* paved the way for an early moment of intensified communist literary exchange, which would peak with Nâzım's return from the Soviet Union in 1928. At the height of his literary fame, Nizamettin, who collaborated with Nâzım and Vâlâ at *Illustrated Monthly*, composed a screenplay about the Turkish War of Independence for Muhsin Ertuğrul's film *A Nation Awakens* (*Bir Millet Uyanıyor*, 1932). The film features a modern-day Davud, an operator for the national underground resistance in and around Istanbul in 1920. Shaped by the history of Turkish and Soviet official entanglements, it offers us a deeper understanding of Nizamettin's itinerary and a contribution to the study of the "historical-revolutionary" Eastern subgenre across the Soviet republic of letters.

Muhsin Ertuğrul, who while in Moscow and Odessa from 1925 to 1927 completed two historical films titled *Tamilla* and *Spartacus*,[78] became a leading figure in early Turkish cinema, though today he is regarded as having made films mainly to support his real interest, the theater.[79]

Ertuğrul was not a member of the TKP, but his travel essays about Russia, published in the daily *Vakit* in August–November 1925, a time "when all the newspapers barked liked dogs against communists," were praised by TKP members as "canny" propaganda.[80] Still considered one of the most important works of early republican cinema, *A Nation Awakens* broke with the theatrical mode of Ertuğrul's earlier films, making extensive use of new techniques such as montage and superimposition.[81] Offering a radically different imagination of revolutionary agency than *Kara Davud*, the screenplay can be said to represent Nizamettin's complete absorption by Kemalism. Though Zarkhi criticized the *Nation* screenplay as "poor" in an interview for *Kino* in 1933, it is unmistakable that certain plot elements served as inspiration for Zarkhi's own screenplay "The Man Who Did Not Kill." During a meeting with Ertuğrul in Istanbul in December 1932, Zarkhi contrasted his own composition of a screenplay in six months to the two-month production time of *A Nation Awakens*, opining that the Turkish film resembled a magician's work.[82]

Published as a short book with the same title in 1932,[83] Nizamettin's screenplay mixed elements of fact and fiction, centering on a minor historical figure named Captain Yahya, who had been mentioned briefly in Mustafa Kemal's *Great Speech* in 1927. In the film's opening scenes, set in 1920, the fictional protagonists Captain Davud and Sergeant Tilki are called to Istanbul from Lapseki in the Dardanelles, where they had participated in the Akbaş arms depot raid conducted by the national forces.[84] The film still on the book cover appears to be a shot of the Turkish forces sailing to the Akbaş depot. This historical allusion offers an interesting point of contrast with Zarkhi's screenplay, reminding the viewer of Turkish support for the Bolsheviks during the Russian Civil War. The Allies had planned to send the stockpiled weapons in the Akbaş depot to the White Army for use in their conflict with the Bolsheviks. In his memoirs, the Soviet representative Aralov recalled how Mustafa Kemal reminded him of the Akbaş depot raid, telling Aralov that the raid amounted to indirect Turkish assistance of the Bolshevik armies.[85]

Immediately upon arrival in Istanbul, identified as "the city of tragedies," Davud and Tilki witness the shooting of a Turkish boy by an English soldier. Later, "by coincidence," they witness the sexual harassment of three veil-wearing girls by French Senegalese soldiers.[86] In each of these

FIGURE 1.2. Book cover of Nizamettin Nazif's screenplay *Bir Millet Uyanıyor* (A nation awakens) (Istanbul: Kanaat Kütüphanesi, n.d. [ca. 1932]). The film was directed by Muhsin Ertuğrul.

encounters, just as Davud and Tilki are about to intervene, a "shadow" abruptly appears and shoots the perpetrators (the English soldier in the first case, the Senegalese soldiers in the second). This same unidentified "shadow who saves national revolutionaries from danger in Istanbul" appears again that same evening to direct Davud and Tilki to a safe house when they are threatened by French soldiers.[87] In contrast with his fifteenth-century namesake in *Kara Davud*, this modern-day Davud is characterized as submissive and sluggish. It turns out that the "shadow" personage is the historical Captain Yahya, an early ally of Mustafa Kemal who led a militia unit in İzmit.

After Yahya defends them in battle against the collaborationist Association of the Friends of England, Duman and Tilki join Yahya's unit but are then captured by the Caliphate Army fighting on the sultan's side. Yahya is killed, Tilki escapes, and Davud and other members of the unit survive when Caliphate Army soldiers refuse an order to execute them. In a dramatic scene containing allusions to *Battleship Potemkin*, these soldiers then join the national resistance instead.[88] The film's conclusion includes documentary footage of the Turkish army and a close-up of the face of Mustafa Kemal superimposed on the Turkish flag.

Abandoning the critique of the fetishism of the despot he developed in *Kara Davud*, in this screenplay Nizamettin celebrated Mustafa Kemal as an original cause of collective social achievement. In a central example of the resort to coincidence as a narrative device, the "shadow" Yahya, whom one can consider a synecdoche of Mustafa Kemal as sovereign leader, transmutes historical contingency into necessity, his unexpected appearance in perilous situations manifesting the intervention of an omniscient will controlling the resistance movement. The film thus affirms Kemal's argument, as presented in the *Great Speech*, that Kemal had designed the national resistance movement and embodied its animating intelligence (a point to which we will return in the following section). Insofar as the entangled revolution was shaped by unpredictable and multidirectional communication and translation involving the use of disguises, ciphers, passwords, and secret messages, Nizamettin's screenplay imagined Kemal as "the great overhearer, the interceptor of all messages, the guarantor that one has the power to beget recognition and that one is recognized only for what is proper, against all false recognition."[89] Representing Yahya as an interceptor of enemy communications, Nizamettin's screenplay described

Kemal as "the antenna of the Ankara radio extending across Turkey to hear everything."⁹⁰

In remarking on the screenplay's loose and untidy structure, critics have questioned the importance granted to a minor historical figure such as Yahya, who was murdered under suspicious circumstances in January 1920.⁹¹ Though Yahya's loyalty was questioned by members of the national resistance, Kemal vindicated him in the *Great Speech*. Incorporating into the book-length edition of *A Nation Awakens* those portions of the *Great Speech* devoted to Yahya, Nizamettin praised the latter as a "clean," "brave soldier of the national struggle." "Those who regard him as a petty outlaw," Nizamettin observed, "do not know that he was attached to [*merbut*] Kemal."⁹² Nizamettin's screenplay might be read as requesting absolution for his past transgressions as a fugitive communist, including his support for Ethem the Circassian's rebellion, for which Kemal denounced Nizamettin in the *Great Speech*.⁹³ If neither the *Great Speech* nor the screenplay for *A Nation Awakens* sheds much light on the circumstances of Yahya's death, that may be because both invoked Kemal as a guarantor of innocence through the power of recognition. In writing the story of a redeemed Yahya, which Kemal would read and approve, Nizamettin obtained that absolution.⁹⁴ More than anything else, *A Nation Awakens* thus stands as a record of the subjective and historical repression of Anatolian Bolshevism and communism as a constitutive condition of the national imaginary and the symbolic in the early 1930s. In its strong contrast with Zarkhi's Russocentric screenplay, it became a precedent for Yutkevich's celebration of Kemal in *Ankara*.

In the 1930s, Nizamettin maintained his friendships with leftist writers and supported their commitment to realism in the literary battles they waged against writers of the literary establishment. During a period defined by the reconstruction of a nation-state with limited resources, the paths of various journalists and writers would cross at Babıali in Istanbul, where the most influential publishing houses operated.⁹⁵ The two communist writers whom Nizamettin married and then divorced, Fatma Nudiye (1932–1933) and Suat Derviş (1934–1938), would remain loyal to the communist movement until their deaths. Despite these personal and professional connections, Nizamettin did not rejoin the TKP underground, and at one point Nâzım suspected that Nizamettin had become a police informant.⁹⁶ Nizamettin was not alone in being absorbed by Kemalism.

The repression of the TKP produced many defections to the Kemalist cadres. While Nizamettin remained a loyal supporter of the Republican People's Party during the transition to the multiparty system (1946–1950) and its aftermath,[97] his comrade Nâzım chose another itinerary. Though Nâzım is known primarily for his introduction of free verse into Turkish poetry, he also made important contributions to Turkish cinema and theater as a screenwriter and director. Though the vaudeville- and operetta-style screenplays he composed under pseudonyms were met with disapproval by both Turkish and Soviet critics, they helped him to earn a living in an era of anticommunist persecution. In 1932, Nâzım collaborated with Nizamettin and Ertuğrul in the filming of *A Nation Awakens*, serving as both assistant director and director of sound recording and arranging for the use of his home, the Midhat Pasha Pavilion, as a filming location.[98] A possible source for Nâzım's influential epic poem about the War of Independence was his discontent with this film's representation of revolutionary agency.

NÂZIM'S TURKISH NATIONALISM: DOMESTICATING MARXISM-LENINISM

Having lived in Soviet Russia in 1922–1924 and 1925–1928 and later during the Cold War years as an émigré, Nâzım is without question the most influential figure in the history of Turkish and Soviet revolutionary entanglements.[99] In my discussion thus far, I have set aside a very conventional literary-historiographical construction of Nâzım as a point of origin. In this section, I challenge another scholarly truism: that by the late 1930s the discourse of anti-imperialism had lost its mobilizing force within the literary international. I will return later to the historical conjuncture of the Popular Front and the Second World War, but here I examine Nâzım's writings from this period for the purpose of tracing the literary representation of the War of Independence across different periods.

Nâzım's literary itinerary during the 1920s and early 1930s (about which I have more to say in chapter 5) might be seen as one of a typical Comintern writer: having composed entire volumes of poetry about the Turkish workers' movement of the late 1920s and early 1930s and anti-imperialist communist struggles in India and China, Nâzım then turned to antifascism and made an important contribution to the international literature of the Popular Front in works such as *Soviet Democracy* (*Sovyet Demokrasisi*, 1936) and *German Fascism and Racism* (*Alman Faşizmi ve Irkçılığı*, 1936).[100] Although this general description of his international literary itinerary is accurate, it does elide the significance of his so-called Eastern writings about the Turkish War of Independence. In examining Nâzım's poems from the 1930s, including "The Gioconda and Si-Ya-U," described as "oriented toward Asia and the anticolonialist struggles," Katerina Clark has suggested that these works advanced a discourse of "red cosmopolitanism" understood as "distinct from Soviet anti-imperialist internationalism."[101] In emphasizing Nâzım's commitment to Soviet anti-imperialism here, I argue that his interwar and Cold War–era critiques of European imperialism in Asia and Africa, including the Italian occupation of Abyssinia, should be read with attention to the shifts in his thematization of the Turkish War of Independence in *Epic of National Liberation Movement* (1939–1941) and later in his autobiographical novel *Life's Good, Brother* (1964). As contributions to a rich body of Turkish and Soviet literary and artistic production about the Turkish War of Independence, these writings are a missing link between what Djagalov calls the first and second phase (post-Bandung) of Soviet and Third World engagements.

"Prison," Régis Debray observes, "was the dissident's second university, his seat of higher learning and greatest moral awareness."[102] Nâzım's former KUTV classmate Şevket Süreyya first encountered Turkish subalternity in prison in Afyon in 1925–1926, an experience that led him to part ways with the TKP.[103] By contrast, Nâzım's episodic incarcerations in the period 1928–1934 and the uninterrupted incarceration from 1938–1950 only deepened his commitment to Turkish communist translation as a grand project. After his own encounter with Turkish subalternity in the Bursa prison in 1933–1934, a period when he served as a member in absentia of the International Bureau of the Association of Writers for the Defense of Culture, Nâzım began composing his epic poems about Ottoman imperial and modern Turkish history. The first of these works, *Epic of Sheik Bedreddin* (*Simavne Kadısı Oğlu Şeyh Bedreddin Destanı*, 1936), reimagined a fifteenth-century peasant uprising led by Börklüce Mustafa, a disciple of Sheik Bedreddin, in the western provinces of the Ottoman Empire.[104] Though, as I shall suggest, Nâzım did not engage in any systematic way with Islamic epistemology in this work, *Epic of Sheik Bedreddin* is an important point in the development of his oeuvre. A second work, *Epic of National Liberation*

Movement, can be read as an effort to mediate local "Eastern" and communist universal histories.

The immediate circumstances of the latter's composition are important. In 1937, at the invitation of Şevket Süreyya, who had joined the Kemalist bureaucracy in the early 1930s, Nâzım attended a dinner party with Turkish government officials, including Minister of Interior Affairs Şükrü Kaya and Chief of State Security Şükrü Sökmensüer. After listening to Nâzım's poem about the Spanish Civil War, "Traveling to Barcelona with the Boat of Ill-Fated Yusuf," Sökmensüer reportedly asked why no one had yet composed an epic about the Turkish War of Independence. Nâzım's biographers, Saime Göksu and Edward Timms, have suggested that this meeting represented Nâzım's final warning from the Turkish state.[105] After refusing to join the Kemalists, in the military trials of 1938 Nâzım was charged with inciting the army and the navy to revolt and given a prison sentence of twenty-eight years. In August of that year, he appealed directly to Mustafa Kemal, asking for justice "from Kemalism and you [*Kemalizmden ve senden*]" in a letter that was never delivered to Kemal, who was then on his deathbed.[106] Beginning *Epic of National Liberation Movement* in the Sultanahmet House of Detention in Istanbul in 1939, Nâzım continued work on the poem following his transfer to the Çankırı and Bursa prisons, completing it in 1941. In a 1939 letter to his uncle Ali Fuat Cebesoy, who had served as the commander of the Western Front during the War of Independence, Nâzım wrote that "by writing this epic, I fulfill not only a duty of literature and history but also of a mobilized soldier's duty."[107] Though both Cebesoy and Kemal's successor, İsmet İnönü, read and admired this work, Nâzım's petitions for amnesty would be unsuccessful.[108] The composition of *Epic of National Liberation Movement* cannot be abstracted from the personally dignified but otherwise desperate circumstances under which it was composed, but that does not mean we should read it as a product of compromise. It must be remembered that the arrival and generalization of communist discourse during the War of Independence gave the war a decisive character for Turkish communists. As I will further emphasize in my reading of the writings of Suat Derviş in chapter 3, the literary politics of the Popular Front produced no meaningful fractures in the Turkish corner of the Soviet republic of letters. It was quite common for Turkish communists to evoke the memory of the entangled Anatolian and Bolshevik Revolutions both in their antifascist party publications of the 1940s and in court during their hearings and trials. After his release in 1950, Nâzım revised the *Epic of National Liberation Movement* for publication, but it did not appear in print in Turkey until 1965, when Yön Publishing House published an edition based on the earliest draft completed in 1941. Nâzım also incorporated the bulk of the original version into his magnum opus *Human Landscapes from My Country* (*Memleketimden İnsan Manzaraları*), composed in prison during the 1940s.[109]

Comprising eight cantos, *Epic of National Liberation Movement* renarrates events in the national struggle described in Mustafa Kemal's *Great Speech*. Beginning with the occupation of Anatolia in 1918–1919, it goes on to describe the national congresses convened in Erzurum and Sivas, the armed conflicts with Greek forces in 1920, and the Turkish victory in 1922. Incorporating quotations from a 1938 edition of the *Great Speech*, it also depicts the contributions of historical and imagined characters, including the day laborer Black Snake, the boatsman İsmail, and the driver Ahmet, among others, who transport explosives, intercept enemy communications, and otherwise support or engage in combat on the front. Extending the Marxian critique of Nizamettin's *Kara Davud* to the republican context and standing clearly in opposition to *A Nation Awakens*, Nâzım's epic offered the people of Turkey a literary representation of their productive power and revolutionary agency. At the same time, in strong contrast with the broadly federalist logic of a nonnational common in *Kara Davud* (and anticipating Frantz Fanon's approach in *The Wretched of the Earth* [1961]), it depicted the War of Independence as a unifying event of national awakening. One might say that in addressing both the people of Turkey and the Kemalist cadre, *Epic of National Liberation Movement* sought to domesticate Turkish communism (along with its persecuted author, sentenced to social death) by treating the discourse of anti-imperialist national liberation as a common denominator of both Kemalism and Marxism-Leninism.

To better understand Nâzım's rewriting of Kemalist historiography, let us return briefly to Mustafa Kemal's *Great Speech*. The address begins with the declaration "On the 19th day of May of the year 1335 AH [1919], I made landfall at Samsun," continuing with a dramatic description of conditions in the aftermath of the First World War.[110] Kemal described his own role in the national resistance as follows:

As the emerging national struggle, which had as its sole goal the deliverance of the nation from foreign invasion, would be crowned with success, it was only a natural and inescapable movement of history that it would realize, step by step until the present day, all the principles and forms of governance based on the national will. The ruling dynast, who as is his wont, sensed this fatal movement of history [*mukadder seyri tarihîyi*], became a merciless enemy of the national struggle from the beginning. I too observed and sensed this fatal movement of history at the beginning. But we [Kemal referring to himself here] did not initially fully disclose and express these sentiments encompassing all the stages to the end.... If it is necessary to summarize my final remarks, I can say that I was obliged to carry in my conscience the great capacity for evolution that I sensed in the conscience and future of the nation like a national secret and bring all our society gradually to execute it. [Bu son sözlerimi hulâsa etmek lâzım gelirse, diyebilirim ki, ben, milletin vicdanında ve istikbalinde ihtisas ettiğim büyük tekâmül istidadını, bir millî sır gibi vicdanımda taşıyarak peyderpey, bütün heyeti içtimaıyemize tatbik ettirmek mecburiyetinde idim.]¹¹¹

Reimagining historical contingency as predestination, Mustafa Kemal depicted the founding of the Turkish republic in teleological terms and authorized his transcendent status as national leader by extolling his ability to recognize and grasp its predestination. One might suggest, drawing on the Marxian concept of alienation, that in the *Great Speech* the condition and combination of labor during the War of Independence "appear[] ... as subservient to and led by an alien will and an alien intelligence—having its *animating unity* [*ihre* seelenhafte Einheit] elsewhere."¹¹² Kemal presented himself as the animating will and intelligence of the people's socially productive labor, and the speech derived its truthfulness from Kemal's abstraction and transcendence as the organizing mind of the nation. Following the analogy Marx suggested linking the capitalist to the Asiatic despot,¹¹³ one might say that just as the capitalist reflects in himself the socially productive power of capital and appears as its transcendent cause, Kemal appears in the *Great Speech* as the embodiment of the nation's unity and the prime mover of the collective labor expended in its name.

Nâzım's most basic technique for rejecting Kemal's fetishistic self-representation in the *Great Speech* is the refusal to focalize him. In two brief appearances on the battlefield, very much as a minor character,

Kemal is referred to only by the third-person pronoun *o*, "he." By contrast, in the opening lines the epic narrator dedicates *Epic of National Liberation Movement* to *onlar*, "them":

> They who are numberless
> > like ants in the earth
> > > fish in the sea
> > > > birds in the air,
>
> who are cowardly
> > brave
> > > ignorant
> > > > sovereign [*hâkim*]
> > > > > and childlike,
>
> and who confound
> > and create,
> > > it is them,
>
> our epic tells only of their adventures.[114]

In the first canto, "The Years 1918 and '19, and the Story of Black Snake," the first successful defense mobilization against French forces in Antep is described through the story of the day laborer Black Snake. Though he physically resembled a black snake, we are told, with his "twig-thin neck" and "big head," Black Snake "lived like a field mouse" in the fields with no "time to think." "Scared as a field mouse," Black Snake "didn't really care / if the heathens held Antep till Doomsday." The animal similes used here establish Black Snake as a form of what Marx called a "species-life" or living "inorganic nature," lacking conscious determination of his life activity.[115] The epic narrator informs us that it was by witnessing a bullet kill a black snake hiding by a rock that Black Snake learned to accept the inevitability of death and joined the fight against the occupiers of Anatolia. Black Snake is thus transformed into what Marx called a "species-being," who can "make his life activity the object of his will and consciousness," a process facilitated by a conscious, purposeful, and necessarily differential relationship to nature as his "inorganic body." We are thus encouraged to conclude that Black Snake's willingness to fight has nothing to do with Mustafa Kemal in particular but is triggered by this critically mimetic relationship to nature, constituting both the "direct means of his life" and the primary domain of his productive activity as a field worker.[116]

In the seventh canto, "August 1922 and Our Women and the Orders of August 6 and the Story of an Instrument and a Man," the epic narrator provides an account of the Battle of Dumlupınar, marking the decisive victory of the Turkish forces. Quoting from Mustafa Kemal's orders of August 6 directing "the First and Second Armies, with their detachments" to move into position, the narrator focuses on just one of "186,326" men operating the "100 motor vehicles / with the total capability of 300 tons" whom Kemal mentions in the *Great Speech*. Imagining the driver Ahmet transporting a supply of arms, the narrator dwells on the relationship between a worker and his instrument as, stuck in the road with a flat tire, Ahmet removes his clothing and fills the tire with it, "reanimating" this mechanical means of production with an item of social necessity otherwise intended to serve the reproduction of his labor-power. "Never / has any human / loved a machine [*âlet*]/ with so much tender hope," the narrator observes.[117] The suggestion is clear: ultimately, Ahmet's affective appropriation of and unification with the instrument of his productive activity are more significant for the outcome of the Battle of Dumlupınar than are the army generals' decisions.

We might say that the combinatory form of *Epic of National Liberation Movement,* grafting together eight distinct cantos, registers the socially productive power of labor developed by each worker and contributes to the demystification of Mustafa Kemal as an agent who personally combines the people's social labor. In the final canto, this collective agency is named "the Turkish people" as an anonymous Turkish soldier from Kayseri gazes at the Aegean "from the south to the north / from the east to the west / with the Turkish people."[118] Anticipating elements of Fanon's writings on national liberation, the epic imagines active participation in combat as constitutive of the nation.[119] In describing each participant's "continuous interchange" with nature and machines, Nâzım imagined a specifically Marxist ontology of the nation, in which human and nature, human and machine are articulated as prostheses of one another.[120] Reminding us of "all the oppressed nations [*mazlum milletler*] fighting against imperialists [*emperyalistler*]," as invoked at the Erzurum Congress of 1919 convened by the supporters of national resistance, it re-represents the War of Independence as a Leninist anti-imperialist struggle. As Corporal Ali puts it in the song sung in the final canto, the struggle is for the annihilation of all forms of oppression: "Annihilate man's servitude to another / this is our call."[121]

Read as a supplement of Nâzım's anticolonial poetry of the early 1930s, *Epic of National Liberation Movement* represents a contribution to the Soviet republic of letters in its imagination of a materialist ontology of national liberation—a contribution whose limits we can recognize in Nâzım's acts of self-censorship—for example, in following the *Great Speech* by describing Ethem the Circassian as a traitor.[122] Where Mustafa Kemal misrepresented the Green Army Association as established to organize a regular army,[123] Nâzım engages in his own misrepresentations by eliding the history of Anatolian Bolshevisms and communisms, including "the story of Mustafa Suphi and his comrades," the subject of a book Nâzım coauthored in 1923 commemorating the fifteen murdered members of the Baku TKP.[124] The fact is that the Muslims of Anatolia, including ethnic Turks, Kurds, Laz, and Circassians, fought for the Ankara government during the War of Independence for a variety of reasons, including political antipathy to the Ottoman government, ethnoreligious antipathy to Greeks and Armenians, fear of being massacred by the Greek occupiers, and compulsory military service, but *Epic of National Liberation Movement* abstracts this historical heterogeneity away, accepting that the nation was the war's telos or final purpose. It is fair to say that its celebratory conclusion revives the fetish of nationalism, making the "conditions of [the nation's] becoming" a result "of its own realization" and a historical necessity.[125]

In emphasizing these limitations, my goal is not, of course, to disvalue Nâzım's project in this work. I would suggest we should embrace that project as an important literary record of the entangled revolutions despite and, in fact, because of those limitations. As mentioned earlier, Nâzım composed his epic under very difficult personal circumstances, and it is reasonable to say that his self-censorship was necessary as a strategic move, enabling him to freely address both the Kemalist cadres and the Turkish people by appealing to the last remaining topic of public discussion to which Turkish communists had any publicly legitimate claim. National-liberatory anti-imperialism provided the only permitted common language for the Turkish communists and the Kemalists. Nâzım's work inhabited this discourse of national liberation in an effort to domesticate the project of the Turkish communists for the Turkish public. By recourse to the secular nationalist idiom, which he sincerely supported, Nâzım delivered a literary representation of the productive power of the people and a materialist image of their subjective formation. We might say that in suggesting a dialectical tension between the national immanence of the past and the "fallen" state of affairs in the republican present, the work implicitly suggested that its readers terminate their service to the Kemalist elites.[126]

Though *Epic of National Liberation Movement* was not published until 1965, copies of the manuscript circulated freely among the Turkish communists. The émigré novelist Fahri Erdinç wrote in his memoirs that during the late 1930s, when he was a student at the Ankara Conservatory, many in his circle of friends received handwritten copies from handlers who had smuggled excerpts out of prison in tins of cheese and olive oil.[127] Vedat Türkali's historical novels *Trust* (*Güven*, 2015) and *One Day All Alone* (*Bir Gün Tek Başına*, 1974) suggest that the circulation of these copies influenced an entire generation of Turkish communists who came of age in the 1940s and the 1950s—an impact whose scope is meaningful even if it ended there because the secular discourse of Turkish nationalism would never fully penetrate the subaltern populations of Anatolia. In the final canto, Nâzım himself appears in the guise of the poet Nurettin Eşfak (one of Nâzım's pen names during this period), who goes to the war front looking to fight. Reciting the lyrics of the Turkish national anthem composed by the Islamist poet Mehmed Akif, Nurettin Eşfak criticizes the latter's appeal to God and his celebration of martyrdom:

"The days God promised us will come."
No.

...

We've promised those days
        to ourselves.[128]

A comparative reading of *Epic of National Liberation Movement* in relation to Nizamettin's historical novel *Kara Davud* might suggest that the absorption of the Ankara communists into the ranks of the Istanbul TKP marked the end of Turkish communist engagement with the social "grammars" of Islam across Anatolia. This in turn might tell us that the failure of Turkish republican communism lay in its reliance on the reach of nationalism, remaining untranslatable across the multiplicity and variety of Islams in the region.[129]

BEYOND ROMANCE AND TRAGEDY: LEGACIES FOR THE POSTCOLONIAL ERA

Emphasizing historical fiction as a neglected genre in the study of the literary international, I have explored the implications of work by Nizamettin and Nâzım for the first and second moments of communist literary exchange between Turkey and the Soviet Union. In their promises and their contradictions, these writings demonstrate that the discourse of Leninist anti-imperialism maintained its influence through the period of the Second World War. In conclusion, I want to turn briefly to a third moment, the mid-1960s, when a remobilized discourse on the Turkish War of Independence was interwoven with an Asian and African anticolonial discourse of emancipation. Where Nizamettin's revised and rebranded edition of *Kara Davud* in 1966 would become a favorite of the nationalist Right during the 1960s and 1970s, Nâzım's *Epic of National Liberation Movement* found its historical moment in the military coup of 1960 and the emergence of socialism as a mass movement with broad support among both the Turkish and Kurdish urban proletariat as well as among students and intellectuals. Under the leadership of the Direction-Revolution (Yön-Devrim) movement, named for the journals *Yön* (1961–1967) and *Devrim* (1969–1971), the articulation of Turkish communism with Kemalist nationalism and secularism would continue into the Cold War era.[130] Doğan Avcıoğlu, the movement's most important ideologue, embraced socialism as an alternative path to rapid economic development (*kalkınma*) and as a necessary step toward completing the project of the Kemalist reforms. Avcıoğlu believed that although the reforms had fallen far short of the necessary structural economic transformation, they had set Turkey on the best possible path. Turning to socialism at a moment when the word *komünist* functioned as a curse, the movement appropriated the discourse of Kemalist nationalism to legitimize and domesticate its own socialist agenda. Blaming Mustafa Kemal's successors for Turkey's postwar regression to neocolonial dependency, the *Yön* writers called for a Second War of Independence (İkinci Kurtuluş Savaşı) against U.S. imperialism and those who collaborated locally with it. Published for the first time by Yön Publishing House in 1965 and the first literary work to be published in Turkey under Nâzım's own name in twenty-seven years, *Epic of National Liberation Movement* could now be reclaimed as a cultural foundation for this new independentist discourse, ensuring that Nâzım would be remembered as a nationalist. Nâzım, who had fled Turkey in 1951 for the Soviet Union via Rumania, would follow these developments in Turkey, working closely with other exiled TKP members, including Dino, Sabiha Sertel, Fahri Erdinç, Hayk and Anjel Açıkgöz, Vartan and Jak İhmalyan, and Gün Benderli, among others. In radio addresses for Our Radio (Bizim Radyo) sponsored by the TKP's External Bureau (Dış Büro) and broadcast in Turkish from Leipzig in East Germany, Nâzım called for a second national liberation movement to free Turkey from the yoke of U.S. imperialism and suggested that resistance to neocolonial dependency represented Mustafa Kemal's true legacy.[131] Meanwhile, in his address at the Tashkent Afro-Asian Writers' Congress in 1958, Nâzım would tell his listeners that "Turkey was the first country to launch a national liberation movement against imperialism in the aftermath of the First World War and to end it with victory,"[132] a point he repeated in a *New World* (*Novyi Mir*) article the same year reporting his impressions of the congress. "Lenin," Nâzım wrote, "called our century the age of socialist and national liberation movements, and ... my country is the first semicolonial country to expel foreign imperialism with the assistance of the Soviet Union."[133]

It is interesting, then, that *Life's Good, Brother*, the autobiographical novel that Nâzım composed during this period and was published in Turkish in 1964 in Bulgaria, offered a radically different representation of the War of Independence, one that refused the common language of Turkish patriotism and nationalism. As a prelude to the full reading of *Life's Good, Brother* that I present in the final chapter of this book, I want to briefly address its thematization of the War of Independence, emphasizing its legacies for the postcolonial era. In many ways anticipating the post-Kemalism that emerged after the 1980s, *Life's Good, Brother* abandoned the argument of Nâzım's contemporaneous writings on the War of Independence as much as his past writings on that topic. It provided an uncensored critical representation of the Kemalist elite, calling for an end to Turkish socialism's "symbiotic" relationship with Kemalism.[134] The novel's dialectical representation of Marxist-Leninist national revolution valuably illuminates Nâzım's role as a mediator of the different phases of

Soviet and Third World entanglement. Tracing "the migration and adaptation of certain topoi and narrative structures" from early twentieth-century proletarian fiction into postcolonial fiction, Djagalov has suggested that Third Worldist writers, including Nâzım, Mulk Raj Anand, and Ngugi wa Thiong'o, remobilized "the international solidarity/foreign utopia topos, the evocation of foreign revolutions as an inspiration for the emancipatory struggles at home."[135] In recasting the topos of the War of Independence and rewriting the narrative structures of both historical-revolutionary Easterns and midcentury epic writing, Nâzım's *Life's Good, Brother* points to another genealogy connecting different phases of the Soviet republic of letters.

Describing the adventures of one Ahmet, a bedridden TKP member hiding in a cottage in Izmir during the communist crackdown of 1925, the novel's nonlinear narrative is organized by Ahmet's memories of travel through Anatolia in 1921 (and, as I discuss at some length in chapter 5, by prolepses to his arrests in the 1930s and 1940s). *Life's Good, Brother* uses the narrative techniques of displacement (metonym) and condensation (metaphor) described by Freud in his analysis of dream-work to describe the foreclosed historical past of Anatolian Bolshevisms and communisms. One of these techniques (displacement) establishes an association of separate yet contiguous events, whereas the other (condensation) imagines the union of multiple events in one.[136] Ahmet's movement in and out of the narrative present through the repetition of motifs is the operation of displacement. A knock on the door of the Izmir cottage in 1925 triggers Ahmet's memory of a knock on the door of a room at an İnebolu inn in 1921.[137] Occupying approximately 20 pages of the 149-page novel, the events of the chronotope of 1921, taking place in Anatolia, are narrated through condensation as each statement provides a compact reference to a rich and layered history.[138] Ahmet encounters an old friend in Ankara at the Kuyulu Coffeehouse, where Şerif Manatov, a founder of the secret TKP, had delivered his lectures on Bolshevism during the summer of 1920.[139] Ahmet and his friend discuss the Ahi brotherhood of craftsmen dating back to the thirteenth century in the towns of central Anatolia. Ahmet's friend tells him: "The Ahis have set up a kind of craftsman-peasant republic, a kind of Bolshevism." The narrative continues: "He suddenly stopped, looked around and whispered: 'The Bolsheviks supply us with guns and gold, but our side fear the Bolsheviks.'"[140] This brief exchange indexes the repressed history of the Bolshevik and Kemalist alliance during the War of Independence and the foreclosed history of communist translation across Anatolia.

A memory of Ahmet's brief meeting with Mustafa Kemal in Ankara is juxtaposed with a memory of the communist crackdown in 1921 and the murder of Mustafa Suphi and his comrades on the Black Sea. Though *Epic of National Liberation Movement* had refused the sublimation of Kemal as transcendent leader, its descriptions of Kemal on the battlefield as a "golden wolf" with "fiery eyes" led in another direction.[141] One cannot help recall those images when reading about Kemal's "steel-blue" eyes and "gold-yellow" hair in *Life's Good, Brother*—descriptions that are followed by a memory of Kemal's violent foreclosure of communism: "Our people are in the hands of the Independence Tribunal. And the bones of the fifteen are off Sürmene, at the bottom of the Black Sea."[142] In ironizing Nâzım's own past representations of Mustafa Kemal, these condensations deployed in *Life's Good, Brother* register the violence of the original relationship of Kemalism with Turkish communism and call implicitly for the Turkish socialists of the 1960s to relinquish their attachments to the former.

Perhaps most importantly, *Life's Good, Brother* refuses to sacralize the War of Independence as an event of historical necessity. It instead represents the Anatolian Revolution as a historically contingent event, haunted from the outset by counterrevolution. During his travels in Anatolia, Ahmet repeatedly remarks the double standard in the implementation of new national laws: in Kastamonu, an Independence Tribunal (İstiklâl Mahkemesi) sentences a peasant to fifteen years' incarceration for consuming alcohol, while the members of the National Assembly in Ankara serve raki at their dinner parties. Ahmet himself receives an allowance ten times that allotted to a regular soldier simply because his uncle is a member of the Assembly. The metaphor of Noah's Ark is used to describe Ankara no less than three times: "Ankara is a Noah's Ark," says Ahmet's friend. "A Noah's Ark floating on the deluge of the collapsed Ottoman Empire. Certainly, it will reach safe haven with its doves, snakes, lions, tigers, wolfs, and lambs all side by side; . . . and there the snakes will eat the doves, the wolves the lambs."[143] Against the grain of the novel's generally realist mode, this metaphor provides the national resistance movement with a mythic dimension, describing it as a re-creation from the ruins of a deadly collapse. Yet the metaphor also refuses to obscure or sanitize the violence of this rebirth, echoing Marx's observation that "force [*die Gewalt*] is the midwife of every old society pregnant with a new one."[144]

Life's Good, Brother, in contrast with both *Epic of National Liberation Movement* and *Human Landscapes from My Country*, refuses to temporalize the failure of the Kemalist revolution as a tragic fall from a pure state of national unity. Nor does it embrace the two-stage revolutionary transformation, with a "bourgeois national-democratic revolution" being followed by a general social revolution, imagined by the Comintern during the 1920s and by the Yön-Devrim movement during the 1960s. Whereas *Epic of National Liberation Movement* represented the Turkish War of Independence as an ideal revolution, offering it universality in its exceptionality as a historical model, the Yön-Devrim movement imagined the sublation of the particular into the universal in Turkey's transformation from national to socialist revolution. Representing a foreclosed future of arrests and crackdowns (about which I will say more in chapter 5), *Life's Good, Brother* rejects all stagist models of development.

Echoing Marx and Engels's suggestion in *The Communist Manifesto* that the discourse of anticommunism predates communist revolution, Nâzım imagines the concrete universality of the entangled (counter)revolution. Neither a late development imposed from without nor a stage to be overcome, failure is a necessary condition or a kind of ineradicable virus at the origin. For Nâzım, revolution is not an event of absolute rupture; rather, it is a continuous striving in the perpetual present of (counter)revolution, despite and against all odds of failure. In this context, we might turn to the support Nâzım expressed for Asian and African anticolonial movements in the poems he composed during his involvement with the Afro-Asian Writers' Bureau from 1958 until his death.[145] Following Gayatri Spivak's discussion of the "failed" attempt in 1946 by W. E. B. Du Bois and Bhimrao Ramji Ambedkar, the architect of the Indian Constitution, to build an alliance between African Americans and the untouchables of India, one might say that Nâzım's articulation of a tricontinental solidarity should be commended for its vision of "a world without colonialism," though the Soviet-sponsored socialist network of conference travel "did not," as Spivak says of Du Bois, "offer him opportunity to get into the struggles interior to colonized space." Not unlike Du Bois's novel *The Dark Princess*, Nâzım's late poetry about Cuba, Tanganyika, and Ghana "reflects the desire to overcome the class-specific problem of access to the subaltern but does not have the resources to imagine a plausible fulfillment."[146]

Life's Good, Brother might then be read as the concrete supplement of Nâzım's more abstract poetic expressions of tricontinental solidarity, articulated in the travel networks of the international Peace Movement and the Afro-Asian Writers' Bureau. It is Nâzım's most substantial intervention into postcolonial literatures, representing national liberation as a historically contingent and inherently dialectical (counter)revolution. In its rejection of Romantic redemption and tragic failure as "affective temporal structures"—or, perhaps more accurately, in its chiasmic inclusion of both narrative emplotments—it can be studied alongside contemporaneous "novels of revolution" addressing the legacies of Marxism-Leninist nationalism, such as Ousmane Sèmbene's *God's Bits of Wood* (1960) and Ayi Kwei Armah's *The Beautyful Ones Are Not Yet Born* (1968).[147] Setting aside Nâzım's earlier idealization of the Turkish War of Independence, his final novel offers a reevaluation of literary and historical legacies for the postcolonial era. In an interview by the Turkish critic Ferit Edgü, the Egyptian Marxist Anouar Abdel-Malek recalled "a remark by Mustafa Kemal that gripped and influenced us very much in Egypt some time ago: 'What shall we do if [as our external critics say] our regime resembles neither socialism nor democracy? We should be proud of this, gentlemen; because we only resemble ourselves.'"[148] Abdel-Malek suggested this remark represented an early imagination of the third way later embraced by the nonaligned postcolonial nations. Exposing as it does the profound contradictions of Kemalist exceptionalism, in this regard Nâzım's late work is perhaps a more useful engagement with "the problematic between Marxism and national liberation" after 1945.[149]

Chapter Two

VÂLÂ NUREDDIN'S COMIC MATERIALISM AND THE SEXUAL REVOLUTION

A history of literary friendships in modern Turkish literature would have to include Vâlâ Nureddin's relationship with Nâzım Hikmet as among the most consequential. Nâzım was accompanied by his friend during his "magic pilgrimage" to Moscow, though the two parted ways in the early 1930s after Vâlâ's split from the TKP. This separation was thematized in Nâzım's poem "You" ("Sen," 1932), which compared Vâlâ's betrayal to a mother's violation of the incest taboo: "You who sell the memories of those days / are like a mother / who sleeps with her son, who sells her daughters' tender flesh!"[1] Though the two reconnected in 1945, Nâzım's fictional autobiography, *Life's Good, Brother*, makes no mention of Vâlâ, depicting the protagonist Ahmet as traveling alone, whereas Vâlâ's contemporaneous biography of Nâzım, *Nâzım Passed from This World* (*Bu Dünyadan Nâzım Geçti*, 1965) provides a detailed account of their journey together. The latter work consolidated Vâlâ's place in Turkish and Soviet scholarship as an authoritative source on Nâzım's life and works during the third moment of intensified communist translation and exchange.

Less widely understood, perhaps, is Vâlâ's role as an equally important mediator of the relationship between Turkish and Soviet literature during the mid-1920s and 1930s: a role he played as novelist, translator, and adapter in works responding to the entangled Anatolian and Bolshevik Revolutions. Born in 1901 in Beirut, Vâlâ Nureddin (1901–1967) moved frequently during his childhood because of his father's employment as an Ottoman state official.² Educated at the prestigious Galatasaray Lycée (Mekteb-i Sultani) and subsequently at the Vienna Imperial Export Academy, he returned to Istanbul in 1917 to work at the newly established Ottoman National Credit Bank (Osmanlı İtibar-ı Milli Bankası). He published his first poems in a literary journal titled serially *The First Book* (*Birinci Kitap*), *The Second Book* (*İkinci Kitap*), and so on, which he coedited with two prominent poets of the syllabic meter, Orhan Seyfi and Yusuf Ziya. With the outbreak of the Turkish War of Independence, Vâlâ traveled with Nâzım through Anatolia to Russia. Studying at KUTV from 1922 to 1925, he married a fellow Armenian student, Anna Mikhailovna, whom he left behind with their newborn daughter, Hatice Süreyya, when he returned to Turkey in 1925 and never saw again.³ Though he briefly took an active role in rebuilding the TKP in the aftermath of the crackdown in 1925, he left the party in 1926 after enduring aggressive police surveillance.⁴

Securing a position at the daily *Evening* (*Akşam*), Vâlâ launched his career as one of the most prolific journalists of the Turkish republican period, contributing a daily column, a short story, and a feuilleton novel under the names "Hatice Süreyya," "Hikâyeci" (Storyteller), and "Vâ-nû."⁵ Praised by prominent republican writers for his "fluent" use of the Turkish language, he developed a witty style under the influence of the Russian émigré writer Arkady Averchenko and the Soviet satirist Mikhail Zoshchenko (about which I say more soon).⁶ Avoiding overtly political topics, his columns addressed social and cultural issues ranging from the implementation of the Turkish language reforms to changing gender relations. Diverging from normative views on the language question, Vâlâ criticized the purging of Arabic and Persian loanwords used in everyday speech, rejecting the artificial borrowing of substitute words and phrases from central Asian Turkic languages.⁷ Describing the larger stake of Vâlâ's journalism as a "critique of everyday life," Tuncay Birkan has valuably argued that his columns should be regarded as a major contribution to the field of republican literature.⁸

Vâlâ would become best known as a prolific translator and adapter of foreign literatures. By the time of his death in 1967, his body of work included more than one hundred feuilleton novels, not only original works but also literary translations and adaptations of works in a variety of genres from detective and crime fiction to the erotic novel originally published in French,

Italian, German, English, and Russian.⁹ His translations from Russian included Maksim Gorky's *The Lower Depths* (*Na dne*, 1902) and *Vassa Zheleznova* (1910) and short stories by Anton Chekhov, Leo Tolstoy, Averchenko, and Zoshchenko. In response to criticism of his work as unoriginal, Vâlâ wrote a series of columns on the importance of translation and adaptation. In a column dated May 8, 1929, for example, he wittily narrated a recent attempt to compose a set of original (*telif*) stories by studying people and events around him, wondering if there was any real difference between an original story based on a conversation overheard on the ferry and an adaptation based on one's recollection of a Russian book.¹⁰ In a preface to his collection of short stories in 1936, he remarked: "Some of my adapted, even translated stories belong more to me than to their authors ... [as] they have been changed and domesticated [*mahallîleştirilmiştir*] to such a degree, whereas some of my original stories carry the mark of foreign literary styles even though they were formed in my brain or perhaps inspired by my life."¹¹ Vâlâ reminded his critics that indigenous stories with "original" plots can be narrated in the "garb" of foreign literary techniques, rejecting their reification as purely original.

Vâlâ regarded adaptation as essential for building a new European civilization, comparing it with the *meşk* lesson common in calligraphy instruction, in which a student copies as closely as possible the writing provided by a teacher. "The *meşk* mimicry of works by foreign masters," Vâlâ remarked, was a necessary step in crafting stories with "European logic [*avrupaî mantıkla*]."¹² Embracing the discourse of republican Occidentalism, he temporarily displaced its East–West binarism by insisting on Russia as a model for Turkish literary culture. Comparing the members of his own literary generation to Alexandr Pushkin as the representative writer of Russian classics, he sought to legitimize the linguistic and literary transformation in Turkey. As Vâlâ saw it, Pushkin had rejected Church Slavonic as the "dead" literary language of the literati and instead composed Western adaptations in the Russian vernacular; similarly, Vâlâ's own contemporaries were carrying out a "classical" revolution in Turkey by rejecting Ottoman Turkish and adapting Western works in the vernacular.¹³

My goal in this chapter is to challenge the secondary role assigned to Vâlâ in Turkish literary history, both as Nâzım's biographer and as a translator and adapter of foreign literatures. Vâlâ's firsthand knowledge of the Soviet Union made him an important informant during Turkish and

Soviet convergence in the 1930s, and he joined Prime Minister İsmet (İnönü)'s entourage during the Turkish state visit to Moscow in 1932, meeting Maksim Gorky there.[14] Though Vâlâ was thus an important participant in the official, state pathway of literary exchange, his activities were not limited to or bound by that first pathway. Blacklisted by his former comrades as an "agent provocateur,"[15] he maintained a legible position on the cultural left of the Kemalist political spectrum. For example, in a column composed after the Menemen incident of 1930, which involved the decapitation of a Turkish lieutenant by rebel dervishes, he argued that the "green danger" was far worse than the "red." Whereas communists wanted a legal party and labor legislation, "the green ones *urgently* want the heads of [all modernists] cut off with a saw."[16] Though he maintained other positions that made clear his separation from the TKP,[17] it was not possible for him to obscure his communist past. In 1941 at the age of forty, he was conscripted for military service in Konya as a penalty for his critical articles on the sinking of a Turkish navy ship in the Mediterranean by a foreign torpedo attack, and he was briefly imprisoned during this period for writing a radio sketch and reading a poem by Nâzım at a public gathering.[18] All this means that the proper name "Vâlâ" has carried an ineradicable surplus in Turkish literary history, circulating as a sign of the entangled revolutions even after his defection from the TKP. This chapter constructs a deeper understanding of Vâlâ's legacy by shifting focus from his (auto) biographical writings to his comparatively understudied literary works.

Regarding Vâlâ's importance to the unofficial pathway of literary exchange, one might point to two ways he brought Turkish and Soviet literatures into conversation in the late 1920s and early 1930s. The first stems from his experience of what Richard Stites called the "sexual revolution" in the Soviet Union and the long shadow that event cast on the thematics of Vâlâ's work, legible in the comic style (the second contribution) that emerged from his translations of Zoshchenko's satirical short stories into Turkish.[19] In examining the latter translations in the next section, I suggest that in them Vâlâ interrupted a developed official discourse on Turkish and Soviet convergence, imagining in Zoshchenko's stories a mirror held up to the failed promise of Kemalist modernization.

In the second section, in reading Vâlâ's neglected erotic historical comedy *Baltacı and Catherine* (*Baltacı ile Katerina*, 1928), unique among Vâlâ's writings in its direct and explicit imagination and specification of an entangled revolution, I suggest, by way of specific attention to this work's comedic elements, that Vâlâ imagined the collapse of both Russian and Ottoman imperial sovereignty through sexual revolution. Together with the two other serialized erotic novel adaptations from the late 1920s and early 1930s alongside which it ought to be read, *Baltacı and Catherine* aimed to liberalize the Turkish republican discourse on gender and sexuality—a project in no way lacking in contradictions. I argue that a study of Vâlâ's unjustifiably neglected writings not only deepens our knowledge of early republican Turkish literature and culture but also provides a more nuanced understanding of the so-called Soviet republic of letters. The entanglement of Vâlâ's writings with the literary cultures of the Soviet Union suggests that genres and forms of exchange across a Soviet republic of letters during this period were not exclusively or even necessarily primarily led by the proletarian novel or revolutionary avant-garde. The historical-revolutionary genres examined in the previous chapter included comedic works along with epic narratives, and representations of sex and gender were as important to this "traveling" literature as were representations of class antagonism and Marxist nationalism.

TRANSLATING ZOSHCHENKO INTO TURKISH

Vâlâ's translations of about a dozen short stories appeared in *Akşam* in a column titled "New Russian Stories" ("Yeni Rus Hikâyeleri") from August 1929 to June 1930. Though he had translated other Russian writers (most importantly, the émigré satirist Arkady Averchenko),[20] his translations of Zoshchenko deserve close attention, for they establish a direct connection between Turkish and Soviet discourses of modernization. Zoshchenko became a favorite of Turkish communist and leftist writers, including Nâzım and Aziz Nesin, casting a shadow of influence on Turkish literary humor that lasted into the late 1940s. Vâlâ's translations of Zoshchenko would be followed by Nâzım's own in the newspaper *New Day (Yeni Gün)*.[21]

Beginning in the mid–nineteenth century with the ascendance of new prose genres, early Ottoman Turkish novelists such as Ahmet Midhat and Recaizade Ekrem turned to satirical humor in an effort to constrain the dynamics of modern national identity. A favored strategy of both Midhat and Ekrem was to ridicule so-called superwesternized Francophile characters.²² Early twentieth-century novelists and nonfiction writers such as Ahmet Rasim, Hüseyin Rahmi, and Ercümend Ekrem followed suit, creating satirical portrayals of both superwesternized and "uncultured" religious characters. These writers remobilized comic devices such as ridicule (*hiciv* or *taşlama*), exaggeration (*mübalağa*), and wordplay, which had been used extensively in both Ottoman court poetry and vernacular folk poetry and performance, in support of Kemalist modernization and secularization.²³ Though Vâlâ was deeply familiar with this Ottoman and early republican satirical tradition, his embrace of the comic came by way of the work of the émigré writer Averchenko and the Soviet satirist Zoshchenko, whom he saw as representing an important emergent comic paradigm in contemporary Russian literature.²⁴ During a period when Turkish translations from Russian were infrequent, Vâlâ introduced these domestically popular Russian writers (to this day, little known elsewhere) to readers who did not read Russian.

Mikhail Zoshchenko (1894–1958), who had worked as a carpenter, police officer, typist, and telephone operator, began his literary career by taking courses at the World Literature Studio and the House of Arts in Petrograd.²⁵ Continuing the prerevolutionary satirical tradition embodied by Averchenko's magazine *New Satyricon* (*Novyi Satirikon*), Zoshchenko's humorous stories focusing on incongruities of Soviet everyday life made him a popular writer in the 1920s.²⁶ Through use of the *skaz* technique, Zoshchenko constructed a highly stylized, colloquial narrator whose idiosyncratic observations made him a character in his own right. Speaking from within the milieu of his uncultured and self-absorbed characters, Zoshchenko's narrator dwells on events of apparent inconsequence (stepping on someone's foot on a crowded street, losing a galosh on the tram) in resistance to the official demand for monumental works about the revolution.²⁷ Despite the hostility this resistance created, Zoshchenko was accepted by the official literary establishment during the 1920s and early 1930s, when humor came to be understood as an essential tool of "participatory critique" and "public self-exposure, self-improvement, and self-discipline."²⁸ (He even participated in the Soviet Writers' Union's tightly controlled and staged touring of the White Sea Canal construction site in 1933, contributing praise of the project to the collaborative documentary volume *Stalin's White Sea-Baltic Canal: History of Construction 1931–1934* (*Belomorsko-Baltiiskii kanal imeni Stalina: Istoriia stroitel'stva 1931–1934 gg.*,

1934). Though Zoshchenko survived the purges of the 1930s, he was expelled from the Soviet Writers' Union (with Anna Akhmatova) in 1946, spending the rest of his life in isolation and poverty. I want to briefly turn to his meeting with Nâzım in 1954 during the poet's exile in the Soviet Union. Nâzım, recalling how he had endured the harsh prison conditions in Turkey by reading and translating Zoshchenko, invited the Soviet satirist to be a guest of honor at the Leningrad premier of his play *The First Day of Bairam* (*Pervyi den' prazdnika*)—a public endorsement that Nâzım offered over the objections of his Soviet colleagues.[29]

Outside of Russian-speaking émigré communities, scholarship in Russian and Soviet literary studies has largely neglected the transnational dimensions of Zoshchenko's work. I examine Vâlâ's translations of Zoshchenko in comparison with Nâzım's translations here to underscore the idiosyncrasy of Vâlâ's literary itinerary that paved the way for the first moment of intensified Turkish and Soviet literary exchange. Vâlâ held that a skilled writer was distinguished by "turns of phrase" (using the French term *tournure* in the Turkish original) rather than by purity of lexicon,[30] and both Vâlâ and Nâzım skillfully reproduced the *skaz* technique by deploying a variety of Turkish colloquialisms, idioms, and archaisms. Whereas in his translations Vâlâ maintained each story's original Soviet context, Nâzım summarily replaced Russian place-names and character names with Turkish substitutes. By thus masking the Russian originals' implicit ambivalence about the Soviet Union, Nâzım's translations became explicitly ironic commentaries on the economic and cultural contradictions of the Turkish republic.

In the story titled "Sincere Simplicity" ("Dushevnaia prostota," 1927, which Nâzım translated into Turkish as "Samimiyet" or "Sincerity"), Zoshchenko's narrator exaggerates the everyday experience of walking a crowded street as if it were an epic battle. When the narrator treads on the foot of a model citizen by mistake, he expects to be scolded or even slapped, but the pedestrian walks on without even noticing. "You stepped on someone, they stepped on you—[you] go on [*Ty nastupil, tebe nastupili—valiai dal'she*]," the narrator concludes.[31] Whereas the humor in the Russian original stems from the self-absorbed narrator's amplification of a trivial occurrence, Nâzım's ironic interpolations add an allegorical quality to the Turkish translation that is absent in the original: "Do you see the sincerity? . . . God knows, even if you were to tread on his head instead of his foot, he'd remain indifferent [*vız gelecek*]! . . . We're a sincere nation, we're a wholehearted nation. So that's that [*vesselam*]!"³² Cathy Popkin has astutely suggested that the subversive significance of "Dushevnaia prostota" lies in its rejection of the official "paradigm" of eventfulness and narratability.³³ Shifting emphasis from the comically defiant, self-absorbed narrator to the pedestrian, Nâzım's translation recasts the story as a woeful allegory of Turkish national oppression.

In another story from 1927, "A Trivial Incident" ("Melkii sluchai," translated by Nâzım into Turkish as "Ehemmiyetsiz Bir Vaka"), Zoshchenko's narrator tells the story of a worker, Vasilii Ivanonich, preparing for the special occasion of attending the theater. When Ivanonich arrives at the theater, the cloakroom attendant refuses to admit him into the arena if he doesn't relinquish his coat. Both Ivanonich and his Turkish counterpart Ahmet Niyazi miss the play entirely because of their inability to pay the required coat check fee. Whereas the Russian original concludes with Ivanovich walking away and spitting in the direction of the cloakroom attendant, the Turkish version ends with Niyazi quarreling with the attendants and then sneaking into the theater after the play is over.³⁴ As Popkin puts it, "We are not called upon to shed tears for the hero" in Zoshchenko's original,³⁵ but Nâzım's allegorical translation invokes precisely this missing pathos: "[Ahmet Niyazi] shouted and clamored, sat until the morning, in front of the closed curtain, inside this great temple of art, without blinking his eyes; he sat and sat, my dear fellows [*efendiciğim*]."³⁶ Sublimating the experience of theater attendance as an unattainable desire, Nâzım's protagonist becomes a tragic rather than a comic hero.

In this way, Nâzım's translations of Zoshchenko can be read as precedents for that moment in the late 1930s in Turkey when the ordinary "little man" (*küçük adam*) of the laboring underclasses in towns and cities became the central figure in the Turkish republican short story.³⁷ Although Vâlâ's Turkish translations, by contrast, maintained the humor of the original stories, they, too, deviated from the Russian originals in ways worth noting. First, Vâlâ rendered the *skaz* narrator as a traditional *meddah* storyteller, a shift that modified Zoshchenko's condensed aesthetics. In Ottoman literary tradition at least since the seventeenth century, *meddah*s were professional urban storytellers who performed in coffeehouses, private households, and the palace. A *meddah*'s improvised performance might incorporate mimicry of a range of speech styles representing social types, and the purpose of its comic exaggerations was to entertain as well as to portray social tensions.³⁸ It is well known that the first Ottoman Turkish novelists, in their deliberate efforts to write novels (*roman* or *hikâye*, used interchangeably) according to the European model, assumed the voice of the traditional *meddah* storyteller. Adopting the conversational *meddah* voice of his predecessors, Vâlâ's hyperbolic narrator is significantly more garrulous and dramatic than Zoshchenko's. In the story "The Cap" ("Shapka," 1927, which Vâlâ translated as "İntizam Avdet Etti" or "Order Is Restored"), Zoshchenko's narrator begins by noting "how far we've stepped forward [*shagnuli vpered*] in ten years." Following his translation of this sentence, Vâlâ interpolates the following: "It's nonsense to call this progress. I mean to say, we rose to the height of a bell tower!"³⁹ In an accompanying footnote, Vâlâ then suggests that the phrase *çankulesi boyu* (height of a bell tower) is the Russian equivalent of the colloquial Turkish phrase *minare boyu* ("height of a minaret," used to describe a vertical distance of approximately ten to twenty meters). This chatty and fanciful *meddah*-like remark is boisterous where the irony of the Russian original is subdued.

Second, Vâlâ's translations of the exaggerated representations of Soviet revolutionary life served as both implicitly and explicitly satirical commentary on the Kemalist reforms. In the story "Oh Teacher ("Uchitel'," 1922, translated as "Heygidi Muallim"), the secondary-school teacher Ivan Semenovich Trupikov is scolded by his students for arriving late to class and for calling on those who are reading newspapers or organizing their stamp collections during his lecture. Amplifying the original Russian's spare and minimal prose, Vâlâ's inflated interpolations ridicule Soviet revolutionary life both thematically and stylistically. A good example is the exchange between the teacher and Semechkin, one of the students reading *Pravda* in class. In the Russian original, when Trupikov calls on him apologetically, Semechkin responds curtly: "What is it? You think I must put away the newspaper? Yes me? Damn it!" Vâlâ's translation replaces the student Semechkin with a student named Nikolai (who is not Vâlâ's invention: Nikolai does also appear in the original story), whose reply to Trupikov goes much further: "What is it? ... My name is called again? Or are you trying to make an allusion [to Czar Nikolai]? ... Or are you trying to prevent me from reading the official newspaper of the government? You're denigrating Bolshevism, ha? You're denigrating the Bolshevik government, ha? Do you know what this would lead to?"[40]

Vâlâ's hyperbolic interpolation modifies the irony of the original, introducing a political schism between students and the teacher, who is represented as a nostalgic supporter of the imperial order. Although in the Russian original Trupikov is apologetic about the necessity of covering the history of Emperor Alexander I's reforms, nothing suggests that he is a counterrevolutionary. Abandoning the original's focus on the erosion of traditional hierarchies, the Turkish translation reinforces the image of Soviet Russia as a country of revolutionary zealotry and intolerance. Vâlâ's narrator includes a concluding note that is entirely absent from the original: "Be aware; don't suppose that I wrote this story because I want to agitate against government 'authority.'"[41] Such a disorderly classroom, he explains, could be acceptable only in the immediate aftermath of the revolution. The Turkish translation thus characterizes the narrator as anxious and defensive, motivated to distance himself from his own story in the face of repression.

We can say that Vâlâ overplays the internal tensions of these stories, in contrast with Nâzım, who masks their ambivalence toward the Soviet Union. Although it is tempting to ascribe this difference to each writer's different position in relation to the Turkish communist movement, I suggest that Vâlâ's translations are not simply or straightforwardly determined in this respect. Zoshchenko's stories were widely read outside the Soviet Union, primarily among Russian émigré communities, as a window onto Soviet everyday life. Vâlâ's narrator refracts that relationship insofar as his references to *inkılâp*, or "revolution," unavoidably evoke the Kemalist reforms. (It is possible that Vâlâ included the defensive note at the end of "Heygidi Muallim" because he was self-conscious about the story's double meaning in suggesting the extremism of the reforms.)

This dynamic is especially legible, even blatant, in Vâlâ's translations of "Fog" ("Tuman," translated as "Ümmîler" ["The Illiterate"]), "Chiromancy" ("Khiromantiia" translated as "Falcı" ["Fortune-teller"]), and "Shapka." Satirizing the Soviet campaign against illiteracy, "Tuman" (1925) relates the story of one Vasilii Ivanovich, who is designated literate though he cannot read and cannot write anything more than his name. It is impossible to read this story without thinking of the Turkish national literacy campaign of the late 1920s, when the National Schools (Millet Mektepleri) were established to instruct adults in reading and writing with the newly adopted Latin alphabet.[42]

In "Shapka," Zoshchenko's narrator makes the depiction of rail travel a vehicle for satire of the Soviet discourse of progress or "striding forward." Recalling an old memory of travel on a train that stopped so that passengers could help the train operator locate his cap, which had been blown away by a gust of wind, the narrator remarks that in the present a train could not afford to stop even if a person were blown off the train: "Time is valuable. We need to keep going."[43] Vâlâ's translation makes the motif of the lost cap, one of Zoshchenko's many allusions to the role played by coats and boots in the works of Gogol and Dostoevsky, into a satire of republican modernization. Popkin suggests that Zoshchenko made the loss of such sartorial items "an act of exposure, of the 'hellish' torments to which citizens are regularly subjected; of real identities beneath scripted roles . . .; of pajama-clad drunks masquerading as men of culture; and, most poignantly, of the arbitrary norms that circumscribe that culture."[44] Throughout the story, Vâlâ translates the Russian term *shapka* using the modern Turkish *şapka*, embellishing with comic details of his own devising, such as a passenger's "brief lecture on the uses of 'şapka'" after the train operator's cap has been recovered.[45] Although the former might seem a straightforward act of translation, the latter interpolation suggests otherwise, given that no reader of Vâlâ's translation could avoid thinking of the republican Hat Revolution (Şapka İnkılâbı) of 1925, which outlawed the fez and the turban and made *şapka* (borrowed from Polish) the modern Turkish word for a Western-style hat.

Describing Turkish modernity by appeal to psychoanalytic theory, the Turkish critic Bülent Somay has suggested that "the Kemalist 'Hat Revolution' . . . symbolically castrated the male population of the incipient nation-in-formation . . . by taking away their 'tall, red, challenging' *fezzes*"[46] and made the *şapka*, or Western hat, central to a new republican masculine subjectivity. Where the misplaced or mixed-up clothing in Zoshchenko's stories appears to comment generally on the arbitrariness of new Soviet social and cultural norms, Vâlâ's Turkish translation orients the disappearance and recovery of the cap specifically toward gender.

Vâlâ, the former communist, thus also used Zoshchenko's uncomplimentary representations of Soviet reality as a cover for satire of the Kemalist discourse of progress and reform. Vâlâ's translations can be understood as precedents for that moment of the early Cold War era in Turkey when literary humor assumed a critical function in the left-oppositional press resisting the single-party system. (Of special importance is the satirical newspaper *Markopaşa* edited by Aziz Nesin, Sabahattin Ali, and Rıfat Ilgaz from November 1946 to September 1949.)[47] If, as Rossen Djagalov writes, the Russian translations of Nesin's "satirical vignettes" would have "immense popularity" in the Soviet Union during the Cold War period, the circulation of Zoshchenko in Turkey in Turkish translation during the interwar years represents an important prehistory of that exchange.[48] Importantly, these stories in translation also undermined an official comparative discourse linking a New Russia and a New Turkey as separate yet equally triumphant engines of modernity during the 1930s.[49] Vâlâ's mediation of Zoshchenko's work by way of a separate itinerary emptied out the abstract discourse of monumental state visits showcasing the epic march to modernity. We might say that in refusing the hierarchical relationship between Russian original and Turkish translation, the doubling dynamic of Vâlâ's translations redoubles the ideal and the real of the entangled revolution, imagining each in its impossible pretense.

But Vâlâ's contributions to the Soviet republic of letters were not limited to translation. The loss of the hat as a phallic signifier in Vâlâ's translation of "Shapka" would become the central thematic of his most original work, the novel *Baltacı and Catherine*, which was neglected by both Turkish and Soviet critics even though it developed the interpolated hyperbole of the Zoshchenko translations into a distinct narrative style. By appeal not to irony but rather to the energies of what Alenka Zupančič calls the "comic proper,"[50] *Baltacı and Catherine* offers us a remarkable representation of the entangled revolution as a sexual revolution in particular. Leaving behind Marxism-Leninism, Vâlâ mobilized another materialist imagination of revolution.

VÂLÂ'S EROTIC COMEDY: REVOLUTION AS THE "MISSING LINK"

In *Life's Good, Brother* and *Nâzım Passed from This World*, respectively, Nâzım and Vâlâ discuss the day they first arrived in Batumi in 1922, encountering nude men and women sunbathing on a beach.[51] Upon reading the manuscript of *Life's Good, Brother*, the Turkish émigré writer Fahri Erdinç reportedly suggested to Nâzım that he modify the description of the women on the beach as "stark naked." "Bigoted people who thirst for our blood," Erdinç suggested, "wait in ambush" to use such "transgressions" against "us." He demanded "for God's sake" that "Nâzım dress these women in underpants." Refusing, Nâzım joked that "it would be difficult to find enough underpants for so many nude [women]."[52]

It is not difficult to see how the fraternal laughter provoked by the punchline of this joke about the opportunism of anticommunists perpetuates one form of masculinism, that of Turkish communist comradeship, in its resistance to another. Erdinç's anxiously traditional conformism and Nâzım's unexamined masculinism represent two complementary tendencies in the work of male Turkish communists, each foreclosing in its own way on substantive critical engagement with questions of gender and sex. By contrast with both Erdinç and Nâzım, and notwithstanding his own limitations as a thinker and writer, Vâlâ was able to confront this masculinism directly and to thematize its phallocentrism in his erotic novels and adaptations of the late 1920s and 1930s.

A historical witness to what we might call the crisis of the imperial father's authority in both the public and the private domain, Vâlâ came of age during a period when traditional intergenerational Muslim family life in Istanbul saw significant social and demographic transformation.[53] Subsequently, during his years at KUTV, Vâlâ also witnessed the dissolution of the patriarchal Russian family structure by revolutionary laws secularizing marriage, simplifying divorce, and legalizing abortion. This legal transformation was a response in part to the social crisis ensuing from the First World War and the civil war, which left millions of orphaned children and widows, and it was accompanied by a rejection of moral and specifically sexual norms among young urban men and women, who saw little value in an older bourgeois conception of romantic love.[54] Building on this discourse of sexual freedom, Eliot Borenstein has emphasized that there was a "second sexual revolution" during the 1920s aiming to subvert the traditional family by another divergent path. Drawing on Russian revolutionary asceticism of the late imperial era, this second, parallel discourse emphasized "all-male," "affiliative" relationships of revolutionary comradeship, celebrating men's freedom from "primitive" familial ties in their renunciation of love.[55]

VÂLÂ NUREDDIN'S COMIC MATERIALISM

Influenced by the first discourse of sexual revolution, Vâlâ narrated more than once an anecdote about the "free love" movement among the KUTV students, who had written on their dormitory beds, "Damn Marriage! Celebrate Free Love!"[56] Vâlâ's situation was further complicated by his marriage while at KUTV to an Armenian student, Anna Mikhailovna, whom he left behind with their newborn daughter, Hatice Süreyya, when he returned to Turkey in 1925 and never saw again.[57] Vâlâ's return to Turkey coincided with the Civil Code of 1926 granting women new family rights pertaining to divorce and child custody—an emancipation unaccompanied by anything resembling a sexual revolution because women were simply reimagined as mothers of a new nation. The code also declared that only a man could be the head of a household, restoring patriarchal authority in the family home, while the image of Mustafa Kemal as father of a new nation reauthorized patriarchy in the public domain. Taking aim at the republican discourse on gender and sexuality, Vâlâ composed numerous erotic novels during this period, including two adaptations of Soviet work, about which I have more to say later. Though the dynamics of the final scenes and passages of *Baltacı and Catherine* do a great deal to undermine its otherwise genuine subversive potential, it must be understood that this novel is unusual both within Vâlâ's oeuvre and within a generalized Soviet republic of letters in its brilliant use of comedy in imagining a true sexual revolution and nonphallocentric social order. Refusing to represent the Bolshevik Revolution as an abstract transcendent ideal, the novel's comic materialism emphasizes the concrete universality of the entangled revolutions, displacing a hierarchical comparative methodology through the humorous doubling of Turkish and Russian characters.

Serialized in *Akşam* from January to March 1928 and published in book form later that year, *Baltacı and Catherine* is set in the mid-1920s at Moscow University and narrated by an unnamed Turkish student in the Department of History. It follows the adventures of Tugan Tuganovski, a Russian professor of Oriental studies, and a group of students curious about what transpired between Grand Vizier Baltacı Mehmed Pasha of the Ottoman Empire and Catherine I of Russia, then Peter the Great's consort, during the Russo-Ottoman War of 1711. This war, also known as the Pruth River Campaign, was long a controversial subject in Ottoman historiography: though the Ottoman army under the command of Grand Vizier Baltacı Mehmed Pasha forced Peter's army to surrender, the peace treaty offered Russia unusually lenient terms. Eighteenth-century historians (most notably Voltaire) noted that Catherine, who had accompanied the czar to the battlefield, played a major role in the peace outcome, sending her jewelry to Baltacı with an envoy conveying a plea.[58] From the eighteenth century to the present, Ottoman Turkish historiography has constructed imaginative interpretations of this episode, usually with the aim of discrediting the grand vizier. As the historian Doğan Gürpınar suggests, a volume of popular history by Ahmet Refik titled *Baltacı Mehmed Pasha and Peter the Great, 1711–1911* (*Baltacı Mehmet Paşa ve Büyük Petro, 1711–1911*) from 1911 was probably one of Vâlâ's sources, providing a freely interpreted version that includes Catherine herself delivering the gifts to Baltacı's tent.[59]

Vâlâ chose this topic at a moment when historical fiction was growing more popular in Turkey, largely under the influence of the novel *Kara Davud* (1927) by Vâlâ's friend and former comrade Nizamettin Nazif, discussed in chapter 1. The dedication included in *Baltacı and Catherine* registers the intertextuality of these two works and the closeness of their authors' friendship: the first volume of *Kara Davud* was addressed to Vâlâ, who reciprocated by dedicating *Baltacı and Catherine* to "my friend and professional and intellectual companion, Nizamettin Nazif, who is the author of our romantic [*romantik*] country's first romantic work *Kara Davud*."[60] As I argued in chapter 1, in narrating the adventures of the warrior Davud during the siege and conquest of Constantinople in 1453, *Kara Davud* extended Marx's critique of the "Asiatic despot" into the Ottoman context. In a column printed on February 16, 1929, Vâlâ commented on Nizamettin's use of the tragic (*dram*) mode by imagining a hero who kills his enemies swiftly and serially "as if he were chopping cucumbers for tzatziki."[61] Vâlâ's *Baltacı and Catherine* also addresses the historical and structural problem of the "fetishism of the despot" but in a comic mode that emphasizes sexual alienation over economic alienation. In other words, the novel shifts its emphasis from the political-economic exceptionality of the despot (as the proprietor of surplus value) to the sexual exceptionality of his jouissance (as the possessor of all women).

Larded with Russian words, place-names, and political references rendered in Ottoman Turkish transliteration and garnished with expository footnotes, *Baltacı and Catherine* serves as a humorously exoticizing tour guide to Russian culture in general and the metropole of Moscow in particular. The novel includes approximately fifty footnotes explaining Russian and Soviet references. Included are notes on "غوسپودین" ("'gospodin,' [which] means monsieur in Russian" [4]), "باریشنیا" ("'baryshnya,' [which] means mademoiselle in Russian" [10]), and "پتروشقا" ("'Petrushka,' [which] means 'Beautiful Petro,' 'Dear Petro' in Russian" [23]; original Ottoman Turkish orthography retained here to give a sense of the work's textuality), among others. In a favorable 1928 review of the novel, the prominent Turkish poet and critic Ahmet Haşim remarked on the novel's "unprecedented orthography and style." For Haşim, Vâlâ's extensive use of Russian words and Turkish exclamations and onomatopoeia created a cinematic effect of "seeing" and "hearing" the events instead of merely reading about them.[62] Comprising a frame narrative and four discrete segments, the novel begins with the Turkish student's presentation of his thesis research about the war of 1711. As the student describes a conversation between Peter the Great and Catherine in bed together as if it were established fact, he is interrupted by Yekaterina Pavlovna, described as the "most beautiful" Russian girl at Moscow University, who criticizes his failure to use scientific method in his research (8). The Turkish student defends his "deductive" historical approach, stating that he is utilizing the same method as the authors of the historical serials published in Istanbul newspapers: "The authors of these works describe everything historical heroes do, including, God forbid, going to the toilet" (16). These self-referential remarks register the novel from the outset as a parody of the republican historical-revolutionary genre.

In the first segment, the narrator continues with his presentation, describing Catherine's attempts to persuade Peter the Great to send her to Baltacı as "gift" during the peace negotiations. Parodying the well-known episode of Davud slapping Sultan Mehmed II in *Kara Davud*, Vâlâ imagines a sadomasochistic relationship between Peter and Catherine. In an early chapter titled "Sadism and Masochism" ("Sadizm ve Mazohizm"), the narrator remarks that although neither Peter nor Catherine knew of the illnesses recognized as "sadism" and "masochism" during the twentieth century, each suffered from one of them. After cursing and beating Catherine, described as admiring "his vulgar and rapacious masculinity when she was ill-treated, slapped, and whipped" (36), Peter agrees to disguise himself as an ordinary Russian soldier and accompany her to the Ottoman side. Escorted by a devout Muslim Tatar soldier, the couple walk through an underground tunnel to the Ottoman camp, are captured by the Janissary guards, and are brought to Baltacı, who demands to be left alone with Catherine in the imperial tent.

As the Turkish narrator reaches the dramatic peak of his presentation, he is interrupted by members of the Cheka (Soviet state security) leading a raid on the university with an order for the arrest of Professor Tuganovski, an event marking the end of the novel's first segment. The Cheka appear to be seeking Tuganovksi's invention, a kind of cinematic time machine, intending to put it to use in police surveillance. Described as a "history gramophone and binocular [*tarih gramafonu ve dürbünü*]," this device operates by connecting to a geological recording and visualization system that Tuganovksi supposedly discovered inside rocks and stones (179). When the machine's controls are set to a specific date, it displays a cinematic projection (including sound) of all events recorded by the earth's surface on that specific date at that particular location.

Vâlâ's technological imagination may have been inspired by the global commercialization of the first "talkies" in 1927.[63] Parodying Turkish and Soviet modernization discourses on "catching up" with industrial civilization, the time-travel device, meanwhile, may have been borrowed from H. G. Wells's novella *The Time Machine* (1895), with which Vâlâ and his futurist Russian contemporaries were familiar.[64] In the novel's second and third segments, Yekaterina Pavlovna, the Turkish narrator, and their Romanian classmate Nik enter the professor's apartment, steal the time machine, and arrange for his escape from the Cheka prison.[65] Via a secret tunnel running from Moscow to Romania, Tuganovski and the students arrive at the principal battlefield of the war of 1711 and begin setting up the time machine. The narrative present in these segments includes details explicitly mirroring the past: for example, Yekaterina Pavlovna is aroused by the pain of her bleeding head after hitting it on something during the tunnel journey to Romania (143), an echo of Catherine masochistically enjoying the burning sensation in her legs while traversing the tunnel to the Ottoman camp (85–86).

In the novel's fourth and final segment, Tuganovski and the students replay the events of the war before they are arrested by the Cheka. The cinematic projection verifies the Turkish narrator's account of past events, including the sexual encounter between Baltacı and Catherine, while an emasculated Peter stands outside the imperial tent, peering through a gap

FIGURE 2.1. Book cover for Vâlâ Nureddin [pseud. Vâ-nû], *Baltacı ile Katerina* (Istanbul: Kitaphane-i Hilmi, 1928).

Focusing on the novel's first part, the book cover for the 1928 edition includes a visual representation of a naked Catherine being whipped by Peter the Great before her visit to Baltacı. The book cover supported the novel's circulation as a kind of humorous Soviet exotica, depicting Peter the Great with a pencil mustache, a belted Russian shirt, and a pet tiger. The representation of Catherine seems to be inspired by the popular image of contemporary White Russian émigré women in Istanbul. Described as *haraşos* (the Russian word for "beautiful") in the press, the émigré women made short haircuts fashionable among Turkish women. Failing to find steady employment in traditional jobs, many Russian refugees opened nightclubs and bars. They also started the trend of sunbathing (*deniz hamamı*) on Istanbul's Florya beach in the summers. See Zafer Toprak, "Istanbulluya Rusyanın Armağanları: Haraşolar," *Istanbul* 1 (1992): 72-79.

in the fabric. The astonished narrator remarks that "we were like invisible people—or spirits—inside the tent, and they were living in their own world unaware of our existence" (229). Though the suspense of this scene is amplified by recourse to a range of literary devices, including embedded narration, in the end it defies the expectations it creates. Although it is implied that Baltacı and Catherine have sexual intercourse, it defers explicit acknowledgment through a series of comic disruptions (about which I will say more soon). What *is* revealed is enough to suggest that Baltacı is given the role of the despot to play, offered unhindered access to the despot's phallic enjoyment, then mocked as not up to the task of fulfilling that role. In a chapter titled "They Can't Get Along in Any Way!" the narrator describes a physically "giant" Baltacı, with "a rough beard" and "a bulky body that is one and a half, two sizes larger than other men," courting an appalled Catherine, who can only be seduced by pain: "He treated her by petting her lovingly and caressing and kissing her. He sprinkled flowers on the bed. Disregarding his own age and rank, he kneeled in front of Catherine, and cried and cried. And I understood that he took pleasure from his self-humiliation in this manner.... As he heard Catherine grumbling in a strange voice, 'My God ... What kind of a man is this?'... he thought he had neglected to do something and became all the more polite" (231). The narrator had earlier described Baltacı keeping the company of young male sexual servants (*civelek*). As the highest-ranking Ottoman representative in the novel, Baltacı embodies the Oriental despot-Father who monopolizes jouissance with his possession of all male and female bodies, including his enemy's mistress.[66] The imperial tent then represents a phantasmatic space beyond the prohibitive law (of castration), where the observing characters and readers expect to find the exceptional, enjoying figure of the despot.

Refusing to fulfill this promise, the novel gives us instead a "perfect gentleman" (225) who sublimates his object of desire into an inaccessible Thing.[67] Surpassing the "effeminate [*efemine*] French chevaliers with narrow waists and pink cheeks" (226), Baltacı is caricatured as a parodic knight in the courtly love tradition.[68] To be sure, one might suggest that Vâlâ purposefully created a refined or "European" Baltacı in an effort to counter the representation of Ottoman rulers as barbaric in Orientalist literature, and there are occasions when the narrator affirms Ottoman culture as a mark of high civilization, contrasting it with an Orientalized

Balkan or Russian way of life.[69] But this temporary redemption of the Ottoman ruler only amplifies the comedy in Baltacı's sublimation of a masochistic, "whorish" Catherine, who enjoys being cursed as a "sukin syn"—Russian phrasing equivalent to "son of a bitch" (73).

"If the trigger of the comic is a split," the psychoanalytic critic Alenka Zupančič has written, "a break-up of an imaginary One (an image of One as wholeness, harmony, completeness, immediacy), this is by no means the whole comic story. . . . The real comedy begins only when the limit the two elements represent to each other starts to function as their most intimate bond and the very territory of their encounter."[70] The mismatch of sexual partners is all the more comical as the captive Catherine's disgruntled responses encourage Baltacı's abjection, in turn deepening her contempt. The comical failure of Catherine and Baltacı's foreplay destroys all images of the despot as "the Great Fucker."[71] Revolution, it suggests, lifts the veil from the despot's phallus and exposes its historical contingency as a privileged signifier. Following Jacques Lacan, who used the metaphor of the "quilting point" or "button tie" to describe the anchoring of the master signifier,[72] one might suggest that the gaps in Baltacı's tent, exposing its comic interior to view, represent the unraveling of this first knot: a displacement of Ottoman imperial phallocentrism as a social discourse.

It would be a mistake to conclude that *Baltacı and Catherine* stops here with the mockery of Baltacı as ineffective ruler—which is after all typical of Ottoman satire (*hiciv*), with its ad hominem attacks on social and political elites.[73] There are multiple modes of comedy in this novel, including derision (or mockery) and comedy proper. Before continuing, I want to briefly distinguish between these modes by appeal to the work of Zupančič.[74] "Derision," Zupančič observes, "is a constellation in which we are shown the Other as not being up to its task (in which we are shown the Other as 'lacking,' malfunctioning, and so on)," while comedy proper shifts focus to "the surplus, material side of this situation." Comedy proper begins with "the surprising appearance of . . . a surplus comic object," implicating characters in amusing mishaps, misunderstandings, and surprising encounters.[75] Whereas derision as a conservative technique aims to restore the symbolic order by reconstituting its imaginary unity, comedy proper plays with a fundamental antagonism, giving it material form as an unruly comic object. In constructing an effeminate Baltacı, this novel certainly uses derision to demystify the myth of the despot. But it does not stop there, with a particularized critique of Baltacı and what he represents. In its specific characteristics and dynamics, I suggest, the comedy of the unruly time machine imagines a structural revolutionary overthrow of phallocentrism.

Let us turn to a substantial example of the critical force of comedy in *Baltacı and Catherine*. In the novel's final segment, while the group watches the time machine's cinematic construction of a mismatched courtship between Baltacı and Catherine, they are spotted by the Chekists pursuing them. Just as the sexual act itself is about to be seen, one of the Chekists accidentally knocks over the time machine, so that it begins to project scrambled images and jumbled sounds. Here is how the Turkish narrator describes this interrupted projection of sexual intercourse:

> Just at that moment, the grand vizier and Catherine, who were lying next to one another on a sofa in a state that can be described as completely naked, ... clamped together as if they were caught in a cyclone and spun around; they became topsy-turvy. As if they were people in a cinema film seized by a raving mad mechanist, they receded into a distance after drawing near; they drew near after receding into a distance. While rolling, they lay down; while lying down, they rolled. They sprang like fish thrown into a hot frying pan. . . . Then, they quickly got up. . . . They quickly moved again. They kissed. And they discussed something, with their syllables getting jumbled.
> (248, SECOND AND THIRD ELLIPSES IN ORIGINAL)

This comic materialism radically desublimates and deforms the abject phallus, which cannot project a coherent, unified image. Though the embedded narration has encouraged the expectation of a sexual act, the anticipated representation of phallic jouissance is not to be, and it disintegrates into the comedy of what, adapting a term from contemporary media culture, we would have to call "glitch." In comedy, Zupančič reminds us, "not only do we (or the comic characters) not get what we asked for, *on top of it* (and not instead of it) we get something we haven't even asked for at all."[76] A key requirement of the genre is to account for this unexpected surplus, which we find in the royalty whose anticipated sexual congress devolves into spinning and bouncing like fish in a frying pan. This transformation of royalty into creaturely physicality is the specific source of laughter here. Such comic exaggeration is not merely destructive of a universal, transcendent notion of sovereignty through the intrusion of its concrete, material side, constituting its truth. The heart of the comic lies rather in the accelerated and immediate connection or "short circuit" established between universal and concrete, high and low.[77]

After one of them has knocked over the time machine, the Chekists demand that the professor reset it and demonstrate how it works. Far more interested in the sexual encounter between Baltacı and Catherine than in Baltacı and Peter's signing of the treaty, they attempt to operate the machine, with the unexpected result that as the couple's scrambled and whirling images reappear on the screen, the novel's narrator discovers himself interpolated into the scene with Baltacı and Catherine:

> How could I not be amazed; I was face to face with my own self. And how? Not like in a mirror reflection.... I was standing in a very different state than the one I am in now, fidgeting. I was staring in one direction with horror.... In the direction where the "imaginary I" ["*hayali ben*"] was looking, the Chekists were pointing their guns at the professor and *baryshnia* [*barişniya*, the Russian word for "young woman" used in the Turkish original to refer to Yekaterina Pavlovna]. But the Chekists and my friends inside the tent were not single individuals. Like me, they were duplicated. (265)

Confused, the narrator turns to the professor, who explains that the Chekists have mistakenly set the time machine to the current year, producing a recording of themselves viewing the distorted image of the sexual encounter at the moment when the Chekists first arrived to arrest them.

Here, the cinematic time machine once again implicates the narrator and other characters in a "surplus" comic situation. Where the novel has to this point maintained fairly clear distinctions between narrative temporalities, here comic confusion short-circuits those temporalities. As mentioned earlier, comedy is distinguished from other modes of humor (including parody, irony, and mockery) by its ligation of mutually exclusive realities in a single frame. In the passage just quoted, the unexpected continuity of past with present, spectator with spectacle, disorients both characters and readers, generating laughter. Following Zupančič, we might say that comic articulation here has an involuted structural and rhetorical form, analogous to the optical-physical dilemma posed by the representation of a Möbius strip, traversing one side of which takes you to its reverse without any crossing. No longer marking a boundary between past and present, the projection screen presents us with a single continuous surface, binding past and present, body and mechanized image, spectator and spectacle, in a continuity with an implausible logic that temporarily works.

For Zupančič, the Möbius strip illustrates the logic of comic articulation in that it "helps us think a singular kind of missing link: not a link that is missing from a chain (which would be thus interrupted), but a link which is missing in a way that enables the very linking of the existing elements, their being bound, attached to one another, their forming a chain, a smooth (causal) sequence."[78] I suggested earlier that Baltacı's abjection both desublimates and deforms the phallus-form. Adding to this, we might suggest that Vâlâ's novel both empties out the image of phallic enjoyment and reinscribes it as a narratological missing link. Thus fused in narrative, a contentless image serves as a point of articulation joining incompatible temporalities.

Refusing to provide an image of phallic enjoyment, the novel then deploys this missing and contentless image as a copula in narrative structure. We might say this deployment amounts to the textual repetition of an originary "missing link" between life and death, body and signification, human sexuality and cultural order. The novel's comic articulations of the intersections of person and machine, subject and object, and the sexual and sociopolitical orders signal a missed human encounter with life that never reveals its secret. Comedy demystifies the phallus-form as a fetishistic symbol whose arbitrariness veils this "traumatic point of linkage" with life.[79]

In Vâlâ's novel, such an entangled revolution not only signals transition to a new political sovereignty but also serves as a kind of wager on the repetition of an impossible passage or articulation between life and death, body and language. The "playing" of the history gramophone-binocular is a game of *fort-da*, destabilizing the phallocentric order by projecting comedy where we expect to find phallic enjoyment. This can be understood as a repetition of the structure of subjective and social origination in primary repression. When the image of enjoyment goes missing, it enacts a subject's (and society's) constituent division and its impossible striving to become whole. At the same time, insofar as each such "play" is a wager on a "Real" that lacks content, it marks an opening to the possibility of radical (Real) difference beyond the fetishism of the phallus.[80] This is to suggest that *Baltacı and Catherine* repeats a subjective and social origination so as to begin again in a time of revolution in both Turkey and the Soviet Union. At least temporarily, this entangled revolution can be imagined as the arrival of a nonphallocentric sexual and gender order.

One might want to distinguish the ironic and comic representations of the entangled revolution in Vâlâ's translations of Zoshchenko and in *Baltacı and Catherine*. Whereas irony derives its force from the clash of the universal ideal with the concrete particular, and Vâlâ's translations of Zoshchenko animate the gap separating the universal idea of revolution and its failed instantiation in both Turkey and Soviet Russia, the comic materialism of *Baltacı and Catherine* binds the universal and the particular on the same plane, making the gramophone-binocular an image of social and sexual origination. Rejecting the philosophical privilege that irony enjoys over comedy, Zupančič reminds us that comic articulation "bets on the possibility of a concrete universal."[81] Each concrete play of a "missing image" in Vâlâ's work makes the impossible realization of (universal) social revolution not a fall or a clash but a necessary risk and trial. Though Vâlâ does not offer a Marxist imagination of revolution here, he mobilizes another materialism, a comic materialism, that wagers on the possibility of a concrete universal, refusing to code revolution as an abstract ideal removed from concrete (corporal or worldly) mediation.

With all that said, we must acknowledge that the subversive potential of Vâlâ's comic materialism ends more or less here. In the end, unable to sustain this missing link as such, *Baltacı and Catherine* concludes by taking refuge in a fantasy of perverse phallic enjoyment. After the Chekists leave with the professor and Nik, the Turkish narrator remains behind with Yekaterina Pavlovna, who turns out to be a descendant of Catherine (via her affair with Baltacı) and a masochist as well. In the narrator's beating and whipping of the Russian girl "as if" she were Catherine, the phallus as fetishistic symbol is restored:

> I whipped Yekaterina Pavlovna with a sadist feeling that awoke in my heart—or more correctly, awakened personally by her in my heart. . . . As I

whipped her, it was as if I whipped and then ... kissed not Yekaterina Pavlovna but her mother's mother's mother's mother's mother's mother's mother's mother's—her great mother eleven generations ago—an exceptional Catherine who is a rarity in a century. Not "as if"! "As if" is superfluous ... I whipped and kissed!! I whipped and kissed Catherine in person for hours and hours. ... And this novel, which is "a novel of betraying the purpose of science in the name of reaching enjoyment as quickly as possible," is finished here.

(287–88, ALL ELLIPSES IN ORIGINAL)

The novel's final scene of perverse sexual criminality recodes the transition from the Ottoman Empire to republican Turkey as a merely political restoration, a substitution for the weak Ottoman father performed by the Turkish republican son, who can occupy the structure of the obscene father-of-enjoyment.[82] As such, the novel's conclusion establishes some continuity with nineteenth-century Ottoman Turkish novels, which in Jale Parla's authoritative account saw "writer-sons" compensating for the weakening authority of the Ottoman fathers by taking fatherlike roles in didactic narratives.[83] In the end, *Baltacı and Catherine* fails to reject this phallocentric and filial tradition of Ottoman Turkish writing, and in refusing to provide a sadistic Soviet counterpart to the Turkish narrator, it suggests a different itinerary for the Bolshevik Revolution. Seizing the history gramophone-binocular, the Chekists boast that by successfully consuming the transgressions of Peter the Great, Rasputin, and Catherine the Second as a form of entertainment, they will now be able to surveil all counterrevolutionaries (268). The Bolshevik band of brothers thus distance themselves from the Russian imperial past while maintaining the myth that the dead father is the sole possessor of unhindered enjoyment. With a logic analogous to that of Freud's account of the primordial father's murder in *Totem and Taboo*, Vâlâ's novel suggests that the Bolshevik Revolution killed the imperial father only to preserve his law prohibiting enjoyment.[84] Notwithstanding differences of temporal location (the imperial past in the Soviet case and the republican present in the Turkish case), this father-of-enjoyment becomes the mythical ground for a phallocentric organization of revolutionary societies in both Turkey and the Soviet Union.

In his sentimentalization of female masochism, Vâlâ eliminates the subject position of the woman. In this context, it is useful to recall Lacan's critique of stereotypical clinical discourses on female passivity: "Female masochism is a fantasy of male desire."[85] Fearful of the (relative) freeing of female desire in Turkey and the Soviet Union in the aftermath of the First World War, Vâlâ recoded femininity as desire for male domination. In the novel's final scene, the omnipotent phallus is retranscendentalized as a fetishistic symbol activated by female consent. Criticizing the fetishism of the phallus-form, Lacan had reminded us that the phallus "doesn't stop not being written." His careful and deliberate phrasing, "doesn't stop not being written," was designed to represent the mystification of the phallus-form as a historical necessity.[86] If as a comic work of fiction *Baltacı and Catherine* works in a critical space in which the phallus "stops not being written [*cesse de ne pas s'écrire*]," it reaches its end at the point where the phallus-form regains its silencing aura: "This novel, which is 'a novel of betraying the purpose of science in the name of reaching enjoyment as quickly as possible,' is finished here" (288).

FROM COMIC SUBVERSION TO BIOPOLITICS: THE LIMITS OF VÂLÂ'S "LEFT MORALITY"

What conclusions can we draw from *Baltacı and Catherine*'s foreclosed comedy for the Soviet republic of letters? While similarly sexualized phallic imagery of the Bolshevik Revolution can also be found in Nâzım Hikmet's avant-garde poetry from the 1920s,[87] *Baltacı and Catherine* is unusual, in a Turkish literary context specifically, in its comic-erotic novelization of the entangled revolution. In this context, we might remind ourselves that the first part of the twentieth century saw unprecedented growth in the production of erotic literature in Turkey and that neither the Soviet revolutionary context as such nor sadomasochistic sexual themes in particular were especially common.[88] In her analysis of republican erotic literature, Fatma Türe reminds us of the popularity of cautionary moral stories and novellas that often ended with the tragic suicide of fallen female characters.[89] Embodying and thematizing the literary and bodily surplus of revolution, *Baltacı and Catherine* inhabits a transnational literary space opened by the Bolshevik Revolution, demonstrating that representations of sex and gender were as important to this "traveling" literature as were representations of class antagonism and Marxist nationalism.

In his analysis of Soviet discourse about sex during the 1920s, Eric Naiman has argued that the Soviet literature of war communism borrowed the metaphor of rape and other images of sexual violence from representations of the Bolshevik Revolution in the Russian literature of the preceding decades.⁹⁰ The sexualized violence of the Bolshevik Revolution in Boris Pil'niak's novel *The Naked Year* (*Golyi god*, 1921), for example, borrowed from such works as Leonid Andreev's story "The Abyss" ("Bezdna," 1902) and Mikhail Artsybashev's novel *Sanin* (1907) as well as from the phallic futurist poetry of the 1910s. Including an ambiguous depiction of rape as well as of a possibly incestuous sibling relationship, *Sanin* represents the sexual humiliation of women as a subversion of conventional morality at the turn of the twentieth century. Identifying the essence of male sexuality with violence, Andreev's "The Abyss" tells the story of a young man who rapes his female companion after witnessing her being gang raped by a group of attackers. Doubtless the obscene content of *Baltacı and Catherine* has its own, somewhat more immediate genealogy in European and Ottoman Turkish works by Voltaire, Freud, Wells, Ahmet Refik, and Nizamettin Nazif. However, insofar as its focus is the eroticization of the entangled revolution, it can be comparatively situated in a constellation with such Soviet Russian works as *The Naked Year* and *The New Woman* (*Femina Nova*, 1918) by Veniamin Stroev, among other reflections on revolution and sexuality.⁹¹ Indeed, the comic materialism of *Baltacı and Catherine* might be read as a temporary interruption of this misogynistic tradition—even as its perverse conclusion, recoding revolution as criminal jouissance, marks the novel's final alignment with and continuation of that tradition. Opening this tradition to comparatism, Vâlâ's novel suggests that contact between Soviet Russian and Turkish literatures during this period cannot be understood by recourse to a hierarchical model of influence. The high and low doubles of Vâlâ's materialist humor articulates Turkish and Russian characters on the same plane, rejecting the universality ascribed to Soviet Russian literary forms in both Turkish literary criticism and contemporary Soviet studies. *Baltacı and Catherine* displaces the critical imagination of (pure) revolution from its home in Soviet Russian literature of the period. Refusing to embody pure difference within the Soviet republic of letters, it imagines in its particularity the limit of (social) revolution, registering the dual birth of the universal and the particular in the entanglements between the Bolshevik and Anatolian Revolutions.

After *Baltacı and Catherine*, Vâlâ composed two erotic literary adaptations based on Soviet sources: *An Obstetrician's Memoir* (*Ebenin Hatıratı*,

1929), based on an unspecified Soviet sexual health manual, and the half-completed *Among Monks and Nuns* (*Rahiplerle Rahibeler Arasında*, 1931), adapting both Antonin Artaud's *The Monk* (*Le moine*, 1931) and Iosif Kallinikov's *Relics* (*Moshchi*, 1925). Including direct echoes of Soviet discourses on sex during the New Economic Plan years, these literary adaptations further illustrate that the forms of exchange with Soviet culture during the interwar period were not mediated only by the genres of revolutionary avant-gardism or the global travels of socialist realism. At the same time, these works represent Vâlâ's attempt to cultivate what he called "left or revolutionary [*inkılapçı*] morality," which harbored deep contradictions.[92] Lacking the comic energy of *Baltacı and Catherine*, these adaptations mobilized an essentialist discourse about sexual difference that reflects modern biopolitics. Examining the transition from monarchical to popular sovereignty in the European context, Eric L. Santner has suggested that the "dethroned" kingly phallus reappears in the modern era as the uncanny creaturely "flesh" of the social body, which "oscillates between the sublime and the abject and calls forth the apparatuses of biopolitical administration."[93] Registering an analogous transition in the Russian and Ottoman Turkish contexts, these adaptations displaced Vâlâ's earlier representation of sex as an indeterminate ontological "missing link" or fundamental unknown of subjectivation. *An Obstetrician's Memoir*, in particular, embraced the discourse of modern science, which sought to control female sex and sexuality for biopolitical ends.

Advertised as an adaptation from "a scientific work by a Russian researcher," *An Obstetrician's Memoir* is framed as a work memoir by a Turkish female obstetrician and gynecologist, "N. N. Khanim," referred to throughout by her initials. In the frame story, she delivers her memoirs to her acquaintance, the journalist Vâ-nû, who publishes them in serialized form in the daily *Akşam*. While some female patients and couples visit her for the abortion of children conceived outside of marriage, others seek advice for the cure of venereal diseases such as syphilis. In one case, a husband requests the treatment of his excessively masculine wife, who physically resembles a man and prefers the company of women; the narrator's advice to the man is that he send his wife for hormonal treatments in Vienna.[94] In another case (included only in the newspaper serial version and excluded from the book), a group of traditional women refuse to allow the narrator-obstetrician to assist in childbirth because she is unmarried, calling in a traditional midwife and thus, it is made clear, risking the lives of both mother and child.⁹⁵

Attacked for the work's obscenity, Vâlâ defended it as medical literature with the purpose of curing "social illnesses [*içtimaî hastalıkları*]."⁹⁶ Though the individual Soviet source or sources of *An Obstetrician's Memoir* are unknown, it is plausible to suggest that it was produced as part of "a popular health advice program known as 'sexual enlightenment' (*polovoe prosveshchenie*)" developed by Soviet physicians in response to the sexual "crisis" of the 1920s. Tracing this program's evolution from the establishment of the People's Commissariat of Public Health (Narkomzdrav) in 1918 to its decline in the early 1930s, Frances Lee Bernstein has noted that Soviet medicine sought to manage the sexual adventurism of the revolutionary years through the production of putatively "expert" knowledge on sex and sexuality. Drawing on outdated theories of glands and nerves common in European endocrinology and psychoneurology, this medical discourse used its ostensibly scientific authority to naturalize and reinforce a binary model of sex and sexuality and reproductive heteronormativity.⁹⁷ This semiautonomous discourse would be supplemented in the 1920s by an official party campaign on childbirth and maternity health that vilified the traditional figure of the midwife and thoroughly medicalized both childbirth and postnatal care.⁹⁸

Modeled after the Swiss Code, the Turkish Civil Code of 1926 outlawed polygamy and granted divorce and child custody rights to both partners in a marriage. Though this women's emancipation went unaccompanied by anything resembling a sexual revolution in Turkey,⁹⁹ a wide variety of original and translated popular marriage manuals and sexual-advice literature were printed by private publishers during the 1920s.¹⁰⁰ Vâlâ's project of cultivating "left or revolutionary morality" developed in this context, against what he called "right or reactionary [*mürteci*] morality," which supported the veiling of women, and against "centrist or conservative morality," which permitted unveiling but kept women under men's control.¹⁰¹ His writings aimed to support the editorial and journalistic work of his friend and colleague Sabiha Zekeriya (Sertel), who would become a leading communist journalist in the 1930s.¹⁰² Sabiha, who came to socialism through a study of August Bebel's *Woman and Socialism* (*Die Frau und der Sozialismus*, 1879) during graduate study at the New York School of Social Work (later the Columbia University School of Social

Work), coedited with her spouse the *Illustrated Monthly (Resimli Ay)*, a magazine-style periodical that from 1929 to 1931 brought together left intellectuals including Vâlâ, Nâzım, and Suat Derviş under Nâzım's leadership. Though the journal is best known for Nâzım's campaign in 1929 against such "idols" of the Turkish literary establishment as Abdülhak Hamit and Mehmet Emin, it covered a wide range of topics, from contemporary family life to fashion trends and social issues such as prostitution. Advocating a public discourse of "equality in morality" (*ahlakta müsavat*), Sabiha's signed and unsigned essays of the period offered a Marxist analysis of the social roots of prostitution, educating her readers about developments in the Soviet Union. (For example, her article on the 1926 Soviet "new marriage laws" affirmed a couple's freedom and autonomy in entering into marriage without the interference of any third party, including immediate family.)[103] In 1926–1927, she also edited the Adorable Monthly (Sevimli Ay) book series "A Book for Ten Piaster" ("10 Kuruşa Bir Kitap"), aimed at preparing young men and women for modern marriage and including such titles as *What Should Every Married Man Know? (Her Evli Erkek Neler Bilmelidir?)* and *What Should Every Married Woman Know? (Her Evli Kadın Neler Bilmelidir?)*. Its manual for married men, for example, argued that "a man who does not ensure his wife's participation in love is no different from an animal." Describing "masculinity as the state of being active and intelligent, creative and proactive," it argued that men derive pleasure from the pleasure they arouse in women, who "enjoy being dominated" in sex.[104] (Vâlâ's novel *Love's First Condition* [*Aşkın Birinci Şartı*], published by the Resimli Ay publishing house in 1930, was an erotic marriage manual aiming to teach husbands the sadomasochistic art of lovemaking so that they could both sexually gratify their wives and protect their marriages against extramarital affairs.)[105] Insofar as the Sevimli Ay series idealized marriage and embraced an essentialist binary model of sexuality, it can be said to have supported the preservation of a phallocentric social order. At the same time, however, the description of lovemaking as "art" and the recognition of women's equal entitlement to pleasure contrast clearly with official republican discourse granting women new rights within the family but desexualizing them as libidinal subjects.

Registering the heterogeneity of the first moment of intensified literary exchange, *An Obstetrician's Memoir* contributed to this marginal public discourse on marital sexual fulfillment by shifting focus to the sexual health of partners. Cases discussed by the narrator include the occurrence of penis captivus during sex between a married woman and her neighbor's son and of female anorgasmia leading a married patient to look for sexual gratification outside marriage.[106] Matters of sex and sexuality, including transgressions of social and sexual conventions, are neither silenced nor punished. One might suggest that the novel's entanglement with Soviet sexual enlightenment contributed to its limited liberalization of a Turkish republican discourse on family and sex originally shaped by modern Islamic and nationalist patriarchal dictates. For example, despite official pro-natalist policies promoting childbirth and criminalizing abortion, the narrator describes an infanticide she performed under threat of death for a woman in an extramarital relationship (62–75) and mentions other cases in which she refused to abort a fetus, but her female patients did so on their own (18–23). Describing an engaged woman who is sent by her fiancée to obtain a letter proving her virginity, the narrator objects to "cruel and humiliating customs and traditions" that "enslave" women (16). While we ought to recognize the novel's openness on taboo subjects, including the subject of female virginity, we should also note the limits of this openness: insofar as the novel represents sex and sexuality as a kind of a feminine dark continent, replete with dangers including syphilis, voyeurism, and homosexuality (not to mention penis captivus), it also constructs modern science as the only legitimate authority on such matters, devoted to producing a heterosexually healthy nation. As its frame narrative concludes, focusing on the doctor's marriage to her publisher Vâ-nû, *An Obstetrician's Memoir* only reinforces a modern, phallocentric structure. "N. N., who knows all the subtleties, irresistible impulses, and defects of sexual relations to such an extent," (121) serves as what as Renata Salecl calls "one of the nominations of the excess called 'primordial father,'" embodying the promise of exceptional jouissance unhindered by the law of castration.[107]

The period from August to November 1930 witnessed Turkey's brief, failed experiment with multiparty politics as the Free Republican Party (Serbest Cumhuriyet Fırkası) was formed under the leadership of Mustafa Kemal's friend Fethi (Okyar), operating with Kemal's endorsement "as loyal opposition" to the ruling Republican People's Party.[108] The public appeal of the new party quickly alarmed Kemal, however, and it was dissolved after only a few months. Opposition to government policies in the

Istanbul dailies and sexually explicit content in the dailies' style and gossip sections triggered the passage of a new press law in July 1931. Severely curtailing freedom of expression, the new law granted the government the right to punish journalists and editors who posed a threat to national interest and public morality. Vâlâ's *Akşam* columns of this period defended the social value of his erotic novels, including "obscene [*açık*]" content.[109] Arguing that contemporary left morality was destined to be normalized, he designated himself as in the vanguard of loosening sexual and gender mores. In a column titled "How Do We Understand Morality?" ("Biz Ahlâkı Nasıl Anlarız?," 1931), he insisted that "a truly moral human maintains his firmness and balance against the possibility of being led astray" and that "the new generation ought to be inculcated with this type of morality."[110]

Joining his former comrades enduring surveillance, harassment, and arrest, Vâlâ was put on trial in August 1931 for offending the public with an erotic novel adaptation titled *Among Monks and Nuns*. Incorporating sections from both Artaud's *The Monk* and Kalinnikov's *Relics*, this feuilleton novel, which was left incomplete, narrates the story of a corrupt monk who serially violates female penitents and nuns in a monastery where same-sex relations and the infanticide of illegitimate children are matters of course.[111] Like the Soviet publisher of *Relics*, Vâlâ considered the novel's obscenity indispensable to exposing the corruption and decadence of religious institutions, but this defense proved ineffective in court. In the end, the sentence of thirty-five days that Vâlâ received brought an end to his engagement with both Soviet sexual discourses and erotic literature.

Today, Vâlâ is known in both Turkish and Soviet scholarship primarily for his acclaimed biography of Nâzım. There can be no doubt that the lionization of Nâzım is a factor in the neglect of Vâlâ's comic-erotic literary itinerary, understood as an archive of the entangled Bolshevik and Anatolian Revolutions. As *Baltacı and Catherine* suggests, Vâlâ was both profoundly attracted by and terrified of the possibility of a true sexual revolution that promised, more than mere sexual adventurism, the destruction of patriarchal phallocentrism. In this novel and the works that followed it, he ended by suppressing the radical possibilities he had recognized. We should recognize that in a Turkey where the republican emancipation of women was *not* also women's sexual liberation, Vâlâ's open engagement with questions of sex and sexuality via Soviet Russia places him on the left side of the cultural-political spectrum. At the same time, however, insofar as he represented feminine sexuality as masochistic, he renaturalized the historical violence that supported the containment of female sexuality for biopolitical ends. Despite this dialectic, or else precisely because of it, Vâlâ's writings do valuably complicate both conventional Turkish and Soviet literary historiographies, not least in recording the real heterogeneity of discourse on sex, gender, and revolution in the Soviet republic of letters.

Though Vâlâ did not write any obscene works after his imprisonment, he continued thematizing the displacement of family as an institution in his romances of the late 1930s and 1940s. Describing republican romances as "popular epics of the new society... distributed across each corner of Anatolia," the literary critic Ömer Türkeş has suggested that "these novels were the social conduct [adab-ı muaşeretinin] manifestoes of the republican generation."[112] Inculcating in Turkish readers new norms of femininity and masculinity, the most popular writers of the period, including Muazzez Tahsin Berkand (1899–1984), Kerime Nadir (1917–1984), and Esat Mahmut Karakurt (1902–1977), idealized love marriages over traditional arranged ones, though each had a different threshold of tolerance for societal transgression, with Berkand's novels refusing to grant unconventional love any happy ending, while Karakurt's romances defended love marriages across both national and class boundaries.[113]

The romances that Vâlâ published (including one under the name of the daughter he abandoned, Hatice Süreyya) varied the conventional romance storyline by depicting ordinary people unwittingly entering incestuous relationships. Vâlâ's use of his daughter's name as a pseudonym memorializes a trauma suffered by many Turkish graduates and instructors at KUTV and their spouses and children, who were separated permanently. These figures include Reşat Fuat Baraner, who served as head of the illegal TKP during the Second World War and left his German wife (Margarete Wilde) and son in Moscow when he returned to Turkey in the late 1930s, and Zehra Kosova, one of the most influential Turkish female graduates of KUTV, who left her newborn daughter in the Soviet Union in 1937.[114] Though Vâlâ refused to represent family fragmentation in the specific context of transnational revolutionary activism, he did not repress it completely. Transposing it into the national context, his romances generalized it by asking the question: What is the social "glue" or minimal condition that holds the symbolic order together, preventing the absolute breakdown of the family structure?

For example, the novella *The Punishment of a Betrayal: Love and Adventure Novel* (*Bir İhanetin Cezası: Aşk ve Macera Romanı*, 1944) is a modern Oedipus tale narrating the adventures of the young man Edip. The Turkish pronunciation of the name "Edip," an Arabic loanword meaning "polite" or "gentlemanly," is close to the Turkish pronunciation of "Ödip," Oedipus. Conceived during an extramarital affair, Edip had been raised by his late father and his father's wife, Servet (Riches), at the request of his birth mother, İffet (Chastity), who feared revenge from her own spouse. Many years later İffet's estranged husband, Osman, devises a scheme to befriend Edip, who is still unaware of the circumstances of his birth, and take him to a brothel where İffet works as a prostitute. At the brothel, İffet and Edip, unaware of their relationship as mother and child, are on the point of having sexual intercourse when İffet is overwhelmed by a surge of maternal affection, and a brief conversation reveals the truth. In contrast with other republican romances that idealize conformist domestic women, *The Punishment of a Betrayal* affirms women occupying morally transgressive positions, such as İffet and Edip's fiancée, Aliye, who are nonetheless "clean in their hearts."[115] In a postrevolutionary world in which good fathers are dead and bad fathers such as Osman are perverse enough to risk the destruction of the symbolic order, this novel seems to suggest that women conserve the paternal function through their maternal "instincts." As in *Baltacı and Catherine*, Vâlâ here recognizes the historical contingency of the phallocentric social order, only to suppress that insight by imagining it a necessary condition.

The family unit comes under threat again in Vâlâ's novel *Under the Weight of the Past: Love and Adventure Novel* (*Mazinin Yükü Altında: Aşk ve Macera Romanı*, 1939), in which agnate siblings fall in love with each other, unaware that they have the same biological father, and plan to marry until their mother intervenes.[116] Finally, Vâlâ's novel *The Man of My Life: Love and Adventure Novel* (*Hayatımın Erkeği: Aşk ve Macera Romanı*, 1939) narrates the adventures of a nineteen-year-old orphan, Nermin, who marries her wealthy employer, Rüştü, unaware that he intends his disfigured brother, who lives in hiding in the house's attic, to consummate the marriage in his place. Suspecting that the man who comes to her room at night is not her husband, Nermin refuses his advances and runs away.

This novel concludes with the brother's death, represented as punishment for male transgression of moral law, while Nermin is praised as having rescued the symbolic order thanks to "innate" morality and ultimately reconciles with a remorseful Rüştü. Rejecting both the closed intrafamilial and the open free exchange of women (that is, prostitution), the novel affirms the exogamous heterosexual marriage alliance as a necessary condition of social reproduction.[117]

In thus representing the phallocentric family as an inalienable social condition, Vâlâ's novels might be described as family romances in a sense made familiar to us by the works of Freud and the research by Lynn Hunt.[118] The estrangement of the family performs a double function in Vâlâ's work, on the one hand defamiliarizing family relationships as uncanny (*unheimlich*), on the other hand familiarizing the stranger as family and thus domesticating the anonymous masses of the nation. Vâlâ composed these works during the period that saw the "Sexual Thermidor" in the Soviet Union, marking the ascendance of the heterosexual reproductive family and the end of the Bolshevik dream of sexual revolution,[119] and although he refused the racial and eugenicist discourses that emerged in Turkey during the Second World War, he also failed to offer a clear alternative. He was publicly criticized by Abidin Dino and Dino's collaborators, who launched a literary campaign in 1939 known as the "Purge" movement (Tasfiye hareketi) against "older" members of the literary establishment for their failure to produce socially engaged literature. In the next chapter, I turn to the socialist-realist novels of Vâlâ's friend and *Illustrated Monthly* colleague Suat Derviş, who more successfully imagined other social possibilities at the limit of the Soviet republic of letters.

PART II

Marxian Form in the Periphery

Modernist Socialist Realisms

Chapter Three

THE PROSTITUTE CEVRIYE AS POSITIVE HERO

Suat Derviş and the Ethics of the
Socialist-Realist Novel

"One's first journey to the Soviet Union undoubtedly evokes more excitement and curiosity than other journeys made to unknown countries," wrote the novelist, journalist, and translator Suat Derviş in *Why Am I a Friend of the Soviet Union?* (*Niçin Sovyetler Birliğinin Dostuyum?*, 1944).[1] Written to counter the dissemination of state-supported fascist propaganda within Turkey, the book was one of two new publications sponsored by the TKP's Legal Communications Committee after a long hiatus from activity.[2] Liquidated in February 1937 by the Comintern under what is known as its "decentralization" (*desantralizasyon*) or "separation" (*separat*) directive, the TKP went dormant during the late 1930s, its members infiltrating Kemalist cultural organizations and launching new literary magazines and journals supporting an antifascist front in Turkey.[3] The defeat of the German army at the Battle of Stalingrad in 1943 marked the revival of TKP underground activism under the leadership of Derviş's spouse and colleague, Reşat Fuat Baraner. *Why Am I a Friend of the Soviet Union?* sought to educate the Turkish public by providing an overview of alliances between Turkey and the Soviet Union dating back to the Turkish War of Independence. Narrated as a travelogue from the midsection on, it included an account of Derviş's travels to the Soviet Union as a journalist in 1937 and 1939. With its description of Soviet Russia as an entirely "different" world that is "incomparable" to "ours,"[4] the book followed the conventions of what Jacques Derrida has called "the rich, brief, intense, and dense tradition of *back from the USSRs*," following André Gide's paradigmatic *Retour de l'U.R.S.S.* (1936).⁵

Contrasting "back from the USSRs" with conventional (secular) travelogues, Derrida productively observes that the former narrate a universal, allegorical journey toward a historical finality of "absolute human culture." He distinguishes the mythic style of these works from other pilgrimage narratives: the place described in *"back from the USSRs"* is not "the archive or seal of an event that has already taken place but rather of a process in progress" of a future in the making.⁶ As an observer of the significant progress in Moscow's development between her two visits, Derviş, too, represented the Soviet Union as an intermediary site of "the conception, gestation, and delivery of the future," as Derrida would put it.⁷ One might say that she accentuated the production and reproduction of this future in her extensive descriptions of improvements in conditions for Soviet women and children. Praising the Soviet Union as a nation of "exemplary" accomplishments in the arts and literature, industry, and agriculture (including collectivization), she also remained silent on the violence of this progress in a manner quite characteristic of many "back from the USSRs." The TKP's attempt to use mythic images of the Soviet Union to interrupt authoritarian and racist wartime discourse in Turkey would cost Derviş her career as a journalist, unable to publish any further columns under her own name.⁸

I begin with this discussion of Derviş's "back from the USSR" because it represents (among other things) the specificity and the difference of the itinerary of Turkish communist women who visited the Soviet Union. Along with the journalist, translator, and editor Sabiha Zekeriya (Sertel) (briefly discussed in the previous chapter), Derviş is one of the most influential communist women writers of the republican period. Unlike Nâzım Hikmet and Vâlâ Nureddin, neither Derviş nor Sabiha was educated at KUTV. Sabiha's contact with the Soviet Union began in 1963 when she settled in Baku, having reached it via Paris, Prague, Budapest, and Leipzig.⁹ Derviş had made her first trip to the Soviet Union as a reporter for *Dawn* (*Tan*) in the summer of 1937, publishing her columns under the title "Travel Notes," later to be incorporated into her "back from the USSR." I suggest that, notwithstanding the brevity of her stay, Derviş would become an important agent of Turkish and Soviet literary exchange during the late

1930s and 1940s. Because this chapter provides an account of this second moment of intensified translation and exchange through Derviş's literary itinerary and political activism, a brief review of her biography is useful.

Born to a Western-educated, elite Ottoman family in Istanbul at the turn of the century, Suat Derviş began her career as a novelist and journalist in her late teens.[10] Her first published poem, "Delirium" ("Hezeyan"), was submitted by her childhood friend Nâzım to the Istanbul newspaper *Alemdar* in 1920 without Derviş's permission. (Derviş would allegedly have a brief love affair with Nâzım during the 1930s.)[11] Her first novels, *Black Book* (*Kara Kitap*, 1920) and *Neither a Sound . . . nor a Breath! (Ne bir Ses . . . Ne bir Nefes!*, 1923), were early examples of Gothic fiction in Turkey, replete with allusions to Goethe's poem "Der Erlkönig" and Schubert's settings of it to music.[12] These openly romantic novels, full of vivid descriptions of isolated mad subjects enclosed in confining spaces, were followed by a series of realist short stories critiquing the modernizing Istanbul elite from a female narrator's point of view.[13]

Derviş went to Berlin in the mid-1920s to study at the Stern Conservatory and returned to the German city from 1930 to 1933, working as a journalist for newspapers and magazines, including *Die Frau und ihre Welt, Das literarische Echo, Tempo*, and *Revue des Monats*.[14] "Thief" ("Hırsız") and "Emine," two short stories published in 1930 in the Sertels' journal *Illustrated Monthly* (*Resimli Ay*), marked the beginning of a shift in Derviş's work in their focus on protagonists of the lower classes and social margins. It is common for critics to propose the year 1933 as a turning point in her work, though it may be more productive to describe this shift as a displacement emerging gradually with the connection to *Illustrated Monthly*, which brought Derviş into the circles of Nâzım, Vâlâ, Sabahattin Ali, and Nizamettin Nazif.[15] Derviş was deeply influenced by Henri Barbusse's "truthful" representation of the First World War in *Le feu* in 1916 and embraced his notion of "proletarian literature" during the late 1920s, a time when the editorial team at *Illustrated Monthly* would introduce this concept to their readership as "revolutionary literature, which aligns with and illuminates the new society developing in the Soviets."[16] Published as a novella by the Resimli Ay publishing house in 1931, Derviş's *Emine* narrates the orphan Emine's precarious life in Istanbul as a hired housekeeper and servant, and the sentimentality of its distant, external narrator risks making Emine an object of pity along with the beggars, pickpockets, and street children populating the *Illustrated Monthly* stories.[17] Despite its limitations, this novella should be regarded as Derviş's most important contribution to the earlier moment of communist translation and literary exchange described in the preceding chapters of this book.

During the 1930s, Derviş composed a number of serialized love novels featuring middle-class or elite heroines and combining critique of the institution of marriage with analysis of modern individualism and the fetishism of money.[18] The representation of urban workers, prostitutes, and street children in the socialist-realist novels that followed in the late 1930s and 1940s was shaped by her work as a journalist and urban ethnographer of the Istanbul underworld. Among Derviş's publications as a journalist, those of special importance include a series of interviews with the titles "Where Do the People of Istanbul Live?," "Our Young Women," "Who Lives Under Istanbul?," "How Do Turkish Women Find Jobs?," and "Master Workmen Who Can't Find Jobs." Produced for the Istanbul dailies *Republic* (*Cumhuriyet*), *Tan*, and *Last Post* (*Son Posta*) and conducted with unemployed men and women, pickpockets, drug abusers, and other residents of Istanbul's shantytowns, these interviews drew attention to the social problems of unemployment, exploitation of labor and absence of protections, and women's issues. In these pieces, Derviş managed to account for her own role as a "representer" of others without collapsing the difference between what Gayatri Spivak has called "representation as political proxy" and "representation as textual portrayal."[19]

During the early 1940s, Derviş's name appeared on the editorial masthead of *New Literature* (*Yeni Edebiyat*), the first "socialist-realist periodical [*toplumcu dergi*]" in Turkey and one that would have a decisive influence on her aesthetics and politics.[20] Published from October 1940 through November 1941, *New Literature* was produced in a bimonthly four-page newspaper format by an editorial team including Baraner (the head of the TKP), Zeki Baştımar, and Abidin Dino, two members of the TKP Central Committee who had recently returned to Turkey from the Soviet Union. Along with other leading journals of the Turkish antifascist literary front, including *S.E.S.*, *Yeni S.E.S.*, and *Küllük* (discussed in chapter 4), *New Literature* sought to fulfill the Comintern directive to launch a literary journal that would be both legal and devoted to influencing Turkish public opinion during the period of "decentralization." During its brief life, it became the banner of a literary school translating into Turkish the key concepts of socialist realism formulated by Maksim Gorky and Andrei Zhdanov in the 1930s, and Derviş's book reviews, which appeared in the column "A Novel in Each Issue" ("Her Sayıda Bir Roman"), are some of the best examples of Turkish Marxist literary criticism to date.

New Literature represented an important turning point in Derviş's life: after her marriage to Baraner in 1940, she would take an active role in the revival of the TKP underground.[21] Following the death of their only son in childbirth, Baraner was summoned to military service in August 1942 (a common fate for many leftist intellectuals, who were also exiled to remote cities in Anatolia). Still on duty but back in Istanbul four months later, he became a deserter, hiding at the home of Derviş's childhood friend Hüseyin Mütena from December 1942 to March 1944. With Derviş's help, Baraner convened a meeting of the TKP Central Committee in June 1943, issuing a group of party bulletins that were distributed secretly to sympathetic students and intellectuals.[22] As thematized in Nâzım's novel *Life's Good, Brother* (discussed in chapters 1 and 5), the government crackdown in March 1944 was triggered by a party bulletin left behind in the Ankara Reserve Conscript School and made public. In addition to copies of these bulletins, the evidence against Baraner included a portable Corona-Zephyr typewriter, a mimeograph, a lithograph, and piles of paper, envelopes, and books that Derviş had unsuccessfully attempted to conceal in suitcases in their friends' homes.[23] The state's repression of this "dangerous" communist writing practice would produce its own massive archive of documents, ranging from the reports of government agents and observers to the confessions and other materials prepared for the trials in 1944.

Something must be said about Derviş's participation in the Turkish underground as a link and carrier of messages from Baraner to the other members of the Central Committee. In this role, Derviş followed in the footsteps of the first republican Turkish communist women.[24] Sabiha Sümbül, who married Salih Hacıoğlu, a communist leader in Ankara, wrote in her unpublished diaries that after the couple moved to Istanbul in 1923, in the disguise of an indigent rural patient she conveyed materials and messages from Hacıoğlu to Şefik Hüsnü, then the TKP leader and a physician: "In order not to draw attention, I'd carry a basket of fruit or a jug of oil. So that the police would think I was a sick patient.... I brought many news and directives to Salih."[25] Lars Lih suggests that Lenin in his early writings imagined *konspiratsiia* not merely as party secrecy but as "the fine art of not getting arrested,"[26] and Turkish women's participation in the communist underground is a fine illustration of this active principle. We might say that Sabiha Sümbül transformed herself into a sign able to signify two different things: a sick patient from the perspective of state authority and a communist message to and messenger for the revolutionary underground.

As a semiotic practice of the control of appearance, in this sense *konspiratsiia* also entailed the play of gender codes. Mihri Belli, Baraner's comrade on the TKP Central Committee, stated in an interview in the early 2000s that during one of his meetings with Derviş in 1943, knowing they were under police surveillance, they had deliberately behaved (at Derviş's request) in a way suggesting they were adulterous lovers. Formed as he was by the traditional Turkish male code of honor, Belli was unsettled by this request for romantic role-play.[27] Without romanticizing the role of women in this context (as it might be said Frantz Fanon risked doing, for example, in his account in "Algeria Unveiled"),[28] we might suggest that this reluctant performance of the roles of an adulterous couple opened a critical space in which such gendered codes of honor were temporarily suspended. However limited in scope such a challenge may have been, among a Turkish communist underground in which traditional Turkish masculinity was still largely unreconstructed, it should be acknowledged as a precedent for the unbinding dynamics of anticolonial nationalism.

Arrested with Baraner, Derviş was given an eight-month prison sentence and Baraner a nine-year sentence in the court trials of 1944.[29] Unable to secure employment with an Istanbul newspaper after her release, Derviş departed for Europe, living in poverty in France, Denmark, West Germany, Switzerland, and Austria from 1953 until 1961. After returning to Turkey in 1961, she continued writing feuilleton novels for newspapers and visited the Soviet Union twice more in 1961 and 1970, two years before her death. Neglected in Turkey until the feminist turn of the 1990s, Derviş's finest serialized novels from the 1940s made their first appearance in book form in French and Russian during the late 1950s and 1960s.[30] Although Derviş's "friendship" with the Soviet Union produced her banishment from both Turkey and the Turkish language as a language of publication, Russian became the host language for the autobiographical *Love Novels* (*Liubovnye romany*, 1969), available only in Russian translation and until recently entirely overlooked in Turkish literary criticism. Set in Istanbul in 1946, this neglected novel traces the daily struggles of Fatma Taran, a persecuted writer who spends her days composing "thoughtless" romances and translating French detective fiction in a desperate attempt to support herself and her jailed twin brother, Fuad, a communist. After being detained in the state prosecutor's office, Fatma vows to stop writing cheap romances and begins a new novel about "a writer who is forced to write love novels."[31]

Like her fictional double Fatma, Derviş published numerous serialized romances between 1944 and 1953. Depicting male and female protagonists who are willing to risk everything in the name of love, these romances hint at the deeper, occluded story of Derviş's decision to pursue a life of activism at the expense of her social privilege as an elite woman. Rejecting her fictional double's negative judgment of Derviş's writings from this period, this chapter focuses on the magnum opus *Phosphorescent Cevriye* (*Fosforlu Cevriye*), best described as a socialist-realist plot interiorized by a romance, which was serialized in the daily *Night Post* (*Gece Postası*) in 1948. Examining this novel's literary, political, and sexual implications for both socialist-realist aesthetics and communist ethics, I trace the itinerary of the most influential of the traveling genres of the Soviet republic of letters within Turkey. Though the antifascist literary front established in Istanbul had dispersed by 1942, Derviş's romances, along with the writings of Dino and Nâzım explored in subsequent chapters, established the remarkable aesthetic legacy of the second moment of communist print revolution. Katerina Clark has argued that during the "ecumenical" years of the Popular Front policy and its aftermath, "the broad adoption of socialist realism did not occur" in the literary international.[32] Much the opposite applies to Turkey, where the 1940s saw intense formal experimentation with socialist realism and Marxist aesthetics.

Phosphorescent Cevriye borrows its title from a Turkish folk song (*türkü*) with the same title composed by Zeki Duygulu in the 1940s.[33] Derviş's intertexual and intermedial novel narrates the love-struck heroine's life in Istanbul during the Second World War and its immediate aftermath. Depicting the life of Cevriye, a street prostitute renowned for her radiant beauty, it tells the story of her unrequited love and self-sacrifice for a mysterious, unnamed fugitive whom she befriends in the streets. Though the nature of the fugitive's crime is never stated anywhere in the novel's three hundred pages, Turkish literary critics have imagined him an illegal communist, whose educated speech and preoccupation with reading and writing distinguish him from a criminal underworld defined by its street argot. Indeed, the unidentified "metal parts" that Cevriye discovers in this unnamed fugitive's hiding place can be sensibly understood as the parts of an underground printing press and as such serve as synecdoches for communist writing practice. *Phosphorescent Cevriye* ends with the fugitive's arrest and Cevriye's death in the act of attempting to dispose of the evidence that would incriminate him, a stockpile of writing machinery.

Despite disagreement about this novel's aesthetic value, Turkish literary criticism has generated a consensus regarding its incompatibility with socialist realism. Though the critic Ahmet Oktay was the first to establish the role of *New Literature* as a pioneering "socialist realist periodical," his analysis in *Sources of Socialist Realism* (*Toplumcu Gerçekçiliğin Kaynakları*, 1986) relies perhaps too heavily on the concepts of "lack" and "belatedness." Attributing all of Derviş's *New Literature* publications directly to Baraner, Oktay suggests that, "to tell the truth, even in writings by R. Fuat Baraner and Z. Baştımar, who are considered the most knowledgeable intellectuals of the 1940s, the discursive mode of the period is not overcome and socialist realist writing is not defined by *its own terminology*."[34] Oktay argues elsewhere that *Phosphorescent Cevriye* is "full of *ideological disabilities*" owing to "the concrete cultural/political/textual circumstances of the 1930s."[35] Drawing an implicitly hierarchical and stagist distinction between "social realism" (*toplumsal* or *sosyal gerçekçilik*) addressed to a broad range of social issues and "socialist realism" (*toplumcu* or *sosyalist gerçekçilik*) focused on class struggle, Şenol Aktürk suggests that *Phosphorescent Cevriye* is a lesser instance of novelistic social realism, surpassed in quality by the work of the socialist-realist writers of the 1950s.[36] Turkish critics who reject socialist realism, meanwhile, praise the novel precisely as a romance that breaks with the work Derviş published in *New Literature*. Such criticism thoroughly neglects the prostitute-heroine's replacement of the archetypal mother of the Soviet socialist-realist novel (as in Maksim Gorky's *The Mother*).[37] Rejecting both of these conclusions, which imagine an inauthentic or absent socialist realism, I argue that *Phosphorescent Cevriye* should be read as a feminist-modernist rewriting of what Katerina Clark calls the "master plot" of the Soviet socialist-realist novel and as a remarkable contribution to Marxist aesthetics.

In the following discussion of debates about socialist realism in Turkey, I establish that Baraner's *New Literature* essays on the "positive type"

THE PROSTITUTE CEVRIYE AS POSITIVE HERO

(*müsbet tip*) and Baştımar's calls for a new literature grounded in folklore established the fundamental principles shaping Derviş's fiction. Through a close reading of *Phosphorescent Cevriye*'s use of oral-speech styles and literary forms and of its feminist rewriting of Gorky, I show that Derviş's "possible aesthetic" of socialist realism upends the conventional view that the 1940s marked the genre's most "closed" or least creative period. Setting aside the opposition of "social realism" to "socialist realism" that is typical in the study of extra-Russian communist literatures, I argue that Derviş's reimagination of the Soviet novel is best described as an example of modernist socialist realism. Emphasizing the pedagogic functioning of her modernist transgressions, the chapter concludes with an analysis of her contributions to Marxist feminism. In contrast with the work of the men among her fellow comrades, Nâzım, Vâlâ, and Gorky, above all, Derviş constructed a concrete image of a nonphallocentric social order structured by feminine enjoyment, imagining a new, universalizable communist ethics of the act.

LITTLE MAGAZINES IN TURKEY: TRANSLATING SOCIALIST REALISM

Most Western and Turkish critics regard the representation of class antagonism as the defining feature of the socialist-realist novel. Drawing on V. I. Lenin's *What Is to Be Done?* and a range of literary works including nineteenth-century Russian radical fiction and religious hagiographies, Clark has emphasized another Leninist dialectic, spontaneity and consciousness, as the genre's motivating conflict. In her influential structuralist study of officially endorsed exemplars of the genre (including Gorky's *The Mother* [1906] and Feodor Gladkov's *Cement* [1925]), Clark conceptualizes the socialist-realist novel as a "single master plot" following the transformation of an undisciplined spontaneous protagonist into a conscious, disciplined revolutionary under the guidance of a party member.[38] *Phosphorescent Cevriye* follows this master plot, representing the transformation of the subaltern Cevriye into a revolutionary actor through her relationship with the fugitive. At the same time, it introduces some noteworthy variations on the structural theme. Before delving into a close reading of this novel, I want to situate it first in the context of debates about socialist realism in Turkey.

In *Why Am I a Friend of the Soviet Union?* Derviş mentions meeting Fedor Panferov and Aleksey Tolstoy during her visit in 1937, noting her high regard for canonical works of Soviet literature, including Mikhail Sholokhov's *Quiet Flows the Don* (1928–1932, 1940), Valentin Kataev's *A White Sail Gleams* (1936), and Nikolai Ostrovsky's *How the Steel Was Tempered* (1934).[39] Her book also provides a brief account of those literary and artistic exchanges between Turkey and the Soviet Union during the 1930s that established the condition of Derviş's own literary production. Despite its repeated crackdown on communist activity, the Turkish state maintained crucial literary and cultural ties with the Soviets during the 1930s.[40] Two prominent ideologues of the Kemalist revolution, Falih Rıfkı and Yakup Kadri, attended the Soviet Writers' Congress in Moscow in 1934. Revisiting Gorky's formulation, Yakup Kadri's address to the congress stated that new epic literatures in revolutionary societies such as Turkey and the Soviet Union ought to be "based on the writings, speeches, and songs of the toiling and working classes, which may seem primitive and vulgar to us."[41] In an article entitled "Soviet Literature" ("Sovyet Edebiyatı"), composed following the congress, Yakup Kadri provided a schematic account of Russian and Soviet literary debates from the late nineteenth century through the revolutionary years. Welcoming the dissolution of the Russian Association of Proletarian Writers and the establishment of the Union of Soviet Writers, Kadri observed that new proletarian Soviet literature displaced an older "vulgar, basic" photographic realism with "healthy, positive, and constructive [*sıhhatli, müsbet ve yapıcı*] models" representing "the ideal socialist world to be reached."[42] Offering a brief overview of new works published since the Bolshevik Revolution, he described Gladkov's *Cement* (1925), Leonid Leonov's *Skutarevsky* (1932), Kataev's *Time, Forward!* (1932), and Sholokhov's *Virgin Soil Upturned* (1932) as examples of new "constructive [*kurucu*]" Soviet literature employing "positive and optimistic realism [*müsbet ve nikbin realizm*]."[43]

An equally noteworthy event was the Exhibition of Fourteen Soviet Painters and Sculptors in Ankara in 1934, which included Isaak Brodskii's *Vladimir Lenin in Smolny* (1930), Alexandr Deineka's *Civil Aviation* (1932), and Sergei Gerasimov's *The Kolkhoz Watchman* (1933).[44] Anonymous reviews in the daily *Nation* (*Ulus*) described these artworks as examples of Soviet "new realist art [*yeni realist sanat*]" and praised them for demystifying "such vague phrases as 'for the people' and 'art addressing the people' for the Turkish public."⁴⁵ Turkish cultural historians emphasize that during the mid-1930s "new Soviet realism" became a reference point for a wide range of Turkish artists and writers, including those who sought to legitimize and popularize the Kemalist revolution through the conservative nationalist ideologies of peasantism (*köycülük*) and populism or popularism (*halkçılık*).⁴⁶ With its aim to reconnect "realism" to a rigorous Marxist critical epistemology and aesthetics, *New Literature* emerged as a corrective to this appropriative discourse, which risked draining such words as *realism*, *the people*, and *peasantry* of their critical force.

A February 15, 1941, editorial titled "What Do We Understand from New Literature?" ("Başlarken: Biz Yeni Edebiyattan Ne Anlıyoruz?") explained that the term *yeni edebiyat*, "new literature," did not represent a search for unprecedented formal originality. Describing Shakespeare, Cervantes, Balzac, Tolstoy, and Gorky as realist writers who had defied time, *New Literature* called for a new Turkish literature reflecting "the social life of its epoch in all its contradictions." "Unfortunately," it continued, "we have not encountered this in our literature until now, so we regard the type of art embracing this view and walking on this road as new."⁴⁷ Extending the work of its Marxist predecessors, including the Sertels' *Illustrated Monthly* and Yusuf Ahıskalı's *S.E.S.*,⁴⁸ *New Literature* was dedicated to effectively translating the emergent concepts of Soviet socialist realism and "Marxist-Leninist aesthetics." Along with official debates on socialist realism, the early 1930s had witnessed the formation of "a canon of Marxist-Leninist aesthetics" in the Soviet Union, led by the work of such intellectuals as Georg Lukács and Mikhail Lifshitz, who assembled the previously unpublished correspondence of Marx with Engels on topics in aesthetics.⁴⁹ As members of the dissolved TKP Central Committee returning from the Soviet Union on the eve of the Second World War, Baraner and Baştımar became important conduits for these debates. The artist and playwright Abidin Dino, who worked at Lenfilm for three years, was also an influential contributor, explicating key concepts of Soviet cinematic socialist realism.

In the pages of *New Literature*, the phrase *hakiki realizm*, "authentic or true realism," was used in place of *sosyalist gerçekçilik*, "socialist realism." Marx and Engels were never mentioned directly, Gorky was occasionally acknowledged, and Baraner published his articles under the pseudonym "Ali Rıza." Short philosophical columns devoted to key concepts of Hegelian

FIGURE 3.1. First page of *Yeni Edebiyat*, no. 9 (February 15, 1941): 1.

philosophy (quality and quantity, negation, the law of the negation of the negation, relative and absolute truth, matter and movement, and others) were published under Suat Derviş's name, though they are often attributed to Baraner. The book reviews and short stories signed by Suat Derviş are her own.[50] Despite the self-censorship of much of this activity, it is clear that the journal's project was to cultivate a theoretical language for socialist realism and Marxist-Leninist aesthetics in Turkish, though the use of a new theoretical translative language disguised or precluded the pursuit of certain ideas. In a debate with Baraner (as Ali Rıza), Dino described the realist artwork "as the kind of artwork that evokes in the consciousness reflections that coincide [*muvazî*] with nature and form a synthesis."[51] Emphasizing the role of consciousness and unconsciousness, Dino sought to account for a level of subjectivism in the creation of realist artwork, but Ali Rıza responded by quibbling over Dino's word *muvazî* (parallel or coincident) and denouncing the idea of an autonomous domain of art distinct from objective reality.[52] As I discuss in the next chapter, Dino would develop his distinct understanding of embodied Marxist realism in his contributions to other journals of the period.

In an editorial titled "Why Are We Debating Realism?" ("Başlarken: Niçin Realizm Münakaşasını Yapıyoruz?"), the editorial team described the debate as "the sole path to practice a people's literature [*halkçı bir edebiyat*] in its full sense, to elevate literature to the people and the people to literature." "To merely mention the people," they continued, "or to touch tangentially on topics that concern the people, is not sufficient for the creation of a serious people's literature and art. In fact, this might completely produce the opposite outcome."[53] Apropos of the gap between the appearance and essence of the real, Ali Rıza explained the "fetish [*fetiş*]" character of the commodity form and its obscuring of a totality of social relations. In this light, "true realism" entails "the analysis of each part in relation to the objective totality [*objektif bütünlüğü*]," as opposed to "naturalism" and to "symbolism, futurism, cubism, and many other isms that are nothing but manifestations of the contemporary social degeneration and crises in art."[54]

Other articles introduced foundational analytic categories of socialist realism, including "type," "positive type," "optimism and pessimism," and "critical realism," as formulated by Gorky and Andrei Zhdanov. In "Literature 1" ("Edebiyat I"), Baştımar described Engels' concept of "type" (*tip*) thus: "According to those who offer a classical definition of realism, in addition to remaining faithful to the accuracy of detail in his work, a writer or a poet ought to create typical characters in typical states and situations; the protagonists . . . ought to take the reasons and motives of their movements from historical and social currents, not from individual desires and passions." Explaining that type is not a rejection of the "individual [*fert*]," Baştımar described it as a synthesis of the general and the particular.[55] Meanwhile, Ali Rıza, elaborating on the concept of "positive and optimistic realism" as formulated by Gorky, Zhdanov, and others, insisted on the limits of "critical realism [*tenkidi realizm*]" depicting negative aspects of social life. A "truly realist" work, he argued, presents a "positive type [*müsbet tip*]" whose struggle with negative social forces provides a pedagogical model for the reader.[56] According to Baştımar, Gorky's early works effectively employed "revolutionary romanticism [*inkılapçı romantizm*]," inspiring "struggle for a new and prosperous society."[57] But neither Ali Rıza nor Baştımar addressed the tension produced by the Zhdanovian demand to combine "the most matter-of-fact, everyday reality with the most heroic prospects."[58]

Where the representation of a heroic political itinerary became a convention of socialist-realist writing for both Soviet writers and critics, the *mode* of heroic representation was as important as its content. As the depiction of a positive hero became the first convention of this genre, its other imperative was to produce a specifically modern literature incorporating oral literary forms accessible to the semiliterate and illiterate masses. Gorky's speech at the First Soviet Writers' Congress stated that "once, in ancient times, the oral [*ustnoe*] artistic compositions of the working people represented the sole organizer of their experience, the embodiment of ideas in imagery and the spur to the working energy of the collective body." Remarking on the unity of working life and artistic representation in ancient societies, Gorky called for a new kind of socialist-realist representation, with the purity of myth extracting "from the sum of a given reality its cardinal idea and embody it in imagery."[59] In this respect, Oktay's emphasis on the socialist-realist commitment to revolutionary romanticism might be said to neglect this imperative to cross the gap separating oral and written cultural forms.[60]

Dino's and Baştımar's *New Literature* essays echoed Gorky's pronouncements about folklore without directly citing them. Noting the inherently artistic character of everyday labor, Dino alluded to the Tantalus myth referenced by Gorky in his remarks in 1934 on the realism of legend.⁶¹ Baştımar's two-part essay "Literature and Folklore" ("Edebiyat ve Folklor") in 1941 described the influence of anonymous oral compositions on the works of Goethe, Dante, and Shakespeare, among others. Describing "people's literature [halk edebiyatı]" as "the first source to be consulted for the creation of a national literature," Baştımar, like Gorky, rejected crude imitation of oral forms; rather, he suggested, "we ought to know how to make good use of [people's literature] by studying it well."⁶² A 1940 poem by the communist poet Hasan İzzettin Dinamo (1909–1989) offered an example of this new literature. Titled "Köroğlu's Folk Song" ("Köroğlunun Türküsü"), it presents the legendary bandit and aşık figure Köroğlu (Son of the Blind Man), who rebelled against the bey of Bolu after the bey blinded his father. Tales and folk songs about Köroğlu had circulated in Anatolia since the seventeenth century, and as this legend became a focus of research in Turkish republican folklore studies during the 1930s and 1940s, Dinamo reclaimed it for a poetry of protest.⁶³

Derviş's contributions to *New Literature* included four short stories about urban workers and a sequence of book reviews (fourteen in total) of Turkish republican fiction of the time. Appealing to these translated concepts of socialist realism, Derviş's reviews criticized Yakup Kadri's *Yaban* (1932, translated as *Stepmother Earth* in 2020) for its naturalism and pessimism and Halide Edib's *Murder in Yolpalas* (*Yolpalas Cinayeti*, 1936) for failing to depict "typical characters."⁶⁴ These reviews alone are an important contribution to Turkish Marxist literary criticism. Though the antifascist literary front led by *New Literature* and other "little magazines" in Istanbul had dissolved by 1942, and Derviş was arrested in 1944 along with Baraner and other TKP members, Derviş drew on her experiences to compose *Phosphorescent Cevriye*, a very significant work of socialist realism, in 1948. Grounded in both Gorky's and Baştımar's calls for a new literature drawing on folklore, Derviş's serialized novel accepted this "law of genre" and then programmatically bent it. Adopting the title of a contemporary folk song performed in taverns, opium dens, and brothels, the novel might be said to have rejected the aura of folkloric authenticity ascribed to the patrimonies of oral literature, while expanding the concept of a "people's literature" to incorporate the oral cultures of Istanbul's underworlds.⁶⁵ Most importantly, as I suggest in my reading of this novel's combination of oral-speech styles and literary forms with realist representation, Derviş's refusal to mimic the Soviet novel produced a revaluation of the positive, specifically female hero as a modernist dialectical image.

CEVRIYE AS SIGN AND SYMBOL: THE POSITIVE HERO AS A DIALECTICAL IMAGE

In his memoir *TKP Intellectuals and Memories* (*TKP Aydınlar ve Anılar*, 1989), the poet Dinamo, a regular contributor to *New Literature*, described the Istanbul underworld of the Second World War years as "an utterly disorderly labyrinthine system": "In addition to a few thousand wretched, poor, hungry, extra-legal people including night thieves, pickpockets, snatchers, drug smugglers, drug addicts, and heroin users, hundreds and thousands of harmful people who were close to the security forces took shelter here and there. More agile and swift specialist crowds who pierced and overcame the adroitness of the police gallivanted on the higher echelons of society. The police were after a few leftists and a few thousand wretched people whose crafts I have listed above."[66]

For Dinamo, an army deserter who lived in hiding in Istanbul from August 1943 to March 1944, it was impossible to draw a clear boundary between lawful and unlawful status in this context. He described an intricate three-tier social structure in which a small group of leftist activists and the marginalized population that Marxism calls the *lumpenproletariat* lived alongside truly criminal and fascistic figures with ties to both the state security forces and the ruling elite. In its setting in the mid-1940s, *Phosphorescent Cevriye* enters this "labyrinthine" world, providing us with a fictional account of the social intersection of leftist activists with the varieties of Istanbul's "wretched."

Narrated in a third-person perspective focalized by Cevriye, this three-hundred-page novel is divided into four chapters, each chapter borrowing a line from the first stanza of the folk song "Phosphorescent Cevriye."[67] The first chapter opens on an evening in the mid-1940s as Cevriye is detained in a Beyoğlu police station with other prostitutes. Cevriye has just returned to Istanbul after serving a year-long prison sentence in Bolu and is evading the conditions set for her parole in order to look for a fugitive she had befriended just before her incarceration. While the prostitutes are transported to the central station for arraignment, at this chapter's end Cevriye's friends stage a brawl to distract the police and help her to escape.

The second, third, and fourth chapters describe Cevriye's first encounter with the fugitive in a series of flashbacks. Homeless and feverish after her release from a hospital where she had an abortion performed, Cevriye fainted in a caique by the Bosphorus Strait and was discovered by the fugitive, who offered her shelter in his attic apartment and tended to her for more than a week, refusing to take advantage of the situation and rejecting her indirect offer to compensate him with sex. During her recovery, Cevriye, by now in love with the fugitive, began leading a new double life as a street prostitute and companion of the fugitive, whom she visited for extended intimate conversations. The third chapter dwells on this emotionally intimate but entirely nonsexual friendship. Their conversations often turn to Cevriye's past as an orphan, but the fugitive reveals next to nothing about himself. Indeed, the words chosen to represent his activities, which include nocturnal errands involving a heavy "package" of some kind and "metal parts" stored in a trunk, are deliberately generic and abstract, leading Cevriye to imagine him a smuggler. Other textual clues, including his educated speech and preoccupation with reading and writing, which distinguish him from a criminal underworld defined by its argot, are designed to suggest that he is a communist engaged in illegal publishing activity.

The fourth and last chapter, "You Are in Mad Love," returns to the narrative present. Cevriye, who learns of the fugitive's arrest and incarceration, is outraged by the prospect that he will be given the death penalty and resolves to work with his relative, Kerim, to destroy the "metal parts" representing evidence against him (293). Lugging these "metal parts" through the streets of Istanbul in a *paket* (which might mean a sack, a wrapped box, or some other type of parcel), Cevriye rows a caique into the Bosphorus, but it capsizes as she tries to throw the *paket* overboard, upon which she falls into the water, hits her head on the caique, and drowns. In the novel's final scene, a fisherman in the distance sings the final stanza of "Phosphorescent Cevriye."

Reading *Phosphorescent Cevriye* alongside Derviş's journalism of the late 1930s, the critic Erol Gökşen has described the interviews "Where Do the People of Istanbul Live?" (*Cumhuriyet*, 1935), "What Is the State of Our Children?" (*Cumhuriyet*, 1935), "Who Lives Under Istanbul?" (*Son Posta*, 1936), and "Our Young Women" (*Tan*, 1937) as primary contributions to the novel's realism.[68] The hardships that Cevriye and her friends endure as homeless children clearly echo the experiences of the children interviewed by Derviş in 1935, while "Typewriter Emine," whom Cevriye meets in prison, is modeled on the office secretaries Derviş interviewed in 1937.[69] This is not to minimize the considerable structural and stylistic differences between Derviş's journalistic prose and her novelistic prose. Where the newspaper interviews are marked by "a purely monologic—abstractly idealized consistency of style" that deliberately positions the journalist and her interviewees "on the same verbal and semantic plane," as Mikhail Bakhtin would put it,[70] *Phosphorescent Cevriye* presents a remarkable literary representation of Turkish language heteroglossia.

Neither Derviş nor most of her Soviet contemporaries were aware of Bakhtin's essay "Discourse in the Novel," which its author composed between 1934 and 1936 when he was a political exile in Kazakhstan, very much on the margin of Soviet cultural life. Nevertheless, in composing *Phosphorescent Cevriye*, Derviş imagined the auditory "imperative of realism" in a manner consonant with Bakhtin's ideas. "The novel," Bakhtin suggested, "must represent all the social and ideological voices of its era, that is, all the era's languages that have any claim to being significant; the novel must be a microcosm of heteroglossia."[71] Considering the specific history of the Turkish republican language reforms, it is unsurprising that Derviş was able to make a similar inference, employing a device used widely in Turkish republican novels devoted to "true realism."[72] At the same time, however, Derviş's representation of dialogized speech can be said to mark a point of divergence between Turkish and Soviet socialist realism.

Though Gorky had employed a variety of speech styles in his early fiction, he strongly opposed the use of regional dialects, slang, idiolects, and ungrammatical speech in the Soviet novel, as he argued in a series of articles published in 1934 immediately preceding the Soviet Writers' Congress. It is in this context that the writer Panferov, whom Derviş met during her visit to the Soviet Union in 1937 and of whose novel *Bruski* she spoke with admiration, ended up playing a central role in the Soviet language controversy of 1934.[73] Criticizing Panferov's "pollution of Russian literary language by undesirable 'local locutions' and by verbal trash in general," Gorky argued for the use of simple and clear language able "to account for the heroic and romantic spirit of the reality that is being created in the Soviet Union."[74] This is not to say that Gorky's views, as set out in these essays, are entirely consistent. Observing "a sort of back-and-forth movement that is not very clear, a hesitation or denegation concerning the status of the language," the critic Régine Robin has suggested that Gorky's support for "popular" literature, on the one hand, cannot be separated from his anxiety about the debasement of literary language, on the other.[75]

For the most part, these Soviet language debates were not transmitted into Turkish letters. In *New Literature*, we can find articles supporting the Kemalist language reforms.[76] Rejecting criticism of some *New Literature* writers for relying on theoretical jargon, Baştımar insisted that the journal was devoted to a "plain and popular language" that is not "vulgar [*amiyane*]." In words that recall Gorky's views, he remarked that "the popular and the vulgar do not mean the same thing" and that "the goal of each newspaper and journal should be to find the level of enlightenment [inherent in the people] [*öz bir münevverlik, bir halk münevverliği*]" through the use of unadorned and accessible language.[77] The monoglot migrant factory workers of Derviş's early socialist-realist novels and her *New Literature* stories stand in contrast with the representation of heteroglossia in *Phosphorescent Cevriye*, understood as a logical extension of the socialist-realist imperative to develop a new literature grounded in orality.[78] In this sense, *Phosphorescent Cevriye*, along with Dino's plays, to which I turn in chapter 4, can be grouped with early Soviet novels such as *The Mother* and *Cement* in their techniques for the representation of linguistic diversity.[79]

Reading *Phosphorescent Cevriye* as a dialogic novel, we can say that as a street prostitute Cevriye serves as both an object of exchange and a mouthpiece, relaying to the fugitive and to the novel's literate reader the speech diversity of the Istanbul underworld, captured in her association with gamblers, pickpockets, drug dealers, and other prostitutes, all from a variety of ethnic and religious backgrounds. In contrast with the novel's third-person narrator and the fugitive, both of whom speak standard Turkish, Cevriye and her friends make abundant use of urban slang. *Phosphorescent Cevriye* represents many Greek and Armenian Christian characters whose only means of survival is their participation in the criminal economy, and Derviş directly simulated the accented Turkish of Greek and Armenian prostitutes and tavern owners on the novel's pages.

For example, Cevriye's Armenian friend Sünbül Dudu, who was once an Ottoman theater actress and now supervises a brothel, speaks in a style combining traces of her own cultural background with those of various men she encounters. "Cevriye, ahçiges kulaklarını bana dört ver," Sünbül tells Cevriye as she reads Cevriye's coffee grounds. "Senin yüreğinin ortalık yerinde çöreklenmis bir yılan gibi, bir şahsı meçhul oturoor . . . Sen şahsen kendisinden fazlacayım mefum oloorsun" (128, ellipses in original; Cevriye, my daughter, prick up your ears. . . . There is a snake in the midst of your heart, an unknown person is sitting there. . . . You're personally extremely in love with him). Here, Sünbül's Armenian ethnolect is marked by the interjection "ahçiges" (my daughter) and a variation on the Turkish idiom "kulaklarını dört açmak" (to open up one's ears fourfold), which incorporates "kulak vermek" (to give an ear) into the phrase "kulaklarını bana dört ver" (give your ears to me fourfold). Her accented pronunciation is represented by the orthography of "oturoor" and "mefum oloorson." Another dimension emerges in Cevriye's remarks on Sünbül's use of "Americanesque [*Amerikanvari*]" words such as "cinfis" (gin fizz), "havaryu Hello" (How are you? Hello), and "Okey" (259), through which Sünbül's speech style serves as a temporal marker, grounding the narrative in the conclusion of the Second World War and the emergence of U.S. hegemony in Turkey.

Cevriye not only serves as a mouthpiece for the diverse speech styles of the Istanbul underworld (and its musical cultures) but also communicates the richness of subaltern practices of reading and inscription, including tattooing and the reading of coffee grounds (something for which she visits Sünbül Dudu frequently). During her conversations with the fugitive, Cevriye frequently appeals to the symbology of folklore, informing him, for example, that a shooting star may signal someone's death (64). Though she is illiterate, she knows other modes of reading and writing. In this sense, Derviş, via Cevriye, can be said to reject the conventional understanding of literacy as only the ability to use letters.

In his fragments "On the Mimetic Faculty" and "Doctrine of the Similar" (1933), Walter Benjamin productively extended the concept of reading to other, older modes of mimetic interpretation. " 'To read what was never written,' " he reflected in the former fragment, "such reading is the most ancient: reading prior to all languages, from the entrails, the stars, or dances."[80] Where literacy in the conventional sense marks the ability to recognize and manage the arbitrary relationships between verbal utterances and written signs, the other literacies of subaltern oral cultures work through an analogical relationship in mimetic correspondence. In contrast with the linear duration of reading verbal signs, the temporality of this mimetic reading is an "instant": "It offers itself to the eye as fleetingly and transitorily as a constellation of stars," Benjamin explained in "Doctrine."[81] Cevriye is both an active interpreter and producer of mimetic correspondences, getting a tattoo of a handcuff on each wrist after the fugitive's arrest, like her namesake in the song "Fosforlu Cevriye."

Focusing only on one dimension of the novel's representation of orality—the use of heteroglossia—critics have analyzed its significance in relation to its third-person narrator, who uses a standard literate register. Tracing the narrator's movement from an external point of view to an internal one, the critic Melahat Gül Uluğtekin has suggested that Derviş sought to enact the ideological transformation of her national-bourgeois readership through the external narrator's gradually more sympathetic identification with Cevriye.[82] The external narrator often marks the difference of her own sociolect by enclosing in quotation marks the words and phrases she borrows from Cevriye and her friends. For example, early in the novel she uses the argot phrase "kodese düşmeden" in quotation marks (14), but as the narration switches to free indirect discourse a few pages later, the narrator's discourse becomes continuous with Cevriye's: "We just got out of the coop, that's no small deal! What a good man Barba is. You need a thousand witnesses that he's a giaour! [*Kodesten çıktık, boru değil! Barba ne iyi adamdır. Gâvur olduğuna bin şahit ister!*]" (29). It is certainly possible to suggest that that this skillful use of free indirect discourse compels the novel's readers to question heteronormative national-bourgeois values regarding women's honor (*namus*), criminality, ethical conduct, and non-Muslim identity. It would be worthwhile to analyze this novelistic use of heteroglossia in relation to Derviş's newspaper interviews from the 1930s, which employ a monologic narrator.[83] But this emphasis ought not overlook the importance of another crucial character in the novel: the fugitive, who embodies communist writing. The implied readers of Derviş's novel are not only members of the national elite but also her fellow communist comrades. The heteroglossia of Derviş's mature work should also be understood as an internal critique of the TKP's failure to reflect on the translatability and untranslatability of Turkish communist language across varieties and registers of the Turkish language more generally. *Phosphorescent Cevriye* can then be read as thematizing the separation of subaltern orality from communist writing for the purpose of fulfilling the socialist-realist master plot.

Although the nameless fugitive, too, is an outlaw, he has no organic connection to the dialogic mimetic oral culture of the Istanbul underworld. "It is as if he's from an entirely different country," remarks the novel's third-person narrator:

> Though he spoke Turkish, it was very different from the language that Cevriye spoke and was accustomed to hear. He did not even use one single word that they used.
>
> The skin of his hands was not roughened. It was evident that he was a human who hadn't done heavy work in his life. His nails were clean; his clothes were clean from top to bottom. He was reading books and also newspapers. That is, he was a literate, schooled man. He was reading a lot and also writing a lot.
>
> (112)

The external narrator's impressions are reinforced by Cevriye, who notices the fugitive's refined sociolect during their first encounter. Hearing him address her with the formal pronoun *siz* (you), "which did not exist in her language" (which knows only the informal *sen*), she thinks to herself: "What a dude [*monşer*, or French *mon chéri* transcribed according to its Turkish pronunciation] we bumped into this evening!" (63).[84] Though his polite formal register causes Cevriye to misrecognize him, she quickly realizes her mistake. Cevriye, who has encountered all kinds of men in Istanbul's "human bazaar," wonders in astonishment: "Are there different kinds of men than dandies and tramps?" (98). Although she sometimes mechanically repeats words and phrases from the literate register of Turkish without understanding their meaning, the "amazing and magical" foreign word *siz* translates across the gap between his literate register and her urban slang, giving her immense pleasure (63). It recognizes her respectfully as a human instead of "a slut [*sürtük*]" (74), and it binds her to the fugitive.[85]

Attempting to guess his city of origin, she remarks that whereas Kerim, the fugitive's relative, speaks with a provincial accent, the fugitive "completely

THE PROSTITUTE CEVRIYE AS POSITIVE HERO

spoke the Istanbul dialect" (195). Used as the basis for the cultivation of a standard written national language, the Istanbul dialect marks something more than a place of origin here: it associates the fugitive with the written language. Cevriye also notes the presence in the fugitive's apartment of bundles or sacks with unidentifiable contents (which the fugitive does not volunteer to describe) and notes that he spends his evenings with "small metal parts" stored in a trunk (77). If, as critical readers of this novel have often suggested, the contents of the sacks are communist books and pamphlets, it is certainly reasonable to suppose that the "metal parts" that Cevriye takes for smuggled goods are components of mechanical writing and printing devices—and that they thus serve as metonyms for communist writing.

Much of the novel's indirection and ambiguity regarding the fugitive's activities may directly reflect the repression in the communist crackdown of 1944, after which Derviş composed it. Although state censorship made it impossible to name the fugitive's crime positively, this did not prevent the communist author from speaking otherwise using the differential logic of signification.[86] Emphasizing the fugitive's difference from other criminal types represented in the novel (gamblers, pimps, thieves, murderers, profiteers, and drug addicts), Derviş conveyed the political nature of his "crime" without positively stating it. She was arguably more ambiguous about the "metal parts," but it is hardly fanciful to suggest that these "metal parts" were writing and printing devices (or components thereof), such as the typewriter, lithograph, and mimeograph that Derviş was caught moving in suitcases, along with books and TKP bulletins, on the eve of her spouse's arrest.[87]

The court documents of the TKP case of 1944 state that Derviş's fugitive spouse Baraner prepared at least five bulletins with her assistance between the summer of 1943 and the winter of 1944 and that they were distributed to different TKP cells in Istanbul and Ankara. These bulletins devoted to "Contemporary Issues" analyzed the fascist politics of the ruling government by examining the activities of a Nazi fifth column in Turkey, the censorship of the press, the government's relation to the Soviets, and fascist agents and German spies in Turkey.[88] In his memoirs, the TKP Central Committee member Mihri Belli describes the committee's attempts to establish printing presses for communist newspapers. Though this plan did not materialize until after 1945, Belli describes a meeting with Dede

Ahmet (Fırıncı) in the summer of 1943, in which the two posed as casual swimmers in the Bosphorus. Informing Belli about the purchase of metal type for minuscule letters, Ahmet handed him some samples underwater, asking him to obtain type for majuscule letters.[89]

"What was he doing every night like this," Cevriye thought to herself about the fugitive, "taking out small metal parts from a trunk?" "He is probably doing some smuggling!" (77). Anticipating Nâzım's novel *Life's Good, Brother*, which thematized the failures of communist writing in relation to the Turkish state, Derviş exposed the limits of this writing in relation to the oral cultures of the dispossessed. On the one hand, in such legal publications as *Why Am I Friend of the Soviet Union?* and in their defenses in court, communist intellectuals used standard national language to address the Turkish people. Their critical discourse aimed to expose the official-national mystification of such floating signifiers as *democracy, the people*, and *national interests* and to legitimize communism as the defender of a "true democracy [*hakiki demokrasi*]."[90] On the other hand, to render Marxist concepts in their writing in such literary publications as *New Literature*, they used a foreignized Turkish interspersed with officially purged Arabic and Persian borrowings and German philosophical loanwords of Latin origin, including *fetiş, concret, abstrai, realite, reel, formel, proses*, and *objektif*. The pedagogic purpose of all these publications was to teach "the people" the fundamentals of Marxist-communist interpretation so that they could read correctly the semiotics of national-capitalist representation (*Darstellung*) and transform themselves into self-representing (*Vertretung*) political agents.[91]

Absorbing the socialist-realist imperative to transcend the gulf between orality and writing, Derviş formalized and thematized that imperative in *Phosphorescent Cevriye* for the purpose of internal critique of Turkish communism. The novel raises profoundly important questions about the (un)translatability of communist political language across different registers and dialects in Turkish. However, it would be mistaken to suggest that *Phosphorescent Cevriye* aims to nullify the pedagogic project of communist writing by presenting it as abstract. Refusing to idealize the subaltern, this novel suggests that Cevriye cannot be imagined as the "'naturally articulate'" speaker of her own oppression. As Spivak points out, "There is no unrepresentable subaltern subject that can know and speak itself."[92] Describing to the fugitive her religious instruction by a neighborhood hodja, Cevriye reveals the ideological coordinates of her own submission to oppression: "God will give us everything we're deprived of in this world, in the other world.... Who knows, perhaps, He'll give me my precious printed silk cloths, the feathery, flowery hats that I gaze at covetously in the Beyoğlu shop windows" (171). In failing to have read critically the fetishism of commodities as well as the conditions of her own sexual and economic exploitation, Cevriye would certainly benefit from a critical Marxist literature focused on her "ideological counterproduction (education)."[93] Indeed, the novel follows what Clark has described as the socialist-realist "master plot," tracing the progress of a positive hero from darkness to social consciousness. But for such a "leap" to occur, Derviş seems to suggest, Turkish communists first need to move past their patronizing approaches to the gendered subaltern.

In adherence to the principles of the socialist-realist master plot, the final scenes of *Phosphorescent Cevriye* suggest that the linguistic-epistemic distance separating communist writing from subaltern orality might be closed. Cevriye, who describes the fugitive as having given her back her "human dignity" (299), is outraged by his arrest and incarceration and by the prospect of the death penalty, and she resolves to do what she can to help by destroying evidence, the "metal parts" (293). As noted earlier, after lugging through the streets of Istanbul a *paket* containing them, she rows a caique into the Bosphorus, but it capsizes as she tries to throw them overboard, and she hits her head on the caique and drowns. The novel's use of what Clark calls the "auxiliary narrative pattern" of death (auxiliary because it is "structurally subordinate to the central plot") conforms with the Soviet novel, in which the positive hero's passage into maturation is represented by their actual and/or symbolic death.[94]

In her final revolutionary act, Cevriye joins the ranks of those Turkish communist women who served as intermediaries among the male party members. The efforts that lead to her death abstract Cevriye's individual personhood and make her a gift offering to the communist underground, her body destroyed by its link to the illicit printing device, her name left behind as the arbitrary sign representing it. What we should also mention is that at the moment that Cevriye drowns, a shooting star appears in the sky and casts its light—that is, its phosphorescence—on the surface of the sea. I have suggested earlier that to read a shooting star as a sign of death is part of the symbology of folklore that the illiterate Cevriye brought to her intimate conversations with the hyperliterate fugitive with whom she had fallen in love. We might describe this convergence of the sinking printing press with the shooting star in the novel's final scenes as an embedded mimetic correspondence incorporating two distinct analogies: one linking Cevriye to that shooting star, another linking her "phosphorescent" beauty to its light on the surface of the sea.

We might say further that this mimetic correspondence is echoed in the song sung by a fisherman as the novel concludes. The lyrics are those of the last stanza of the folk song "Fosforlu Cevriye," which gave the novel its title. "I'm a sand of the seas / I'm a scale of the fish / Open your bosom, Cevriye / I too am a servant of God" (302). If we can read this linking of the novel *Phosphorescent Cevriye* to the folk song that shares its name as a mimetic correspondence at the generic level, it is fair to say that on behalf of the novel, the fisherman's song, as an artifact of subaltern culture, unequivocally affirms the illiterate Cevriye as a revolutionary heroine foreignized by her contact with communist hyperliteracy.

I want to propose that as both a symbol of subaltern orality and a sign of communist writing, the figure of Cevriye in *Phosphorescent Cevriye* is a dialectical image in Benjamin's sense of that term. Susan Buck-Morss's description of this concept is usefully lucid: "It is a way of seeing that crystallizes antithetical elements by providing the axes for their alignment.... [The] unfolding of concepts in their 'extremes' can be visualized as antithetical polarities of axes that cross each other, revealing a 'dialectical image' at the null point, with its contradictory 'moments' as axial fields."[95] The dialectical image marks a momentary intersection of oppositional elements without eliminating their difference. As "the sign of a messianic arrest [*Stillstellung*] of happening,"[96] the dialectical image of the positive hero arrests historical time and momentarily redeems the world.

I suggest that we consider Derviş's informed and specific work with this dialectical image of the positive hero a significant contribution to both Turkish and Soviet socialist realism. Clark has explained the common critical view that the Soviet novel represented a failed form by pointing to the "modal schizophrenia" or "dissonance" of Soviet socialist realism, its grafting of mythic discourse into realist discourse, as an obstacle to critical assimilation.[97] On this view, in attempting to close the distance separating oral and literary forms, the Soviet novel fatally submerged the novel in myth and historical time in epic. Here we are also reminded of Robin's description of socialist realism as an "impossible aesthetic," resistant to critical assimilation in "the nature of the particular combination that it put into figures: epics, heroic narratives, legendary-verse chronicles that take on the forms of verisimilitude, realism, and representation." "Having set out in search of authentic representation," Robin concludes, "this fiction ends up, in the Zhdanovian period, by figuring Neoplatonic ideas or essences, by killing any 'text effect.'"[98]

We can accept that socialist realism became a frozen aesthetic in the Soviet Union without discounting Derviş's work with that aesthetic, which was no merely derivative translation into Turkey and Turkish. Indeed, her work deserves to be called a possible aesthetic. We should affirm it along with the work of Bertolt Brecht and Bakhtin, who for Robin represent the aesthetic trajectories marginalized in and by Soviet socialist realism. *Phosphorescent Cevriye*'s literary figuration of orality is not Clark's "modal dissonance" but a deliberate, temporary relief of modal tension in which the image of the positive hero is rendered at the intersection of orality and literacy. It is not the annulment of historical time but the suspension of that time for an instant. Most importantly, Derviş's possible aesthetic does not rationalize the violent "auxiliary narrative pattern" of death in its fulfillment of the master plot. Borrowing Stephen Cohen's description of Stalinism as "two towering and inseparable mountains, a mountain of national accomplishments alongside a mountain of crimes," Robin suggests that the Soviet aesthetic of the positive hero maintained the enthusiasm for this order by concealing the tragic price "paid for the construction of socialism, the lost generation, the uncertainty of the future."[99] Derviş's novel refuses to domesticate the *Unheimlichkeit* of the positive hero foreignized by both communist writing and death. Insofar as the dialectical arrest of historical time occurs in *Phosphorescent Cevriye* at the expense of "blasting" its medium, the subaltern woman's body, it exposes the absolute gravity and urgency of the ethicopolitical work to be done across the epistemic divide between communist vanguardism and the gendered subaltern.

REWRITING GORKY: THE FEMININE JOUISSANCE AND THE COMMUNIST ETHICS OF THE ACT

I have thus far argued that the specific contribution of Derviş's *Phosphorescent Cevriye* lies in her reimagination of the positive hero as a dialectical image spanning the divide separating subaltern orality from communist writing. The literary-archaeological work of this chapter demonstrates that Derviş's brilliant manipulation of genre conventions was rooted in a deep understanding of those conventions. As stated previously, I have set aside here the term *social realism*, commonly used in the study of extra-Soviet communist literatures, to suggest instead that Derviş's deviant aesthetics is best described as *modernist socialist realism*. This term is more useful than its alternatives because of the way it recognizes and respects the historical categories by which communist authors of the period crafted their work. At the same time, the estrangement produced by the amalgamation of these conventionally oppositional categories establishes a productive critical distance, affirming these authors' formal deviation as a creative surplus or excess rather than coding them as a lack or deficiency. As I have suggested, the modernist sensibilities of Derviş's novel are best understood in the context of her commitment to the translation of communism across "idiomatic" and "standard" linguistic modes or registers.[100] In this respect, her work shares space with those of her fellow communist writers, including Dino, who also pursued a project of epistemological transformation of the subaltern and the communist vanguard.

While it is important to recognize Derviş's contributions to a shared project of Marxist "aesthetic education," it would be mistaken to neglect her departure from her comrades where matters of gender and sexuality are concerned. Shifting focus to her feminist rewriting of the socialist-realist master plot, I examine in this section the implications of her aesthetic for both Marxist feminism and communist ethics.

Anyone familiar with Gorky's novel *The Mother* (1906) would recognize the crucial similarities between Cevriye and Pelageya Nilovna Vlasova, both of whom rise to action by serving as "messengers" of revolutionary literature. Influenced by her son Pavel's illegal Bolshevik revolutionary activism under the czarist regime, the illiterate Nilovna supports the Bolshevik youth first by carrying revolutionary leaflets, concealed under her clothes, into the factory where her son had once worked. At *The Mother*'s end, having delivered forbidden books, newspapers, and leaflets to a nearby village, she is caught and beaten by gendarmes while carrying a suitcase full of printed and duplicated copies of a militant speech Pavel had delivered in court before being sent to prison. (Notably, the novel remarks on the use of different print and duplicating processes, such as the use of a hectograph.) Where the new (translative) political lexicon employed by

Pavel and other Bolshevik youth often seem foreign to Nilovna and other members of the older generation, her "self-translation" into an activist serves to naturalize and domesticate a new political language and identity.

Documents in the State Archive of the Russian Federation reveal that after Derviş's visit to the Soviet Union in 1937, VOKS mailed copies of *The Mother* and other Soviet classics in French and German translation to her.[101] Although both Gorky and Derviş traced the progression of a female positive hero from the world of orality into literacy, it was Derviş who imagined in the place of the Mother a prostitute who aborts a pregnancy (80). We might say that first and foremost this rewriting subverts the myth of the "Great Family" integral to the Soviet socialist-realist novel. Here it is useful to recall Clark's observation that "the political parable of the socialist realist novel was... patterned by the basic myth of Stalinist political culture, in which the working out of th[e] dialectic [of spontaneity and consciousness] accorded with the myth of the 'Great Family.'"[102] In Gorky's prerevolutionary classic, the Mother completes her transformation through the understanding that "all are family [*vse—rodnye*], all are children of one mother [*vse—deti odnoi materi*]";[103] her progress entails learning to embrace not only her kin but all revolutionary youth. In the Soviet novel of subsequent decades, Gorky's plot was modified to incorporate the representation of male positive heroes and mentors outside of family relations. However, it still perpetuated the myth of the Great Family, albeit in modified form: "in terms of an ongoing hierarchy of 'fathers,' or highly 'conscious' members of the vanguard, and 'sons,' or highly 'spontaneous' positive figures who were nurtured to political consciousness by the 'fathers.'" Clark suggests that this "myth confirmed symbolically both the purity of the line of succession from Lenin, the original 'father,' and the assured progress toward Communism."[104]

In portraying a prostitute in the role of the positive hero, Derviş refuses to model a communist collective on the heteronormative, phallocentric family. Diverging from the thematic structure of the Soviet novel, she also makes love a central theme of the master plot. Pavel's comrade Nikolai's remarks on love in *The Mother* offer a marked contrast with *Phosphorescent Cevriye*: love "reduces a revolutionary's energy—it always does! . . . There's no one we could walk alongside without perverting our faith, and we should never forget that our mission isn't small gains, but only complete victory."[105] Representing lovers separated from one another by imprisonment, exile, and death, *The Mother* is a typical example of the socialist-realist genre supporting the (Freudian) sublimation of sexual desires. Suggesting implicitly that the realization of revolution would mark the attainment of exceptional, uncastrated jouissance, the Soviet novel fails to imagine a structurally different alternative to phallic jouissance. Through a brief close reading of the complex, asexual, yet ecstatic relationship between Cevriye and the fugitive, I will show that Derviş provides a concrete image of an alternative social order structured by feminine enjoyment. Refusing to reproduce the paternal structure of the mentor–disciple relationship grounded in a morality of the superego, *Phosphorescent Cevriye* points to the possibility of a new communist subjectivity and ethics of the act.

The figure of the prostitute was used widely in the nineteenth-century Ottoman Turkish novel to represent the seductive dangers of modern translation and commodification for Muslim Turkish subjects. A commodity in the expanding world of commodities, in works by Ahmed Midhat Efendi, Namık Kemal, and Recaizade Ekrem the prostitute figure often leads male protagonists to their downfall.[106] Though this allegorical, moralistic mode of representation persisted in early republican novels, the translation of works by Aleksandra Kollontai (1872–1952) and August Bebel presented the possibility of understanding prostitution as a social institution. Kollontai's speech on prostitution in 1921 was serialized in Turkish translation in 1922 in the newspaper *New Life* (*Yeni Hayat*), published by the People's Communist Party of Turkey (Türkiye Halk İştirakiyun Fırkası, THIF). Countering "the bourgeois academics of the Lombroso-Tarnovsky school" who regarded prostitution as an inborn vice, Kollontai described it as "*a social phenomenon [sotsial'noe iavlenie]*" resulting from women's economic dependency in bourgeois family and marriage.[107]

As the regulation of prostitution became a subject of public debate in republican Turkey during the 1920s and 1930s, Sabiha Zekeriya (Sertel), the Turkish translator of Bebel's book *Women and Socialism*, composed numerous articles in the *Illustrated Monthly*. Pointing to Soviet Russia as a model for supporting women's employment, she emphasized the impossibility of eradicating prostitution by mere legislative or moral measures.[108] According to Sabiha, there were three social causes of prostitution in bourgeois society: first, the patriarchal organization of the economy that bars women from the professions offers no viable employment options to unmarried and divorced women who need to earn their own living; second, the "white slave trade"; and, third, the ideology of bourgeois gender, which compelled poor women to "sell themselves" in exchange for jewelry, clothing, and beauty products. Sabiha emerged as a strong supporter of women's economic independence as well as of their "moral equality [*ahlakta müsavat*]" with men, rejecting the conflation of women's sexual and moral freedom with prostitution.[109]

As a contribution to this Marxist-feminist critique of patriarchy, *Phosphorescent Cevriye* emphasizes that the prostitute is *not* an exception to "honorable" women: rather, the prostitute typifies all women's objectification and commodification in a modernizing patriarchal Turkey connected into the global capitalist economy of the war period. Sitting at the dinner table with the fugitive, Cevriye pities married women: "'Among husbands, there must be such burdensome, dumpy, bad-tempered, foolish ones [*ne sakiller, ne gebeşler, ne huysuzlar, ne andavallılar vardır*],' she thought.... Even if their husbands are dotard, sulky, good-for-nothing, or peevish, they have to spend their lives with them" (96). By contrast with the lifelong imprisonment of married women, Cevriye feels free—though it is impossible to overlook the irony of this remark in light of the novel's representation of systematic male violence against prostitutes in the criminal underground. For Derviş, Cevriye and married women are the inverted doubles of each another in a society where sexual difference cuts across other forms of social stratification, subordinating women to men by a range of different patriarchal arrangements, from bourgeois marriage to arranged marriage to the keeping of mistresses to prostitution.

Cevriye's nonsexual friendship with the fugitive challenges the phallocentrism of gender and sexual relations in the national order. Though initially Cevriye attempts to arouse him, he maintains a friendly distance, refusing any sexual encounters (137). As their friendship develops, she can no longer "do in front of him her vulgar, carnal flirtatious acts, which drove other men crazy, or utter her obscene, arousing witticisms; she forgot all the tricks and skills she used to sell her womanhood" (118). Insofar as the figure of the prostitute is associated here with a set of deceptive feminine bodily gestures and speech-acts, the prostitute is not understood as an exception to (hetero)normative femininity: rather, embodying the dynamic of phallocentric sexual relations in their purity, she reveals the essence of femininity as masquerade within the hegemonic order. In this respect, Derviş anticipates Jacques Lacan's conceptualization of femininity as masquerade (based on Joan Riviere's essay "Womanliness as Masquerade," 1929).

For Lacan, both men and women undergo the primordial loss of castration in their emergence as subjects in a phallocentric society, and the symbolic order operates by veiling this lack in different ways. Insofar as the phallus becomes the signifier of this loss in a patriarchal social context, men and women occupy structurally different positions: whereas masculinity is a pretense for *having* the phallus, women, defined by their anatomical lack, are ascribed the role of *being* the phallus for men. Femininity in a phallocentric social context can be understood as a masquerade to the extent that it entails adorning the body and covering up what one lacks in making oneself an object for men's fantasy and possession: "It is for what she is not that she expects to be desired as well as loved."[110] Cevriye's inability to perform her usual act marks the opening of a critical space in which the violent contingency of woman's masquerade is exposed and temporarily annulled.

The fugitive's attic apartment is a liminal space in which the phallocentric social order is both criticized and displaced by a (positive) imagination of another sexuation and enjoyment. What binds Cevriye to the fugitive is not merely his caregiving during her illness but also his recognition of her as a dignified subject: "He respected Cevriye," writes the narrator. "He was the first human not to separate Cevriye from... honorable [*namuslu*] women. He said 'You' [*Siz*, the formal second-person pronoun in Turkish] to Cevriye" (116). It is true that Cevriye, who is objectified for the satisfaction of male sexual desire, is sometimes the recipient of exceptional acts of kindness and generosity from the Greek tavern owner Barba and other men in the underworld. But benevolence does not in itself require the recognition of another as an end in herself.[111] To be sure, Cevriye's love for the fugitive includes an imaginary dimension: to an extent, she falls in love with the affirmative mirror image or ideal ego of herself that he reflects back to her. Yet Cevriye's love does not remain *only* in this register. Rather, it assumes a dimension of the Real, which is of specific interest here.

In attempting to explain the absence of a sexual relationship between Cevriye and the fugitive, critics have described the fugitive's attic apartment as a purgatory for the "sinful" Cevriye, who assumes bodily asceticism and spiritual purification there.[112] Operating within the milieu of an elite moralizing readership, the novel's narrator appears to encourage this interpretation: "Cevriye, who gave her body to anyone, loved him with an unexpected spiritual virginity." "In his room, next to him, the sparkles in her hair resembled the glitters painted around the images of angels on cheap postcards, creating a divine halo above her hair" (175). Undoubtedly, this image of an angelic (Christian) icon of newfound moral chastity makes the sex worker Cevriye more palatable to an elite moralizing national readership. However, we would be mistaken to let that implied reader bound our interpretation. Although in her nonsexual relationship with the fugitive, Cevriye exits the phallocentric (an)economy of jouissance, this does not mean she has no further relation to enjoyment. Cevriye loves the fugitive as she loves God, "regarding him so sublime that she did not expect anything from him in return for her feelings, just as she would not hope for a response from God for her affection, love, and respect" (174). Borrowing the stock imagery of the moth and candle from Sufist mystical literature, the narrator describes Cevriye as a moth casting herself into the flame of the beloved (91).[113] During an exchange of gifts with the fugitive, Cevriye expresses her gratitude with a traditional gesture, kissing the fugitive's hand—a gesture that she then compares to an act of worship, awakening in her an unprecedented, "painfully intense" feeling of "happiness and pleasure" (190). Drawing on psychoanalytic theory, we might suggest that the religious-mystical codification of Cevriye's love in these instances is interesting and meaningful in its representation of the structural possibility of another (nonphallic) jouissance.

Describing in *Encore* the mystic's ecstatic experience as "feminine jouissance," Lacan writes: "It's like for Saint Teresa—you need but go to Rome and see the statue by Bernini to immediately understand that she's coming. There's no doubt about it."[114] In its reliance on the archetype of the mystic, Lacan's late work is useful in explicating the alternative sexuation and enjoyment imagined by Derviş (though, unlike Lacan, Derviş makes use of the symbology of both Christian and Sufist mystical traditions). For Lacan, women, like men, are subject to the primordial loss of castration in a phallocentric social context, but they are not "wholly hemmed in by the phallic function": "the phallus is . . . the signifier of Man," not of Woman. Precisely because the phallocentric order cannot *entirely* assimilate her difference, woman marks the possibility of establishing another relation to the Real of primordial loss and to enjoyment. While no woman (or man) is compelled to invest in this other path of subjectivation, its fortuitous emergence entails "the forging of *a new master signifier*" of the representation of primordial loss.[115] In the feminine structure, no ready-made, single, fixed signifier is available; depending on one's culture or subculture, it may appear in the form of God, art, or music. In Cevriye's case, the fugitive becomes this master signifier, and in refusing to relate to him by the terms of the symbolic order (that is, as phallus), Cevriye locates him topographically in the Real, relating to him as an unattainable Other.

The feminine structure marks the establishment of a fundamentally different relation to the master signifier, creating a different economy of enjoyment. Whereas in the masculine structure the prohibitive master signifier of the Father's "No!" fundamentally closes off and limits man's desire, the master signifier in the feminine structure does not establish such a negative boundary. Hemmed into the symbolic, man channels desire into the closed set of women in the masculine structure, but this experience of phallic jouissance is masturbatory, finite, and dissatisfying. In the phallocentric order, man invests his partner insofar as she stands in for the (prohibited) object cause of his desire, and woman relates to him insofar as he "serve[s] as prop for the phallus for her."[116] Phallic enjoyment is finite because it is supported by the fantasy of a primordial Father who escapes castration. Its experience is a disappointment measured against the exceptional (that is, uncastrated) jouissance of the Father, who is imagined to experience true enjoyment.

Derviş's thematization of prostitution reveals the fragility of a phallic economy of enjoyment. When Cevriye is not with the fugitive, she continues to work as a prostitute: "Apart from the life she spent in that secret, mysterious room, in that attic apartment on the Necatibey Street, Cevriye was again the old Cevriye.... She was tramping the streets and giving her love and womanhood to whoever wanted it in dark, secluded living quarters, cheap rentals, and fire ruins" (120). During these sexual encounters, Cevriye invests her partners as phallus (as money or sometimes as "the organ as instrument of the [phallic] signifier"),[117] while men relate to her as a mere fetish object. Imagined as an obscene social act, the sexual encounter with a prostitute is supported by a fantasy of the Father's exceptional jouissance. The prohibitive moral law of the Father, which paradoxically achieves transgression at its moment of foundation, can dominate the symbolic order only by permitting clandestine immoral enjoyment in the underworld.

In providing something more than mere critique of the phallocentric order, *Phosphorescent Cevriye* imagines an alternative (an)economy of feminine enjoyment. Cevriye's asexual relation with the fugitive shows that the feminine jouissance is a "jouissance of love." Like the ecstasy of a religious mystic, it is asexual "and yet ... *of* and *in* the body,"[118] marked by an experience of satisfaction of the drives: "feeling herself drunk even when she did not put a drink in her mouth," Cevriye was filled with "intense excitement" (120). The field of feminine jouissance is not bound: eliminating the fantasy of a prohibitive Father, the feminine structure opens the possibility of infinite enjoyment. ("Infinite" does not denote here quality or quantity; rather, it describes the open, unhindered field of relation to the Other.)[119] Though the experience of feminine jouissance is ineffable, language is an indispensable medium in the feminine structure. It is not necessary to converse with an objectified (small) other in a phallic sexual encounter, but as Cevriye's long conversations with the fugitive demonstrate, there is no Real love relationship without dialogized discourse. Derviş's nuanced representation of heteroglossia assumes new significance as a marker of the feminine "jouissance of speech."[120]

Put another way, Cevriye's asexual relationship with the fugitive does not represent bodily asceticism but rather marks the imagination of another, nonphallic sexuation and enjoyment. Derviş's feminist rewriting productively interrupts the phallocentrism of her Turkish and Soviet contemporaries, including Gorky, Vâlâ, Nâzım, and Nizamettin Nazif.[121] At the same time, it makes a contribution to Marxist feminism by supplementing the foundational work of Kollontai, who was marginalized for her efforts to theorize the "riddle of love" and sexual enjoyment. In the essay "Make Way for Winged Eros!" ("Dorogu krylatomu erosu!," 1923), Kollontai had offered a Marxist analysis of love relations from ancient kinship communities to the revolutionary present, arguing that "the task of proletarian ideology is not to drive Eros from social life but to rearm him according to the new social formation." Kollontai's concept of "Wingless Eros" served as a critique of phallic jouissance in "momentary and joyless sexual relations which were bought (as in the case of prostitution) or stolen (as in adultery)" in bourgeois culture. Her alternative concept of "Winged

Love," meanwhile, was an attempt to imagine nonphallocentric sexuation through a sublation of the dialectic between body and soul, sex and love: according to Kollontai, the Winged Love of proletarian society would be based on sexual attraction, but the person experiencing it would acquire "the inner qualities necessary to the builders of a new culture—sensitivity, responsiveness and the desire to help others."[122] Notwithstanding her valuable critique of phallic jouissance, Kollontai can be said to have approached love only in its imaginary and symbolic registers, specifically in her formulation of a new love–comradeship (*liubov'– tovarishchestvo*) relation. Circumventing the question of desire's fundamental extramorality, she imagined a necessary consonance between desire and the social good. An excerpt from Kollontai's writings on love that appeared in the *Illustrated Monthly* suggests that the imagination of Winged Love shaped some of Sabiha's thinking.[123] Whereas historical circumstances in the Soviet Union prevented Kollontai from theorizing love more freely, Derviş's precarious position in Turkey paradoxically made it possible for her to push Marxist feminist writing beyond its limits. Refusing to be bound by Kollontai's sublimation of the drives into the proletarian symbolic, she represented the trials of feminine desire in the Real.

I argue that Derviş's imagination of feminine jouissance has important implications for the imagination of a new communist morality. Although Clark does not examine at length the moral function of the mentor–disciple relationship in the Soviet novel, we can draw some conclusions based on her semiotic analysis of the socialist-realist master plot. Clark observes that "fathers," embodying transcendent revolutionary consciousness, are described in the Soviet novel as "august," "stern," and "vigilant" (yet also "loving"), while "sons" are characterized as "brave" and "hotheaded." Following Freud's analysis of the leader in *Group Psychology and the Analysis of the Ego*, Clark notes that the mentor figure is represented as alone, even when he is part of a family, and without any other libidinal attachments.[124]

Building on this passing reference to Freud, we might suggest that what is at stake in the socialist-realist master plot is the representation of a communist morality grounded in the superego. If the father figure in the Soviet novel represents in psychoanalytic terms the Ego-Ideal, "the agency whose gaze I try to impress with my ego image, the big Other who watches over me and impels me to give my best, the ideal I try to follow and actualize," then "superego is this same agency in its vengeful, sadistic, punishing aspect."[125] Superego is an effect of social law's foundational violence, marking its excess or its fundamental lack, which cannot be absorbed and legitimized by a legal framework. As the ferociously irrational double of social law, superego makes excessive demands on the subject, producing guilt over impossible fulfillment even in the absence of formal transgression.

The Marxist Lacanian philosopher Slavoj Žižek has usefully differentiated the operation of the superego under Stalinism from its function in traditional power. Whereas "in traditional power," Žižek suggests, "the superego is active clandestinely[,] ... in the 'totalitarian' order, it takes over the public space, and so called 'warm humanity' [or we might say 'stern love'] appears as the private feature of people to whom the necessity of History imposes the accomplishments of obscene horrors."[126] In the socialist-realist novel, we might say, the father's "stern love" and "taut voice" not only register literary convention but also represent the benevolent appearance of superegoic totalitarian law in the private sphere.[127] The literary representation of the father as Ego-Ideal finds its ultimate, sadistic historical truth in the public figure of Stalin administering the purges. I suggest that what is problematic here is not limited to the Soviet novel's "fetishistic disavowal" of this obscene violence in its imagination of ideal communism. The ethics of socialist realism is flawed, fundamentally so, because its moral lesson entails the instruction of the "disciple-son" in becoming an instrument of fundamentally obscene paternal authority. Its master plot ascribes final moral agency to the father/mentor, reducing communist ethics to itemized codes, prohibitions, and laws to be obeyed under the father's eye.[128]

Establishing a love relationship instead of a mentor–disciple relationship between Cevriye and the fugitive, Derviş's novel imagines another communist ethics of the act. Refusing to be bound by the dictates of the patriarchal national order and those of the party, Cevriye pursues the "law" of her own desire to the end. She is compelled to help the fugitive, but the absolute necessity of this decision is not based on any moral exemplar; that is, her revolutionary act is not obedience to the fugitive's command. Deriving its necessity from the contingency of her open, indeterminate relation to the fugitive, the absolute freedom of her act retroactively creates the conditions of its own legitimacy.[129] The novel imagines the ethical imperative of her act as a singular universality that is its own measure. We might say that it is precisely in this rewriting of the master plot that Derviş remained true to Lenin. Revisiting the Lenin of the war years, as he was "thrown into an open situation" and compelled to act, Žižek observes that "with Lenin, as with Lacan, the point is that *revolution ne s'autorise que d'elle-même.*"[130] If the thematic structure of the Soviet novel served to legitimize "the purity of the line of succession from Lenin, the original 'father,'"[131] Derviş's modernist socialist realism suggests the possibility of another relation to Lenin's legacy, one grounded in the feminine structure of the revolutionary act.

LOOKING BACK, LOOKING FORWARD: LEGACIES FOR THE 1960S

In this chapter, I have explored the communist "print revolution" of the 1940s in the Turkish corner of the literary international. As a supplement to existing scholarship on the Soviet republic of letters, this study demonstrates that the 1940s represented not a period of contraction but a moment of intense formal experimentation in the outer periphery of the literary international. I have refused to subsume this literary production under the narrow category of a "Comintern aesthetics," arguing instead that Derviş's feminist modernist rewriting of the Soviet novel represents a major contribution to Marxist aesthetics by a neglected "Eastern" woman writer.

I want to conclude by addressing the implications of Derviş's work for scholarly periodization of the literary international. Until republication of her serialized novels in book form began in the late 1960s, Derviş's writings had been largely forgotten in Turkey. That a younger generation of leftist activists knew her only as "the wife of the TKP general secretary Reşat Fuat" was a source of deep frustration for her.[132] On the other side of the Turkish-Soviet border in 1953, meanwhile, in a *Pravda* article describing the repression of 1951–1953, Derviş's jailed husband was introduced to the Soviet public as "the spouse of the famous Turkish writer Suat Derviş."[133] Following the Russian language anthologization of excerpts from her writings in the 1940s, Russian translations of *Phosphorescent Cevriye* and *Prisoner of Ankara* (*Ankara Mahpusu*) were published by the Foreign Literature Publishing House in 1957 and 1960, a moment when Soviet outreach to Afro-Asian writers was also accelerating.[134] Derviş's Russian translator,

THE PROSTITUTE CEVRIYE AS POSITIVE HERO

Radii Fish, wrote in his memoirs that in 1956 Derviş had sent him newspaper clippings of *Phosphorescent Cevriye* along with her corrections.[135] Though Derviş did not attend the Afro-Asian Writers' Conference in Tashkent in 1958, she was an active participant in the Soviet and Third World literary engagements during her exile in Europe. In a little-known public letter sent to the Soviet Preparatory Committee of the conference, she expressed her support for decolonization in Africa and Asia and emphasized the need to overcome distrust between nations, urging writers to work in unison to defend peace.[136] In Tashkent in 1958, Derviş's "heartfelt greetings" were read to the delegates along with the congratulatory telegrams from Gamal Abdel Nasser, Pham Van Dong, and other prominent leaders.[137] In an interview in 1961, P. A. Chuvikov, director of the Foreign Literature Publishing House, stated that Derviş was among its "regular guests and correspondents."[138] In March of that year, Derviş visited Moscow as a guest of the Soviet Writers' Union, an event rarely mentioned by Derviş's Turkish biographers.[139]

The Soviet connections that Derviş forged during the Cold War are key to the gaps in our knowledge of her life and body of work. Turkish sources have said little about the circumstances of her escape from Turkey in 1953, but Fish's memoirs inform us of the grim details of the difficult journey made by train via Italy.[140] Because the original Turkish manuscript of Derviş's autobiographical *Love Novels* has never been found, the Russian edition published in Moscow in 1969 remains our sole source of knowledge about this important work. *Love Novels* affords us a view of Derviş's life on the eve of the arrests in December 1946, when she would be detained for more than a month.[141] A rewriting of Sophocles's *Antigone*, *Love Novels* describes a novelist condemned to "social death" for refusing to abandon her communist twin brother, Fuat, in prison. In its portrayal of the positive heroine's everyday life under police surveillance, this work offers an uncensored imagination of the communist ethics of the act, registering Derviş's articulation of a modernist socialist-realist aesthetic in her later work.

More broadly, the Russian afterlives of Derviş's writings matter because they suggest a constellational relation between the communist translation of the 1940s and the Afro-Asian literatures of the Cold War era. In chapter 1 of this book, through a study of Nâzım's writings, I explored several neglected continuities across the interwar, the Second World War, and

Cold War eras. The publication history of Derviş's writings and, more generally, her exilic itinerary support this exploration from another angle. Setting aside the conventional understanding of the Cold War era as a historical rupture, we might say that the literary internationalism of the 1960s left us an uncannily plural temporality that still harbors both the foreclosed promise of 1920 and that of 1940. In a meeting with the editors of the journal *Soviet Woman* (*Sovetskaia zhenshchina*) in 1961, which had published a Russian translation of her short story "Thief" ("Vorovka"; "Hırsız"), Derviş was asked why the protagonist of *Phosphorescent Cevriye* was a "fallen woman." Describing the oppression under which she had composed this novel, Derviş stated that the figure of Cevriye served as an "outlet to pour out her own suppressed feelings." A Russian attendee, whose notes at this meeting survived, described *Phosphorescent Cevriye* as "a sui generis [*svoeobraznyi*] work of protest by the authoress."[142] Indeed, it was exactly that and one with universalizing implications both for the era in which it was composed and for the era in which it was translated.

Chapter Four

ABIDIN DINO'S PEASANT THEATER AND THE SOVIET *FAKTURA*

Estranging Socialist Realism

> The weakest point of Kemalism is the peasant question.
>
> —FAKHRI, "KOMPARTIIA TURTSII V BOR'BE ZA MASSY," 1933

Though the paths of Suat Derviş and the painter and playwright Abidin Dino crossed in Paris in 1953, these former TKP comrades did not develop much of a relationship during their exile. Having been criticized harshly by Derviş's spouse, Reşat Fuat Baraner, in the party newspaper *New Literature* (*Yeni Edebiyat*) during a public exchange about realism in the early 1940s, Dino was uncooperative when Derviş came to Paris to seek help navigating émigré life in France.¹ The fact that two of the most important literary figures of the TKP's decentralization period did not associate with each other does not, of course, mean that their work cannot be associated in interesting ways. Derviş's modernist arrest of socialist-realist aesthetics aimed to bridge the space separating TKP print culture from the illiterate urban subaltern, where Dino mobilized a modernist socialist-realist aesthetic to represent the rural subaltern in the Turkish countryside. Each writer imagined a pedagogical project that would extend the literary culture of Turkish communism and Soviet socialism to its excluded outside: what one might call, borrowing Gayatri Spivak's phrase, an "aesthetic education."²

Born in 1913 in Istanbul, Dino came from a prominent landowning family from the Ottoman province of Janina, which today connects northwestern Greece to southern Albania.³ His paternal grandfather and namesake, Abidin Pasha, had served as the Ottoman minister of foreign affairs in 1880 and as the governor of Adana from 1880 to 1885, where he was granted substantial pastureland as compensation for his service.[4] (In 1942, Dino would be exiled to Adana.) While Dino's social background resembles those of Nâzım Hikmet, Nizamettin Nazif, and Baraner, all of whom belonged to the Ottoman Balkan elite, his itinerary was ultimately quite different from theirs.

A former director of the Ottoman Audit Office, Dino's father moved his family to Europe after the Balkan Wars (1912–1913) to seek compensation for the family lands in Janina that were ceded to Greece.[5] The youngest of five siblings, Dino spent the First World War years and their immediate aftermath in Switzerland, France, and Greece, coming under the influence of family members active in the arts, including his brothers, Ali and Arif, a cartoonist and a painter, respectively. After returning to Istanbul in 1925 and leaving high school prematurely in 1930, he became a caricature artist and book illustrator who was widely admired in Istanbul's bohemian communities. After meeting Nâzım and Nizamettin, both of whom were involved with the leftist *Illustrated Monthly* (*Resimli Ay*) during the late 1920s and early 1930s, Dino created the illustrations for a number of Nâzım's books, including the poetry collection *The City That Lost Its Voice* (*Sesini Kaybeden Şehir*, 1931) and the screenplay *A Funeral Home* (*Bir Ölü Evi*, 1932). Dino's illustrations of Nâzım's *Epic of National Liberation Movement* and *Life's Good, Brother* show that his work with Nâzım spanned the different stages of their respective lives in exile.

In October 1933, Dino, then twenty years old, joined the "d Group" of four painters and a sculptor orchestrating a sensational public exhibition of cubist-constructivist drawings in a hat store in Istanbul's Beyoğlu district, aiming to "habituate the Turkish people to new art [*yeni sanat*]."[6] Naming themselves after the fourth letter of the Latin alphabet to mark their succession from the three major modern art movements of the nineteenth and twentieth centuries to date, the d Group rejected the impressionism of their predecessors and imagined a dynamic "living" art responsive to the modernization of the republican era.[7] The exhibit's convergence with the tenth-anniversary celebrations of the Turkish Republic would bring Dino an unexpected opportunity when the d Group met with the Soviet film director Sergei Yutkevich, who had traveled to Istanbul for the anniversary celebrations. Impressed by Dino's black-and-white portraits of the hashish lodges (*esrar tekkeleri*) of the Tophane district, Yutkevich arranged for Dino to visit the Soviet Union in 1934 to work as a set designer (*khudozhnik*) at Lenfilm.⁸ As we will see, this interval in the Soviet Union, which extended to three years, deeply shaped Dino's aesthetic and political itineraries. In addition to attending the dress rehearsals of Vsevolod Meyerhold's staging of *The Queen of Spades* (*Pikovaia dama*), Dino collaborated with Yutkevich in the production of the films *The Miners* (*Shakhtery*, 1936) and *The Man with the Gun* (*Chelovek s ruzh'em*, 1938). Returning to Turkey in 1938 via Paris, Dino would join the TKP a year later, overseeing the party's "press affairs in Istanbul" and contributing in important ways to a second intensification of Marxist-Leninist translation during the period of decentralization.⁹ As I argued in chapter 3, the wide range of literary and artistic newspapers and magazines published during this period by party members and antifascist sympathizers extended the concepts of socialist realism into a Turkish context.

The purpose of this chapter is to examine Dino's mobilization of Soviet literary and cinematic concepts in his multimedia work of the 1940s about the Turkish countryside. As I suggest in the following two sections, Dino's essays in antifascist magazines of the period, including *S.E.S.*, *Yeni S.E.S.*, and *New Literature*, as well as his paintings and the plays he composed after his return from the Soviet Union (and before he emigrated in 1952) helped to shape a discourse about *halk sanatı*, or "folk arts." Not just a witness to the transformation of twentieth-century European and Soviet art but also a participant through his collaboration with Pablo Picasso, Gertrude Stein, and Paul Robeson, Dino has been the subject of many a biographical study, but there exists little criticism about his work. Ahmet Oktay recognized Dino as a leading figure in Turkish literary circles of the late 1930s and early 1940s but assessed Dino's "folkmania" mostly critically, assigning him responsibility for the emergence of a schematically vulgar social realism in Turkish literature. According to Oktay, Dino's mistake, "which cannot be overemphasized," lay "in the substitution of a peasantist discourse for a working class discourse and the misapprehension of this discourse as socialism."¹⁰ In a later assessment, Oktay did soften this earlier criticism, connecting Dino's "folkmania" to the antifascist front in Turkey, but he still failed to consider the aesthetic principles of Dino's work as shaped by Soviet cinematic socialist realism.¹¹

Rejecting Oktay's assessment, I argue that Dino's work represents an important moment of Turkish and Soviet literary exchange, expanding the translatability of Marxism-Leninism by turning to a common language of objects in place of the common language of nationalism. Like his *New Literature* colleagues Zeki Baştımar and Reşat Fuat Baraner, Dino was influenced by Maksim Gorky and Andrei Zhdanov's formulations of Soviet socialist realism, but he was also attracted to the Soviet concepts of *faktura*, or "texture" and materiality, which Emma Widdis suggests enjoyed a broad range of reference, including "textures and materials of set design but also ... its objects." Widdis argues persuasively that the cinematic representation of *faktura* in the Soviet films of the 1920s and early 1930s attempted to shape a new sensory Soviet subject who would relate to the material world in dynamically embodied ways.[12] Addressing Dino's work as a set designer in the Soviet Union under the patronage of Yutkevich, the first section of this chapter shows that Dino's turn to Turkish folk poetry and handicrafts cannot be understood independently of his work with filmic *faktura* at Lenfilm. In his essay in 1939 about the seventeenth-century minstrel Karacaoğlan and the early twentieth-century poet and playwright Vladimir Mayakovsky and in his controversial paintings of Balıkesir clay ewers (*ibrik*), Dino explored the peasant's tactile, embodied experience of the material world as a model for a new revolutionary sensory subject in Turkey.[13] Although the limits of Dino's engagement, I suggest, can be located in its Orientalist representation of "primitive sensations,"[14] Dino saw this tactile knowledge of the world as endowing peasants with critical awareness of their dispossession in a semifeudal regime. Turkish folk poetry and traditional peasant theater were important in this context because they had already articulated such a critical social epistemology. Exiled from Istanbul to Mecitözü in northern Anatolia in 1942 and then to Adana from 1943 to 1945, Dino would compose *Baldy* (*Kel*) and *The Inheritors* (*Verese*), two plays drawing on his experience with peasant theater at the Adana People's House (Halkevi) as well as on his participation in Yutkevich's studio school at Lenfilm.[15] I argue that despite their suppression, these plays, in their creation of a modernist socialist-realist "instructive theater,"[16] are Dino's most important contribution to Turkish republican communism and to a Soviet republic of letters. Contemporaneous with Mao's Talk at the Yan'an Conference, these works show that the conceptualization and practice of popular literature across the literary international had plural genealogies. Both plays thematized theatrical *faktura* but refused to represent an ethnographically tactile subject, focusing on the dispossessed peasantry's purposeful destruction of objects such as commoditized animals, coins, and discarded goods and their defamiliarizing use of other objects, such as women's shoes and animal skins. Dino mobilized the modernist estrangement (*ostranenie*) of theatrical objects and the dialogic form of the peasant theater to educate his rural spectators about the conditions of their exploitation and the emancipation made possible by proletarianization and collective farming. In exploring the equivalency of Yutkevich's studio school with vernacular theater and suggesting a translatability between oral protest forms and Marxist-Leninist critique, Dino's project is inassimilable to those of the Kadro intellectuals (about whom I say more soon), the peasantists, or his TKP comrades who regarded rural subalternity as "prepolitical." Instead, devising a singular strain of formalist socialist realism, Dino imagined in place of the Marxian proletariat another universal revolutionary subject: the dispossessed, deterritorialized rural subaltern of the Anatolian countryside. As I suggest in concluding this chapter, Dino's work found its most significant literary response in the novels and short stories of his young collaborator in Adana, the Kurdish bard Kemal Sadık Göğceli, later known as Yaşar Kemal, whose stories and novels reimagined the Çukurova subaltern and their sensory-subjective and critical-epistemological relationships to the material world in new, hybrid, modernist socialist-realist forms.

RETURNING TO ANATOLIA BY WAY OF LENINGRAD AND DONBASS

Dino had published two surrealistic short stories in 1934 thematizing the urban subaltern of Istanbul's multiethnic underworld,[17] but the representation of the rural subaltern became the main focus of his work only after his return from the Soviet Union a few years later. In a little-known but remarkable essay titled "Letter to Turkish Artists" ("Pis'mo k turetskim khudozhnikam") and published in *Iskusstvo* in 1934 with color reproductions of drawings and designs brought back from Turkey, Yutkevich described his "discovery" of Dino and other artists and imagined himself the "Christopher Columbus" of a new Turkish art world. Praising Dino's drawings and sketches *The Fingers* and *Hashish Nightmares*, Yutkevich admired "these strangest phantasmagoric combinations," comparing the fingers "cut off from the hand" to "Major Kovalev's runaway nose" in

Gogol's "The Nose" and the "anthropoid" forms of Dino's hashish smokers to H. G. Wells's Martians.[18] (Though Yutkevich did not use the concept of movement, which was key to the cinema theory of Sergei Eisenstein, in this essay, while in Istanbul he made a point of telling Dino that Dino's drawings captured "movement [*hareket* or *dvizhenie*]" and that he should become a filmmaker.)[19] However, he also criticized the drawings as lacking rootedness in the "living reality" of Anatolia and called on Dino and his contemporaries to reflect the authentic reality of the new Turkish nation. Yutkevich was correct to observe that the Western-educated d Group artists did not initially participate in the national debate of the moment about "the people" (*halk*) of the Turkish countryside.[20] Because Dino's writings intervened in this national debate after his return from the Soviet Union, though, I provide a brief overview of different ways that Anatolia was imagined in the discourse of the early republican period.

In the 1930s, a populist discourse emerged targeting the perceived remoteness of the Kemalist elite. Faced with the local effects of the global economic crisis and with uprisings in the majority-Kurdish regions of eastern and southeastern Anatolia, Mustafa Kemal focused on expanding and consolidating the single-party rule of the Republican People's Party (RPP). Former TKP members, including Vedat Nedim, Şevket Süreyya, and İsmail Hüsrev (the latter two educated at KUTV), played important roles in shaping official discourse from 1932 to 1934. Leaving the TKP in the late 1920s and joining the Kemalists, they formed the Kadro group with other intellectuals, including the novelist Yakup Kadri, arguing for the necessity of a vanguard cadre to spread the Kemalist revolution through the countryside.[21]

In his influential autobiography, *The Man in Search of Water* (*Suyu Arayan Adam*, 1959), modeled on Jean-Jacques Rousseau's *The Confessions* (1782–1789), Şevket Süreyya described his Kemalist "conversion" in Afyon prison in 1926–1927. Where Rousseau (who followed the *Confessions* of St. Augustine) described a philosophical "illumination" while walking to Vincennes to visit Diderot in prison, Süreyya described an epiphany about the limits of communism in Turkey following his encounters with imprisoned Turkish peasants.[22] In contrast with Rousseau's representation of a mythical noble savagery corrupted by the vices of civilization, Süreyya and his Kadro colleagues represented rural subalternity as a dark, sluggish human mass crushed by "merciless nature."[23]

This image had its origin in Yakup Kadri's novel *Stepmother Earth* (*Yaban*, 1932, trans. 2020), an influential work of early republican literature that imagines the Turkish countryside in explicitly Conradian terms as a "heart of darkness."[24] Presented as the memoir of a retired Ottoman officer hiding in a village in central Anatolia during the Turkish War of Independence and designed to alarm its elite urban readership about the depravity of conditions in the countryside, the novel described the extreme alienation of its modern narrator from the "barbaric" religious villagers and their indifference to the nationalist project. In their advocacy of land redistribution and other state interventions, the Kadro intellectuals took a similar stance, arguing that vanguardist teachers and bureaucrats should develop and incorporate the Anatolian periphery by introducing techniques for large-scale organization and cooperation into the villages.[25]

When the Kadro group lost Mustafa Kemal's favor in 1934, a group of educators and bureaucrats including Nusret Köymen, İsmail Hakkı Tonguç, and Sait Aydoslu assembled around the influential journal *Ideal* (*Ülkü*) published by the Ankara People's House, articulating a peasantist ideology in their work.[26] Wary of the effects of urbanization, mechanization, and proletarianization, these thinkers—the "peasantists"—viewed the Turkish peasants as Rousseau might have, lavishing praise on their incorruptible morality and idyllic stability. To empower villagers in their "struggle against nature," the peasantists proposed a new mode of education in the villages, including formalized instruction in farming, animal husbandry and fishing, beekeeping and carpentry, among other agricultural and vocational skills.[27] The Village Institutes (Köy Enstitüleri), established in 1940 and then gradually dissolved from 1946 to 1954, recruited and trained a generation of peasant teachers to staff these new vocational elementary schools in the villages. The People's Houses established in various Anatolian cities and towns during the 1930s and 1940s also became important sites for advancing the peasantists' agenda. Organizing the visits of urban writers and artists to local towns and villages, the People's Houses introduced country people to the city elite while imagining in their periodicals and published books an authentic national folklore of vernacular arts and crafts.[28]

Whereas the peasantists turned to educational uplift to empower the peasantry in its struggle with nature, the TKP Action Program (Türkiye Komünist Fırkası Faaliyet Programı) in 1931 had demanded the abolition of all exploitative social relations in the Turkish countryside.[29] The TKP's organizational work during the early republican era was limited to workers in industrialized cities such as Istanbul, Izmir, Bursa, Adana, Zonguldak, and Samsun,[30] but the Vienna Congress proceedings of 1926 and the Action Program in 1931 show that the party recognized the urgency of the rural question. According to the latter program, "The independence war failed to lead to a peasant revolution [köylülük inkılâbı]" because "the level of class consciousness of the peasantry was low and it was deprived of the leadership of the Anatolian working class."[31] Criticizing the feudal relations of production in the eastern Kurdish provinces and objecting to large landholdings and semicapitalist farming in the West and South, it described the pauperization and dispossession of small peasants by usurers and large-scale farming operations and demanded land-redistribution reforms. Although the Action Program imagined the Kurdish rebellions of the 1920s as counterrevolutionary resistance led by religious tribal leaders under the influence of British and French imperialism, it recognized the Kurds' right to self-determination, and in this it parted ways with both the peasantists and the Kadro intellectuals supporting republican Turkification.[32]

Though the *Illustrated Monthly* was not a party journal, and though Nâzım himself led an opposition group inside the TKP in 1929, his essays, poems, and book reviews in the journal extended elements of this political discourse into the aesthetic domain. Nâzım supported emerging socialist writers, including Sabahattin Ali and Sadri Ertem, whose short stories thematized the state-sanctioned oppression and expropriation of Turkish peasants.[33] At the same time, his conceptualization of literary history during this period followed a crude stagism. Embracing Soviet constructivism and futurism, Nâzım rejected both the traditional *aruz* meter of Ottoman court poetry and the syllabic meter of folk poetry, mobilizing free verse in his poems about city life and industrialization. For him, this new poetry registering "the magnificent symphony of the city" represented a sublation of "the monotonic sounds of the peasant and shepherd economy" in folk poetry.[34] In its use of both the *aruz* and syllabic meters, *Epic of Sheik Bedreddin* (1936), an epic prose poem about a fifteenth-century peasant uprising, marks Nâzım's abandonment of this crude stagism. At the thematic level, while Nâzım recognized the Turkish countryside as a liminal space, in mobilizing the metaphor of a traveling train for the new nation, his magnum opus *Human Landscapes from My Country* (composed during the 1940s) prioritized representation of the urban and provincial upper and lower classes instead of the rural subaltern cut off from the connecting line of the railway.[35] More generally, the translation and mediation of key concepts of Soviet socialist realism by Baştımar, Baraner, and Dino, who returned from the Soviet Union in the late 1930s, would prompt deeper engagement with oral literary cultures. The conscription of former and current TKP members and sympathizers into military service in the early 1940s and the exile of influential party members such as Dino to remote corners of Anatolia would reconnect the TKP to the Turkish countryside, reestablishing continuity with the neglected legacy of Anatolian Bolshevisms and communisms examined in chapter 1.

Lacking any formal training in art, Dino's early aesthetic was shaped by his encounter with Ottoman and Byzantine imperial art forms, including Islamic calligraphy and miniature painting and Byzantine mosaics.[36] One can observe Dino's early interest in material objects in a posthumously published humorous screenplay dating to the 1930s, which constructs a fantastic dialogue between two discarded objects, an empty can of dolma and a raki bottle.[37] However, no specific interest in Marxist aesthetics is detectable in Dino's work prior to his time in the Soviet Union. Despite government suppression of leftist publications and a general shortage of paper during the Second World War, the late 1930s and early 1940s saw a flourishing of antifascist journals and magazines in Istanbul and Anatolian cities as magazines closed by Turkish security forces under martial law relaunched under new titles.[38] Joining the TKP in 1939, Dino played a leading role in the operations of some of the most significant of such magazines, including *S.E.S., Yeni S.E.S., Küllük*, and *New Literature*, exerting significant influence on TKP sympathizers among the literary youth of the "1940s generation."[39]

In addressing the peasant question, Dino's essays during this period distinguished the TKP's Marxist approach from the "return to soil literature [*toprağa avdet edebiyatı*]" of Turkish peasantists. Criticizing Yakup Kadri's *Stepmother Earth* and Reşat Nuri's *The Wren* (*Çalıkuşu*, 1922), Dino rejected the "unsystematic, individualist" romanticization of pastoral life by republican writers who imagined village life as an escape from the social decay of capitalist development. Comparing these elites to Marie Antoinette, "who enjoyed dressing up as a peasant girl with ribbons," Dino argued for the mechanization of agriculture and the industrialization of the Turkish countryside to free the peasants from their feudal living conditions.[40] Along with his rejection of the artificial mimicry of folk forms, these arguments echoed the views of his comrades Baraner and Baştımar, as expressed in *New Literature* (discussed in chapter 3).

We should remember that Dino conducted a heated public exchange with Baraner after the latter criticized Dino's definition of realist art "as the kind of artwork that evokes in the consciousness reflections that coincide [*muvazî*] with nature and form a synthesis."[41] In objecting to Dino's use of the words *muvazî* (parallel or coincident) and *nisbî* (relative), Baraner was concerned about anti-Marxist interpretation of the idea that each individual artist offers a relative representation of the truth. As we have seen, Baraner wore the literary hat for strictly tactical reasons, and some saw in the stridency of this criticism a tendency to Stalinist totalitarianism.[42] What Baraner, Haydar Seçkin, and others imagined as "surrealistic" or "idealist" in Dino's work is better understood as an attempt to formulate some internal laws of aesthetic creativity under capitalism. It was mistaken then and would be mistaken now to suggest that Dino's emphasis on the autonomy of aesthetics and his recognition of the subjective and sensory constitution of an individual artist alongside objective determination are incompatible with the foundational principles of Marxism.[43] Representing a different intellectual and creative trajectory than those of Baraner and Baştımar, Dino's writings introduced a set of concepts borrowed from his collaborators at Lenfilm, including "thingness" (*eşya*), "three-dimensionality" (*üç buutlu*, orthography, in the original), and "sense" (*his*). Among other things, this borrowing suggests that Turkish socialist-realist discourse was actively influenced by Soviet cinematic socialist realism in the late 1930s and early 1940s. Without rejecting the value of studying state or international institutional agendas, including those of the Comintern or MORP, we can recognize that individuals like Dino, who lived his life at the intersection of a precarious communist organization with such transnational institutions, helped to shape the afterlives of Soviet aesthetic discourses in Turkey.

For Dino, handcrafted objects and folk poetry could furnish models for a new socialist-realist art because they exhibited no investment in the separation of the aesthetic from everyday life, including politics, and in this freedom they modeled a new tactile art suited to a revolutionary sensory subject. In the *New Literature* essay "Art and the People" ("Halk ve San'at," 1940), Dino praised "the people for their consideration of art as an absolute aspect of everyday life," suggesting that "the color pleasure evoked by the patterns in a peasant's socks can only be matched by the pleasure evoked by flowers."[44] In "Work and Art" ("İş ve San'at," 1939), Dino addressed the embodied relationship of older artisans to their handcrafted objects (*eşya*), declaring that "under each blow [of the hammer], the work became a source of happiness for the eye, the head, and the arm." Accompanied by Dino's black-and-white illustration of a human hand, the essay rejected capitalist production of arbitrary and ugly objects in the pursuit of profit, demanding a return to "a work ethic of love [*iş aşkı*]."[45] And in the essay "Stop!" (1939), Dino narrated the story of a poor rural shoe shiner in a remote village who went to extraordinary lengths to obtain a handmade shoeshine stand produced by an elderly craftsman just before his death.[46] Expressing his admiration of the songs sung in the fields and the patterns woven into peasant women's aprons, Dino contrasted the "alive and vital existence of art" in the Turkish village to art's abstracted consumption in city exhibits and concert halls.[47]

This is not just about the supersession of aesthetic autonomy but also about a new sensory subject "handling" the world, so to speak, in newly embodied ways. *Mücessem* and *üç buutlu*, or "three-dimensionality," are key terms in these essays, where they refer not only to the depiction of "the human in a state of movement [*hareket*] connected to the entities surrounding him through a web of material and spiritual interests" but also to a sensory corporeal poetics.[48] In 1939, Dino described a "kinship" between the revolutionary poetics of Vladimir Mayakovsky and the seventeenth-century minstrel (*aşık*) Karacaoğlan, comparing the former's poetic act of "licking away the microbes of consumption with the tongue of the posters" to the latter's "playing the *saz* to seek remedy for remediless afflictions." Dino argued that the purpose of true art is "to be an art of living, to relieve [*ferahlatmak*] what is seen and heard and to give form and unity to what is seen, heard, and thought."[49] In another essay on the dialectical materialism of Gustave Flaubert's realism, he quoted Flaubert's declaration that "[he] likes works that have the smell of sweat."[50] Like Flaubert's sweat-smelling works or the licking tongue of Mayakovsky's posters, the sensory imagery of Turkish folk poetry modeled a newly embodied realism.

Departing from the tradition of court poetry, the vernacular poetry of fifteenth-century Turkish minstrels developed as a form of entertainment for profane gatherings (that is, separated from ritualistic ceremonious contexts). The "earthy realism" of folk poetry describes love, hopelessness, and disappointment by appeal to the gendered body, nature, and everyday life, including the carnal sensual activities of kissing, biting, and so on.[51] Discussing oral folk poetry that he had recorded during a village visit, Dino quoted a quatrain comparing Istanbul's Bosphorus Strait to "the cleavage of dark breasts" and another that described suffering through natural analogies for writing: "even if the seas became ink / . . . / and the trees become pens / my suffering could not be expressed." Yet another described hopelessness through analogy to the labor of "planting crops that refuse to grow."[52]

Dino performed no particularly close reading of such excerpts, but he selected them to highlight the folk poets' aptitude for what the Russian formalist Viktor Shklovsky called "enstrangement," or "transferring an object from its usual sphere of experience to a new one, a kind of semantic change."[53] Like Shklovsky and other formalists who were influenced by the study of folklore, Dino saw poetic language as deeply textural, though he understood such *faktura* as produced by imagistic concretion more than by the insertion of local dialects.[54] Dino's prose in these essays mimicked the style of this materialist multisensory "three-dimensional" poetry, and he compared this poetics to the construction of a cathedral or a mosque from stone.[55] We can infer, though Dino never put it so directly, that Turkish folk poetry represented the possibility of unalienated subjectivity and a new tactile relationship to language imagined as the equivalent of a peasant's or craftsman's toolbox. A concrete metaphoric language rooted in the world, a cosmology shaped by the interactions of embodied humanity with the environment: all this implicitly rejected the mind–body split of the dualistic Cartesian subject and the modern imagination of language as an arbitrary system of signs. Decisively rejected here is the usurping of nature in European Romantic poetry, the substitutive metaphors transfigured and sublimated to describe interior states or ideal concepts and to exercise subjective mastery of the objective world.[56] The earthly realism of Dino's selections ground the human in the rhythms of the natural world, closing the distance between nature and the (gendered) body. This embodied realism is genuinely "three dimensional," and it establishes a translational equivalence between Marxist materialism and a subaltern episteme even as it is compromised by Orientalist primitivism.

I have suggested that Dino's materialist folk aesthetics was shaped by his work as a set designer at Lenfilm, which he began after arriving in Leningrad by way of Odessa and Moscow in September 1934. Films produced by the studio during this period included Fridrikh Ermler and Yutkevich's *Counterplan* (*Vstrechnyi*, 1932), Georgii and Sergei Vasil'ev's *Chapaev* (1934), and Grigorii Kozintsev and Leonid Trauberg's *Maksim's Youth* (*Iunost' Maksima*, 1934)—films celebrated, in Robert Bird's words, as "the most authoritative models for the future cinema of socialist realism."[57] Established in 1918 and reorganized by decrees several times during the 1920s and 1930s, Lenfilm was directed by Adrian Piotrovskii from 1928 until his arrest and execution in 1937. A former member of the Russian formalist group OPOIaZ, Piotrovskii, along with Iurii Tynianov and Boris Eikhenbaum, had taught at the State Institute for the History of the Arts (Gosudarstvennyi institut istorii iskusstv) in Leningrad during the 1920s and contributed to the influential volume *The Poetics of Cinema* (*Poetika kino*, 1927).[58] As Bird puts it, Piotrovskii's directorial tenure at Lenfilm "sought to combine the formal sophistication of the Moscow avant-gardists with narrative accessibility."[59] Piotrovskii's collaborators in these efforts included members of the avant-garde film collective Factory of the Eccentric Actor (Fabrika ekstsentricheskogo aktera, FEKS), including the directors Kozintsev and Trauberg, the set designer Evgenii Enei, and the cinematographer Andrei Moskvin.[60] Rejecting the ornamental excess of costume dramas, the historical films made by the FEKS collective, including *The Overcoat* (*Shinel'*, 1926), *SVD* (*Soiuz velikogo dela*, 1927), and *New Babylon* (*Novyi Vavilon*, 1929), were deeply invested in the formal composition of elements of set, lighting, and camera configuration designed to make the viewer "feel" the epoch in what Widdis calls a new "haptic" spectatorship.[61]

Following the All-Union Party Conference on Film in Moscow in 1928 and the centralizing reorganization of the Soviet film industry, filmmakers came under pressure to produce films "intelligible to the millions" by thematizing the heroic contributions of remarkable ordinary figures.[62] A former painter and set designer who trained with Sergei Eisenstein in the Meyerhold Theater Workshop and a founding member of the original FEKS collective in 1922, Yutkevich rejoined his colleagues at Lenfilm in

1928 as the emergence of the "heroic" cinema of the 1930s got underway.[63] Though the FEKS members had to observe the socialist-realist thematic and formal conventions of the 1930s, that does not mean that some avant-garde practices did not continue. Drawing on his experience at the Meyerhold Theater as well as in FEKS and the Experimental Film Collective (known by its Russian acronym EKKIu), Yutkevich would found a workshop at Lenfilm in 1935 that served as a studio school for actors, cameramen, and set designers, including Dino.[64] This collaborative approach to production, crucial in shaping what Widdis calls "Soviet cinema's materialist project,"[65] underwrote continued cinematic explorations of the revolutionary sensory subject through the 1930s. Whereas films of the late 1920s had emphasized the materiality of the mise-en-scène in exploring the Soviet subject's embodied relationship to the world, those of the 1930s addressed both proper socialist sensations *and* feelings by mobilizing an adapted visual grammar. The role of the *khudozhnik*, or set designer, in shaping the materialist aesthetics of Soviet cinema was of great importance across the entire period.

Scholars including Gennadii Miasnikov, Widdis, and Eleanor Rees have emphasized the centrality of set design for film production in the 1920s and 1930s.[66] Rejecting the excessively "decorative" theatrical set design of prerevolutionary Russian films and the stylized antirealism of German expressionist cinema, early Soviet designers emphasized authenticity and realism. The production of three-dimensional cinematic space was a priority typified by Sergei Kozlovksii's suggestion that set designers be referred to as "architects" to emphasize that they worked with spatial volume, not just surfaces.[67] Widdis's survey of debates on Soviet set design demonstrates the dialectical tension between this emphasis on three-dimensionality and filmic *faktura*.[68]

With its roots in the Soviet avant-garde, the concept of *faktura* required "textures and materials of set design, but also its objects" be made palpable to the cinematic spectator.[69] Influenced by both Shklovsky's writings and Marx's reflections on the sensory subject in the Notebooks of 1844, Soviet filmmakers explored the *faktura* of cinema as a three-dimensional embodied encounter with the world on screen.[70] The use of textiles, patterned surfaces, and both handcrafted and mass-produced industrial objects expressed the embodied relationship of the Soviet citizen to socialist materiality, but Soviet critics reviewing the films of the late 1920s characterized their "poetic" approach to such objects as politically immature and deviantly formalist: in 1937, I. Manevich criticized Yutkevich's metonymic use of textiles and manufacturing equipment in portraying Komsomol workers at a lace factory in his film *Lace* (*Kruzheva*, 1928). Praising the film *Counterplan* as a turning point in Yutkevich's body of work, by contrast, Manevich declared that whereas in earlier work "things . . . were eclipsing people and dominating the frame completely," in *Counterplan* "things [*veshchi*] and people changed places."[71] By the early 1930s, representing rounded three-dimensional individual heroes as feeling subjects was a declared goal of Soviet filmmakers,[72] though that did not mean abandoning the material conditions of Soviet subjectivity (for example, in a late film such as *The Miners*).

Though Dino's correspondence includes more than five hundred letters sent to various family members during this period, these letters, collected by his nephew Rasih Nuri İleri (1920–2014) are currently unavailable to researchers.[73] Information about Dino's Soviet years can be found in several interviews conducted in the 1980s and 1990s. A competent speaker of French in addition to his native Turkish, Dino appears to have learned Russian during his work on the set of Erast Garin's film *Marriage* (*Zhenit'ba*, 1936), adapted from Gogol's play of the same title. Of this experience, Dino observed that "the rehearsals, in which each line was repeated at least ten times before the shooting, turned out to be an excellent language school." Employed by Lenfilm on a permanent contract, Dino joked that he and the other artists led materially comfortable lives as members of a Soviet "artistocracy," while acknowledging as a witness to the political aftermath of the murder of Sergei Kirov the terror produced by intensifying Stalinist repression. Dino recounted how Enei, whom Dino described as one of Lenfilm's most accomplished set designers, calmly informed Dino that he (Enei) was being sent to a Siberian labor camp.[74]

Dino attributed the success of directors such as Eisenstein and Yutkevich to their careers as artists. Noting that Eisenstein sketched his films in storyboard format, Dino ascribed his own success at Lenfilm to an ability to draw quickly.[75] This account confirms film historians' description of Soviet set design as a two-step process in which sketches of the entire screenplay were followed by set construction from décor to props and costumes.[76] These interviews also provide us with useful information about the film *The Miners* (which I discuss more fully later). In general, we can

FIGURE 4.1. Décor model titled "The Railway Station" ("Vokzal") created by Abidin Dino and Olga Pchel'nikova for Sergei Yutkevich's film *The Miners* (*Shakhtery*, 1936).
Source: RGALI f. 3070, op. 1, ed. khr. 1514, l. 1.

say that Dino's mobilization of such concepts as "movement" (*hareket*), "three-dimensionality" (*üç boyutluluk*), *faktura* or "thingness" (*eşya*), and "living art" (*canlı san'at*) in his essays published in Turkey extended the materialist aesthetic of Soviet cinema into Turkish folk poetry and crafts. Though there is no evidence that Dino worked on any "Eastern" films while at Lenfilm, his engagement with Turkish peasant arts can be read as consonant with the Oriental peasant *faktura* of such films as Nikoloz Shengelaia's *Eliso* (1928), Viktor Turin's *Turksib* (1929), Mikhail Kalatozov's *Salt for Svanetia* (*Sol' Svanetii*, 1930), and Yutkevich's *Ankara* (1933).

Widdis emphasizes the "haptic" visual grammar of images of manual labor and ritual dance in Soviet Easterns, shaped by the anthropological and linguistic research of Alexandr Luria, Lev Vygotsky, and Nikolai Marr. The tactile Orientalism of such films focused on the backward conditions of impoverished and illiterate Islamic minorities in the domestic

East, celebrating their "primitive" sensory engagement with the world as an aspect of their resilience and their "prelogical" concrete knowledge of the world as a condition of embodied revolutionary awakening.[77] Though Widdis does not discuss Yutkevich's *Ankara*, the film fits this description, using representations of manual labor and dance to construct rural Anatolia as deeply impoverished yet full of elemental energy,[78] the movements of sword-bearing *zeibek* dancers embodying the resilience of peasants and tactile peasant knowledge as a foundation of Turkish national independence. It makes sense that Soviet Easterns contributed to Dino's turn to folk arts during the decentralization period, though, as I suggest, his involvement with peasant theater in Adana helped him to overcome their Orientalism.

In concluding this section, I want to address the controversial paintings completed for the state-sponsored Second Country Tour (İkinci Yurt Gezisi) of Turkish artists in 1939, which followed the Comintern's directive to join the cultural organizations of the ruling RPP.[79] The paintings were exhibited in Balıkesir in September 1939 and subsequently included in the First State Art and Sculpture Exhibit (Birinci Devlet Resim ve Heykel Sergisi) in Ankara as well as in state exhibits in 1942 and 1944, though only one of them, titled *Balıkesir Testisi*, has survived and is currently held by the Ankara Cartography Museum (Haritacılık Müzesi).[80] These paintings were widely criticized as strange, idiosyncratic, and extravagant and ridiculed for their depiction of "toilet ewers [*abdesthane ibrikleri*]."[81] When three paintings by Dino were reproduced in the literary journal *New Man* (*Yeni Adam*), the journal's editor İsmail Hakkı Baltacıoğlu and the critic Nurullah Ataç exchanged public letters with each other and with Dino.[82] Ataç attacked the paintings as abstract and elitist, while Baltacıoğlu defended Dino as an artist "not going toward but belonging to the people," declaring that "abstraction [*mücerred*]" was integral to traditional Turkish decorative arts. In his own response, Dino rejected Ataç's characterization and reminded his critics that ewers are material and "everyday objects in the peasants' lives": "When a peasant feels thirsty while working in the field," he wrote, "he drinks water from an ewer." "He washes his dead relatives with water poured from the same ewer; in short, the ewer is a unique companion of the peasant from childhood to old age. If this were not the case, he would not shape, polish, and decorate it with his own hands."[83]

MARXIAN FORM IN THE PERIPHERY

In Dino's painting *Balıkesir Testisi* (figure 4.2), the formal contiguity of the yellow peppers and the ewer is echoed by the contiguity of the spout's and handle's contours and the inclining leaves. In *Portre?* (figure 4.3), we can see the continuity of the ewer with the natural world extended to the peasant girl as gendered subaltern, whose body, positioned against the same striped and floral-patterned background, echoes the shape of the ewer.

FIGURE 4.2. Abidin Dino, *Balıkesir Testisi*, 1939, oil on canvas, 60 × 63 centimeters, exhibited in the Cartography Museum of the General Directorate of Mapping (Harita Genel Müdürlüğü Haritacılık Müzesi), Ankara, Turkey, https://www.harita.gov.tr/muze-resim-galerisi.

FIGURE 4.3. Abidin Dino, *Portre?*, 1939, as reproduced in the journal *Güzel Sanatlar*
Source: Ahmet Muhip Dranas, "Resimde Ümanizma," *Güzel Sanatlar* 2 (May 1940): 142.

The original painting has not survived. This black-and-white photograph was included in Ahmet Muhip Dranas's article on the First State Art and Sculpture Exhibit.

These paintings are not conventional still lifes or portraits but mimetic explorations of relationships between the rural subject and the natural world in which the texture of heavy brush strokes deliberately indexes painting as a handicraft just like textile embroidering or the potter's production of an ewer. We might say that Dino's work thus reimagines the use-value of painting, setting aside the tension between what Walter Benjamin called the "cult value" or "aura" of a work of art and its "exhibition value."[84] Though Dino's rural *faktura* was rejected by some of his TKP colleagues, an open letter in *Yeni Adam* by one "M. Oğuz" correctly identified the aims of Dino's embodied materialist aesthetic, commenting that "the meaning of Dino's ewers" could be found in dancing to traditional music, an experience in which "one could hold by hand [*elle tutulabilecekti*] the joyful pride bursting from the faces of the people."[85]

Dino's "folkmania" would continue to be misunderstood as an intellectual regression and obstacle to a universalizing Turkish Left literature and thought. While recognizing the formative nature of Dino's time in the Soviet Union and Europe, Oktay, for example, mistook the choice of such topics as "peasants' socks" as pandering to an unworldly viewer.[86] In taking more seriously the relationship of Dino's materialist aesthetics to Soviet cinematic socialist realism, I have also suggested that the tactile Orientalism of Dino's writings and paintings of the decentralization period ultimately compromise and limit this work. In the following two sections, I show how Dino, unlike his Soviet contemporaries, successfully broke with the ontological imagination of the rural subaltern, specifically in the plays he composed during his exile in Adana, and how this break makes Dino a remarkable figure in the Soviet republic of letters. Refusing any longer to romanticize rural subalterns as undivided affective-sensory subjects who know and represent themselves, Dino in Adana imagined instead divided critical-epistemological subjects entangled in "networks of power, desire, and interest."[87] Recognizing the revolutionary necessity of educational mediation and abandoning the avant-garde understanding of aesthetics as direct action, Dino went on to organize an important if short-lived program of aesthetic education.[88]

THE AFTERLIVES OF YUTKEVICH'S STUDIO SCHOOL: DINO'S PEASANT THEATER

In September 1942, Dino was arrested for his involvement in antifascist activities and exiled to Mecitözü, near the city of Çorum in the Black Sea region. As mentioned in the introduction, influential Turkish generals and cabinet members, dreaming of a federalist Turkist state crossing central Asia, had argued for joining the Second World War as a German ally. For the seven years following the declaration of martial law in Istanbul and Thrace in November 1940, the Turkish state maintained complete control of the press, monitoring news coverage in the dailies and censoring and closing leftist publications. Writers for a growing number of anti-fascist literary journals, some of which were deliberately licensed for the purpose of surveilling left political activities, were detained, arrested, and exiled to remote towns in Anatolia.[89] When Dino arrived at Mecitözü, a site of political exile since the late Ottoman era, he encountered its small Alevi peasant community who served as field workers in the paddies of landowners. As Dino wrote in his posthumously published memoirs, he was welcomed as an exiled oppositional figure by religious and other local leaders who had endured persecution by both the Ottoman state and the Turkish republic.[90] After seven months in Mecitözü, Dino was approved in 1943 to continue his exile in Adana, where his family owned pastureland. Marrying Güzin Dikel (the doctoral assistant of the German scholar Eric Auerbach during the latter's residence in Turkey) that same year, Dino wrote for the newspaper *Türksözü* until May 1945, when he was drafted for military service in Kayseri.[91]

Adana in the 1950s was compared to both Ottoman Egypt and the western United States during the so-called frontier period.[92] Situated in the fertile Çukurova (Cilicia) Delta plain of the eastern Mediterranean, it was transformed during the late nineteenth century as the Ottoman state sedentarized Kurdish and Turkmen pastoralists, coercing them into farming cotton as an export crop, and settled Muslim emigrants from the Balkans and Russian Empire in the area. Home to a substantial Armenian population subject to deportation and genocide in the early twentieth century, Adana was occupied after the First World War by French forces, who faced an insurrection from the Muslim landowners who had appropriated Armenian homes and land. During the early republican period, the Turkish state continued the Ottoman practice of forced resettlement and pursued the commercial production of both cotton and wheat. After the Second World War, agriculture in Adana was consolidated and mechanized under the U.S. Marshall Plan, which, along with rapid population growth, led to the dispossession and proletarianization of sharecroppers and small farmers and their mass migration to urban centers.

Arriving in Adana on the eve of this transformation, Dino witnessed its "vanishing history" as both a landowner and a communist playwright. Employed at *Türksözü* as the night editor, he became its de facto editor in chief, writing columns, editing the cultural section, doing page design, and translating war news from foreign presses and radio broadcasts. Though he was warned by Ferit Celal Güven, the owner of *Türksözü* and an RPP representative, "not to let red writing appear anywhere except in the daily's title typeset in red font," Dino's columns reporting on the Allies' successes and the Nazis' losses maintained a continuity with his antifascist publications in Istanbul before his exile.[93] Where his essays on the Ottoman imperial architect Sinan's stonework constructions developed an earlier Marxist historicization of Ottoman classical aesthetics, his discussion of the folk art of *tekerleme* (jingle) as "realism with the most extraordinary elements" illustrated his Gorkyean folk realism with examples collected from Çukurova.[94]

This is not to suggest that Dino was untransformed by exile. Régis Debray observes in "Socialism: A Life-Cycle" (2007) that "the two privileged evolutionary niches of the revolutionary socialist were prison and exile. Prison, to concentrate; exile, to campaign."[95] Whereas for Debray foreign exile was an important condition of a cosmopolitan socialist print culture, Dino's domestic exile showed him the limits of such Marxist-Leninist hyperliteracy. Nor can we assimilate Dino's experience to the views of either Eisenstein or Sergei Tretyakov, who substituted a proximate "haptic knowledge" of Eastern materiality for the visual pleasures of Orientalist exotica.[96] For Eisenstein, film "penetrated matter," while Tretyakov believed his factographic writing about China could make his readers "touch" and "feel" China as if they were present there.[97] Dino's time in the Anatolian borderlands did not overcome representational distance but rather widened it in a specific sense as in Adana he came to reject the self-proximate, unified (non)representation of an ontologically illiterate peasant. As a member of the village and theater committees of the Adana People's House, Dino formed an informal internal collective that included his spouse, Güzin, who was writing a doctoral thesis on the nineteenth-century French realist novel under Erich Auerbach's supervision; the socialist-realist writer Orhan Kemal, recently released from prison in Bursa; Dino's exiled brother Arif; and the young Kurdish *aşık* Kemal Sadık Göğceli, later known as Yaşar Kemal.[98] Naming this group "the Adana school," Dino articulated their goal as a new realist representation of the

Turkish peasant trapped between exploitative social relations including landlordism, usury, and debt bondage, on the one hand, and the ecological crisis of a malaria epidemic, on the other.

In an essay published years later, in 1994, Yaşar Kemal remarked that in Adana Dino had made and then destroyed in frustration many black-and-white and pastel drawings and monochrome watercolor and gouache paintings depicting nomads (*yörükler*) and farmhands (*ırgatlar*). The pastel works portrayed the father, mother, and child units of nomadic families as figures of indigeneity, bearing oblong faces atop bodies of straight and angled lines. The watercolor and gouache portraits deformed the figures of aging men and women using deliberately thickened and broken strokes. Yaşar Kemal recalled that he had wondered at the time at Dino's negation of the expansive and brightly colorful natural diversity of the Çukurova plain.[99] However, one might suggest that this dull oppositional mode, in its implicit refusal of haptic visuality, is a vivid record of Dino's transformation during the period. In the encounter with a "dispersed and dislocated" cognitive rural subject caught between "the formation of a (descriptive) class and the nonformation of a (transformative) class," Dino opted against depicting the Turkish peasantry as irrational savages or canny subalterns, as would have been in line with the available peasantist discourses of the era (as discussed previously).[100] Dino's turn to the peasant theater instead recognized the subaltern in Adana as a thinking subject whose negation by capitalist representation (*Darstellung*) could be mediated by the theatrical presentation of objects. Though ultimately this engagement with the peasant theater in Adana would be suppressed, its history can be understood as an afterlife of Soviet cinematic socialist realism in Turkey.

During his Istanbul years, Dino had published relatively little on the Turkish theater, but one essay in particular, "How Will the Turkish Theater Be Born?" ("Türk Tiyatrosu Nasıl Doğacak?," 1939), is a significant methodological statement. In this essay, Dino praised the institutionalization of modern Turkish theater under the leadership of Muhsin Ertuğrul while lamenting the loss of important fundamentals. Declaring that "the raucous deceitfulness of European Romanticism" had become a stage norm, he advocated a return to commedia dell'arte and the character realism of Molière. Emphasizing the contiguity of these realist comedic traditions and the popular urban theater (*ortaoyunu*), Dino argued that "Turkish traditional theater is the epitome of the newest theater," suggesting that actors should be trained in the vernacular realist technique of improvisation (*doğaçlama*).[101]

At the Adana People's House, collaborating with the amateur theater enthusiasts who performed a repertoire of Western-style plays approved by Ankara for the cultivation of morality and national citizenship,[102] Dino explored a tradition of village plays (*köy seyirlik oyunları*). Though village plays represent a discrete tradition, not to be conflated with the popular urban *ortaoyunu* and shadow theater that had developed in Ottoman urban centers, they did share some features with *ortaoyunu*, being performed in open areas and using very few props. Performed during the harvest and livestock-mating seasons and other transitional moments, village plays followed stock plots with themes of death and regeneration.[103] In April–May 1943, Dino's group went to the nearby villages of Baklalı and Gerdan to observe performances and perform their own village plays, titled "Quinine" ("Kinin") and "Gamble" ("Kumar"), about quinine price gouging in Baklalı and gambling in Gerdan, respectively. While Pertev Naili (Boratav), a close friend of Dino in France, claimed that "Quinine" inspired the Baklalı villagers to action against price gouging,[104] no direct records of these performances survived the suppression of the group by local state authorities, though Dino published an extant account of the visits to the villages in the April–May 1943 issues of *Görüşler*, the monthly periodical of the Adana People's House.

Arguing that traditional village plays served as the foundation of urban popular theater (*ortaoyunu*), Dino suggested that their "backwardness in dramaturgy" meant they could serve as a point of departure, if not a destination, and emphasized improvisation as key to true realism. He outlined "a three-step method" for the generalization and institutionalization of a new peasant theater (*köy tiyatrosu*) across Turkey:

    A. A few theoretical speeches [addressing];
        1. the psychological impetus of theater;
        2. psychology of acting
        3. psychology in local [*yerli*] theater.
    B. Rehearsals;
        1. collective thinking of the subject
        2. improvisational performance of this subject
        3. critique [*kritik*].

C. Performance in the village;
   1. watching and studying village plays
   2. the performance of the [rehearsed] play by members of the theater branch who are trained according to the principles of village theater, with spontaneous participation of the peasants.[105]

Dino proposed that a peasant theater group should begin by conceptually exploring "the psychological impetus of theater, psychology of acting, and psychology in local theater." Next, it should collectively discuss and determine the subject of a play, followed by improvisation-based rehearsal and critique. After rehearsal, the group should visit a village, study its local theater, and perform its own play, actively involving the villagers in the performance. Dino described an "unartificial" and "nonplastic" acting style and imagined "actor-writers" fulfilling a social responsibility by addressing issues of importance in a specific village.[106] Each Turkish province, he proposed in another essay, might form a core group furnishing guidance to amateur theater groups and coordinating their activities via literary figures living in urban centers.[107]

Though Dino accomplished none of this project, his vision should be recognized as a contribution to the Soviet republic of letters. In considering both his essays and his posthumously published and republished peasant plays, which I discuss in the following section, I suggest that Dino's methodology actively and creatively reimagined the principles of acting formulated by Yutkevich at Lenfilm. I have already mentioned Yutkevich's Lenfilm workshop and its function as a studio school for young filmmakers and designers, including Dino. Relinquishing the conventional role of the master director around which the creative process was centripetally organized, Yutkevich presented the workshop as a collaborative occasion for discussion, rehearsal, and critique of each film by the entire production team. "Perhaps also with my help," as Dino put it, Yutkevich developed a distinctive production style during this period, involving extensive improvisational rehearsal, for which Dino's work at Lenfilm included providing décor models.[108] Dino's account is consistent with the "Declaration of the First Artistic Workshop" ("Deklaratsiia pervoi khudozhestvennoi masterskoi," 1935) describing a three-stage method incorporating planning, rehearsal, and shooting.[109]

In his essay "Great Outlook" ("Bol'shaia perspektiva," 1937), Yutkevich suggested the contributions of his workshop's format to a new acting style.

Criticizing earlier montage cinema for eliding the actor's creativity and recognizing the significance of Stanislavsky's and Nemirovich-Danchenko's acting methods for both Russian and world theater, Yutkevich argued that Soviet cinema should prioritize the actor and a new dialectical acting method. Rather than casting actors only once a screenplay was complete, he proposed that actors should join the playwright, the director, and other members of a creative team right from the start. He emphasized rehearsing an entire screenplay prior to shooting film but suggested that rehearsal should not rely on memorization, and he suggested that "the significance, weightiness, and impressiveness of a particular actor's image" was a matter of internal "expressiveness" as well as external appearance.[110] As an example, Yutkevich cited his work with the actor Vladimir Lukin, cast as the lead, Mat'ev Bobylev, in *The Miners*, a failed theater actor who in A. Kapler's screenplay is a fictionalized representation of Alexei Stakhanov. In Donbass in Ukraine, where the film was shot, Lukin had worked with a Stakhanovite miner for a week before the shooting, and Lukin's monologues in the film, from his recitation of excerpts from Shakespeare's *King Lear* to a description of new and more productive coal-mining techniques, were delivered with an expressiveness displacing the tension between manual and mental labor and embodying the new socialist man as both artist and physical worker.[111] During the month and a half of rehearsals, the actors deliberately socialized with the production team.

Although *The Miners* is not considered Yutkevich's best work, it clearly contributed a great deal to his theory of acting, and Dino's own short-lived workshop and its program for actor training extended and adapted Yutkevich's theory to a Turkish context, where the task, as Dino saw it, was to educate the subaltern. Dino saw a new acting style as emerging from the improvisational comic realism of *ortaoyunu* and the village play, a style he described in "Notes on a Village Play" ("Bir Köy Oyunu Notları," 1943) as "live writing [*canlı yazı*]" more effective than newspapers, radio, or movies in reaching rural populations. Indeed, Dino imagined a "theater mobilization [*temsil seferberliği*]" of "live-writing squads" deploying "a comedy bombardment of live writing" in the battle against social problems as well as malaria and typhus.[112] Thus imagining village theater as an extension of communist writing into oral literature, Dino metaphorized embodied spectatorial participation in such contexts as modes of reading that were key to shaping consciousnesses. In the next section, I turn to *Baldy* and

The Inheritors, two published but unperformed plays that serve as useful records of Dino's modernist socialist-realist aesthetic education project.

FORMALIST SOCIALIST REALISM AS SUBALTERN EDUCATION

Published in 1944 by the Türksözü Publishing House in a limited edition of five hundred copies that were confiscated by the police, *Baldy* included a note explaining the limited print run as reflecting Dino's limited resources rather than any aspiration to reach only "elite" readers (*seçkinler*). Composed in 1942, the play's three acts loosely follow a socialist-realist master plot, with the coffeehouse proprietor Ali organizing the dispossessed peasants of Mecitözü to work in a new coal mine over the objections of the landlord and local shop owner (*aktar*), Siyamettin Efendi, who embodies interlinked modes of exploitation. Having through usury and extralegal coercion appropriated the paddy of a large farm as well as the small holdings of a number of peasants, Siyamettin also owns the only store in town, selling the peasants seeds in return for half of each peasant's earnings per harvest.[113] Combined with the debt that the peasants incur by taking goods from his store, these arrangements have ended up costing peasants both their homes and their land, leading them to sharecropping (*ortakçı*) or work as Siyamettin's farmhands (*ırgat*) and increasing their exposure to malaria. This play depicts spontaneous acts of peasant resistance to the local patriarchal order, including attacks on farmhand recruiters, the beating and murder of an agha, and the elopement of Siyamettin's store clerk, Abdullah, with the daughter of a retired Ottoman official exiled to Mecitözü. While the play affirms these acts of defiance, an affirmation enacted by Ali joining the peasants laboring at Siyamettin's rice farm, it also clearly suggests that real change can come only through the proletarianization of the peasants and the mine's role in structural development.

A prime intertext for *Baldy* is Yutkevich's film *The Miners*, set in the Donbass region and observing the transformation of Horlivka into a beautiful socialist city. Its subplot, focused on international espionage and a saboteur's arrest, finds a counterpart in Dino's satire in *Baldy* of the exiled Ottoman official, once a member of Sultan Abdülhamid II infamous spying network, who files false reports on the ostensibly illegal activities of Ali and the others. Here, of course, Dino also borrowed the comic devices of the Turkish village theater, which furnish the satire of other elite characters, such as the civil engineer who arrives to conduct a land survey and whose gustatory fixation on pickles comically undermines his social authority (30). *Baldy* also draws on the obscene jokes and noisy brawls found in shadow plays, *ortaoyunu*, and village plays alike—for example, in a subplot involving an adulterous local woman's quarrel with a male Istanbul theater actor over the actor's putative love affair with the woman's husband (51–53), which culminates in the woman and the actor eloping together. More consequential, perhaps, is the way *Baldy* mobilizes general tropes of the Stalinist novel and film, most importantly the production narrative promising technological mastery over wild nature, while remaining embedded in local reality, describing the discovery of brown-coal reserves near Mecitözü in 1942 and the major earthquake in December of that year.

Though a significant mass of Turkish criticism exists on village novels, Dino's plays have often been neglected,[114] and his biographer, Güzel, is alone in noting his successful representation of heteroglossia. As Dino explained in a note to *Baldy*'s readers, the phonetic rather than traditional orthography of the 1944 edition was intended to register regional pronunciations, with *ofis* (office) written *opis*, *vefat* (death) written *mefat*, and *belediye* (municipality) written *velediye* (111). The local social fabric also includes urban or otherwise elite speech styles, from the Istanbul vernacular of Ali and an otherwise unnamed exile referred to as "Garip" (Stranger) to the formal, somewhat archaic Ottoman Turkish of the exiled officials, marked by its Arabic and Persian loanwords and phrases. The uneducated, accented speech of the peasants is signaled by such letter substitutions as *h* for *k* (thus *yoh* for *yok*) and *i* for *e* (thus *vir* for *ver* and *get* for *git*). While heteroglossia is certainly important in *Baldy*, it is only one aspect of this play's commitment to dialogic exchange. In the discussion that follows, focused on the coffeehouse as a main setting and on the "eccentric" construction of the play's positive hero, Ali, I argue that Dino developed a hybrid, rewriting the aesthetic formula of Soviet national literatures as vernacular rather than national in form and modernist socialist realist in content.[115] In using the dialogic form of the village play to construct a nonidealized destructive and self-destructive positive hero, *Baldy* imagined a socialist-realist *Bildung* that displaced the hierarchical relationship of leader to led and training the subaltern to use reason freely.

Remember that in "How Will the Turkish Theater Be Born?," Dino had praised the dialogic relationship of spectator to performer in the traditional Turkish theater. He suggested that the improvisational style of Turkish theater performed on an unmarked stage in an open area closed the gap between "represented truth" and "the real world." "In traditional shadow theater and *ortaoyunu*," he wrote, "insofar as there is realism, there is merriness [*neşe*], which obliterates almost entirely the ego [*benlik*] of the spectators and actors." "I say almost entirely," Dino clarified, "otherwise, we would end up pointing a gun at Iago and yell at Desdemona not to drop her handkerchief."[116] Both the self-absorption of high-spirited spectatorship and the subsequent separation of the self are important here: where the first unifies actors and spectators, the second permits the spectator to reflect analytically and critically on the representation. In this respect, we might say that Dino saw the dynamic of Yutkevich's collaborative workshop in the dialogic structure of traditional Turkish theater.

The coffeehouse is consequential as the main setting in *Baldy*. While events occur in other public locations as well, including a barbershop, the town train station and cemetery, and a communal sleeping area on Siyamettin's farm, the play begins and ends at the coffeehouse with the monologues of an intoxicated Ali. In contrast with the conventional unity of action in Western drama, the most important events, including Süleyman Agha's murder, the wrongful arrest of Kel (Baldy) as the murderer, the sudden death of Ali's mother, Abdullah's elopement, and a major earthquake, all take place offstage and are reported by characters at the coffeehouse. Insofar as this approach makes discourse the main "action" on stage, it lends the play an episodic structure. A key event unifying the plot, if loosely, is Ali's departure from the coffeehouse to join the peasants working at Siyamettin's farm at the end of act 2. Even here, we are not transferred to the farm field but to the communal sleeping area at the end of a workday as a farmworker dying of malaria is looked after by the others.

The first editorial in Dino's journal *Küllük*, launched in 1940 and named for a coffeehouse in Istanbul frequented by writers and artists, described the village coffeehouse as "the true temple of the village" and its "main strategic center," where folk poets and storytellers delivered their performances and where local, national, and world news was recited, heard, discussed, and recirculated. Observing the coffeehouse's social diversity as a gendered public space, Dino described its oral culture as a supplement to communist writing:

> The state of crops is discussed at the coffeehouse.
> The news of a girl's abduction reaches the coffeehouse.
> "So and so is shot" is announced at the coffeehouse.
> The tax agent visits the coffeehouse.
> The moneylender makes up his scheme at the coffeehouse. . . .
> The news of the 1940 war reached Turkish peasants through the coffeehouse speakers.[117]

We can say that the coffeehouse in *Baldy* is marked by Dino's imagination of Mecitözü subalternity as critical-discursive subjectivity. Where the essays and paintings discussed earlier celebrated the three-dimensionality of folk arts as bridging the separation of everyday use from cult value, politics from aesthetics, Dino's new concept of village theater activated a three-dimensional participatory spectatorship, while maintaining the distinction between real and representation, praxis and theory.

We might say that Dino's goal for performances of *Baldy* was to three-dimensionally unify spectators and actors, transporting the spectators to Ali's coffeehouse and encouraging them to participate in onstage conversations in the roles of critical discursive subjects. Dino did not intend this unification as a mode of absorption or self-forgetfulness but imagined the spectators in the coffeehouse as embedded in a heterogeneous collective discursive space, the space of the village theater as such. In thus reflecting and doubling the space of the coffeehouse, I suggest, Dino's peasant theater emphasized the oral public use of reason in the Kantian sense as a discontinuous but necessary condition of revolutionary action.[118] Rejecting the political immediacy of revolutionary art as imagined by both Soviet constructivism and, differently, Soviet socialist realism, Dino embraced the mediacy of village theater as both a subaltern *Publikum* and a site of Marxist "aesthetic education" for the Anatolian subaltern and the elite vanguard alike.

In the coffeehouse proprietor Ali, *Baldy* presents a just "positive hero" without idealizing that hero as a model or authority in transmitting knowledge. In the opening monologue addressed to an unnamed patron, the inebriated Ali declares that he dislikes trade and all forms of buying and selling (4), adding that after his wife's death he had sold both his house and his land to the first bidder, unconcerned with profit. He would like to rid himself of his remaining possessions, Ali declares, and the only reason he hasn't done so is to deny his acquisitive older customers any opportunity to acquire them (4). Ali deliberately misuses or abuses these items, such as a wedding suit he makes a point of wearing while laboring at Siyamettin's farm (70). In refusing an offer to buy his deceased wife's patent leather shoes, Ali declares that he "threw one shoe into a well and kept the other," taking it from a sack to display to the play's audience (4). (This shoe eventually accompanies Ali to Siyamettin's farm, and when he returns to the coffeehouse, he offers it a toast: "Now we're alone, brother Ali. . . . Together with one patent leather shoe" [102].)

This use of props by Ali can be distinguished from the conventions of the traditional village play. Scholars of the village theater, including Dino, see the few props of the traditional village play as registers of symbolic value, including spiritual esoteric value, exceeding their function as everyday objects. For the peasant spectator, the dark sheepskin of an actor's costume might symbolize winter or death, while a white costume might represent regeneration. A male actor can play a bride just by wearing a skirt and a headscarf, without disguising his mustache. The prop's function is basically mimetic, a relation of similitude and affinity whose stylization in the village theater has been imagined as anticipating the modernist theater of Antonin Artaud and the constructivist theater of Meyerhold.[119] Dino's village theater, in contrast, deliberately employs props as estranged commodities, marking the ghostly objectivity of human labor, rather than as animistic tokens or handicraft *faktura*.

In the withholding, abuse, destruction, and fire sale of his possessions, all of which reject the rules of exchange, Ali is a figure of contrast with his customers' commodity fetishism and with the mercantile Siyamettin Efendi, who appropriates the surplus value produced by the peasants and whose store stocks even trash items such as shattered mirrors and used underwear as objects of potential exchange. "You come to my store," Siyamettin states, "and look at every corner. People think something is unusable and unsellable—it is sellable . . . a rusty shaving blade, an eyeless sewing needle, broken liquor glasses, pictures of women cut from old magazines. . . . What great notebooks we made and sold from ablution paper" (15). As Siyamettin tells Garip, the mysterious Istanbulite: "It is haram to leave these [peasants] any property.... The challenge is to let them live without killing them" (17–18).

On this point, Ali's behavior toward Siyamettin is deliberately antagonistic. Siyamettin asks Ali to reuse the paper bags in which Siyamettin sells sugar cubes in the store, but Ali burns them instead (15). When a relative of Süleyman Agha arrives and makes a spectacle of buying chocolate, cigarettes, and Turkish delight for everyone present, Ali ejects him from the coffeehouse, throws his money in the trash, and gives the treats to a street beggar (61–62). Even Ali's drunkenness, the farm labor for which he volunteers, and the malaria he contracts in the process can be read as deliberate abuses of a possession (69–70).

These defiances of modern capitalist rationality—understood as production, self-reproduction, or the accumulation of wealth—are "eccentricities" or "attractions," as the FEKS collective developed that concept in the 1920s. *Baldy* mediates the socialist-realist master plot through the modernist estrangement of the positive hero and his stage props. In thus borrowing the formalist-eccentric technique of the "impeded form," Dino "extends the period of time taken by the audience to perceive an object and complicates the whole process of perception."[120] The dissociation of the positive hero and his props from their milieu and their recontextualization—as the coffeehouse proprietor becomes a farmworker, a red shoe becomes a drinking companion, and money becomes trash—serves to block spectatorial absorption in realism, "baring the device," so to speak, while raising critical questions about the representation of the real. In *Baldy*, such estrangement serves to denaturalize the semifeudal relations of economic and social domination in the Turkish countryside and mark them as historically contingent.

Contrasted with spontaneous acts of violence directed at persons, from the knife attack on the recruiter to the murder of Süleyman Agha, Ali's eccentric expenditure of objects, money, and his own body is aimed at the system of capitalist representation (*Darstellung*), including commodity fetishism and the fetishistic representation of the agha as creator and guarantor of surplus value. Registering the historical contingency of both the commodity form and private property, Ali's conversations with two Alevi peasants named Hasan and Hüseyin articulate collectivist forms of proprietorship in their place. Hasan and Hüseyin propose a subaltern communism based on the practice of *imece*, or common labor and collective production.[121] "When a house is burned down at ours," Hasan and Hüseyin explain, "some bring wood and others nails[;] ... there is no separateness [ayrı gayrı] among us" (69). The peasant dying of malaria, meanwhile, reminds the other farmworkers that "earth is an integral [yekpare] body" evading attempts to divide and appropriate it, whether through imperial war or internal state violence (79–80). Finally, the earthquake taking place offstage reminds everyone present of the fundamental inalienability of the earth.

Again, my argument here is that in *Baldy* and *The Inheritors*, another posthumously published and neglected play, Dino extended Yutkevich's cinematic socialist realism into the Turkish countryside and that this extension represents a contribution to a Soviet republic of letters.[122] I have already mentioned the criticism Dino faced from his TKP comrades for the "surrealistic" transgressions of his *New Literature* essays. *Surrealistic* is the clearly wrong word for Dino's imagination of a "possible socialist realist aesthetic" displacing the ideological opposition of formalism and socialist realism, a polarity that has long since been challenged in Soviet studies. In his study of the "total art of Stalinism," for example, Boris Groys rejected the Western scholarly elevation of an emancipatory Soviet avant-garde over propagandistic socialist realism, which was cast as a villain, arguing that socialist realism was "a laying bare of the avant-garde device and not merely a negation of it." In the contiguity of the "demiurgical" creator of the Soviet avant-garde and the positive hero of socialist realism, Groys presents Stalinism as satisfying "the fundamental avant-garde demand that art cease representing life and begin transforming it by means of a total aesthetico-political project."[123] We can say that in representing neither a genealogical continuity nor a dialectical transition from formalism to socialist realism but rather a hybrid aesthetic, Dino's project, like that of Suat Derviş, mediated the translation of Marxist-Leninist concepts into a subaltern orality.

Other scholarship in Slavic studies has set aside Groys's arguably monolithic representation of the avant-garde and overemphasis on the modernist origins of Soviet socialist realism, focusing instead on the social and political conditions of socialist-realist aesthetics understood as something more than a canon of texts. Evgeny Dobrenko, for example, suggests that the transformative institutionalization of socialist-realist aesthetics was accomplished by substituting literary and filmic representation for the real, producing an ideal socialism as materialized reality, and "derealizing" and nullifying the everyday life of "dreary workdays, routine daily labor, and a life of hardship and inconvenience."[124] In the case of Turkey, we can say that Kemalism as a representational order proved unable to develop a similarly totalizing and pure mass aesthetic as the materialization of an idealized nationalist reality, while the repression of Turkish communism blocked any institutionalization of socialist realism. However, this structural difference does not and should not prevent us from seeing in both Derviş's and Dino's hybrid and nontotalizing aesthetics an itinerary of socialist realism in translation.

In other ways, Dino's village theater might be considered a counterpart of Brecht's epic theater. Lars Kleberg has offered a useful typology of theater as naturalist, stylized, ritual, constructivist, or epic based on how each form models the relationship between stage and auditor. Whereas the ritualized total theater of Proletkult, for example, requested the unification of the spectator and actor on stage, the constructivist theater of Meyerhold demanded their unification in the auditorium, treating the spectator as an object to be shaped by the artist and the stage as a platform for "*real*, model actions" "to be emulated in life outside the theatre." The instructive theater of Brecht, by contrast, maintained a distinction between stage and auditorium, treating the audience as a rational subject and refusing spectators any homogeneous group identity. As an example in the Soviet context, Kleberg suggests the unrealized performance of Tretyakov's *I Want a Child* (*Khochu rebenka*) intended to include questions from the audience and responses during the performance.[125] Though state repression would prevent Dino from continuing to develop his village theater, the essays I have discussed here and the plays written for performance in discursive public spaces (such as coffeehouses) clearly distinguish that project from a ritual theater in Kleberg's sense in that they substituted dialogic collective discussion and "critique" for the participatory festival or parade of socialist-realist film.[126] Articulating a translational equivalence linking Yutkevich's studio school to the village subalternity and incorporating formalism in a heterological rather than a dialectical manner, Dino developed an instructive theater from within a genealogy of socialist realism.

Dino's village theater project can and should be contextualized in relation to the efforts made by other Marxist anticolonial intellectuals to pursue educational activism. In his readings of the work of Antonio Gramsci,

W. E. B. Du Bois, Frantz Fanon, Aimé Césaire, and Gayatri Chakravorty Spivak, among others, Ben Conisbee Baer has argued that "the mind-bending poison of an educative relation, in which the entire colonized society becomes a cruel schoolroom spawning nightmares, retains a rare potential to be used medicinally to help heal the wounds it has participated in inflicting." Baer emphasizes that democratic national liberation requires a training of consciousness in the social habits of democracy and that such an educational program requires an education of educators who do not share a cultural formation with subaltern groups.[127] Where the National Schools (Millet Mektepleri) and to an extent the Village Institutes of the Kemalist state adopted Enlightenment-style common schooling in overwriting the language, religion, and culture of rural populations with a fabricated Turkish ethnicity, Dino's village theater was designed to intervene in such internal colonization by activating and training the critical-discursive capacity of the rural subaltern as a self-governing subject.

THE FUTURES OF THE "ADANA SCHOOL": YAŞAR KEMAL'S *FAKTURA*

Dino's village theater was repressed, but the legacy of the "Adana school" he formed with Güzin and Arif Dino and the writers Orhan Kemal and Yaşar Kemal is still legible today. I want to conclude this chapter by suggesting that the career of Yaşar Kemal represents both an endpoint and a new beginning of the aesthetic genealogy I have traced from Yutkevich to Dino. Born around 1926 in the Turkmen village of Hemite, to which his family had immigrated from eastern Anatolia after the First World War, Yaşar Kemal achieved a reputation as a bard and collector of Kurdish and Turkish epics and dirges of the Adana region while he was still young, his first book published by the Adana People's House in 1943.[128] Kemal knew the essays on folk arts and poetry that Dino had published in Istanbul, and he welcomed the news that the Dino brothers would be exiled in Adana. Although the Dinos' intellectual and material support for Kemal is widely recognized, their influence on his work has received less attention.[129] As I have suggested, Dino's plays can be read as substituting the figure of the Adana farmworker, as a dispossessed universalized subject, in place of the universal revolutionary subject of Marx and Engels's proletariat. Yaşar Kemal's early stories and novellas use another kind of engagement with objects and *faktura* to build on Dino's accomplishment by reimagining Dino's subalterns as not only epistemological subjects but also desiring subjects.

The early story "The Baby" ("Bebek," 1950), for example, describes the newborn child of a sharecropper named İsmail, a child not yet given a name, who is nursed by other women in his village after the death of his mother. In this story, the infant is presented as a thing or a surplus, unwanted object carried by İsmail while he is working in the field and from one village woman to another—but it is a thing whose existence is maintained.[130] Set alongside the almost purely negative abuse and destruction of objects in Dino's *Baldy*, we can see in "Bebek" a positivization of that negation: a dynamic also observable in the decrepit titular object of Kemal's story "Mattress" ("Yatak," 1952), which its vagrant narrator drags from one sleeping place to another. The mattress is not solely an index of its narrator's poverty because it is also marked by sexual desire, in the pride with which he conceals it from a woman he finds attractive.[131] Objects are also central in Kemal's early novella *The Pomegranate Tree on the Knoll* (*Hüyükteki Nar Ağacı*, 1951) and in many other works from his five decades of writing, including *Three Anatolian Legends* (*Üç Anadolu Efsanesi*, 1967), *The Legend of Mount Ararat* (*Ağrıdağı Efsanesi*, published in 1970 and illustrated by Dino), and *The Legend of the Thousand Bulls* (*Bin Boğalar Efsanesi*, 1971)—his "magic realist" novels from the late 1960s and 1970s, in which he adroitly evaded the primitivist Orientalism that compromised Dino's early journalism.[132] Where Dino's work in Adana progressed from a sensory-ontological to a critical-epistemological representation of the peasant, Kemal's work resolved that tension in the imagination of a divided rural subject with a positively embodied relationship to nature. Haydar Usta's ironwork in *The Legend of the Thousand Bulls*, Karacaoğlan's *saz*, and Halil's fallow deer in *Three Anatolian Legends* register an embodied sensory relationship to animate nature and the material world and at the same time function as an impossible object cause of desire in the Lacanian sense.[133] In thus completely dismantling the hierarchy of the relation of formal to informal schooling, Kemal surpassed the work of his mentor.

One might say that Kemal's literary development of modernist socialist realism also represents the missing chapter in Erich Auerbach's work *Mimesis*, famously composed in Istanbul in the early 1940s, and that

Dino's Adana school or "educational *imece*" represents an unacknowledged scene of comparative literature in Turkey.[134] Such a literary genealogy would also contribute to recent debates on peripheral realisms, featuring calls by Joe Cleary, Colleen Lye, and Jed Esty for attention to realism in postcolonial studies and transnational modernist studies.[135] Breaking with the vulgar materialist approach to literary form advanced by Franco Moretti and the Warwick Collective, Cleary provides a compelling account of the dissolution of British and French realisms and the emergence of European modernism in the context of early twentieth-century imperial histories. "However conceived," Cleary writes, modernism "was essentially the literature of an interregnum between the dissolution of one kind of European world-ordering imperialism and the consolidation of a new kind of US-Soviet imperialism in its place."[136] While Cleary's account is a valuable intervention on behalf of the political mediation of literary form, it neglects the history of nineteenth-century realisms outside western Europe, with the exception of Russia. In general, although scholars of peripheral realisms recognize the significance of Soviet socialist realism, they tend to treat it as an "orthodoxy," and sometimes the engagement ends there.

The history of what I have called "entangled revolutions" suggests that during the interwar period the emergence, consolidation, and translation of socialist realism (and its variants, including proletarian realism) were shaped by the decline of the Ottoman and Russian Empires, the discourses of Soviet anti-imperialism, and the "global moment" of 1920. Extending Cleary's account further, one might suggest that early twentieth-century realisms were also "an attempted sublation of [global nineteenth-century] realism into more spatially and cognitively expansive forms," but not in the same way as modernist aesthetics.[137] Modernism and realism, responding to similar structural pressures, formed the ossified critical polarity so familiar to us from the writings of Brecht, Benjamin, Adorno, and Lukács in the 1930s, but this is not the end of the story. The less well-known or altogether little-known writings of these figures' Turkish contemporaries also have a place in this debate. To rehistoricize them would be to expand our understanding of Marxian aesthetics and to address its neglect of non-European contributions on similar questions.

Another contemporary matter is represented by the European theories of new materialism and object-oriented ontology recently embraced in historical scholarship on the Turkish countryside. In such work, the dissipation of the subject into flows, intensities, and other figures borrowed from the work of Gilles Deleuze and his interpreters have reproduced the primitivism rejected so powerfully by Gayatri Chakravorty Spivak in the essay "Can the Subaltern Speak?" The work of Dino and Yaşar Kemal is also part of the foreclosed legacy of Ankara communism examined in chapter 1, and their specific engagement with *faktura* and objects registers what Alenka Zupančič calls "the form of existence of the contradiction . . . at work in the very existence of objects as objects" as well as in the subject as the agent of change through education and politics.[138]

Though Dino's exile in France lasted until his death in 1993, he remained involved in Turkish art, literature, and politics. Under the leadership of the TKP Soviet representative İsmail Bilen, the Our Radio (Bizim Radyo) station was established in Leipzig, Germany, broadcasting in Turkish from 1958 on. Following the TKP secretary Zeki Baştımar's arrival in Leipzig from Turkey in 1961, the party's External Bureau was formed with Dino, Nâzım, Baştımar, Bilen, and Aram Pehlivanyan as members. Following Nâzım's death, Dino parted ways with the External Bureau, but he attended the TKP conference in Leipzig in 1962, the first general meeting of the party since the late 1940s. Reflecting on his formation at Lenfilm in relation to the goals of Bizim Radyo and rearticulating the principles of his project of instructive theater, Dino emphasized the importance of reaching Turkish villagers with new techniques and "bold forms."[139] From January 1959 to September 1964, Dino wrote radio dialogues for the station, adapting the comic villager figures of İbiş and the Old Man from the nineteenth-century *tuluat* theater and addressing issues such as the Turkish military coup of 1960, U.S. imperialism, and local and national elections from a TKP perspective. The conversations Dino staged between the naive and unworldly İbiş and the canny Memiş in their accented and stylized peasant speech supported the newly established Workers' Party of Turkey (Türkiye İşçi Partisi), calling on listeners to join a united front of peasants, workers, and opposition groups against İnönü government policies and the growing influence of the Justice Party (Adalet Partisi).[140] On a visit to Moscow in January 1966 to attend an exhibition of his work at the Central House of Writers (Tsentralnyi dom literatov) and to deliver a lecture at the Moscow State University's Institute of Asian and African Studies, Dino met with Yutkevich, Garin, Khesya Lokshina, and other former colleagues for the first time in twenty-eight years,[141] and when the May 1968 movement came, he celebrated the new pedagogies it imagined for revolutionizing education through and as *imece*, or "collective work." "The purpose of educational collective work [*eğitim imecesi*] is not merely transmission of knowledge by those who know to those who don't," Dino observed; it "reflects instead a decision to collectively search and find values, truths, and knowledge."[142]

Chapter Five

IN THE SHADOW OF LENIN

Nâzım Hikmet's Prose Poetics of Seriality and the Time of (Post)communism

> I believed all my life in the rapid establishment of communism. I was certain that it would happen during my lifetime. I had thought so up until a year ago. But now I understand that tens, hundreds of years are needed to establish communism. . . . The time span I mention is necessary for the construction of the new man, the extraordinary man [*neobyknovennogo cheloveka*]! I see this man, and how pleasing he is to me! All of us communists were a little impatient; we thought that we could speed up the time of development of human consciousness. But no matter how much a prospective father wishes to hasten the birth of his child, he needs to wait nine months; otherwise, a miscarriage happens.
>
> —NÂZIM HIKMET

In May 1963, a few weeks before Nâzım's death, his comrade and collaborator Abidin Dino received an envelope enclosing the manuscript of Nâzım's last novel, which was serialized at the same time in the influential Soviet literary magazine *Znamia* in a Russian translation titled *Romantika: Roman*.[1] On the envelope was written in capital letters: "Yaşamak Güzel Şey Be Kardeşim" ("It's Good to Live, eh Brother"—or as the English translators of this novel have rendered it, "Life's Good, Brother").[2] It appears that Nâzım wished to retitle *Romantika* shortly before his death, making use of an expression uttered by the novel's protagonist in his rare moments of bliss. This affirmative new title offers a striking contrast with the novel's tragic plot as well as its original ironic title. Though the serialized French translation appeared in Louis Aragon's journal *La lettres françaises* under the title *Les romantiques* with Dino's illustrations, the first Turkish edition was published in Sofia, Bulgaria, in 1964 with Nâzım's proposed new title, and a censored edition with the new title would appear in Turkey in 1967.[3] As I suggest in this chapter, whereas the transnational history of the publication of *Life's Good, Brother* in multiple languages and editions illustrates the precarious condition of suppressed Turkish communist literature during the

Cold War years, the uncanny doubling of its title registers Nâzım's complex relation to the communist project.

Nâzım has appeared in one form or another in each chapter of this book because his life and oeuvre mark an event in Turkish and comparative literary history embodying the force of the entangled Anatolian and Bolshevik Revolutions. I want to be clear that in using the term *event* here, I am not referring only to Nâzım's towering literary influence on his Turkish and global contemporaries. Perhaps more importantly, Nâzım's life and work represent a generalization of communism among sections of the urban proletariat and secular lower- and middle-class students and professionals in Turkey. As the Turkish émigré Şekibe Yamaç reminds us in her poetic dictionary, in Turkey Nâzım's best-known verses are frequently quoted in a manner similar to the recitation of proverbs (*darb-ı mesel*).[4] Under state suppression, the clandestine circulation of Nâzım's verses provided an anonymous, collective linguistic fund of Turkish communism—belonging at once to everyone and to no one, with Nâzım's specific authorship being of secondary importance or of no importance at all. Even today, when leftists quote Nâzım's poems (something they often do anonymously, without attribution), they are not only quoting the work of the great poet Nâzım Hikmet but also invoking a common linguistic currency of Turkish communism. The dissolution of Nâzım's authorial proper name and the becoming-language of his verse in this mode of circulation mark both the horizon and limit of Turkish communism as I discussed it in the introduction and chapter 1.

Much ink has been spilled concerning Nâzım's role across the Soviet republic of letters. Examining his writings in the shadow of Comintern aesthetics and politics, comparative scholarship in the United States has traced his contributions to an international literature of the Popular Front during the mid-1930s and to tricontinental postcolonial literatures during the 1950s. Recent approaches to Nâzım in the context of Comintern and Soviet-sponsored literary institutions are useful in balancing the nationalistic interpretation of his legacy in Turkey. Emphasizing the transnational dimensions of the production of the discourse of Turkish national liberation, I suggested in chapter 1 that his neglected writings about the Turkish War of Independence are crucial in understanding his role as a missing link between the interwar and post–Second World War anti-imperialist discourses across the Soviet republic of letters. Whereas my earlier discussion addressed the thematic representation of the War of Independence, my goal in this chapter is to delineate Nâzım's contribution to Marxist aesthetics. Through a reading of his party writings on communist journalism in relation to his literary works, I establish that the Leninist concept of seriality formed the core principle of Nâzım's socialist-realist aesthetics. Rejecting the characterization of Asian and African writers as latecomers to the Marxist debates on genre and form, I argue that Nâzım's prose poetics of seriality represents another "origin" of this debate.

It is well known that Nâzım was deeply transformed by his encounter with Russian futurism and documentary cinema during his KUTV years. His first poem in free verse, "The Eyeballs of the Hungry" ("Açların Gözbebekleri"), was composed in Moscow in 1922 to honor the famine victims he encountered during his travel by train. Mimicking the structure of a poem likely by Vladimir Mayakovsky that Nâzım had read in a Russian newspaper, this poem also invoked Soviet cinematographic techniques in manipulating typeface dimensions to suggest camera movement:[5]

> *Not a few*
>   not five or ten
>   thirty million
>   **hungry**
>   **of ours!**[6]

Nâzım's use of free verse, typographic experimentation, and a new domain of Marxist-internationalist literary themes would revolutionize Turkish poetics. To emphasize only his relation to Mayakovsky and the Soviet avant-garde, however, is to remain at the surface of the relevant issues. In making use of Nâzım's recently published correspondence and reports on communist journalism in the TKP archive, and in suggesting that V. I. Lenin (more than Mayakovsky) was a key influence in Nâzım's literary writings, this chapter aims to move beyond the perfunctory, generalizing study of the relation between his literary aesthetics and his revolutionary activism.[7] Of central importance among his party writings is a report titled "Newspaper: A Collective Organizer" ("Gazete Kollektif Bir Teşkilatçı," 1925), which drew extensively on the Turkish translations of Lenin's article "Where to Begin" ("S chego nachat'?," 1901) and book *What Is to Be Done?* (*Chto delat'?*, 1902).[8] Through a reading of this report in the next section, I argue that Nâzım borrowed from Lenin the notion of serial writing that established the principles of both his party activism and his poetics from the late 1920s to the 1960s. Reading Nâzım's magnum opus *Human Landscapes from My Country* in the light of his prison letters to Kemal Tahir during the 1940s, I show that this epic novel in verse, depicting more than two hundred characters, makes an original contribution to Marxist aesthetics with its additive assemblage of a collective revolutionary subject. If, as Katerina Clark has argued, Lenin's *What Is to Be Done?* provided the framework for the "master plot" of the Soviet novel, this chapter shows that Lenin's book was a generative "origin" for socialist-realist aesthetics in more than one way.

Approaching *Life's Good, Brother* as a metanovel of Nâzım's entire body of work, the chapter's final section addresses the continuities and shifts in Nâzım's prose poetics of seriality during the 1960s. Composed toward the end of Nâzım's life, on the eve of socialist and postcolonial revolutions across the globe, *Life's Good, Brother* thematized the failure of a group of Turkish communists to establish an effective underground press. In this work that mobilizes modernist narrative techniques, including nonlinear dual narration and free indirect discourse, Nâzım reimagined the logic of seriality shaping his socialist-realist aesthetics. Both the young Lenin and the younger Nâzım had imagined a communist "underground," in the broader sense, modeled structurally on writing imagined as a uniform and homogeneous continuum. But in *Life's Good, Brother*, Nâzım broke with Lenin and with his own earlier poetic and political formulations, offering an indirect critique of the positivist grammatology of such a "connective" model and imagining another seriality in its place. Dispersed in time and space, the differential and discontinuous transnational communism imagined by Nâzım in *Life's Good, Brother* can be read as both an anticipation and an interruption of the postcommunism of our own time.

NÂZIM'S JOURNALISM

"Socialism," Régis Debray has written, "was born with a printers' docket around its neck.... Book, school, newspaper: for the party militant, the greatest emphasis lay on the third."[9] Describing his daily routine at KUTV, Nâzım's poem "My Nineteenth Year" ("19 Yaşım," 1931) emblematized one of socialism's "tools of transmission," capitalizing and repeating the word *book* (*kitap*) no less than nine times:

> Fish soup, training for rifle marksmanship, theater, and ballet
> BOOK..
> Fix your bayonet and stand guard by the potato truck.
> BOOK...BOOK..
> Matter, consciousness, exploitation, surplus value [*fazlakiymet*]
> BOOK..BOOK...BOOK..
> Manicure:
> no,
> tooth brush:
> yes.
> BOOK..BOOK...BOOK..[10]

The personal history of Nâzım's activism, meanwhile, demonstrates the central importance of the newspaper for the party militant. Literary critics have neglected the significance of Nâzım's journalism, though it constituted the main area of his contribution to the TKP from the very start. Upon arriving in Batumi in 1921, he joined the editorial board of the party journal *New World* (*Yeni Dünya*) and published *Commons* (*İştirak*) and the *Red Daily* (*Kızıl Gazete*) with Vâlâ Nureddin, Şevket Süreyya, and Ali Cevat Emre.[11] As Nâzım had suggested on his KUTV registration form when asked about his employment plans upon graduation, he had decided on a career in "communist journalism."[12] Shortly after the proclamation of the Turkish Republic, he returned to Istanbul in 1924, working for the party journal *Light* (*Aydınlık*).

The year 1925 saw the suppression of all political opposition in Turkey under nationwide emergency measures imposed to crush major Kurdish uprisings. The influential Communist Party publications *Aydınlık* and *Sickle and Hammer* (*Orak Çekiç*) were closed in March 1925, and a wave of arrests and detentions began after the TKP's issuing of May Day proclamations for distribution to workers. In August 1925, after being tried in absentia and given a fifteen-year jail sentence, Nâzım escaped from Izmir to the Soviet Union.[13] In "Newspaper: A Collective Organizer," the report written following his escape, Nâzım analyzed the blow dealt to the party's organizational structure by the arrests that year. This understudied document provides a valuable account of the Leninist concepts and ideas that informed his party work and poetic writings through the Second World War years.

Observing the "scattered," "inelastic" state of party organization, Nâzım's report suggested that the absence of strong links among town committees in Anatolia and between the Central Committee in Istanbul and those town committees posed "artisanal limitations" that had pushed the party toward "economism [*ekonomizm*]."[14] Nâzım used the Turkish term *zanaatkârlık* to translate Lenin's Russian *kustarnichestvo*, a word rendered in English by Lars T. Lih as "artisanal limitations." Derived from the Russian word *kustar'*, meaning "artisan" or "handicraftsman," *kustarnichestvo* captures the provincial and fragmentary nature of local party relations, marking the first stage of institutional development toward a modernized nationwide network. Translating and paraphrasing passages from Lenin's article "Where to Begin" (1901), later incorporated into his booklet *What Is to Be Done?* (1902), Nâzım extended Lenin's analysis of the Russian Social Democratic Party at the turn of the century to the TKP in 1925. As Lih notes, Lenin had composed these texts during a period of mass student and worker demonstrations and strikes, aiming to organize the Russian Social Democratic Party on the model of the Social Democratic Party in Germany. Following Karl Kautsky's Erfurt Program, which conceptualized social democracy as "a merger of socialism and the worker movement," Lenin prescribed to the party the task of preparing workers for leadership and the takeover of state power as a class, emphasizing the newspaper as a key medium for the transformation of "spontaneous" activity into "conscious," purposeful political mobilization.[15]

Closely following Lenin's argument in "Where to Begin," Nâzım affirmed in "Newspaper" the growth of worker activism in Turkish factories, proposing that "what is to be done now is to propel the proletarian class and working people to political struggle without neglecting the economic struggle." "If it is not possible to hear such political voices among the people and proletarian masses today," Nâzım wrote, "it is because they have neither a tribune [*kürsüye*] to cry out from nor an audience who could hear their voices" ("Gazete," 47). Here Nâzım closely echoes Lenin, who wrote in "Where to Begin": "We must not be discouraged by the fact that the voice of political exposure is today so feeble, timid, and infrequent. This is not because of a wholesale submission to police despotism, but because those who are able and ready to make exposures have no tribune [*tribuny*] from which to speak, no eager and encouraging audience, they do not see anywhere among the people that force to which it would be worth while directing their complaint against the 'omnipotent' Russian Government."[16] For both Lenin and Nâzım, the proletariat is ready for a political newspaper that will also reach the peasants and handicraftsmen through the working class.

For both Lenin and Nâzım, a nationwide "political newspaper is not only an agitator but also an extraordinarily powerful, collective organizer" ("Gazete," 46; Lenin: "Gazeta—ne tol'ko kollektivnyi propagandist i kollektivnyi agitator, no takzhe i kollektivnyi organizator" ["S chego nachat'?," 11].) It establishes links between the center and towns and between different towns, creating a "network of agents" ("set' agentov" in Russian; "gazete ajanları" in Nâzım's rendering) who form a "skeleton" of a unified party organization, collecting and assessing news material, promoting distribution, and influencing and/or organizing revolutionary action ("S chego nachat'?," 12; "Gazete," 46). Participation in journalistic work disciplines party members in the techniques of *konspiratsiia*, or secrecy, essential to avoid arrest. It introduces flexibility into party organization, making the organization adaptable to changing historical circumstances and tactics of state repression. A nationwide political newspaper introduces a kind of "double-consciousness" into each party member in the provinces, enabling them to assess their role in a broader national context. It transposes the noise of "spontaneous outbursts [*stikhiinykh vzryvov*]" into "meaningful" political speech, establishing a new symbolic order within the autocratic order that promises recognition to those repressed by the state ("Where to Begin," 24; "S chego nachat'?," 13).

In his study *A Marxist Philosophy of Language* (2006), Jean-Jacques Lecercle observes the absence of robust Marxist debate on questions of language. In his analysis of the writings of Valentin Voloshinov, Joseph Stalin, and Pier Paolo Pasolini, among others, he ascribes special importance to another of Lenin's pamphlets, "On Slogans" ("K lozungam"). Composed in July 1917 in the midst of struggle between the Bolsheviks and the Provisional Government (supported by the Socialist-Revolutionary and Menshevik leaders of the Soviets), "On Slogans" rejected the slogan "All the Power to the Soviets" as inappropriate and ineffective for the counter-revolutionary July Days. Providing a "concrete analysis of a concrete situation," this pamphlet, as Lecercle reads it, provides us with the fundamentals of a Marxist materialist theory of language that might profitably be counterposed to what he calls "Chomskyan naturalism" and "Habermasian irenism."[17]

"On Slogans" is certainly one of Lenin's most important essays, combining concrete analysis of a historical conjuncture with political analysis formulating strategy and tactics. Yet Lecercle's emphasis on this pamphlet does come at the expense of "Where to Begin," published fifteen years earlier, and its anticipation of the arguments Lecercle values in the later work. In "Where to Begin," Lenin had already suggested that the production of a common newspaper could train "the most talented political party leaders capable, at the right moment, of releasing the slogan [dat' lozung] for the decisive struggle" ("Where to Begin," 24; "S chego nachat'?," 13). Perhaps more importantly, the Lenin of "Where to Begin" had also imagined a communist underground modeled structurally on writing pictured as a uniform and homogeneous continuum, as something that connects. This latter point is an important one: for both Lenin and Nâzım, a newspaper is not just a publication medium for the representation of reality. In its seriality, which extends it through both space and time, the newspaper's form draws its force from and materializes in print the structure of repetition inherent in writing.

In emphasizing the constitution of a national political community in repeated performances of reading, writing, publishing, and distributing publications, Lenin and Nâzım not only anticipated the media theories of the newspaper made famous by Marshall McLuhan and Benedict Anderson but also drew implicitly on a European tradition of grammatological thought. Like Jean-Jacques Rousseau and Étienne Bonnot de Condillac, important representatives of this tradition, the young Lenin and Nâzım value writing mainly as that which provides a record of and perhaps restitution for something missing. For Rousseau, writing's supplemental character recuperates a lost idealized state of nature;[18] for Lenin and Nâzım, it realizes revolution as a historical finality. For both Lenin and Nâzım, writing not only connects dispersed interlocutors but also restores the imagined continuity disrupted by arrest and other forms of state repression, including death.

Rousseau famously wrote in the *Confessions*, "My decision to write and hide myself is precisely the one that suits me."[19] In the works of Lenin and

Nâzım as well, writing is understood as a technique of *konspiratsiia*, or spectralization, for avoiding arrest and maintaining clandestine activity in the underground. Rendering himself an arbitrary sign, the revolutionary subject under surveillance learns to play with external appearance; this process is (doubly) spectralizing in the case of newspaper work because its secret writing is transitory and ephemeral at best. The metaphors that Lenin uses, "thread," "skeleton," and "scaffolding," also emphasize this connective and extensive spectralization and represent spectrality as a transitory condition to be overcome by the pure event of revolution. Responding to the critics who charged him with "armchair theorizing" and "bookishness," Lenin argued that "the scaffolding is not needed after one starts to live in the building, the scaffolding is built out of inferior material, the scaffolding is put up for a short time and is tossed into the furnace once the building is completed even in crude fashion."[20] This is an imagination of revolution as an event of immediacy, of communication without an intermediary.

"We must dream!," Lenin wrote in *What Is to Be Done?*—quoting a passage by Dmitri Pisarev from "Blunders of Immature Thought" ("Promakhi nezreloi mysli") on the contribution of dreaming to the accomplishment of actual goals. Drawing an analogy between writing and the construction of a building, Lenin in a sense gave away his own dream: "When the bricklayers put down bricks in different places of an immense and unprecedented structure,—is it merely a 'paper' exercise to provide a thread that will help them find the correct place for each brick, that shows the final goal of the common work, making it possible to put to proper use not only every brick but every fragment of a brick, so that they join together with the ones proceeding and following to form a completed and all-embracing line?"[21] Promising a "leap" from the spectral textuality of writing represented by such metaphors as "paper" and "thread" to the concrete materiality of revolution embodied in "brick building," Lenin reiterated again the importance of writing as a supplement. Resisting the idiomaticity inherent in language, he also imagined here the construction of a totality of fragments comprising a uniform and homogeneous national unity.[22]

The events of the Great War precipitated a major shift in Lenin's writings on revolution.[23] Dealing with the difficulty of party organization under a repressive regime, Nâzım directly echoed Lenin's imagination of a national political newspaper in the prerevolutionary writings, presenting a new report on the question of the press at the TKP's Vienna Congress in 1926. The congress proceedings included debates concerning the frequency of publication of such a newspaper as well as its content, and they recorded a resolution to publish a weekly, including sections devoted to national and international news, agitation, propaganda, and party discipline.[24] In the tumultuous aftermath of the Vienna Congress, this newspaper project failed to materialize. The TKP suffered another blow in 1927 when the secretary of the Executive Committee, Vedat Nedim, delivered all the party literature in his possession to the government, provoking a wave of repression that included the TKP leader Şefik Hüsnü's arrest.

By this time, Nâzım was in the Soviet Union, but he returned to Turkey in August 1928. After another wave of repression engulfed the party in the spring of 1929, Nâzım convened a secret meeting on Pavli Island on the Marmara Sea and formed an opposition within the TKP that targeted Şefik Hüsnü and his associates. In a report dated April 12, 1931, submitted to the Comintern, the opposition described a plan to centralize and unify party work by publishing a secret weekly newspaper that would serve as "a collective organizer."[25] In a report in 1935, the poet Nail V. Çakırhan, a former member of the opposition and a graduate of KUTV, described the principles approved at the Pavli gathering as "word-by-word translations from Lenin." Çakırhan wrote, "It is possible to collect the opposition's essentials under the following three main lines: (a) the grounding of the party on production cells [*istihsal hücreleri*]; (b) a professional, revolutionary cadre [*profesyonel, revolüsyoner kadro*] in the party organization; (c) a central, secret, political newspaper to be distributed across all Turkey."[26] In his memoirs, the influential poet Hasan İzzettin Dinamo describes a meeting with Ruşen Zeki in Ankara in the early 1930s, where he learned of the opposition's plan to print two journals in Syria and distribute them to Turkish intellectuals, peasants, and workers. Handing Dinamo two small medicine bottles of invisible ink, Ruşen Zeki had recruited Dinamo to write for these journals at Nâzım's request.[27]

With the arrests in 1934, Nâzım's attempt to publish an all-Turkey party newspaper was thwarted once more. Conflict between Şefik Hüsnü's associates and the opposition culminated in the expulsion of dissident party members in 1934, Nâzım among them. The Comintern decided to decentralize and then liquidate the TKP in 1937, and Nâzım was arrested and tried in the army and navy cases of 1938. This was the end of Nâzım's dream for an all-Turkey party newspaper, at least for the moment.

NÂZIM'S POETICS OF SERIALITY

Nâzım's poetic writings during this period were aimed directly at supporting his newspaper project. In a posthumously published interview, Nâzım remarked that the state repression of the 1930s prevented him from reciting his poems to Turkish workers at public readings: "The only way [to make them available] was to have them printed." He understood his poems of the 1930s as marked by the regime of the printing press, appearing as "the poet's conversation with one or a couple of people in a quiet voice."[28] In one of these "silent" poems, titled "Next in Line" ("Sıradaki"), Nâzım aimed to cultivate the subjectivity of "one of a million in millions," "a rank-and-file soldier," who willingly gives up his singularity to become part of a unified, connected social body. Describing the Turkish worker as a purely corporal subject with physical needs, Nâzım imagined this working body as a link to the realization of a materialist social ontology: "He drinks water with his mouth, he walks on his feet / For him, there is only work that begins, ends, and begins."[29] Borrowing Lenin's metaphor of "a completed and all-embracing line," another poem, titled "Death of the One Next in Line" ("Sıradakinin Ölümü"), described the logic of connective seriality and substitutability:

> He was neither in the front
> >nor in the back
> >>he was in line
> >>>on our line . .
> And when the bloody head of the one next to him fell down on his shoulder
> >>>>when his turn came
> >>>>>he counted his number . . .[30]

Like Lenin, Nâzım recognized the disruption of seriality by death, while imagining its restoration by substitutability.

A volume authored by Nâzım with Çakırhan in 1930, *1 + 1 = One* (*1 + 1 = Bir*), meanwhile, provided another symbol of serial communist writing.

The volume's title signified not only the fusion of two poets' work but also the additive, serial, uniform structure of Leninist organization, with the linguistic sign "One" marking a totalizing unity. The seriality represented by the title's mathematical equation may be understood as an example of the "bad" or "spurious infinite [*das Schlecht-Unendliche*]" conceptualized by Hegel. Contrasting the "true infinite [*das wahrhafte Unendliche*]" of reason with the bad infinite of understanding, Hegel suggested that the latter posits a mutually exclusive relationship between the universal and the particular. For Hegel, the true infinite is precisely that which lacks any external measure or boundary, encompassing the particular as a moment of its universality.[31] Nâzım's title offers a mathematical notation of this false universality bound by the particular, positing a transcendent universal "One" abstracted from the additive particulars (1 + 1).

Composed while Nâzım was in prison in the late 1930s and early 1940s, *Human Landscapes from My Country* is rarely studied in relation to Nâzım's earlier poetic and political writings, though it represents his most significant attempt to realize the Leninist dream of serial writing on a large scale, extending from the party and the proletariat to the nation and the world. The prison letters that Nâzım exchanged with Kemal Tahir between 1940 and 1950 reveal that Nâzım thought deeply about the composition of this modern "epic novel" in verse. In contrast with his influential contemporary Georg Lukács, Nâzım called for a new direction in Marxist aesthetics that would break with the novelistic representation of "types," emphasizing in its place the collective interlinked revolutionary subject of twentieth-century social movements.

Nâzım regarded the traditional novelistic construction of individual types or heroes as an anachronism and viewed the emergence of the novel as inseparable from the emergence of the nation and the scaling effects of communication and transportation technologies. In composing novels about small groups of individuals and families, the great realists of the nineteenth century, such as Honoré de Balzac and Leo Tolstoy, managed to successfully depict a totality of social relations within a given nation. But in an age of socialism that was also an age of "aviation and motor technology," Nâzım saw little value in producing national variations of these earlier novel forms and character types. Though he thought the novel's historical development as a literary form lacked dynamism, he felt it

FIGURE 5.1. Book cover for the first edition of Nâzım Hikmet and Nail V., *1+1= Bir* (Istanbul: İlhami Matbaası, 1930).

necessary to include novelistic elements in his modern epic, observing in one letter to Tahir that "the new human interactions that are born or about to be born ... require a newer form, a higher modality ... that incorporates elements of the novel while remaining distinct from it." Addressing not just his fellow countrymen, but also the "world [*dünya*]" beyond them, he aspired to invent a new Marxist form as an original contribution to world literature. The inherent brevity of verse seemed especially useful in that it offered the writer the opportunity to describe each character concretely as a "human [*insan*]" rather than as a schematic type, without resorting to digression, *and* at the same time include an agglomeration of different protagonists in an unbounded mode.[32]

Rethinking Nâzım's prison letters in relation to his earlier writings, one might say that in the 1940s Nâzım was exploring the construction of a literary "scaffold" or an "all-embracing line" that could serially connect members of the party, the nation, and the world. Rewriting the mathematical logic of the title of his book with Çakırhan, we might represent this new serial writing by the notation $1 + 1 + 1 + \ldots$, a symbol of "spurious infinity" in the Hegelian sense. Narrating the life stories of two groups of Turkish travelers on their way from Istanbul to Ankara in the first-class and third-class cars of two separate trains and including roughly two hundred characters in total from such groups as imprisoned party members, war profiteers, workers, and peasants, *Human Landscapes* offered a panorama of republican Turkey. As Nâzım saw it, the socialist revolution of the twentieth century required that his "undisciplined" prose poem include an international dimension.[33] Accordingly, *Human Landscapes* incorporated the tale of Zoya Kosmodemyanskaya, an eighteen-year-old Soviet partisan fighter brutally killed by the Nazis in 1941. As I have argued elsewhere, the anonymous narrator, who has no characterological role to play in the poem's plot, might best be described as a transcriptionist, recording the inner speech of the nation and its beyond, now in direct testimonial quotation, now in free indirect discourse.[34] It is regrettable that scholarship in comparative literary studies has failed to account for the contributions of "Eastern" Marxists to the realism debates during the 1940s. Deeply aware of his belatedness in relation to his French, Russian, and Soviet predecessors, Nâzım invented a new Marxist form of seriality during a period in which he could not practice political journalism.[35]

We might describe *Human Landscapes* as another example of modernist socialist realism:

>Haydar Pasha Station,
>spring 1941,
>>>3 p.m.
>
>On the steps, sun
>>fatigue
>>>and confusion.
>
>A man
>>stops on the steps
>>>thinking about something.
>
>Thin.
>Scared.
>His nose is long and pointed,
>and his cheeks are pockmarked.
>The man on the steps,
>>Master Galip,
>>>is famous for thinking strange thoughts:
>
>"If I could eat sugar wafers every day," he thought
>>>when he was 5.
>
>"If I could go to school," he thought
>>at 10.
>
>............................
>And now standing on the steps
>he's lost
>>in the strangest of thoughts:
>
>"When will I die?
>Will my blanket cover me when I die?"
>>>he thinks.
>
>............................
>Spring comes to Haydar Pasha Station
>with the smell of fish in the sea
>>and bedbugs on the floor.
>
>Baskets and saddlebags
>>go up and down,

>   stopping to rest
>   on the steps.
>
> A child
>   about five
>   comes down the steps with a policeman.
> There is no record of his birth,
> but his name is Kemal.³⁶

In contrast with Lukács, who famously privileged epic narration over description,³⁷ Nâzım's serial, additive writing in *Human Landscapes* maintains both modes, ascribing each mode a different functionality. Description in each discrete moment supports the linear epic narration without being completely subsumed under it, emphasizing the assemblage or "montage" of different parts. *Human Landscapes* imagines a mobile heterogeneous collective subject of becoming-socialism, offering a useful counterpoint to Lukács, who rejected the "one-dimensional" modernist technique of montage. "The details [in montage] may be dazzlingly colorful," wrote Lukács, "but the whole will never be more than an unrelieved grey on grey."³⁸ Without abandoning his commitment to the representation of objective totality, Nâzım demonstrated the usefulness of "montage" for a new socialist-realist aesthetics drawing on Lenin's notion of seriality. He supplemented the pedagogic project of his TKP comrades by thematizing the ethical act of giving oneself to a socialist seriality.

Human Landscapes was certainly not Nâzım's final experimentation with serial writing. Given the persistence of his commitment to a communist press during his years in Turkey, one would expect *Life's Good, Brother*, the fictional autobiography composed toward the end of his life, to reflect these concerns. And they do—but with a twist. In this final work narrating the serial failures of a group of TKP members to establish an effective underground party press in the mid-1920s and early 1940s, Nâzım would reimagine another revolutionary subject and temporality. In *Life's Good, Brother*, he would reject the substance of both the young Lenin's and his own earlier formulations and the emphasis they placed on writing as primarily continuous and connective. Nâzım would also offer an indirect critique of what we might call the *positivist grammatology* of those earlier models and the imagination of something else in its place.

ANOTHER REVOLUTIONARY WRITING

In light of Nâzım's attempt to write a "supranovel [*romanüstü*]" or "a novel that will become something other than a novel [*romandan başka bir birşey olacak roman*]," it might be surprising that by the late 1950s he had embraced the conventional form of the novel.[39] However, it would be a mistake to regard *Life's Good, Brother* as a regression. In an undated letter to Tahir, Nâzım observed that unlike the capitalist and peasant types who were overrepresented in twentieth-century world literature, the figure of the communist had not yet been exhausted.[40] Narrating the life stories of a group of "typical" Turkish communists, *Life's Good, Brother* seeks to close this gap in literary history. It is regrettable that this novel is read almost exclusively for its biographical significance.[41] In its brilliant rewriting of the socialist-realist master plot, *Life's Good, Brother* represents an important shift in Nâzım's prose poetics of seriality and a major new contribution to the "possible aesthetic" of socialist realism.[42]

Composed during a period of de-Stalinization and relative liberalization in the Soviet literary establishment,[43] *Life's Good, Brother* is set in the Aegean city of Izmir on the eve of the first major wave of repression of Turkish communists in May 1925. It follows the KUTV-educated caricature artist Ahmet, who has relocated to Izmir following a TKP directive to establish an underground press with the help of a factory worker and fellow party member, İsmail. Hiding in İsmail's cottage as the arrests begin, Ahmet digs a hole in the cottage's floor for concealing a printing machine, a project he compares to "digging his own grave."[44] With the promised deliveries of press equipment and supplies blocked by the crackdown, and made claustrophobic by days spent in the cottage, Ahmet leaves for a walk and is bitten by a stray dog. Developing a fever and anxious about the possibility of contracting rabies, he orders İsmail to kill him and bury him in the hole in the cottage floor if worst comes to worst.

As the Russian title *Romantika* clearly suggests, this novel is an ironic account of an immobilized revolutionary, bedridden and delirious, experiencing a distortion of time. According to a letter dated September 14, 1925, sent by Nâzım to the head of the TKP, Şefik Hüsnü, Nâzım himself had been instructed to found a city committee in Izmir in the period just before the arrests in 1925.[45] Working closely with the lathe operator İsmail Hakkı to establish party cells among the railroad workers of Izmir, Nâzım reported in his letter that he had set up a secret underground cellar in

Izmir for storing party literature. The fictional character Ahmet's being bitten by a dog appears to be a fictional allusion to the adaptation of a French play titled *The Lighthouse Keepers* (*Gardiens de phare*, 1905), directed by Muhsin Ertuğrul in Istanbul in the 1910s and 1920s.[46]

Continuing Nâzım's lifelong practice of formal experimentation, *Life's Good, Brother* makes notable use of a modernist narrative technique, shifting back and forth between Ahmet and İsmail's first-person narration and free indirect style as episodes in the story take place in different past and future moments.[47] The events of the narrative present are interrupted, for example, by Ahmet's delirious analepses depicting his travels in Anatolia in 1921 and his years at KUTV from 1922 and 1924. Equally noteworthy are the prolepses depicting İsmail's periodic arrests and prison sentences in Turkey in the late 1930s and 1940s. To the extent that continuity is maintained across sudden shifts from one narrator and chronotope to another, it is through the repetition of a set of motifs. A relatively early passage in the novel provides an illustration of its paratactic texture and episodic structure:

> I got up. I took a chalk from my charcoal set. I drew six lines behind the door. Six white lines.
> —What's that, Ahmet?
> —Today is the sixth day [since the dog bite], İsmail.
> —By God, brother, you're crazy.
> (He lit a cigarette. He threw one at Ahmet. He doesn't like this kid's state. He won't get rabies, but the boy will be beside himself for forty days.)
> İsmail blew out the lamp. In the dark, Ahmet can see the six white lines on the door.
>
> On the seventh day, Anushka saw the lines I had drawn on the dacha door:
> —What are these, Ahmet?
> —It's our seventh day. So we have thirteen days left, Anushka.
> —Then what?
> —Then, you know, your leave is over, my vacation ends. We'll go back to Moscow...
> (26; 27–28, ELLIPSES IN ORIGINAL)

Several subtle yet deliberate narrative shifts occur here: first, in the parenthesized passage Ahmet's first-person narration yields to İsmail's unvoiced inner speech in free indirect style. Next, focalization shifts back to Ahmet in the third-person narration that follows the parenthesis: "İsmail blew out the lamp. In the dark, Ahmet can see the six white lines on the door." The passage concludes in Ahmet's first-person narration again: "On the seventh day, Anushka saw the lines I had drawn on the dacha door." Narration jumps from the chronotope of Izmir in 1925 to the summer of 1924 in a Moscow exurb, where Ahmet vacations with his lover, Anushka, before returning to Turkey. Refusing a unified narrative perspective and linear narrative temporality, the fractured surface of this passage is stitched together using motifs, the repetition of the act of drawing lines and the shadowing of the cottage by the dacha maintaining continuity across gaps in time and space.

The motifs of enclosed space and line drawing also support the flashes forward to the year 1943, when three party cell members, Kerim, İsmail, and Ziya, are tortured at the Istanbul Police Headquarters for possessing and exchanging a typewriter and printing paper intended for use in communist publication activity (134; 148). İsmail is kept in solitary confinement, while Kerim is locked in "the coffin [*tabutluk*]," a tight, narrow space not much larger than a human body, and Ziya is trussed and hung from a window as if "crucified" (144; 180). As Ahmet puts it ironically, all the torture and suffering were for little more than "waxed paper and an old typewriter." With its sticky letter *D* key, the typewriter cannot even print the Turkish word for revolution, *Devrim* (144; 180). Just as in the narrative past and present in the Moscow dacha and the Izmir cottage, where Ahmet counts each day by drawing a line on the door, İsmail scratches a line on the wall in his cell. Indeed, the only acts of writing by the revolutionaries include the lines and the multiplication sign that Ahmet draws on the door of Anushka's dacha and on the cottage door in Izmir as well as the lines scratched by İsmail on a prison wall in 1943. It is as if the revolutionaries assembled a new kind of writing machine to replace the broken typewriter (or in the chronotope of 1925 the missing printing supplies), one that operates with the notational line symbols and the multiplication sign. Most of the book's twenty-six chapter titles are direct references to these acts of writing: "The Seventh Line in Anushka's Dacha," "The First Line at Police Headquarters," "The Twenty-Fifth Line in Izmir," "The Tenth Line in Anushka's Dacha," "Multiplication Sign: X," and so on.

Together, these lines and the multiplication sign can be understood as a symbol of encoded communication systems that Turkish communists used under arrest, such as the Morse signals tapped on radiator pipes by the Military Academy students placed in solitary confinement in 1938 for admiring Nâzım's poetry and/or possessing a Turkish translation of Carlo Cafiero's summary of *Capital*.[48] They may also be understood as a diagram of the novel's master plot and as a map of the logic of an alternative communist writing and temporality that Nâzım imagines in this work, replacing both Lenin's and his own youthful formulations. Where Lenin had imagined writing as a continuous and connecting thread, these separate line segments cum gaps stand for repetitions of failure, the failure of a uniform, national communist press in the face of poor strategy, police repression, and torture. We might also imagine them as comprising a kind of diagram of the novel's syntagmatic (or sequential) organization in much the same sense. And we might imagine the X or multiplication sign that Ahmet draws on the cottage door as suggesting the paradigmatic (or selective) shape of the novel as a whole. In the chapter titled "Multiplication Sign: X," Ahmet marks his recovery from illness by drawing a large X with "its four points touching the four corners of the door" over the thirty-two lines representing the thirty-two days he had spent ill in the cottage (144; 181). More than just a symbol, this X stands for the narratological structure of negation, a "cross-shaped reversal of properties that rhetoricians call chiasmus," in the words of the literary critic Paul de Man.[49]

To this we must add the programmatically paratactic writing style that Nâzım chose and his intricately nonlinear storytelling. An illustration of the novel's style is provided by the passage I cited earlier in this section. It is a paratactic arrangement of brief, truncated phrases and sentence fragments that makes minimal use of grammatical conjunctions to suggest relationships. The novel continually introduces and accentuates gaps at the level of syntax and narrative organization, refusing to eliminate them. (Censored Turkish editions of the novel published in Turkey from 1967 to this day emphasize such gaps at another level insofar as the removed content is marked by parenthetical or bracketed ellipses.[50])

Certain narrative temporal shifts in the story, meanwhile, tend to negate revolutionary statements and actions when they appear. The novel begins with a scene in which Ahmet meets with İsmail in the narrative present of 1925 in Izmir, but it almost immediately shifts proleptically forward to 1938, when we learn of İsmail's arrest in a way that underscores the futility of what is happening in 1925: "Thirteen years later, in 1938, in the Ankara military prison they would throw him in solitary for six months. . . .

İsmail would remember this night—how the blanket prickled his chin, how Ahmet kept trying but couldn't blow out the lamp" (12; 9–10). When Ahmet has a flashback to the Turkish War of Independence in 1922, he imagines a horseman from Adana fighting the Greeks in Izmir. "Where is he now, in 1925?," he asks in an intimation of the foreclosure of the Anatolian Revolution. "Working on which big landowner's farm? A sharecropper?" (9; 6). While researching the impact of the October Revolution at the KUTV library in 1923, Ahmet glances at issues of *Pravda* published in 1922, with headlines juxtaposing reports on the famine during the Russian Civil War with news of the revolution's fifth anniversary (32; 34). And during his stay in his lover Anushka's dacha in the chronotope of 1924, Ahmet counts down each day remaining before he will be sent to Turkey. This countdown draws criticism from Anushka, who objects, "When I'm watching a real good play, I don't think about how much longer it will last. I watch it as if it'll never end" (117; 144).

Just as important acts and events are foreclosed by such narrative temporal shifts, so are the novel's characters pursued by their impending deaths: Petrosian, the cancer-stricken Armenian student at KUTV, has been told he has nine months left to live (98; 119). Si-Ya-U, the Chinese student, returns to China knowing that those who returned before him were arrested and decapitated upon crossing the border. At age sixty, Ahmet is shadowed by his own death in the novel's final chapter, "My Guests," where his last words are, "If I could just live five more years..." (149; 187, ellipses in original). We might take the hole that Ahmet digs in the cottage floor as a synecdoche for the novel itself in that every character, every event is emptied of its revolutionary significance and spectralized as a hollow sign through these analepses and prolepses. In contrast with Lenin's account of spectrality, in *Life's Good, Brother* such a "hauntology" is a perpetual state, one that it regards as impossible to overcome. Nâzım's ironic representation diverges from the conventional construction of the positive hero as a "Neoplatonic idea" or a frozen "archetype."[51] Representing a protagonist who fails to transcend the spectral materiality of writing, the novel reimagines a possible socialist-realist aesthetic in which "the text effect" is not absorbed by "the thesis effect."

One would be forgiven at this point for the reasonable assumption that in Nâzım's imagination all this represents the futility of communism itself and that it thus represents Nâzım's break with communism. After all, at one point Ahmet explicitly derides his own communist commitment as "romantika" and explicitly questions the value of revolutionary romanticism: "For years my life has been romantika [the Russian *romantika*, meaning "romance" or "romanticism," is here rendered in Turkish transliteration]. Kerim's, too, and the lives of many people I don't know but will come to know, and Suphi's, Petrosian's, Marusa's, and Anushka's—all romantika" (141; 176).⁵² But this assumption would be mistaken. The X that Ahmet draws on the cottage door, the chiasmus, is not just an ironic structure. As a rhetorical figure of inversion, it also stands for the logic of specularity, or repetition, that propels the novel into the future that this novel *also* imagines. We can trace this logic of repetition in the way that Ahmet's place is taken by—in the way he is doubled and substituted for—other "positive heroes" in the novel's different, layered chronotopes: Anushka, İsmail, Ziya, Kerim, Agop, Neriman, and others. While each arrest, disappearance, or death stands for an end, it also stands for this structure of repetition in a way that maintains its promise even in the face of failure.

I suggested earlier that both Lenin and Nâzım associated repetition with writing, but whereas Lenin imagined writing as connective, continuous, and homogeneous, the Nâzım of *Life's Good, Brother* imagines it as differential, as what the philosopher Jacques Derrida called a "seriality without paradigm," in which each repetition is an irregular, contingent iteration across a gap.⁵³ In this context, there is no horizon to cross, no revolution imminent, no determinate end at all, which, of course, makes for the starkest contrast with Lenin. The repetition of failed revolutionary activity within each chronotope does not conform to the pattern of any Marxist-Leninist evolutionary historical paradigm, nor does it imply in any way the possibility of a revolutionary leap. In contrast with the "bad infinity" of $1 + 1 = $ *One* or *Human Landscapes*, the irregular seriality in *Life's Good, Brother* represents "true infinity" in the Hegelian sense. Encompassing the finite instead of contrasting with it, the true infinite, for Hegel, lacks any external ground or measure, involving an endlessly self-reflexive relation to itself. Contemporary readers of Hegel emphasize that the structure of true infinity is best represented by an open circle with a gap rather than by a closed circle.⁵⁴ Imagining revolution as a contingent (im)possibility in each chronotope, the novel represents it as an incomplete process of becoming, or a "not-all," which harbors in itself the condition of its possibility and failure. The endlessness of revolutionary becoming in each chronotope spills into the next, sustaining a "restless," irregular communist seriality without transcendence.

My argument here is that *Life's Good, Brother* accepts and affirms this nonfinality, this infinitude of revolution, despite the disappointment and failure it represents, and that this acceptance of nonfinality need *not* represent a rejection of communism. Imagining a gathering of the novel's characters distributed in its different chronotopes, the aged Ahmet observes in the novel's final chapter, "My Guests," "I have guests: Anushka, İsmail, Ahmet, Neriman, Marusa, Ziya, Si-Ya-U.... My guests haven't aged. They are still the age they were when I last saw them" (149; 187). Ahmet reads a poem of his own to this group of "guests" at this point:

I'm a communist [*Komünistim*],

> I'm love from head to toe,
> Love [*Sevda*]: to see, to think, to understand,
> Love: a newborn, advancing light
> Love: to hitch a swing to the stars,
> Love: to cast steel in a sweat,

I'm a communist [*Komünistim*],
> I'm love from head to toe . . .

(149; 187, TRANSLATION MODIFIED, ELLIPSES IN ORIGINAL)

Whereas Ahmet's earlier, repeated failure to compose a poem parallels the novel's negation of communist writing, this final poem in free verse and in the Turkish vernacular is the only nonfailed (I hesitate to use the word *successful*) act of communist writing in *Life's Good, Brother*.[55] The modernist form of the socialist-realist novel invokes the open, irregular seriality of a transnational communist collective, but poetry as a genre is in no way necessarily antithetical to that: on the contrary, as a kind of rewriting of Nâzım's earlier poems from the 1930s, this final poem supports the novel's arrested socialist-realist master plot, in this case in embracing a communist ontology produced by and through the irregular series.[56] The lines "I'm a communist / I'm love from head to toe," repeated twice, must be read not only as a "yes" but also as a doubled "yes," a repeated or iterated "yes," a doubled affirmation of this novel's arrested and failed communist writing. This double affirmation is doubly significant if we remember that in all editions of the book published in Turkey since 1967, "Komünistim" has been replaced with "Emekçiyim," or "I'm a worker."[57] Resisting the effacement of the loanword *komünist* as a curse (*küfür*) by Turkish anticommunism, Nâzım's poem embraces and generalizes it as a fundamental form of subjectivity grounded in relationality.

AFTER (POST)COMMUNISM

Recognizing Nâzım's importance as an "Asian intermediary," recent scholarship on Comintern aesthetics has re-read his avant-garde poetry from the 1920s and 1930s through the lens of Comintern politics. There is no doubt that Nâzım's contributions to the field of Comintern aesthetics were crucial ones. However, as I have argued both in this chapter and throughout the book, this fact should not obscure Nâzım's and his comrades' distinct contributions to the form and theory of socialist-realist aesthetics in the subsequent decades. Simply put, Nâzım's poetic itinerary cannot be understood independently of his party work for the TKP. Like the work of both his Soviet and his Turkish contemporaries, Nâzım's political journalism and literary writings return us to the "urtext" of *What Is to Be Done?* to open up another future for socialist-realist aesthetics. As Nâzım commented provocatively in a lecture at Leipzig University in 1958 describing Picasso as a socialist realist, "As long as the message is communist, let there be millions of different forms."[58] Refusing any fixed opposition of modernism to realism of the kind that Lukács, for example, insisted on in "The Ideology of Modernism" in 1955,[59] Nâzım embraced the possibilities of modernist socialist realism.

What conclusions might we draw for today from the legacy of Nâzım's work? First, as what we might call a free retranslation, instead of a literal transplantation, and as a radical reconceptualization of Lenin's early writings, Nâzım's literary production across several decades represents the Soviet republic of letters as a dynamic space of translation. His imagination of a new prose poetics of seriality, in all of its dynamic shifting and variation, should be recognized as an aesthetic genealogy in its own right. His prison correspondence with Tahir, meanwhile, should be considered a missing supplement to the influential volume *Aesthetics and Politics* published by New Left Books, which remains the principal sourcebook for the study of Marxist literary theory in the Anglophone academy.[60]

My second conclusion here concerns the scattered publication history of Nâzım's writings, which invite a new practice of literary archaeology. Through its thematization of the line symbols and with its own translational and publication history, *Life's Good, Brother* embodies the censorship, loss, dispersion, and destruction of the Turkish communist archive recounted in this book. Following the legacy of Nâzım's final work, my goal in *Writing in Red* has been to uncover and trace the itineraries and legacies of this arrested writing and its interpretive communities, who were imprisoned for possessing copies of manuscripts, books, waxed paper, movable type, or typewriters. In their "allusive" and coded representations of communist writing, *Life's Good, Brother* and the other works I have discussed ask not to be read at all if they are not to be read closely and at depth, in both language and history.[61] In depicting characters who become underground signs, the critical-representational reading these works ask for is both comparative and "afformative," demanding the gift of infinite seriality.[62]

My third observation here concerns periodization in the literary international. The aesthetic itineraries of Nâzım and other writers examined in this book demonstrate that the Cold War literary field cannot be understood without accounting for the literary and political legacies of the 1920s and 1940s. As Mustai Karim, secretary of the Bashkir Writers' Union, Konstantin Simonov, member of the administrative board of the Soviet Writers' Union, and Radii Fish, literary translator of Turkish works into Russian, wrote in a coauthored *Pravda* article in 1966, the year 1965 marked an important turning point as writers from Turkey and the Soviet Union made meaningful contact for the first time since the late 1930s.[63] Influential writers such as Aziz Nesin, Yaşar Kemal, Melih Cevdet Anday, and Nevzat Üstün traveled to Moscow in the summer of 1965 to attend a symposium of the Afro-Asian Writers Association, a visit reciprocated by the Soviet writers' visit to Istanbul and Ankara in December of that year.

The frequency of both such semiofficial and private visits during the late 1960s and 1970s spurred the translation of Turkish works into Russian and other Turkic languages as well as the translation of Russian, Kyrgyz, and Kazakh works into Turkish. (For example, Fish may have obtained the manuscript of Derviş's *Love Novels* during his meeting with Derviş in Istanbul in 1966, arranged by Üstün. A collection of Üstün's poetry was subsequently translated into Russian by Fish and published in 1969 by Progress Publishers, the leading Soviet publisher of Afro-Asian works.

Meanwhile, Oğuz Akkan, owner of the progressive Cem Publishing House in Istanbul, published the collected works of the Kyrgyz writer Chingiz Aitmatov and invited the latter to Turkey in September 1975.)[64] The holdings of the Russian State Archive of Literature and Art (Rossiiskii gosudartsvennyi arkhiv literatury i iskusstvo) demonstrate that the Turkish publishers Salim Şengil and Akkan contacted the Soviet embassy in Ankara and the Soviet Writers' Union in Moscow in an attempt to obtain manuscripts of Nâzım's writings.[65] In his role as president of the Turkish Writers' Union, Cengiz Tuncer contacted the deputy chairman of the Foreign Commission of the Soviet Writers' Union, A. A. Kosorukov, in 1968 to request copies of Turkish books published in Russian for an exhibit in Istanbul.[66] For the influential novelist Orhan Kemal, imprisoned with Nâzım during the 1940s, royalties generated by Russian editions of his novels represented an important source of income while he was being persecuted for his communist activities.[67] Another influential writer, Rıfat Ilgaz (a former contributor to *New Literature* and a member of "the 1940s generation"), complained that though he was invited to the Afro-Asian Writers' Conference in Tashkent in 1968, Soviet Turcologists had not translated his work into Russian, and his work had been listed last in a recent Russian anthology of contemporary Turkish poetry.[68]

If the legacies of Nâzım and other figures examined in this book shaped a third moment of intensified translation and literary production both within and outside Turkey, Nâzım distinguished himself by refusing to represent the 1960s through an "emplotment" of what David Scott has elsewhere called revolutionary "romance."[69] Rejecting both romance and tragedy, Nâzım offered in *Life's Good, Brother* a new realist emplotment of the past, present, and future beyond optimism and pessimism. I have concluded this book with my treatment of *Life's Good, Brother* because in registering the uncanny sedimented time of the literary international, Nâzım's final work also anticipated the postcommunism of our own time, well before postcommunism's official arrival.

In a book about Nâzım's paintings, *Nâzım Hikmet: Portraits* (*Nâzım Hikmet: Portreler*, 2001), Nâzım's stepson, Memet Fuat, describes Nâzım's unusual approach to reading a book, which might be considered as good a description of how Nâzım wrote later in his life as it is of how he read: "My mother would say that Nâzım would read a section each from the beginning, middle, and end of a book, and he'd restart from the beginning only if he liked [what he read]. She would be amazed: 'How does one read a book whose ending one knows!' But that is how Nâzım read."[70] Imagine this nonlinear habit of reading generalized in the composition of a novel whose prolepses and analepses constantly iterate communism's foreclosed future. Composed toward the end of his life, on the eve of socialist revolutions across the globe, Nâzım's untimely novel addresses us from within a postcommunism before postcommunism.

For Nâzım, the temporality of revolution is neither rupture, as for the revolutionary avant-garde, nor the past present of a Benjaminian *Neuzeit*; rather, it is a foreclosed future within the past. Coming from the past (rather than from the future), postcommunism stands not for a simple surpassing of communism but for a necessary condition at the historical inception of the revolutionary movement. In anticipating and dwelling on postcommunism as such a necessary historical condition, Nâzım's prose poetics of seriality opens a liminal space in our own counterrevolutionary historical present. The poet who began his literary career as a futurist leaves us with a new model of a "positive hero" who willingly takes their turn in the here and now, in the shadow of perpetual failure.

CONCLUSION

In the Anteroom of History

"The ship with a hundred masts, / Where is the port it sails for?"[1] The protagonist of Nâzım's novel *Life's Good, Brother* repeats these lines to himself as he narrates his journey to Bolshevik Russia and the journeys of others, including the fifteen founding members of the Baku Turkish Communist Party murdered at sea in January 1921. These lines furnished the epigraph in the introduction of this book and marked its commencement with the clandestine travels of Nâzım Hikmet, Vâlâ Nureddin, Nizamettin Nazif, and others across the Black Sea. Where other scholars of this history and its geographic, geopolitical, and geocultural spaces have imagined a "single common international ocean" linking them to Moscow, I have sought to amplify the voices of Turkish writers who both imagined and experienced a Soviet republic of letters in a quite different way.[2]

The lines drawn by Ahmet and İsmail in *Life's Good, Brother*, the narrow streets through which Cevriye lugs parcels of communist publications in *Phosphorescent Cevriye*, the spiral (*sarmal*) facial lines in Dino's peasant drawings, and Vâlâ's cinematic screen in *Baltacı and Catherine*—these line forms representing a passage between life and death, past and present, revolution and (counter)revolution are spatial figures of the Soviet republic of letters in the works examined in this book. *Writing in Red* has argued that the Soviet republic of letters is not (only) an imagined literary international mediated by Soviet and Comintern-sponsored institutions and not a mere site of cultural diplomacy between the two countries but (also) a liminal boundary space, perhaps best imagined in the shape of a Möbius strip. For those born in the entangled Anatolian and Bolshevik Revolutions and responding to the entanglement's call in their Turkish writings, the encounter with Soviet Russia and Russian literary works represented a journey to the interior exteriority of the Anatolian Revolution, displacing the hierarchical relationship of convention elevating Russian originality over Turkish derivativeness. Emphasizing the "dual birth" of the entangled Anatolian and Bolshevik Revolutions, *Writing in Red* has argued that the history of the Soviet republic of letters cannot be understood without accounting for the imagination of revolution as universal in the non-Russian languages of Eurasia.

Though I have emphasized the concrete universality of Turkish communist translation and literary production, there are other narratives that cut across this book. *Writing in Red* can be read as an alternative transnational account of Turkish literary modernity through its connections with Soviet Russia or as a description of the neglected afterlives-in-translation of the works of N. A. Zarkhi, Mikhail Zoshchenko, Maksim Gorky, Sergei Yutkevich, and V. I. Lenin. It can also be read as a literary and cultural history of the TKP, one of the oldest communist parties in the Middle East. In this respect, the book offers a major contribution to a domain of area studies scholarship that has neglected literary and artistic production. The literary archaeology I have employed as a mode in this book owes little to the conventional disciplinary hierarchies of area studies, where modern literature often ranks last. Reminding us that the form of the novel, along with the newspaper and little magazines, functioned as a technology of communist print revolution in Turkey and elsewhere, *Writing in Red* restores a missing literary and cultural history for students of world communism.

As a contribution to the study of transnational modernism and peripheral realism, *Writing in Red* demonstrates that the oppositional categories of the avant-garde and popular literature, modernism and socialist realism that have shaped the history of western European literatures do not adequately capture the dynamics of Turkish communist and formerly communist literary production. Despite their familiarity with the Soviet and international avant-garde, Nizamettin and Vâlâ turned deliberately to historical fiction, though this turn cannot be understood as a simple rejection of the literary avant-garde. In making use of unfamiliar orthographies and futurist topoi such as the "history gramophone and binocular," they devised original estranging devices for use in historical fiction, establishing that genres of literary exchange during the interwar years were not exclusively avant-garde ones. Along these lines, in this book I have imagined a significantly expanded understanding of Marxist aesthetics and its neglect of non-European contributions. In displacing a now ossified critical polarization of realism and modernism, Nâzım's prose poetics of seriality, Suat Derviş's feminist modernist socialist realism, and Abidin Dino's formalist socialist realism suggest both other pasts and other futures for Marxian form and realist aesthetics. Reading these authors' formal experimentation in the light of their concrete political struggles, I have shown that their hybrid literary production reflects the pursuit of a nonhierarchical "aesthetic education" in the vernacular that aimed to produce self-governing subjects.

Finally (last but not least), *Writing in Red* can be read as a narrative of the entangled Anatolian and Bolshevik Revolutions and of the long shadow that the global moment of 1920 cast on the history of the twentieth century, spanning the interwar, Second World War, and Cold War years. In this respect, the book is a contribution to postcolonial scholarship that has recently begun to explore its Soviet genealogies. The ambivalences, tensions, and promises of the Turkish and Soviet anti-imperialist alliance discussed in this book offer a corrective supplement to such efforts, which risk abstracting and idealizing a Soviet "invention" of postcolonial studies.

This book is also motivated by my deep respect for the extensive personal suffering of so many of its protagonists and for their remarkable achievements in circumstances that so many others did not survive. As I was finishing it, Russia invaded and occupied Ukraine, and the looting and plundering of parliamentary democratic institutional structures in Turkey accelerated to new heights. This book's ethos is best described as a variation on Siegfried Kracauer's concept of "anteroom thinking." In the posthumously published *History*, originally drafted contemporaneously with Nâzım's *Life's Good, Brother*, Kracauer imagined a mode of historical thinking that could affirm the historically contingent without sacrificing the value of philosophical abstraction and speculation. For Kracauer, anteroom thinking entailed placing "the timeless and the temporal," the general and the particular, and the empirical and the ideal into contact without subsuming the former term under the latter in any of these formulations.[3] I have consciously acted as Kracauer's ambiguous historian in describing the concrete universal of revolution imagined in the works of Nizamettin Nazif, Vâlâ Nureddin, Suat Derviş, Abidin Dino, and Nâzım Hikmet, but without conflating their horizons of expectation with our own in a postrevolutionary historical present. Indeed, my target was a "terra incognito in the hollows between the lands we know."[4]

NOTES

ABBREVIATIONS

GARF   Gosudarstvennyi arkhiv Rossiiskoi Federatsii (State Archive of the Russian Federation), Moscow.
IISH   International Institute of Social History, Amsterdam, Netherlands.
RGALI   Rossiiskii gosudarstvennyi arkhiv literatury i iskusstva (Russian State Archive of Literature and Art), Moscow.
RGASPI   Rossiiskii gosudarstvennyi arkhiv sotsial'no-politicheskoi istorii (Russian State Archive for Social-Political History), Moscow.
TBMM   Türkiye Büyük Millet Meclisi (Grand National Assembly of Turkey), Ankara.
TÜSTAV   Türkiye Sosyal Tarih Araştırma Vakfı (Turkish Social History Research Foundation), Istanbul.

INTRODUCTION. REVOLUTIONARY ENTANGLEMENTS ACROSS TURKEY AND THE SOVIET UNION: AN OVERVIEW

1. On this journey, see the Turkish translation of the Comintern representative M. Gol'man's report in Erden Akbulut and Mete Tunçay, *Türkiye Halk İştirakiyun Fırkası (1920–1923)*, rev. ed. (Istanbul: TÜSTAV, 2016), 441–45. For the Russian original, see M. Gol'man, "Prakticheskie zamechaniia o kominternovskoi rabote

INTRODUCTION

v Turtsii," TÜSTAV Comintern Archival Fond 1, CD 33, Folder 2_6, File 720-737, esp. 735 (quoted).
2. On the concept of the "Soviet republic of letters," about which I say more soon, see Rossen Djagalov, "The Red Apostles: Imagining Revolutions in the Global Proletarian Novel," *Slavic and East European Journal* 61, no. 3 (2017): 396–422.
3. The Republic Monument is a common point of reference in historical scholarship on Turkish and Soviet convergences. While there is some disagreement concerning the identity of the Soviet figure represented in the monument, the Turkish historian Mehmet Perinçek establishes that it is Aralov; see Mehmet Perinçek, "Anıttaki Ruslar Kim?," *Aydınlık*, January 9, 2012, https://www.aydinlik.com.tr/arsiv/mehmet-perncek-anttaki-ruslar-kim.
4. Adeeb Khalid, "Central Asia Between the Ottoman and Soviet Worlds," *Kritika: Explorations in Russian and Eurasian History* 12, no. 2 (2011): 470–76, https://doi.org/10.1353/kri.2011.0028.
5. For a historical survey of this period, see Erik J. Zürcher, *Turkey: A Modern History* (London: I. B. Tauris, 2004), 133–65. On Istanbul under occupation, see Nur Bilge Criss, *Istanbul Under Allied Occupation, 1918–1923* (Boston: Brill, 1999). On the history of the Turkish War of Independence, see Sabahattin Selek, *Anadolu İhtilâli*, 2 vols. (Istanbul: Kastaş Yayınları, 1987).
6. See Uygur Kocabaşoğlu and Metin Berge, *Bolşevik İhtilâli ve Osmanlılar* (Ankara: Kebikeç Yayınları, 1994), 223–26; and George S. Harris, *The Communists and the "Kadro" Movement: Shaping Ideology in Atatürk's Turkey* (Istanbul: ISIS, 2002), 20.
7. On the foundational role of the Bolshevik Revolution in the making of modern Turkey, see Emel Akal, "Rusya'da 1917 Şubat ve Ekim Devrimlerinin Türkiye'ye Etkileri/Yansımaları," in *Modern Türkiye'de Siyasî Düşünce*, ed. Tanıl Bora and Murat Gültekingil, vol. 8: *Sol*, ed. Murat Gültekingil (Istanbul: İletişim, 2007), 114–37; and Şefik Hüsnü, "Teşrînisânî İhtilâli ve Türkiye," *Aydınlık*, no. 27 (November 1924), reprinted in Şefik Hüsnü, *Toplumsal Sınıflar, Türkiye Devrimi ve Sosyalizm*, ed. Gökhan Atılgan, translit. Şeyda Oğuz (Istanbul: Yordam Kitap, 2017), 304–10. For a valuable survey of coverage of the February and October Revolutions in the Istanbul and Ankara press between 1917 and 1922, see Kocabaşoğlu and Berge, *Bolşevik İhtilâli ve Osmanlılar*. Whereas press coverage from 1917 to 1918 focused on the revolution's impact on the peace process, a shift occurred during the Turkish War of Independence from 1919 to 1922 that we might describe as a cathexis of Bolshevism as "the Eastern Ideal."
8. For an account of this alliance, see Stefanos Yerasimos, *Türk-Sovyet İlişkileri: Ekim Devriminden "Milli Mücadele"ye* (Istanbul: Gözlem Yayınları, 1979); Mehmet Perinçek, *Atatürk'ün Sovyetler'le Görüşmeleri (Sovyet Arşiv Belgeleriyle)* (Istanbul: Kaynak, 2005); Bülent Gökay, *Soviet Eastern Policy and Turkey, 1920–1991* (New York: Routledge, 2006); and Samuel J. Hirst, "Transnational Anti-imperialism and the National Forces: Soviet Diplomacy and Turkey, 1920–23," *Comparative Studies of South Asia, Africa, and the Middle East* 33, no. 2 (2013): 214–26, https://doi.org/10.1215/1089201X-2322498.
9. Leonid and Friedrich, *Angora: Freiheitskrieg der Türkei* (Berlin: Vereinigung internationaler Verlagsanstalten, 1923), 34. The Russian graphic artist Evgenii E. Lansere, who visited Ankara in the summer of 1922 at the invitation of the Soviet representative Aralov, chronicled his visit in E. E. Lansere, *Leto v Angore: Risunki i zametki iz*

INTRODUCTION

dnevnika poezdki v Anatoliiu letom 1922 g. (Leningrad: Izdatel'stvo Brokgauz-Efron, 1925). On the French journalist and Comintern representative Magdeleine Marx's account of her trip to Ankara, see Magdeleine Marx, *Istanbul 1921–Ankara 1922: Makaleler-Anılar*, trans. Ahmet Şensılay (Istanbul: TÜSTAV, 2007).

10. Hirst, "Transnational Anti-imperialism," 215.
11. On language as force, see Jacques Derrida, "Signature Event Context," in *Margins of Philosophy*, trans. Alan Bass (Chicago: University of Chicago Press, 1982), 307–30. For recent historical scholarship on the communist press in the Middle East, see Burak Sayim, "Transregional by Design: The Early Communist Press in the Middle East and Global Revolutionary Networks," *Journal of Global History*, online December 13, 2022, https://doi.org/10.1017/S1740022822000250.
12. On the generalization of such words as *amele* (worker), *zahmetkeş* (toiler), and *şura* (council) during this period, see Emel Akal, *Milli Mücadelenin Başlangıcında Mustafa Kemal, İttihat Terakki ve Bolşevizm*, rev. ed. (Istanbul: İletişim, 2012), 92–93. See also Leonid and Friedrich, *Angora*, 38.
13. Claude Lévi-Strauss, *Introduction to the Work of Marcel Mauss*, trans. Felicity Baker (London: Routledge & Kegan Paul, 1987), 54–55, 64.
14. James Siegel, *Naming the Witch* (Stanford, CA: Stanford University Press, 2006), 44, 214.
15. Nâzım Hikmet, *Yaşamak Güzel Şeydir Kardeşim: Roman* (Sofia, Bulgaria: Narodna Prosveta, 1964), 29; Nâzım Hikmet, *Life's Good, Brother: A Novel*, trans. Mutlu Konuk Blasing (New York: Persea, 2013), 31 (translation modified). This imagination of Soviet Russia as the externalized and negated communist interiority of the Anatolian Revolution recalls the type of spatial fold and inversion that Derrida suggested we call "invagination," which he described as "the inverted reapplication of the outer edge to the inside of a form." Jacques Derrida, "Living On," trans. James Hulbert, in Harold Bloom, Paul de Man, Jacques Derrida, Geoffrey Hartman, and J. Hillis Miller, *Deconstruction and Criticism* (New York: Continuum, 2004), 97.
16. Nâzım and Vâlâ were students at KUTV with Lahouti, Sidqi, and San from 1922 to 1925.
17. For a history of world communism and its "global moments," see Stephen A. Smith, ed., *The Oxford Handbook of the History of Communism* (New York: Oxford University Press, 2014).
18. For the quoted phrases, see Jean-François Fayet, "1919," in *The Oxford Handbook of the History of Communism*, ed. Smith, 114, 119.
19. Nergis Ertürk, "Baku, Literary Common," in *Futures of Comparative Literature: ACLA State of the Discipline Report*, ed. Ursula Heise (London: Routledge, 2017), 141–44.
20. Katerina Clark, *Eurasia Without Borders: The Dream of a Leftist Literary Commons, 1919–1943* (Cambridge, MA: Harvard University Press, 2021), 1–8.
21. On Charara, see Fadi A. Bardawil, "Dreams of a Dual Birth: Socialist Lebanon's World and Ours," in "Marxism, Communism, and Translation," ed. Nergis Ertürk and Özge Serin, special issue of *boundary 2* 43, no. 3 (2016): 313–35. On the "dual birth" of the universal and the particular, see Nergis Ertürk and Özge Serin, "Marxism, Communism, and Translation: An Introduction," in "Marxism, Communism, and Translation," ed. Ertürk and Serin, 21–25.

INTRODUCTION

22. Sources I have consulted on the history of Turkish communisms include George S. Harris, *The Origins of Communism in Turkey* (Stanford, CA: Hoover Institution Press, 1967); Harris, *Communists and the "Kadro" Movement*; Mete Tunçay, *Türkiye'de Sol Akımlar (1908–1925)*, vol. 1, rev. and exp. ed. (Istanbul: İletişim, 2009); Akbulut and Tunçay, *Türkiye Halk İştirakiyun Fırkası*; Hamit Erdem, *1920 Yılı ve Sol Muhalefet* (Istanbul: Sel Yayıncılık, 2010); and Emel Akal, *Moskova-Ankara-Londra Üçgeninde: İştirakiyuncular, Komünistler ve Paşa Hazretleri* (Istanbul: İletişim, 2013). On the late nineteenth-century emergence of socialist currents among diverse populations of the Ottoman Empire, see Mete Tunçay and Erik Jan Zürcher, eds., *Socialism and Nationalism in the Ottoman Empire, 1876–1923* (London: I. B. Tauris, 1994).
23. Harris, *Communists and the "Kadro" Movement*, 40, 50, 45.
24. On Galiev, see Alexandre A. Bennigsen and S. Enders Wimbush, *Muslim National Communism in the Soviet Union: A Revolutionary Strategy for the Colonial World* (Chicago: University of Chicago Press, 1979).
25. "Yeşil Ordu Talimatnamesi," in Akbulut and Tunçay, *Türkiye Halk İştirakiyun Fırkası*, 34–35.
26. On gift economy, see Marcel Mauss, *The Gift: The Form and Reason for Exchange in Archaic Societies*, trans. W. D. Halls (London: Routledge, 1990). On the Islamic practice of almsgiving, see Azim Nanji, "Almsgiving," in *Encyclopaedia of the Qur'ān*, ed. Jane Dammen McAuliffe, Brill Online, 2015, http://referenceworks.brillonline.com/entries/encyclopaedia-of-the-quran/almsgiving-EQCOM_00008. The Green Army supported governmental redistribution of wealth. Although it recognized the lawful ownership of jewelry and other nonessential luxury items currently in one's possession, it called for passing new laws to prevent such accumulation in the future. The Green Army also considered itself an ally of the Red Army. For a complete program of the Green Army Association, see "Yeşil Ordu Nizamnamesi," in Akbulut and Tunçay, *Türkiye Halk İştirakiyun Fırkası*, 28–30.
27. "Erkâni Harbiyei Umumiye Reisi İsmet Beyin, Vaziyeti Umumiye Hakkında Beyanatı ve bu Hususta Cereyan Eden Müzakere," July 8, 1920, 224–25, TBMM 1. Dönem, 2. Cilt, 30. Birleşim, Zabıt Ceridesi (Minutes), https://www.tbmm.gov.tr/tutanaklar/TUTANAK/TBMM/d01/c002/tbmm01002030.pdf.
28. Uygur Kocabaşoğlu, "Milli Mücadelenin Sözcülerinden: *Anadolu'da Yeni Gün*," *Ankara Üniversitesi SBF Dergisi* 36, no. 1 (1981): 184–85.
29. Nadi was also influenced by the former Ottoman minister Enver Pasha, who traveled with Grigorii Zinov'ev to attend the First Congress of the Peoples of the East. Enver founded the Union of Islamic Revolutionary Societies (İslam İhtilal Cemiyetleri İttihadı) in Berlin in the summer of 1920 to assist and unify peoples of Islam in their struggle against imperialists and capitalists. On the alliance of the exiled Committee of Union and Progress leaders Enver and Talaat Pashas with the Bolsheviks, see Tunçay, *Türkiye'de Sol Akımlar (1908–1925)*, 1:258–84; and Akal, *Milli Mücadelenin Başlangıcında*, 81–125.
30. Yunus Nadi, "Yeni Hayat," *Anadolu'da Yeni Gün*, September 16, 1920, quoted in Kerim Sadi, *Türkiye'de Sosyalizmin Tarihine Katkı* (Istanbul: İletişim, 1994), 436.
31. For other publications coding Bolshevism as anti-imperialism during this period, see an anonymous editorial entitled "Bolsheviks and Us" ("Bolşevikler ve Biz") published in the Kastamonu newspaper *Açıksöz* on July 12, 1920: "Bolshevism

INTRODUCTION

[Bolşeviklik], which shines as the sun of deliverance and salvation, and which will save the weak and defeated nations from the great subjugation and cruelty of a rapacious and greedy Europe, is not a stranger to our nation, which has faced new calamities and new consolations every day for a number of years now. As imperialist Europe crushed us under its feet of cruelty and scorn, we bound ourselves to the East and Bolshevism [Şarka ve Bolşevikliğe] with deeper and sincerer affection, and finally, we decided to deliver our lives and ourselves by accepting this esteemed and exalted principle" (quoted in Kocabaşoğlu and Berge, *Bolşevik İhtilâli ve Osmanlılar*, 278–79).

32. "Türkiye Komünist Partisi Umumî Nizamnamesi," June 1920, in Akbulut and Tunçay, *Türkiye Halk İştirakiyun Fırkası*, 117.
33. "Türkiye Komünist Partisi Beyannamesi," July 14, 1920, in Akbulut and Tunçay, *Türkiye Halk İştirakiyun Fırkası*, 120–21.
34. "İstihzah takriri münasebetiyle İsmet Beyefendi ile Fevzi ve Mustafa Kemal Paşa Hazeratının Vaziyeti Askeriye, Siyasiye ve Dahiliye Hakkında Beyanatları," May 29, 1920, 48, TBMM 1. Dönem, 1. Cilt, 21. Birleşim, Gizli Celse Zabıtları (Closed Session Minutes), https://www.tbmm.gov.tr/tutanaklar/TUTANAK/GZC/d01/CILT01/gcz01001021.pdf. On Mustafa Kemal's negotiations with Bolshevik representatives during the War of Independence, see Perinçek, *Atatürk'ün Sovyetler'le Görüşmeleri*, 27–163.
35. "Bursa Mebusu ve Diyarbekir İstiklal Mahkemesi Azası Şeyh Servet Efendinin Komünizm Propagandası Yaptığına Dair Şifre Telgraflar," January 22, 1921, 334, TBMM 1. Dönem, 1. Cilt, 136. Birleşim, Gizli Celse Zabıtları, https://www.tbmm.gov.tr/tutanaklar/TUTANAK/GZC/d01/CILT01/gcz01001136.pdf.
36. The editorial was unsigned, but its authorship by Mustafa Kemal is undisputed. See [Mustafa Kemal], "Cereyanlar," *Hakimiyet-i Milliye*, October 9, 1920, reprinted in *Kurtuluş Savaşı'nın İdeolojisi: "Hakimiyeti Milliye" Yazıları*, ed. Hadiye Bolluk (Istanbul: Kaynak, 2003), 85.
37. [Mustafa Kemal], "Rus Bolşevizmi Türk Komünizmi," *Hakimiyet-i Milliye* 1, no. 65 (October 16, 1920): 1, Ankara Üniversitesi Gazeteler Veritabanı, http://gazeteler.ankara.edu.tr/dergiler/milli_kutup/1541/1541_3/0006.pdf.
38. [Mustafa Kemal], "İki Komünizm," *Hakimiyet-i Milliye* 1, no. 64 (October 12, 1920): 1, Ankara Üniversitesi Gazeteler Veritabanı, http://gazeteler.ankara.edu.tr/dergiler/milli_kutup/1541/1541_3/0004.pdf.
39. See the declaration of the official TKP in Akbulut and Tunçay, *Türkiye Halk İştirakiyun Fırkası*, 66, emphasizing the same points as the *National Sovereignty* editorials regarding the absence of a native ruling capitalist class in Turkey. The official TKP aimed to end the political exploitation of the people by members of the state bureaucracy; in the economic sphere, it supported the state ownership of large industries and the protection of private property for small businesses, landowners, and peasants.
40. Mustafa Kemal, "Cereyanlar," 87.
41. "Bursa Mebusu ve Diyarbekir," January 22, 1921, 335, TBMM, Gizli Celse Zabıtları.
42. On the rising anticommunist tide in the Assembly in 1921, see Akal, *Moskova-Ankara-Londra Üçgeninde*, 365–442.
43. The specifics of these murders—especially whether other political agents (such as Mustafa Kemal or the commander of the Eastern Front, Kazım Karabekir) were

INTRODUCTION

involved in planning them and recruiting the assassins—are still unresolved. On the history of the Baku TKP and its founding leader, Mustafa Suphi, see Yavuz Aslan, *Türkiye Komünist Fırkası'nın Kuruluşu ve Mustafa Suphi: Türkiye Komünistlerinin Rusya'da Teşkilâtlanması (1918–1921)* (Ankara: Türk Tarih Kurumu, 1997).

44. *28–29 Kanun-i Sani 1921: Karadeniz Kıyılarında Parçalanan Mustafa Suphi ve Yoldaşlarının İkinci Yıldönümleri* (Moscow: Kızıl Şark Matbaası, 1923).

45. Hüseyin Ragıp, "Sağdan Sola Doğru," March 8, 1921, in *Kurtuluş Savaşı'nın İdeolojisi*, ed. Bolluk, 122.

46. See Mustafa Kemal's usage of *serseri* in "Bursa Mebusu ve Diyarbekir," 333, TBMM, Gizli Celse Zabıtları. He echoed the anticommunist declaration of the Society for the Protection of Sacred Values (Muhafaza-i Mukaddesat Cemiyet) founded in Erzurum in January 1921, which described communists as "lowly people" with "unknown parentage" and "dirty pasts" and communism as "meslek-i kâfirane," or "a path of infidelity" (quoted in Akal, *Moskova-Ankara-Londra Üçgeninde*, 367). For the complete text of the declaration, see Dursun Ali Akbulut, *Albayrak Olayı: Milli Mücadele Başlarında Halk Hükûmeti Kurma Girişimi (Erzurum 1920)* (Istanbul: Temel Yayınları, 2006), 98–101.

47. For an influential anticommunist publication from the 1940s, see R. Oğuz Türkkan, *Kızıl Faaliyet!* (Istanbul: Bozkurtçu Yayını, 1943). Also, it was common to call a Turkish communist a "Bolshevik" into the 1960s. See Vedat Türkali's novel *Bir Gün Tek Başına* (Istanbul: Kurtiş, 1989), set on the eve of the military coup in 1960; the former TKP member Kenan is routinely teased by his friend for being a "Bolshevik."

48. *Oxford English Dictionary*, s.v. "curse, v.," http://www.oed.com.ezaccess.libraries.psu.edu/view/Entry/46133.

49. On the Quranic meaning of *kufr*, see Camilla Adang, "Belief and Unbelief," in *Encylopaedia of the Qurʾān*, ed. McAuliffe, Brill Online, http://referenceworks.brillonline.com.ezaccess.libraries.psu.edu/entries/encyclopaedia-of-the-quran/belief-and-unbelief-EQCOM_00025. See also Elsaid M. Badawi and Muhammad Abdel Haleem, *Arabic–English Dictionary of the Qurʾanic Usage* (Leiden: Brill, 2008), s.v. "كفر, kufr [v. n.]."

50. Tekin Erer, "Göründüğü Yerde Ezmeliyiz," in *Kızıl Tehlike*, vol. 2 (Istanbul: As, 1967), 189–90.

51. Siegel, *Naming the Witch*, 216–17.

52. "Bursa Mebusu ve Diyarbekir," January 22, 1921, 326, TBMM, Gizli Celse Zabıtları.

53. For this letter, see Akal, *Moskova-Ankara-Londra Üçgeninde*, 368–69.

54. I am suggesting that *komünist* works as a special kind of curse or insult, like the performative *witch* described in Siegel's book *Naming the Witch*. On "excitable" or "injurious" speech, see Judith Butler, *Excitable Speech: A Politics of the Performative* (New York: Routledge, 1997), 36. On the curse as a speech-act, see Giorgio Agamben, *The Sacrament of Language: An Archaeology of the Oath* (Homo Sacer II, 3), trans. Adam Kotsko (Stanford, CA: Stanford University Press, 2011), esp. 54–72. Agamben emphasizes the differential relationship between oath and curse: "Oath and perjury, bene-diction and male-diction correspond to this double possibility inscribed in the *logos*, in the experience by means of which the living being has been constituted as speaking being. Religion and law technicalize this anthropogenic experience of the word in the oath and the curse as historical

institutions, separating and opposing point by point truth and lie, true name and false name, efficacious formula and incorrect formula" (70). The Quranic concept of *küfür* might be understood similarly as the institutionalization of an inherent division in God's word (*kalam*), though my emphasis (via Siegel) is on something else here: namely, the social effects of a curse as a speech-act producing a state of radical negativity.

55. For example, see Erdem, *1920 Yılı ve Sol Muhalefet*, 9. See also Akal, *Milli Mücadelenin Başlangıcında*, 23.
56. On "significant geographies," see Karima Laachir, Sara Marzagora, and Francesca Orsini, "Significant Geographies," *Journal of World Literature* 3, no. 3 (2018): 290–310, https://doi.org/10.1163/24056480-00303005.
57. On the KUTV curriculum, see Lana Ravandi-Fadai, "'Red Mecca'—the Communist University for Laborers of the East (KUTV): Iranian Scholars and Students in Moscow in the 1920s and 1930s," *Iranian Studies* 48, no. 5 (2015): 715, https://dx.doi.org/10.1080/00210862.2015.1058640. See also Vâlâ Nureddin's memoir *Bu Dünyadan Nâzım Geçti* (1965; reprint, Istanbul: Cem Yayınevi, 1980), 294–300. Established in 1921 in the model of Sverdlov Communist University, KUTV aimed to train revolutionary cadres from both the Soviet East and the neighboring countries, including Persia, Afghanistan, Turkey, China, and India. The curriculum covered the history of the "East" through a study of works of Soviet Orientalism. (In his memoir, Vâlâ mentions attending the lectures of Lev Vaks, who would later compose a textbook on "the history of national-bourgeois revolutions in the East" [288].) Ravandi-Fadai emphasizes that some KUTV graduates who stayed in the Soviet Union became researchers and bibliographers, shaping in crucial ways the development of Soviet Orientalism and foreign policy during the late 1920s and 1930s.

Specifically on the Turkish section of KUTV opened in 1925, see James H. Meyer, "Children of Trans-empire: Nâzım Hikmet and the First Generation of Turkish Students at Moscow's Communist University of the East," *Journal of the Ottoman and Turkish Studies Association* 5, no. 2 (Fall 2018): 195–218, https://doi.org/10.2979/jottturstuass.5.2.12. Nâzım and Vâlâ had initially enrolled in the French section. Comprising an eclectic group of students, the Turkish section included former Ottoman prisoners of war, Turkish youth from the Black Sea borderlands, and the descendants of Russian-born Muslims who had immigrated to Istanbul during the late imperial era. See Meyer, "Children of Trans-empire, 212–13. On the Arab section, see Masha Kirasirova, "The 'East' as a Category of Bolshevik Ideology and Comintern Administration: The Arab Section of the Communist University of the Toilers of the East," *Kritika: Explorations in Russian and Eurasian History* 18, no. 1 (2017): 7–34, https://doi.org/10.1353/kri.2017.0001. On KUTV as an important institutional point of entry into the Soviet literary sphere, see Rossen Djagalov, *From Internationalism to Postcolonialism: Literature and Cinema Between the Second and Third Worlds* (Montreal: McGill-Queen's University Press, 2020), 43–52.
58. Erdem, *1920 Yılı ve Sol Muhalefet*, 15–31.
59. See Çağlar Keyder, *State and Class in Turkey: A Study in Capitalist Development* (London: Verso, 1987), esp. 81–82. For the TKP leader Şefik Hüsnü's examination of social classes and political discourse in the early 1920s, see the collection of his *Aydınlık* essays in Şefik Hüsnü, *Toplumsal Sınıflar, Türkiye Devrimi ve Sosyalizm*, ed. Gökhan Atılgan, translit. Şeyda Oğuz (Istanbul: Yordam Kitap, 2017).

INTRODUCTION

60. On the history of the TKP during the republican period, see Mete Tunçay, *Türkiye'de Sol Akımlar (1925–1936)*, vol. 2, rev. and exp. ed. (Istanbul: İletişim, 2009).
61. "Foreclosure" is used in the psychoanalytic sense here and throughout the book. Describing a more radical form of negation than repression or disavowal, foreclosure entails the ejection of a portion of reality from the symbolic order as if it had never existed in the first place. For a useful explication of this concept, see Bruce Fink, *A Clinical Introduction to Lacanian Psychoanalysis: Theory and Technique* (Cambridge, MA: Harvard University Press, 1997), 75–101.
62. A close confidante of Mustafa Kemal and the editor in chief of the semiofficial daily *National Sovereignty*, Falih Rıfkı (Atay) served as a deputy in the National Assembly from 1923 to 1950. He first visited the Soviet Union in October 1930, accompanying Minister of External Affairs Tevfik Rüştü (Aras). For a collection of his articles on New Russia first published as a series in *National Sovereignty*, see Falih Rıfkı, *Yeni Rusya* (Ankara: Hakimiyet-i Milliye Matbaası, 1931). In *Moskova-Roma*, Rıfkı chronicled his second visit to the Soviet Union in May 1932 as a member of Prime Minister İsmet İnönü's delegation. See Falih Rıfkı, *Moskova-Roma* (Istanbul: Muallim Ahmet Halit Kitaphanesi, 1932). Yakup Kadri, who was also a close friend of Mustafa Kemal and a deputy in the Assembly, composed a series of articles titled "Ankara, Moscow, Rome" for *Kadro* (Cadre) between June 1932 and April 1933, chronicling his visit to the Soviet Union as a member of the prime minister's delegation.
63. On this point, see also Özge Serin, "The Use-Value of Idioms: The Language of Marxism and Language as Such," in "Marxism, Communism, and Translation," ed. Ertürk and Serin, 298–99.
64. A third pathway of literary and cultural exchange was established by Soviet Muslim émigrés who moved to Turkey after the Bolshevik Revolution, but the histories of nineteenth-century Russian Muslim and twentieth-century Soviet Muslim immigration to Turkey are not addressed in this book. For a historical overview of literary and cultural production by émigré intellectuals, see Lowell Bezanis, "Soviet Muslim Emigrés in the Republic of Turkey," *Central Asian Survey* 13, no. 1 (1994): 59–180.
65. For an account of Soviet cultural diplomacy, see Michael David-Fox, *Showcasing the Great Experiment: Cultural Diplomacy and Western Visitors to the Soviet Union, 1921–1941* (New York: Oxford University Press, 2012).
66. For a survey of VOKS's activities with respect to Turkey, see Raşid Tacibayev, *Kızıl Meydan'dan Taksim'e: Siyasette, Kültürde ve Sanatta Türk-Sovyet İlişkileri (1925–1945)* (Istanbul: Truva, 2004), 166–221. For a useful account of Turkish and Soviet literary and cultural relations during the interwar period, see A. K. Sverchevskaia, *Sovetsko-turetskie kul'turnye sviazi, 1925–1981* (Moscow: Nauka, 1983); Mehmet Perinçek, *Türk-Rus Diplomasisinden Gizli Sayfalar: Siyaset-Askeriye-Ekonomi-Kültür-Bilim-Spor* (Istanbul: Analiz Basın Yayın, 2011); and Dimitır Vandov, *Atatürk Dönemi Türk-Sovyet İlişkileri* (Istanbul: Kaynak, 2014).
67. On the official ties between the Republic of Turkey and the Soviet Union, see Samuel J. Hirst, "Anti-Westernism on the European Periphery: The Meaning of Soviet-Turkish Convergence in the 1930s," *Slavic Review* 72, no. 1 (Spring 2013): 32–53, https://www.jstor.org/stable/10.5612/slavicreview.72.1.0032.

INTRODUCTION

68. *Türkiye Bibliyografyası: Hususî Neşriyat (1928-1938)*, vol. 2 (Istanbul: Devlet Basımevi, 1939), 667–74. One of the most important translators of the period was Haydar Rifat (Yorulmaz) (1877–1942), a lawyer who never became a TKP member. In addition to translating work by Marx, Engels, Kropotkin, Lenin, and Stalin, he translated Russian classics by Dostoevsky, Turgenev, Tolstoy, and Chekhov during the 1930s (which were most likely retranslations of French and German translations). For a list of his translations, see Şakir Babacan, "Sosyalist Eserler Mütercimi Haydar Rifat Yorulmaz," master's thesis, Istanbul University, 2014, 84–85, https://tez.yok.gov.tr/UlusalTezMerkezi/tezDetay.jsp?id=ok4AepJhYI3uvtIQAXeCDA&no=wJRV1hwI8f4V4PqCwzeq8Q. Other notable translators of the period who did not have party affiliation include Samizade Süreyya (who likely retranslated work by Pushkin, Turgenev, and Chekhov from English and French translations), Ali Kâmi Akyüz (who retranslated Tolstoy from French), and the influential literary historian Mustafa Nihat Özön (who retranslated Dostoevsky, Gorky, and Sholokhov from French). During the 1940s, important translators who translated directly from Russian included the émigré Nihal Yalaza Taluy and Erol Güney. For a useful survey, see Altan Aykut, "Türkiye'de Rus Dili ve Edebiyatı Çalışmaları," *Ankara Üniversitesi Dil ve Tarih-Coğrafya Fakültesi Dergisi* 46, no. 2 (2006): 1–27.

69. Samuel J. Hirst, "Soviet Orientalism Across Borders: Documentary Film for the Turkish Republic," *Kritika: Explorations in Russian and Eurasian History* 18, no. 1 (2017): 35–61.

70. Katerina Clark, *Moscow, the Fourth Rome: Stalinism, Cosmopolitanism, and the Evolution of Soviet Culture, 1931–1934* (Cambridge, MA: Harvard University Press, 2011), 13.

71. On Nail Vahdeti's life, see Nail Çakırhan, *Anılar*, interview by Erden Akbulut (Istanbul: TÜSTAV, 2008). On *Illustrated Monthly*, see its publisher Sabiha Sertel's memoir *Roman Gibi (Anılar)* (Istanbul: Ant Yayınları, 1969), 87–182; for the English translation, see Sabiha Sertel, *The Struggle for Modern Turkey*, ed. Tia O'Brien and Nur Deriş, trans. David Selim Sayers and Evrim Emir-Sayers (London: I. B. Tauris, 2019), 47–104. On the importance of *Illustrated Monthly* for Turkish literary history, see Ahmet Oktay's classical account *Toplumcu Gerçekçiliğin Kaynakları: Sosyalist Realizm Üstüne Eleştirel Bir Çalışma* (1986; reprint, Istanbul: İthaki, 2008), 315–25. For a more comprehensive general account of authorship during the early republican era, see Tuncay Birkan, *Dünya ile Devlet Arasında Türk Muharriri, 1930–1960* (Istanbul: Metis, 2018).

72. Nâzım Hikmet, "19 Yaşım," in *Sesini Kaybeden Şehir* ([Istanbul]: Remzi Kitaphanesi, 1931), 44–49.

73. See Nâzım Hikmet, "Yeni Şairlere Dair," *Resimli Ay* 6, no. 9 (November 1929): 40.

74. On archival records pertaining to decentralization, see *Vedat Türkali ile "Güven" Üzerine: Desantralizasyon, Separat Kararları Belgeleri* (Istanbul: TÜSTAV, 2000), 39–64. Proposed in 1936, the decentralization order was ratified by the Comintern in early 1937. Apparently, just before the Comintern representative Genrik Valetskii (Henryk Walecki) announced the Comintern order to the TKP representatives, he remarked: "Don't mistake me for an agent of Mustafa Kemal." For the quoted statement from Valetskii, see Vedat Türkali, *Güven*, 2 vols. (Istanbul: Ayrıntı Yayınları, 2015), 1:637. Türkali's two-volume novel *Güven* narrates the

story of a group of Turkish university students who try but fail to join the TKP in the late 1930s and early 1940s.
75. On Turkey during the Second World War, see Cemil Koçak, *Türkiye'de Millî Şef Dönemi (1938–1945)*, 2 vols. (Istanbul: İletişim, 1996); and Onur İşçi, *Turkey and the Soviet Union During World War II* (London: I. B. Tauris, 2020).
76. On Baraner, see Ersin Tosun, *Reşat Fuat Baraner: Yaşamı, Çalışmaları, Anılar* (Istanbul: TÜSTAV, 2013). On Baştımar, see Erden Akbulut, *Zeki Baştımar: Yaşam Öyküsü, Mektuplar, Yazılar* (Istanbul: TÜSTAV, 2009).
77. See Anton Chekhov, *Maske*, trans. Zeki Baştımar (Istanbul: Remzi Kitabevi, 1938); and Leo Tolstoy, *Harb ve Sulh*, trans. Zeki Baştımar (Istanbul: Milli Eğitim Basımevi, 1943–1949). (Nâzım's name did not appear on the cover of his and Baştımar's translation of *War and Peace*.) The Tolstoy translation was published in a series titled Translations from World Literature (Dünya Edebiyatından Tercümeler) launched by the Translation Bureau under the auspices of the statesman Hasan Âli Yücel, who advocated a new cultural politics of "Turkish humanism" (*Türk humanizması*) during his tenure as minister of education from 1938 to 1946. During the 1950s, Baştımar also published book-length general introductions on the lives and works of Chekhov and Tolstoy. See Zeki Baştımar, *Çehov'un Hayat ve Sanat Hikayesi* (Istanbul: Yenigün Yayınları, n.d. [ca. 1950s]); and Zeki Baştımar, *L. Tolstoy: Hayatı, Eserleri, Fikirleri* (Istanbul: Yenigün Yayınları, n.d. [ca. 1950s]).
78. For Derviş's autobiographical account of her Berlin years, see Suat Derviş, *Anılar, Paramparça* (Istanbul: İthaki, 2017), 53–123.
79. Suat Derviş, *Niçin Sovyetler Birliğinin Dostuyum?* (Istanbul: Arkadaş Matbaası, 1944).
80. Bonnie S. McDougall, *Mao Zedong's "Talks at the Yan'an Conference on Literature and Art": A Translation of the 1943 Text with Commentary* (Ann Arbor: University of Michigan Center for Chinese Studies, 1980).
81. Emma Widdis, "*Faktura*: Depth and Surface in Early Soviet Set Design," *Studies in Russian and Soviet Cinema* 3, no. 1 (2009): 13.
82. Türkali, *Güven*, 1:393.
83. On the use of literature as "mask" by Turkish communists, see, for example, the influential anticommunist İlhan Darendelioğlu's book *Türkiye'de Komünist Hareketleri: Solcular, Sosyalistler, Marksistler ve Komünistler*... (Istanbul: Bedir Yaynevi, 1973), 199. For criticism from the Turkish Left, see the collection of interviews with prominent Turkish leftist journalists, critics, and scholars in Levent Cinemre and Ruşen Çakır, eds., *Sol Kemalizme Bakıyor: Röportaj* (Istanbul: Metis, 1991).
84. Oktay, *Toplumcu Gerçekçiliğin Kaynakları*, 291–393. For other influential works of Marxist literary criticism from the post–Second World War era, see İbrahim Tatarlı and Rıza Mollof, *Marksist Açıdan Türk Romanı: Hüseyin Rahmi'den Fakir Baykurt'a* (Istanbul: Habora Kitabevi, 1969); and Fethi Naci, *100 Soruda Türkiye'de Roman ve Toplumsal Değişme* (Istanbul: Gerçek Yayınevi, 1981).
85. "In Turkish criticism," writes the critic Nurdan Gürbilek, "it has become a reflex to begin by pointing to an absence." Gürbilek's essay is a valuable critique of this tendency. See Nurdan Gürbilek, "'The *Orijinal* Turkish Spirit,'" in *The New Cultural Climate in Turkey: Living in a Shop Window*, trans. Victoria Holbrook (London: Zed, 2011), 167. Though Turkish communists often lamented their

INTRODUCTION

belatedness in relation to Soviet communism, there was no similar hierarchical relation structuring Turkey's official relations with the Soviet state. Whereas Soviet representatives idealized Bolshevik Russia as a "savior" of Turkey, the Turkish side rejected such paternalism.

86. Oktay, *Toplumcu Gerçekçiliğin Kaynakları*, 33, 38.
87. One might regard Nâzım's volumes of poetry in the 1930s as his attempt to form a Leninist "party literature," though this concept is limited in its usefulness, given that Nâzım led an oppositional faction within the TKP, which led to his expulsion in 1934.
88. Steven S. Lee, "Introduction: Comintern Aesthetics—Space, Form, History," in *Comintern Aesthetics*, ed. Amelia M. Glaser and Steven S. Lee (Toronto: University of Toronto Press, 2020), 3.
89. The phrase "magic pilgrimage" is an allusion to Claude McKay's memoir *A Long Way from Home*, ed. Gene Andrew Jarret (New Brunswick, NJ: Rutgers University Press, 2007), 121.
90. For an explication of this point, see Ertürk and Serin, "Marxism, Communism, and Translation: An Introduction," 3–4.
91. Slavoj Žižek, *The Parallax View* (Cambridge, MA: MIT Press, 2006), 34.
92. On the American legacies of the Bolshevik Revolution, see Kate A. Baldwin, *Beyond the Color Line and the Iron Curtain: Reading Encounters Between Black and Red, 1922–1963* (Durham, NC: Duke University Press, 2002); and Steven S. Lee, *The Ethnic Avant-Garde: Minority Cultures and World Revolution* (New York: Columbia University Press, 2015). On the Bolshevik Revolution as world revolution, see Anindita Banerjee and Jenifer Presto, "Foreword: World Revolution," in "The 1917 Revolution and Its Ripple Effects (Anniversary Forum)," ed. Anindita Banerjee and Jenifer Presto, special issue of *Slavic and East European Journal* 61, no. 3 (2017): 394–95. On the Soviet imagination of China and Sino-Russian relations during the interwar years, see Edward Tyerman, *Internationalist Aesthetics: China and Early Soviet Culture* (New York: Columbia University Press, 2022).
93. Susan Buck-Morss, "Theorizing Today: The Post-Soviet Condition," *Log* 11 (2008): 30, https://www.jstor.org/stable/41765180.
94. See Khalid, "Central Asia Between the Ottoman and Soviet Worlds"; Michael A. Reynolds, *Shattering Empires: The Clash and Collapse of the Ottoman and Russian Empires, 1908–1918* (Cambridge: Cambridge University Press, 2011); James H. Meyer, *Turks Across Empires: Marketing Muslim Identity in the Russian–Ottoman Borderlands, 1856–1914* (New York: Oxford University Press, 2014); Mustafa Tuna, *Imperial Russia's Muslims: Islam, Empire, and European Modernity, 1788–1914* (Cambridge: Cambridge University Press, 2015); and Lâle Can, *Spiritual Subjects: Central Asian Pilgrims and the Ottoman Hajj at the End of Empire* (Stanford, CA: Stanford University Press, 2020). For a thorough conceptualization of *histoire croisée* and its influence in the human and social sciences during the past two decades, see Michael Werner and Bénédicte Zimmermann, "Beyond Comparison: *Histoire Croisée* and the Challenge of Reflexivity," *History and Theory* 45, no. 1 (February 2006): 30–50.
95. Christine Philliou, "Introduction: USSR South: Postcolonial Worlds in the Soviet Imaginary," *Comparative Studies of South Asia, Africa, and the Middle East* 33,

no. 2 (2013): 198, https://doi.org/10.1215/1089201X-2322480. For recent historical scholarship on Russian and Arabic cultural and political ties, see Eileen Kane, Masha Kirasirova, and Margaret Litvin, eds., *Russian-Arab World: A Documentary History* (Oxford: Oxford University Press, 2023).

96. The prefaces Tunçay wrote for past editions of *Türkiye'de Sol Akımlar (1908–1925)* (Left movements in Turkey [1908–1925], originally published in 1967) are included in the most recent revised and expanded edition of 2009. They provide a useful account of the challenges faced by an academic historian of Turkish republican communism during the Cold War era.

97. For an account of this collaboration, see Zülfikar Özdoğan, "Uluslararası Sosyal Tarih Enstitütüsü (USTE) ve Türkiye Koleksiyonları," *Kebikeç* 25 (2008): 27–44. The Bulgarian-born TKP member Bilal Şen (1920–2017) played a leading role in the identification and reproduction of TKP documents in the RGASPI archive. For an account of his involvement in the TKP, see Bilal Şen, *Anılar-Notlar*, ed. Erden Akbulut and Ersin Tosun, exp. 2nd ed. (Istanbul: TÜSTAV, 2019).

98. "Comparative Studies of South Asia, Africa, and the Middle East: Mission Statement," *Comparative Studies of South Asia, Africa, and the Middle East* 33, no. 2 (2013): 135, https://doi.org/10.1215/1089201X-2322336.

99. Suad Dervish, *Liubovnye romany*, trans. Radii Fish (Moscow: Izdatel'stvo TsK VLKSM "Molodaia gvardiia," 1969); Nergis Ertürk, "*Aşk Romanları* (*Liubovnye romany*) ve Düşündürdükleri: Rusça'da Çeviri Bir Suat Derviş Romanı," *Birikim*, no. 389 (September 2021): 92–104.

100. For the phrase "catastrophic success," see Geoffrey Lewis, *The Turkish Language Reform: A Catastrophic Success* (New York: Oxford University Press, 1999).

101. Anna Krakus and Cristina Vatulescu, "Foucault in Poland: A Silent Archive," *Diacritics* 47, no. 2 (2019): 72–105, esp. 75, 89.

102. On "the limit of enunciability," see Krakus and Vatulescu, "Foucault in Poland," 92. On the concept of "literary archaeology," see Toni Morrison's foundational essay "The Site of Memory," in *Inventing the Truth: The Art and Craft of Memoir*, ed. William Zinsser (Boston: Houghton Mifflin, 1987), 101–24. See also Jenny Sharpe, *Ghosts of Slavery: A Literary Archeology of Black Women's Lives* (Minneapolis: University of Minnesota Press, 2003). On the practice of reading "along the archival grain," see Ann Laura Stoler, *Along the Archival Grain: Epistemic Anxieties and Colonial Common Sense* (Princeton, NJ: Princeton University Press, 2009). The "literary archaeology" pursued in this book must be understood in relation to the signifying history of "communism" and "Bolshevism" and the structure of anticommunist violence discussed in the first section of this introduction.

103. For seminal work on modern Turkish literature, see Güzin Dino, *La genèse du roman turc au XIXe siècle* (Paris: Publications orientalistes de France, 1973); Ahmet Ö. Evin, *Origins and Development of the Turkish Novel* (Minneapolis: Bibliotheca Islamica, 1983); Berna Moran, *Türk Romanına Eleştirel Bir Bakış*, 3 vols. (Istanbul: İletişim, 1983–1994); Jale Parla, *Babalar ve Oğullar: Tanzimat Romanının Epistemolojik Temelleri* (Istanbul: İletişim, 1990); and Nurdan Gürbilek, *Kör Ayna, Kayıp Şark* (Istanbul: Metis, 2004). In *Step ve Bozkır: Rusça ve Türkçe Edebiyatta Doğu-Batı Sorunu ve Kültür* (Istanbul: İletişim, 2016), Murat Belge provides a valuable comparative study of Russian and Turkish literatures through the lens

INTRODUCTION

of westernization. For more recent work in English on the epistemic transformation of modern Turkish literature in relation to European philological, linguistic, and philosophical discourses, see Laurent Mignon, *Neither Shiraz nor Paris: Papers on Modern Turkish Literature* (Istanbul: Gorgias, 2010); Nergis Ertürk, *Grammatology and Literary Modernity in Turkey* (New York: Oxford University Press, 2011); Erdağ Göknar, *Orhan Pamuk, Secularism, and Blasphemy: The Politics of the Turkish Novel* (London: Routledge, 2013); Özen Nergis Dolcerocca, ed., "Beyond World Literature: Reading Ahmet Hamdi Tanpınar Today," special issue of *Middle Eastern Literatures* 20, no. 2 (2017); and Ayşe Özge Koçak Hemmat, *The Turkish Novel and the Quest for Rationality* (Leiden, Netherlands: Brill, 2019). For a valuable recent study that examines Turkish "westernization" through the lens of U.S. literary and cultural influence, see Perin E. Gürel, *The Limits of Westernization: A Cultural History of America in Turkey* (New York: Columbia University Press, 2017).

104. See, for example, Laurent Mignon, "A Pilgrim's Progress: Armenian and Kurdish Literatures in Turkish and the Rewriting of Literary History," *Patterns of Prejudice* 48, no. 2 (2014): 182–200; Laurent Mignon, *Hüzünlü Özgürlük: Yahudi Edebiyatı ve Düşüncesi Üzerine Yazılar* (Istanbul: Gözlem Gazetecilik, 2014); Laurent Mignon, *Edebiyatın Sınırlarında: Türkçe Edebiyat, Gürcistan ve Cengiz Aytmatov'a Dair* (Istanbul: Evrensel Basım Yayın, 2016); Mehmet Fatih Uslu and Fatih Altuğ, *Tanzimat ve Edebiyat: Osmanlı İstanbulu'nda Modern Edebi Kültür* (Istanbul: Türkiye İş Bankası, 2014); Hülya Adak, *Halide Edib ve Siyasal Şiddet: Ermeni Kırımı, Diktatörlük ve Şiddetsizlik* (Istanbul: Bilgi Üniversitesi Yayınları, 2016); and Ceyhun Arslan, *The Ottoman Canon and the Construction of Arabic and Turkish Literatures* (Edinburgh: Edinburgh University Press, forthcoming). For a comparative study of modern Turkish literature in relation to modern Mexican and Bengali literatures, see Ian Almond, *World Literature Decentered: Beyond the "West" Through Turkey, Mexico, and Bengal* (New York: Routledge, 2022).

105. For a critical explication of post-Kemalism as the dominant paradigm in Turkish studies since the 1980s, see İlker Aytürk, "Post-post-Kemalizm: Yeni Bir Paradigmayı Beklerken," *Birikim* 319 (November 2015): 34–47.

106. For an example of work representing this first approach and focusing on the Vsemirnaia Literatura (World Literature) Publishing House founded by Maksim Gorky in 1918, see Maria Khotimsky, "World Literature, Soviet Style: A Forgotten Episode in the History of the Idea," *Ab Imperio* 3, no. 3 (2013): 119–54, https://doi.org/10.1353/imp.2013.0075. See also Michael David-Fox, *Crossing Borders: Modernity, Ideology, and Culture in Russia and the Soviet Union* (Pittsburgh: University of Pittsburgh Press, 2015); and Clark, *Moscow, the Fourth Rome*.

107. On the concept of the Soviet republic of letters, see Djagalov, "The Red Apostles," 398, 400. See also Katerina Clark, "The Soviet Project of the 1930s to Found a 'World Literature' and British Literary Internationalism," *Modern Language Quarterly* 80, no. 4 (2019): 403–25. For another useful conceptualization of the Soviet republic of letters as a "literary international," see Samuel Gold Hodgkin, "Lāhūtī: Persian Poetry in the Making of the Literary International, 1906–1957," PhD diss., University of Chicago, 2018. Through a study of Lahuti's works and career as a "literary representative," Hodgkin convincingly argues that the shared

legacy of Persianate literary forms and cultural sensibilities shaped the literary common of Soviet Eastern internationalism across Central Eurasia.

108. See Clark, *Eurasia Without Borders*, charting "the varied patterns of 'diffusion'" of Soviet texts and emphasizing "the dialectic of integration and disintegration in the movement for an internationalist left literature that would span all Eurasia" (354).

109. For a similar critique, see Samuel Hodgkin, *Persianate Verse and the Poetics of Eastern Internationalism* (Cambridge: Cambridge University Press, forthcoming). Hodgkin's valuable study explores the original use of Persianate poetics and "persistent forms" by Eastern writers.

110. Hans Günther, "Die Lebensphasen eines Kanons—am Beispiel des sozialistischen Realismus," in *Kanon und Zensur: Beiträge zur Archäologie der literarischen Kommunikation II*, ed. Jan Assmann and Aleida Assmann (Munich: Fink, 1987), 138–48, esp. 138 (quote).

111. Boris Groys, *The Total Art of Stalinism: Avant-Garde, Aesthetic Dictatorship, and Beyond*, trans. Charles Rougle (Princeton, NJ: Princeton University Press, 1992).

112. On aesthetic education, see Gayatri Chakravorty Spivak, *An Aesthetic Education in the Era of Globalization* (Cambridge, MA: Harvard University Press, 2012).

113. On peripheral realisms, see Joe Cleary, Jed Esty, and Colleen Lye, eds., "Peripheral Realisms," special issue of *Modern Language Quarterly* 73, no. 3 (2012).

114. See Robert J. C. Young, *Postcolonialism: An Historical Introduction* (2001; reprint, Malden, MA: Blackwell, 2008). For the quoted phrase, see Hannah Arendt, "The Decline of the Nation-State and the End of the Rights of Man," in *The Origins of Totalitarianism* (New York: Harcourt, 1976), 267. Although scholarship by Walter D. Mignolo and Madina Tlostanova in so-called decolonial studies has addressed Russian and Ottoman differences, its treatment of these imperial formations as "dewesternization" projects could be characterized as essentialist and identitarian. This scholarship has not been useful to me. See Walter D. Mignolo, *The Politics of Decolonial Investigations* (Durham, NC: Duke University Press, 2021).

115. Djagalov, *From Internationalism to Postcolonialism*; Lydia H. Liu, "The Eventfulness of Translation: Temporality, Difference, and Competing Universals," *Translation: A Transdisciplinary Journal* 4 (Spring 2014): 147–70; Hala Halim, "Lotus, the Afro-Asian Nexus, and Global Comparatism," *Comparative Studies of South Asia, Africa, and the Middle East* 32, no. 3 (2012): 563–83; Monica Popescu, *At Penpoint: African Literatures, Postcolonial Studies, and the Cold War* (Durham, NC: Duke University Press, 2020). For a nuanced exploration of the East-West divide in relation to eastern Europe, see Anita Starosta, *Form and Instability: Eastern Europe, Literature, Postimperial Difference* (Evanston, IL: Northwestern University Press, 2016). On the usefulness and the limitations of the postcolonial paradigm for the study of the Caucasus, see Leah Feldman, *On the Threshold of Eurasia: Revolutionary Poetics in the Caucasus* (Ithaca, NY: Cornell University Press, 2018).

116. On "the Soviet creation of postcolonial studies," see Robert J. C. Young, "The Soviet Invention of Postcolonial Studies," *boundary 2* 50, no. 2 (2023): 133–56.

1. THE TURKISH WAR OF INDEPENDENCE IN LITERATURE AND FILM: LIMITS OF MARXIST-LENINIST NATIONALISM AND LEGACIES FOR THE POSTCOLONIAL ERA

1. Samuel J. Hirst, "Soviet Orientalism Across Borders: Documentary Film for the Turkish Republic," *Kritika: Explorations in Russian and Eurasian History* 18, no. 1 (2017): 44, https://doi.org/10.1353/kri.2017.0002. On the Soviet Eastern genre, see Hirst's useful account in general. See also Michael G. Smith, "Cinema for the 'Soviet East': National Fact and Revolutionary Fiction in Early Azerbaijani Film," *Slavic Review* 56, no. 4 (Winter 1997): 645–78, analyzing the "national realist" style of Soviet Eastern films "as a darker underside to the socialist realist equation" (646).
2. "Millî Mücadele Filmi...," *Cumhuriyet*, December 15, 1932, 3; see also "İnkılâbımızın Mükemmel Filmi Nasıl Olacak?," *Vakit*, December 15, 1932, 10.
3. Nihad Sâmi Banarlı, *Devlet ve Devlet Terbiyesi* (Istanbul: Kubbealtı, 1985), 155.
4. For the first book edition of the serialized French original, see Claude Farrère, *L'homme qui assassina: Roman* (Paris: Société d'éditions littéraires et artistiques, Librairie P. Ollendorff, [1910?]). For its Russian translation, see Klod Farrer, *Chelovek, kotoryi ubil...* (Paris: Franko--russkaia pechat', 1921). For a Turkish translation of a French play based on Farrère's novel, see Peyami Safa, *Meçhul Katil!* (Istanbul: Resimli Maarif İdaresi, 1341 [1925]).
5. Sergei Iutkevich, *Sobranie sochinenii v trekh tomakh*, vol. 2: *Put'*, ed. M. Z. Dolinskii (Moscow: Iskusstvo, 1991), 85.
6. For the original typeset screenplay, see N. Zarkhi and S. Iutkevich, "Chelovek, kotoryi ne ubil," RGALI f. 2003, op. 1, d. 61 and d. 62. For published excerpts, see N. Zarkhi and S. Iutkevich, "Chelovek, kotoryi ne ubil," *Kino*, August 16, 1933; N. Zarkhi and S. Iutkevich, "Chelovek, kotoryi ne ubil," *Kino*, August 22, 1933; and N. Zarkhi and S. Iutkevich, "Chelovek, kotoryi ne ubil," *Sovetskoe kino*, no. 8 (August 1933): 28–39.
7. Smith, "Cinema for the 'Soviet East,'" 666–69. For a brief comparative discussion of "The Man Who Did Not Kill" in relation to Nikoloz Shengelaia's historical-revolutionary Eastern titled 26 Commissars (26 komissarov) of 1932, about the execution of twenty-six Baku commissars in 1918, see D. Matskin, "Tema molodoi Turtsii," *Sovetskoe kino*, no. 9 (September 1933): 15–26, esp. 26.
8. A. K. Sverchevskaia, *Sovetsko-turetskie kul'turnye sviazi, 1925–1981* (Moscow: Nauka, 1983), 34–35. Khikmet's transformation from a superwesternized dandy into a nationalist hero would have been implausible for Turkish readers of the screenplay, which might have contributed to the termination of the project. The unredeemable figure of the "superwesternized" dandy has been a subject of ridicule in modern Turkish literature dating back to the late nineteenth century.
9. For the Russian translation, see Mustafa Kemal, *Put' novoi Turtsii, 1919–1927*, 4 vols. (Moscow: Litizdat NKID, 1929–1934).
10. Sergei Iutkevich and Leo Arnshtam, dirs., *Türkiye'nin Kalbi Ankara* (Lenfilm and Turkish Ministry of Education, 1934), https://www.tccb.gov.tr/ata_ozel/video/. Prime Minister İsmet İnönü delivered a speech celebrating Turkish and Soviet friendship in the documentary.

1. THE TURKISH WAR OF INDEPENDENCE IN LITERATURE AND FILM

11. For my analysis of Lenin's concept of national self-determination as described in his early twentieth-century articles and philosophical notebooks, see Nergis Ertürk, "Lenin via Cavid: Towards a Communism of Other-Determination," *Interventions: International Journal of Postcolonial Studies* 18, no. 5 (2016): 627–50. For Lenin's description of partitioned Turkey as an "oppressed" country, see V. I. Lenin, "The Second Congress of the Communist International," in *Collected Works*, vol. 31, trans. and ed. Julius Katzer (Moscow: Progress, 1966), 218, 240–41; V. I. Lenin, "II kongress Kommunisticheskogo Internatsionala," in *Polnoe sobranie sochinenii*, vol. 41, 5th ed. (Moscow: Gosudarstvennoe izdatel'stvo, 1963), 218, 242.
12. S. I. Aralov, *Bir Sovyet Diplomatının Türkiye Hatıraları*, trans. Hasan Âli Ediz (Istanbul: Burçak Yayınevi, 1967), 231.
13. "Session 17: Trade Unions (20 November)," in *Toward the United Front: Proceedings of the Fourth Congress of the Communist International, 1922*, ed. and trans. John Riddell (Leiden, Netherlands: Brill, 2012), 619.
14. M. N. Roy, "The Turkish Victory," *International Press Correspondence* 2, no. 89 (October 17, 1922): 672. For other discussions of the War of Independence in Comintern publications, see Doğu Perinçek, ed., *Komintern Belgelerinde Türkiye*, vol. 1: *Kurtuluş Savaşı ve Lozan* (Istanbul: Kaynak, 1993). See also Doğu Perinçek, ed., *Lenin Stalin Mao'nun Türkiye Yazıları* (Istanbul: Kaynak, 1991).
15. Here I draw on Vahram Ter-Matevosyan, *Turkey, Kemalism, and the Soviet Union: Problems of Modernization, Ideology, and Interpretation* (Cham, Switzerland: Palgrave Macmillan, 2019), 173–230, which provides a valuable account of Soviet discourses on "Kemalism," the "Turkish national movement," and "new Turkey" from the early 1920s through the 1960s. On the history of Marxist-Leninist Orientology, see Michael Kemper, "Red Orientalism: Mikhail Pavlovich and Marxist Oriental Studies in Early Soviet Russia," *Die Welt des Islams* 50 (2010): 435–76.
16. On the distinction between the inner and outer (domestic and foreign) East, see Masha Kirasirova, "The 'East' as a Category of Bolshevik Ideology and Comintern Administration: The Arab Section of the Communist University of the Toilers of the East," *Kritika: Explorations in Russian and Eurasian History* 18, no. 1 (2017): 7–34, https://doi.org/10.1353/kri.2017.0001.
17. Rossen Djagalov, *From Internationalism to Postcolonialism: Literature and Cinema Between the Second and Third Worlds* (Montreal: McGill-Queen's University Press, 2020), 32–64, 112, 12, 72.
18. On the representation of the War of Independence in modern Turkish literature, see "Türk Romanında Kurtuluş Savaşı Özel Sayısı," special issue of *Türk Dili*, no. 298 (July 1, 1976); İnci Enginün, Zeynep Kerman, and Selim İleri, eds., *Kurtuluş Savaşı ve Edebiyatımız* (Istanbul: Oğlak, 1998); and Mürşit Balabanlılar, ed., *Türk Romanında Kurtuluş Savaşı: İnceleme* (Istanbul: Türkiye İş Bankası Kültür Yayınları, 2003).
19. Iutkevich, *Sobranie sochinenii v trekh tomakh*, 2:90. Nâzım was incarcerated in the Sultanahmet House of Detention in the spring of 1933 before his transfer to the Bursa prison; see Nail Çakırhan, *Anılar*, interview by Erden Akbulut (Istanbul: TÜSTAV, 2008), 48–49. He would be incarcerated in Sultanahmet again in 1938 and 1939.
20. N. A. Zarkhi, "Fil'ma o Turtsii," *Kino*, January 28, 1933.

1. THE TURKISH WAR OF INDEPENDENCE IN LITERATURE AND FILM

21. There is little scholarship about Nizamettin's life and works. For brief biographical accounts of his life, see İbrahim Alâettin Gövsa, "Tepedelenlioğlu, Nizameddin Nazif," in *Türk Meşhurları Ansiklopedisi* (Istanbul: Yedigün, 1946), 378–79; and Erden Akbulut and Mete Tunçay, *İstanbul Komünist Grubu'ndan (Aydınlık Çevresi) Türkiye Komünist Partisi'ne, 1919–1926*, 3 vols. (Istanbul: TÜSTAV, 2012–2013), 1:394. For an interview with Nizamettin about his pursuit of journalism as a career, see Nizamettin Nazif Tepedelenlioğlu, "Anket: Zoraki Muharrir," interview by M. Niyazi Acun, *Uyanış* 45, no. 2014-329 (March 28, 1935): 278–79, 284. On Tepedelenli Ali Pasha, see K. E. Fleming, *The Muslim Bonaparte: Diplomacy and Orientalism in Ali Pasha's Greece* (Princeton, NJ: Princeton University Press, 1999).
22. On Anatolian communisms and Bolshevisms, see the introduction. On Nizamettin's communist activities in Anatolia, see George S. Harris, *The Origins of Communism in Turkey* (Stanford, CA: Hoover Institution Press, 1967), 87–88, 108; Bülent Gökay, *Soviet Eastern Policy and Turkey, 1920–1991* (London: Routledge, 2006), 32–33; Erden Akbulut and Mete Tunçay, *Türkiye Halk İştirakiyun Fırkası (1920–1923)*, rev. ed (Istanbul: TÜSTAV, 2016), 192, 229–30, 384–85; and Emel Akal, *Moskova-Ankara-Londra Üçgeninde: İştirakiyuncular, Komünistler ve Paşa Hazretleri* (Istanbul: İletişim, 2013), 371–72, 410–11, and 490. On Nizamettin's arrest and trial, see also Feridun Kandemir, *Atatürk'ün Kurduğu Türkiye Komünist Partisi ve Sonrası* (Istanbul: Nejat Ağbaba, [1966]), 182.
23. For the official Soviet records of the meeting between Upmal and Mustafa Kemal on January 24, 1921, see Mehmet Perinçek, *Atatürk'ün Sovyetler'le Görüşmeleri (Sovyet Arşiv Belgeleriyle)* (Istanbul: Kaynak, 2005), 262–80.
24. Akbulut and Tunçay, *Türkiye Halk İştirakiyun Fırkası*, 298.
25. During this period, Nizamettin also contributed to another weekly, *Voice of the East (Şarkın Sesi)*, calling on Turkish peasants to support an Eastern anti-imperialist alliance. Only one issue of this paper has survived. See Akbulut and Tunçay, *Türkiye Halk İştirakiyun Fırkası*, 295, 306, 307–8, 313.
26. "Türkiye Halk İştirakiyun Fırkası'nın Büyük Millet Meclisi Hükümetine Beyannamesi," *Yeni Hayat* 1, no. 3 (April 1, 1338 [1922]), in *THİF Yayın Organı: "Yeni Hayat" (Mart-Eylül 1922)*, ed. Hamit Erdem (Istanbul: TÜSTAV, 2017), 86–89.
27. "Maksadımız," *Yeni Hayat* 1, no. 1 (March 18, 1338 [1922]), in *THİF Yayın Organı*, ed. H. Erdem, 51.
28. A. Nâzım, "Söz ve Hak," *Yeni Hayat* 1, no. 17 (July 22, 1338 [1922]), in *THİF Yayın Organı*, ed. H. Erdem, 358–61.
29. Nizamettin Nazif, "Anadolu," *Yeni Hayat* 1, no. 12 (June 10, 1338 [1922]), in *THİF Yayın Organı*, ed. H. Erdem, 267–68.
30. Nizamettin Nazif, "Anadolu Nasıl Yaşıyor?," *Yeni Hayat* 1, no. 14 (June 24, 1338 [1922]), in *THİF Yayın Organı*, ed. H. Erdem, 300–304 (quote on 303).
31. Nizamettin Nazif, "Ölüm Sultanlığa," *Yeni Hayat* 1, nos. 20–21 (September 29, 1338 [1922]), in *THİF Yayın Organı*, ed. H. Erdem, 427–29.
32. Leonid and Friedrich, *Angora: Freiheitskrieg der Türkei* (Berlin: Vereinigung internationaler Verlagsanstalten, 1923), 59. For the congress proceedings, see Akbulut and Tunçay, *Türkiye Halk İştirakiyun Fırkası*, 355–81.
33. "Session 20. The Eastern Question (23 November)" and "Appendix: Resolutions and Statements," in *Toward the United Front*, ed. Riddell, 725, 1180–88.

1. THE TURKISH WAR OF INDEPENDENCE IN LITERATURE AND FILM

34. On Nizamettin's journey to Russia, see Akbulut and Tunçay, *Türkiye Halk İştirakiyun Fırkası*, 441–45. After his return to Turkey, the party asked Nizamettin to unify and lead the communist youth groups in Istanbul and Ankara, an effort that failed due to conflict with the Istanbul group. See Salih Hacıoğlu's letter dated September 1, 1923, in Akbulut and Tunçay, *İstanbul Komünist Grubu'ndan*, 1:293–94. On Nizamettin's Izmir activities, see the letter dated July 18, 1924, by the Soviet ambassador in Izmir in Akbulut and Tunçay, *İstanbul Komünist Grubu'ndan*, 2:79–80.
35. On Nizamettin's arrest, see "Ankara İstiklâl Mahkemesi, Hülâsa-i Hüküm Tezkeresi," in Akbulut and Tunçay, *İstanbul Komünist Grubu'ndan*, 3:19–20.
36. For example, see the collection of newspaper articles from 1959 chronicling Nizamettin's experiences in Ankara during the War of Independence, which make no mention of his communist activities: Nizamettin Nazif Tepedelenlioğlu, *Bilinmeyen Taraflariyle Atatürk* (Istanbul: Yeni Çığır Kitabevi, 1959).
37. Nizamettin Nazif Tepedelenlioğlu, "Nizamettin Nazif Tepedelenlioğlu Cevap Veriyor: Ahmet Cevat Emre'nin Moskova Hatıraları Dolayısiyle," *Yeni Tarih Dünyası* 6 (May 1965): 168.
38. For a brief useful history of the historical fiction genre, see Levent Cantek, "Türkiye'de Tarihi Çizgi Romanlar: Kılıçbaz Kahramanlar," *Toplumsal Tarih* 118 (October 2003): 14–23. The French Orientalist Léon Cahun's study *Introduction à l'histoire de l'Asie* (1896) and novel *La bannière bleue* (1877), translated by the Ottoman Turkologist Necib Asım in 1900 and 1912, respectively, served as important sources of this genre (Cantek, "Türkiye'de Tarihi Çizgi Romanlar," 21). For a valuable discussion of the "grand national narrative" (*büyük ulusal anlatı*) of Turkish historical fiction, see Murat Belge, *Genesis: "Büyük Ulusal Anlatı" ve Türklerin Kökeni* (Istanbul: İletişim, 2009). Both Cantek and Belge address the novels of the Turkish communist writer Kemal Tahir from the post–Second World War era, but they fail to account for Nizamettin and Vâlâ. (Cantek briefly mentions Nizamettin without accounting for his communist past.)
39. On the Pardaillan series as a model for *Kara Davud*, see Cantek, "Türkiye'de Tarihi Çizgi Romanlar," 21.
40. Jean-Paul Sartre, *Les mots* (Paris: Gallimard, 1964), 109; Jean-Paul Sartre, *The Words: The Autobiography of Jean-Paul Sartre*, trans. Bernard Frechtman (New York: Vintage, 1981), 132–33.
41. Regarding Dino's illustration of the *Kara Davud* serials, see Rasih Nuri İleri, "Abidin Dino Hakkında Bir Kronoloji Denemesi," *Güldiken*, no. 4 (1994): 12. I have not encountered this claim in any other source, so for the time being it cannot be corroborated.
42. Unless otherwise noted, citations to *Kara Davud* refer to the first book editions: Nizamettin Nazif, *Kara Davud*, vol. 1 (Istanbul: Türk Matbaası, 1928); Nizamettin Nazif, *Kara Davud*, vol. 2 (Istanbul: Amedi Matbaası, 1928); and Nizamettin Nazif, *Kara Davut: Üçüncü Kitap*, vol. 3 (Istanbul: Kanaat Kütüphanesi, 1930).
43. Nizamettin Nazif, *Kara Davud*, 2:19.
44. On the public outrage, see Zeki Taştan, "Cumhuriyet Dönemi Tarihî Romancılığımızda Dikkat Çekici Bir Eser: *Kara Davut* ve Devrinde Uyandırdığı Akisler," in *II. Kayseri ve Yöresi Kültür, Sanat ve Edebiyat Bilgi Şöleni (10–12*

1. THE TURKISH WAR OF INDEPENDENCE IN LITERATURE AND FILM

Nisan 2006): Bildiriler, ed. Mustafa Argunşah (Kayseri: Erciyes Üniversitesi, 2007), 576–88.
45. See Ahmet Haşim, "Palavra Edebiyatı," in *Bütün Eserleri*, vol. 2: *Bize Göre/İkdam'daki Diğer Yazıları*, ed. İnci Enginün and Zeynep Kerman (Istanbul: Dergâh, 1991), 81–82; and Ahmet Haşim, "Büyük Bir Efsaneci," in *Bütün Eserleri*, 2:169–70.
46. Nâzım Hikmet, "Yeni Çıkan Kitaplar: *Kara Davut*," *Resimli Ay* 6, no. 4 (June 1929): 34, reprinted in *Yazılar 1: Sanat, Edebiyat, Kültür, Dil* (Istanbul: Adam, 1991), 17–19.
47. Franco Moretti, *Atlas of the European Novel, 1800–1900* (Verso: London, 1998), 38.
48. For a historical account of this period, see Halil Inalcik, *The Ottoman Empire: The Classical Age 1300–1600* (London: Phoenix, 1973), 17–34.
49. For the quoted phrase, see Inalcik, *The Ottoman Empire*, 23.
50. On the despotic state machine, see Gilles Deleuze and Félix Guattari, *Anti-Oedipus: Capitalism and Schizophrenia*, trans. Robert Hurley, Mark Seem, and Helen R. Lane (Minneapolis: University of Minnesota Press, 2000), 192–222.
51. Kara Davud and Mehmed II first meet early in the novel, when the young Mehmed is serving as governor of Manisa province, and Mehmed tortures Kara Duman for trespassing on reserved hunting lands. Hearing Duman's cries for help, Davud saves Duman's life, defeating Mehmed in a duel.
52. For the quoted phrase, see Georg Lukács, *The Historical Novel*, trans. Hannah Mitchell and Stanley Mitchell (Lincoln: University of Nebraska Press, 1983), 77. Lukács described historical fiction as an exemplary genre in which "the novel reaches its closest point to the epic" (36) and pointed to Walter Scott as "a model for the objective presentation of contending historical forces" (77–78). Nizamettin's novel is closer to the Romantic examples of the genre, offering what Lukács called "a moralizing fable intended to demonstrate the superiority of virtue over vice" (78).
53. For the quoted phrases about Davud, see Nizamettin Nazif, *Kara Davud*, 1:43, emphasis in the original. On Sultan Mehmed II's order of a three-day pillage, see Nizamettin Nazif, *Kara Davud*, 1:389.
54. Nizamettin Nazif, *Kara Davud*, 2:9.
55. See, for example, Halim Kara, "Mazinin Edebi Temsili: Tarihsel Romanda Fatih'in Karakterizasyonu," in *Edebiyatın Omzundaki Melek: Edebiyatın Tarihle İlişkisi Üzerine Yazılar*, ed. Zeynep Uysal (Istanbul: İletişim, 2011), 337–80, esp. 348–50.
56. Nizamettin Nazif, *Kara Davud*, 2:10, emphasis in the original.
57. For the revised version, see Nizamettin Nazif Tepedelenlioğlu, *Kara Davud* (Istanbul: Ak Kitabevi, 1966), 418. Whereas the original edition of 1928 offers an exaggerated representation of Kara Davud as an epic hero with both subhuman (animal) and superhuman (godlike) characteristics, the revised edition of 1966 provides a more realistic description, eliminating the climactic action of Davud slapping Mehmed II.
58. Nizamettin Nazif, *Kara Davud*, 1:205, 208; Tepedelenlioğlu, *Kara Davud*, 22, 225, 226.
59. Karl Marx, *Grundrisse: Foundations of the Critique of Political Economy (Rough Draft)*, trans. Martin Nicolaus (New York: Penguin, 1993), 472–74; Karl Marx,

1. THE TURKISH WAR OF INDEPENDENCE IN LITERATURE AND FILM

Grundrisse, part 2, in *MEGA* II/1.2, 380–81, MEGAdigital, Berlin-Brandenburgische Akademie der Wissenschaften, http://telota.bbaw.de/mega/#.

60. Karl Marx, *Capital: A Critique of Political Economy*, vol. 1, trans. Ben Fowkes (New York: Penguin, 1990), 450; Karl Marx, *Das Kapital*, vol. 1, in *MEGA* II/5, 268–69, MEGAdigital, Berlin-Brandenburgische Akademie der Wissenschaften, http://telota.bbaw.de/mega/#.

61. On the possibility of extending the Marxian concept of fetishism to the Asiatic mode of production, see Étienne Balibar, "On the Basic Concepts of Historical Materialism," in Louis Althusser et al., *Reading Capital*, trans. Ben Brewster (London: Verso, 2009), 244–46. The novel also criticizes the use of slave labor on the Venetian ships; see Nizamettin Nazif, *Kara Davud*, 1:299–300.

62. Nâzım Hikmet, "Yeni Çıkan Kitaplar: *Kara Davut*," 34. For the dedication, see Nizamettin Nazif, *Kara Davut: Üç Cilt Bir Arada* (Istanbul: Resimli Ay Matbaası, 1929), 213. The abridged Resimli Ay edition of 1929 concludes with Davud's election as the ruler of Lesbos. Though Nâzım's critique addressed the abridged edition, it can productively be extended to the original edition.

63. Marx, *Grundrisse*, 473; Marx, *Grundrisse*, part 2, 381.

64. Nizamettin Nazif, *Kara Davud*, 2:433.

65. On the conflicts between Soviet representatives and the THIF members, see Akbulut and Tunçay, *Türkiye Halk İştirakiyun Fırkası*, 298–313, 403–20. For the phrase "Anatolian primitives," see George S. Harris, *The Communists and the "Kadro" Movement: Shaping Ideology in Atatürk's Turkey* (Istanbul: ISIS, 2002), 45.

66. Moretti, *Atlas of the European Novel*, 33, 46, 43.

67. Nizamettin Nazif, *Kara Davud*, 1:135.

68. Nizamettin Nazif, *Kara Davud*, 1:154, 136. In the 1966 edition, the Turkish translation of "Dirican" is provided in the main text with no mention of its Kurdish origin (Tepedelenlioğlu, *Kara Davud*, 149). Eliminating the note about *kasr*, Nizamettin describes it as a "stone tower" in the main text, refusing to identify it as a specific type of Kurdish residence (Tepedelenlioğlu, *Kara Davud*, 168). The erasure of Kurdish in the revised edition is not systematic, however, as other references to Kurdish people and languages are preserved (Tepedelenlioğlu, *Kara Davud*, 95, 105, 168).

69. Moretti, *Atlas of the European Novel*, 40, emphasis in original. Borrowing Gayatri Spivak's special use of the term *lexicalization*, one might say that Nizamettin's novel aimed to "lexicalize" subaltern practices with these documentations. "To *lexicalize*," Spivak writes, "is to separate a linguistic item from its appropriate grammatical system into the conventions of another grammar." Her example is from W. E. B. Du Bois, *The Souls of Black Folk*: "At the head of each chapter, Du Bois takes a line of African spiritual and writes it in the European musical notation. There we have the desire to convert the performative into performance—an active cultural idiom lexicalized into the encyclopedia or the museum—that is at the core of it." Gayatri Chakravorty Spivak, "Harlem," *Social Text* 22, no. 4 (2004): 118, 125.

70. In the text, "Alevi" and "Qizilbash" are used interchangeably. Beginning in the fifteenth century, the term *kızılbaş* or *qizilbash* (crimson head) appeared in Ottoman historical documents referring to the nomadic tribes in eastern Anatolia who opposed sedentary Ottoman rule. It referred to the crimson headdress worn

1. THE TURKISH WAR OF INDEPENDENCE IN LITERATURE AND FILM

by tribe members to represent their adherence to the Twelve Imams and their spiritual leader Sheik Haydar. Marginalized as heretics by the Ottomans, who adhered to Sunni Islam, the Qizilbash embraced a syncretic, heterodox Islam incorporating elements of local Anatolian folklore. In the modern era, the name "Alevi" (follower of Ali) is used instead. Comprising ethnic Turks, Kurds, and Zaza Alevi (Dersimli), Alevis in Turkey represent approximately 15 percent of the population and have been subject to systematic discrimination by the Turkish state and the Sunni majority. On Alevi identity, see Irène Mélikoff, "Bektashi/Kızılbaş: Historical Bipartition and Its Consequences," in *Alevi Identity: Cultural, Religious, and Social Perspectives*, ed. Tord Olsson, Elisabeth Özdalga, and Catharina Raudvere (London: Taylor and Francis, 2005), 1–8; and M. Hakan Yavuz, *Islamic Political Identity in Turkey* (New York: Oxford University Press, 2003), 65–79. Turkish historiography has conventionally emphasized Alevi support for the Kemalist republic, but more recent research rejects such claims. See Hamit Bozarslan, "Alevism and the Myths of Research: The Need for a New Research Agenda," in *Turkey's Alevi Enigma: A Comprehensive Overview*, ed. Paul J. White and Joost Jongerden (London: Brill, 2003), 3–16.

71. In the 1966 revised edition, Nizamettin added the phrase "Alevi Turk" as a descriptor of the people of Arguvan, presumably to resolve the ambiguous ethnic identity of Davud's wife. Compare Nizamettin Nazif, *Kara Davut: Üçüncü Kitap*, 146, and Tepedelenlioğlu, *Kara Davud*, 567.
72. Nizamettin Nazif, "Anadolu Nasıl Yaşıyor?," 303.
73. See Akbulut and Tunçay, *Türkiye Halk İştirakiyun Fırkası*, 296, 314–17. Nizamettin's article also offered a forceful critique of Farrère, who visited Turkey in 1922. Its anti-French tone displeased the Ankara government at a time when it sought to secure its southern borders through negotiations with the French.
74. For the quoted phrase, see Smith, "Cinema for the 'Soviet East,'" 647.
75. For the quoted phrase, see Etienne [sic] Balibar, "The Nation Form: History and Ideology," trans. Chris Turner, in Etienne Balibar and Immanuel Wallerstein, *Race, Nation, Class: Ambiguous Identities* (London: Verso, 1991), 96. For an explication of Kemalist nationalist discourse during the War of Independence and the early republican era, see Ahmet Yıldız, *"Ne Mutlu Türküm Diyebilene": Türk Ulusal Kimliğinin Etno-seküler Sınırları (1919–1938)* (Istanbul: İletişim, 2001), esp. 124–26.
76. For the quoted phrase, see Özge Serin, "The Use-Value of Idioms: The Language of Marxism and Language as Such," in "Marxism, Communism, and Translation," ed. Nergis Ertürk and Özge Serin, special issue of *boundary 2* 43, no. 3 (2016): 296.
77. See Nizamettin Nazif, *Kara Davud*, 1:3–4.
78. *Tamilla* is an adaptation of Ferdinand Duchêne's novel *Thamil'la* (1907). On the reception of these films, see Âlim Şerif Onaran, *Muhsin Ertuğrul'un Sineması* (Ankara: Saim Toraman Matbaası, 1981), 127–31. On Ertuğrul's contributions to Turkish cinema and theater, see A. A. Guseinov, *Mukhsin Ertugrul v teatre i kino* (Moscow: Nauka, 1990); and Efdal Sevinçli, *Meşrutiyet'ten Cumhuriyet'e Sinemadan Tiyatroya: Muhsin Ertuğrul* (Istanbul: Broy, 1987).
79. For a critical assessment of Ertuğrul and the first generation of Istanbul City Theater actors and actresses who shaped early republican cinema, see Nijad

1. THE TURKISH WAR OF INDEPENDENCE IN LITERATURE AND FILM

Özön, *Türk Sineması Tarihi: Dünden Bugüne (1896–1960)* (Istanbul: Ekicigil Matbaası, 1962), 60, 109–15.

80. See Vedat Nedim's report dated August 30, 1925, in Akbulut and Tunçay, *İstanbul Komünist Grubu'ndan*, 3:69. Ertuğrul's essays described his visits to the Moscow Public Library, Tretyakov Gallery, and other important cultural sites, introducing Turkish readers to the history of Russian theater and avant-garde art. Ertuğrul visited the Soviet Union again in 1934, chronicling his travels in the theater journal *Darülbedayi* from October 1934 to March 1935. For an extensive discussion of Muhsin Ertuğrul's travel essays, see Nergis Ertürk, "Türkiye ve Rusya Hattında Muhsin Ertuğrul," introduction to Muhsin Ertuğrul, *Moskova Notları*, ed. Tuncay Birkan (Istanbul: Can, 2023), 13–37.
81. See Onaran, *Muhsin Ertuğrul'un Sineması*, 197–206. Breaking with past practice, for *A Nation Awakens* Ertuğrul also cast actors without professional theater training.
82. Onaran, *Muhsin Ertuğrul'un Sineması*, 152.
83. Nizamettin Nazif, *Bir Millet Uyanıyor* (Istanbul: Kanaat Kütüphanesi, n.d. [ca. 1932]).
84. See Muhsin Ertuğrul, dir., *Bir Millet Uyanıyor* (İpek Film, 1932), https://www.youtube.com/watch?v=NhiBXtvY19g.
85. Aralov, *Bir Sovyet Diplomatının Türkiye Hatıraları*, 129–30.
86. Nizamettin Nazif, *Bir Millet Uyanıyor*, 42–43, 48.
87. Nizamettin Nazif, *Bir Millet Uyanıyor*, 54. For an interesting response to the negative representation of French and British characters in the film, see U.S. ambassador Charles H. Sherril's report "Document Concerning the Turkish Movie 'The Awakening of a Nation,'" in *The Turkish Cinema in the Early Republican Years*, ed. Rifat N. Bali (Istanbul: ISIS, 2007), 21–22. Sherril remarked that the Soviet ambassador and he "could safely be invited to be present" at a private screening of the film as "it has no criticism of the United States or Russia" (22).
88. On the film's allusion to *Battleship Potemkin*, see Özön, *Türk Sineması Tarihi*, 97.
89. James T. Siegel, *Fetish, Recognition, Revolution* (Princeton, NJ: Princeton University Press, 1997), 173.
90. Nizamettin Nazif, *Bir Millet Uyanıyor*, 63.
91. Özön, *Türk Sineması Tarihi*, 96.
92. Nizamettin Nazif, *Bir Millet Uyanıyor*, 70.
93. Gazi Mustafa Kemal, *Nutuk (1927)* (Istanbul: Yapı Kredi Yayınları, 2011), 466. For an English translation, see Gazi Mustafa Kemal, *A Speech Delivered by Mustafa Kemal Atatürk, 1927* (Istanbul: Turkish Ministry of Education Printing Plant, 1963), 452.
94. Mustafa Kemal read the screenplay before the film was shot and agreed to appear in the film. See Erman Şener, *Kurtuluş Savaşı ve Sinemamız* (N.p.: Dizi Yayınları, 1970), 43.
95. For Nizamettin's collaboration with other leftist writers, see Kemal Sülker, *Nâzım Hikmet'in Gerçek Yaşamı*, 6 vols. (Istanbul: Yalçın Yayınları, 1987–1989), 3:254–67. Nizamettin joined Nâzım, Suat Derviş, and others in 1935 to commemorate the legacy of Kemal Ahmed, a journalist colleague who had died in poverty in 1934. See also Tuncay Birkan, *Dünya ile Devlet Arasında Türk Muharriri, 1930–1960* (Istanbul: Metis, 2018), 354. Offering a nuanced analysis of Nizamettin's contributions to the public debate in 1936 about "national literature," Birkan also

1. THE TURKISH WAR OF INDEPENDENCE IN LITERATURE AND FILM

reminds us that his columns about the Spanish Civil War expressed support for the republican Popular Front (274–75, 494).
96. Sülker, *Nâzım Hikmet'in Gerçek Yaşamı*, 2:240.
97. See Nizamettin Nazif, *Topuna Birden: Umumî Bir Cevap* (Istanbul: Tanin Matbaası, 1946).
98. See Oğuz Makal, *Beyaz Perdede ve Sahnede Nâzım Hikmet* (Istanbul: Kalkedon, 2015), 86.
99. The biographical details of Nâzım's life in exile are well known. An entire industry of biography and memoir about Nâzım now thrives. For an authoritative account in Russian (which was later translated into Turkish), see A. A. Babaev, *Nazym Khikmet: Zhizn' i tvorchestvo* (Moscow: Nauka, 1975). For a valuable source in Turkish, see the six volumes of Sülker, *Nâzım Hikmet'in Gerçek Yaşamı*. For sources in English, see Mutlu Konuk Blasing, *Nâzım Hikmet: The Life and Times of Turkey's World Poet* (New York: Persea, 2013); and Saime Göksu and Edward Timms, *Romantic Communist: The Life and Work of Nazım Hikmet* (New York: St. Martin's, 1999). For a recent biography that draws extensively on understudied Russian archival materials, see James H. Meyer, *Red Star Over the Black Sea: Nâzım Hikmet and His Generation* (Oxford: Oxford University Press, 2023).
100. After his return to Turkey, Nâzım led a successful left oppositional group within the TKP. Accused of being a "Trotskyist police agent," he was expelled from the TKP in 1933 but then readmitted in 1939. See Erden Akbulut, "Nâzım Hikmet, TKP ve O Yıllar," in *Nâzım'ın Cep Defterlerinde Kavga, Aşk ve Şiir Notları (1937–1942)*, ed. Mehmet Ulusel et al. (Istanbul: Yapı Kredi Yayınları, 2018), 19–21.
101. Katerina Clark, "European and Russian Cultural Interactions with Turkey: 1910s–1930s," *Comparative Studies of South Asia, Africa, and the Middle East* 33, no. 2 (2013): 208, https://doi.org/10.1215/1089201x-2322489. In *Eurasia Without Borders: The Dream of a Leftist Literary Commons, 1919–1943* (Cambridge, MA: Harvard University Press, 2021), however, Clark appears to have abandoned this distinction.
102. Régis Debray, "Socialism: A Life Cycle," *New Left Review* 46 (July–August 2007): 24.
103. Şevket Süreyya Aydemir, *Suyu Arayan Adam* (Ankara: Öz Yayınları, 1959), 400.
104. See Nâzım Hikmet, *Simavne Kadısı Oğlu Şeyh Bedreddin Destanı* (Istanbul: Yeni Kitapçı, 1936). For my analysis of *Epic of Sheik Bedreddin*, see Nergis Ertürk, *Grammatology and Literary Modernity in Turkey* (New York: Oxford University Press, 2011), 166–75. Born sometime between 1359 and 1364 CE, Bedreddin was an unorthodox Muslim scholar whose imagination of common property ownership was blamed for the uprising crushed in 1420 by Mehmed I, who sentenced Bedreddin to death afterward.
105. Göksu and Timms, *Romantic Communist*, 135–36.
106. For a copy of this letter, see Sülker, *Nâzım Hikmet'in Gerçek Yaşamı*, 5:206–7. As a member of the press corps covering Mustafa Kemal, Nizamettin witnessed firsthand the futility of attempts to rescue Nâzım (Sülker, *Nâzım Hikmet'in Gerçek Yaşamı*, 5:63–67).
107. For a copy of this letter, see Orhan Koloğlu, "100. Doğum Yıldönümünde Nâzım Hikmet," *Tarih ve Toplum* 37, no. 217 (2002): 18.

1. THE TURKISH WAR OF INDEPENDENCE IN LITERATURE AND FILM

108. In a letter to the novelist Kemal Tahir dated August 25, 1941, Nâzım claimed that both his uncle and President İnönü had read and admired the epic. See Nâzım Hikmet, *Kemal Tahir'e Mahpusaneden Mektuplar* (Ankara: Bilgi, 1968), 110.
109. On the publication history of *Epic of National Liberation Movement*, see Göksu and Timms, *Romantic Communist*, 232–33. It is included in book 2 of *Human Landscapes* as an unpublished epic composed by the imprisoned poet Cemâl (a figure standing for Nâzım himself). The waiter Mustafa has a handwritten copy of "the prison epic" and reads it aloud to the cook and the headwaiter of a first-class train traveling from Istanbul to Ankara in 1941. The ironic narration moves back and forth between scenes of collective reading and conversations among first-class passengers (who are war profiteers) about the military successes of Nazi Germany.

    After his release from prison in 1950, Nâzım thought that the epic of national liberation was the only portion of *Human Landscapes* that could survive government censorship, so he revised it for publication under the title "Kuvâyi Milliye: Destan" (Epic of the national forces). Though the owner of the İnkılap Bookstore purchased the rights for its publication, it remained unpublished. Excerpts from *Epic of National Liberation Movement* appeared in literary magazines and anthologies during the 1940s and 1950s, but a complete version based on the original draft did not appear in print in Turkey until 1965. For this edition, see Nâzım Hikmet, *Kurtuluş Savaşı Destanı* (Istanbul: Yön, 1965). Unless otherwise noted, page numbers cited in this chapter's notes refer to this edition. An annotated edition based on the final manuscript prepared by Nâzım in 1950 was published in 1968 by Cevdet Kudret, including black-and-white illustrations by Dino. For this version, see Nâzım Hikmet, *Kuvâyi Milliye: Destan* (Ankara: Bilgi, 1968).

    The 1965 edition was published under the title *Epic of the War of Independence*, but in his letter correspondence and conversations Nâzım often referred to this work as "Milli Kurtuluş Hareketi Destanı," or "Epic of National Liberation Movement," unless he was using the shortened title "Milli Destan," or "National Epic." Following Nâzım, I use the title *Epic of National Liberation Movement*, which accurately reflects his Leninist politics. On Nâzım's use of this title, see Nâzım Hikmet, *Piraye'ye Mektuplar*, vol. 1, ed. Memet Fuat (Istanbul: Adam, 1998), 306; Nâzım Hikmet, *Kemal Tahir'e Mahpusaneden Mektuplar*, 90, 110, 139–40; and Gün Benderli, *Su Başında Durmuşuz: Anılar* (Istanbul: Belge, 2003), 283.
110. For valuable rhetorical and discursive analyses of the *Great Speech*, see Taha Parla, *Türkiye'de Siyasal Kültürün Resmî Kaynakları*, vol. 1, *Atatürk'ün "Nutuk" 'u* (Istanbul: İletişim, 1991); Hülya Adak, "National Myths and Self-Na(rra)tions: Mustafa Kemal's *Nutuk* and Halide Edib's *Memoirs* and *The Turkish Ordeal*," *South Atlantic Quarterly* 102, nos. 2–3 (2003): 509–27; and Toni Alaranta, "Mustafa Kemal Atatürk's Six-Day Speech of 1927: Defining the Official Historical View of the Foundation of the Turkish Republic," *Turkish Studies* 9, no. 1 (2008): 115–29. Parla suggests that *Nutuk* might be read as a bildungsroman of the Turkish nation (30).
111. Gazi Mustafa Kemal, *Nutuk*, 17–18; Gazi Mustafa Kemal, *A Speech*, 11–12, translation significantly modified.
112. Marx, *Grundrisse*, 470; Marx, *Grundrisse*, part 2, 377. See also Serin, "The Use-Value of Idioms," 295–96.

1. THE TURKISH WAR OF INDEPENDENCE IN LITERATURE AND FILM

113. See Marx, *Capital*, 1:451–52; and Marx, *Das Kapital*, 1:271, describing the effects of simple coordination "in the gigantic structures erected by the ancient Asiatics, Egyptians, Etruscans, etc.": "This power of Asiatic and Egyptian kings, of Etruscan theocrats, etc. has in modern society been transferred to the capitalist, whether he appears as an isolated individual or, as in the case of joint-struck companies, in combination with others." Later in this section, Marx addresses the differences between "free" buying and selling of labor-power under capitalism and direct relations of domination and servitude "in ancient times, in the Middle Ages, and in modern colonies" (452).
114. Nâzım Hikmet, *Kurtuluş Savaşı Destanı*, 7; Nâzım Hikmet, *Human Landscapes from My Country: An Epic Novel in Verse*, trans. Randy Blasing and Mutlu Konuk (New York: Persea, 2002), 150. For quotations, I cite both *Kurtuluş Savaşı Destanı* and *Human Landscapes from My Country*, into which the *Epic of National Liberation Movement* was incorporated. (For more on this incorporation, see note 109.) I have on occasion silently modified the quotations from the English translation.
115. Nâzım Hikmet, *Kurtuluş Savaşı Destanı*, 10, 11; *Human Landscapes*, 152–53, 154. For the quoted phrase "species-life," see Karl Marx, "Economic and Philosophic Manuscripts of 1844," in *Karl Marx and Frederick Engels: Collected Works*, vol. 3: *Marx and Engels 1843–1844* (London: Lawrence and Wishart, 2010), 275.
116. For the quoted phrases from Marx, see Marx, "Economic and Philosophic Manuscripts of 1844," 275–76.
117. Nâzım Hikmet, *Kurtuluş Savaşı Destanı*, 60–61, 64; *Human Landscapes*, 186, 190.
118. Nâzım Hikmet, *Kurtuluş Savaşı Destanı*, 75.
119. See Frantz Fanon, "On National Culture," in *The Wretched of the Earth*, trans. Richard Philcox (New York: Grove Press, 2004), 167–68.
120. For the quoted phrase, see Marx, "Economic and Philosophic Manuscripts of 1844," 276. See also Erkan Irmak, *Kayıp Destan'ın İzinde: "Kuvâyi Milliye" ve "Memleketimden İnsan Manzaraları" 'nda Milliyetçilik, Propaganda ve İdeoloji* (Istanbul: İletişim, 2011), 43–115, which treats the epic as a "frozen" work of propaganda celebrating Mustafa Kemal. Whereas Irmak observes a notable difference between *Epic of National Liberation Movement* and *Human Landscapes*, I argue in the chapter text that Nâzım's decisive break with the Kemalist national episteme is best registered by his final novel *Life's Good, Brother*.
121. Nâzım Hikmet, *Kurtuluş Savaşı Destanı*, 17, 75.
122. Nâzım Hikmet, *Kurtuluş Savaşı Destanı*, 28; *Human Landscapes*, 157.
123. Gazi Mustafa Kemal, *Nutuk*, 413–14; *A Speech*, 401–3. Mustafa Kemal also misrepresented Nâzım Bey, one of the founders of the Green Army Association and People's Communist Party of Turkey, as a foreign agent (*Nutuk*, 439–40; *A Speech*, 428).
124. The reference to the missing "story of Mustafa Suphi and his comrades" in *Human Landscapes* (175) registers Nâzım's self-censorship. For the commemorative book on Suphi, see *28–29 Kanun-i Sani 1921: Karadeniz Kıyılarında Parçalanan Mustafa Suphi ve Yoldaşlarının İkinci Yıldönümleri* (Moscow: Kızıl Şark Matbaası, 1923).
125. For the quoted phrases, see Marx, *Grundrisse*, 460. Compare Marx's discussion of capital's "original accumulation" in *Grundrisse*, 459–60, and *Grundrisse*, part 2, 368–69.

1. THE TURKISH WAR OF INDEPENDENCE IN LITERATURE AND FILM

126. In the epic's sixth canto, Kâzım from Kartal, who had killed a traitorous translator during the War of Independence, is described as a dignified man who "didn't get any land or apartments... when the fighting ended." His itinerary registers the gap between the War of Independence and its failed republican aftermath (Nâzım Hikmet, *Kurtuluş Savaşı Destanı*, 56; *Human Landscapes*, 174).
127. Fahri Erdinç, *Kalkın Nazım'a Gidelim: Anılar* (Istanbul: Varlık, 1987), 25–26.
128. Nâzım Hikmet, *Kurtuluş Savaşı Destanı*, 71; *Human Landscapes*, 195.
129. Though Nâzım's poetics borrowed from Perso-Arabic literary genres of the past, he did not engage systematically with Islamic thought. Faik Bercâvi, who was imprisoned in Bursa with Nâzım during the 1930s, wrote in his memoirs that he showed Nâzım a manuscript draft of his book *Socialism in Islam* in 1937. Nâzım apparently responded jokingly: "Brother Faik, if I were a little mulla like you and knew Arabic, perhaps I'd write an epic about the birth and spread of Islam. But to be frank, these kinds of topics don't interest me very much." Bercâvi notes that at the Afro-Asian Writers' Congress in Cairo in 1962 Nâzım discussed Arab-Islamic socialisms in an interview with Fawzi Sulaiman. *Socialism in Islam* represents an important deviation from the secular "prejudice" of Turkish republican communism. See A. Faik Bercâvi, *İslâmda Sosyalizm* (Istanbul: Işık Basımevi, 1946); and for his memoirs, see A. Faik Bercâvi, *Nâzım'la 1933–1938 Yılları* (Istanbul: Adam Yayınları, 1995), 82.
130. On the history of the Yön-Devrim movement, see Gökhan Atılgan, *Kemalizm ile Marksizm Arasında Geleneksel Aydınlar: Yön-Devrim Hareketi* (Istanbul: Yordam, 2008); and Özgür Mutlu Ulus, *The Army and the Radical Left in Turkey: Military Coups, Socialist Revolution, and Kemalism* (London: I. B. Tauris, 2011), 20–42.
131. On Nâzım's radio journalism between 1958 and 1963, see the collection Nâzım Hikmet, *Bizim Radyoda Nâzım Hikmet*, ed. Anjel Açıkgöz (Istanbul: TÜSTAV, 2002).
132. Nâzım Hikmet, "Asya, Afrika Yazarları Toplantısı Konuşması" (1958), *Yarına Doğru*, no. 8 (June 1974): 5.
133. Mehmet Perinçek, "Bilinmeyen Yazıları ve Belgelerle Nâzım Hikmet'in Orta Asya Seyahati," *Toplumsal Tarih*, no. 281 (May 2017): 72.
134. For a critical explication of the symbiotic relationship between Marxism and Kemalism, see the contributions in Levent Cinemre and Ruşen Çakır, eds., *Sol Kemalizme Bakıyor: Röportaj* (Istanbul: Metis, 1991).
135. Djagalov, *From Internationalism to Postcolonialism*, 113.
136. On condensation and displacement, see Sigmund Freud, *The Interpretation of Dreams*, trans. James Strachey (New York: Avon, 1998), 311–44.
137. Nâzım Hikmet, *Yaşamak Güzel Şeydir Kardeşim: Roman* (Sofia, Bulgaria: Narodna prosveta, 1964), 39–40; Nâzım Hikmet, *Life's Good, Brother: A Novel*, trans. Mutlu Konuk Blasing (New York: Persea, 2013), 44.
138. See, for example, Nâzım Hikmet, *Yaşamak Güzel Şeydir*, 45–55, 56–63; *Life's Good*, 48–63, 65–74.
139. Akal, *Moskova-Ankara-Londra Üçgeninde*, 97.
140. Nâzım Hikmet, *Yaşamak Güzel Şeydir*, 51; *Life's Good*, 58.
141. Nâzım Hikmet, *Kurtuluş Savaşı Destanı*, 69.
142. Nâzım Hikmet, *Yaşamak Güzel Şeydir*, 48; *Life's Good*, 55.
143. Nâzım Hikmet, *Yaşamak Güzel Şeydir*, 47, 54; *Life's Good*, 53, 62.
144. Marx, *Capital*, 1:916; Marx, *Das Kapital*, 1:601.

145. Gül Bilge Han, "Nâzım Hikmet's Afro-Asian Solidarities," *Safundi* 19, no. 3 (2018): 284–305, https://doi.org/10.1080/17533171.2018.1470814.
146. Gayatri Chakravorty Spivak, "Du Bois in the World: Pan-Africanism and Decolonization," *b20: an online journal*, December 2018, https://www.boundary2.org/2018/12/spivakondubois/#_ftnref7.
147. For an analysis of "affective temporal structures" in African "novels of revolution," see Monica Popescu, *At Penpoint: African Literatures, Postcolonial Studies, and the Cold War* (Durham, NC: Duke University Press, 2020), 107–44.
148. Pertev Naili Boratav et al., *Kültür Emperyalizmi Üstüne Konuşmalar* (Istanbul: Ataç Kitabevi, 1967), 64.
149. For an influential analysis of the relationship between Marxism and national liberation, see Anouar Abdel-Malek, "Marxism and National Liberation: A Statement of the Theoretical Problem," in *Social Dialectics*, vol. 2: *Nation and Revolution*, trans. Mike Gonzalez (London: Macmillan, 1981), 78–114.

2. VÂLÂ NUREDDIN'S COMIC MATERIALISM AND THE SEXUAL REVOLUTION

1. Nâzım Hikmet, "Sen," in *Gece Gelen Telgraf* (Istanbul: Muallîm Ahmet Halit Kütüphanesi, 1932), 63.
2. Sources consulted for Vâlâ's biography include Vâlâ Nureddin [pseud. Vâ-nû], *Bu Dünyadan Nâzım Geçti* (1965; reprint, Istanbul: Cem Yayınevi, 1980) (subsequent citations of works by Vâlâ Nureddin under the pseudonym Vâ-nû give just "Vâ-nû" for the author's name); Müzehher Vâ-nû, *Bir Dönemin Tanıklığı*, 2nd ed. (Istanbul: Sosyal Yayınlar, 1997); Sündüs Nureddin, "Ağabeyime ait biografik malûmat," 1968, IISH, Vâlâ Nureddin Papers, no. 88; and Selçuk Atay, *Vâlâ Nurettin Vâ-nû: İnsan ve Eser* (Ankara: Etkin Yayınevi, 2012). See also the newspaper columns by Vâlâ: "Seyahat Mektupları: Berut'ta Eski Hatıralarım," *Akşam*, July 13, 1930, 3; "Nasıl Muharrir Oldum?," *Akşam*, November 1, 1932, 9; and "Anadoluda Seyahat," *Akşam*, November 7, 1932, 9.
3. On Vâlâ's first marriage, see Vâ-nû, *Bu Dünyadan Nâzım Geçti*, 329. See also Yıldız Sertel, *Ardımdaki Yıllar* (Istanbul: İletişim, 2001), 259; and Atay, *Vâlâ Nurettin*, 380–81.
4. At KUTV, Vâlâ served as a member of the troika leading the Turkish group. He apparently had a conflict with another Turkish student, Server Hayreddin, for which the latter was punished and sent into exile. The events surrounding Server Hayreddin's exile and eventual death seem to have divided the Turkish students at KUTV into two camps; see Erden Akbulut and Mete Tunçay, *İstanbul Komünist Grubu'ndan (Aydınlık Çevresi) Türkiye Komünist Partisi'ne, 1919–1926*, 3 vols. (Istanbul: TÜSTAV, 2012–2013), 2:278, 280–82, 284, 288–92. The archival records show that Vâlâ distanced himself from the party by the spring of 1926. In a letter dated May 26, 1926, the TKP leader Şefik Hüsnü described Vâlâ as a member of an oppositional group led by Ahmet Cevad; see Akbulut and Tunçay, *İstanbul Komünist Grubu'ndan*, 3:185.
5. Published from 1918 to the present, *Akşam* is one of the oldest newspapers in Turkey. Though it was supportive of Mustafa Kemal's Republican People's Party

2. VÂLÂ NUREDDIN'S COMIC MATERIALISM

during the republican period, it refused to publish editorials overtly critical of the Democratic Party (Demokrat Partisi) when the latter assumed power in 1950. After the death of its founding editor, Necmettin Sadak, in 1953, *Akşam* became a lifestyle and gossip paper. Vâlâ worked for *Akşam* in 1927–1933, 1937–1954, and 1957–1958. On the history of this newspaper, see Nurhan Kavaklı, *Bir Gazetenin Tarihi: "Akşam"* (Istanbul: Yapı Kredi Yayınları, 2005).

6. See Hikmet Feridun's interview of Şükûfe Nihal in "Edebiyatımız Ne Halde?," *Akşam*, April 23, 1929, 1, and of Necip Fazıl in "Edebiyatımız Ne Halde?," *Akşam*, May 7, 1929, 2.

7. In his book review of *Türk Dili İçin* (For the Turkish language), an influential philological study by the Kazan Tatar émigré Sadri Maksudi, Vâlâ rejected Maksudi's "dream" of unification of different Turkic language; see Vâ-nû, "Yeni Neşriyat: 'Türk Dili İçin' İsmindeki Kıymetli Eser," *Akşam*, March 6, 1931, 7. See also his columns in *Akşam* rejecting the proposals to substitute Tatar words for centuries-old Arabic loanwords (for example, *ötkünç* for *hikâye*, "story"): Vâ-nû, "Hariçten Gazel Memnudur!," *Akşam*, March 31, 1931, ; "'Su' Kelimesini Türkçeden Kovmalı mı?" *Akşam*, April 1, 1931, 3; "Tatar Irktaşlarımıza Bir Tavsiye," *Akşam*, April 2, 1931, 3.

Vâlâ changed his position in the aftermath of the First Language Congress in October 1932, calling for the linguistic and cultural unity of Turkic peoples across the world. See Vâ-nû, "Türkiye Haricindeki Irkdaşlarımızla Hars Münasebeti," *Akşam*, October 13, 1932, 3. The contradictions of his linguistic writings did not go unnoticed; see Vâ-nû, "Ben Dönek Değilim," *Akşam*, October 17, 1932, 3–4, for his polemic against the Turkish racist ideologue Nihal Atsız.

8. Tuncay Birkan, "Vâ-nû: Bir Fıkracının Edebiyatçı Olarak Portresi," in Vâ-nû, *Fikir ve Sanat Âlemimize Bu Hürriyet Kâfi Değildir*, ed. Tuncay Birkan (Istanbul: Can, 2021), 28. See also Vâ-nû, *Asri Rüyalar, Fetiş Rejimler*, ed. Tuncay Birkan (Istanbul: Can, 2021).

9. Vâlâ's translations from European literatures included Boccaccio's *Decameron*; Zoltán Ambrus's version of the Griselda tale, *La vraie patience de Grisélidis*; Joseph Conrad's "The Informer"; and E. T. A. Hoffmann's "Der Sandmann," to name only a few. Vâlâ most likely translated Boccaccio and Ambrus from French translations (instead of from the respective Italian and Hungarian originals). There is relatively little critical scholarship on him. An important exception is Atay, *Vâlâ Nurettin*, which includes a comprehensive bibliography.

10. Vâ-nû, "Adaptasyon Korkusu," *Akşam*, May 8, 1929, 3.

11. Vâ-nû, preface to *Benim ve Onların Hikâyeleri* (Istanbul: Resimli Ay, 1936), 3.

12. Vâ-nû, "Adaptasyon," *Akşam*, April 23, 1929, 3.

13. Vâ-nû, "Biz Klasiğiz Galiba," *Akşam*, June 14, 1929, 3. For other columns on Pushkin, see Vâ-nû, "Bir Kitap Kapanırken," *Akşam*, June 3, 1930, 3; and Vâ-nû, "Istanbul Şivesi mi? 'Yüksek Türkçe' mi?," *Akşam*, December 28, 1930, 3.

14. Vâlâ wrote proudly that among the group of writers and journalists invited (which included Yunus Nadi, Ruşen Eşref, and Yakup Kadri), he was the only one able to communicate with Gorky in Russian (that is, without an interpreter). See Vâ-nû, "Maksim Gorki ile Mülâkat," *Akşam*, May 13, 1932, 3.

15. See "Belge 38: *Orak Çekiç*'in Oniki Sayısı," in Mete Tunçay, *Türkiye'de Sol Akımlar (1925–1936)*, vol. 2 (Istanbul: İletişim, 2009), 523.

2. VÂLÂ NUREDDIN'S COMIC MATERIALISM

16. Vâ-nû, "Sağaaa Bak!!!," *Akşam*, December 30, 1930, 3, emphasis in original. On December 23, 1930, a group of young dervishes organized an uprising in the town of Menemen to restore the caliphate, beheading Lieutenant Mustafa Fehmi Kubilay, who had been deployed to suppress the rebellion.
17. For instance, Vâlâ rationalized the regime of private property as a historical necessity, supporting investments in construction, trade, and industrialization to generate capital and develop the nation. See Vâ-nû, "Haspaya Yakışır," *Akşam*, June 28, 1931, 3; and Vâ-nû, "'Pauperist' Zihniyeti," *Akşam*, June 29, 1931, 3.
18. On Vâlâ's exile to Konya, see M. Vâ-nû, *Bir Dönemin Tanıklığı*, 13–26.
19. Richard Stites, *The Women's Liberation Movement in Russia: Feminism, Nihilism, and Bolshevism, 1860–1930* (Princeton, NJ: Princeton University Press, 1990).
20. Vâlâ's first published book was a collection of short stories by Averchenko about love relationships translated into Turkish and published in 1927. See Arkady Averchenko, *Aşk Nizamnamesinin Yedi Maddesi*, trans. Vâlâ Nureddin [pseud. Vâ-nû] (Istanbul: Cumhuriyet Matbaası, 1927). Averchenko (1881–1925) left Soviet Russia in 1920 and lived in Istanbul between 1920 and 1922 before moving to Prague. The former communist Hasan Âli Ediz, who emerged as a prolific translator of Russian and Soviet literatures during the late 1930s, also published a collection of translations of Averchenko's short stories entitled *Sahtekârsız Memleket* (Country without a counterfeiter) in 1955. The frame stories in this collection thematized the economic downturn in revolutionary Russia, offering an indirect satirical critique of the economic crises in Turkey in 1946 and 1954. See Arkady Averchenko, *Sahtekârsız Memleket*, trans. Hasan Âli Ediz (Istanbul: Akbaba, [1955]).
21. Nâzım's translations were published under the pseudonym "Ben" or "I." Ediz also published Turkish translations of short stories by Zoshchenko in 1941 and 1958; for a collection including all of his Zoshchenko translations, see Mikhail Zoshchenko, *Çarın Çizmeleri*, trans. Hasan Âli Ediz ([Istanbul]: Altın Kitaplar, 1970). Unaware that Vâlâ first introduced Zoshchenko to Turkish readers, most readers of Zoshchenko in contemporary Turkey would compare the Russian writer to the great Turkish humorist Aziz Nesin. For Nesin's discussion of Zoshchenko's legacy, see Aziz Nesin, "*Çarın Çizmeleri*'nin Yayını Dolayısıyla Zoşçenko Olayından Alınacak Ders," in *Sanat Yazıları: Yazılar* (Istanbul: Nesin Yayınevi, 2011), 333–36.
22. Şerif Mardin, "Super Westernization in Urban Life in the Ottoman Empire in the Last Quarter of the Nineteenth Century," in *Turkey: Geographical and Social Perspectives*, ed. Peter Benedict, Erol Tümertekin, and Fatma Mansur (Leiden, Netherlands: Brill, 1974), 403–46.
23. On the Turkish tradition of literary humor, see Aziz Nesin, *Cumhuriyet Döneminde Türk Mizahı: Düzyazı* (Istanbul: Akbaba Yayınları, 1973); Ferit Öngören, *Cumhuriyet Dönemi Türk Mizahı ve Hicvi (1923–1983)* (Ankara: Türkiye İş Bankası Kültür Yayınları, 1983); and Levent Cantek and Levent Gönenç, *Muhalefet Defteri: Türkiye'de Mizah Dergileri ve Karikatür* (Istanbul: Yapı Kredi Yayınları, 2017).
24. Vâ-nû, "Edebî Mevzular," *Akşam*, February 16, 1929, 3.
25. On Zoshchenko's biography and the complex history of the reception of his writings from the 1920s to the present, see Linda Hart Scatton, *Mikhail Zoshchenko: Evolution of a Writer* (Cambridge: Cambridge University Press, 1993); and

Gregory Carleton, *The Politics of Reception: Cultural Constructions of Mikhail Zoshchenko* (Evanston, IL: Northwestern University Press, 1998).

26. On the liberal, anti-Bolshevik humor of *Satirikon / Novyi Satirikon* that lasted from 1908 to 1918, see Lesley Milne, "*Novyi Satirikon*, 1914–1918: The Patriotic Laughter of the Russian Liberal Intelligentsia During the First World War and the Revolution," *Slavonic and East European Review* 84, no. 4 (2006): 639–65. The magazine writers' satirical treatment of topical events established an important precedent for Zoshchenko.
27. On this point, see Cathy Popkin, *The Pragmatics of Insignificance: Chekhov, Zoshchenko, Gogol* (Stanford, CA: Stanford University Press, 1993), 58–59. For a useful contextualization of Zoshchenko's writings in relation to both Russian and Western theories of *skaz*, see Jeremy Hicks, *Mikhail Zoshchenko and the Poetics of Skaz* (Nottingham, U.K.: Astra Press, 2000).
28. Serguei Alex. [sic] Oushakine, "'Red Laughter': On Refined Weapons of Soviet Jesters," *Social Research* 79, no. 1 (2012): 205.
29. On Nâzım's meeting with Zoshchenko, see Vera Tuliakova-Khikmet, *Poslednii razgovor s Nazymom* (Moscow: Vremia, 2009), 53–62. The Turkish communist Faik Bercâvi wrote in his memoirs that he cotranslated Zoshchenko's short stories with Nâzım when the two were inmates in the Bursa prison in 1933–1934; see A. Faik Bercâvi, *Nâzım'la 1933–1938 Yılları* (Istanbul: Adam Yayınları, 1995), 73–74. These translations apparently appeared in the daily *Last Post* (*Son Posta*) in 1936 (five years after the *Yeni Gün* ones), though they are not included in the contemporary Adam and YKY editions of Nâzım's collected works.
30. Vâ-nû, "Kelimecilikten Tabirciliğe," *Akşam*, November 30, 1929, 3.
31. For the Russian originals of Zoshchenko's short stories cited in this section, see Mikhail Zoshchenko, *Sobranie sochinenii*, vol. 1: *Rasskazy i fel'etony* (Moscow: TERRA, 1994). For "Dushevnaia prostota," see *Sobranie sochinenii*, 1:392–93.
32. For Nâzım's translations of Zoshchenko's stories cited in this section, see Mikhail Zoshchenko, *Çeviri Hikayeler*, trans. Nâzım Hikmet (Istanbul: Adam, 1987). For "Samimiyet," see *Çeviri Hikayeler*, 66–67.
33. Popkin, *The Pragmatics of Insignificance*, 67–68.
34. In the Russian original, Ivanonich is eventually allowed admittance by a second cloak attendant, but he rejects this offer because he has missed most of the play. See Mikhail Zoshchenko, "Melkii sluchai," in *Sobranie sochinenii*, 1:370–73; and Mikhail Zoshchenko, "Ehemmiyetsiz Bir Vaka," in *Çeviri Hikayeler*, 68–70.
35. Popkin, *The Pragmatics of Insignificance*, 71.
36. Zoshchenko, "Ehemmiyetsiz Bir Vaka," trans. Nâzım Hikmet, 70.
37. On the little man as an icon in modern Turkish literature, see Ahmet Oktay, *Cumhuriyet Dönemi Edebiyatı, 1923–1950* (Ankara: Etiş, 1993), 123–25. Turkish literary historians consider the short story writer Sait Faik as the initiator and popularizer of this development.
38. On the *meddah* tradition, see Özdemir Nutku, "On *Aşıks* (Tale Singers) and *Meddahs* (Story Tellers)," in *The Traditional Turkish Theater*, ed. Mevlüt Özhan (Ankara: Turkish Ministry of Culture Publications, 1999), 53–68.
39. Mikhail Zoshchenko, "İntizam Avdet Etti," trans. Vâla Nureddin [pseud. Hikâyeci], *Akşam*, August 19, 1929, 6; Mikhail Zoshchenko, "Shapka," in *Sobranie sochinenii*, 1:408.

2. VÂLÂ NUREDDIN'S COMIC MATERIALISM

40. Mikhail Zoshchenko, "Heygidi Muallim," trans. Vâlâ Nureddin [pseud. Hikâyeci], *Akşam*, August 6, 1929, 6; Mikhail Zoshchenko, "Uchitel'," in *Sobranie sochinenii*, 1:123.
41. Zoshchenko, "Heygidi Muallim."
42. Mikhail Zoshchenko, "Ümmîler," trans. Vâlâ Nureddin [pseud. Hikâyeci], *Akşam*, August 12, 1929, 6; Mikhail Zoshchenko, "Tuman," in *Sobranie sochinenii*, 1:291–92; Mikhail Zoshchenko, "Falcı," trans. Vâlâ Nureddin [pseud. Hikâyeci], *Akşam*, August 11, 1929, 6.
43. Zoshchenko, "Shapka," in *Sobranie sochinenii*, 1:409.
44. Popkin, *The Pragmatics of Insignificance*, 84.
45. Zoshchenko, "İntizam Avdet Etti," 6.
46. Bülent Somay, *The Psychopolitics of the Oriental Father: Between Omnipotence and Emasculation* (New York: Palgrave Macmillan, 2014), 155.
47. See Levent Cantek, *"Markopaşa": Bir Mizah ve Muhalefet Efsanesi* (Istanbul: İletişim, 2001).
48. Rossen Djagalov, *From Internationalism to Postcolonialism: Literature and Cinema Between the Second and the Third Worlds* (Montreal: McGill-Queen's University Press, 2020), 109.
49. On the official discourse on "New Russia," see the introduction.
50. Alenka Zupančič, *The Odd One In: On Comedy* (Cambridge, MA: MIT Press, 2008).
51. See Nâzım Hikmet, *Life's Good, Brother: A Novel*, trans. Mutlu Konuk Blasing (New York: Persea, 2013), 28–29; and Vâ-nû, *Bu Dünyadan Nâzım Geçti*, 196.
52. Fahri Erdinç, *Kalkın Nazım'a Gidelim: Anılar* (Istanbul: Varlık, 1987), 125, 127.
53. On the social transformation of the Ottoman Turkish family, see Alan Duben and Cem Behar, *Istanbul Households: Marriage, Family, and Fertility 1880–1940* (Cambridge: Cambridge University Press, 1991). For an authoritative account of the absence of the Ottoman father in Tanzimat literature, see Jale Parla, *Babalar ve Oğullar: Tanzimat Romanının Epistemolojik Temelleri* (Istanbul: İletişim, 1990).
54. The Bolshevik feminist Aleksandra Kollontai's writings and novels (about which I say more in chapter 3) were influential in shaping the Soviet discourse on love and sex. For a discussion of the new sexual ethos among the youth, see Stites, *The Women's Liberation Movement in Russia*; and Gregory Carleton, *Sexual Revolution in Bolshevik Russia* (Pittsburgh, PA: University of Pittsburgh Press, 2005).
55. Eliot Borenstein, *Men Without Women: Masculinity and Revolution in Russian Fiction, 1917–1929* (Durham, NC: Duke University Press, 2000), 7, 18.
56. Vâ-nû, "Seyahat Mektupları: Milli Ahlâklar [Fransa'da ve Rusya'da Aşk]," *Akşam*, September 26, 1930, 3; and Vâ-nû, *Bu Dünyadan Nâzım Geçti*, 314–15.
57. See note 3.
58. For Voltaire's account, see Voltaire, *Histoire de Charles XII, roi de Suede*, rev. ed. (London, 1773), 218–20, Gale, Eighteenth Century Collections Online, link.gale.com/apps/doc/CB0132733556/ECCO?u=psucic&sid=bookmark-ECCO&xid=037cbf6f&pg=1; and Voltaire, *History of Charles XII, King of Sweden*, trans. Winifred Todhunter (London: J. M. Dent, 1912), 220–22. For the eighteenth-century official Ottoman court historian Raşid's account of the same events, see Râşid Mehmed Efendi and Çelebizâde İsmaîl Âsım Efendi, *Târih-i Râşid ve Zeyli*, vol. 2, ed. Abdülkadir Özcan et al. (Istanbul: Klasik, 2013), 860.

2. VÂLÂ NUREDDIN'S COMIC MATERIALISM

59. See Doğan Gürpınar, "Double Discourses and Romantic Ottomanism: The Ottoman Empire as a 'Foreign Country,'" *International Journal of Turkish Studies* 17, nos. 1–2 (2011): 44. For the relevant passage in *Baltacı Mehmed Pasha and Peter the Great*, see Ahmet Refik, *Baltacı Mehmed Paşa ve Büyük Petro, 1711–1911* (Istanbul: Matbaa-i Hayriye ve Şürekâsı, 1327 [1911]), 78. Ahmet Refik's rendering of the events is based on his misquotation of a phrase from the following passage of Voltaire's *Histoire de Charles XII*: "The Vice-Chancellor [of Peter the Great] wrote a letter to the Grand Vizir in his master's name, which the Czarina, in spite of the Emperor's prohibition, carried into the tent to him, and after many prayers, tears and argument [*ayant, après bien des priéres, des conteftations & des larmes, obtenu qu'il la fignât*] she prevailed on him to sign it; she then took all her money, all her jewels and valuables, and what she could borrow from the generals, and having collected by this means a considerable present, she sent it with the Czar's letter to Osman Aga, lieutenant to the Grand Vizir" (*History of Charles XII*, 222; *Histoire de Charles XII*, 218).

    Ahmet Refik renders "ayant, après bien des priéres, des conteftations & des larmes, obtenu qu'il la fignât" as "ricalar ve niyazlar, tebessümler ve gözyaşlarıyla ikna ederek muahedeye imza etmeye razı ettikten sonra" (after persuading him to sign the treaty with pleas and prayers, smiles and tears). The scandal of Ahmet Refik's translation is that he inserts it into a description of Catherine going to Baltacı's tent to "persuade him to sign the treaty with pleas and prayers, smiles and tears." No such act appears in Voltaire's text, where the clause quoted refers to an exchange between Catherine and Peter the Great.

60. See Nizamettin Nazif, *Kara Davud*, vol. 1 (Istanbul: Türk Matbaası, 1928), 2; and Vâ-nû, *Baltacı ile Katerina* (Istanbul: Kitaphane-i Hilmi, 1928), 2. Subsequent page citations to this edition of *Baltacı ile Katerina* are given parenthetically in the text.

61. Vâ-nû, "Edebî Mevzular." Vâlâ borrowed the quoted phrase from his contemporary Aka Gündüz.

62. See Ahmet Haşim, "*Baltacı ile Katerina*," in *Bütün Eserleri*, vol. 2: *Bize Göre/İkdam'daki Diğer Yazıları*, ed. İnci Enginün and Zeynep Kerman (Istanbul: Dergâh, 1991), 184.

63. Foreign sound films began to be screened in Turkey in 1929. The first domestic sound film was *Istanbul Sokaklarında* (In the streets of Istanbul, 1931) by Muhsin Ertuğrul. Turkish film critics (such as Nezih Erdoğan and Canan Balan) productively discuss works of modern Turkish literature to examine the new "techniques of the observer" in Turkey, though they seem to overlook Vâlâ's *Baltacı and Catherine*.

64. On Wells's influence on Russian futurists, see Anindita Banerjee, *We Modern People: Science Fiction and the Making of Russian Modernity* (Middletown, CT: Wesleyan University Press, 2013), 66–80. Vâlâ's translations of Wells's short stories "In the Avu Observatory" and "The Valley of Spiders" appeared in *Akşam* during this period. See H. G. Wells, "Rasathanede Bir Vak'a," trans. Vâlâ Nureddin [pseud. Hikâyeci], *Akşam*, January 18, 1929, 6; and H. G. Wells, "Örümceklerin Hücumu," trans. Vâlâ Nureddin [pseud. Hikâyeci], *Akşam*, January 7, 1931, 9.

65. In his memoirs, Vâlâ describes how the TKP seal was stolen from his and Nâzım's belongings in a hotel room in Batumi shortly after their arrival there. Both

2. VÂLÂ NUREDDIN'S COMIC MATERIALISM

Nâzım and Vâlâ were detained and interrogated by Cheka in 1922 (*Bu Dünyadan Nâzım Geçti*, 215–17).

66. "All the organs of all the subjects, all the eyes, all the mouths, all the penises, all the vaginas, all the ears, and all the anuses become attached to the full body of the despot, as though to the peacock's tail of a royal train," write Deleuze and Guattari in their account of the despot; see Gilles Deleuze and Félix Guattari, *Anti-Oedipus: Capitalism and Schizophrenia*, trans. Robert Hurley, Mark Seem, and Helen R. Lane (Minneapolis: University of Minnesota Press, 2000), 210. In *The Psychopolitics of the Oriental Father*, Somay offers a valuable Marxist-Lacanian analysis of the father figure in Ottoman and modern Turkish cultures, including a nuanced consideration of the ways its role exceeds both Freud's and Lacan's approaches. The foundational myths of ancient Turkic and Ottoman cultures "*do not have a Brothers' pact conspiring for patricide as a starting point for civilisation*," Somay observes, but this does not mean that psychoanalytic theory is irrelevant. "The original Freudian reading of the tale of Oedipus," Somay continues, "has nothing to do with patricide at all, except as a passing reference, its necessary and sufficient condition being having been born to, and raised by, a mother submitting to male domination, to the phallic function. This condition is fulfilled on both sides of the East/West divide, since male domination is more primal than the fundamental difference between Greco-Roman and Asiatic/Middle Eastern civilizations" (52, 53, emphasis in original).

67. On sublimation as the elevation of the object "to the dignity of the Thing," see Jacques Lacan, *The Seminar of Jacques Lacan: The Ethics of Psychoanalysis, 1959–1960, Book VII*, ed. Jacques-Alain Miller, trans. Dennis Porter (New York: Norton, 1992), 112. For a useful explication of Lacan's concept of sublimation, see Marc de Kesel, *Eros and Ethics: Reading Jacques Lacan's Seminar VII*, trans. Sigi Jöttkandt (Albany: State University of New York Press, 2009), 163–203.

68. On courtly love as a practice of aesthetic sublimation, see Lacan, *The Seminar of Jacques Lacan: Book VII*, 139–54. Baltacı's knightly subservience to masochistic, "whorish" Catherine is a parodic allusion to this tradition, in which the sublimated love object is emptied of her personhood and elevated to the status of an "extimate" Thing.

69. The narrator praises the education Baltacı received in the Ottoman palace school during his youth. In an earlier passage, the narrator compares himself with his "rude and fat friend, [Nik], from the Balkans," who does not know how to treat a woman respectfully. Mentioning his privileged background as the son of an Ottoman governor, the narrator writes: "I was taught good manners [*konak terbiyesi*] during my childhood" (Vâ-nû, *Baltacı ile Katerina*, 144).

70. Zupančič, *The Odd One In*, 122.

71. Lacan, *The Seminar of Jacques Lacan: Book VII*, 307.

72. On *point de capiton*, or "quilting point," see Jacques Lacan, "The Subversion of the Subject and the Dialectic of Desire in the Freudian Unconscious," in *Écrits: The First Complete Edition in English*, trans. Bruce Fink in collaboration with Héloïse Fink and Russell Grigg (New York: Norton, 2006), 681. It is the point at which "the signifier stops the otherwise indefinite sliding of signification" (681), creating the necessary illusion of a stable meaningfulness.

2. VÂLÂ NUREDDIN'S COMIC MATERIALISM

73. On Ottoman satire, see Öngören, *Cumhuriyet Dönemi Türk Mizahı ve Hicvi*, 137–60.
74. Zupančič's work, which draws on Hegel, Freud, and Lacan, is especially useful to me in the precision of its analysis of the comic in relation to the foundational problematic of phallocentrism as Vâlâ thematized it. Though a reader of this chapter might also recall Mikhail Bakhtin's writings on revolution and the obscene, the fact is that Vâlâ's novel cannot be read as a carnivalesque celebration of bodily becoming and renewal in the tradition of the pagan and medieval Christian festival. More usefully and more appropriately for my purposes here, Zupančič's focus is on ancient Greek and modern French comedy. The associated comic devices of the double and accelerated exaggeration appeared in traditional Ottoman modes of performance, including the Karagöz shadow theater and the *ortaoyunu*, and, in fact, some of the literary works central to Zupančič's analysis, such as the comedies of Molière, were among the first to be translated into Turkish during the nineteenth century. On Karagöz theater, see Metin And, *Karagöz: Turkish Shadow Theatre* (Ankara: Dost Yayınları, 1975).
75. Zupančič, *The Odd One In*, 91, 92.
76. Zupančič, *The Odd One In*, 132, emphasis in original.
77. Zupančič, *The Odd One In*, 59.
78. Zupančič, *The Odd One In*, 56.
79. Zupančič, *The Odd One In*, 204.
80. For a valuable explication of repetition in primary repression and the game of *fort-da*, see Zupančič, *The Odd One In*, 161–73. Compare Henri Bergson's discussion of the comic as "something mechanical encrusted on the living" in *Laughter: An Essay on the Meaning of the Comic*, trans. Cloudesley Brereton and Fred Rothwell (New York: Macmillan, 1914), 37. Rejecting the privilege Bergson gave to vital force over mechanized repetition, both Zupančič and Vâlâ embrace the irreducibility of the comic dimension of human subjectivity.
81. Zupančič, *The Odd One In*, 59. On the privileging of irony, see Charles Baudelaire, "On the Essence of Laughter (and, in General on the Comic in the Plastic Arts)," in *The Painter of Modern Life and Other Essays*, ed. and trans. Jonathan Mayne (London: Phaidon, 1964), 147–65.
82. Vâlâ's imagination here captures some aspects of Turkish republican psychopolitics. For an analysis of Mustafa Kemal as "the primordial father reborn," see Somay, *The Psychopolitics of the Oriental Father*, 139–57.
83. Parla, *Babalar ve Oğullar*, 19–20.
84. Compare this representation with Soviet literature of the 1920s discussed in Borenstein, *Men Without Women*.
85. Jacques Lacan, "Guiding Remarks for a Convention on Female Sexuality," in *Écrits*, 615. On Lacan's understanding of masochism and sadism as (structurally) male perversion, see Bruce Fink, "Perversion," in *Perversion and the Social Relation*, ed. Molly Anne Rothenberg, Dennis A. Foster, and Slavoj Žižek (Durham, NC: Duke University Press, 2003), 38–67. Spelling *perversion* as "père-version" in French (meaning "a turn or appeal to the father"), Lacan suggests that the term should not be used to classify "deviant" sexual behavior but rather to describe a *"staging or making believe regarding the paternal function"*; the pervert who has not worked through the Oedipal complex seeks to enact the (prohibitive) paternal

2. VÂLÂ NUREDDIN'S COMIC MATERIALISM

law so as to set limits to an overbearing jouissance (Fink, "Perversion," 44, emphasis in original).
86. Lacan quoted in Zupančič, *The Odd One In*, 204–5. For the original citation, see Jacques Lacan, "Knowledge and Truth," in *The Seminar of Jacques Lacan: On Feminine Sexuality, the Limits of Love, and Knowledge, Book XX, Encore 1972–1973*, ed. Jacques-Alain Miller, trans. Bruce Fink (New York: Norton, 1999), 94.
87. For example, see Nâzım's constructivist poem "To Become a Machine" ("Makinalaşmak," 1923), in which he describes sexual coupling with a machine: "I'm going mad / to take each dynamo / under me! My salivary tongue is licking the copper wires." His poem "Regarding Art" ("San'at Telakkisi," 1929), meanwhile, considers revolutionary production as superior to human sexual reproduction. For these poems, see Nâzım Hikmet, *835 Satır* (Istanbul: Muallim Ahmet Halit Kitaphanesi, 1929), 15–16, 29–30.
88. In the aftermath of the Second Constitutional Revolution of 1908 in the Ottoman Empire, publication of a new kind of erotic literature grew significantly. In their study of Ottoman court poetry as well as of Karagöz shadow theater, dream interpretation, and medical and sexual treatises, including *bâhnâme*s (books of coitus/lust), cultural historians such as Walter Andrews, Mehmet Kalpaklı, Selim Kuru, and Dror Ze'evi have demonstrated the richness and variegation of erotic and sexual literature in the Ottoman Empire before the nineteenth-century Tanzimat era. The nineteenth century marked a shift to a binary model of sexuality that represented same-sex relations as a disease. The forms and genres of erotic literature were transformed during this period as translations and adaptations of modern European works were popularized. On Ottoman discourses, see Walter G. Andrews and Mehmet Kalpaklı, *The Age of Beloveds: Love and the Beloved in Early-Modern Ottoman and European Culture and Society* (Durham, NC: Duke University Press, 2005); and Dror Ze'evi, *Producing Desire: Changing Sexual Discourse in the Ottoman Middle East, 1500–1900* (Berkeley: University of California Press, 2006). On the Second Constitutional period, see Irvin Cemil Schick, "Print Capitalism and Women's Sexual Agency in the Late Ottoman Empire," *Comparative Studies of South Asia, Africa, and the Middle East* 31, no. 1 (2011): 196–216; and Burcu Karahan, "Repressed in Translation: Representation of Female Sexuality in Ottoman Erotica," *Journal of Turkish Literature* 9 (2012): 30–45. Vâlâ's exaggerated use of the sadomasochistic theme seems to be inspired in part by Sabiha Zekeriya's writings during this period (discussed more later in this chapter).
89. Fatma Türe, *Facts and Fantasies: Images of Istanbul Women in the 1920s* (Tyne, U.K.: Cambridge Scholars, 2015). An important exception is a popular series titled *A Thousand and One Kisses* (*Bin Bir Buse*), whose editing was attributed to Mehmed Rauf. Published weekly in 1923 and 1924 as a twenty-four-page fascicle, each of the sixteen episodes included brief, humorous erotic tales about the sexual adventures of an affluent heterosexual westernized elite in Istanbul. See Ömer Türkoğlu, ed., *1923–24 İstanbul'undan Erotik Bir Dergi: "Bin Bir Buse,"* with an introduction by Irvin Cemil Schick (Istanbul: Kitap Yayınevi, 2005). Though the comic mode is used subversively in *Bin Bir Buse*, none of the stories thematize the Soviet context. Each chance encounter between different sexual partners generates a surprising (surplus) outcome in the stories, subverting the myth of unity in love, revealing sex to be a "missing link" or an impossible encounter.

90. Eric Naiman, *Sex in Public: The Incarnation of Early Soviet Ideology* (Princeton, NJ: Princeton University Press, 1997), esp. 59–63.
91. Naiman, *Sex in Public*, 63–64.
92. See Vâ-nû, "Ahlâk Telâkkilerindeki Müteharriklik," *Akşam*, June 21, 1931, 3–4. For a valuable critique of Vâlâ's biological essentialism as represented in his newspaper articles, see Aylin Özman, "Domesticated Souls: Vâlâ Nureddin (Vâ-Nû) on Womanhood," *Turkish Studies* 8, no. 1 (2007): 137–50; and Aylin Özman, "The Image of 'Woman' in Turkish Political and Social Thought: On the Implications of Social Constructionism and Biological Essentialism," *Turkish Studies* 11, no. 3 (2010): 445–64.

    Özman examines the contribution of Vâlâ's writings (mainly from the 1940s and 1950s) to republican discourse on gender and sex, though she does not account for their connection to Soviet Russia. Though I reach a similar conclusion about Vâlâ's gender essentialism, I follow a divergent path: in my view, Vâlâ's writings from the late 1920s and early 1930s held a promise on which they ultimately failed to deliver and must be grasped in their multidimensionality in this sense.
93. Eric L. Santner, *The Royal Remains: The People's Two Bodies and the Endgames of Sovereignty* (Chicago: University of Chicago Press, 2011), 81.
94. Vâ-nû, *Ebenin Hatıratı* (Istanbul: Kanaat Kütüphanesi, 1929), 59. For the book advertisement, see "Yeni Neşriyat," *Akşam*, October 22, 1929, 2. This novel was serialized in *Akşam* from February 12 to May 26, 1929, with an abridged and revised version published as a book later that year. Unless noted otherwise, I quote from the book version.
95. See the installments of *Ebenin Hatıratı* published in *Akşam* from April 16 to April 21, 1929.
96. Vâ-nû, "Edebiyatta Ahlâk," *Akşam*, March 4, 1929, 3.
97. Frances Lee Bernstein, *The Dictatorship of Sex: Lifestyle Advice for the Soviet Masses* (DeKalb: Northern Illinois University Press, 2007), 4.
98. Tricia Starks, *The Body Soviet: Propaganda, Hygiene, and the Revolutionary State* (Madison: University of Wisconsin Press, 2008), 135–61.
99. For the text of the law, see "Türk Kanunu medenisi," Kanun no. 743, February 17, 1926, *Türkiye Büyük Millet Meclisi Tutanak Dergisi*, https://www.tbmm.gov.tr/tutanaklar/KANUNLAR_KARARLAR/kanuntbmmc004/kanuntbmmc004/kanuntbmmc00400743.pdf. For an analysis of gender inequalities in the law, see Zehra F. Arat, "Kemalism and Turkish Women," *Women and Politics* 14, no. 4 (1994): 57–80. On the denial of Turkish women's sexuality, see Ayşe Kadıoğlu, "Cinselliğin İnkârı: Büyük Toplumsal Projelerin Nesnesi Olarak Türk Kadınları," in *75 Yılda Kadınlar ve Erkekler*, ed. A. B. Hacımirzaoğlu (Istanbul: Türk Tarih Vakfı Yayınları, 1998), 89–100.
100. For an extensive bibliography of popular sex-advice literature (including translations and pseudotranslations) published in Turkey from the late Ottoman period through the 1960s, see Müge Işıklar-Koçak, "Problematizing Translated Popular Texts on Women's Sexuality: A New Perspective on the Modernization Project in Turkey from 1931 to 1959," PhD diss., Istanbul Bosphorus University, 2007, 360–413.
101. Vâ-nû, "Ahlâk Telâkkilerindeki Müteharriklik."

2. VÂLÂ NUREDDIN'S COMIC MATERIALISM

102. For accounts of her life, see Sabiha Sertel, *Roman Gibi (Anılar)* (Istanbul: Ant Yayınları, 1969); and Yıldız Sertel, *Annem: Sabiha Sertel Kimdi Neler Yazdı* (Istanbul: Yapı Kredi Yayınları, 1994). Sabiha's TKP membership is referenced in a secret report dated 1943 in Sabiha's personal file at the Russian State Archive of Socio-Political History based on information provided by Marat (alias for İsmail Bilen): "She drew our attention as a sympathizer of our party after her return to Turkey [from the United States] and was admitted into the TKP ranks in 1935." See Belov, "İlmühaber," January 6, 1943, TÜSTAV file no. 495-266-23-2. I am grateful to Erden Akbulut for furnishing me with a copy of the Turkish translation of this report.
103. Sabiha Zekeriya, "Ahlakta Müsavat İsteriz," *Resimli Ay* 6, no. 1 (March 1929): 6. Sabiha's writings on prostitution are discussed in chapter 3. On "Russia's new marriage laws," see Sabiha Zekeriya, "Rusya'nın Yeni İzdivaç Kanunları," *Resimli Ay* 4, no. 4 (June 1927): 27–29. On Sabiha's *Resimli Ay* essays, see A. Holly Shissler, "Womanhood Is Not For Sale: Sabiha Zekeriya Sertel Against Prostitution and for Women's Employment," *Journal of Middle East Women's Studies* 4, no. 3 (2008): 12–30, esp. 24. For a useful account of Sabiha's feminism, see Aylin Özman and Ayça Bulut, "Sabiha (Zekeriya) Sertel: Kemalizm, Marksizm ve Kadın Meselesi," *Toplum ve Bilim* 96 (2003): 184–218.
104. *What Should Every Married Man Know?* is quoted in Türe, *Facts and Fantasies*, 194. For the original, see *Her Evli Erkek Neler Bilmelidir?* (Istanbul: Sevimli Ay Matbaası, 1927), 45.
105. Vâ-nû, *Aşkın Birinci Şartı* (Istanbul: Resimli Ay, 1930). The title page describes Vâlâ as "nâkili" (the one who transfers), suggesting that this book was an adaptation. Though Sabiha appears to be an important interlocutor for Vâlâ's erotic writings during this period, the two had a public dispute in 1931. In a humorous *Akşam* column calling for "women masculinists," Vâlâ defended the rights of men who work hard to provide for their families and criticized women for treating men as "money-making machines." In her response, Sabiha reminded Vâlâ of age-old patriarchy barring women's participation in public life. "Socialism," she concluded, "makes the most powerful pledge for the kind of equality that you and I both want." See [Sabiha Zekeriya], "Kadın Maskulinistler," *Cumhuriyet*, May 27, 1930, 2; and [Sabiha Zekeriya], "Ev Erkeği Olmak İstiyen 1000 Delikanlıya, ve Rehberleri Va.Nu Beye!," *Cumhuriyet*, June 5, 1930, 2.
106. Vâ-nû, *Ebenin Hatıratı*, 32–44, 23–32; subsequent page citations are given parenthetically in the text.
107. Renata Salecl, introduction to *Sexuation*, ed. Renata Salecl (Durham, NC: Duke University Press, 2000), 9.
108. Feroz Ahmad, *Turkey: The Quest for Identity* (Oxford: Oneworld, 2005), 87.
109. Vâ-nû, "Venüs'e Don Giydirilir mi?," *Akşam*, April 27, 1930, 3.
110. Vâ-nû, "Biz Ahlâkı Nasıl Anlarız?," *Akşam*, March 17, 1931, 3.
111. In his court defense, Vâlâ stated that one portion of the novel had been borrowed from a French novel and another from a Russian novel, though he declined to provide more specific information. See "Neşriyat Davası Son Safhasında," *Vakit*, August 18, 1931, 1–2. The feuilletons published in *Akşam* from June 12 to July 16, 1931, follow closely the first, second, and sixth chapters of Antonin Artaud's *Le moine* (1931), which was an adaptation of Matthew Lewis's *The Monk* (1796). In

2. VÂLÂ NUREDDIN'S COMIC MATERIALISM

the feuilletons published after July 17, 1931, Vâlâ seems to draw on Iosif Kallinikov's *Relics* (1925) in describing the promiscuous affairs of nuns and monks in a Russian monastery. On *Relics*, see Carleton, *Sexual Revolution*, 136-37.

112. Ömer Türkeş, "Güdük Bir Edebiyat Kanonu," in *Modern Türkiye'de Siyasî Düşünce*, ed. Tanıl Bora and Murat Gültekingil, vol. 2: *Kemalizm*, ed. Ahmet İnsel (Istanbul: İletişim, 2001), 436-37.
113. On this point and for a more detailed comparative analysis of these figures, see Alpay Doğan Yıldız, *Popüler Türk Romanları: Kerime Nadir-Esat Mahmut Karakurt-Muazzez Tahsin Berkand, 1930-1950* (Istanbul: Dergah, 2009).
114. See Ersin Tosun, *Reşat Fuat Baraner: Yaşamı, Çalışmaları, Anılar* (Istanbul: TÜSTAV, 2013), 8-9; and Zehra Kosova, *Ben İşçiyim*, ed. Zihni T. Anadol (Istanbul: İletişim, 1996), 108-9. Here it is important to mention that foreign spouses of Turkish communist men were subject to sexual violence in Turkey: Mustafa Suphi's Russian wife, Meryem Suphi, most likely died after being sold to sexual slavery in Trabzon, where her husband and other TKP comrades were murdered in 1921. See "Abdülkadir Yoldaşın Layihası Kopyası," in *TKP MK 1920-1921 Dönüş Belgeleri*, trans. Yücel Demirel, 2 vols. (Istanbul: TÜSTAV, 2004), 2:161-62. For a valuable multigenerational study of family and love relations of Chinese revolutionaries in Russia and on "romance" as a metaphor for Sino-Soviet relations, see Elizabeth McGuire, *Red at Heart: How Chinese Communists Fell in Love with the Russian Revolution* (New York: Oxford University Press, 2018). A social and cultural history of this kind remains to be written about Turkish revolutionaries.
115. Vâlâ Nureddin [pseud. Hatice Süreyya], *Bir İhanetin Cezası: Aşk ve Macera Romanı* (Istanbul: Arif Bolat Kitabevi, 1944), 6, 90.
116. Vâ-nû, *Mazinin Yükü Altında: Aşk ve Macera Romanı* (Istanbul: İnkılâp Kitabevi, 1939).
117. Vâ-nû, *Hayatımın Erkeği: Aşk ve Macera Romanı* (Istanbul: İnkılap Kitabevi, 1939). On the "political economy" of sex, see Gayle Rubin's influential essay "The Traffic in Women: Notes on the 'Political Economy' of Sex," in *Toward an Anthropology of Women*, ed. Rayna R. Reiter (New York: Monthly Review Press, 1975), 157-210.
118. See Sigmund Freud, "Family Romances," in *The Standard Edition of the Complete Psychological Works of Sigmund Freud*, vol. 9: *1906-1908: Jensen's "Gradiva" and Other Works*, trans. and ed. James Strachey (London: Hogarth Press, 1959), 235-41; and Lynn Hunt, *The Family Romance of the French Revolution* (Berkeley: University of California Press, 1992).
119. Stites, *The Women's Liberation Movement in Russia*, 376.

3. THE PROSTITUTE CEVRIYE AS POSITIVE HERO: SUAT DERVIŞ AND THE ETHICS OF THE SOCIALIST-REALIST NOVEL

1. Suat Derviş, *Niçin Sovyetler Birliğinin Dostuyum?* (Istanbul: Arkadaş Matbaası, 1944), 13, published with the subtitle *Niçin Sovyet Rusyaya Hayranım?* (Why do I admire Soviet Russia?).
2. See Mihri Belli, *Mihri Belli'nin Anıları:"İnsanlar Tanıdım"* (Istanbul: Milliyet Yayınları, 1989), 85.
3. On decentralization, see the introduction.

3. THE PROSTITUTE CEVRIYE AS POSITIVE HERO

4. Derviş, *Niçin Sovyetler Birliğinin Dostuyum?*, 13.
5. Jacques Derrida, "Back from Moscow, in the USSR," in *Politics, Theory, and Contemporary Culture*, ed. Mark Poster, trans. Mary Quaintaire (New York: Columbia University Press, 1993), 198, emphasis in the original.
6. Derrida, "Back from Moscow, in the USSR," 212, 209.
7. Derrida, "Back from Moscow, in the USSR," 222.
8. On Derviş's use of pseudonyms after 1944, see Zihni T. Anadol, "Suat Derviş ile Konuşmalar...," *Yazın* 12, no. 59 (March 1994): 16–17.
9. Sabiha became a target of anticommunist violence because of her leftist columns in the daily *Tan* and was forced to leave Turkey with her family in 1950.
10. Derviş's birth year has been recorded in different sources as 1901 or 1903 or 1905. Her father, İsmail Derviş, was an obstetrician at the maternity clinic founded in 1892 by Besim Ömer. Her mother, Hesna, was the daughter of an enslaved Circassian woman raised at Sultan Abdülaziz's court. Sources consulted on Derviş's biography include Rasih Nuri İleri, "Yakın Tarihimizden Portreler: Suat Derviş—Saadet Baraner," in *Kırklı Yıllar 1: En Büyük Tehlike (Faris Erkman); Niçin Sovyetler Birliğinin Dostuyum? (Suat Derviş)*, ed. Rasih Nuri İleri (Istanbul: TÜSTAV, 2002), 128–65; Behçet Necatigil, "Dünya Kadın Yılında Suat Derviş Üzerine Notlar," in *Nesin Vakfı Edebiyat Yıllığı 1976* (Istanbul: Tekin Yayınları, 1976), 593–609; İbrahim Tatarlı, "Ölümünün 10. Yıldönümünde Suat Derviş Üzerine Bir İnceleme," in *Nesin Vakfı Edebiyat Yıllığı 1983* (Istanbul: Kardeşler Basımevi, 1983), 607–12; Saliha Paker and Zehra Toska, "Yazan, Yazılan, Silinen ve Yeniden Yazılan Özne: Suat Derviş'in Kimlikleri," *Toplumsal Tarih* 39 (March 1997): 11–22; and Liz Behmoaras, *Suat Derviş: Efsane Bir Kadın ve Dönemi* (Istanbul: Remzi Kitabevi, 2008). For useful bibliographies of Derviş's publications in Turkey, see Oya Körpe, "Suat Derviş'in Hayatı, Edebî Kişiliği ve Eserleri Üzerine Bir İnceleme," master's thesis, Dokuz Eylül Üniversitesi, 2001, 161–80; and Serdar Soydan, "Suat Derviş ve Eserleri," in Suat Derviş, *Bu Roman Olan Şeylerin Romanıdır* (Istanbul: İthaki, 2018), 247–65.
11. In an interview by İbrahim Tatarlı, Derviş stated that Nâzım's poem "Her Shadow" ("Gölgesi") was dedicated to her (Tatarlı, "Ölümünün 10. Yıldönümünde," 610). Regarding Nâzım and Derviş's brief love affair during the 1930s, see İbrahim Balaban, *Nâzım Hikmet'le Yedi Yıl* (Istanbul: Berfin, 2003), 167–69.
12. Republished in 1946 in Latin lettering, *Neither a Sound... nor a Breath!* is a prose adaptation of "Der Erlkönig," featuring a female protagonist caught in a love triangle between a father and son. See Suat Derviş, *Ne bir Ses... Ne bir Nefes! Milli Roman* (1923; reprint, Istanbul: Inkılâp Kitabevi, 1946).
13. For a collection of her short stories, see Suat Derviş, *Hepimiz Birbirimizin Örneğiyiz*, ed. Zehra Toska (Istanbul: Oğlak, 1998).
14. For this chronology, see Soydan, "Suat Derviş ve Eserleri," 251. Derviş was in Berlin during the Weimar years, which saw a boom in photojournalism. Little is known about her publications in Germany. For a brief news report about her in the *Vossische Zeitung*, see "Die Gotteslästerung," *Das Unterhaltungsblatt der Vossischen Zeitung*, no. 188 (August 13, 1927): 1. This report states that the Derviş, "who is also known in Germany," was charged with blasphemy by the Istanbul Criminal Court and (along with her publisher Ahmed İhsan Bey) received a suspended sentence of one month in prison because she had compared religion to

3. THE PROSTITUTE CEVRIYE AS POSITIVE HERO

opium in an article in the journal *Servet-i Fünun*. For an interview with Derviş, see "Gespräche mit Suad Derwisch," *Die Frau und ihre Welt*, January 17, 1929, 3. For an essay on the "emancipation" of Turkish women, see Suad Derwish, "Der entzauberte Harem," *Revue des Monats* 6 (1931–1932): 62–66. Derviş's constrained account of Turkish modernization in this essay is focused on women of her own social class and ends up reproducing, rather than displacing, the habits of German Orientalism. For her review of Nâzım's poetry, see Suad Derwisch, "Nazim Hikmet," *Die Literatur: Monatsschrift für Literatur-freunde* 33 (June 1931): 498–500. For Derviş's autobiographical account of her Berlin years, see Suat Derviş, *Anılar, Paramparça* (Istanbul: İthaki, 2017), 53–123.

15. Derviş returned to Turkey following her father's death in 1932 and the election of Hitler as chancellor in 1933. On the year 1933 as a turning point in her work, see Paker and Toska, "Yazan, Yazılan, Silinen ve Yeniden Yazılan Özne," 18.
16. For Derviş's account of her composition of *Emine* under Barbusse's influence, see Suad Derwich, "Hommage d'un écrivain Turc," *Europe* 33, nos. 119–20 (November–December 1955): 89–90. She would translate *Le feu* into Turkish in 1970. For the quoted definition of "proletarian literature" (*proleterya edebiyatı*), see "Dünyanın Büyük Yazıcılarından Hanri Barbüs Proleter Edebiyatını Nasıl Tarif Ediyor?," *Resimli Ay* 7, no. 7 (September 1930): 11, 37–38.
17. Suat Derviş, *Emine* (Istanbul: Resimli Ay, 1931). For the earlier story, see Suat Derviş, "Emine," *Resimli Ay* 6, no. 12 (February 1930): 34–35.
18. For example, see her novel *Nothing* (*Hiç*), which was serialized in 1935 and published in book form in 1939.
19. Gayatri Chakravory Spivak, "Can the Subaltern Speak?," in *Can the Subaltern Speak? Reflections on the History of an Idea*, ed. Rosalind C. Morris (New York: Columbia University Press, 2010), 21–78.
20. For the quoted phrase, see Ahmet Oktay, *Toplumcu Gerçekçiliğin Kaynakları: Sosyalist Realizm Üstüne Eleştirel Bir Çalışma* (1986; reprint, Istanbul: İthaki, 2008), 409.
21. Divorced three times and married four times, Derviş was married to Nizamettin Nazif between 1934 and 1938 and to Baraner from 1940 until his death in 1968. Born in 1902 in Salonica to a mother who was a cousin of Mustafa Kemal Atatürk, Baraner joined a TKP cell in 1925 when he was a student at Istanbul University. He went to Germany to study chemical engineering on a government fellowship from 1925 to 1928. Between 1928 and 1937, he lived in Turkey and the Soviet Union, becoming the party secretary in 1935. Returning to Turkey in 1937, Baraner would never reunite with his first wife, Margarete Wilde, a German communist, who remained in the Soviet Union with their toddler son. Respected for having survived brutal police torture during the crackdown in Turkey in 1944, Baraner published books on the Spanish Civil War and the Chinese Civil War and translated Engels's *Anti-Dühring* and Henri Lefebvre's writings on Marx during the 1960s. On Baraner's life and publications, see Ersin Tosun, *Reşat Fuat Baraner: Yaşamı, Çalışmaları, Anılar* (Istanbul: TÜSTAV, 2013).
22. During this period, the TKP also sponsored the publication of two books addressed to the general public: Derviş's *Why Am I a Friend of the Soviet Union?* and Baraner's *The Greatest Danger* (*En Büyük Tehlike*). The latter, warning the Turkish public of the dangers of fascism, was published under Faris Erkman's

3. THE PROSTITUTE CEVRIYE AS POSITIVE HERO

name. On the official documents of the crackdown on the TKP in 1944, including the full texts of the indictment and the sentencing record, see Rasih Nuri İleri, ed., *Kırklı Yıllar 2: 1944 TKP Davası* (Istanbul: TÜSTAV, 2003).

23. See "T.C. Ankara Garnizon Komutanlığı 1 No. Askeri Mahkemesi Esas 945/2, Karar 945/7: Gerekçeli Hüküm," in *Kırklı Yıllar 2*, ed. R. İleri, 116-17, 217-19.
24. The founding members of the clandestine TKP established in Ankara in the summer of 1920 included two women, Cemile Selim Nevşirvanova and Fatma Salih Hacıoğlu, the spouses of Ziynetullah Nevşirvanov and Salih Hacıoğlu, respectively. When these women (along with Cemile's sister, Rahime) attended a meeting with all-male members of the Popular Group in November 1920, the more traditionalist members of the Popular Group decided not to join the party merger that would produce the People's Communist Party of Turkey (Türkiye Halk İştirakiyun Fırkası, THIF). Fatma Hacıoğlu passed away in 1922, and in that same year Nevşirvanova moved to the Soviet Union, along with her spouse and sister, as a representative of Turkish communist women. Salih Hacıoğlu married Sabiha Sümbül, and the couple lived in Istanbul from 1923 until 1928, when they also moved to the Soviet Union. For more on the THIF, see the introduction to this book. On women's involvement in the clandestine TKP and THIF, see Erden Akbulut and Mete Tunçay, *Türkiye Halk İştirakiyun Fırkası (1920-1923)*, rev. ed. (Istanbul: TÜSTAV, 2016), 179-81. For an autobiographical account of Nevşirvanova's activism between 1912 and 1922, see Cemile Selim Nevşirvanova, "Göç Anıları," in *Milli Azadlık Savaşı Anıları*, ed. Erden Akbulut (Istanbul: TÜSTAV, 2006), 95-105. For an excerpt from Sabiha Sümbül's diary, see Akbulut and Tunçay, *Türkiye Halk İştirakiyun Fırkası*, 137-42.
25. Sabiha Sümbül quoted in Akbulut and Tunçay, *Türkiye Halk İştirakiyun Fırkası*, 139.
26. Lars T. Lih, *Lenin Rediscovered: "What Is to Be Done?" in Context* (Chicago: Haymarket, 2008), 447.
27. For Belli's account of this meeting, see Behmoaras, *Suat Derviş*, 187-88.
28. For Fanon's analysis of women's (un)veiling during the Algerian War of Independence, see Frantz Fanon, "Algeria Unveiled," in *A Dying Colonialism*, trans. Haakon Chevalier (New York: Grove Press, 1965), 35-68.
29. See "T.C. Ankara Garnizon Komutanlığı 1 No. Askeri Mahkemesi Esas 945/2, Karar 945/7," in *Kırklı Yıllar 2*, ed. R. İleri, 127, 224. Because Derviş had been detained for eight months before her trial, she was released immediately. Baraner was released in a general amnesty in 1950, then arrested again the following year and sentenced to seven more years. The couple reunited in 1961.
30. *For Zeynep* (*Zeynep İçin*, originally serialized in *Haber* in 1946) and *As If Mad* (*Çılgın Gibi*, originally serialized in *Yeni Sabah* in 1945) appeared in French translation under the titles *Le prisonnier d'Ankara* (Paris: Éditeurs français réunis, 1957) and *Les ombres du yali* (Paris: Éditeurs français réunis, 1958), respectively, and under the name "Suat Derwich." *Çılgın Gibi* appeared in book form in Turkey in 1945, but *Ankara Mahpusu* did not follow until 1968. I discuss the Russian editions of Derviş's romances in the final section of this chapter.
31. Suad Dervish, *Liubovnye romany*, trans. Radii Fish (Moscow: Izdatel'stvo TsK VLKSM "Molodaia gvardiia," 1969), 144; this edition includes a pink inside cover with the Turkish title *Aşk Romanları*. *Liubovnye romany* is rarely mentioned in

3. THE PROSTITUTE CEVRIYE AS POSITIVE HERO

Turkish bibliographies of Derviş's works. For Derviş's own brief reference to it, see Kemal Bisalman, "Suat Derviş İçin," *Yeditepe Sanat Dergisi* 171 (July 1970): 5. See also Serdar Soydan, "Suat Derviş'in Gözleri," *K24*, March 21, 2019, https://t24.com.tr/k24/yazi/suat-dervis-in-gozleri,2207.

32. Katerina Clark, *Eurasia Without Borders: The Dream of a Leftist Literary Commons, 1919–1943* (Cambridge, MA: Harvard University Press, 2021), 29–30.
33. This song is also known in Turkey by its first line, "Karakolda Ayna Var" (There is a mirror in the police station). The Turkish adjective *fosforlu*, which I translated into English as "phosphorescent," is difficult to render in English. Whereas in English *phosphorescent* is used in a scientific sense to describe a process of light emission, the Turkish *fosforlu* can be used colloquially to describe a glowing object. For example, the everyday term for a highlighter pen is *fosforlu kalem*. It can also be used in urban slang to mean "gaudily dressed and heavily made up." The heroine Cevriye has the nickname "Fosforlu" because of her radiant beauty.
34. Oktay, *Toplumcu Gerçekçiliğin Kaynakları*, 384, emphasis in original.
35. Ahmet Oktay, "*Fosforlu Cevriye*: Aşkın Yarattığı Erdem," in *Türkiye'de Popüler Kültür* (Istanbul: Yapı Kredi Yayınları, 1993), 198, emphasis in original.
36. Şenol Aktürk, "Toplumcu Gerçekçi Yönüyle Suat Derviş'in Romanlarına Bakış," *Journal of Academic Social Science Studies* 5, no. 3 (2012): 1–33.
37. For critical essays on this novel, see Günseli Sönmez İşçi, ed., *Yıldızları Seyreden Kadın: Suat Derviş Edebiyatı* (Istanbul: İthaki, 2015). For a valuable essay in this volume addressing the novel's socialist realism, see Erendiz Atasü, "Suat Derviş'te Tutku ve Siyasal Bilinç: *Fosforlu Cevriye* ve *Ankara Mahpusu* Romanları Üstüne Bir İnceleme," 31–45.
38. Katerina Clark, *The Soviet Novel: History as Ritual*, 3rd ed. (Bloomington: Indiana University Press, 2000), 5–24.
39. Derviş, *Niçin Sovyetler Birliğinin Dostuyum?*, 38–41.
40. Derviş, *Niçin Sovyetler Birliğinin Dostuyum?*, 7.
41. Yakup Kadri, "Moskova Edebiyat Kongrasında," *Kadro: Aylık Fikir Mecmuası*, no. 33 (September 1934): 32, reprinted in *Kadro: Aylık Fikir Mecmuası: Tıpkı Basım (19–36. Sayılar)*, vol. 2: *1933–1934*, ed. Özgür Erdem (Istanbul: İleri, 2011), 1804.
42. Yakup Kadri, "Sovyet Edebiyatı," *Kadro: Aylık Fikir Mecmuası*, nos. 35–36 (December 1934–January 1935): 34, 31, reprinted in *Kadro*, ed. Erdem, 2:1900, 1897.
43. Yakup Kadri, "Sovyet Edebiyatı," 33, reprinted in *Kadro*, ed. Erdem, 1899.
44. "Savyet Resim ve Heykel Sergisi," *Ulus*, December 21, 1934, 2. On Turkish painters' reception of this exhibition, see Özge Karagöz, "Of Modernist Painting and Statist Economy: Nurullah Berk on the Soviet Art Exhibition in Turkey, 1934–35," *Journal of the Ottoman and Turkish Studies Association* 8, no. 2 (2021): 271–80, https://www.muse.jhu.edu/article/859843.
45. For the first quoted phrase, see "Ankara'da Bir Sovyet Resim Sergisi," *Ulus*, December 11, 1934, 5, and for the second phrase, see "Sovyet Sanat Sergisi," *Ulus*, December 20, 1934, 3. The use of the term *new realism* is consistent with its mobilization in Soviet discourses of this period. Régine Robin emphasizes "little mention" of the term *socialist realism* in the Soviet Writers' Congress of 1934: "There is little mention of the notion itself, whereas much is said about the new aesthetic to be established, about what Soviet literature should be; and the old realism is frequently opposed to a new realism that is not otherwise extensively characterized. I am

3. THE PROSTITUTE CEVRIYE AS POSITIVE HERO

stressing this point because the secondary literature, both in Russian and in English, often gives the impression that the definition of SR dominated the discussions." Régine Robin, *Socialist Realism: An Impossible Aesthetic*, trans. Catherine Porter (Stanford, CA: Stanford University Press, 1992), 44.

46. On this point and for a broader literary and cultural history of this period, see Oktay, *Toplumcu Gerçekçiliğin Kaynakları*. See also chapter 4.
47. "Başlarken: Biz Yeni Edebiyattan Ne Anlıyoruz?," *Yeni Edebiyat*, no. 9 (February 15, 1941): 1–2.
48. Published intermittently between 1938 and 1941, the literary journal *S.E.S.: San'at, Edebiyat, Sosyoloji Aylık Mecmua* (Art, literature, and sociology monthly journal), which was retitled *Yeni S.E.S.* (New S.E.S.) in 1939, brought together leftist writers and artists during the Second World War.
49. For an account of the Soviet literary debates of the 1930s, see Katerina Clark and Galin Tihanov, "Soviet Literary Theory in the 1930s: Battles Over Genre and the Boundaries of Modernity," in *A History of Russian Literary Theory and Criticism: The Soviet Age and Beyond*, ed. Evgeny Dobrenko and Galin Tihanov (Pittsburgh: University of Pittsburgh Press, 2011), 109–43.
50. Rasih Nuri İleri, preface to *Yeni Edebiyat 1940–1941: Sosyalist Gerçekçilik*, ed. Suphi Nuri İleri (Istanbul: Scala, 1998), 11.
51. Abidin Dino, "Realizme Dair Notlar," *Yeni Edebiyat*, no. 5 (December 15, 1940): 1, 3. Regarding this debate, see also chapter 4.
52. See Reşat Fuat Baraner [pseud. Ali Rıza], "Realizme Dair Notlar Münasebetiyle," *Yeni Edebiyat*, no. 5 (December 15, 1940): 1, 3.
53. "Başlarken: Niçin Realizm Münakaşasını Yapıyoruz?," *Yeni Edebiyat*, no. 7 (January 15, 1941): 1, reprinted in *Yeni Edebiyat 1940–1941*, ed. S. İleri, 53.
54. For the first quoted phrase, see Baraner, "Realizme Dair Notlar Münasebetiyle"; for a critique of naturalism, see Abidin Dino, "Realizm Notları," *Yeni Edebiyat*, no. 7 (January 15, 1941): 2, reprinted in *Yeni Edebiyat 1940–1941*, ed. S. İleri, 46; and for the last quoted phrase rejecting the avant-garde, see Zeki Baştımar, "Şairin Sesi," *Yeni Edebiyat*, no. 5 (December 15, 1940): 1.
55. Zeki Baştımar, "Edebiyat I," *Yeni Edebiyat*, no. 15 (May 15, 1941): 1, 3.
56. Reşat Fuat Baraner [pseud. Ali Rıza], "Edebî Eserde Müsbet Tip," *Yeni Edebiyat*, no. 13 (April 15, 1941): 1; see also the editorial "Başlarken: Bedbinler ve Nikbinler," *Yeni Edebiyat*, no. 1 (October 5, 1940): 1.
57. Zeki Baştımar, "Edebiyat III," *Yeni Edebiyat*, no. 19 (August 1, 1941): 1–2.
58. Andrei Zhdanov quoted in Clark, *The Soviet Novel*, 34. For the Russian original, see A. A. Zhdanov, "Rech' sekretaria TsK VKP(b) A. A. Zhdanova," in *Pervyi vsesoiuznyi s"ezd sovetskikh pisatelei 1934: Stenograficheskii otchet* (Moscow: Sovetskii pisatel', 1990), 4.
59. Maksim Gorky, "Soviet Literature," in Maksim Gorky et al., *Soviet Writers' Congress, 1934: The Debate on Socialist Realism and Modernism in the Soviet Union* (London: Lawrence and Wishart, 1977), 52 (translation slightly modified), 44; Maksim Gor'kii, "Doklad A.M. Gor'kogo o sovetskoi literature," in *Pervyi vsesoiuznyi s"ezd sovetskikh pisatelei 1934*, 13, 10.
60. Oktay, *Toplumcu Gerçekçiliğin Kaynakları*, 133.
61. See Abidin Dino, "Halk ve San'at," *Yeni Edebiyat*, no. 2 (October 26, 1940): 1, 3; Dino, "Realizm Notları."

3. THE PROSTITUTE CEVRIYE AS POSITIVE HERO

62. Zeki Baştımar, "Edebiyat ve Folklor," *Yeni Edebiyat*, no. 20 (August 15, 1941): 1, 3; see also Zeki Baştımar, "Edebiyat ve Folklor II," *Yeni Edebiyat*, no. 21 (September 1, 1941): 1–2.
63. Hasan İzzettin Dinamo, "Köroğlunun Türküsü," *Yeni Edebiyat*, no. 3 (November 15, 1940): 4. For an influential early folkloric study of the epic of Köroğlu, see Pertev Naili, *Köroğlu Destanı* (Istanbul: Evkaf Matbaası, 1931). For a more extensive discussion of Turkish oral literature and socialist realism, see chapter 4.
64. Suat Derviş, "Her Sayıda Bir Roman: *Yaban*," *Yeni Edebiyat*, no. 1 (October 5, 1940): 3; and Suat Derviş, "Her Sayıda Bir Roman: *Yolpalas Cinayeti*," *Yeni Edebiyat*, no. 7 (January 15, 1941): 3, reprinted in *Yeni Edebiyat 1940–1941*, ed. S. İleri, 276.
65. For brief biographical information about Zeki Duygulu, the composer of the folk song "Fosforlu Cevriye," see Yılmaz Öztuna, "Duygulu [Zekî]," in *Büyük Türk Mûsikîsi Ansiklopedisi*, vol. 1: *A–L* (Ankara: Kültür Bakanlığı, 1990), 234–36.
66. Hasan İzzettin Dinamo, *TKP Aydınlar ve Anılar* (Istanbul: Yalçın, 1989), 84–85.
67. Suat Derviş, *Fosforlu Cevriye* (Istanbul: May, 1968); subsequent page citations to this edition of the novel are given parenthetically in the text.
68. Erol Gökşen, "Suat Derviş'in Gazete Yazıları Işığında *Fosforlu Cevriye*'yi Okuma Denemesi," *Roman Kahramanları*, no. 18 (April–June 2014): 91–95.
69. On the character of Typewriter Emine, see Derviş, *Fosforlu Cevriye*, 244. For Derviş's interview of homeless children, see Suat Derviş, "Çocuklarımız Ne Halde? 6—Kurtulan Çocuklara Göre," *Cumhuriyet*, August 27, 1935, 7–8. For her interview of office secretaries, see Suat Derviş, "Kızlarımız: Bu Daktilo Kız Hayatından Niçin Şikâyetçi," *Tan*, November 15, 1937, 7.
70. M. M. Bakhtin, "Discourse in the Novel," in *The Dialogic Imagination: Four Essays*, ed. Michael Holquist, trans. Caryl Emerson and Michael Holquist (Austin: University of Texas Press, 1981), 372, 373.
71. Bakhtin, "Discourse in the Novel," 411.
72. For an analysis of heteroglossia in the conservative modernist Peyami Safa's writings during this period, see Nergis Ertürk, *Grammatology and Literary Modernity in Turkey* (New York: Oxford University Press, 2011), 135–58. It is likely that the specific circumstances of Derviş's life also shaped her representations of the Istanbul underworld. In her loosely autobiographical novel *Liubovnye romany*, the protagonist Fatma Taran lives in a basement apartment near a brothel and a gambling house in a back alley of Beyoğlu during the mid-1940s and mentions the conversations of pimps, prostitutes, and gamblers that she could hear from her window overlooking the street. See Dervish, *Liubovnye romany*, 15; and Behmoaras, *Suat Derviş*, 204–8.
73. Derviş, *Niçin Sovyetler Birliğinin Dostuyum?*, 38
74. Maksim Gorky quoted in Robin, *Socialist Realism*, 166, 169. For the Russian original of the first quoted phrase, see Maksim Gor'kii, "Po povodu odnoi diskussii," *Literaturnaia gazeta*, January 28, 1934, 2; for the second quoted phrase, see Maksim Gor'kii, "Otkrytoe pis'mo A. S. Serafimovichu," *Literaturnaia gazeta*, February 15, 1934, 1. For a useful account of the language debates in 1934, see Robin, *Socialist Realism*, 51–55, 165–90.
75. Robin, *Socialist Realism*, 182. Gorky delivered a speech at the peasant writers' congress in 1929, calling for new peasant writers to draw from "the inexhaustible treasury of the popular Russian language" (quoted in Robin, *Socialist Realism*, 182).

3. THE PROSTITUTE CEVRIYE AS POSITIVE HERO

76. See, for example, "Başlarken: Eski Harflerin Liselerde Öğretilmesi Doğru mudur?," *Yeni Edebiyat*, no. 2 (October 26, 1940): 1, opposing the journalist Ahmet Emin Yalman's public proposal to begin the instruction of the Ottoman Turkish alphabet in high schools. Refusing a wholesale rejection of the past, the editorial nevertheless argued that the Turkish language reforms demonstrated the necessary dialectical movement of history. See also Suat Derviş, "Fıkra: Dil Bayramı," *Yeni Edebiyat*, no. 22 (September 15, 1941): 1, reprinted in *Yeni Edebiyat 1940–1941*, ed. S. İleri, 190.
77. Zeki Baştımar, "Bir Az Tevazu," *Yeni Edebiyat*, no. 14 (May 1, 1941): 1, 4. See also Reşat Fuat Baraner [pseud. Ali Rıza], "Halkçı Edebiyatta Şekil," *Yeni Edebiyat*, no. 2 (October 26, 1940): 2, in which Baraner argued that "people's literature [*halkçı edebiyat*] should not descend to the level of the lowest reader" but rather aim to elevate the intellectual level of its readership.
78. In her proletarian novel *Bu Roman Olan Şeylerin Romanıdır* (1937), for example, the use of *pavrika* instead of *fabrika* for "factory" is the only lexical marker distinguishing the working-class characters from the narrator. With the exception of a few minor characters (a disabled former factory worker, a German engineer, and a male criminal who appear briefly in the novel), all the major characters speak standard Istanbul vernacular.
79. Walter Benjamin's book review of the German translation of *Cement* in 1927 praised the linguistic achievement of both the Russian original and the German translation (specifically their use of the Bolshevik argot); see Walter Benjamin, "Review of Gladkov's *Cement*," trans. Rodney Livingstone, in *Walter Benjamin: Selected Writings*, vol. 2, part 1: *1927–1930*, ed. Michael W. Jennings, Howard Eiland, and Gary Smith, trans. Rodney Livingstone and others (Cambridge, MA: Harvard University Press, 1999), 47–49. Hans Günther writes that *Cement* "became a movable palimpsest" as it went through multiple stages of "stylistic 'refinement'" during the 1930s. See Hans Günther, "Soviet Literary Criticism and the Formulation of the Aesthetics of Socialist Realism, 1932–1940," in *A History of Russian Literary Theory and Criticism*, ed. Dobrenko and Tihanov, 97.
80. Walter Benjamin, "On the Mimetic Faculty," trans. Edmund Jephcott, in *Walter Benjamin: Selected Writings*, vol. 2, part 2: *1931–1934*, ed. Michael W. Jennings, Howard Eiland, and Gary Smith, trans. Rodney Livingstone and others (Cambridge, MA: Harvard University Press, 2005), 722; Walter Benjamin, "Über das mimetische Vermögen," in *Gesammelte Schriften*, vol. 2.1, ed. Rolf Tiedemann and Hermann Schweppenhäuser (Frankfurt: Suhrkamp, 1977), 213.
81. Walter Benjamin, "Doctrine of the Similar," trans. Michael Jennings, in *Walter Benjamin: Selected Writings*, vol. 2, part 2, 695–96; Walter Benjamin, "Lehre vom Ähnlichen," in *Gesammelte Schriften*, vol. 2.1, 206.
82. See Melahat Gül Uluğtekin, "İzlek ve Biçem İlişkisi Açısından Suat Derviş Romanlarının Türk Edebiyatındaki Yeri," PhD diss., Bilkent University, 2010, 192–96.
83. The novel's external narrator may be read as a double of the journalist narrator in Derviş's newspaper interviews. Although in the interviews Derviş domesticated the alterity of the urban working class and subaltern groups by replacing "their brute heteroglossia" with her own "single-imaged, 'ennobled' language" (Bakhtin, "Discourse in the Novel," 410), she also depicted herself as an elite figure. For

3. THE PROSTITUTE CEVRIYE AS POSITIVE HERO

example, the published account of her interview of a group of female factory workers includes their criticism of Derviş: "You women who don't work at a factory talk out of your hat [*bol keseden atarsınız*]." See Suat Derviş, "Türk Kadını Nasıl İş Bulur? Erkeğin İşi Kadından Çoçuğa mı Geçiyor?" *Tan*, January 6, 1937, 7. In an interview of a disabled beggar, Derviş acknowledged her complicity in the beggar's exploitation: "I gave him money not because he was begging but because he gave me a topic to write about; I put in his hand a small tip, or more accurately, a small share from the money I will earn from his story." See Suat Derviş, "Hayattan Hikayeler: Neden Dileniyormuş?," *Tan*, August 31, 1937, 6. Despite such self-critical constructions, it is fair to say that these interviews largely foreclose the imagination of any truly meaningful relation to alterity. The external narrator in *Phosphorescent Cevriye* speaks for the most part from the same milieu as this journalist narrator, but the novel's use of dialogized heteroglossia represents a more plausible opening to alterity. See also Suat Derviş, "İstanbul'un Altında Kimler Yaşıyor?," *Son Posta*, June 25, 1936, 7.

84. It was common for westernized Ottoman elites to address one another with the French phrase *mon chéri*.

85. Cevriye borrows unfamiliar words from the archaic literate register of Ottoman Turkish, interspersing them into her speech to impress the fugitive. For example, during her stay in the hospital she hears an older patient use the phrase *emraz tabibi* (doctor of illnesses). Considering this "a great word," she deploys it "to appear refined" in her first exchange with the fugitive (Derviş, *Fosforlu Cevriye*, 71). In "Translation as Culture," Spivak emphasizes the need for a Bangla-Bangla dictionary "from idiom to standard": "I want to say, with particular emphasis, that what the largest part of the future electorate needs, in order to accede, in the longest run, to democracy rather than have their votes bought and sold, is practical, simple, same-language dictionaries that will help translate idiom into standard, in all these languages." See Gayatri Chakravorty Spivak, "Translation as Culture," in *An Aesthetic Education in the Era of Globalization* (Cambridge, MA: Harvard University Press, 2012), 255.

86. On the differential logic of signification, see Ferdinand de Saussure, *Course in General Linguistics*, ed. Charles Bally and Albert Sechehaye, with Albert Reidlinger, trans. Roy Harris (Chicago: Open Court, 1995), 118: "In a language there are only differences, *and no positive terms*. . . . In a sign, what matters more than any idea or sound associated with it is what other signs surround it" (emphasis in original).

87. See "T.C. Ankara Garnizon Komutanlığı 1 No. Askeri Mahkemesi Esas 945/2, Karar 945/7: Gerekçeli Hüküm," in *Kırklı Yıllar 2*, ed. R. İleri, 217–24.

88. For summaries of these bulletins in the official court proceedings, see "T.C. Ankara Garnizon Komutanlığı 1 No. Askeri Mahkemesi Esas 945/2, Karar 945/7: Gerekçeli Hüküm," in *Kırklı Yıllar 2*, ed. R. İleri, 105–17. There are no original copies of these documents in the TÜSTAV archive.

89. Belli, *Mihri Belli'nin Anıları*, 217–18.

90. For Baraner's court defense, see "T.C. Ankara Garnizon Komutanlığı 1 No. Askeri Mahkemesi Esas 945/2, Karar 945/7: Gerekçeli Hüküm," in *Kırklı Yıllar 2*, ed. R. İleri, 118–25. The prosecutor described Baraner's defense as "wordplay": "The defendant engages in wordplay by claiming that they want to be populist, statist,

3. THE PROSTITUTE CEVRIYE AS POSITIVE HERO

and antifascist and that the TKP wants to work with the Republican People's Party to make Turkey a friend of the Soviet Union" (123).
91. Spivak, "Can the Subaltern Speak?," 33.
92. Spivak, "Can the Subaltern Speak?," 40, 42.
93. For the quoted phrase, see Rosalind C. Morris, "Dialect and Dialectic in 'The Working Day' of Marx's *Capital*," in "Econophonia: Music, Value, and Forms of Life," ed. Gavin Steingo and Jairo Moreno, special issue of *boundary 2* 43, no. 1 (2016): 246.
94. Clark, *The Soviet Novel*, 178.
95. Susan Buck-Morss, *The Dialectics of Seeing: Walter Benjamin and the Arcades Project* (Cambridge, MA: MIT Press, 1991), 210.
96. Walter Benjamin, "On the Concept of History," trans. Harry Zohn, in *Walter Benjamin: Selected Writings*, vol. 4: *1938–1940*, ed. Howard Eiland and Michael W. Jennings, trans. Edmund Jephcott and others (Cambridge, MA: Harvard University Press, 2003), 396; Walter Benjamin, "Über den Begriff der Geschichte," in *Gesammelte Schriften*, vol. 1.2, 703.
97. Clark, *The Soviet Novel*, 37.
98. Robin, *Socialist Realism*, xxiii, 298.
99. Robin, *Socialist Realism*, xxiii (quoting Cohen), xxvii.
100. Spivak, "Translation as Culture," 255.
101. "Otchet o prebyvanii v SSSR turetskoi pisatel'nitsy Suad Dervish, perepiska ee i zapisi besed," GARF f. R-5283, op. 4, d. 237, l. 1–4. *The Mother* was retranslated into Ottoman Turkish (from a French translation) by İsmail Müştak (Mayakon) and Muhiddin (Birgen) in 1911. It is unknown if Derviş had access to the Ottoman Turkish edition.
102. Katerina Clark, "Socialist Realism *with* Shores: The Conventions for the Positive Hero," in *Socialist Realism Without Shores*, ed. Thomas Lahusen and Evgeny Dobrenko (Durham, NC: Duke University Press, 1997), 29.
103. Maksim Gorky, *The Mother*, trans. Hugh Aplin (Surrey, U.K.: Alma, 2015), 361; Maksim Gor'kii, *Mat'*, in *Polnoe sobranie sochinenii*, vol. 8: *1906–1910* (Moscow: Nauka, 1970), 339.
104. For the quoted material in this sentence and the previous one, see Clark, "Socialist Realism *with* Shores," 29.
105. Gorky, *The Mother*, 312–13; Gor'kii, *Mat'*, 295. On the rare use of the "auxiliary narrative pattern" of love in the Soviet novel, see Clark, *The Soviet Novel*, 182–85. For a similar characterization of love relationships within the TKP, see Emin Karaca's interview of Mihri Belli in Emin Karaca, *Eski Tüfeklerin Sonbaharı* (Istanbul: Toplumsal Dönüşüm Yayınları, 1996). Belli remarked that "we did not have tolerance of love relationships between young girls and boys under the sacred roof of the party" (41). Belli married Sevim Tarı, whom he met in prison in the aftermath of the communist crackdown of 1951.
106. On the Tanzimat novel, see Ertürk, *Grammatology and Literary Modernity in Turkey*, 31–69.
107. Aleksandra Kollontai, *Prostitutsiia i mery borb'y s nei: Rech' na III vserossiiskom soveshchanii zaveduiushchikh gubzhenotdelami* (Moscow: Gosudarstvennoe izdatel'stvo, 1921), 7; Alexandra Kollontai, "Prostitution and Ways of Fighting It," in *Selected Writings of Alexandra Kollontai*, trans. Alix Holt (Westport, CT: Lawrence

3. THE PROSTITUTE CEVRIYE AS POSITIVE HERO

Hill, 1977), 264, emphasis in the original. For the serialized Turkish translation of Kollontai's speech delivered at the Third All-Russian Conference of the Heads of the Regional Women's Departments in 1921, see "Fahişelik ve Onunla Mübareze Çareleri: M. Kollontay Tarafından İrad Olunan Nutuktan!," in *THİF Yayın Organı: "Yeni Hayat" (Mart–Eylül 1922)*, ed. Hamit Erdem (Istanbul: TÜSTAV, 2017), 70–71, 95–96, 107–9, 120–21, 150–51, 197–98. The serialization appeared from March 25 to May 6, 1922.
108. For Sabiha's discussion of Soviet Russia as a model, see Sabiha Zekeriya, "Kadınlık Satılamaz," *Resimli Ay* 3, no. 35 (January 1927): 24–25. For her analysis of prostitution, see her unsigned article "Bu Kadını Nasıl Kurtarabiliriz? Fuhuşun Önüne Nasıl Geçilir?," *Resimli Ay* 7, no. 9 (January 1, 1931): 15–16. See also Sabiha Zekeriya, "Zehra Arzuhalini Yazdım Fakat Verecek Makam Bulamıyorum," *Resimli Ay* 1, no. 6 (July 1924): 2–4; and Sabiha Zekeriya, "Gerzeli Ayşe," *Resimli Ay* 6, no. 3 (May 1929): 12–14, 39. For an historical account of prostitution in Turkey, see Mark David Wyers, *"Wicked" Istanbul: The Regulation of Prostitution in the Early Turkish Republic* (Istanbul: Libra, 2012).
109. [Sabiha Zekeriya], "Ahlakta Müsavat İsteriz," *Resimli Ay* 6, no. 1 (March 1929): 6.
110. Jacques Lacan, "The Signification of the Phallus," in *Écrits: The First Complete Edition in English*, trans. Bruce Fink in collaboration with Héloïse Fink and Russel Grigg (New York: Norton, 2006), 583. On the concept of the masquerade, see Stephen Heath, "Joan Riviere and the Masquerade," in *Formations of Fantasy*, ed. Victor Burgin, James Donald, and Cora Kaplan (London: Routledge, 1986), 45–61.
111. Regarding respect, Kant writes: "Rational beings are called persons because their nature already marks them out as an end in itself, that is, as something that may not be used merely as a means, and hence so far limits all choice (and is an object of respect)." See Immanuel Kant, *Groundwork of the Metaphysics of Morals*, trans. and ed. Mary J. Gregor (Cambridge: Cambridge University Press, 1998), 37/4:428.
112. See, for example, Oktay, *"Fosforlu Cevriye."*
113. The story of the moth and candle, first allegorized by the tenth-century mystic Mansur al-Hallaj, is used in Rumi's works; see Annemarie Schimmel, *Rumi's World: The Life and Work of the Great Sufi Poet* (Boston: Shambhala, 1992), 89.
114. Jacques Lacan, "God and Woman's Jouissance," in *The Seminar of Jacques Lacan: On Feminine Sexuality, the Limits of Love and Knowledge, Book XX, Encore 1972–1973*, ed. Jacques-Alain Miller, trans. Bruce Fink (New York: Norton, 1999), 76.
115. For the quoted phrases, see Bruce Fink, *The Lacanian Subject: Between Language and Jouissance* (Princeton, NJ: Princeton University Press, 1995), 107, 115, 116, emphasis in original. My discussion of phallic and feminine jouissance in this section draws on Fink's work. The adjectives *masculine* and *feminine* here describe different subjectivities; there is nothing that prevents a biological man from investing the feminine structure or vice versa.
116. Fink, *The Lacanian Subject*, 121.
117. Fink, *The Lacanian Subject*, 120.
118. Fink, *The Lacanian Subject*, 120, emphasis in original.
119. On the finitude of phallic jouissance and infinitude of feminine jouissance, see Alenka Zupančič, "The Case of the Perforated Sheet," in *Sexuation*, ed. Renata Salecl (Durham, NC: Duke University Press, 2000), 282–96. Zupančič writes: "To

3. THE PROSTITUTE CEVRIYE AS POSITIVE HERO

use Jean-Claude Milner's formula, 'the infinite is that which says no to the exception to the finite.' 'Infinite' refers to the structure or topology of enjoyment and not to its quantity (or quality). Infinite *jouissance* is that which puts an end to 'exceptional enjoyment' in all meanings of the words" (296).

120. On the jouissance of speech, see Jacques-Alain Miller, "Of Distribution Between the Sexes," *Psychoanalytical Notebooks*, no. 11 (2003): 25.
121. On Vâlâ and Nâzım, see chapter 2. One might also mention here a neglected novel entitled *Arm in Arm (Kolkola*, 1944) by Nizamettin Nazif (Derviş's former spouse), criticizing the contradictions of new republican morality in Turkey. Naci, the novel's protagonist, supports a "truly European" morality based on monogamous heterosexual love. Describing marriage as a frivolous formality, Naci argues that because women enjoy being dominated by men, strong masculinity is essential for maintaining a stable long-term relationship in an unmarried couple. See Nizamettin Nazif, *Kolkola* (Istanbul: Semih Lûtfi Kitabevi, 1944), 252–53.
122. Alexandra Kollontai, "Make Way for Winged Eros: A Letter to Working Youth," in *Selected Writings of Alexandra Kollontai*, 291–92, 289; Aleksandra Kollontai, "Dorogu krylatomu erosu!," *Molodaia gvardiia*, no. 3.10 (May 1923): 124, 122.
123. Aleksandra Kollontai [as Mm. Kollontay], "Asrî Kadına Göre Aşkın Manası Nedir?," *Resimli Ay* 7, no. 9 (January 1, 1931): 9.
124. Clark, "Socialist Realism *with* Shores," 41.
125. Slavoj Žižek, *How to Read Lacan* (New York: Norton, 2006), 80.
126. Slavoj Žižek, "Superego by Default," in *The Metastases of Enjoyment: Six Essays on Women and Causality* (London: Verso, 2005), 81–82.
127. For the quoted phrases describing Zhukhrai in Nikolai Ostrovsky's novel *How the Steel Was Tempered*, see Clark, "Socialist Realism *with* Shores," 35.
128. For a valuable essay making a similar argument through a reading of Valentin Kataev's *Son of the Regiment*, see Sergei Zimovets, "*Son of the Regiment*: Deus ex Machina," trans. John Henriksen, in *Socialist Realism Without Shores*, ed. Lahusen and Dobrenko, 191–202.
129. For a valuable discussion of the difference between superegoic morality and ethics of the act in Kant's writings, see Alenka Zupančič, *Ethics of the Real: Kant and Lacan* (New York: Verso, 2011).
130. Slavoj Žižek, introduction to V. I. Lenin, *Revolution at the Gates: A Selection of Writings from February to October 1917*, ed. with an introduction and afterword by Slavoj Žižek (London: Verso, 2011), 6, 8.
131. Clark, "Socialist Realism *with* Shores," 29.
132. Regarding Derviş's objection to her introduction as Baraner's wife at a meeting in 1970, see Behmoaras, *Suat Derviş*, 276–77.
133. See O. Orestov, "Sudebnaia rasprava s turetskimi patriotami," *Pravda*, October 25, 1953, 6. The following sources provide some sense of Derviş's reputation in Soviet Russia prior to the Cold War. For a reference to Derviş's antifascist *Tan* columns in the Soviet press, see "Germanskie intrigi v Turtsii," *Pravda*, March 3, 1937, 5. For an article emphasizing her feminist contributions, see E. Gal'perina, "Turetskie pisateli v Moskve," *Literaturnaia gazeta*, no. 58 (October 20, 1939): 4; this article also discussed other Turkish writers, such as Sadri Ertem and Şükrü Esmer, who, along with Derviş, traveled to Moscow with the Turkish delegation

3. THE PROSTITUTE CEVRIYE AS POSITIVE HERO

to attend the All-Union Agricultural Exhibition. For a Russian translation of her short story "Hasan Çavuş'un Oğlu" (1936), see Suad Dervish, "On ili ne on?," in *Turetskie rasskazy: Sbornik*, ed. L. V. Nikulin (Moscow: Gosudarstvennoe izdatel'stvo "Khudozhestvennaia literatura," 1940), 214–20. For a Russian translation of her short story "The City Where I Was Born" ("Doğduğum Şehir") and translations of excerpts from *Emine* and *Why Am I a Friend of the Soviet Union?*, see L. N. Starostov and E. V. Sumin, eds., *Literaturnaia khrestomatiia na turetskom iazyke* (Moscow: Voennyi institut inostrannykh iazykov, 1954), 321–45. The editors of this volume write in their introduction that "these works date from the mature period of the authoress's oeuvre and do not have anything in common with her earlier semimystical publications" (viii). To characterize *Emine* as one of Derviş's mature works is mistaken.

134. For the first Russian edition of *Phosphorescent Cevriye*, see Suad Dervish, *Fosforicheskaia Dzhevrie*, trans. Radii Fish (Moscow: Izdatel'stvo inostrannoi literatury, 1957).The 1958 Russian edition of *Fosforicheskaia Dzhevrie*, published by the Novosibirsk Book Publishing House, is mentioned in a bibliography of Turkish books published in Russian translation in the Soviet Union between 1958 and 1968. This bibliography was distributed to attendees of the decennial anniversary Afro-Asian Writers' Conference in Tashkent in 1968. See Oktay Akbal, "Sovyetlerde Türk Edebiyatı," *Yeditepe Sanat Dergisi* 151 (November 1968): 14. For the Bulgarian edition of the novel in Turkish, see Suat Derviş, *Fosforlu Cevriye* (Sofia, Bulgaria: Narodna prosveta, 1962). For the Azeri edition, see Suad Derviş, *Fosforlu Cevriyə*, trans. Bəhram Cəfərov (Baku: Azərbaycan Dövlət Nəşriyyatı, 1964). For the Russian edition of *Ankara Mahpusu*, see Suad Dervish, *Ankarskii uznik: Roman*, trans. Radii Fish (Moscow: Izdatel'stvo inostrannoi literatury, 1960); for the Azeri edition, see Suad Derviş, *Ankara mahbusu: Roman* (Baku, Azerbaijan: Gənclik, 1973).

135. See Radii Fish, *Pisateli Turtsii: Knigi i sud'by* (Moscow: Sovetskii pisatel', 1963), 158.

136. See Derviş's published letter in "Pochta podgotovitel'nogo komiteta," *Informatsionnyi biulleten' Sovetskogo podgotovitel'nogo komiteta po sozyvu Konferentsii pisatelei stran Azii i Afriki*, no. 3 (July 1958): 17.

137. See V. Maevskii and A. Ivakhnenko, "Konferentsiia pisatelei stran Azii i Afriki: Krepit' sviazi mezhdu kul'turoi Vostoka i Zapada," *Pravda*, October 12, 1958, 4. For Derviş's article "In the Name of Trust," calling for the formation of a new united front at the Tashkent Conference, see Suad Dervish, "Vo imia doveriia," *Literaturnaia gazeta*, no. 121 (October 9, 1958): 4.

138. "Knigi 1960-go," *Literaturnaia gazeta*, no. 18 (February 9, 1961): 1.

139. "Otchet perevodchika o prebyvanii v SSSR Suad Dervish s 2 po 20 Marta 1961 g.," RGALI f. 631, op. 26, ed. khr. 5608, l. 1–11.

140. Derviş left Turkey in 1953 with her sister Hamiyet, who held a Danish passport acquired during her marriage to a Danish citizen. According to Radii Fish, who recounts his conversations with Hamiyet and Derviş, Turkish authorities were reluctant to issue Derviş a passport but acquiesced when Hamiyet threatened to call on the Danish embassy for assistance. The sisters hoped to travel to Milan by train, but at the Greek border near the village of Çakmak Derviş was removed

4. ABIDIN DINO'S PEASANT THEATER

from the train and taken to a district police station in Edirne, while Hamiyet continued on to Milan, where she planned to contact the Danish embassy. Derviş, informed that her detention had been a mistake, was released with approval to leave Turkey in the evening and hired a carriage to take her to the train station. Traveling at night alone with two men on a sixty-kilometer road that wound along the side of a steep cliff, Derviş was terrified when the carriage paused at a bridge: "You know, I am not a coward ... but at that moment I said goodbye to life in my thoughts. I remembered [the Turkish writer] Sabahattin Ali's story, he was killed not far from where we were. What else could the 'mistake' of removing me from the train mean? But the driver gave water to the horses, and we moved on. Maybe something hindered them, maybe the conversation with my sister about her Danish passport scared them; we had purposefully conversed loudly. The next day my sister, who could barely stand still and was in a state of great excitement, met me at the Milan train station." See Fish, *Pisateli Turtsii*, 170–71; and Radii G. Fish, *Turetskie dnevniki: Vstrechi, razmyshleniia* (Moscow: Nauka, 1977), 122–23.

141. On the modernist socialist realism of *Love Novels*, see Nergis Ertürk, "Aşk Romanları (*Liubovnye romany*) ve Düşündürdükleri: Rusça'da Çeviri Bir Suat Derviş Romanı," *Birikim*, no. 389 (September 2021): 92–104.
142. "Otchet perevodchika," RGALI f. 631, op. 26, ed. khr. 5608, l. 7.

4. ABIDIN DINO'S PEASANT THEATER AND THE SOVIET *FAKTURA*: ESTRANGING SOCIALIST REALISM

1. See Liz Behmoaras, *Suat Derviş: Efsane Bir Kadın ve Dönemi* (Istanbul: Remzi Kitabevi, 2008), 222–25; and *TKP MK Dış Bürosu 1962 Konferansı* (Istanbul: TÜSTAV, 2002), 18.
2. See Gayatri Chakravorty Spivak, introduction to *An Aesthetic Education in the Era of Globalization* (Cambridge, MA: Harvard University Press, 2012), 1–34. See also Ben Conisbee Baer, *Indigenous Vanguards: Education, National Liberation, and the Limits of Modernism* (New York: Columbia University Press, 2019).
3. Biographical sources I have consulted include Rasih Nuri İleri, "Abidin Dino Hakkında Bir Kronoloji Denemesi," *Güldiken*, no. 4 (1994): 11–15; Zeynep Avcı, *A'dan Z'ye Abidin Dino* (Istanbul: Yapı Kredi Yayınları, 2000); M. Şehmus Güzel, *Abidin Dino ile Söyleşiler; Yazılar: Hayat ve Sanat* (Istanbul: Pêrî, 2006); M. Şehmus Güzel, *Abidin Dino: Üç Kitap (1913–1993)*, 3 vols. (Istanbul: Kitap Yayınevi, 2007–2008); Jean-Pierre Deleage, *Abidin Dino ya da Kanatlanan El*, trans. Samih Rifat (Istanbul: Yapı Kredi Yayınları, 2007); Abidin Dino and Güzin Dino, *Güzin Dino–Abidin Dino Mektupları (1952–1973)*, ed. Defne Asal Er and Handan Akdemir (Istanbul: İş Bankası Kültür Yayınları, 2004); and Güzin Dino, *Gel Zaman Git Zaman: Abidin Dino'lu Yıllar* (Istanbul: Can, 2000).
4. A prominent figure in Albanian national historiography, Abidin Pasha joined a group of Ottoman Albanian intellectuals and deputies who opposed the cession of the Ottoman territories in Janina to the Greeks in 1877. For a brief account of the Dino family's involvement in the Albanian League in the late nineteenth century, see Bülent Bilmez and Nathalie Clayer, "A Prosopographic Study on Some

4. ABIDIN DINO'S PEASANT THEATER

'Albanian' Deputies to the First Ottoman Parliament," in *The First Ottoman Experiment in Democracy*, ed. Christoph Herzog and Malek Sharif (Würzburg, Germany: Ergon, 2010), 175–77.
5. İleri, "Abidin Dino Hakkında Bir Kronoloji Denemesi," 11.
6. For the quoted phrase, see Hikmet Feridun's interview of the sculptor Zühtü (Müridoğlu) in *Akşam*, October 10, 1933, 4. The d Group's exhibition of black-and-white drawings (*desen*) was a novelty for its Turkish attendees; see the report in *Akşam*, October 9, 1933, 4.
7. For an account of Turkish modernist art, see Nilüfer Öndin, *Cumhuriyet'in Kültür Politikası ve Sanat (1923–1950)* (Istanbul: İnsancıl Yayınları, 2003). On the d Group, see Nihal Elvan, ed., *d Grubu = D Group, 1933–1951* (Istanbul: Yapı Kredi Yayınları, 2002); and Zeynep Yasa Yaman, "1930–1950 Yılları Arasında Kültür ve Sanat Ortamına Bir Bakış: d Grubu," PhD diss., Hacettepe University, 1992.
8. Güzel, *Abidin Dino ile Söyleşiler*, 29. For Yutkevich's account of his meeting with Dino, Nurullah Cemal, and other contemporary artists, including Fikret Mualla, see Sergei Iutkevich, "Pis'mo k turetskim khudozhnikam," *Iskusstvo* 2 (1934): 71–86.
9. For Dino's TKP position, see *TKP MK Dış Bürosu 1962 Konferansı*, 17.
10. Ahmet Oktay, *Toplumcu Gerçekçiliğin Kaynakları: Sosyalist Realizm Üstüne Eleştirel Bir Çalışma* (1986; reprint, Istanbul: İthaki, 2008), 325, 298. See also Yalçın Küçük, *Aydın Üzerine Tezler, 1830–1980*, vol. 4 (Istanbul: Tekin Yayınevi, 1986), 35–93.
11. Ahmet Oktay, "Abidin Dino Bir 'Yazar,'" in *Abidin Dino Bir Dünya*, ed. Zeynep Avcı (Istanbul: Sakıp Sabancı Müzesi, 2007), 57–65.
12. Emma Widdis, "*Faktura*: Depth and Surface in Early Soviet Set Design," *Studies in Russian and Soviet Cinema* 3, no. 1 (2009): 13; Emma Widdis, *Socialist Senses: Film, Feeling, and the Soviet Subject, 1917–1940* (Bloomington: Indiana University Press, 2017).
13. Abidin Dino, "Karacaoğlan: Cehenneme Ateş Götürmeyi Tavsiye Eden Şair," *Yeni S.E.S.*, November 1939, 5. For the paintings, see İlhan Berk et al., *Yurt Gezileri ve Yurt Resimleri (1938–1943)*, ed. Amélie Edgü (Istanbul: Milli Reasürans T.A.Ş., 1998), 125.
14. Widdis, *Socialist Senses*, 165.
15. Abidin Dino, *Kel* (Adana: Türksözü Basımevi, 1944); and Abidin Dino, *Verese*, in *Verese Kel: Oyunlar* (Istanbul: Adam, 1996), 95–165.
16. For this concept, see Lars Kleberg, *Theatre as Action: Soviet Russian Avant-Garde Aesthetics*, trans. Charles Rougle (London: MacMillan, 1993), 103–13.
17. See Abidin Dino, *Yeditepe Öyküleri*, ed. Mürşit Balabanlılar (Istanbul: İş Bankası Kültür Yayınları, 2002), 13–38.
18. Iutkevich, "Pis'mo k turetskim khudozhnikam," 79. I am grateful to Kate Antanovich for her translation of this essay into English. Dino would use the same reference to Christopher Columbus to describe Yutkevich in his first published article in the Soviet Union; see Abidin Dino, "Ankara—Moskva," *Sovetskoe iskusstvo*, no. 46 (October 5, 1934): 3.
19. M. Şehmus Güzel, *Abidin Dino: Üç Kitap (1913–1993)*, vol. 1: *Birinci Kitap (1913–1942)* (Istanbul: Kitap Yayınevi, 2007), 182.
20. It is fair to state that at the third d Group exhibit held in June 1934, one could begin to discern the influence of this national debate on some members' artwork.

4. ABIDIN DINO'S PEASANT THEATER

Dino contributed a painting titled *The Saz Poet* (*Saz Şairi*). For a review of this exhibit, see Eşref Fehim, "D. Grupunun 3'üncü Sergisi Yeni Ressamın Gücünü Gösteriyor," *Yeni Adam* 1, no. 26 (June 25, 1934): 7.

21. On the Kadro movement, see İlhan Tekeli and Selim İlkin, *Bir Cumhuriyet Öyküsü: Kadrocuları ve "Kadro" 'yu Anlamak* (Istanbul: Tarih Vakfı Yurt Yayınları, 2003). Shaped by the Anatolian Bolshevik movement (discussed in chapter 1), İsmail Hüsrev traveled to Bolshevik Russia with Nizamettin Nazif to attend the Congress of the Young Communist International in October 1922.
22. Şevket Süreyya Aydemir, *Suyu Arayan Adam* (Ankara: Öz Yayınları, 1959), 400.
23. Şevket Süreyya, review of Yakup Kadri, *Yaban*, *Kadro*, no. 18 (June 1933): 85.
24. Yakup Kadri, *Yaban* (Istanbul: Muallim Ahmet Halit Kütüphanesi, 1932). For the English translation, see Yakup Kadri Karaosmanoğlu, *Stepmother Earth*, trans. Mark David Wyers (N.p.: Milet, 2020). A more literal translation of the title would be "The Alien."
25. See İsmail Hüsrev, "Türk Köylüsünü Topraklandırmalı. Fakat Nasıl?," *Kadro*, no. 23 (November 1933): 33–39, reprinted in *Kadro: Aylık Fikir Mecmuası: Tıpkı Basım (19–36. Sayılar)*, vol. 2: *1933–1934*, ed. Özgür Erdem (Istanbul: İleri, 2011), 1277–83. Framed as the memoirs of a retired teacher, Şevket Süreyya Aydemir's novel *Toprak Uyanırsa: Ekmeksizköy Öğretmeninin Hatıraları* (Istanbul: Remzi Kitabevi, 1963) is a literary thematization of past Kadro proposals, representing the "awakening" and development of a fictional central Anatolian village by a retired teacher.
26. Asım Karaömerlioğlu, *Orada Bir Köy Var Uzakta: Erken Cumhuriyet Döneminde Köycü Söylem* (Istanbul: İletişim, 2006), 51–85.
27. On the Village Institutes, see M. Asım Karaömerlioğlu, "The Village Institutes Experience in Turkey," *British Journal of Middle Eastern Studies* 25, no. 1 (1998): 47–73; and Fay Kirby, *Türkiye'de Köy Enstitüleri*, trans. Niyazi Berkes (Ankara: İmece, 1962). For an account by one of the institutes' well-known graduates, see Mahmut Makal, *Köy Enstitüleri ve Ötesi* (Istanbul: Çağdaş Yayınları, 1979).
28. Arzu Öztürkmen, *Türkiye'de Folklor ve Milliyetçilik* (Istanbul: İletişim, 1998).
29. "Türkiye Komünist Fırkası Faaliyet Programı" (1931), in Mete Tunçay, *Türkiye'de Sol Akımlar (1925–1936)*, vol. 2 (Istanbul: İletişim, 2009), 372–93. The program was submitted to the Comintern in 1929 and approved in 1930. It was published with a preface in January 1931.
30. *Türkiye Komünist Partisi 1926 Viyana Konferansı*, trans. and translit. Sinan Dervişoğlu (Istanbul: TÜSTAV, 2004), 151.
31. "Türkiye Komünist Fırkası Faaliyet Programı," 387. The analysis of the Turkish countryside in İsmail Hüsrev's book *Turkish Village Economics* (*Türkiye Köy İktisadiyatı*, 1934) bears some similarities to the TKP program. Though both the TKP and the Kadro group advocated for land redistribution, each called for different steps for its implementation. See İsmail Hüsrev, *Türkiye Köy İktisadiyatı: Bir Millî İktisat Tetkiki* (Istanbul: Matbaacılık ve Neşriyat Türk Anonim Şirketi, 1934).
32. According to İsmail Hüsrev, "There are Kurdish-speaking tribes and Turkish groups who are forced to speak Kurdish," but these groups do not form a common nation (*Türkiye Köy İktisadiyatı*, 182). On the role of the Village Institutes in the Turkification of the countryside, see Karaömerlioğlu, *Orada Bir Köy Var Uzakta*, 73, 101–4.

33. For example, see Sabahattin Ali, "Orman Hikâyesi," *Resimli Ay* 7, no. 7 (September 1930): 22–24, 38. Nâzım praised Sabahattin Ali's realist representation of "peasant psychology with all of its conservative and progressive aspects" as well as his thematization of primitive accumulation; see [Nâzım Hikmet], "Bugünün İstidadı, Yarının Kuvveti," *Resimli Ay* 7, no. 7 (September 1930): 35. Sabahattin Ali's critical representation of state officials in his short stories and novels distinguished him from the Kadro writers, who envisioned a vanguardist state developing the countryside.
34. [Nâzım Hikmet], "Mecmuamıza Şiir Gönderen Şairlerle Hasbıhal," *Resimli Ay* 6, no. 8 (October 1929): 35. Narrating the downfall of a proletarianized peasant protagonist, Nâzım's short story "I Wrote My Execution Decree with My Own Blood" revealed his Marxist prejudice against "individualist" "peasant mentality" and folk literature. Refusing to join the collective organization of other workers, the protagonist Mehmet Efe loses his factory job and becomes a vagrant, alcoholic folk singer. See Nâzım Hikmet [pseud. Orhan], "Kendi Hûnumla Yazdım Ben Hükmü İdamımı," *Resimli Ay* 7, no. 6 (August 1930): 22–24.
35. For more on Nâzım's poetics, see chapters 1 and 5.
36. Güzel, *Abidin Dino*, 1:86, 104, 115.
37. Dino, *Yeditepe Öyküleri*, 91–101. Before his time in the Soviet Union, Dino contributed drawings and caricatures to the weekly *Yeni Adam*, founded by the pedagogue İsmail Hakkı Baltacıoğlu in January 1934. On Baltacıoğlu's engagement with traditional arts, see Nergis Ertürk, "Surrealism and Turkish Script Arts," *Modernism/modernity* 17, no. 1 (2010): 47–60.
38. For a valuable survey of the leftist magazines and periodicals of this period, see M. Bülent Varlık, *1940'ların Dergileri*, 5 vols. (Istanbul: TÜSTAV, 2020–2023). For a firsthand account of Dino's leadership in literary journals and battles of the period, see Hasan İzzettin Dinamo, *İkinci Dünya Savaşı'ndan Edebiyat Anıları* (Istanbul: De Yayınevi, 1984); and Ömer Faruk Toprak, *Duman ve Alev* (Istanbul: May Yayınları, 1968), 211–15. See also Abidin Dino and Sait Faik, "1940 Kuşağı'nın Ortak Bildirisi," in Sâlah Birsel, *Gandhi ya da Hint Kirazının Gölgesinde* (Istanbul: Yapı Kredi Yayınları, 1993), 97–101 (originally published in the daily *Tan*, January 24, 1940).
39. On the 1940s generation, see Hikmet Altınkaynak, *Edebiyatımızda 1940 Kuşağı* (Istanbul: Yaylacık Basımevi, 1977); and Mehmed Kemal, *Acılı Kuşak: Anılar, Söyleşiler, Denemeler* (Istanbul: Çağdaş, 1977).
40. For the quoted phrases in this sentence and the previous one, see Abidin Dino, "Halk San'atı," *Yeni Edebiyat*, no. 19 (August 1, 1941): 1, 4. For a collection of Dino's essays, see Abidin Dino, *Toplu Yazılar (1938–1994): Edebiyat, Sanat, Politika*, ed. Turgut Çeviker (Istanbul: Everest, 2018). See in particular the essay "Avdet Edebiyatı," 151–55 (originally published in *Yeni S.E.S.* in 1940).
41. Abidin Dino, "Realizme Dair Notlar," *Yeni Edebiyat*, no. 5 (December 15, 1940): 1, 3.
42. Rasih Nuri İleri, preface to *Yeni Edebiyat 1940–1941: Sosyalist Gerçekçilik*, ed. Suphi Nuri İleri (Istanbul: Scala, 1998), 12–15.
43. On Marxist aesthetics, see Georg Lukács, "Marx and Engels on Aesthetics," in *Writer and Critic and Other Essays*, ed. and trans. Arthur Kahn (Lincoln, NE: iUniverse, an Authors Guild Backprint.com edition, 2005), 61–88. For Dino's

emphasis on the unconscious (*tahtelşuur*) and five senses, see Dino, "Realizme Dair Notlar," 1, 3.
44. Abidin Dino, "Halk ve San'at," *Yeni Edebiyat*, no. 2 (October 26, 1940): 3.
45. Abidin Dino, "İş ve San'at," *S.E.S.*, no. 3 (August 1939): 5.
46. Abidin Dino, "Stop!," *Yeni S.E.S.*, no. 2 (December 1939): 5.
47. Abidin Dino, "Köy ve Sanat," *S.E.S.*, no. 4 (September 1939): 5, 23.
48. Abidin Dino, "Mücessem Sinema," *Yeni Edebiyat*, no. 17 (June 15, 1941): 3. For Dino's discussion of Rumi's "three-dimensional" poetry, see Dino, "İş ve San'at," 5.
49. Dino, "Karacaoğlan," 5. In the description "licking away," Dino is alluding to Mayakovsky's poem "At the Top of My Voice" ("Vo ves' golos"): "the poet / licked up / consumption's spit-wads / with the raspy tongue of his posters." See Vladimir Mayakovsky, "At the Top of My Voice," in *Selected Poems*, trans. James H. McGavran III (Evanston, IL: Northwestern University Press, 2013), 152.
50. Abidin Dino, "Gustave Flaubert ve Realizm," in *Toplu Yazılar*, 195 (originally published in *Yeni S.E.S.* in 1941).
51. İlhan Başgöz, "Love Themes in Turkish Folk Poetry," *Review of National Literatures*, no. 4 (1973): 106, 110.
52. Dino, "Köy ve Sanat," 5, 23.
53. Victor Shklovsky, "Art, as Device," trans. Alexandra Berlina, *Poetics Today* 36, no. 3 (2015): 171. For the Russian original, see Viktor Shklovskii, "Iskusstvo, kak priem," in *Poetika: Sborniki po teorii poeticheskogo iazyka*, ed. Viktor Shklovskii (1919; reprint, Zug, Switzerland: Inter Documentation, 1967), 101–14. In an oft-quoted passage, Shklovsky wrote: "Art exists in order to restore the sensation of life, in order to make us feel things, in order to make a stone stony" ("Art, as Device," 162; "Iskusstvo, kak priem," 105). On Turkish folk poetry's use of parallelisms, see Erman Artun, *Âşıklık Geleneği ve Âşık Edebiyatı* (Istanbul: Akçağ, 2001), 115–22.
54. On the influence of folklore studies on Russian formalists, see Jessica Merrill, *The Origins of Russian Literary Theory: Folklore, Philology, Form* (Evanston, IL: Northwestern University Press, 2022), esp. 57–69.
55. Dino, "Köy ve Sanat," 5, 23.
56. On European Romantic poetry, see Paul de Man, "The Rhetoric of Temporality," in *Blindness and Insight: Essays in the Rhetoric of Contemporary Criticism*, 2nd ed. (Minneapolis: University of Minnesota Press, 1997), 187–228.
57. Robert Bird, "Lenfilm: The Birth and Death of an Institutional Aesthetic," in *A Companion to Russian Cinema*, ed. Birgit Beumers (Malden, MA: Wiley, 2016), 75. My account of Lenfilm in this section draws on Bird's essay. On the cultural and intellectual life of Leningrad during the 1920s and 1930s, see Katerina Clark, *Petersburg: Crucible of Cultural Revolution* (Cambridge, MA: Harvard University Press, 1995). For useful surveys of Soviet cinema, see Jay Leyda, *Kino: A History of the Russian and Soviet Film*, 3rd ed. (Princeton, NJ: Princeton University Press, 1983); and Denise J. Youngblood, *Movies for the Masses: Popular Cinema and Soviet Society in the 1920s* (New York: Cambridge University Press, 1992).
58. B. M. Eikhenbaum, ed., *The Poetics of Cinema*, ed. Richard Taylor, trans. Richard Taylor and others (Oxford: RPT, 1982). For the Russian original, see B. M. Eikhenbaum, ed., *Poetika kino* (Moscow: Kinopechat'', 1927).
59. Bird, "Lenfilm," 73.

60. As former members of the experimental theater workshop FEKS in 1921, these young artists had drawn inspiration from the futurism of Mayakovsky, street posters and circus performances, and Meyerhold's constructivist theater, embracing a new art practice of eccentric "attractions." By 1925, FEKS had evolved into a workshop for actor training. For the FEKS manifesto of 1922 and other archival documents pertaining to the film collective, see Ian Christie and John Gillett, eds., *Futurism/Formalism/FEKS: "Eccentrism" and Soviet Cinema, 1918–1936* (London: British Film Institute, 1978). See also Oksana Bulgakowa, *FEKS: Die Fabrik des Exzentrischen Schauspielers* (Berlin: Potemkin Press, 1996); and Maria Natasha Corrigan, "Soviet Eccentrism: 'A Can-Can on the Tightrope of Logic,'" PhD diss., University of California, Santa Barbara, 2015.
61. Regarding FEKS films "making the historical contemporary," see Yuri Tynyanov, "On FEKS," in *The Film Factory: Russian and Soviet Cinema in Documents*, ed. Richard Taylor and Ian Christie, trans. Richard Taylor (Cambridge, MA: Harvard University Press, 1988), 257–59 (originally published as "O FEKSakh" in *Sovetskii ekran* in 1929). For Widdis's discussion of "haptic" looking in relation to the FEKS films, see Widdis, *Socialist Senses*, 51–79. For a visual analysis of FEKS films through the cameraman Moskvin's camera and lighting work, see Philip Cavendish, *The Men with the Movie Camera: The Poetics of Visual Style in Soviet Avant-Garde Cinema of the 1920s* (New York: Berghahn, 2013), 196–240.
62. First used in a Central Committee resolution on literature in 1925, the phrase "intelligible to the millions" became popular in the late 1920s. On its mobilization in the context of Soviet cinema, see "Party Cinema Conference Resolution: The Results of Cinema Construction in the USSR and the Tasks of Soviet Cinema," in *The Film Factory*, ed. Taylor and Christie, 212.
63. On Yutkevich's life and works, see Dmitrii Moldavskii, *S Maiakovskim v teatre i kino: Kniga o Sergee Iutkeviche* (Moscow: Vserossiiskoe teatral'noe obshchestvo, 1975). On his early years, see Sergei Yutkevich, "Teenage Artists of the Revolution," in *Cinema in Revolution: The Heroic Era of the Soviet Film*, ed. Luda Schitzer, Jean Schnitzer, and Marcel Martin, trans. David Robinson (New York: Hill and Wang, 1973), 11–41.
64. See Bird, "Lenfilm," 77; Moldavskii, *S Maiakovskim v teatre i kino*, 149–56; and Sergei Iutkevich, "Pervyi god raboty kinomasterskoi," *Iskusstvo kino*, no. 1 (January 1936): 33–37. Rejecting specialization in film production, Yutkevich's report on the first year of the workshop praised the collective organization of filmmaking in cinema's early days.
65. Widdis, *Socialist Senses*, 298.
66. For useful historical accounts drawing extensively on archival materials, see Gennadii Miasnikov, *Ocherki istorii sovetskogo kinodekoratsionnogo iskusstva (1918–1930)* (Moscow: VGIK, 1975); and Gennadii Miasnikov, *Ocherki istorii sovetskogo kinodekoratsionnogo iskusstva (1931–1945)* (Moscow: VGIK, 1979). In addition to Widdis's groundbreaking work in *Socialist Senses* and "Faktura," cited earlier, see Emma Widdis, "Cinema and the Art of Being: Towards a History of Early Soviet Set Design," in *A Companion to Russian Cinema*, ed. Beumers, 314–36. See also Eleanor Rees, *Designing Russian Cinema: The Production Artist and the Material Environment in Silent Era Film* (London: Bloomsbury Academic, 2023).

67. S. V. Kozlovskii and N. M. Kolin, *Khudozhnik-arkhitektor v kino* (Moscow: Teakinopechat', 1930), quoted in Widdis, "Faktura," 10. The constructivist influence on Russian stage set represents an important prehistory of the debates on film in the 1930s; see John E. Bowlt, "Constructivism and Russian Stage Drama," *Performing Arts Journal* 1, no. 3 (1977): 62–84.
68. Widdis, "Faktura," 10.
69. Widdis, "Faktura," 13. For a rich essay tracing the discursive shifts in *faktura* from 1912 to 1922 in the writings of the Russian avant-garde, see Maria Gough, "Faktura: The Making of the Russian Avant-Garde," *RES: Anthropology and Aesthetics* 36 (1999): 33–59; see also Christina Kiaer, *Imagine No Possessions: The Socialist Objects of Russian Constructivism* (Cambridge, MA: MIT Press, 2005).
70. For Shklovsky's discussion of *faktura* in relation to Tatlin's work in 1921, see Victor Shklovsky, "On Faktura and Counter-reliefs," trans. Eugenia Lockwood, in *Tatlin*, ed. Larissa Zhadova (New York: Rizzoli, 1988), 341–42; Viktor Shklovskii, "O fakture i kontrrel'efakh," in *Gamburgskii schet, 1914–1933* (Moscow: Sovietskii pisatel', 1990), 98–100. Describing *faktura* as "the main distinguishing feature of that particular world of specially constructed objects the totality of which we ... call art," Shklovsky articulated the purpose of art as the creation of a "continuous and thoroughly palpable" "faktura-thing [*veshch' fakturnuiu*]" ("On Faktura," 341; "O fakture," 99). For Shklovsky, the *faktura* object made possible a new sensory mode of living and relating to the world. For his emphasis on the staging and altering of filmic material, see Victor Shklovsky, "The Semantics of Cinema," in *The Film Factory*, ed. Taylor and Christie, 131–33; Viktor Shklovskii, "Semantika kino," *Kino-zhurnal A.R.K.* 8–9 (1925): 5, reprinted in Viktor Shklovskii, *Za 60 let: Raboty o kino* (Moscow: Iskusstvo, 1985), 30–32. Criticizing Dzigo Vertov's cine-eye for failing to produce a three-dimensional encounter with filmic material, Shklovksy wrote that "in their frames objects [*veshchi*] are impoverished because there is no tendentious (in the artistic sense of this word) attitude towards the object" ("The Semantics of Cinema," 133; "Semantika kino," 32).
71. I. Manevich, "V bor'be za realisticheskii obraz," *Iskusstvo kino*, no. 9 (September 1937): 5, 11.
72. Widdis, *Socialist Senses*, 227–64. See also Anna Toropova, *Feeling Revolution: Cinema, Genre, and the Politics of Affect Under Stalin* (New York: Oxford University Press, 2020).
73. Regarding these letters, see Güzel, *Abidin Dino*, 1:210.
74. Dino quoted in Güzel, *Abidin Dino*, 1:190, 207–8, 192–93. For Yutkevich's account of the rehearsals for *Marriage*, see Iutkevich, "Pervyi god raboty kinomasterskoi," 33–34. After being "exiled to Kazakhstan for several years," Enei returned to movie production during the 1940s. See Jamie Miller, *Soviet Cinema: Politics and Persuasion Under Stalin* (London: I. B. Tauris, 2010), 88.
75. Güzel, *Abidin Dino*, 1:190. For examples of Dino's sketches for *The Miners*, see Rasih Nuri İleri, *Sahne ve Kostüm Tasarımı: Abidin Dino / Scenery and Costume Design: Abidin Dino* (Istanbul: Yapı Kredi Yayınları, 2005), 28–29.
76. Widdis, "Cinema and the Art of Being," 322–23.
77. Widdis, *Socialist Senses*, 193; for Widdis's discussion of Soviet Easterns, see chapters 5 and 8 of *Socialist Senses*. For an earlier discussion of Soviet Orientalism in my book, see chapter 1.

4. ABIDIN DINO'S PEASANT THEATER

78. *Ankara*'s middle section is set in the old village of Ankara, depicting narrow and irregular stone streets and cramped dwellings surrounded by rugged mountains. The sequence of shots includes women and children cleaning wool, an old man building a brick wall, men carrying heavy jars, a barber cutting hair, a seamster sewing pants, children and adults selling animals, and men idling and smoking cigarettes. With an intertitle announcing a segment about a traditional *zeibek* dance performed for the Soviet visitors, the film turns romantically ethnographic, with close-ups emphasizing the dancer's embodied resilience and tactile knowledge, linking the dance to national independence through the images of a statue of an armed Turkish soldier and one of a peasant woman holding a cannonball. See Sergei Iutkevich and Leo Arnshtam, dirs., *Türkiye'nin Kalbi Ankara* (Lenfilm and Turkish Ministry of Education, 1934), https://www.tccb.gov.tr/ata_ozel/video/.
79. For a useful account of the Country Tours, see Murat Ural, "Cumhuriyet'in Romansı: Ressamlar Yurt Gezisinde (1938–1943)," in Berk et al., *Yurt Gezileri ve Yurt Resimleri (1938–1943)*, 20–61. Although Dino welcomed the Country Tours for establishing a potential "contact zone" for Turkish artists and peasants, he wondered if they too closely resembled "the travels of tourists to Africa for lion hunting" (Dino, "Stop!," 21).
80. See Ural, "Cumhuriyet'in Romansı," 20–21, 53.
81. For "toilet ewers," see İsmail Hakkı Baltacıoğlu, "Abidin Dino'ya Açık Mektup," *Servet-i Fünun*, no. 2267-572 (November 23, 1939): 2. The other descriptions are given in Ahmet Muhip Dranas, "Cumhuriyet Halk Partisinin Anadolu Resim Gezileri," *Güzel Sanatlar*, no. 4 (1942): 76.
82. See the dossier "Abidin Dino'nun İbrikleri," *Yeni Adam*, no. 264 (January 18, 1940): 10–13, 17.
83. Nurullah Ataç, "Bir Mektup İ. H. Baltacıoğlu'na," *Yeni Adam*, no. 264 (January 18, 1940): 11–12; İsmail Hakkı Baltacıoğlu, "Nurullah Ataç'a Mektup," *Yeni Adam*, no. 264 (January 1940): 13, 17; Abidin Dino, "Bir Açık Mektup Daha," *Yeni Adam*, no. 264 (January 18, 1940): 12.
84. Walter Benjamin, "The Work of Art in the Age of Its Technological Reproducibility: Second Version," trans. Edmund Jephcott and Harry Zohn, in *Walter Benjamin: Selected Writings*, vol. 3: *1935–1938*, ed. Howard Eiland and Michael W. Jennings (Cambridge, MA: Harvard University Press, 2006), 106–8. Like Benjamin, Dino concluded his essay with a comparative discussion of architecture and film, imagining the latter as tactile three-dimensional art.
85. M. Oğuz, "Bir Anlayış!," *Yeni Adam*, no. 268 (February 15, 1940): 9. For Abidin Nesimi's criticism of Dino during this period, see Abidin Nesimi, *Yılların İçinden* (Istanbul: Gözlem, 1977), 182–83.
86. Oktay, *Toplumcu Gerçekçiliğin Kaynakları*, 324.
87. For the quoted phrase, see Gayatri Chakravorty Spivak, "Can the Subaltern Speak?," in *Can the Subaltern Speak?: Reflections on the History of an Idea*, ed. Rosalind C. Morris (New York: Columbia University Press, 2010), 23.
88. On Dino's discussion of art as direct action, see Dino, "Karacaoğlan," 5; and Abidin Dino, "Harp ve Sanat," in *Toplu Yazılar*, 167–70 (originally published in *Yeni Edebiyat* in 1941). Treating Karacaoğlan as more than just a lyric poet, Dino emphasized his protest of the beys' feudalism and proposed both Mayakovsky

4. ABIDIN DINO'S PEASANT THEATER

and Karacaoğlan as models of a new rebellion (*isyan*) literature capable of weaponizing the power of words against an inegalitarian social order.
89. For an account of the Turkish press during the Second World War, see O. Murat Güvenir, *İkinci Dünya Savaşında Türk Basını: Siyasal İktidarın Basını Denetlemesi ve Yönlendirmesi* (Istanbul: Gazeteciler Cemiyeti, 1991).
90. Abidin Dino, *Kızılbaş Günlerim* (Istanbul: Sel Yayıncılık, 2001), 21–22.
91. M. Şehmus Güzel, *Abidin Dino: Üç Kitap (1913–1993)*, vol. 2: *İkinci Kitap (1942–1952)* (Istanbul: Kitap Yayınevi, 2008), 105, 248. During Dino's military service in Kayseri, which lasted through January 1946, Güzin moved to Ankara to work as a docent in the School of Language and History-Geography at Ankara University.
92. On the socioeconomic history of the Adana region, see Çağlar Keyder, *State and Class in Turkey: A Study in Capitalist Development* (London: Verso, 1987), 138–39, 206; Meltem Toksöz, *Nomads, Migrants, and Cotton in the Eastern Mediterranean: The Making of the Adana-Mersin Region, 1850–1908* (Leiden, Netherlands: Brill, 2010); and Chris Gratien, *The Unsettled Plain: An Environmental History of the Late Ottoman Frontier* (Stanford, CA: Stanford University Press, 2022).
93. Güzel, *Abidin Dino*, 2:77–79. For his *Türksözü* columns, see Abidin Dino, *Adana Yazıları*, ed. Murat Baycanlar (Adana: Karahan Kitabevi, 2013).
94. For the quoted phrase, see Dino, "Çukurova Tekerlemesi," in *Adana Yazıları*, 40. Regarding his Adana essays on Sinan, see Dino, *Adana Yazıları*, 28–47. For Dino's discussion of Sinan in the Istanbul journal *Yeni Yol* in 1940, see Abidin Dino, "Hümanizma Dönüş: Hayır! Hümanizma Gidiş: Evet!," in *Toplu Yazılar*, 108–13.
95. Régis Debray, "Socialism: A Life-Cycle," *New Left Review* 46 (July–August 2007): 24.
96. Widdis, *Socialist Senses*, 181.
97. Eisenstein quoted in Widdis, *Socialist Senses*, 195. On Tretyakov's factographic writing about China, see Edward Tyerman, *Internationalist Aesthetics: China and Early Soviet Culture* (New York: Columbia University Press, 2022), 20–28.
98. On the Adana school, see Abidin Dino, "Yaşar Kemal," in *Toplu Yazılar*, 245–53; Abidin Dino, "'Adana Okulu'ndan Günümüze," in *Toplu Yazılar*, 255–61; G. Dino, *Gel Zaman Git Zaman*, 103–5; and Yaşar Kemal, *Yaşar Kemal Kendini Anlatıyor: Alain Bosquet ile Görüşmeler* (Istanbul: Yapı Kredi Yayınları, 1990), 54–62, 93–97, 112–13.
99. Yaşar Kemal, "Mutluluğun Resmini Yapan Adam, Abidin Dino," in *Ustadır Arı: Yazılar/Konuşmalar*, ed. Alpay Kabacalı (Istanbul: Can, 1995), 160. The essay was first published in French in 1994. For Dino's Adana paintings and drawings, see Avcı, *Abidin Dino Bir Dünya*, 162–79.
100. For the quoted phrases, see Spivak, "Can the Subaltern Speak?," 29, 31.
101. Abidin Dino, "Türk Tiyatrosu Nasıl Doğacak?," *Yeni S.E.S.*, November 1939, 17, 21. For his theater reviews during his Istanbul years, see Abidin Dino, "Üç Film ve Bir Piyes," *Yeni Edebiyat*, no. 8 (February 1, 1941): 1–2; and Abidin Dino, "Hamlet," *Yeni Edebiyat*, no. 24 (October 15, 1941): 1–2.
102. On the theater branch of the Adana People's House and Dino's contributions, see Nurhan Tekerek, *Cumhuriyet Dönemi'nde Adana'da Batı Tarzı Tiyatro Yaşamı (1923–1990)* (Ankara: Türk Tarih Kurumu Basımevi, 1997), 72–102.
103. On traditional village plays, see Metin And, *A History of Theatre and Popular Entertainment in Turkey* (Ankara: Forum, 1963–1964); and Nurhan Tekerek, *Köy Seyirlik Oyunları* (Istanbul: Mitos Boyut, 2008).

4. ABIDIN DINO'S PEASANT THEATER

104. Pertev Naili Boratav, *100 Soruda Türk Halk Edebiyatı* (Istanbul: Gerçek, 1988), 223–24.
105. Abidin Dino, "Halkevinde Köy Tiyatrosu," *Görüşler*, no. 52 (April 1943): 14.
106. Dino, "Halkevinde Köy Tiyatrosu," 14.
107. Abidin Dino, "Bir Köy Oyunu Notları," *Görüşler*, no. 53 (May 1943): 13–14.
108. Güzel, *Abidin Dino*, 1:200.
109. The declaration states:

    The basis for the workshop's work is a general plan. After the final correction of the script, each directing team makes their preliminary presentation, which is heard and discussed by the entire group, and after the creative director's approval, work with the designer, cameraman, and composer begins.

    The director and the designer finalize the decors for all the scenes and use them to rehearse with the actors. And only after the final presentation of the rehearsed main scenes of the film, and perhaps also some trial shoots, the director ... finalizes the working version of the script that serves as the basis for the final plan of the shooting period.

    "Deklaratsiia pervoi khudozhestvennoi masterskoi pod khudozhestvennym rukovodstvom S. Iutkevicha," in *Iz istorii Lenfil'ma*, vol. 4, ed. Nina Gornitskaia (Leningrad: Iskusstvo, 1975), 136–37.
110. Sergei Iutkevich, "Bol'shaia perspektiva," *Iskusstvo kino*, no. 12 (December 1937): 44, 54, 51.
111. Iutkevich, "Bol'shaia perspektiva," 54–55. On the shooting of *The Miners*, see also Moldavskii, *S Maiakovskim v teatre i kino*, 154–61.
112. Dino, "Bir Köy Oyunu Notları," 13–14.
113. Dino, *Kel*, 17–18; subsequent page citations to the 1944 edition are given parenthetically in the text.
114. For an important example of the genre, see Mahmut Makal, *Bizim Köy: Köy Öğretmeninin Notları* (Istanbul: Varlık, 1950). On Turkish village literature, see Carole Rathbun, *The Village in the Turkish Novel and Short Story, 1920 to 1955* (The Hague, Netherlands: Mouton, 1972); Guzine Dino, "The Turkish Peasant Novel, or the Anatolian Theme," trans. Joan Grimbert, *World Literature Today* 60, no. 2 (1986): 266–75; Taner Timur, *Osmanlı-Türk Romanında Tarih, Toplum ve Kimlik* (Istanbul: Afa Yayıncılık), 87–193; and Erkan Irmak, *Eski Köye Yeni Roman* (Istanbul: İletişim, 2018).
115. On Soviet national literatures, see Kathryn Douglas Schild, "Between Moscow and Baku: National Literatures at the 1934 Congress of Soviet Writers," PhD diss., University of California, Berkeley 2010.
116. Dino, "Türk Tiyatrosu Nasıl Doğacak?," 17.
117. Abidin Dino, "Küllük Beyannamesi," in *Toplu Yazılar*, 118 (originally published in *Küllük* in 1940).
118. Immanuel Kant, "An Answer to the Question: What Is Enlightenment?," trans. James Schmidt, in *What Is Enlightenment? Eighteenth-Century Answers and Twentieth-Century Questions*, ed. James Schmidt (Berkeley: University of California Press, 1996), 58–64.
119. Tekerek, *Köy Seyirlik Oyunları*, 95–105, 140–42, 103–4.

4. ABIDIN DINO'S PEASANT THEATER

120. Vladimir Nedobrovo, "The Eccentricism of FEKS," trans. Richard Sherwood, in *Futurism/Formalism/FEKS*, ed. Christie and Gillett, 19. Ali's wasteful consumption may remind some readers of Georges Bataille's imagination of unproductive expenditure, but *Baldy* clearly points to proletarianization as the condition of structural transformation. See Georges Bataille, "The Notion of Expenditure," in *Visions of Excess: Selected Writings, 1927–1939*, ed. Allan Stoekl, trans. Allan Stoekl, with Carl R. Lovitt and Donald M. Leslie Jr. (Minneapolis: University of Minnesota Press, 1985), 116–29.
121. Dino first encountered the concept of *imece* in Balıkesir in 1939 and used it in his writings during the 1940s and 1960s. For an early discussion, see Dino, "İş ve San'at," 5.
122. Composed in the late 1940s and set during the Second World War, *The Inheritors* is focused on the spendthrift son of a pasha, Paşazade (possibly based on Dino's elder brother Ahmet), who lives on rent from the family pastureland in Adana. Like *Baldy*, it features heteroglossia and the destructive estrangement of commodity objects, suggesting that farmworkers crushed by absentee landowners, semifeudal renters, agrarian capitalist intermediaries, and corrupt state bureaucrats will be emancipated by proletarianization and collective farming. The play mobilizes another formalist technique of embedded representation, incorporating characters' dream scenes as well as scenes taking place in the city cinema hall and a photography shop (Dino, *Verese*, 122, 133, 165).
123. Boris Groys, *The Total Art of Stalinism: Avant-Garde, Aesthetic Dictatorship, and Beyond*, trans. Charles Rougle (Princeton, NJ: Princeton University Press, 1992), 44, 36.
124. Evgeny Dobrenko, *Political Economy of Socialist Realism*, trans. Jesse M. Savage (New Haven, CT: Yale University Press, 2007), 5, 14.
125. Kleberg, *Theatre as Action*, 112–13, 76, 113, 111.
126. Although parades appear in the final scenes of both plays, with the peasants heading to the mine and the dying farmworker Kadri dreaming of a collectivist farm, *Baldy* concludes with Ali in the coffeehouse, and *The Inheritors* concludes with Hasan and the others viewing Kadri's body in the street. On the translation and adaptation of Brecht's works and theories in Turkey after the 1960s, see Ela E. Gezen, *Brecht, Turkish Theater, and Turkish-German Literature: Reception, Adaptation, and Innovation After 1960* (Rochester, NY: Camden House, 2018).
127. Baer, *Indigenous Vanguards*, 17, 20.
128. Kemal Sadık Göğceli, *Ağıtlar 1* (Adana: Türksözü Matbaası, 1943). On Yaşar Kemal's life, see Yaşar Kemal, *Yaşar Kemal Kendini Anlatıyor*.
129. For a useful survey of Yaşar Kemal's oeuvre, see Laurent Mignon, "Yaşar Kemal," in *Turkish Novelists Since 1960*, ed. Burcu Alkan and Çimen Günay-Erkol (Detroit: Gale Cengage Learning, 2014), 156–71. Important criticism includes the essays in Ahmet Ö. Evin, ed., "Yaşar Kemal," special issue of *Edebiyât: Journal of Near Eastern Literatures* 5, nos. 1–2 (1980); Arif Dirlik, "'Like a Song Gone Silent': The Political Ecology of Barbarism and Civilization in *Waiting for the Barbarians* and *The Legend of the Thousand Bulls*," *Diaspora* 1, no. 3 (1991): 321–52; Altan Gökalp et al., *Yaşar Kemal'i Okumak: İnceleme*, trans. Nedret Tanyolaç Öztokat and Erdim Öztokat (Istanbul: Adam Yayınları, 1999); and Fethi Naci, *Yaşar Kemal'in Romancılığı* (Istanbul: Yapı Kredi, 2004).

4. ABIDIN DINO'S PEASANT THEATER

130. Yaşar Kemal, "Bebek," in *Sarı Sıcak* (Istanbul: Varlık, 1952), 12–44. *The Baby* was first published in 1950 in the daily *Cumhuriyet*. *Sarı Sıcak* (Yellow heat, translated into English under the title *Anatolian Tales* by Thilda Kemal in 1968) is Yaşar Kemal's first published collection of short stories.
131. Yaşar Kemal, "Yatak," in *Sarı Sıcak*, 45–52.
132. Yaşar Kemal, *Hüyükteki Nar Ağacı* (Istanbul: Toros, 1982), composed in 1951 but first published in 1982; Yaşar Kemal, *Üç Anadolu Efsanesi: Köroğlu'nun Meydana Çıkışı, Karacaoğlan, Alageyik* (Istanbul: Ararat, 1967); Yaşar Kemal, *Ağrıdağı Efsanesi* (Istanbul: Cem, 1970); and Yaşar Kemal, *Bin Boğalar Efsanesi* (Istanbul: Cem, 1971).
133. For Yaşar Kemal's discussion of the importance of objects in his work, see Yaşar Kemal, *Yaşar Kemal Kendini Anlatıyor*, 149–52.
134. On the concept of "revolutionary educational *imece*," see Abidin Dino, "Devrimci Eğitim İmecesi," in *Toplu Yazılar*, 822 (originally published in *Ant* in 1968). Güzin corresponded with Auerbach regularly during this period. Moving beyond the nationalist appropriation of Anatolian folk traditions by Auerbach's other students, Yaşar Kemal saw the possibility of another Marxist humanism in the epics and legends of Turkmen and Kurdish nomadic tribes and subaltern villagers.
135. Joe Cleary, Jed Esty, and Colleen Lye, eds., "Peripheral Realisms," special issue of *Modern Language Quarterly* 73, no. 3 (2012).
136. Joe Cleary, "Realism After Modernism and the Literary World-System," in "Peripheral Realisms," ed. Cleary, Esty, and Lye, 261. For the Warwick Collective's account of critical irrealism, see Warwick Research Collective [Sharae Deckard et al.], "The Question of Peripheral Realism," in *Combined and Uneven Development: Towards a New Theory of World-Literature* (Liverpool: Liverpool University Press, 2015), 49–80.
137. Cleary, "Realism After Modernism," 268.
138. Alenka Zupančič, *What Is Sex?* (Cambridge, MA: MIT Press, 2017), 122. It is also useful to recall Antonio Gramsci's critique of Renaissance "immanentist philosophies": "Their weakness is demonstrated in the educational field, in that the immanentist philosophies have not even attempted to construct a conception which could take the place of religion in the education of children"; see Antonio Gramsci, *Selections from the Prison Notebooks*, trans. Quintin Hoare and Geoffrey Nowell Smith (London: International, 1971), 329, qtd. in Baer, *Indigenous Vanguards*, 38.
139. See *TKP MK Dış Bürosu 1962 Konferansı*, 30. Dino also emphasized the need for reliable new data about the Turkish countryside, promising to send the Leipzig group recently published materials (*TKP MK Dış Bürosu 1962 Konferansı*, 28). A report he published in French in 1964 on "the conditions of land reform" reviewed recent economic studies of Turkey, examining inequalities in land distribution in the context of postwar development. See Abidin Dino, "Türkiye'de 'Tarımsal' Reform Olanakları," trans. Gülten Kazgan, in *Toplu Yazılar*, 728–47 (Turkish translation first published in *Yeni Ufuklar* in 1965).
140. For the digital proofs of a two-volume collection of Dino's Bizim Radyo scripts, see Abidin Dino, "İbiş ile Memiş-1" and "İbiş ile Memiş-2," 2005, TÜSTAV. Unfortunately, they remain unpublished. According to the TKP member Hayk Açıkgöz, the Turkish writer Fahri Erdinç also contributed to the production of

İbiş and Memiş radio dialogues on Bizim Radyo. See Hayk Açıkgöz, *Anadolulu Bir Ermeni Komünistin Anıları* (Istanbul: Belge Yayınları, 2006), 508. On İbiş and the Old Man, see Metin And, *Drama at the Crossroads* (Istanbul: ISIS Press, 1991), 148. Beginning in the 1950s, the Yeşilçam film industry produced a series of popular comedies using İbiş and Memiş as stock characters.

141. On this visit, see Sergei Iutkevich, "'Ia vstrechaiu Abidina...,'" *Literaturnaia gazeta*, no. 16 (February 5, 1966), 2; and Dino and Dino, *Güzin Dino-Abidin Dino Mektupları*, 20–25. Dino also designed the book cover for the Russian translation of Orhan Kemal's collection of short stories *Mstitel'naia volshebnitsa: Rasskazy*, trans. S. I. Uturgauri (Moscow: Nauka, 1967).

142. Dino, "Devrimci Eğitim İmecesi," in *Toplu Yazılar*, 822. See also Abidin Dino, "Geleceğe Dönük Köy-Kent Enstitüleri," in *Toplu Yazılar*, 882–86 (originally published in *Forum* in 1970).

5. IN THE SHADOW OF LENIN: NÂZIM HIKMET'S PROSE POETICS OF SERIALITY AND THE TIME OF (POST)COMMUNISM

1. Nazym Khikmet, *Romantika: Roman*, trans. L. Starostova, *Znamia* 33, no. 4 (April 1963): 35–77; and Nazym Khikmet, *Romantika, roman: Okonchanie*, trans. L. Starostova *Znamia* 33, no. 5 (May 1963): 43–92. For the first book edition in Russian, see Nazym Khikmet, *Romantika: Roman*, trans. L. Starostova (Moscow: Sovetskii pisatel', 1964).

2. Abidine Dino, "Nazım Hikmet, mon ami de la Sublime Porte," *Lettres françaises*, no. 989 (August 1–7, 1963): 7.

3. For the book edition in French, see Nâzım Hikmet, *Les romantiques (La vie est belle, mon vieux...): Roman*, trans. Munevver Andaç (Paris: Éditeurs français réunis, 1964). For the Turkish editions, see Nâzım Hikmet, *Yaşamak Güzel Şeydir Kardeşim: Roman* (Sofia, Bulgaria: Narodna prosveta, 1964); and Nâzım Hikmet, *Yaşamak Güzel Şey Bekardeşim* (Istanbul: Gün, 1967). On the publication of Nâzım's collected works (including this novel) in Bulgaria under the editorship of Ekber Babaev, see Sabri Tata, *Türk Komünistlerinin Bulgaristan Macerası* (Istanbul: Boğaziçi Yayınları, 1993), 27–31.

4. Ziya Yamaç and Şekibe Yamaç, *Nâzım Hikmet Aramızda* (Istanbul: Hasat Yayınları, 1992), 49–79. Nâzım's poetry thematized this opening to anonymity; see Nergis Ertürk, *Grammatology and Literary Modernity in Turkey* (New York: Oxford University Press, 2011), in particular the chapter "Nâzım's Ghostwriting," 159–81. On the widespread practice of anonymous quotation of Nâzım's poetic lines in the obituaries of Turkish communist youth killed during the 1970s and 1980s, see Jill Stockwell, "A Shared Longing: Rewriting Nâzım Hikmet in Turkish and Turkish-German Literature, 1963–2017," PhD diss., Princeton University, 2017, 37, 63.

5. On this point, see Mutlu Konuk Blasing, *Nâzım Hikmet: The Life and Times of Turkey's World Poet* (New York: Persea, 2013), 53. For Şevket Süreyya's account of a public screening of Vsevolod Pudovkin's documentary film *Golod... Golod... Golod...* in the summer of 1922 in Moscow, see Şevket Süreyya, "Polemik: Benerji Kendini Niçin Öldürdü?," *Kadro: Aylık Fikir Mecmuası*, no. 4 (April 1932): 31, facsimile in *Kadro: Aylık Fikir Mecmuası: Tıpkı Basım (1–18. Sayılar)*, vol. 1: *1932–1933*, ed.

5. IN THE SHADOW OF LENIN

Özgür Erdem (Istanbul: İleri Yayınları, 2011), 189. Nâzım supposedly wrote the poem the morning after the screening.

6. Nâzım Hikmet, "Açların Gözbebekleri," in *835 Satır* (Istanbul: Muallim Ahmet Halit Kitaphanesi, 1929), 17, spacing, italics, and bold type in the original.
7. For a useful discussion of the relationship between Nâzım's poetics and politics, see Mutlu Konuk Blasing, "Nâzım Hikmet and Ezra Pound: 'To Confess Wrong Without Losing Rightness,'" *Journal of Modern Literature* 33, no. 2 (2010): 1–23.
8. Nâzım Hikmet, "Gazete Kollektif Bir Teşkilatçı," in Erden Akbulut, *Komintern Belgelerinde Nâzım Hikmet* (Istanbul: TÜSTAV, 2002), 45–47.
9. Régis Debray, "Socialism: A Life-Cycle," *New Left Review* 46 (July–August 2007): 7, 16.
10. Nâzım Hikmet, "19 Yaşım," in *Sesini Kaybeden Şehir* ([Istanbul]: Remzi Kitaphanesi, 1931), 46–47, spacing and use of two and three suspension points in the original.
11. Erden Akbulut, "Nâzım Hikmet Üzerine Yeni Belgeler," *Kıyı*, no. 275 (2012): 29.
12. Akbulut, "Nâzım Hikmet Üzerine Yeni Belgeler," 29. See also "Registratsionnyii list," RGASPI f. 495, op. 266, d. 47, l. 155.
13. Akbulut, *Komintern Belgelerinde Nâzım Hikmet*, 36.
14. Nâzım Hikmet, "Gazete Kollektif Bir Teşkilatçı," 45; subsequent page citations are given parenthetically in the text. By "economism," both Lenin and Nâzım meant a socialist program supporting a restriction of the worker movement to economic struggle for higher wages and improved work conditions. Lenin was critical of the economists' "surrender" of the political struggle to the bourgeoisie. See Lars T. Lih, *Lenin Rediscovered: "What Is to Be Done?" in Context* (Chicago: Haymarket, 2008), 706–13.
15. Lih, *Lenin Rediscovered*, 435, 457, 6.
16. V. I. Lenin, "Where to Begin," in *Collected Works*, vol. 5, ed. Victor Jerome, trans. Joe Fineberg and George Hanna (Moscow: Foreign Languages Publishing House, 1961), 21–22; V. I. Lenin, "S chego nachat'?," in *Polnoe sobranie sochinenii*, vol. 5, 5th ed. (Moscow: Gosudarstvennoe izdatel'stvo, 1959), 10. Subsequent page citations to both "Where to Begin" and "S chego nachat'?" are given parenthetically in the text.
17. Jean-Jacques Lecercle, *A Marxist Philosophy of Language*, trans. Gregory Elliott (Leiden, Netherlands: Brill, 2006), 103, 104.
18. Jacques Derrida, *Of Grammatology*, trans. Gayatri Chakravorty Spivak, 40th anniv. ed. (Baltimore, MD: Johns Hopkins University Press, 2016), 172–73.
19. Rousseau quoted in Derrida, *Of Grammatology*, 154.
20. V. I. Lenin, *What Is to Be Done? Burning Questions of Our Movement*, in Lih, *Lenin Rediscovered*, 823; V. I. Lenin, *Chto delat'? Nabolevshie voprosy nashego dvizheniia*, in *Polnoe sobranie sochinenii*, vol. 6, 5th ed. (Moscow: Gosudarstvennoe izdatel'stvo, 1959), 165.
21. Lenin, *What Is to Be Done?*, 829, 821; *Chto delat'?*, 171, 163.
22. Compare Walter Benjamin's image of a whole text (or textual whole) in "The Task of the Translator," trans. Harry Zohn, in *Walter Benjamin: Selected Writings*, vol. 1: *1913–1926*, ed. Marcus Bullock and Michael W. Jennings, trans. Rodney Livingstone and others (Cambridge, MA: Harvard University Press, 2002), 260:

5. IN THE SHADOW OF LENIN

"Fragments of a vessel that are to be glued together must match one another in the smallest details, although they need not be like one another."
23. As Étienne Balibar puts it, Lenin never abandoned the idea of world communist revolution as historically necessary: "At the price of an extreme tension, this coexisted and sought linkage with a strategic 'empiricism,' an 'analysis of concrete situations'" that recognized the "plurality of forms" of struggle. See Etienne Balibar, "The Philosophical Moment in Politics Determined by War: Lenin 1914–16," in *Lenin Reloaded: Toward a Politics of Truth*, ed. Sebastian Budgen, Stathis Kouvelakis, and Slavoj Žižek (Durham, NC: Duke University Press, 2007), 211. Where such "strategic empiricism" describes the mode of Lenin's performative theory of slogans, the examination of translation and Latinization in the later writings revised Lenin's prerevolutionary understanding of writing as secondary supplement. On Lenin's imagination of revolutionary writing as force in the later works, see Nergis Ertürk, "Toward a Literary Communism: The 1926 Baku Turcological Congress," *boundary 2* 40, no. 2 (2013): 183–213.
24. *Türkiye Komünist Partisi 1926 Viyana Konferansı*, trans. and translit. Sinan Dervişoğlu (Istanbul: TÜSTAV, 2004), 56–61.
25. Akbulut, *Komintern Belgelerinde Nâzım Hikmet*, 155–58.
26. Nail V. Çakırhan quoted in Akbulut, *Komintern Belgelerinde Nâzım Hikmet*, 187.
27. See Hasan İzzettin Dinamo, *TKP Aydınlar ve Anılar* (Istanbul: Yalçın Yayınları, 1989), 19–20; and Hasan İzzettin Dinamo, "Nâzım Hikmet'le Birlikte Kurduğumuz İllegal(!) Örgüt," *Türkiye Yazıları Dergisi* 1 (1977): 29–30. Ruşen Zeki served as a member of the THIF established in Ankara, contributing to the party newspaper *Yeni Hayat*, edited by Nizamettin Nazif, during the Turkish War of Independence.
28. Kemal Sülker, *Şair Nâzım Hikmet* (Istanbul: May Yayınları, 1976), 173. For a thematic study of Nâzım's poetry, see Şükran Kurdakul and Sennur Sezer, *Nâzım, Dünya ve Biz* (Istanbul: Evrensel, 2002).
29. Nâzım Hikmet, "Sıradaki," in *Sesini Kaybeden Şehir*, 34.
30. Nâzım Hikmet, "Sıradakinin Ölümü," in *Sesini Kaybeden Şehir*, 36, spacing and use of two and three suspension points in the original. For another engagement with Lenin during this period, see Nâzım's pamphlet *Postscript to the Bedreddin Epic: On the National Pride* (*Simavne Kadısı Oğlu Şeyh Bedreddin Destanı'na Zeyl: Millî Gurur*, 1936), in which he responded to the criticisms of his poem *Epic of Sheik Bedreddin* by translating and quoting passages from Lenin's essay "On the National Pride of the Great Russians" (1914).
31. Georg Wilhelm Friedrich Hegel, *The Science of Logic*, trans. and ed. George di Giovanni (Cambridge: Cambridge University Press, 2010), 108–25.
32. Nâzım Hikmet, *Kemal Tahir'e Mahpusaneden Mektuplar* (Ankara: Bilgi, 1968), 254, 197, 255, 263, 340–41, 83, 100.
33. Nâzım Hikmet, *Kemal Tahir'e Mahpusaneden Mektuplar*, 312, 314.
34. Ertürk, *Grammatology and Literary Modernity in Turkey*, 178–79.
35. For other works of criticism that address the originality of *Human Landscapes*, see Ahmet Oktay, "Memleketimden İnsan Manzaraları Üstüne Notlar," in *Şairin Kanı* (Istanbul: Yapı Kredi Yayınları, 2001), 17–36; and Erkan Irmak, *Kayıp Destan'ın İzinde: "Kuvâyi Milliye" ve "Memleketimden İnsan Manzaraları"'nda Milliyetçilik, Propaganda ve İdeoloji* (Istanbul: İletişim, 2011), 151–55, 237–52.

5. IN THE SHADOW OF LENIN

36. Nâzım Hikmet, *Human Landscapes from My Country: An Epic Novel in Verse*, trans. Randy Blasing and Mutlu Konuk (New York: Persea, 2002), 3–4, translation modified.
37. Georg Lukács, "Narrate or Describe?," in *Writer and Critic and Other Essays*, ed. and trans. Arthus Kahn (Lincoln, NE: iUniverse, Inc., an Authors Guild Backprint.com edition, 2005), 110–48.
38. Georg Lukács, "Realism in the Balance," trans. Rodney Livingstone, in Theodor Adorno et al., *Aesthetics and Politics*, with an afterword by Fredric Jameson, translation ed. Ronald Taylor (London: Verso, 1980), 43.
39. Nâzım Hikmet, *Kemal Tahir'e Mahpusaneden Mektuplar*, 356, 360.
40. Nâzım Hikmet, *Kemal Tahir'e Mahpusaneden Mektuplar*, 263–66.
41. For example, see A. A. Babaev, *Nazym Khikmet: Zhizn' i tvorchestvo* (Moscow: Nauka, 1975); Hikmet Akgül, *Nâzım Hikmet: Siyasi Biyografi* (Istanbul: Chiviyazilari Yayınevi, 2002); and Emin Karaca, *Nâzım Hikmet Şiirinde Gizli Tarih* (Istanbul: Destek Yayınevi, 2011), 131–54. Important exceptions include Konuk Blasing, *Nâzım Hikmet*, 243–54, and Svetlana N. Uturgauri, "Nâzım Hikmet'in Düzyazı Sanatı," trans. E. Zeynep Günal, Nâzım Hikmet Kültür Merkezi, "Sol Kültür," n.d., https://www.nhkm.org.tr/nazim-hikmetin-duzyazi-sanati/, which provide a literary analysis of the novel's modernist narratological devices.
42. On the (im)possible aesthetic of socialism realism, see Régine Robin, *Socialist Realism: An Impossible Aesthetic*, trans. Catherine Porter (Stanford, CA: Stanford University Press, 1992), 292–95.
43. For a useful historical account of the period, see Evgeny Dobrenko and Ilya Kalinin, "Literary Criticism During the Thaw," in *A History of Russian Literary Theory and Criticism: The Soviet Age and Beyond*, ed. Evgeny Dobrenko and Galin Tihanov (Pittsburgh: University of Pittsburgh Press, 2011), 184–206.
44. Nâzım Hikmet, *Yaşamak Güzel Şeydir Kardeşim*, 24, 29; Nâzım Hikmet, *Life's Good, Brother: A Novel*, trans. Mutlu Konuk Blasing (New York: Persea, 2013), 25, 32. Subsequent page citations are given parenthetically in the text, with the first page numeral referencing the 1964 Turkish original and the second referencing the 2013 English translation by Mutlu Konuk Blasing; note citations also refer to these two editions. Where necessary, I have silently modified the English translations to provide renderings more directly reflecting the original.
45. Akbulut, *Komintern Belgelerinde Nâzım Hikmet*, 41–43.
46. The intertextuality is clear when Ahmet remarks to İsmail in one of their exchanges that he has watched Ertuğrul's production of this play (Nâzım Hikmet, *Yaşamak Güzel Şeydir Kardeşim*, 25; *Life's Good*, 25). Nâzım's spouse, Vera Tuliakova-Khikmet, writes in her memoirs that Nâzım had a recurrent nightmare in which he was attacked by ferocious dogs and that this experience shaped the composition of *Life's Good, Brother*. See Vera Tuliakova-Khikmet, *Poslednii razgovor s Nazymom* (Moscow: Vremia, 2009), 156–57.
47. According to Oğuz Makal, Nâzım's use of nonlinear temporality may have been inspired by Alain Resnais's films *Hiroshima mon amour* (1959) and *L'année dernière à Marienbad* (1961); see Oğuz Makal, *Beyaz Perdede ve Sahnede Nâzım Hikmet* (Istanbul: Kalkedon, 2015), 28–29. It might be useful to point to another genealogy. Nâzım had used the "flash-forward" technique in a film he directed in Istanbul in 1937. Titled *Journey to the Sun* (*Güneşe Yolculuk*), the film depicts a

5. IN THE SHADOW OF LENIN

young amnesiac who recovers his memory seventeen years after losing it in the Turkish War of Independence. *Journey to the Sun* appears to be an adaptation of Fridrikh Ermler's Soviet silent film *Fragment of an Empire* (*Oblomok imperii*, 1929), depicting an amnesiac Russian soldier's recovery of his memory ten years after its loss in the Russian Civil War.

48. A. Kadir, *1938 Harp Okulu Olayı ve Nâzım Hikmet: Anı* (Istanbul: Can Yayınları, 1993), 49–50.

49. Paul de Man, "Rhetoric of Tropes (Nietzsche)," in *Allegories of Reading: Figural Language in Rousseau, Nietzsche, Rilke, and Proust* (New Haven, CT: Yale University Press, 1979), 113.

50. In the 1967 Gün Yayınları edition of *Yaşamak Güzel Şey Bekardeşim*, for example, half a paragraph concerning Mustafa Kemal's use of the Kurdish rebellions as an alibi for the suppression of all opposition is elided (10), and the identical elision can be found in a 2011 Yapı Kredi Yayınları edition: see Nâzım Hikmet, *Yaşamak Güzel Şey Be Kardeşim* (Istanbul: Yapı Kredi Yayınları, 2011), 9. In the Gün edition, a conversation between İsmail and Neriman about class warfare, which ends with İsmail singing a proletarian anthem, is elided (134). The Yapı Kredi edition includes most of this censored conversation but omits the song (101). Although in most instances the Yapı Kredi edition uses bracketed ellipses to mark the censored text, the elision of this song is not marked at all. Other examples of elision and modification include the substitution of the word *sosyalist* for *komünist* in several places in the text. An entire history of the discourse of anticommunism in Turkey could be written via a comparative reading of these elisions.

51. Robin, *Socialist Realism*, 293.

52. Upon completing the manuscript of *Life's Good, Brother* at Zekeriya and Sabiha Sertels' apartment in Vienna, Nâzım apparently remarked: "Isn't it romantika? What unnecessary arguments we had, how pointless were our imprisonments.... We squabbled over who wrote a declaration, informed on one another, and then as if we did a great job, we suffered for months, years in prison: all romantika." Quoted in Zekeriya Sertel, *Nâzım Hikmet'in Son Yılları* (Istanbul: Milliyet Yayınları, 1978), 284–85.

53. Jacques Derrida, "Living On," trans. James Hulbert, in Harold Bloom et al., *Deconstruction and Criticism* (New York: Continuum, 2004), 130.

54. For a useful discussion of Hegel's concept of "true infinity" in relation to the Derridean *différance* and Lacanian "not-all," see Mark C. Taylor, "Infinite Restlessness," in *Hegel and the Infinite: Religion, Politics, and Dialectic*, ed. Slavoj Žižek, Clayton Crockett, and Creston Davis (New York: Columbia University Press, 2011), 91–113; and Slavoj Žižek, "Hegel and Shitting: The Idea's Constipation," in *Hegel and the Infinite*, ed. Žižek, Crockett, and Davis, 221–32.

55. In the chronotope of Izmir in 1925, Ahmet spends his days reading an unidentified book of poems left behind by Ziya, memorizing the line "The ship with a hundred masts, where is the port it sails?" (Nâzım Hikmet, *Yaşamak Güzel Şeydir Kardeşim*, 19; *Life's Good*, 18). He attempts a poem of his own modeled on this line, using the *aruz* and syllabic meters, but fails (55; 64). In the chronotope of 1922–1924 in Moscow, Ahmet repeatedly quotes the opening lines of Rumi's Persian poem *Masnavi* in Turkish translation to his lover, Anushka: "Listen to the

reed-flute's lament, it grieves its separation [*Dinle neyden ki hikâyet kılmada, ayrılıklardan şikâyet kılmada*]." Ahmet then translates the lines into Russian while remarking that he would not write a love (*sevda*) poem if he were a poet (55, 66, 129; 64, 79, 161). Ahmet's skepticism about poetry might be said to ironize Nâzım's lifelong commitment to it. The novel's concluding poem, which can be understood as a modern *nazire* (parallel poem) version of *Masnavi*'s opening lines, registers the importance of Sufist poetry to Nâzım, though, as I argue in chapter 1, his engagement with Islamic tradition was not methodical.

56. In her memoirs, the TKP member Gün Benderli describes witnessing Nâzım's composition of the poem "Polish Letters" ("Lehistan Mektubu") during his visit to Prague in 1953. Collecting drafts of the poem that Nâzım had discarded, Benderli "took away from him the papers filled with parallel lines and repeated stanzas." The content of a typical page in Benderli's possession looked something like this:

Ben böyle uzun boyluyum
|||| |||| |||
|||| ||||

See Gün Benderli, *Su Başında Durmuşuz: Anılar* (Istanbul: Belge, 2003), 233–37. For a valuable exploration of the relationship between communism and poetry in the Greek context, see Stathis Gourgouris, "Communism and Poetry," *Gramma* 8 (2008): 43–54.

57. In the typescript of "Romantika" in the holdings of the International Institute of Social History as well as in the Sofia edition of 1964, the repeating first and seventh lines, "I'm a communist," appear as "Komünistim." See Nâzım Hikmet, "Romantika," manuscript, c. 1962, 142, IISH, Türkiye Birleşik Komünist Partisi Archives, no. 448. Whereas in the Russian and French translations, we find "Kommunist ia" (*Romantika* [1964], 215) and "Je suis communiste" (*Les romantiques*, 260), respectively, in the English translation we find "I'm a worker" (*Life's Good*, 187).

58. Nâzım Hikmet quoted in Aleksandr Fevral'skii, "Nazym Khikmet," in *Zapiski rovesnika veka* (Moscow: Sovetskii pisatel', 1976), 382–83.

59. Georg Lukács, "The Ideology of Modernism," in *The Meaning of Contemporary Realism*, trans. John Mander and Necke Mander (London: Merlin Press, 1962), 23–24.

60. Adorno et al., *Aesthetics and Politics*. The first edition was published by New Left Books in 1977.

61. On "allusive reading," see Stockwell, "A Shared Longing." Compare Rudolf Mrázek's analysis of "concentrated" communist writing in the Nazi concentration camp Terezín, established in Bohemia for European Jews, and the Dutch colonial camp Boven Digoel, established in New Guinea for the imprisonment of Indonesian communists: Rudolf Mrázek, "Lenin of the Camps: Radical Translation in Colonial Digoel and Nazi Terezín," in "Marxism, Communism, and Translation," ed. Nergis Ertürk and Özge Serin, special issue of *boundary 2* 43, no. 3 (2016): 133–58.

62. Contrasting the terms *afformation*, *afformance*, and *afformative* with the terms *performation*, *performance*, and *performative*, Werner Hamacher describes an imperformative mode of language whose operation is to "let this thing enter into

the realm of positings" without being present in "the field of positive manifestation." For Hamacher, "afformance 'is' the event of forming, itself formless, to which all forms and all performative acts remain exposed." See Werner Hamacher, "Afformative, Strike: Benjamin's 'Critique of Violence,'" trans. Dana Hollander, in *Walter Benjamin's Philosophy: Destruction and Experience*, ed. Andrew Benjamin and Peter Osborne (London: Routledge, 1994), 128.

63. Mustai Karim, Konstantin Simonov, and Radii Fish, "Cherez tridtsat' let...," *Pravda*, February 27, 1966, 5. For an account of their visit to Ankara written by two secretaries of the Soviet embassy, see RGALI f. 631, op. 27, ex. 146, l. 1–3.
64. For Fish's letter to A. A. Kosorukov to host Üstün and his wife in June 1968, see RGALI f. 631, op. 27, ex. 591, l. 18. Fish mentions that Üstün is an active participant of the Afro-Asian writers' movement and that he is involved with the preparation of an international youth festival in Istanbul, to which Soviet writers would be invited. For an account of Aitmatov's visit written by the first secretary of the Soviet embassy in Ankara, see RGALI f. 631, op. 27, ex. 1854, l. 17–19; and for Akkan's invitation, see RGALI f. 631, op. 27, ex. 1854, l. 20.
65. Regarding Şengil's appeal to the Soviet embassy in Ankara regarding Nâzım manuscripts in February 1966, see RGALI f. 631, op. 27, ex. 146, l. 4. Regarding Akkan's request in 1975 to access Nâzım's archive, see RGALI f. 631, op. 27, ex. 1854, l. 23. For Akkan's own account of his visit to Moscow that year, see Oğuz Akkan, preface to Nâzım Hikmet, *Yayınlanmamış Eserler*, ed. Oğuz Akkan (Istanbul: Cem, 1977), 5–6.
66. RGALI f. 631, op. 27, ex. 591, l. 8.
67. For the appeal made by Orhan Kemal's wife to the Soviet consul in Istanbul in August 1968, see RGALI f. 631, op. 27, ex. 591, l. 43.
68. For Ilgaz's exchange with the Soviet consul in Istanbul in November 1968 after his return from the Afro-Asian Writers' Conference in Tashkent, see RGALI f. 631, op. 27, ex. 591, l. 44–45.
69. David Scott, *Conscripts of Modernity: The Tragedy of Colonial Enlightenment* (Durham, NC: Duke University Press, 2004), 7.
70. Memet Fuat, *Nâzım Hikmet: Portreler* (Istanbul: Yapı Kredi Yayınları, 2001), 54.

CONCLUSION: IN THE ANTEROOM OF HISTORY

1. Nâzım Hikmet, *Life's Good, Brother: A Novel*, trans. Mutlu Konuk Blasing (New York: Persea, 2013), 64.
2. The quoted phrase is from Katerina Clark, *Eurasia Without Borders: The Dream of a Leftist Literary Commons, 1919–1943* (Cambridge, MA: Harvard University Press, 2021), 5.
3. Siegfried Kracauer, *History: The Last Things Before the Last*, completed after the death of the author by Paul Oskar Kristeller (Princeton, NJ: Markus Wiener, 1995), 191–217, 211, 216. Tuncay Birkan's Turkish translation of this book introduced me to Kracauer's final work, which explores the relationship between photography and history. For Birkan's own insightful engagement with this work, see Tuncay Birkan, *Dünya ile Devlet Arasında Türk Muharriri, 1930–1960* (Istanbul: Metis, 2018), 36–42.
4. Kracauer, *History*, 217.

BIBLIOGRAPHY

ARCHIVES

Gosudarstvennyi arkhiv Rossiiskoi Federatsii (GARF, State Archive of the Russian Federation), Moscow.
International Institute of Social History (IISH), Amsterdam, Netherlands.
Türkiye Birleşik Komünist Partisi (United Communist Party of Turkey) Archives.
Vâlâ Nureddin Papers.
Rossiiskii gosudarstvennyi arkhiv literatury i iskusstva (RGALI, Russian State Archive of Literature and Art), Moscow.
Rossiiskii gosudarstvennyi arkhiv sotsial'no-politicheskoi istorii (RGASPI, Russian State Archive for Social-Political History), Moscow.
Türkiye Büyük Millet Meclisi (TBMM, Grand National Assembly of Turkey), Ankara.
Gizli Celse Zabıtları (Closed Session Minutes).
Zabıt Ceridesi (Minutes).
Türkiye Sosyal Tarih Araştırma Vakfı (TÜSTAV, Turkish Social History Research Foundation), Istanbul.

OTHER SOURCES

Abdel-Malek, Anouar. "Marxism and National Liberation: A Statement of the Theoretical Problem." In *Social Dialectics*, vol. 2: *Nation and Revolution*, translated by Mike Gonzalez, 78–114. London: Macmillan, 1981.
"Abidin Dino'nun İbrikleri." *Yeni Adam*, no. 264 (January 18, 1940): 10–13, 17.
Açıkgöz, Hayk. *Anadolulu Bir Ermeni Komünistin Anıları*. Istanbul: Belge Yayınları, 2006.

BIBLIOGRAPHY

Adak, Hülya. *Halide Edib ve Siyasal Şiddet: Ermeni Kırımı, Diktatörlük ve Şiddetsizlik.* Istanbul: Bilgi Üniversitesi Yayınları, 2016.

———. "National Myths and Self-Na(rra)tions: Mustafa Kemal's *Nutuk* and Halide Edib's *Memoirs* and *The Turkish Ordeal.*" *South Atlantic Quarterly* 102, nos. 2–3 (2003): 509–27.

Adang, Camilla. "Belief and Unbelief." In *Encylopaedia of the Qurʾān*, edited by Jane Dammen McAuliffe. Brill Online. http://referenceworks.brillonline.com.ezaccess.libraries.psu.edu/entries/encyclopaedia-of-the-quran/belief-and-unbelief-EQCOM_00025.

Adorno, Theodor, Walter Benjamin, Ernst Bloch, Bertolt Brecht, and Georg Lukács. *Aesthetics and Politics.* With an afterword by Fredric Jameson. Translation edited by Ronald Taylor. London: Verso, 1980.

Agamben, Giorgio. *The Sacrament of Language: An Archaeology of the Oath* (Homo Sacer II, 3). Translated by Adam Kotsko. Stanford, CA: Stanford University Press, 2011.

Ahmad, Feroz. *Turkey: The Quest for Identity.* Oxford: Oneworld, 2005.

Ahmet Haşim. *Bütün Eserleri.* Vol. 2: *Bize Göre/İkdam'daki Diğer Yazıları.* Edited by İnci Enginün and Zeynep Kerman. Istanbul: Dergâh, 1991.

Ahmet Refik. *Baltacı Mehmed Paşa ve Büyük Petro, 1711–1911.* Istanbul: Matbaa-i Hayriye ve Şürekâsı, 1327 [1911].

Akal, Emel. *Milli Mücadelenin Başlangıcında Mustafa Kemal, İttihat Terakki ve Bolşevizm.* Rev. ed. Istanbul: İletişim, 2012.

———. *Moskova-Ankara-Londra Üçgeninde: İştirakiyuncular, Komünistler ve Paşa Hazretleri.* Istanbul: İletişim, 2013.

———. "Rusya'da 1917 Şubat ve Ekim Devrimlerinin Türkiye'ye Etkileri/Yansımaları." In *Modern Türkiye'de Siyasî Düşünce*, edited by Tanıl Bora and Murat Gültekingil, vol. 8: *Sol*, edited by Murat Gültekingil, 114–37. Istanbul: İletişim, 2007.

Akbal, Oktay. "Sovyetlerde Türk Edebiyatı." *Yeditepe Sanat Dergisi* 151 (November 1968): 14.

Akbulut, Dursun Ali. *Albayrak Olayı: Milli Mücadele Başlarında Halk Hükûmeti Kurma Girişimi (Erzurum 1920).* Istanbul: Temel Yayınları, 2006.

Akbulut, Erden. *Komintern Belgelerinde Nâzım Hikmet.* Istanbul: TÜSTAV, 2002.

———. "Nâzım Hikmet, TKP ve O Yıllar." In *Nâzım'ın Cep Defterlerinde Kavga, Aşk ve Şiir Notları (1937–1942)*, edited by Mehmet Ulusel, Handan Durgut, Erden Akbulut, and Yeşim Bilge, 11–21. Istanbul: Yapı Kredi Yayınları, 2018.

———. "Nâzım Hikmet Üzerine Yeni Belgeler." *Kıyı*, no. 275 (2012): 25–44.

———. *Zeki Baştımar: Yaşam Öyküsü, Mektuplar, Yazılar.* Istanbul: TÜSTAV, 2009.

Akbulut, Erden, and Mete Tunçay. *İstanbul Komünist Grubu'ndan (Aydınlık Çevresi) Türkiye Komünist Partisi'ne, 1919–1926.* 3 vols. Istanbul: TÜSTAV, 2012–2013.

———. *Türkiye Halk İştirakiyun Fırkası (1920–1923).* Rev. ed. Istanbul: TÜSTAV, 2016.

Akgül, Hikmet. *Nâzım Hikmet: Siyasi Biyografi.* Istanbul: Chiviyazilari Yayınevi, 2002.

Akkan, Oğuz. Preface to Nâzım Hikmet, *Yayınlanmamış Eserler*, 5–6.

Aktürk, Şenol. "Toplumcu Gerçekçi Yönüyle Suat Derviş'in Romanlarına Bakış." *Journal of Academic Social Science Studies* 5, no. 3 (2012): 1–33.

Alaranta, Toni. "Mustafa Kemal Atatürk's Six-Day Speech of 1927: Defining the Official Historical View of the Foundation of the Turkish Republic." *Turkish Studies* 9, no. 1 (2008): 115–29.

BIBLIOGRAPHY

Almond, Ian. *World Literature Decentered: Beyond the "West" Through Turkey, Mexico, and Bengal.* New York: Routledge, 2022.
Altınkaynak, Hikmet. *Edebiyatımızda 1940 Kuşağı.* Istanbul: Yaylacık Basımevi, 1977.
Anadol, Zihni T. "Suat Derviş ile Konuşmalar. . . ." *Yazın* 12, no. 59 (March 1994): 16–17.
And, Metin. *Drama at the Crossroads.* Istanbul: ISIS Press, 1991.
———. *A History of Theatre and Popular Entertainment in Turkey.* Ankara: Forum, 1963–1964.
———. *Karagöz: Turkish Shadow Theatre.* Ankara: Dost Yayınları, 1975.
Andrews, Walter G., and Mehmet Kalpaklı. *The Age of Beloveds: Love and the Beloved in Early-Modern Ottoman and European Culture and Society.* Durham, NC: Duke University Press, 2005.
"Ankara'da Bir Sovyet Resim Sergisi." *Ulus*, December 11, 1934, 5.
Aralov, S. I. *Bir Sovyet Diplomatının Türkiye Hatıraları.* Translated by Hasan Âli Ediz. Istanbul: Burçak Yayınevi, 1967.
Arat, Zehra F. "Kemalism and Turkish Women." *Women and Politics* 14, no. 4 (1994): 57–80.
Arendt, Hannah. "The Decline of the Nation-State and the End of the Rights of Man." In *The Origins of Totalitarianism*, 267–302. New York: Harcourt, 1976.
Arslan, Ceyhun. *The Ottoman Canon and the Construction of Arabic and Turkish Literatures.* Edinburgh: Edinburgh University Press, forthcoming.
Artun, Erman. *Âşıklık Geleneği ve Âşık Edebiyatı.* Istanbul: Akçağ, 2001.
Aslan, Yavuz. *Türkiye Komünist Fırkası'nın Kuruluşu ve Mustafa Suphi: Türkiye Komünistlerinin Rusya'da Teşkilâtlanması (1918–1921).* Ankara: Türk Tarih Kurumu, 1997.
Ataç, Nurullah. "Bir Mektup İ. H. Baltacıoğlu'na." *Yeni Adam*, no. 264 (January 18, 1940): 11–12.
Atasü, Erendiz. "Suat Derviş'te Tutku ve Siyasal Bilinç: *Fosforlu Cevriye* ve *Ankara Mahpusu* Romanları Üstüne Bir İnceleme." In Sönmez İşçi, *Yıldızları Seyreden Kadın*, 31–45.
Atay, Selçuk. *Vâlâ Nurettin Vâ-nû: İnsan ve Eser.* Ankara: Etkin Yayınevi, 2012.
Atılgan, Gökhan. *Kemalizm ile Marksizm Arasında Geleneksel Aydınlar: Yön-Devrim Hareketi.* Istanbul: Yordam, 2008.
Avcı, Zeynep, ed. *Abidin Dino Bir Dünya.* Istanbul: Sakıp Sabancı Müzesi, 2007.
———. *A'dan Z'ye Abidin Dino.* Istanbul: Yapı Kredi Yayınları, 2000.
Averchenko, Arkady. *Aşk Nizamnamesinin Yedi Maddesi.* Translated by Vâlâ Nureddin [pseud. Vâ-nû]. Istanbul: Cumhuriyet Matbaası, 1927.
———. *Sahtekârsız Memleket.* Translated by Hasan Âli Ediz. Istanbul: Akbaba, [1955].
Aydemir, Şevket Süreyya. *Suyu Arayan Adam.* Ankara: Öz Yayınları, 1959.
———. *Toprak Uyanırsa: Ekmeksizköy Öğretmeninin Hatıraları.* Istanbul: Remzi Kitabevi, 1963.
Aykut, Altan. "Türkiye'de Rus Dili ve Edebiyatı Çalışmaları." *Ankara Üniversitesi Dil ve Tarih-Coğrafya Fakültesi Dergisi* 46, no. 2 (2006): 1–27.
Aytürk, İlker. "Post-post-Kemalizm: Yeni Bir Paradigmayı Beklerken." *Birikim* 319 (November 2015): 34–47.
Babacan, Şakir. "Sosyalist Eserler Mütercimi Haydar Rifat Yorulmaz." Master's thesis, Istanbul University, 2014. https://tez.yok.gov.tr/UlusalTezMerkezi/tezDetay.jsp?id=ok4AepJhYI3uvtIQAXeCDA&no=wJRV1hwI8f4V4PqCwzeq8Q.

BIBLIOGRAPHY

Babaev, A. A. *Nazym Khikmet: Zhizn' i tvorchestvo*. Moscow: Nauka, 1975.
Baer, Ben Conisbee. *Indigenous Vanguards: Education, National Liberation, and the Limits of Modernism*. New York: Columbia University Press, 2019.
Bakhtin, Mikhail. "Discourse in the Novel." In *The Dialogic Imagination: Four Essays*, edited by Michael Holquist, translated by Caryl Emerson and Michael Holquist, 259–422. Austin: University of Texas Press, 1981.
———. *Rabelais and His World*. Translated by Helene Iswolsky. Bloomington: Indiana University Press, 1984.
Balaban, İbrahim. *Nâzım Hikmet'le Yedi Yıl*. Istanbul: Berfin, 2003.
Balabanlılar, Mürşit, ed. *Türk Romanında Kurtuluş Savaşı: İnceleme*. Istanbul: Türkiye İş Bankası Kültür Yayınları, 2003.
Balan, Canan. "Imagining Women at the Movies: Male Writers and Early Film Culture in Istanbul." In *Doing Women's Film History: Reframing Cinemas, Past and Future*, edited by Christine Gledhill and Julia Knight, 53–65. Urbana: University of Illinois Press, 2015.
Baldwin, Kate A. *Beyond the Color Line and the Iron Curtain: Reading Encounters Between Black and Red, 1922–1963*. Durham, NC: Duke University Press, 2002.
Balibar, Étienne [or Etienne]. "The Nation Form: History and Ideology." Translated by Chris Turner. In Etienne Balibar and Immanuel Wallerstein, *Race, Nation, Class: Ambiguous Identities*, 86–106. London: Verso, 1991.
———. "On the Basic Concepts of Historical Materialism." In Louis Althusser, Étienne Balibar, Roger Establet, Pierre Macherey, and Jacques Rancière, *Reading Capital*, translated by Ben Brewster, 223–345. London: Verso, 2009.
———. "The Philosophical Moment in Politics Determined by War: Lenin 1914–16." In *Lenin Reloaded: Toward a Politics of Truth*, edited by Sebastian Budgen, Stathis Kouvelakis, and Slavoj Žižek, 207–21. Durham, NC: Duke University Press, 2007.
Baltacıoğlu, İsmail Hakkı. "Abidin Dino'ya Açık Mektup." *Servet-i Fünun*, no. 2267-572 (November 23, 1939): 2.
———. "Nurullah Ataç'a Mektup." *Yeni Adam*, no. 264 (January 18, 1940): 13, 17.
Banarlı, Nihad Sâmi. *Devlet ve Devlet Terbiyesi*. Istanbul: Kubbealtı, 1985.
Banerjee, Anindita. *We Modern People: Science Fiction and the Making of Russian Modernity*. Middletown, CT: Wesleyan University Press, 2013.
Banerjee, Anindita, and Jenifer Presto. "Foreword: World Revolution." In "The 1917 Revolution and Its Ripple Effects (Anniversary Forum)," ed. Anindita Banerjee and Jenifer Presto, special issue of *Slavic and East European Journal* 61, no. 3 (2017): 394–95.
Baraner, Reşat Fuat [pseud. Ali Rıza]. "Edebî Eserde Müsbet Tip." *Yeni Edebiyat*, no. 13 (April 15, 1941): 1.
———. "Halkçı Edebiyatta Şekil." *Yeni Edebiyat*, no. 2 (October 26, 1940): 2.
———. "Realizme Dair Notlar Münasebetiyle." *Yeni Edebiyat*, no. 5 (December 15, 1940): 1, 3.
Bardawil, Fadi A. "Dreams of a Dual Birth: Socialist Lebanon's World and Ours." In Ertürk and Serin, "Marxism, Communism, and Translation," 313–35.
Başgöz, İlhan. "Love Themes in Turkish Folk Poetry." *Review of National Literatures*, no. 4 (1973): 99–114.
"Başlarken: Bedbinler ve Nikbinler." *Yeni Edebiyat*, no. 1 (October 5, 1940): 1.

BIBLIOGRAPHY

"Başlarken: Biz Yeni Edebiyattan Ne Anlıyoruz?" *Yeni Edebiyat*, no. 9 (February 15, 1941): 1–2.
"Başlarken: Eski Harflerin Liselerde Öğretilmesi Doğru mudur?" *Yeni Edebiyat*, no. 2 (October 26, 1940): 1.
"Başlarken: Niçin Realizm Münakaşasını Yapıyoruz?" *Yeni Edebiyat*, no. 7 (January 15, 1941): 1. Reprinted in S. İleri, *Yeni Edebiyat 1940–1941*, 52–53.
Baştımar, Zeki. "Bir Az Tevazu." *Yeni Edebiyat*, no. 14 (May 1, 1941): 1, 4.
———. *Çehov'un Hayat ve Sanat Hikayesi*. Istanbul: Yenigün Yayınları, n.d. [ca. 1950s].
———. "Edebiyat I." *Yeni Edebiyat*, no. 15 (May 15, 1941): 1, 3.
———. "Edebiyat III." *Yeni Edebiyat*, no. 19 (August 1, 1941): 1–2.
———. "Edebiyat ve Folklor." *Yeni Edebiyat*, no. 20 (August 15, 1941): 1, 3.
———. "Edebiyat ve Folklor II." *Yeni Edebiyat*, no. 21 (September 1, 1941): 1–2.
———. *L. Tolstoy: Hayatı, Eserleri, Fikirleri*. Istanbul: Yenigün Yayınları, n.d. [ca. 1950s].
———. "Şairin Sesi." *Yeni Edebiyat*, no. 5 (December 15, 1940): 1–2.
Bataille, Georges. "The Notion of Expenditure." In *Visions of Excess: Selected Writings, 1927–1939*, edited by Allan Stoekl, translated by Allan Stoekl, with Carl R. Lovitt and Donald M. Leslie Jr., 116–29. Minneapolis: University of Minnesota Press, 1985.
Baudelaire, Charles. "On the Essence of Laughter (and, in General on the Comic in the Plastic Arts)." In *The Painter of Modern Life and Other Essays*, edited and translated by Jonathan Mayne, 147–65. London: Phaidon, 1964.
Behmoaras, Liz. *Suat Derviş: Efsane Bir Kadın ve Dönemi*. Istanbul: Remzi Kitabevi, 2008.
Belge, Murat. *Genesis: "Büyük Ulusal Anlatı" ve Türklerin Kökeni*. Istanbul: İletişim, 2009.
———. *Step ve Bozkır: Rusça ve Türkçe Edebiyatta Doğu-Batı Sorunu ve Kültür*. Istanbul: İletişim, 2016.
Belli, Mihri. *Mihri Belli'nin Anıları: "İnsanlar Tanıdım."* Istanbul: Milliyet Yayınları, 1989.
Benderli, Gün. *Su Başında Durmuşuz: Anılar*. Istanbul: Belge, 2003.
Benjamin, Walter. "Doctrine of the Similar." Translated by Michael Jennings. In Benjamin, *Walter Benjamin: Selected Writings*, vol. 2, part 2: *1931–1934*, 694–98.
———. *Gesammelte Schriften*. Vol. 2.1. Edited by Rolf Tiedemann and Hermann Schweppenhäuser. Frankfurt: Suhrkamp, 1977.
———. "Lehre vom Ähnlichen." In Benjamin, *Gesammelte Schriften*, vol. 2.1, 204–10.
———. "On the Concept of History." Translated by Harry Zohn. In *Walter Benjamin: Selected Writings*, vol. 4: *1938–1940*, edited by Howard Eiland and Michael W. Jennings, 389–400. Cambridge, MA: Harvard University Press, 2003.
———. "On the Mimetic Faculty." Translated by Edmund Jephcott. In Benjamin, *Walter Benjamin: Selected Writings*, vol. 2, part 2: *1931–1934*, 720–22.
———. "Review of Gladkov's *Cement*." Translated by Rodney Livingstone. In *Walter Benjamin: Selected Writings*, vol. 2, part 1: *1927–1930*, edited by Michael W. Jennings, Howard Eiland, and Gary Smith, 47–49. Cambridge, MA: Harvard University Press, 1999.
———. "The Task of the Translator." Translated by Harry Zohn. In *Walter Benjamin: Selected Writings*, vol. 1: *1913–1926*, edited by Marcus Bullock and Michael W. Jennings, 253–63. Cambridge, MA: Harvard University Press, 2002.

———. "Über den Begriff der Geschichte." In *Gesammelte Schriften*, vol. 1.2, edited by Rolf Tiedemann and Hermann Schweppenhäuser, 691–704. Frankfurt: Suhrkamp, 1974.

———. "Über das mimetische Vermögen." In Benjamin, *Gesammelte Schriften*, vol. 2.1, 210–13.

———. *Walter Benjamin: Selected Writings*. Vol. 2, part 2: *1931–1934*. Edited by Michael W. Jennings, Howard Eiland, and Gary Smith. Translated by Rodney Livingstone and others. Cambridge, MA: Harvard University Press, 2005.

———. "The Work of Art in the Age of Its Technological Reproducibility: Second Version." Translated by Edmund Jephcott and Harry Zohn. In *Walter Benjamin: Selected Writings*, vol. 3: *1935–1938*, edited by Howard Eiland and Michael W. Jennings, 101–33. Cambridge, MA: Harvard University Press, 2006.

Bennigsen, Alexandre A., and S. Enders Wimbush. *Muslim National Communism in the Soviet Union: A Revolutionary Strategy for the Colonial World*. Chicago: University of Chicago Press, 1979.

Bercâvi, A. Faik. *İslâmda Sosyalizm*. Istanbul: Işık Basımevi, 1946.

———. *Nâzım'la 1933–1938 Yılları*. Istanbul: Adam Yayınları, 1995.

Bergson, Henri. *Laughter: An Essay on the Meaning of the Comic*. Translated by Cloudesley Brereton and Fred Rothwell. New York: Macmillan, 1914.

Berk, İlhan, Levent Çalıkoğlu, Ferit Edgü, Turan Erol, and Murat Ural. *Yurt Gezileri ve Yurt Resimleri (1938–1943)*. Edited by Amélie Edgü. Istanbul: Milli Reasürans T.A.Ş., 1998.

Bernstein, Frances Lee. *The Dictatorship of Sex: Lifestyle Advice for the Soviet Masses*. DeKalb: Northern Illinois University Press, 2007.

Beumers, Birgit, ed. *A Companion to Russian Cinema*. Malden, MA: Wiley, 2016.

Bezanis, Lowell. "Soviet Muslim Emigrés in the Republic of Turkey." *Central Asian Survey* 13, no. 1 (1994): 59–180.

Bilmez, Bülent, and Nathalie Clayer. "A Prosopographic Study on Some 'Albanian' Deputies to the First Ottoman Parliament." In *The First Ottoman Experiment in Democracy*, edited by Christoph Herzog and Malek Sharif, 151–85. Würzburg, Germany: Ergon, 2010.

Bird, Robert. "Lenfilm: The Birth and Death of an Institutional Aesthetic." In Beumers, *A Companion to Russian Cinema*, 66–91.

Birkan, Tuncay. *Dünya ile Devlet Arasında Türk Muharriri, 1930–1960*. Istanbul: Metis, 2018.

Bisalman, Kemal. "Suat Derviş İçin." *Yeditepe Sanat Dergisi* 171 (July 1970): 5, 13.

Bolluk, Hadiye, ed. *Kurtuluş Savaşı'nın İdeolojisi: "Hakimiyeti Milliye" Yazıları*. Istanbul: Kaynak, 2003.

Boratav, Pertev Naili [*see also* Pertev Naili]. *100 Soruda Türk Halk Edebiyatı*. Istanbul: Gerçek, 1988.

Boratav, Pertev Naili, Abidin Dino, Güzin Dino, Ferit Edgü, and Anouar Abdel-Malek. *Kültür Emperyalizmi Üstüne Konuşmalar*. Istanbul: Ataç Kitabevi, 1967.

Borenstein, Eliot. *Men Without Women: Masculinity and Revolution in Russian Fiction, 1917–1929*. Durham, NC: Duke University Press, 2000.

Bowlt, John E. "Constructivism and Russian Stage Drama." *Performing Arts Journal* 1, no. 3 (1977): 62–84.

BIBLIOGRAPHY

Bozarslan, Hamit. "Alevism and the Myths of Research: The Need for a New Research Agenda." In *Turkey's Alevi Enigma: A Comprehensive Overview*, edited by Paul J. White and Joost Jongerden, 3–16. London: Brill, 2003.
Buck-Morss, Susan. *The Dialectics of Seeing: Walter Benjamin and the Arcades Project.* Cambridge, MA: MIT Press, 1991.
———. "Theorizing Today: The Post-Soviet Condition." *Log* 11 (2008): 23–31. https://www.jstor.org/stable/41765180.
Bulgakowa, Oksana. *FEKS: Die Fabrik des Exzentrischen Schauspielers.* Berlin: Potemkin Press, 1996.
Butler, Judith. *Excitable Speech: A Politics of the Performative.* New York: Routledge, 1997.
Çakırhan, Nail. *Anılar.* Interview by Erden Akbulut. Istanbul: TÜSTAV, 2008.
Can, Lâle. *Spiritual Subjects: Central Asian Pilgrims and the Ottoman Hajj at the End of Empire.* Stanford, CA: Stanford University Press, 2020.
Cantek, Levent. *"Markopaşa": Bir Mizah ve Muhalefet Efsanesi.* Istanbul: İletişim, 2001.
———. "Türkiye'de Tarihi Çizgi Romanlar: Kılıçbaz Kahramanlar." *Toplumsal Tarih* 118 (October 2003): 14–23.
Cantek, Levent, and Levent Gönenç. *Muhalefet Defteri: Türkiye'de Mizah Dergileri ve Karikatür.* Istanbul: Yapı Kredi Yayınları, 2017.
Carleton, Gregory. *The Politics of Reception: Cultural Constructions of Mikhail Zoshchenko.* Evanston, IL: Northwestern University Press, 1998.
———. *Sexual Revolution in Bolshevik Russia.* Pittsburgh, PA: University of Pittsburgh Press, 2005.
Cavendish, Philip. *The Men with the Movie Camera: The Poetics of Visual Style in Soviet Avant-Garde Cinema of the 1920s.* New York: Berghahn, 2013.
Chekhov, Anton. *Maske.* Translated by Zeki Baştımar. Istanbul: Remzi Kitabevi, 1938.
Christie, Ian, and John Gillett, eds. *Futurism/Formalism/FEKS: "Eccentrism" and Soviet Cinema, 1918–1936.* London: British Film Institute, 1978.
Cinemre, Levent, and Ruşen Çakır, eds. *Sol Kemalizme Bakıyor: Röportaj.* Istanbul: Metis, 1991.
Clark, Katerina. *Eurasia Without Borders: The Dream of a Leftist Literary Commons, 1919–1943.* Cambridge, MA: Harvard University Press, 2021.
———. "European and Russian Cultural Interactions with Turkey: 1910s–1930s." *Comparative Studies of South Asia, Africa, and the Middle East* 33, no. 2 (2013): 201–13. https://doi.org/10.1215/1089201X-2322489.
———. *Moscow, the Fourth Rome: Stalinism, Cosmopolitanism, and the Evolution of Soviet Culture, 1931–1941.* Cambridge, MA: Harvard University Press, 2011.
———. *Petersburg, Crucible of Cultural Revolution.* Cambridge, MA: Harvard University Press, 1995.
———. "Socialist Realism with Shores: The Conventions for the Positive Hero." In Lahusen and Dobrenko, *Socialist Realism Without Shores*, 27–50.
———. *The Soviet Novel: History as Ritual.* 3rd ed. Bloomington: Indiana University Press, 2000.
———. "The Soviet Project of the 1930s to Found a 'World Literature' and British Literary Internationalism." *Modern Language Quarterly* 80, no. 4 (2019): 403–25.

Clark, Katerina, and Galin Tihanov. "Soviet Literary Theory in the 1930s: Battles Over Genre and the Boundaries of Modernity." In Dobrenko and Tihanov, *A History of Russian Literary Theory and Criticism*, 109–43.
Cleary, Joe. "Realism After Modernism and the Literary World-System." In Cleary, Esty, and Lye, "Peripheral Realisms," 255–68.
Cleary, Joe, Jed Esty, and Colleen Lye, eds. "Peripheral Realisms." Special issue of *Modern Language Quarterly* 73, no. 3 (2012).
"Comparative Studies of South Asia, Africa, and the Middle East: Mission Statement." *Comparative Studies of South Asia, Africa, and the Middle East* 33, no. 2 (2013): 135. https://doi.org/10.1215/1089201X-2322336.
Corrigan, Maria Natasha. "Soviet Eccentrism: 'A Can-Can on the Tightrope of Logic.'" PhD diss., University of California, Santa Barbara, 2015.
Criss, Nur Bilge. *Istanbul Under Allied Occupation, 1918–1923*. Boston: Brill, 1999.
Darendelioğlu, İlhan. *Türkiye'de Komünist Hareketleri: Solcular, Sosyalistler, Marksistler ve Komünistler* . . . . Istanbul: Bedir Yayınevi, 1973.
David-Fox, Michael. *Crossing Borders: Modernity, Ideology, and Culture in Russia and the Soviet Union*. Pittsburgh, PA: University of Pittsburgh Press, 2015.
——. *Showcasing the Great Experiment: Cultural Diplomacy and Western Visitors to the Soviet Union, 1921–1941*. New York: Oxford University Press, 2012.
Debray, Régis. "Socialism: A Life-Cycle." *New Left Review* 46 (July–August 2007): 5–28.
De Kesel, Marc. *Eros and Ethics: Reading Jacques Lacan's Seminar VII*. Translated by Sigi Jöttkandt. Albany: State University of New York Press, 2009.
"Deklaratsiia pervoi khudozhestvennoi masterskoi pod khudozhestvennym rukovodstvom S. Iutkevicha." In *Iz istorii Lenfil'ma*, vol. 4, edited by Nina Gornitskaia, 128–37. Leningrad: Iskusstvo, 1975.
Deleage, Jean-Pierre. *Abidin Dino ya da Kanatlanan El*. Translated by Samih Rifat. Istanbul: Yapı Kredi Yayınları, 2007.
Deleuze, Gilles, and Félix Guattari. *Anti-Oedipus: Capitalism and Schizophrenia*. Translated by Robert Hurley, Mark Seem, and Helen R. Lane. Minneapolis: University of Minnesota Press, 2000.
De Man, Paul. "The Rhetoric of Temporality." In *Blindness and Insight: Essays in the Rhetoric of Contemporary Criticism*, 2nd ed., 187–228. Minneapolis: University of Minnesota Press, 1997.
——. "Rhetoric of Tropes (Nietzsche)." In *Allegories of Reading: Figural Language in Rousseau, Nietzsche, Rilke, and Proust*, 103–18. New Haven, CT: Yale University Press, 1979.
Derrida, Jacques. "Back from Moscow, in the USSR." In *Politics, Theory, and Contemporary Culture*, edited by Mark Poster, translated by Mary Quaintaire, 197–235. New York: Columbia University Press, 1993.
——. "Living On." Translated by James Hulbert. In Harold Bloom, Paul de Man, Jacques Derrida, Geoffrey Hartman, and J. Hillis Miller, *Deconstruction and Criticism*, 75–176. New York: Continuum, 2004.
——. *Of Grammatology*. Translated by Gayatri Chakravorty Spivak. 40th anniv. ed. Baltimore, MD: Johns Hopkins University Press, 2016.
——. "Signature Event Context." In *Margins of Philosophy*, translated by Alan Bass, 307–30. Chicago: University of Chicago Press, 1982.

BIBLIOGRAPHY

Derviş, Suat [see also Dervish, Suad; Derwich, Suat; Derwisch, Suad; Derwish, Suad]. *Anılar, Paramparça*. Istanbul: İthaki, 2017.
———. *Ankara mahbusu: Roman*. Baku, Azerbaijan: Gənclik, 1973.
———. *Bu Roman Olan Şeylerin Romanıdır*. Istanbul: İthaki, 2018.
———. "Çocuklarımız Ne Halde? 6—Kurtulan Çocuklara Göre." *Cumhuriyet*, August 27, 1935, 7-8.
———. *Emine*. Istanbul: Resimli Ay, 1931.
———. "Emine." *Resimli Ay* 6, no. 12 (February 1930): 34-35.
———. "Fıkra: Dil Bayramı." *Yeni Edebiyat*, no. 22 (September 15, 1941): 1. Reprinted in S. İleri, *Yeni Edebiyat 1940-1941*, 190.
———. *Fosforlu Cevriye*. Sofia, Bulgaria: Narodna prosveta, 1962.
———. *Fosforlu Cevriye*. Istanbul: May, 1968.
———. *Fosforlu Cevriyə*. Translated by Bəhram Cəfərov. Baku, Azerbaijan: Azərbaycan Dövlət Nəşriyyatı, 1964.
———. "Hayattan Hikayeler: Neden Dileniyormuş?" *Tan*, August 31, 1937, 6.
———. *Hepimiz Birbirimizin Örneğiyiz*. Edited by Zehra Toska. Istanbul: Oğlak, 1998.
———. "Her Sayıda Bir Roman: *Yaban*." *Yeni Edebiyat*, no. 1 (October 5, 1940): 3.
———. "Her Sayıda Bir Roman: *Yolpalas Cinayeti*." *Yeni Edebiyat*, no. 7 (January 15, 1941): 3. Reprinted in S. İleri, *Yeni Edebiyat 1940-1941*, 272-77.
———. *Hiç: Edebi Roman*. Istanbul: İnkılâp Kitabevi, 1939.
———. "Hırsız." *Resimli Ay* 7, no. 8 (October 1930): 33-35.
———. "İstanbul'un Altında Kimler Yaşıyor?" *Son Posta*, June 25, 1936, 7.
———. "Kızlarımız: Bu Daktilo Kız Hayatından Niçin Şikâyetçi." *Tan*, November 15, 1937, 7.
———. *Ne bir Ses . . . Ne bir Nefes! Milli Roman*. 1923. Reprint. Istanbul: İnkılâp Kitabevi, 1946.
———. *Niçin Sovyetler Birliğinin Dostuyum?* Istanbul: Arkadaş Matbaası, 1944.
———. "Pochta podgotovitel'nogo komiteta." *Informatsionnyi biulleten' Sovetskogo podgotovitel'nogo komiteta po sozyvu Konferentsii pisatelei stran Azii i Afriki*, no. 3 (July 1958): 17.
———. "Türk Kadını Nasıl İş Bulur? Erkeğin İşi Kadından Çoçuğa mı Geçiyor?" *Tan*, January 6, 1937, 7.
Dervish, Suad [see also Derviş, Suat]. *Ankarskii uznik: Roman*. Translated by Radii Fish. Moscow: Izdatel'stvo inostrannoi literatury, 1960.
———. *Fosforicheskaia Dzhevrie*. Translated by Radii Fish. Moscow: Izdatel'stvo inostrannoi literatury, 1957.
———. *Liubovnye romany*. Translated by Radii Fish. Moscow: Izdatel'stvo TsK VLKSM "Molodaia gvardiia," 1969.
———. "On ili ne on?" In *Turetskie rasskazy: Sbornik*, edited by L. V. Nikulin, 214-20. Moscow: Gosudarstvennoe izdatel'stvo "Khudozhestvennaia literatura," 1940.
———. "Vo imia doveriia." *Literaturnaia gazeta*, no. 121 (October 9, 1958): 4.
Derwich, Suat [see also Derviş, Suat]. "Hommage d'un écrivain Turc." *Europe* 33, nos. 119-20 (November-December 1955): 89-90.
———. *Les ombres du yali*. Paris: Éditeurs français réunis, 1958.
———. *Le prisonnier d'Ankara*. Paris: Éditeurs français réunis, 1957.
Derwisch, Suad [see also Derviş, Suat]. "Nazim Hikmet." *Die Literatur: Monatsschrift für Literatur-freunde* 33 (June 1931): 498-500.

Derwish, Suad [*see also* Derviş, Suat]. "Der entzauberte Harem." *Revue des Monats* 6 (1931–1932): 62–66.
Dinamo, Hasan İzzettin. *İkinci Dünya Savaşı'ndan Edebiyat Anıları*. Istanbul: De Yayınevi, 1984.
———. "Köroğlunun Türküsü." *Yeni Edebiyat*, no. 3 (November 15, 1940): 4.
———. "Nâzım Hikmet'le Birlikte Kurduğumuz İllegal (!) Örgüt." *Türkiye Yazıları Dergisi* 1 (1977): 25–39.
———. *TKP Aydınlar ve Anılar*. Istanbul: Yalçın Yayınları, 1989.
Dino, Abidin. *Adana Yazıları*. Edited by Murat Baycanlar. Adana: Karahan Kitabevi, 2013.
———. "Ankara—Moskva." *Sovetskoe iskusstvo*, no. 46 (October 5, 1934): 3.
———. "Bir Köy Oyunu Notları." *Görüşler*, no. 53 (May 1943): 13–14.
———. "Halkevinde Köy Tiyatrosu." *Görüşler*, no. 52 (April 1943): 14.
———. "Halk San'atı." *Yeni Edebiyat*, no. 19 (August 1, 1941): 1, 4.
———. "Halk ve San'at." *Yeni Edebiyat*, no. 2 (October 26, 1940): 1, 3.
———. "Hamlet." *Yeni Edebiyat*, no. 24 (October 15, 1941): 1–2.
———. "İş ve San'at." *S.E.S.*, no. 3 (August 1939): 5.
———. "Karacaoğlan: Cehenneme Ateş Götürmeyi Tavsiye Eden Şair." *Yeni S.E.S.*, November 1939, 5.
———. *Kel*. Adana: Türksözü Basımevi, 1944.
———. *Kızılbaş Günlerim*. Istanbul: Sel Yayıncılık, 2001.
———. "Köy ve Sanat." *S.E.S.*, no. 4 (September 1939): 5, 23.
———. "Mücessem Sinema." *Yeni Edebiyat*, no. 17 (June 15, 1941): 1, 3.
——— [Abidine Dino]. "Nazım Hikmet, mon ami de la Sublime Porte." *Lettres françaises*, no. 989 (August 1–7, 1963): 7.
———. "Realizme Dair Notlar." *Yeni Edebiyat*, no. 5 (December 15, 1940): 1, 3.
———. "Realizm Notları." *Yeni Edebiyat*, no. 7 (January 15,1941): 2. Reprinted in S. İleri, *Yeni Edebiyat 1940–1941*, 45–47.
———. "Stop!" *Yeni S.E.S.*, no. 2 (December 1939): 5, 21.
———. *Toplu Yazılar (1938–1994): Edebiyat, Sanat, Politika*. Edited by Turgut Çeviker. Istanbul: Everest, 2018.
———. "Türk Tiyatrosu Nasıl Doğacak?" *Yeni S.E.S.*, November 1939, 17, 21.
———. "Üç Film ve Bir Piyes." *Yeni Edebiyat*, no. 8 (February 1, 1941): 1–2.
———. "Verese." In *Verese Kel: Oyunlar*, 95–165. Istanbul: Adam, 1996.
———. *Yeditepe Öyküleri*. Edited by Mürşit Balabanlılar. Istanbul: İş Bankası Kültür Yayınları, 2002.
Dino, Abidin, and Güzin Dino. *Güzin Dino–Abidin Dino Mektupları (1952–1973)*. Edited by Defne Asal Er and Handan Akdemir. Istanbul: İş Bankası Kültür Yayınları, 2004.
Dino, Abidin, and Sait Faik. "1940 Kuşağı'nın Ortak Bildirisi." In Sâlah Birsel, *Gandhi ya da Hint Kirazının Gölgesinde*, 97–101. Istanbul: Yapı Kredi Yayınları, 1993.
Dino, Güzin. *Gel Zaman Git Zaman: Abidin Dino'lu Yıllar*. Istanbul: Can, 2000.
———. *La genèse du roman turc au XIXe siècle*. Paris: Publications orientalistes de France, 1973.
———. "The Turkish Peasant Novel, or the Anatolian Theme." Translated by Joan Grimbert. *World Literature Today* 60, no. 2 (1986): 266–75.

BIBLIOGRAPHY

Dirlik, Arif. "'Like a Song Gone Silent': The Political Ecology of Barbarism and Civilization in *Waiting for the Barbarians* and *The Legend of the Thousand Bulls*." *Diaspora* 1, no. 3 (1991): 321–52.
Divitçioğlu, Sencer. *Asya Üretim Tarzı ve Osmanlı Toplumu*. Istanbul: Sermet Matbaası, 1967.
Djagalov, Rossen. *From Internationalism to Postcolonialism: Literature and Cinema Between the Second and Third Worlds*. Montreal: McGill-Queen's University Press, 2020.
———. "The Red Apostles: Imagining Revolutions in the Global Proletarian Novel." *Slavic and East European Journal* 61, no. 3 (2017): 396–422.
Dobrenko, Evgeny. "The Disaster of Middlebrow Taste, or, Who 'Invented' Socialist Realism?" In Lahusen and Dobrenko, *Socialist Realism Without Shores*, 135–64.
———. *Political Economy of Socialist Realism*. Translated by Jesse M. Savage. New Haven, CT: Yale University Press, 2007.
Dobrenko, Evgeny, and Natalia Jonsson-Skradol, eds. *Socialist Realism in Central and Eastern European Literatures: Institutions, Dynamics, Discourses*. London: Anthem Press, 2018.
Dobrenko, Evgeny, and Ilya Kalinin. "Literary Criticism During the Thaw." In Dobrenko and Tihanov, *A History of Russian Literary Theory and Criticism*, 184–206.
Dobrenko, Evgeny, and Galin Tihanov, eds. *A History of Russian Literary Theory and Criticism: The Soviet Age and Beyond*. Pittsburgh, PA: University of Pittsburgh Press, 2011.
Dolcerocca, Özen Nergis, ed. "Beyond World Literature: Reading Ahmet Hamdi Tanpınar Today." Special issue of *Middle Eastern Literatures* 20, no. 2 (2017).
Dranas, Ahmet Muhip. "Cumhuriyet Halk Partisinin Anadolu Resim Gezileri." *Güzel Sanatlar*, no. 4 (1942): 75–85.
———. "Resimde Ümanizma." *Güzel Sanatlar*, no. 2 (1940): 131–56.
Duben, Alan, and Cem Behar. *Istanbul Households: Marriage, Family, and Fertility 1880–1940*. Cambridge: Cambridge University Press, 1991.
"Dünyanın Büyük Yazıcılarından Hanri Barbüs Proleter Edebiyatını Nasıl Tarif Ediyor?" *Resimli Ay* 7, no. 7 (September 1930): 11, 37–38.
Eikhenbaum, B. M., ed. *The Poetics of Cinema*. Edited by Richard Taylor. Translated by Richard Taylor and others. Oxford: RPT, 1982.
———, ed. *Poetika kino*. Moscow: Kinopechat', 1927.
Elvan, Nihal, ed. *d Grubu = D Group, 1933–1951*. Istanbul: Yapı Kredi Yayınları, 2002.
Enginün, İnci, Zeynep Kerman, and Selim İleri, eds. *Kurtuluş Savaşı ve Edebiyatımız*. Istanbul: Oğlak, 1998.
Erdem, Hamit. *1920 Yılı ve Sol Muhalefet*. Istanbul: Sel Yayıncılık, 2010.
———, ed. *THİF Yayın Organı: "Yeni Hayat" (Mart–Eylül 1922)*. Istanbul: TÜSTAV, 2017.
Erdem, Özgür, ed. *Kadro: Aylık Fikir Mecmuası: Tıpkı Basım (1–18. Sayılar)*. Vol. 1: 1932–1933. Istanbul: İleri, 2011.
———, ed. *Kadro: Aylık Fikir Mecmuası: Tıpkı Basım (19–36. Sayılar)*. Vol. 2: 1933–1934. Istanbul: İleri, 2011.
Erdinç, Fahri. *Kalkın Nazım'a Gidelim: Anılar*. Istanbul: Varlık, 1987.

Erdoğan, Nezih. "The Spectator in the Making: Modernity and Cinema in Istanbul, 1896–1928." In *Orienting Istanbul: Cultural Capital of Europe?*, edited by Deniz Göktürk, Levent Soysal, and İpek Türeli, 129–43. London: Routledge, 2010.
Erer, Tekin. *Kızıl Tehlike*. Vol. 2. Istanbul: As, 1967.
Ertuğrul, Muhsin, dir. *Bir Millet Uyanıyor*. İpek Film, 1932. https://www.youtube.com/watch?v=NhiBXtvY19g.
Ertürk, Nergis. "*Aşk Romanları (Liubovnye romany)* ve Düşündürdükleri: Rusça'da Çeviri Bir Suat Derviş Romanı." *Birikim*, no. 389 (September 2021): 92–104.
———. "Baku, Literary Common." In *Futures of Comparative Literature: ACLA State of the Discipline Report*, edited by Ursula Heise, 141–44. London: Routledge, 2017.
———. *Grammatology and Literary Modernity in Turkey*. New York: Oxford University Press, 2011.
———. "Lenin via Cavid: Towards a Communism of Other-Determination." *Interventions: International Journal of Postcolonial Studies* 18, no. 5 (2016): 627–50.
———. "Surrealism and Turkish Script Arts." *Modernism/modernity* 17, no. 1 (2010): 47–60.
———. "Toward a Literary Communism: The 1926 Baku Turcological Congress." *boundary 2* 40, no. 2 (2013): 183–213.
———. "Türkiye ve Rusya Hattında Muhsin Ertuğrul." Introduction to Muhsin Ertuğrul, *Moskova Notları*, ed. Tuncay Birkan, 13–37. Istanbul: Can, 2023.
Ertürk, Nergis, and Özge Serin, eds. "Marxism, Communism, and Translation." Special issue of *boundary 2* 43, no. 3 (2016).
———. "Marxism, Communism, and Translation: An Introduction." In Ertürk and Serin, "Marxism, Communism, and Translation," 1–26.
Eşref Fehim,. "D. Grupunun 3'üncü Sergisi Yeni Ressamın Gücünü Gösteriyor." *Yeni Adam* 1, no. 26 (June 25, 1934): 7.
Evin, Ahmet Ö. *Origins and Development of the Turkish Novel*. Minneapolis: Bibliotheca Islamica, 1983.
———, ed. "Yaşar Kemal." Special issue of *Edebiyât: Journal of Near Eastern Literatures* 5, nos. 1–2 (1980).
Falih Rıfkı. *Moskova-Roma*. Istanbul: Muallim Ahmet Halit Kitaphanesi, 1932.
———. *Yeni Rusya*. Ankara: Hakimiyet-i Milliye Matbaası, 1931.
Fanon, Frantz. "Algeria Unveiled." In *A Dying Colonialism*, translated by Haakon Chevalier, 35–68. New York: Grove Press, 1965.
———. *The Wretched of the Earth*. Translated by Richard Philcox. New York: Grove Press, 2004.
Farrer, Klod [*see also* Farrère, Claude]. *Chelovek, kotoryi ubil*. . . . Paris: Frankorusskaia pechat', 1921.
Farrère, Claude [*see also* Farrer, Klod]. *L'homme qui assassina: Roman*. Paris: Société d'éditions littéraires et artistiques, Librairie P. Ollendorff, [1910?].
Fayet, Jean-François. "1919." In Smith, *The Oxford Handbook of the History of Communism*, 109–24.
Feldman, Leah. *On the Threshold of Eurasia: Revolutionary Poetics in the Caucasus*. Ithaca, NY: Cornell University Press, 2018.
Fethi Naci. *100 Soruda Türkiye'de Roman ve Toplumsal Değişme*. Istanbul: Gerçek Yayınevi, 1981.
———. *Yaşar Kemal'in Romancılığı*. Istanbul: Yapı Kredi Yayınları, 2004.

BIBLIOGRAPHY

Fevral'skii, Aleksandr. "Nazym Khikmet." In *Zapiski rovesnika veka*, 319–89. Moscow: Sovetskii pisatel', 1976.
Fink, Bruce. *A Clinical Introduction to Lacanian Psychoanalysis: Theory and Technique*. Cambridge, MA: Harvard University Press, 1997.
———. *The Lacanian Subject: Between Language and Jouissance*. Princeton, NJ: Princeton University Press, 1995.
———. "Perversion." In *Perversion and the Social Relation*, edited by Molly Anne Rothenberg, Dennis A. Foster, and Slavoj Žižek, 38–67. Durham, NC: Duke University Press, 2003.
Fish, Radii G. *Pisateli Turtsii: Knigi i sud'by*. Moscow: Sovetskii pisatel', 1963.
———. *Turetskie dnevniki: Vstrechi, razmyshleniia*. Moscow: Nauka, 1977.
Fleming, K. E. *The Muslim Bonaparte: Diplomacy and Orientalism in Ali Pasha's Greece*. Princeton, NJ: Princeton University Press, 1999.
Freud, Sigmund. "Family Romances." In *The Standard Edition of the Complete Psychological Works of Sigmund Freud*, vol. 9: *1906–1908: Jensen's "Gradiva" and Other Works*, translated and edited by James Strachey, 235–41. London: Hogarth Press, 1959.
———. *The Interpretation of Dreams*. Translated by James Strachey. New York: Avon, 1998.
Gabrilovich, Evgeny, and Sergei Yutkevich. *A Film Trilogy About Lenin*. Translated by Nadezhda Burova. Moscow: Progress, 1985.
Gal'perina, E. "Turetskie pisateli v Moskve." *Literaturnaia gazeta*, no. 58 (October 20, 1939): 4.
Gazi Mustafa Kemal [*see also* Mustafa Kemal]. *Nutuk* (1927). Istanbul: Yapı Kredi Yayınları, 2011.
———. *A Speech Delivered by Mustafa Kemal Atatürk, 1927*. Istanbul: Turkish Ministry of Education Printing Plant, 1963.
"Germanskie intrigi v Turtsii." *Pravda*, March 3, 1937, 5.
"Gespräche mit Suad Derwisch." *Die Frau und ihre Welt*, January 17, 1929, 3.
Gezen, Ela E. *Brecht, Turkish Theater, and Turkish-German Literature: Reception, Adaptation, and Innovation After 1960*. Rochester, NY: Camden House, 2018.
Göğceli, Kemal Sadık. *Ağıtlar 1*. Adana: Türksözü Matbaası, 1943.
Gökalp, Altan, Güzin Dino, Jean-Pierre Deleage, Nedim Gürsel, Daniel Rondeau, Timour Muhidine, Carole Gündoğar, et al. *Yaşar Kemal'i Okumak: İnceleme*. Translated by Nedret Tanyolaç Öztokat and Erdim Öztokat. Istanbul: Adam Yayınları, 1999.
Gökay, Bülent. *Soviet Eastern Policy and Turkey, 1920–1991*. New York: Routledge, 2006.
Göknar, Erdağ. *Orhan Pamuk, Secularism, and Blasphemy: The Politics of the Turkish Novel*. London: Routledge, 2013.
Gökşen, Erol. "Suat Derviş'in Gazete Yazıları Işığında *Fosforlu Cevriye*'yi Okuma Denemesi." *Roman Kahramanları*, no. 18 (April–June 2014): 91–95.
Göksu, Saime, and Edward Timms. *Romantic Communist: The Life and Work of Nazım Hikmet*. New York: St. Martin's, 1999.
Gor'kii, Maksim [*see also* Gorky, Maksim]. "Doklad A.M. Gor'kogo o sovetskoi literature." In *Pervyi vsesoiuznyi s"ezd sovetskikh pisatelei 1934*, 5–18.
———. *Mat'*. In *Polnoe sobranie sochinenii*, vol. 8: *1906–1910*, 5–346. Moscow: Nauka, 1970.

——. "Otkrytoe pis'mo A. S. Serafimovichu." *Literaturnaia gazeta*, February 15, 1934, 1.
——. "Po povodu odnoi diskussii." *Literaturnaia gazeta*, January 28, 1934, 2.
Gorky, Maksim [*see also* Gor'kii, Maksim]. *The Mother*. Translated by Hugh Aplin. Surrey, U.K.: Alma, 2015.
——. "Soviet Literature." In Maksim Gorky, Karl Radek, Nikolai Bukharin, Andrey Zhdanov, and others, *Soviet Writers' Congress, 1934: The Debate on Socialist Realism and Modernism in the Soviet Union*, 27–69. London: Lawrence and Wishart, 1977.
"Die Gotteslästerung." *Das Unterhaltungsblatt der Vossischen Zeitung*, no. 188 (August 13, 1927): 1.
Gough, Maria. "Faktura: The Making of the Russian Avant-Garde." *RES: Anthropology and Aesthetics* 36 (1999): 33–59.
Gourgouris, Stathis. "Communism and Poetry." *Gramma* 8 (2008): 43–54.
Gövsa, İbrahim Alâettin. "Tepedelenlioğlu, Nizameddin Nazif." In *Türk Meşhurları Ansiklopedisi*, 378–79. Istanbul: Yedigün, 1946.
Gramsci, Antonio. *Selections from the Prison Notebooks*. Translated by Quintin Hoare and Geoffrey Nowell Smith. London: International, 1971.
Gratien, Chris. *The Unsettled Plain: An Environmental History of the Late Ottoman Frontier*. Stanford, CA: Stanford University Press, 2022.
Groys, Boris. *The Total Art of Stalinism: Avant-Garde, Aesthetic Dictatorship, and Beyond*. Translated by Charles Rougle. Princeton, NJ: Princeton University Press, 1992.
Günther, Hans. "Die Lebensphasen eines Kanons—am Beispiel des sozialistischen Realismus." In *Kanon und Zensur: Beiträge zur Archäologie der literarischen Kommunikation II*, edited by Jan Assmann and Aleida Assmann, 138–48. Munich: Fink, 1987.
——. "Soviet Literary Criticism and the Formulation of the Aesthetics of Socialist Realism, 1932–1940." In Dobrenko and Tihanov, *A History of Russian Literary Theory and Criticism*, 90–108.
Gürbilek, Nurdan. *Kör Ayna, Kayıp Şark*. Istanbul: Metis, 2004.
——. "'The *Orijinal* Turkish Spirit.'" In *The New Cultural Climate in Turkey: Living in a Shop Window*, translated by Victoria Holbrook, 167–97. London: Zed, 2011.
Gürel, Perin E. *The Limits of Westernization: A Cultural History of America in Turkey*. New York: Columbia University Press, 2017.
Gürpınar, Doğan. "Double Discourses and Romantic Ottomanism: The Ottoman Empire as a 'Foreign Country.'" *International Journal of Turkish Studies* 17, nos. 1–2 (2011): 39–63.
Guseinov, A. A. *Mukhsin Ertugrul v teatre i kino*. Moscow: Nauka, 1990.
Güvenir, O. Murat. *İkinci Dünya Savaşında Türk Basını: Siyasal İktidarın Basını Denetlemesi ve Yönlendirmesi*. Istanbul: Gazeteciler Cemiyeti, 1991.
Güzel, M. Şehmus. *Abidin Dino ile Söyleşiler; Yazılar: Hayat ve Sanat*. Istanbul: Pêrî, 2006.
——. *Abidin Dino: Üç Kitap (1913–1993)*. Vol. 1: *Birinci Kitap (1913–1942)*. Istanbul: Kitap Yayınevi, 2007.
——. *Abidin Dino: Üç Kitap (1913–1993)*. Vol. 2: *İkinci Kitap (1942–1952)*. Istanbul: Kitap Yayınevi, 2008.
Halim, Hala. "Lotus, the Afro-Asian Nexus, and Global Comparatism." *Comparative Studies of South Asia, Africa, and the Middle East* 32, no. 3 (2012): 563–83.

BIBLIOGRAPHY

Hamacher, Werner. "Afformative, Strike: Benjamin's 'Critique of Violence.'" Translated by Dana Hollander. In *Walter Benjamin's Philosophy: Destruction and Experience*, edited by Andrew Benjamin and Peter Osborne, 110–38. London: Routledge, 1994.
Han, Gül Bilge. "Nâzım Hikmet's Afro-Asian Solidarities." *Safundi* 19, no. 3 (2018): 284–305. https://doi.org/10.1080/17533171.2018.1470814.
Harris, George S. *The Communists and the "Kadro" Movement: Shaping Ideology in Atatürk's Turkey*. Istanbul: ISIS, 2002.
——. *The Origins of Communism in Turkey*. Stanford, CA: Hoover Institution Press, 1967.
Haydar Rifat. *Bolşeviklik Âlemi*. Istanbul: Şirketi Mürettibiye Matbaası, 1932.
Heath, Stephen. "Joan Riviere and the Masquerade." In *Formations of Fantasy*, edited by Victor Burgin, James Donald, and Cora Kaplan, 45–61. London: Routledge, 1986.
Hegel, Georg Wilhelm Friedrich. *The Science of Logic*. Translated and edited by George di Giovanni. Cambridge: Cambridge University Press, 2010.
Her Evli Erkek Neler Bilmelidir? Istanbul: Sevimli Ay Matbaası, 1927.
Hicks, Jeremy. *Mikhail Zoshchenko and the Poetics of Skaz*. Nottingham, U.K.: Astra Press, 2000.
Hikmet Feridun. "Edebiyatımız Ne Halde?" (interview of Şükûfe Nihal). *Akşam*, April 23, 1929, 1.
——. "Edebiyatımız Ne Halde?" (interview of Necip Fazıl). *Akşam*, May 7, 1929, 2.
Hirst, Samuel J. "Anti-Westernism on the European Periphery: The Meaning of Soviet-Turkish Convergence in the 1930s." *Slavic Review* 72, no. 1 (Spring 2013): 32–53. https://www.jstor.org/stable/10.5612/slavicreview.72.1.0032.
——. "Soviet Orientalism Across Borders: Documentary Film for the Turkish Republic." *Kritika: Explorations in Russian and Eurasian History* 18, no. 1 (2017): 35–61. https://doi.org/10.1353/kri.2017.0002.
——. "Transnational Anti-imperialism and the National Forces: Soviet Diplomacy and Turkey, 1920–23." *Comparative Studies of South Asia, Africa, and the Middle East* 33, no. 2 (2013): 214–26. https://doi.org/10.1215/1089201X-2322498.
Hodgkin, Samuel. "Lāhūtī: Persian Poetry in the Making of the Literary International, 1906–1957." PhD diss., University of Chicago, 2018.
——. *Persianate Verse and the Poetics of Eastern Internationalism*. Cambridge: Cambridge University Press, forthcoming.
Hunt, Lynn. *The Family Romance of the French Revolution*. Berkeley: University of California Press, 1992.
Hüseyin Ragıp. "Sağdan Sola Doğru" (March 8, 1921). In Bolluk, *Kurtuluş Savaşı'nın İdeolojisi*, 116–24.
İleri, Rasih Nuri. "Abidin Dino Hakkında Bir Kronoloji Denemesi." *Güldiken*, no. 4 (1994): 11–15.
——. *Sahne ve Kostüm Tasarımı: Abidin Dino / Scenery and Costume Design: Abidin Dino*. Istanbul: Yapı Kredi Yayınları, 2005.
——, ed. *Kırklı Yıllar 1: En Büyük Tehlike (Faris Erkman); Niçin Sovyetler Birliğinin Dostuyum? (Suat Derviş)*. Istanbul: TÜSTAV, 2002.
——, ed. *Kırklı Yıllar 2: 1944 TKP Davası*. Istanbul: TÜSTAV, 2003.
——. Preface to S. İleri, *Yeni Edebiyat 1940–1941*, 9–15.
İleri, Suphi Nuri, ed. *Yeni Edebiyat 1940–1941: Sosyalist Gerçekçilik*. Istanbul: Scala, 1998.

Inalcik, Halil. *The Ottoman Empire: The Classical Age 1300–1600*. London: Phoenix, 1973.
"İnkılâbımızın Mükemmel Filmi Nasıl Olacak?" *Vakit*, December 15, 1932, 10.
Irmak, Erkan. *Eski Köye Yeni Roman*. Istanbul: İletişim, 2018.
———. *Kayıp Destan'ın İzinde: "Kuvâyi Milliye" ve "Memleketimden İnsan Manzaraları" 'nda Milliyetçilik, Propaganda ve İdeoloji*. Istanbul: İletişim, 2011.
İşçi, Onur. *Turkey and the Soviet Union During World War II*. London: I. B. Tauris, 2020.
Işıklar-Koçak, Müge. "Problematizing Translated Popular Texts on Women's Sexuality: A New Perspective on the Modernization Project in Turkey from 1931 to 1959." PhD diss., Istanbul Bosphorus University, 2007.
İsmail Hüsrev. *Türkiye Köy İktisadiyatı: Bir Millî İktisat Tetkiki*. Istanbul: Matbaacılık ve Neşriyat Türk Anonim Şirketi, 1934.
———. "Türk Köylüsünü Topraklandırmalı. Fakat Nasıl?" *Kadro*, no. 23 (November 1933): 33–39. Reprinted in Ö. Erdem, *Kadro*, vol. 2: *1933–1934*, 1277–83.
Iutkevich, Sergei [*see also* Yutkevich, Sergei]. "Bol'shaia perspektiva." *Iskusstvo kino*, no. 12 (December 1937): 43–59.
———. "'Ia vstrechaiu Abidina. . . .'" *Literaturnaia gazeta*, no. 16 (February 5, 1966): 2.
———. "Pervyi god raboty kinomasterskoi." *Iskusstvo kino*, no. 1 (January 1936): 33–37.
———. "Pis'mo k turetskim khudozhnikam." *Iskusstvo* 2 (1934): 71–86.
———. *Sobranie sochinenii v trekh tomakh*. Vol. 2: *Put'*, edited by M. Z. Dolinskii. Moscow: Iskusstvo, 1991.
Iutkevich, Sergei, and Leo Arnshtam, dir. *Türkiye'nin Kalbi Ankara*. Lenfilm and Turkish Ministry of Education, 1934. https://www.tccb.gov.tr/ata_ozel/video/.
Kadıoğlu, Ayşe. "Cinselliğin İnkârı: Büyük Toplumsal Projelerin Nesnesi Olarak Türk Kadınları." In *75 Yılda Kadınlar ve Erkekler*, edited by A. B. Hacımirzaoğlu, 89–100. Istanbul: Türk Tarih Vakfı Yayınları, 1998.
Kadir, A. *1938 Harp Okulu Olayı ve Nâzım Hikmet: Anı*. Istanbul: Can, 1993.
Kallinikov, Iosif. *Moshchi: Roman*. 4 vols. 2nd ed. Moscow: Krug, [ca. 1920s].
Kandemir, Feridun. *Atatürk'ün Kurduğu Türkiye Komünist Partisi ve Sonrası*. Istanbul: Nejat Ağbaba, [1966].
Kane, Eileen, Masha Kirasirova, and Margaret Litvin, eds. *Russian-Arab World: A Documentary History*. Oxford: Oxford University Press, 2023.
Kant, Immanuel. "An Answer to the Question: What Is Enlightenment?" Translated by James Schmidt. In *What Is Enlightenment? Eighteenth-Century Answers and Twentieth-Century Questions*, edited by James Schmidt, 58–64. Berkeley: University of California Press, 1996.
———. *Groundwork of the Metaphysics of Morals*. Translated and edited by Mary J. Gregor. Cambridge: Cambridge University Press, 1998.
Kara, Halim. "Mazinin Edebi Temsili: Tarihsel Romanda Fatih'in Karakterizasyonu." In *Edebiyatın Omzundaki Melek: Edebiyatın Tarihle İlişkisi Üzerine Yazılar*, edited by Zeynep Uysal, 337–80. Istanbul: İletişim, 2011.
Karaca, Emin. *Eski Tüfeklerin Sonbaharı*. Istanbul: Toplumsal Dönüşüm Yayınları, 1996.
———. *Nâzım Hikmet Şiirinde Gizli Tarih*. Istanbul: Destek Yayınevi, 2011.
Karagöz, Özge. "Of Modernist Painting and Statist Economy: Nurullah Berk on the Soviet Art Exhibition in Turkey, 1934–35." *Journal of the Ottoman and Turkish Studies Association* 8, no. 2 (2021): 271–80. https://www.muse.jhu.edu/article/859843.

BIBLIOGRAPHY

Karahan, Burcu. "Repressed in Translation: Representation of Female Sexuality in Ottoman Erotica." *Journal of Turkish Literature* 9 (2012): 30–45.
Karaömerlioğlu, M. Asım. *Orada Bir Köy Var Uzakta: Erken Cumhuriyet Döneminde Köycü Söylem*. Istanbul: İletişim, 2006.
——. "The Village Institutes Experience in Turkey." *British Journal of Middle Eastern Studies* 25, no. 1 (1998): 47–73.
Karaosmanoğlu, Yakup Kadri. *Stepmother Earth*. Translated by Mark David Wyers. N.p.: Milet, 2020.
Karim, Mustai, Konstantin Simonov, and Radii Fish. "Cherez tridtsat' let. . . ." *Pravda*, February 27, 1966, 5.
Kavaklı, Nurhan. *Bir Gazetenin Tarihi: "Akşam."* Istanbul: Yapı Kredi Yayınları, 2005.
Kemper, Michael. "Red Orientalism: Mikhail Pavlovich and Marxist Oriental Studies in Early Soviet Russia." *Die Welt des Islams* 50 (2010): 435–76.
Keyder, Çağlar. *State and Class in Turkey: A Study in Capitalist Development*. London: Verso, 1987.
Khalid, Adeeb. "Central Asia Between the Ottoman and Soviet Worlds." *Kritika: Explorations in Russian and Eurasian History* 12, no. 2 (2011): 451–76. https://doi.org/10.1353/kri.2011.0028.
Khotimsky, Maria. "World Literature, Soviet Style: A Forgotten Episode in the History of the Idea." *Ab Imperio* 3, no. 3 (2013): 119–54. https://doi.org/10.1353/imp.2013.0075.
Kiaer, Christina. *Imagine No Possessions: The Socialist Objects of Russian Constructivism*. Cambridge, MA: MIT Press, 2005.
Kirasirova, Masha. "The 'East' as a Category of Bolshevik Ideology and Comintern Administration: The Arab Section of the Communist University of the Toilers of the East." *Kritika: Explorations in Russian and Eurasian History* 18, no. 1 (2017): 7–34. https://doi.org/10.1353/kri.2017.0001.
Kirby, Fay. *Türkiye'de Köy Enstitüleri*. Translated by Niyazi Berkes. Ankara: İmece, 1962.
Kleberg, Lars. *Theatre as Action: Soviet Russian Avant-Garde Aesthetics*. Translated by Charles Rougle. London: MacMillan, 1993.
"Knigi 1960-go." *Literaturnaia gazeta*, no. 18 (February 9, 1961): 1.
Kocabaşoğlu, Uygur. "Milli Mücadelenin Sözcülerinden: *Anadolu'da Yeni Gün*." *Ankara Üniversitesi SBF Dergisi* 36, no. 1 (1981): 179–203.
Kocabaşoğlu, Uygur, and Metin Berge. *Bolşevik İhtilâli ve Osmanlılar*. Ankara: Kebikeç Yayınları, 1994.
Koçak, Cemil. *Türkiye'de Millî Şef Dönemi (1938–1945)*. 2 vols. Istanbul: İletişim, 1996.
Koçak Hemmat, Ayşe Özge. *The Turkish Novel and the Quest for Rationality*. Leiden, Netherlands: Brill, 2019.
Kollontai, Aleksandra [see also Kollontai, Alexandra]. "Asrî Kadına Göre Aşkın Manası Nedir?" *Resimli Ay* 7, no. 9 (January 1, 1931): 9.
——. "Dorogu krylatomu erosu!" *Molodaia gvardiia*, no. 3.10 (May 1923): 111–24.
——. *Prostitutsiia i mery bor'by s nei: Rech' na III vserossiiskom soveshchanii zaveduiushchikh gubzhenotdelami*. Moscow: Gosudarstvennoe izdatel'stvo, 1921.
Kollontai, Alexandra [see also Kollontai, Aleksandra]. "Make Way for Winged Eros: A Letter to Working Youth." In Kollontai, *Selected Writings of Alexandra Kollontai*, 276–92.

———. "Prostitution and Ways of Fighting It." In Kollantai, *Selected Writings of Alexandra Kollontai*, 261–75.
———. *Selected Writings of Alexandra Kollontai*. Translated with an introduction and commentaries by Alix Holt. Westport, CN: Lawrence Hill, 1977.
Koloğlu, Orhan. "100. Doğum Yıldönümünde Nâzım Hikmet." *Tarih ve Toplum* 37, no. 217 (2002): 13–19.
Konuk Blasing, Mutlu. "Nâzım Hikmet and Ezra Pound: 'To Confess Wrong Without Losing Rightness.'" *Journal of Modern Literature* 33, no. 2 (2010): 1–23.
———. *Nâzım Hikmet: The Life and Times of Turkey's World Poet*. New York: Persea, 2013.
Körpe, Oya. "Suat Derviş'in Hayatı, Edebî Kişiliği ve Eserleri Üzerine Bir İnceleme." Master's thesis, Dokuz Eylül Üniversitesi, 2001.
Kosova, Zehra. *Ben İşçiyim*. Edited by Zihni T. Anadol. Istanbul: İletişim, 1996.
Kozlovskii, S. V., and N. M. Kolin. *Khudozhnik-arkhitektor v kino*. Moscow: Teakinopechat', 1930.
Kracauer, Siegfried. *History: The Last Things Before the Last*. Completed after the death of the author by Paul Oskar Kristeller. Princeton, NJ: Markus Wiener, 1995.
Krakus, Anna, and Cristina Vatulescu. "Foucault in Poland: A Silent Archive." *Diacritics* 47, no. 2 (2019): 72–105.
Küçük, Yalçın. *Aydın Üzerine Tezler, 1830–1980*. Vol. 4. Istanbul: Tekin Yayınevi, 1986.
Kurdakul, Şükran, and Sennur Sezer. *Nâzım, Dünya ve Biz*. Istanbul: Evrensel, 2002.
Laachir, Karima, Sara Marzagora, and Francesca Orsini. "Significant Geographies." *Journal of World Literature* 3, no. 3 (2018): 290–310. https://doi.org/10.1163/24056480-00303005.
Lacan, Jacques. *Écrits: The First Complete Edition in English*. Translated by Bruce Fink in collaboration with Héloïse Fink and Russell Grigg. New York: Norton, 2006.
———. "God and Woman's Jouissance." In Lacan, *The Seminar of Jacques Lacan, Book XX, Encore*, 64–77.
———. "Guiding Remarks for a Convention on Female Sexuality." In Lacan, *Écrits*, 610–20.
———. "Knowledge and Truth." In Lacan, *The Seminar of Jacques Lacan, Book XX, Encore*, 90–103.
———. *The Seminar of Jacques Lacan: The Ethics of Psychoanalysis, 1959–1960, Book VII*. Edited by Jacques-Alain Miller. Translated by Dennis Porter. New York: Norton, 1992.
———. *The Seminar of Jacques Lacan: On Feminine Sexuality, the Limits of Love and Knowledge, Book XX, Encore 1972–1973*. Edited by Jacques-Alain Miller. Translated with notes by Bruce Fink. New York: Norton, 1999.
———. "The Signification of the Phallus." In Lacan, *Écrits*, 575–84.
———. "The Subversion of the Subject and the Dialectic of Desire in the Freudian Unconscious." In Lacan, *Écrits*, 671–702.
Lahusen, Thomas. "Socialist Realism in Search of Its Shores: Some Historical Remarks on the 'Historically Open Aesthetic System of the Truthful Representation of Life.'" In Lahusen and Dobrenko, *Socialist Realism Without Shores*, 5–26.
Lahusen, Thomas, and Evgeny Dobrenko, eds. *Socialist Realism Without Shores*. Durham, NC: Duke University Press, 1997.
Lansere, E. E. *Leto v Angore: Risunki i zametki iz dnevnika poezdki v Anatoliiu letom 1922 g*. Leningrad: Izdatel'stvo Brokgauz-Efron, 1925.

BIBLIOGRAPHY

Lecercle, Jean-Jacques. *A Marxist Philosophy of Language*. Translated by Gregory Elliott. Leiden, Netherlands: Brill, 2006.
Lee, Steven S. *The Ethnic Avant-Garde: Minority Cultures and World Revolution*. New York: Columbia University Press, 2015.
———. "Introduction: Comintern Aesthetics—Space, Form, History." In *Comintern Aesthetics*, edited by Amelia M. Glaser and Steven S. Lee, 3–28. Toronto: University of Toronto Press, 2020.
Lenin, V. I. "II kongress Kommunisticheskogo Internatsionala." In *Polnoe sobranie sochinenii*, vol. 41, 5th ed., 213–67. Moscow: Gosudarstvennoe izdatel'stvo, 1963.
———. *Chto delat'? Nabolevshie voprosy nashego dvizheniia*. In *Polnoe sobranie sochinenii*, vol. 6, 5th ed., 2–192. Moscow: Gosudarstvennoe izdatel'stvo, 1959.
———. "S chego nachat'?" In *Polnoe sobranie sochinenii*, vol. 5, 5th ed., 3–13. Moscow: Gosudarstvennoe izdatel'stvo, 1959.
———. "The Second Congress of the Communist International." In *Collected Works*, vol. 31, translated and edited by Julius Katzer, 213–63. Moscow: Progress, 1966.
———. *What Is to Be Done? Burning Questions of Our Movement*. In Lars T. Lih, *Lenin Rediscovered: "What Is to Be Done?" in Context*, 671–840. Chicago: Haymarket, 2008.
———. "Where to Begin." In *Collected Works*, vol. 5, edited by Victor Jerome, translated by Joe Fineberg and George Hanna, 13–24. Moscow: Foreign Languages Publishing House, 1961.
Leonid and Friedrich. *Angora: Freiheitskrieg der Türkei*. Berlin: Vereinigung internationaler Verlagsanstalten, 1923.
———. *Ankara 1922: İki Komintern Gözlemcisinin Kurtuluş Savaşı Değerlendirmesi*. Translated by Gizem Gürtürk. Istanbul: Kaynak, 1994.
Lévi-Strauss, Claude. *Introduction to the Work of Marcel Mauss*. Translated by Felicity Baker. London: Routledge & Kegan Paul, 1987.
Lewis, Geoffrey. *The Turkish Language Reform: A Catastrophic Success*. New York: Oxford University Press, 1999.
Leyda, Jay. *Kino: A History of the Russian and Soviet Film*. 3rd ed. Princeton, NJ: Princeton University Press, 1983.
Lih, Lars T. *Lenin Rediscovered: "What Is to Be Done?" in Context*. Chicago: Haymarket, 2008.
Liu, Lydia H. "The Eventfulness of Translation: Temporality, Difference, and Competing Universals." *Translation: A Transdisciplinary Journal* 4 (Spring 2014): 147–70.
Lukács, Georg. *The Historical Novel*. Translated by Hannah Mitchell and Stanley Mitchell. Lincoln: University of Nebraska Press, 1983.
———. "The Ideology of Modernism." In *The Meaning of Contemporary Realism*, translated by John Mander and Necke Mander, 17–46. London: Merlin Press, 1962.
———. "Narrate or Describe?" In Lukács, *Writer and Critic and Other Essays*, 110–48.
———. "Marx and Engels on Aesthetics." In Lukács, *Writer and Critic and Other Essays*, 61–88.
———. "Realism in the Balance." Translated by Rodney Livingstone. In Theodor Adorno et al., *Aesthetics and Politics*, 28–59.
———. *Writer and Critic and Other Essays*. Edited and translated by Arthur Kahn. Lincoln, NE: iUniverse, an Authors Guild Backprint.com edition, 2005.
Maevskii, V., and A. Ivakhnenko. "Konferentsiia pisatelei stran Azii i Afriki: Krepit' sviazi mezhdu kul'turoi Vostoka i Zapada." *Pravda*, October 12, 1958, 4.

BIBLIOGRAPHY

Makal, Mahmut. *Bizim Köy: Köy Öğretmeninin Notları*. Istanbul: Varlık, 1950.
———. *Köy Enstitüleri ve Ötesi*. Istanbul: Çağdaş Yayınları, 1979.
Makal, Oğuz. *Beyaz Perdede ve Sahnede Nâzım Hikmet*. Istanbul: Kalkedon, 2015.
Manevich, I. "V bor'be za realisticheskii obraz." *Iskusstvo kino*, no. 9 (September 1937): 3–13.
Mardin, Şerif. "Super Westernization in Urban Life in the Ottoman Empire in the Last Quarter of the Nineteenth Century." In *Turkey: Geographical and Social Perspectives*, edited by Peter Benedict, Erol Tümertekin, and Fatma Mansur, 403–46. Leiden, Netherlands: Brill, 1974.
Marx, Karl. *Capital: A Critique of Political Economy*. Vol. 1. Translated by Ben Fowkes. New York: Penguin, 1990.
———. "Economic and Philosophic Manuscripts of 1844." In *Karl Marx and Frederick Engels: Collected Works*, vol. 3: *Marx and Engels 1843–1844*, 229–346. London: Lawrence and Wishart, 2010.
———. *Grundrisse*. Part 2. In *MEGA* II/1.2, MEGAdigital, Berlin-Brandenburgische Akademie der Wissenschaften. http://telota.bbaw.de/mega/#.
———. *Grundrisse: Foundations of the Critique of Political Economy (Rough Draft)*. Translated by Martin Nicolaus. New York: Penguin, 1993.
———. *Das Kapital*. Vol. 1. In *MEGA* II/5, MEGAdigital, Berlin-Brandenburgische Akademie der Wissenschaften. http://telota.bbaw.de/mega/# .
Marx, Magdeleine. *Istanbul 1921–Ankara 1922: Makaleler-Anılar*. Translated by Ahmet Şensılay. Istanbul: TÜSTAV, 2007.
Matskin, D. "Tema molodoi Turtsii." *Sovetskoe kino*, no. 9 (September 1933): 15–26.
Mauss, Marcel. *The Gift: The Form and Reason for Exchange in Archaic Societies*. Translated by W. D. Halls. London: Routledge, 1990.
Mayakovsky, Vladimir. *Selected Poems*. Translated by James H. McGavran III. Evanston, IL: Northwestern University Press, 2013.
McDougall, Bonnie S. *Mao Zedong's "Talks at the Yan'an Conference on Literature and Art": A Translation of the 1943 Text with Commentary*. Ann Arbor: University of Michigan Center for Chinese Studies, 1980.
McGuire, Elizabeth. *Red at Heart: How Chinese Communists Fell in Love with the Russian Revolution*. New York: Oxford University Press, 2018.
McKay, Claude. *A Long Way from Home*. Edited by Gene Andrew Jarret. New Brunswick, NJ: Rutgers University Press, 2007.
Mehmed Kemal. *Acılı Kuşak: Anılar, Söyleşiler, Denemeler*. Istanbul: Çağdaş, 1977.
Mélikoff, Irène. "Bektashi/Kızılbaş: Historical Bipartition and Its Consequences." In *Alevi Identity: Cultural, Religious, and Social Perspectives*, edited by Tord Olsson, Elisabeth Özdalga, and Catharina Raudvere, 1–8. London: Taylor and Francis, 2005.
Memet Fuat. *Nâzım Hikmet: Portreler*. Istanbul: Yapı Kredi Yayınları, 2001.
Merrill, Jessica. *The Origins of Russian Literary Theory: Folklore, Philology, Form*. Evanston, IL: Northwestern University Press, 2022.
Meyer, James H. "Children of Trans-empire: Nâzım Hikmet and the First Generation of Turkish Students at Moscow's Communist University of the East." *Journal of the Ottoman and Turkish Studies Association* 5, no. 2 (Fall 2018): 195–218. https://doi.org/10.2979/jottturstuass.5.2.12.
———. *Red Star Over the Black Sea: Nâzım Hikmet and His Generation*. Oxford: Oxford University Press, 2023.

BIBLIOGRAPHY

———. *Turks Across Empires: Marketing Muslim Identity in the Russian-Ottoman Borderlands, 1856–1914.* New York: Oxford University Press, 2014.
Miasnikov, Gennadii. *Ocherki istorii sovetskogo kinodekoratsionnogo iskusstva (1918–1930).* Moscow: VGIK, 1975.
———. *Ocherki istorii sovetskogo kinodekoratsionnogo iskusstva (1931–1945).* Moscow: VGIK, 1979.
Mignolo, Walter D. *The Politics of Decolonial Investigations.* Durham, NC: Duke University Press, 2021.
Mignon, Laurent. *Edebiyatın Sınırlarında: Türkçe Edebiyat, Gürcistan ve Cengiz Aytmatov'a Dair.* Istanbul: Evrensel Basım Yayın, 2016.
———. *Hüzünlü Özgürlük: Yahudi Edebiyatı ve Düşüncesi Üzerine Yazılar.* Istanbul: Gözlem Gazetecilik, 2014.
———. *Neither Shiraz nor Paris: Papers on Modern Turkish Literature.* Istanbul: Gorgias, 2010.
———. "A Pilgrim's Progress: Armenian and Kurdish Literatures in Turkish and the Rewriting of Literary History." *Patterns of Prejudice* 48, no. 2 (2014): 182–200.
———. "Yaşar Kemal." In *Turkish Novelists Since 1960,* edited by Burcu Alkan and Çimen Günay-Erkol, 156–71. Detroit: Gale Cengage Learning, 2014.
Miller, Jacques-Alain. "Of Distribution Between the Sexes." *Psychoanalytical Notebooks,* no. 11 (2003): 9–27.
Miller, Jamie. *Soviet Cinema: Politics and Persuasion Under Stalin.* London: I. B. Tauris, 2010.
"Millî Mücadele Filmi...." *Cumhuriyet,* December 15, 1932, 3.
Milne, Lesley. "*Novyi Satirikon,* 1914–1918: The Patriotic Laughter of the Russian Liberal Intelligentsia During the First World War and the Revolution." *Slavonic and East European Review* 84, no. 4 (2006): 639–65.
Moldavskii, Dmitrii. *S Maiakovskim v teatre i kino: Kniga o Sergee Iutkeviche.* Moscow: Vserossiiskoe teatral'noe obshchestvo, 1975.
Moran, Berna. *Türk Romanına Eleştirel Bir Bakış.* 3 vols. Istanbul: İletişim, 1983–1994.
Moretti, Franco. *Atlas of the European Novel, 1800–1900.* London: Verso, 1998.
Morris, Rosalind C. "Dialect and Dialectic in 'The Working Day' of Marx's *Capital.*" In "Econophonia: Music, Value, and Forms of Life," edited by Gavin Steingo and Jairo Moreno, special issue of *boundary 2* 43, no. 1 (2016): 219–48.
Morrison, Toni. "The Site of Memory." In *Inventing the Truth: The Art and Craft of Memoir,* edited by William Zinsser, 101–24. Boston: Houghton Mifflin, 1987.
Mrázek, Rudolf. "Lenin of the Camps: Radical Translation in Colonial Digoel and Nazi Terezín." In Ertürk and Serin, "Marxism, Communism, and Translation," 133–58.
Mustafa Kemal [*see also* Gazi Mustafa Kemal]. "Cereyanlar." *Hakimiyet-i Milliye,* October 9, 1920. Reprinted in Bolluk, *Kurtuluş Savaşı'nın İdeolojisi,* 84–87.
———. "İki Komünizm." *Hakimiyet-i Milliye* 1, no. 64 (October 12, 1920): 1. Ankara Üniversitesi Gazeteler Veritabanı. http://gazeteler.ankara.edu.tr/dergiler/milli_kutup/1541/1541_3/0004.pdf.
———. *Put' novoi Turtsii, 1919–1927.* 4 vols. Moscow: Litizdat NKID, 1929–1934.
———. "Rus Bolşevizmi Türk Komünizmi." *Hakimiyet-i Milliye* 1, no. 65 (October 16, 1920): 1. Ankara Üniversitesi Gazeteler Veritabanı. http://gazeteler.ankara.edu.tr/dergiler/milli_kutup/1541/1541_3/0006.pdf.

Naiman, Eric. *Sex in Public: The Incarnation of Early Soviet Ideology*. Princeton, NJ: Princeton University Press, 1997.
Nanji, Azim. "Almsgiving." In *Encyclopaedia of the Qurʾān*, edited by Jane Dammen McAuliffe. Brill Online, 2015. http://referenceworks.brillonline.com/entries/encyclopaedia-of-the-quran/almsgiving-EQCOM_00008.
Nâzım Hikmet [*see also* Nazym Khikmet]. *835 Satır*. Istanbul: Muallim Ahmet Halit Kitaphanesi, 1929.
———. "Asya, Afrika Yazarları Toplantısı Konuşması" (1958). *Yarına Doğru*, no. 8 (June 1974): 3–9.
———. *Bizim Radyoda Nâzım Hikmet*. Edited by Anjel Açıkgöz. Istanbul: TÜSTAV, 2002.
———. "Bugünün İstidadı, Yarının Kuvveti." *Resimli Ay* 7, no. 7 (September 1930): 35.
———. "Gazete Kollektif Bir Teşkilatçı." In E. Akbulut, *Komintern Belgelerinde Nâzım Hikmet*, 45–47.
———. *Gece Gelen Telgraf*. Istanbul: Muallîm Ahmet Halit Kütüphanesi, 1932.
———. *Human Landscapes from My Country: An Epic Novel in Verse*. Translated by Randy Blasing and Mutlu Konuk. New York: Persea, 2002.
———. *Kemal Tahir'e Mahpusaneden Mektuplar*. Ankara: Bilgi, 1968.
——— [pseud. Orhan]. "Kendi Hûnumla Yazdım Ben Hükmü İdamımı." *Resimli Ay* 7, no. 6 (August 1930): 22–24.
———. *Kurtuluş Savaşı Destanı*. Istanbul: Yön, 1965.
———. *Kuvâyı Milliye: Destan*. Ankara: Bilgi, 1968.
———. *Life's Good, Brother: A Novel*. Translated by Mutlu Konuk Blasing. New York: Persea, 2013.
———. "Mecmuamıza Şiir Gönderen Şairlerle Hasbıhal." *Resimli Ay* 6, no. 8 (October 1929): 35.
———. *Piraye'ye Mektuplar*. Vol. 1. Edited by Memet Fuat. Istanbul: Adam, 1998.
———. "Putları Yıkıyoruz, No. 1: Abdülhak Hâmit." *Resimli Ay* 6, no. 4 (June 1929): 24–25.
———. *Les romantiques (La vie est belle, mon vieux . . .): Roman*. Translated by Munevver Andaç. Paris: Éditeurs français réunis, 1964.
———. *Sesini Kaybeden Şehir*. [Istanbul]: Remzi Kitaphanesi, 1931.
———. *Simavne Kadısı Oğlu Şeyh Bedreddin Destanı*. Istanbul: Yeni Kitapçı, 1936.
———. *Simavne Kadısı Oğlu Şeyh Bedreddin Destanı'na Zeyl: Millî Gurur*. Istanbul: Yeni Kitapçı, 1936.
———. *Yaşamak Güzel Şey Bekardeşim*. Istanbul: Gün, 1967.
———. *Yaşamak Güzel Şey Be Kardeşim*. Istanbul: Yapı Kredi Yayınları, 2011.
———. *Yaşamak Güzel Şeydir Kardeşim: Roman*. Sofia, Bulgaria: Narodna prosveta, 1964.
———. *Yayınlanmamış Eserler*. Edited by Oğuz Akkan. Istanbul: Cem, 1977.
———. "Yeni Çıkan Kitaplar: *Kara Davut*." *Resimli Ay* 6, no. 4 (June 1929): 34. Reprinted in *Yazılar 1: Sanat, Edebiyat, Kültür, Dil*, 17–19. Istanbul: Adam, 1991.
———. "Yeni Şairlere Dair." *Resimli Ay* 6, no. 9 (November 1929): 40.
Nazym Khikmet [*see also* Nâzım Hikmet]. *Romantika: Roman*. Translated by L. Starostova. *Znamia* 33, no. 4 (April 1963): 35–77.
———. *Romantika: Roman*. Translated by L. Starostova. Moscow: Sovetskii pisatel', 1964.
———. *Romantika, roman: Okonchanie*. Translated by L. Starostova. *Znamia* 33, no. 5 (May 1963): 43–92.

BIBLIOGRAPHY

Nâzım Hikmet and Nail V. *1 + 1 = Bir*. Istanbul: İlhami Matbaası, 1930.
Necatigil, Behçet. "Dünya Kadın Yılında Suat Derviş Üzerine Notlar." In *Nesin Vakfı Edebiyat Yıllığı 1976*, 593–609. Istanbul: Tekin Yayınları, 1976.
Nedobrovo, Vladimir. "The Eccentricism of FEKS." Translated by Richard Sherwood. In Christie and Gillett, *Futurism/Formalism/FEKS*, 17–20.
Nesimi, Abidin. *Yılların İçinden*. Istanbul: Gözlem, 1977.
Nesin, Aziz. *Cumhuriyet Döneminde Türk Mizahı: Düzyazı*. Istanbul: Akbaba Yayınları, 1973.
——. *Sanat Yazıları: Yazılar*. Istanbul: Nesin Yayınevi, 2011.
"Neşriyat Davası Son Safhasında." *Vakit*, August 18, 1931, 1–2.
Nevşirvanova, Cemile Selim. "Göç Anıları." In *Milli Azadlık Savaşı Anıları*, edited by Erden Akbulut, 95–105. Istanbul: TÜSTAV, 2006.
Nizamettin Nazif [*see also* Tepedelenlioğlu, Nizamettin Nazif]. *Bir Millet Uyanıyor*. Istanbul: Kanaat Kütüphanesi, n.d. [ca. 1932].
——. *Kara Davud*. Vol. 1. Istanbul: Türk Matbaası, 1928.
——. *Kara Davud*. Vol. 2. Istanbul: Amedi Matbaası, 1928.
——. *Kara Davut: Üç Cilt Bir Arada*. Istanbul: Resimli Ay Matbaası, 1929.
——. *Kara Davut: Üçüncü Kitap*. Vol. 3. Istanbul: Kanaat Kütüphanesi, 1930.
——. *Kolkola*. Istanbul: Semih Lûtfî Kitabevi, 1944.
——. *Topuna Birden: Umumî Bir Cevap*. Istanbul: Tanin Matbaası, 1946.
Nutku, Özdemir. "On *Aşıks* (Tale Singers) and *Meddahs* (Story Tellers)." In *The Traditional Turkish Theater*, edited by Mevlüt Özhan, 53–68. Ankara: Turkish Ministry of Culture Publications, 1999.
Oğuz, M. "Bir Anlayış!" *Yeni Adam*, no. 268 (February 15, 1940): 9.
Oktay, Ahmet. "Abidin Dino Bir 'Yazar.'" In Avcı, *Abidin Dino Bir Dünya*, 57–65.
——. *Cumhuriyet Dönemi Edebiyatı, 1923–1950*. Ankara: Etiş, 1993.
——. "*Fosforlu Cevriye*: Aşkın Yarattığı Erdem." In *Türkiye'de Popüler Kültür*, 198–200. Istanbul: Yapı Kredi Yayınları, 1993.
——. "*Memleketimden İnsan Manzaraları* Üstüne Notlar." In *Şairin Kanı*, 17–36. Istanbul: Yapı Kredi Yayınları, 2001.
——. *Toplumcu Gerçekçiliğin Kaynakları: Sosyalist Realizm Üstüne Eleştirel Bir Çalışma*. 1986. Reprint. Istanbul: İthaki, 2008.
Onaran, Âlim Şerif. *Muhsin Ertuğrul'un Sineması*. Ankara: Saim Toraman Matbaası, 1981.
Öndin, Nilüfer. *Cumhuriyet'in Kültür Politikası ve Sanat (1923–1950)*. Istanbul: İnsancıl Yayınları, 2003.
Öngören, Ferit. *Cumhuriyet Dönemi Türk Mizahı ve Hicvi (1923–1983)*. Ankara: Türkiye İş Bankası Kültür Yayınları, 1983.
Orestov, O. "Sudebnaia rasprava s turetskimi patriotami." *Pravda*, October 25, 1953, 6.
Orhan Kemal. *In Jail with Nâzım Hikmet*. Translated by Bengisu Rona. London: Saqi, 2010.
——. *Mstitel'naia volshebnitsa: Rasskazy*. Translated by S. I. Uturgauri. Moscow: Nauka, 1967.
Oushakine, Serguei Alex. "'Red Laughter': On Refined Weapons of Soviet Jesters." *Social Research* 79, no. 1 (2012): 189–216.
Özdoğan, Zülfikar. "Uluslararası Sosyal Tarih Enstitütüsü (USTE) ve Türkiye Koleksiyonları." *Kebikeç* 25 (2008): 27–44.

Özman, Aylin. "Domesticated Souls: Vâlâ Nureddin (Vâ-Nû) on Womanhood." *Turkish Studies* 8, no. 1 (2007): 137–50.

———. "The Image of 'Woman' in Turkish Political and Social Thought: On the Implications of Social Constructionism and Biological Essentialism." *Turkish Studies* 11, no. 3 (2010): 445–64.

Özman, Aylin, and Ayça Bulut. "Sabiha (Zekeriya) Sertel: Kemalizm, Marksizm ve Kadın Meselesi." *Toplum ve Bilim* 96 (2003): 184–218.

Özön, Nijad. *Türk Sineması Tarihi: Dünden Bugüne (1896–1960)*. Istanbul: Ekicigil Matbaası, 1962.

Öztuna, Yılmaz. "Duygulu [Zekî]." In *Büyük Türk Mûsikîsi Ansiklopedisi*, vol. 1: *A–L*, 234–36. Ankara: Kültür Bakanlığı, 1990.

Öztürkmen, Arzu. *Türkiye'de Folklor ve Milliyetçilik*. Istanbul: İletişim, 1998.

Paker, Saliha, and Zehra Toska. "Yazan, Yazılan, Silinen ve Yeniden Yazılan Özne: Suat Derviş'in Kimlikleri." *Toplumsal Tarih* 39 (March 1997): 11–22.

Parla, Jale. *Babalar ve Oğullar: Tanzimat Romanının Epistemolojik Temelleri*. Istanbul: İletişim, 1990.

Parla, Taha. *Türkiye'de Siyasal Kültürün Resmî Kaynakları*. Vol. 1: *Atatürk'ün "Nutuk" 'u*. Istanbul: İletişim, 1991.

"Party Cinema Conference Resolution: The Results of Cinema Construction in the USSR and the Tasks of Soviet Cinema." In Taylor and Christie, *The Film Factory*, 208–20.

Perinçek, Doğu, ed. *Komintern Belgelerinde Türkiye*. Vol. 1: *Kurtuluş Savaşı ve Lozan*. Istanbul: Kaynak, 1993–1995.

———, ed. *Lenin Stalin Mao'nun Türkiye Yazıları*. Istanbul: Kaynak, 1991.

Perinçek, Mehmet. "Anıttaki Ruslar Kim?" *Aydınlık*, January 9, 2012. https://www.aydinlik.com.tr/arsiv/mehmet-perncek-anttaki-ruslar-kim.

———. *Atatürk'ün Sovyetler'le Görüşmeleri (Sovyet Arşiv Belgeleriyle)*. Istanbul: Kaynak, 2005.

———. "Bilinmeyen Yazıları ve Belgelerle Nâzım Hikmet'in Orta Asya Seyahati." *Toplumsal Tarih*, no. 281 (May 2017): 66–80.

———. *Türk-Rus Diplomasisinden Gizli Sayfalar: Siyaset-Askeriye-Ekonomi-Kültür-Bilim-Spor*. Istanbul: Analiz Basın Yayın, 2011.

Pertev Naili [*see also* Boratav, Pertev Naili]. *Köroğlu Destanı*. Istanbul: Evkaf Matbaası, 1931.

Pervyi vsesoiuznyi s"ezd sovetskikh pisatelei 1934: Stenograficheskii otchet. Moscow: Sovetskii pisatel', 1990.

Philliou, Christine. "Introduction: USSR South: Postcolonial Worlds in the Soviet Imaginary." *Comparative Studies of South Asia, Africa, and the Middle East* 33, no. 2 (2013): 197–200. https://doi.org/10.1215/1089201X-2322480.

Popescu, Monica. *At Penpoint: African Literatures, Postcolonial Studies, and the Cold War*. Durham, NC: Duke University Press, 2020.

Popkin, Cathy. *The Pragmatics of Insignificance: Chekhov, Zoshchenko, Gogol*. Stanford, CA: Stanford University Press, 1993.

Ram, Harsha. "The Scale of Global Modernisms: Imperial, National, Regional, Local." *PMLA* 131, no. 5 (2016): 1372–85.

Râşid Mehmed Efendi and Çelebizâde İsmaîl Âsım Efendi. *Târih-i Râşid ve Zeyli*. Vol. 2. Edited by Abdülkadir Özcan, Yunus Uğur, Baki Çakır, and Ahmet Zeki İzgöer. Istanbul: Klasik, 2013.

BIBLIOGRAPHY

Rathbun, Carole. *The Village in the Turkish Novel and Short Story, 1920 to 1955.* The Hague, Netherlands: Mouton, 1972.

Ravandi-Fadai, Lana. "'Red Mecca'—the Communist University for Laborers of the East (KUTV): Iranian Scholars and Students in Moscow in the 1920s and 1930s." *Iranian Studies* 48, no. 5 (2015): 713–27. https://dx.doi.org/10.1080/00210862.2015.1058640.

Rees, Eleanor. *Designing Russian Cinema: The Production Artist and the Material Environment in Silent Era Film.* London: Bloomsbury Academic, 2023.

Reynolds, Michael A. *Shattering Empires: The Clash and Collapse of the Ottoman and Russian Empires, 1908–1918.* Cambridge: Cambridge University Press, 2011.

Riddell, John, ed. *To See the Dawn: Baku, 1920—First Congress of the Peoples of the East.* New York: Pathfinder, 2010.

———, ed. *Toward the United Front: Proceedings of the Fourth Congress of the Communist International, 1922.* Translated by John Riddell. Leiden, Netherlands: Brill, 2012.

Robin, Régine. *Socialist Realism: An Impossible Aesthetic.* Translated by Catherine Porter. Stanford, CA: Stanford University Press, 1992.

Roy, M. N. "The Turkish Victory." *International Press Correspondence* 2, no. 89 (October 17, 1922): 671–72.

Rubin, Gayle. "The Traffic in Women: Notes on the 'Political Economy' of Sex." In *Toward an Anthropology of Women*, edited by Rayna R. Reiter, 157–210. New York: Monthly Review Press, 1975.

Sabahattin Ali. "Orman Hikâyesi." *Resimli Ay* 7, no. 7 (September 1930): 22–24, 38.

Sabiha Zekeriya [*see also* Sertel, Sabiha]. "Ahlakta Müsavat İsteriz." *Resimli Ay* 6, no. 1 (March 1929): 6.

———. "Bu Kadını Nasıl Kurtarabiliriz? Fuhuşun Önüne Nasıl Geçilir?" *Resimli Ay* 7, no. 9 (January 1, 1931): 15–16.

———. "Ev Erkeği Olmak İstiyen 1000 Delikanlıya, ve Rehberleri Va.Nu Beye!" *Cumhuriyet*, June 5, 1930, 2.

———. "Gerzeli Ayşe." *Resimli Ay* 6, no. 3 (May 1929): 12–14, 39.

———. "Kadınlık Satılamaz." *Resimli Ay* 3, no. 35 (January 1927): 24–25.

———. "Kadın Maskulinistler." *Cumhuriyet*, May 27, 1930, 2.

———. "Rusya'nın Yeni İzdivaç Kanunları." *Resimli Ay* 4, no. 4 (June 1927): 27–29.

———. "Zehra Arzuhalini Yazdım Fakat Verecek Makam Bulamıyorum." *Resimli Ay* 1, no. 6 (July 1924): 2–4.

Sadi, Kerim. *Türkiye'de Sosyalizmin Tarihine Katkı.* Istanbul: İletişim, 1994.

Safa, Peyami. *Meçhul Katil!* Istanbul: Resimli Maarif İdaresi, 1341 [1925].

Salecl, Renata. Introduction to Salecl, *Sexuation*, 1–9.

———, ed. *Sexuation.* Durham, NC: Duke University Press, 2000.

Santner, Eric L. *The Royal Remains: The People's Two Bodies and the Endgames of Sovereignty.* Chicago: University of Chicago Press, 2011.

Sartre, Jean-Paul. *Les mots.* Paris: Gallimard, 1964.

———. *The Words: The Autobiography of Jean-Paul Sartre.* Translated by Bernard Frechtman. New York: Vintage, 1981.

Saussure, Ferdinand de. *Course in General Linguistics.* Edited by Charles Bally and Albert Sechehaye, with Albert Reidlinger. Translated by Roy Harris. Chicago: Open Court, 1995.

"Savyet Resim ve Heykel Sergisi." *Ulus*, December 21, 1934, 2.

Sayim, Burak. "Transregional by Design: The Early Communist Press in the Middle East and Global Revolutionary Networks." *Journal of Global History*, online December 13, 2022. https://doi.org/10.1017/S1740022822000250.

Scatton, Linda Hart. *Mikhail Zoshchenko: Evolution of a Writer*. Cambridge: Cambridge University Press, 1993.

Schick, Irvin Cemil. "Print Capitalism and Women's Sexual Agency in the Late Ottoman Empire." *Comparative Studies of South Asia, Africa, and the Middle East* 31, no. 1 (2011): 196–216.

Schild, Kathryn Douglas. "Between Moscow and Baku: National Literatures at the 1934 Congress of Soviet Writers." PhD diss., University of California, Berkeley, 2010.

Schimmel, Annemarie. *Rumi's World: The Life and Work of the Great Sufi Poet*. Boston: Shambhala, 1992.

Scott, David. *Conscripts of Modernity: The Tragedy of Colonial Enlightenment*. Durham, NC: Duke University Press, 2004.

Şefik Hüsnü. *Toplumsal Sınıflar, Türkiye Devrimi ve Sosyalizm*. Edited by Gökhan Atılgan. Transliterated by Şeyda Oğuz. Istanbul: Yordam Kitap, 2017.

Selek, Sabahattin. *Anadolu İhtilâli*. 2 vols. Istanbul: Kastaş Yayınları, 1987.

Şen, Bilal. *Anılar-Notlar*. Edited by Erden Akbulut and Ersin Tosun. Exp. 2nd ed. Istanbul: TÜSTAV, 2019.

Şener, Erman. *Kurtuluş Savaşı ve Sinemamız*. N.p.: Dizi Yayınları, 1970.

Serin, Özge. "The Use-Value of Idioms: The Language of Marxism and Language as Such." In Ertürk and Serin, "Marxism, Communism, and Translation," 287–312.

Sertel, Sabiha [see also Sabiha Zekeriya]. *Roman Gibi (Anılar)*. Istanbul: Ant Yayınları, 1969.

——. *The Struggle for Modern Turkey*. Edited by Tia O'Brien and Nur Deriş. Translated by David Selim Sayers and Evrim Emir-Sayers. London: I. B. Tauris, 2019.

Sertel, Yıldız. *Annem: Sabiha Sertel Kimdi Neler Yazdı*. Istanbul: Yapı Kredi Yayınları, 1994.

——. *Ardımdaki Yıllar*. Istanbul: İletişim, 2001.

Sertel, Zekeriya. *Nâzım Hikmet'in Son Yılları*. Istanbul: Milliyet Yayınları, 1978.

Sevinçli, Efdal. *Meşrutiyet'ten Cumhuriyet'e Sinemadan Tiyatroya: Muhsin Ertuğrul*. Istanbul: Broy, 1987.

Şevket Süreyya. "Polemik: Benerji Kendini Niçin Öldürdü?" *Kadro: Aylık Fikir Mecmuası*, no. 4 (April 1932): 31–39. Facsimile in Ö. Erdem, *Kadro*, vol. 1: 1932–1933, 189–97.

S"ezd narodov vostoka, Baku 1–8 sent. 1920 g: Stenograficheskie otchety. Petrograd: Communist International Publishing House, 1920.

Sharpe, Jenny. *Ghosts of Slavery: A Literary Archeology of Black Women's Lives*. Minneapolis: University of Minnesota Press, 2003.

Sherril, Charles H. "Document Concerning the Turkish Movie 'The Awakening of a Nation.'" In *The Turkish Cinema in the Early Republican Years*, edited by Rifat N. Bali, 21–23. Istanbul: ISIS, 2007.

Shissler, A. Holly. "Womanhood Is Not for Sale: Sabiha Zekeriya Sertel Against Prostitution and for Women's Employment." *Journal of Middle East Women's Studies* 4, no. 3 (2008): 12–30.

Shklovskii, Viktor [see also Shklovsky, Victor]. "Iskusstvo, kak priem." In *Poetika: Sborniki po teorii poeticheskogo iazyka*, edited by Viktor Shklovskii, 101–14. 1919. Reprint. Zug, Switzerland: Inter Documentation, 1967.

BIBLIOGRAPHY

———. "O fakture i kontrrel'efakh." In *Gamburgskii schet, 1914–1933*, 98–100. Moscow: Sovietskii pisatel', 1990.

———. "Semantika kino." *Kino-zhurnal A.R.K.* 8–9 (1925): 5. Reprinted in Viktor Shklovskii, *Za 60 let: Raboty o kino*, 30–32. Moscow: Iskusstvo, 1985.

Shklovsky, Victor [*see also* Shklovkii, Viktor]. "Art, as Device." Translated and introduced by Alexandra Berlina. *Poetics Today* 36, no. 3 (2015): 151–74.

———. "On *Faktura* and Counter-reliefs." Translated by Eugenia Lockwood. In *Tatlin*, edited by Larissa Zhadova, 341–42. New York: Rizzoli, 1988.

———. "The Semantics of Cinema." In Taylor and Christie, *The Film Factory*, 131–33.

Siegel, James T. *Fetish, Recognition, Revolution*. Princeton, NJ: Princeton University Press, 1997.

———. *Naming the Witch*. Stanford, CA: Stanford University Press, 2006.

Smith, Michael G. "Cinema for the 'Soviet East': National Fact and Revolutionary Fiction in Early Azerbaijani Film." *Slavic Review* 56, no. 4 (Winter 1997): 645–78.

Smith, Stephen A., ed. *The Oxford Handbook of the History of Communism*. New York: Oxford University Press, 2014.

Somay, Bülent. *The Psychopolitics of the Oriental Father: Between Omnipotence and Emasculation*. New York: Palgrave Macmillan, 2014.

Sönmez İşçi, Günseli, ed. *Yıldızları Seyreden Kadın: Suat Derviş Edebiyatı*. Istanbul: İthaki, 2015.

"Sovyet Sanat Sergisi." *Ulus*, December 20, 1934, 3.

Soydan, Serdar. "Suat Derviş'in Gözleri." *K24*, March 21, 2019. https://t24.com.tr/k24/yazi/suat-dervis-in-gozleri,2207.

———. "Suat Derviş ve Eserleri." In Derviş, *Bu Roman Olan Şeylerin Romanıdır*, 247–65.

Spivak, Gayatri Chakravorty. *An Aesthetic Education in the Era of Globalization*. Cambridge, MA: Harvard University Press, 2012.

———. "Can the Subaltern Speak?" In *Can the Subaltern Speak? Reflections on the History of an Idea*, edited by Rosalind C. Morris, 21–78. New York: Columbia University Press, 2010.

———. "Du Bois in the World: Pan-Africanism and Decolonization." *b20: an online journal*, December 2018. https://www.boundary2.org/2018/12/spivakondubois/#_ftnref7.

———. "Harlem." *Social Text* 22, no. 4 (2004): 113–39.

———. Introduction to Spivak, *An Aesthetic Education in the Era of Globalization*, 1–34.

———. "Translation as Culture." In Spivak, *An Aesthetic Education in the Era of Globalization*, 241–55.

Starks, Tricia. *The Body Soviet: Propaganda, Hygiene, and the Revolutionary State*. Madison: University of Wisconsin Press, 2008.

Starosta, Anita. *Form and Instability: Eastern Europe, Literature, Postimperial Difference*. Evanston, IL: Northwestern University Press, 2016.

Starostov, L. N., and E. V. Sumin, eds. *Literaturnaia khrestomatiia na turetskom iazyke*. Moscow: Voennyi institut inostrannykh iazykov, 1954.

Stites, Richard. *The Women's Liberation Movement in Russia: Feminism, Nihilism, and Bolshevism, 1860–1930*. Princeton, NJ: Princeton University Press, 1990.

BIBLIOGRAPHY

Stockwell, Jill. "A Shared Longing: Rewriting Nâzım Hikmet in Turkish and Turkish-German Literature, 1963–2017." PhD diss., Princeton University, 2017.
Stoler, Ann Laura. *Along the Archival Grain: Epistemic Anxieties and Colonial Common Sense*. Princeton, NJ: Princeton University Press, 2009.
Sülker, Kemal. *Nâzım Hikmet'in Gerçek Yaşamı*. 6 vols. Istanbul: Yalçın Yayınları, 1987–1989.
———. *Şair Nâzım Hikmet*. Istanbul: May Yayınları, 1976.
Sverchevskaia, A. K. *Sovetsko-turetskie kul'turnye sviazi, 1925–1981*. Moscow: Nauka, 1983.
Tacibayev, Raşid. *Kızıl Meydan'dan Taksim'e: Siyasette, Kültürde ve Sanatta Türk-Sovyet İlişkileri (1925–1945)*. Istanbul: Truva, 2004.
Taştan, Zeki. "Cumhuriyet Dönemi Tarihî Romancılığımızda Dikkat Çekici Bir Eser: *Kara Davut* ve Devrinde Uyandırdığı Akisler." In *II. Kayseri ve Yöresi Kültür, Sanat ve Edebiyat Bilgi Şöleni (10–12 Nisan 2006): Bildiriler*, edited by Mustafa Argunşah, 576–88. Kayseri: Erciyes Üniversitesi, 2007.
Tata, Sabri. *Türk Komünistlerinin Bulgaristan Macerası*. Istanbul: Boğaziçi Yayınları, 1993.
Tatarlı, İbrahim. "Ölümünün 10. Yıldönümünde Suat Derviş Üzerine Bir İnceleme." In *Nesin Vakfı Edebiyat Yıllığı 1983*, 607–12. Istanbul: Kardeşler Basımevi, 1983.
Tatarlı, İbrahim, and Rıza Mollof. *Marksist Açıdan Türk Romanı: Hüseyin Rahmi'den Fakir Baykurt'a*. Istanbul: Habora Kitabevi, 1969.
Taylor, Mark C. "Infinite Restlessness." In Žižek, Crockett, and Davis, *Hegel and the Infinite*, 91–113.
Taylor, Richard, and Ian Christie, eds. *The Film Factory: Russian and Soviet Cinema in Documents*. Translated by Richard Taylor. Cambridge, MA: Harvard University Press, 1988.
Tekeli, İlhan, and Selim İlkin. *Bir Cumhuriyet Öyküsü: Kadrocuları ve "Kadro" 'yu Anlamak*. Istanbul: Tarih Vakfı Yurt Yayınları, 2003.
Tekerek, Nurhan. *Cumhuriyet Dönemi'nde Adana'da Batı Tarzı Tiyatro Yaşamı (1923–1990)*. Ankara: Türk Tarih Kurumu Basımevi, 1997.
———. *Köy Seyirlik Oyunları*. Istanbul: Mitos Boyut, 2008.
Tepedelenlioğlu, Nizamettin Nazif [*see also* Nizamettin Nazif]. "Anket: Zoraki Muharrir." Interview by M. Niyazi Acun. *Uyanış* 45, no. 2014-329 (March 28, 1935): 278–79, 284.
———. *Bilinmeyen Taraflariyle Atatürk*. Istanbul: Yeni Çığır Kitabevi, 1959.
———. *Kara Davud*. Istanbul: Ak Kitabevi, 1966.
———. "Nizamettin Nazif Tepedelenlioğlu Cevap Veriyor: Ahmet Cevat Emre'nin Moskova Hatıraları Dolayısiyle." *Yeni Tarih Dünyası* 6 (May 1965): 167–68, 176.
Ter-Matevosyan, Vahram. *Turkey, Kemalism, and the Soviet Union: Problems of Modernization, Ideology, and Interpretation*. Cham, Switzerland: Palgrave Macmillan, 2019.
Tevetoğlu, Fethi. *Türkiye'de Sosyalist ve Komünist Faâliyetler (1910–1960)*. Ankara: Ayyıldız Matbaası, 1967.
Timur, Taner. *Osmanlı-Türk Romanında Tarih, Toplum ve Kimlik*. Istanbul: Afa Yayıncılık.
TKP MK 1920–1921 Dönüş Belgeleri. Translated by Yücel Demirel. 2 vols. Istanbul: TÜSTAV, 2004.

BIBLIOGRAPHY

TKP MK Dış Bürosu 1962 Konferansı. Istanbul: TÜSTAV, 2002.
Toksöz, Meltem. *Nomads, Migrants, and Cotton in the Eastern Mediterranean: The Making of the Adana-Mersin Region, 1850–1908.* Leiden, Netherlands: Brill, 2010.
Tolstoy, Leo. *Harb ve Sulh.* Translated by Zeki Baştımar. Istanbul: Milli Eğitim Basımevi, 1943–1949.
Toprak, Ömer Faruk. *Duman ve Alev.* Istanbul: May Yayınları, 1968.
Toprak, Zafer. "Istanbulluya Rusyanın Armağanları: Haraşolar." *Istanbul* 1 (1992): 72–79.
Toropova, Anna. *Feeling Revolution: Cinema, Genre, and the Politics of Affect Under Stalin.* New York: Oxford University Press, 2020.
Tosun, Ersin. *Reşat Fuat Baraner: Yaşamı, Çalışmaları, Anılar.* Istanbul: TÜSTAV, 2013.
Tuliakova-Khikmet, Vera. *Poslednii razgovor s Nazymom.* Moscow: Vremia, 2009.
Tuna, Mustafa. *Imperial Russia's Muslims: Islam, Empire, and European Modernity, 1788–1914.* Cambridge: Cambridge University Press, 2015.
Tunçay, Mete. *Türkiye'de Sol Akımlar (1908–1925).* Vol. 1. Rev. and exp. ed. Istanbul: İletişim, 2009.
———. *Türkiye'de Sol Akımlar (1925–1936).* Vol. 2. Rev. and exp. ed. Istanbul: İletişim, 2009.
Tunçay, Mete, and Erik Jan Zürcher, eds. *Socialism and Nationalism in the Ottoman Empire, 1876–1923.* London: I. B. Tauris, 1994.
Türe, Fatma. *Facts and Fantasies: Images of Istanbul Women in the 1920s.* Tyne, U.K.: Cambridge Scholars, 2015.
"Türk Romanında Kurtuluş Savaşı Özel Sayısı." Special issue of *Türk Dili*, no. 298 (July 1, 1976).
Türkali, Vedat. *Bir Gün Tek Başına.* Istanbul: Kurtiş, 1989.
———. *Güven.* 2 vols. Istanbul: Ayrıntı Yayınları, 2015.
———. *Komünist.* Istanbul: Gendaş, 2001.
Türkeş, Ömer. "Güdük Bir Edebiyat Kanonu." In *Modern Türkiye'de Siyasî Düşünce*, edited by Tanıl Bora and Murat Gültekingil, vol. 2: *Kemalizm*, edited by Ahmet İnsel, 425–48. Istanbul: İletişim, 2001.
Türkiye Bibliyografyası: Hususî Neşriyat (1928–1938). Vol. 2. Istanbul: Devlet Basımevi, 1939.
"Türkiye Komünist Fırkası Faaliyet Programı" (1931). In Tunçay, *Türkiye'de Sol Akımlar (1925–1936)*, 2:372–93.
Türkiye Komünist Partisi 1926 Viyana Konferansı. Translation and transliteration by Sinan Dervişoğlu. Istanbul: TÜSTAV, 2004.
Türkkan, R. Oğuz. *Kızıl Faaliyet!* Istanbul: Bozkurtçu Yayını, 1943.
Türkoğlu, Ömer, ed. *1923–24 İstanbul'undan Erotik Bir Dergi: "Bin Bir Buse."* With an introduction by Irvin Cemil Schick. Istanbul: Kitap Yayınevi, 2005.
28–29 Kanun-i Sani 1921: Karadeniz Kıyılarında Parçalanan Mustafa Suphi ve Yoldaşlarının İkinci Yıldönümleri. Moscow: Kızıl Şark Matbaası, 1923.
Tyerman, Edward. *Internationalist Aesthetics: China and Early Soviet Culture.* New York: Columbia University Press, 2022.
Tynyanov, Yuri. "On FEKS." In Taylor and Christie, *The Film Factory*, 257–59.
Uluğtekin, Melahat Gül. "İzlek ve Biçem İlişkisi Açısından Suat Derviş Romanlarının Türk Edebiyatındaki Yeri." PhD diss., Bilkent University, 2010.

BIBLIOGRAPHY

Ulus, Özgür Mutlu. *The Army and the Radical Left in Turkey: Military Coups, Socialist Revolution, and Kemalism*. London: I. B. Tauris, 2011.

Ural, Murat. "Cumhuriyet'in Romansı: Ressamlar Yurt Gezisinde (1938–1943)." In Berk et al., *Yurt Gezileri ve Yurt Resimleri (1938–1943)*, 20–61.

Uslu, Mehmet Fatih, and Fatih Altuğ. *Tanzimat ve Edebiyat: Osmanlı İstanbulu'nda Modern Edebi Kültür*. Istanbul: Türkiye İş Bankası, 2014.

Uturgauri, Svetlana N. "Nâzım Hikmet'in Düzyazı Sanatı." Translated by E. Zeynep Günal. Nâzım Hikmet Kültür Merkezi, "Sol Kültür," n.d. https://www.nhkm.org.tr/nazim-hikmetin-duzyazi-sanati/.

Vâlâ Nureddin [pseud. Hatice Süreyya]. *Bir İhanetin Cezası: Aşk ve Macera Romanı*. Istanbul: Arif Bolat Kitabevi, 1944.

Vâlâ Nureddin [pseud. Vâ-nû]. "Adaptasyon." *Akşam*, April 23, 1929, 3.

———. "Adaptasyon Korkusu." *Akşam*, May 8, 1929, 3.

———. "Ahlâk Telâkkilerindeki Müteharriklik." *Akşam*, June 21, 1931, 3–4.

———. "Anadoluda Seyahat." *Akşam*, November 7, 1932, 9.

———. *Aşkın Birinci Şartı*. Istanbul: Resimli Ay, 1930.

———. *Asri Rüyalar, Fetiş Rejimler*. Edited by Tuncay Birkan. Istanbul: Can, 2021.

———. *Baltacı ile Katerina*. Istanbul: Kitaphane-i Hilmi, 1928.

———. "Ben Dönek Değilim." *Akşam*, October 17, 1932, 3–4.

———. *Benim ve Onların Hikâyeleri*. Istanbul: Resimli Ay, 1936.

———. "Bir Kitap Kapanırken." *Akşam*, June 3, 1930, 3.

———. "Biz Ahlâkı Nasıl Anlarız." *Akşam*, March 17, 1931, 3.

———. "Biz Klasiğiz Galiba." *Akşam*, June 14, 1929, 3.

———. *Bu Dünyadan Nâzım Geçti*. 1965. Reprint. Istanbul: Cem Yayınevi, 1980.

———. *Ebenin Hatıratı*. Istanbul: Kanaat Kütüphanesi, 1929.

———. "Edebî Mevzular." *Akşam*, February 16, 1929, 3.

———. "Edebiyatta Ahlâk." *Akşam*, March 4, 1929, 3.

———. *Fikir ve Sanat Âlemimize Bu Hürriyet Kâfi Değildir*. Edited by Tuncay Birkan. Istanbul: Can, 2021.

———. "Hariçten Gazel Memnudur!" *Akşam*, March 31, 1931, 3.

———. "Haspaya Yakışır." *Akşam*, June 28, 1931, 3.

———. *Hayatımın Erkeği: Aşk ve Macera Romanı*. Istanbul: İnkılâp Kitabevi, 1939.

———. "İstanbul Şivesi mi? 'Yüksek Türkçe' mi?" *Akşam*, December 28, 1930, 3.

———. "Kelimecilikten Tabirciliğe." *Akşam*, November 30, 1929, 3.

———. "Maksim Gorki ile Mülâkat." *Akşam*, May 13, 1932, 3.

———. *Mazinin Yükü Altında: Aşk ve Macera Romanı*. Istanbul: İnkılâp Kitabevi, 1939.

———. "Nasıl Muharrir Oldum?" *Akşam*, November 1, 1932, 9.

———. "'Pauperist' Zihniyeti." *Akşam*, June 29, 1931, 3.

———. "Sağaaa Bak!!!" *Akşam*, December 30, 1930, 3.

———. "Seyahat Mektupları: Berut'ta Eski Hatıralarım." *Akşam*, July 13, 1930, 3.

———. "Seyahat Mektupları: Milli Ahlâklar [Fransa'da ve Rusya'da Aşk]." *Akşam*, September 26, 1930, 3.

———. "'Su' Kelimesini Türkçeden Kovmalı mı?" *Akşam*, April 1, 1931, 3.

———. "Tatar Irktaşlarımıza Bir Tavsiye." *Akşam*, April 2, 1931, 3.

———. "Türkiye Haricindeki Irkdaşlarımızla Hars Münasebeti." *Akşam*, October 13, 1932, 3.

———. "Venüs'e Don Giydirilir mi?" *Akşam*, April 27, 1930, 3.

BIBLIOGRAPHY

———. "Yeni Neşriyat: 'Türk Dili İçin' İsmindeki Kıymetli Eser." *Akşam*, March 6, 1931, 7.
Vandov, Dimitır. *Atatürk Dönemi Türk-Sovyet İlişkileri*. Istanbul: Kaynak, 2014.
Vâ-nû, Müzehher. *Bir Dönemin Tanıklığı*. 2nd ed. Istanbul: Sosyal Yayınlar, 1997.
Varlık, M. Bülent. *1940'ların Dergileri*. 5 vols. Istanbul: TÜSTAV, 2020-2023.
Vedat Türkali ile "Güven" Üzerine: Desantralizasyon, Separat Kararları Belgeleri. Istanbul: TÜSTAV, 2000.
Voltaire. *Histoire de Charles XII, roi de Suede*. Rev. ed. London, 1773. Gale, Eighteenth Century Collections Online. link.gale.com/apps/doc/CB0132733556/ECCO?u=psu cic&sid=bookmark-ECCO&xid=037cbf6f&pg=1.
———. *History of Charles XII, King of Sweden*. Translated by Winifred Todhunter. London: J. M. Dent, 1912.
Warwick Research Collective [Sharae Deckard, Nicholas Lawrence, Neil Lazarus, Graeme Macdonald, Upamanyu Pablo Mukherjee, Benita Parry, and Stephen Shapiro]. "The Question of Peripheral Realism." In *Combined and Uneven Development: Towards a New Theory of World-Literature*, 49-80. Liverpool: Liverpool University Press, 2015.
Wells, H. G. "Örümceklerin Hücumu." Translated by Vâlâ Nureddin [pseud. Hikâyeci]. *Akşam*, January 17, 1931, 9.
———. "Rasathanede Bir Vak'a." Translated by Vâlâ Nureddin [pseud. Hikâyeci]. *Akşam*, January 18, 1929, 6.
Werner, Michael, and Bénédicte Zimmermann. "Beyond Comparison: *Histoire Croisée* and the Challenge of Reflexivity." *History and Theory* 45, no. 1 (February 2006): 30-50.
Widdis, Emma. "Cinema and the Art of Being: Towards a History of Early Soviet Set Design." In Beumers, *A Companion to Russian Cinema*, 314-36.
———. "*Faktura*: Depth and Surface in Early Soviet Set Design." *Studies in Russian and Soviet Cinema* 3, no. 1 (2009): 5-32.
———. *Socialist Senses: Film, Feeling, and the Soviet Subject, 1917-1940*. Bloomington: Indiana University Press, 2017.
Wyers, Mark David. *"Wicked" Istanbul: The Regulation of Prostitution in the Early Turkish Republic*. Istanbul: Libra, 2012.
Yakup Kadri [*see also* Karaosmanoğlu, Yakup Kadri]. *Ankara*. Ankara: Hakimiyeti Milliye Matbaası, 1934.
———. "Moskova Edebiyat Kongrasında." *Kadro: Aylık Fikir Mecmuası*, no. 33 (September 1934): 27-32. Reprinted in Ö. Erdem, *Kadro*, vol. 2: *1933-1934*, 1799-804.
———. "Sovyet Edebiyatı." *Kadro: Aylık Fikir Mecmuası*, nos. 35-36 (December 1934-January 1935): 28-34. Reprinted in Ö. Erdem, *Kadro*, vol. 2: *1933-1934*, 1894-900.
———. *Yaban*. Istanbul: Muallim Ahmet Halit Kütüphanesi, 1932.
Yamaç, Ziya, and Şekibe Yamaç. *Nâzım Hikmet Aramızda*. Istanbul: Hasat Yayınları, 1992.
Yasa Yaman, Zeynep. "1930-1950 Yılları Arasında Kültür ve Sanat Ortamına Bir Bakış: d Grubu." PhD diss., Hacettepe University, 1992.
Yaşar Kemal. *Ağrıdağı Efsanesi*. Istanbul: Cem, 1970.
———. *Bin Boğalar Efsanesi*. Istanbul: Cem, 1971.
———. *Hüyükteki Nar Ağacı*. Istanbul: Toros, 1982.
———. "Mutluluğun Resmini Yapan Adam, Abidin Dino." In *Ustadır Arı: Yazılar/Konuşmalar*, edited by Alpay Kabacalı, 157-62. Istanbul: Can, 1995.

BIBLIOGRAPHY

——. *Sarı Sıcak*. Istanbul: Varlık, 1952.
——. *Üç Anadolu Efsanesi: Köroğlu'nun Meydana Çıkışı, Karacaoğlan, Alageyik*. Istanbul: Ararat, 1967.
——. *Yaşar Kemal Kendini Anlatıyor: Alain Bosquet ile Görüşmeler*. Istanbul: Yapı Kredi Yayınları, 1990.
Yavuz, M. Hakan. *Islamic Political Identity in Turkey*. New York: Oxford University Press, 2003.
Yerasimos, Stefanos. *Türk-Sovyet İlişkileri: Ekim Devriminden "Milli Mücadele"ye*. Istanbul: Gözlem Yayınları, 1979.
Yetkin, Çetin. *Siyasal İktidar Sanata Karşı*. Istanbul: Bilgi, 1970.
Yıldız, Ahmet. *"Ne Mutlu Türküm Diyebilene": Türk Ulusal Kimliğinin Etno-seküler Sınırları (1919–1938)*. Istanbul: İletişim, 2001.
Yıldız, Alpay Doğan. *Popüler Türk Romanları: Kerime Nadir-Esat Mahmut Karakurt-Muazzez Tahsin Berkand, 1930–1950*. Istanbul: Dergah, 2009.
Young, Robert J. C. *Postcolonialism: An Historical Introduction*. 2001. Reprint. Malden, MA: Blackwell, 2008.
——. "The Soviet Invention of Postcolonial Studies." *boundary 2* 50, no. 2 (2023): 133–56.
Youngblood, Denise J. *Movies for the Masses: Popular Cinema and Soviet Society in the 1920s*. New York: Cambridge University Press, 1992.
Yunus Nadi. "Yeni Hayat." *Anadolu'da Yeni Gün*, September 16, 1920.
Yutkevich, Sergei [*see also* Iutkevich, Sergei]. "Teenage Artists of the Revolution." In *Cinema in Revolution: The Heroic Era of the Soviet Film*, edited by Luda Schnitzer, Jean Schnitzer, and Marcel Martin, translated by David Robinson, 11–41. New York: Hill and Wang, 1973.
Zarkhi, N. A. "Fil'ma o Turtsii." *Kino*, January 28, 1933.
Zarkhi, N., and S. Iutkevich. "Chelovek, kotoryi ne ubil." *Kino*, August 16, 1933.
——. "Chelovek, kotoryi ne ubil." *Kino*, August 22, 1933.
——. "Chelovek, kotoryi ne ubil." *Sovetskoe kino*, no. 8 (August 1933): 8–39.
Ze'evi, Dror. *Producing Desire: Changing Sexual Discourse in the Ottoman Middle East, 1500–1900*. Berkeley: University of California Press, 2006.
Zhdanov, A. A. "Rech' sekretaria TsK VKP(b) A. A. Zhdanova." In *Pervyi vsesoiuznyi s"ezd sovetskikh pisatelei 1934*, 2–5.
Zimovets, Sergei. "*Son of the Regiment*: Deus ex Machina." Translated by John Henriksen. In Lahusen and Dobrenko, *Socialist Realism Without Shores*, 191–202.
Žižek, Slavoj. "Hegel and Shitting: The Idea's Constipation." In Žižek, Crockett, and Davis, *Hegel and the Infinite*, 221–32.
——. *How to Read Lacan*. New York: Norton, 2006.
——. Introduction to V. I. Lenin, *Revolution at the Gates: A Selection of Writings from February to October 1917*, edited with an introduction and afterword by Slavoj Žižek, 1–12. London: Verso, 2011.
——. *The Parallax View*. Cambridge, MA: MIT Press, 2006.
——. "Superego by Default." In *The Metastases of Enjoyment: Six Essays on Women and Causality*, 54–85. London: Verso, 2005.
Žižek, Slavoj, Clayton Crockett, and Creston Davis, eds. *Hegel and the Infinite: Religion, Politics, and Dialectic*. New York: Columbia University Press, 2011.

BIBLIOGRAPHY

Zoshchenko, Mikhail. *Çarın Çizmeleri*. Translated by Hasan Âli Ediz. [Istanbul]: Altın Kitaplar, 1970.
———. *Çeviri Hikayeler*. Translated by Nâzım Hikmet. Istanbul: Adam, 1987.
———. "Falcı." Translated by Vâlâ Nureddin [pseud. Hikâyeci]. *Akşam*, August 11, 1929, 6.
———. "Heygidi Muallim." Translated by Vâlâ Nureddin [pseud. Hikâyeci]. *Akşam*, August 6, 1929, 6.
———. "İntizam Avdet Etti." Translated by Vâlâ Nureddin [pseud. Hikâyeci]. *Akşam*, August 19, 1929, 6.
———. *Sobranie sochinenii*. Vol. 1: *Rasskazy i fel'etony*. Moscow: TERRA, 1994.
———. "Ümmîler." Translated by Vâlâ Nureddin [pseud. Hikâyeci]. *Akşam*, August 12, 1929, 6.
Zupančič, Alenka. "The Case of the Perforated Sheet." In Salecl, *Sexuation*, 282–96.
———. *Ethics of the Real: Kant and Lacan*. New York: Verso, 2011.
———. *The Odd One In: On Comedy*. Cambridge, MA: MIT Press, 2008.
———. *What Is Sex?* Cambridge, MA: MIT Press, 2017.
Zürcher, Erik J. *Turkey: A Modern History*. London: I. B. Tauris, 2004.

INDEX

ABC of Communism, The (Bukharin and Preobrazhensky), 45
Abdel-Malek, Anouar, 75
Abdülhak Hamit, 105
Abidin Pasha, 273n4
"Abyss, The" (Andreev), 102
Açıkgöz, Anjel, 71
Açıkgöz, Hayk, 71
Adak, Hülya, 30
Adana, socioeconomic history, 173–74
"Adana School," 165, 174–75, 187–91
Adana Türksözü publishing house, 29
Adorno, Theodor, 32, 189
aesthetic education, 32
aesthetics: of avant-garde, 172; Comintern, 26; for Dino, 161; Marxian, 32–34; Marxist-Leninist, 33, 40, 42, 125; modern-realist, 19; in *Phosphorescent Cevriye*, 120; socialist realism and, 138–39
Afro-Asian Writers' Congress: Afro-Asian writers' movement and, 33, 74–75, 248n129; decennial anniversary conference, 216–17, 272n134; Derviş and, 151; Nâzım at, 71

agrarian mode, of literary production, 19
Ahıskalı, Yusuf, 123
Ahmet Haşim, 47
Ahmet Mithat Efendi, 80, 142
Ahmet Rasim, 81
Ahmet Refik, 90, 103, 254n59
Akal, Emel, 28
Akbulut, Erden, 28
Akkan, Oğuz, 217
Akşam (newspaper), 89
Alemdar (newspaper), 115
Alevis, 173, 242n70; representation of, 51, 53–54, 184–85
Ali, Sabahattin, 19, 87, 160
Ali Nâzım (Resmor), 45, 247n23
Ali Rıza (pen name), 125. *See also* Baraner, Reşat Fuat
All-Union Society for Cultural Relations with Foreign Countries (VOKS), 17
Altuğ, Fatih, 30
Among Monks and Nuns (Rahiplerle Rahibeler Arasında) (Vâlâ), 103
Anadolu'da Yeni Gün (newspaper). *See New Day in Anatolia*

INDEX

Anatolian Revolution (*Anadolu İhtilali*), 225n15; Bolshevism and, 15; dual birth of the universal and the particular and, 7, 102, 220; entanglements of, 3, 5, 7, 37; as social revolution, 15

Anatolia region: in *Ankara—the Heart of Turkey*, 54; Baku communists in, 12; communist refugees from, 1; Dino return to, 157–72; in *Kara Davud*, 48, 53, 55; in *New Life*, 44–45, 54; rejection of Bolshevism in, 10; rejection of communism in, 10

Anday, Melih Cevdet, 216

Anderson, Benedict, 199

Andreev, Leonid, 102

Andrews, Walter, 257n88

Anglocentrism, in postcolonial studies, 41

Ankara People's House, 159

Ankara—the Heart of Turkey (Yutkevich), 17, 168, 280n28; Anatolia region in, 54; as collaborative production, 40

anteroom thinking, 221–22

anticommunism: communist archives and, 28–31; Kemal and, 14; speech-act of, 13–14

antifascist literary front, 21, 113, 116, 155, 161, 172, 272n133

Antigone (Sophocles), 151

anti-imperialism, 4, 8–9, 61–70, 226n31

Aragon, Louis, 192

Aralov, Semen, 3, 40, 57

archaeology. *See* literary archaeology

area studies: Cold War, 27; hierarchies of, 220; scholarship on, 29–31; Slavic, 2, 27–32

Armah, Ayi Kwei, 75

Armenians: dispossession of, 131–32; in *Phosphorescent Cevriye*, 131–32

Arnshtam, Leo O., 39–40

Artaud, Antonin, 103, 107

Artsybashev, Mikhail, 102

assimilation: in *Kara Davud*, 55; politics of, 55

Ataç, Nurullah, 169

Atatürk, Mustafa Kemal. *See* Mustafa Kemal

Atsız, Nihal, 47

Auerbach, Erich, 174, 188–89

avant-garde: aesthetics of, 172; categories of, 220; film, 165; international, 20, 220; literary, 221; Marxist-Leninist, 42; modernist, 26; poetry, 101, 215; revolutionary, 80, 103, 218; Soviet, 37, 165–66, 185, 194, 220

Avcıoğlu, Doğan, 70

Averchenko, Arkady, 80

Aydınlık (newspaper), 196

Aydoslu, Sait, 159

"back from the USSRs" (as genre), 113–14

Baer, Ben Conisbee, 187

Bakhtin, Mikhail, 32, 130, 256n74

Baku communists, 12, 16

Baku Congress. *See* First Congress of the Peoples of the East

Baldy (*Kel*) (Dino), 29, 156, 179, 181, 185–87; heteroglossia, 180; positive hero in, 182–84

Balibar, Étienne, 287n23

Balıkesir Testisi (Dino), 170

Balkan Wars, 154

Baltacı and Catherine (Vâlâ Nureddin), 21, 87–88, 102–3, 109; Bolshevik Revolution and, 101; book cover, 93; comic elements of, 95–97; comic materialism in, 96–99; criticism of, 95; entangled revolutions in, 79–80, 98–99; as erotic historical comedy, 79–80; female masochism in, 100–101; fetishism of the despot in, 90; footnotes in, 91; gender themes in, 80; narration in, 92, 94–95, 255n69; Orientalist themes in, 94–95; phallocentrism in, 98–100; as satire, 95; serialization of, 89; sexuality themes in, 80, 99–101; subversive elements of, 89; in transnational literary space, 101

Baltacı Mehmed Pasha and Peter the Great, 1711–1911 (Ahmet Refik), 90

Baltacıoğlu, İsmail Hakkı, 169

Balzac, Honoré de, 203

INDEX

Baraner, Reşat Fuat (Ali Rıza), 1, 18, 108, 120, 156; arrest of, 118, 127; criticism of Dino, 153, 162; Derviş and, 113; Kemal and, 22

Barbusse, Henri, 115

Baştımar, Zeki, 1, 18, 116, 120, 156, 190; education, 22; *New Literature*, 125–27; on socialist realism, 125–26

Battle of Stalingrad, 113

Beautiful Ones Are Not Yet Born, The (Armah), 75

Bebel, August, 104, 142

Bekir, İlhami, 19

Belli, Mihri, 118, 135–36

Benderli, Gün, 71

Benjamin, Walter, 132–33, 189

Bercavi, Faik, 248n129

Berkand, Muazzez Tahsin, 108

Bernstein, Frances Lee, 104

Bilen, İsmail, 190

Bird, Robert, 165

Birikim (journal), 29

Birkan, Tuncay, 77, 291n3

Bizim Radyo, 71, 190, 284n140

Black Book (Derviş), 115

bodily ascetism, 144–45

Bolshevik Revolution, 100; aftermath of, 2; *Baltacı and Catherine* and, 101; dual birth of the universal and the particular and, 7, 102, 220; entanglements of, 3, 5, 7, 37; print technologies after, 4–5; sexualized violence of, 102; universalizing accounts of, 15

Bolshevism: Anatolian Revolution and, 15; in Anatolia region, 10; as anti-imperialism, 226n.31; Islamic, 8; Kemal on, 10; Nadi on, 8–9; re-purposing of term, 12; Turkish communism as distinct from, 11; Turkish War of Independence and, 5

Borenstein, Eliot, 88

Brecht, Bertolt, 32, 186, 189

Brodskii, Isaak, 122

Buck-Morss, Susan, 27, 138

Bukharin, Nikolai, 45

Bulgaria, 71, 234n97, 272n134, 285n3

Bureau of the Association of Writers for the Defense of Culture, 62

Butayev, Ilan, 40

Cahun, Léon, 46

"Cap, The" (Zoshchenko), 84

Cebesoy, Ali Fuat, 63

Cement (Gladkov), 121–22

censorship: in *Kara Davud*, 55–56; in Turkey, 107, 135, 211

Césaire, Aimé, 187

Chapaev (G. Vasil'ev and S. Vasil'ev), 165

Charara, Waddah, 7

Chekhov, Anton, 17, 78; *The Mask*, 22

"Chiromancy" (Zoshchenko), 85

Chuvikov, P. A., 151

City That Lost Its Voice, The (Nâzım), 154

Civil Aviation (Deineka), 122

Clark, Katerina, 6–7, 31, 62, 195; auxiliary narrative pattern of death, 137; on father figures, 148; on Popular Front policy, 119; on socialist realism, 121, 138

Cleary, Joe, 189

Cohen, Stephen, 139

Cold War: area studies for, 27; Turkey during, 28

comic materialism: in *Baltacı and Catherine*, 96–99; Zupančič on, 98. *See also* erotic historical comedies

Comintern: aesthetics, 26; decentralization directive of, 21, 201–2, 231n74; era of, 31; *New Literature* and, 116–17; Turkish Communist Party and, 31, 113

communism: in Anatolia region, 10; archives of, 216; Congress of the Third Communist International, 46; in *Epic of National Liberation Movement*, 64; fake, 12; foreclosures of, 6, 16, 73, 230n61; Fourth Congress of the Third Communist International, 1, 40, 46; Islam and, 8; under Kemal, 6, 11; language politics and, 6, 23; Nâzım and, 212–13; People's Communist Party of Turkey,

communism (*continued*)
1, 44, 46; print revolution and, 150; repression of, 61; translation and, 33; Turkish War of Independence and, 5, 28. *See also* anticommunism; postcommunism; Turkish Communist Party
communist: ethics of the act, 139–50; re-purposing of term, 12
Communist Manifesto, The (Marx and Engels), 74
Communist University of the Toilers of the East (KUTV), 1, 15, 41, 229n57, 249n4; in Nâzım's work, 108, 195–96, 212; sexual relations and marriage at, 77, 89, 108
comparative literature, literary archaeology and, 27–32
concrete universality, 220; of entangled revolutions, 74, 89; of Turkish literary production, 16–27
Confessions, The (Rousseau), 158, 199–200
constructivism, 160
Counterplan (Yutkevich), 165, 167
counterrevolution, revolution and, 73
curse. *See küfür*

Darendelioğlu, İlhan, 28
Debray, Régis, 174
decentralization (*desantralizasyon*), of TKP, 21, 201–2, 231n74
Deineka, Alexandr, 122
Deleuze, Gilles, 48
democracy, as floating signifier, 136
Derrida, Jacques, 114, 213, 225n15
Derviş, Suat, 2, 19–20, 60, 105, 110; arrest of, 118, 127; Baraner and, 113; *Black Book*, 115; contributions to Marxist feminism, 148; dialectical image of positive hero, 32; Dino and, 153; early life, 115; *Illustrated Monthly* and, 115–16; as journalist, 114–15; as Lenin loyalist, 150; *Love Novels*, 29, 118–19, 151, 216; *Neither a Sound . . . nor a Breath!*, 115; *New Literature* and, 116–17, 127–28; Panferov and, 130–31;

Prisoner of Ankara, 150; publication history of, 152; serial novels by, 116, 118–19; visit to Soviet Union, 141; *Why Am I a Friend of the Soviet Union?*, 23, 113, 122, 136. *See also* Phosphorescent Cevriye
desantralizasyon. *See* decentralization
despotic state machine, in *Kara Davud*, 48
despotism, fetishism of, 50–51, 56
Deymer, Şefik Hüsnü. *See* Şefik Hüsnü
d Group, 154
dialectical image, positive hero as, 128–52
Dikel, Güzin, 174
Dinamo, Hasan İzzettin, 127–28, 201
Dino, Abidin, 2, 19–20, 47, 110, 116, 221; Adana School, 165, 174–75, 187–91; aesthetic of, 161; antifascist front and, 116, 119, 155, 161; arrest of, 172–73; *Baldy*, 29, 156, 179–87; *Balıkesir Testisi*, 170; Baraner criticism of, 153, 162; Bizim Radyo and, 191, 284n40; book illustrations of, 47, 154, 163, 192, 240n41, 246n109; Derviş and, 153; in d Group, 154–55; early years of, 153–54; educational *imece* for, 189, 191; embodied Marxism of, 125; exile to Adana, 154, 156, 173–74; *faktura* for, 156–57, 164, 166–67; *The Fingers*, 157; folkmania for, 172; Gorky as influence in, 156; *Hashish Nightmares*, 157; *The Inheritors*, 156, 185, 283n122; marriage of, 174; *New Literature* and, 123, 125; object use for, 163; peasant theater, 172–79; *Portre?*, 171; return to Anatolia, 157–72; "sense" for, 162; tactile Orientalism of, 172; "thingness" for, 162; "three-dimensionality" for, 162; Yutkevich and, 154–55
Direction-Revolution movement (Yön-Devrim movement), 70, 74
"Discourse on the Novel" (Bakhtin), 130
Djagalov, Rossen, 31, 33, 41, 87
Dobrenko, Evgeny, 185–86
Dostoevsky, Fyodor, 17

INDEX

dual birth of the universal and the particular, 2, 7, 102, 220
Du Bois, W. E. B., 34, 74, 187, 242n69
Duygulu, Zeki, 119

East (*Vostok*), 4, 38, 41
Eastern genre, 37
"Eastern Ideal" (Şark Mefkuresi), 4
East-West binarism, 78
Ebenin Hatıratı (Vâlâ). *See Obstetrician's Memoir, An*
Ego-Ideal, 149
Eisenstein, Sergei, 174
embodied realism, 164–65
Emre, Ali Cevat, 196
Enei, Evgenii, 165
Engels, Friedrich, 45, 74; on socialist realism, 125–26
entangled revolutions: in *Baltacı and Catherine*, 79–80, 98–99; concrete universality of, 74, 89; history of, 189. *See also* Anatolian Revolution; Bolshevik Revolution
Enver Pasha, 226n29
Epic of National Liberation Movement (Nâzım), 20, 42, 62–63, 65–66, 154, 246n109; combinatory form of, 67; composition of, 68; *Great Speech* and, 64; *Kara Davud* and, 69–70; literary legacy of, 69–70; Marxist national ontology in, 68; Mustafa Kemal in, 73; revision of, 64; socialism and, 70; Soviet republic of letters and, 68
Epic of Sheik Bedreddin (Nâzım), 62, 160–61
equality, in morality, 105, 143
Erdem, Hamit, 28
Erdinç, Fahri, 69, 71, 88
Erer, Tekin, 13
"Erlkönig, Der" (Goethe), 115
Ermler, Fridrikh, 165
erotic historical comedies, *Baltacı and Catherine* as, 79–80, 87–101
Ertem, Sadri, 19, 160
Ertuğrul, Muhsin, 17, 175, 254n63; *A Nation Awakens*, 56–61; *Spartacus*, 56; *Tamilla*, 56

Erzurum Congress of 1919, 67
estrangement (*ostranenie*), 164
Ethem the Circassian, 8, 12; in *Great Speech*, 68; *New World*, 44
ethics of the act, 23, 31, 121; communist, 139–50; Derviş and, 139–50; feminine jouissance and, 139–50
Eurasian literary international, establishment of, 6–7
Eurasia Without Borders (Clark), 6–7
Europocentrism, 30
exceptionalism, Turkish, 75

fake communism, 12
faktura, for Dino, 156–57, 164, 166–67
Falih Rıfkı (Atay), 17, 122, 230n62
Fanon, Frantz, 34, 64, 118, 187
Farrère, Claude, 37–38
father figures, 148, 255n69
Fatma Nudiye, 60
FEKS film collective, 165–66
female masochism, 100–101
feminine jouissance: Derviş and, 139–50; ethics of the act and, 139–50
fetishism: in *Baltacı and Catherine*, 90; of the despot, 50–51, 56; in *Great Speech*, 65–66; in *Kara Davud*, 50–51, 56
film, avant-garde in, 165. *See also* historical-revolutionary films; *specific films*
Fingers, The (Dino), 157
finite seriality. *See* infinite seriality
First Congress of the Peoples of the East, 6, 8–9, 33–34
First Soviet Writers' Congress, 126
First World War: global moment of 1920 after, 3; Kemalist Turkey after, 3
Fish, Radii, 151, 216
floating signifiers: democracy as, 136; in global moment of 1920, 3–5; miscoding of, 16; negation of, 12
"Fog" (Zoshchenko), 85
folk arts, 155
folklore, in *New Literature*, 126–27
folk poetry, 160, 164
foreclosures: of communism, 6, 16, 73, 230n61; of revolution, 212

formalism: socialist realism and, 157, 179–87, 221; as subaltern education, 179–87
Fosforlu Cevriye (Derviş). *See* Phosphorescent Cevriye
"Fosforlu Cevriye" (folk song), 138
Fourteen Points, 3
Fourth Congress of the Third Communist International, 1, 40, 46
France, in Turkish War of Independence, 4, 13
Francocentrism, in postcolonial studies, 41
Free Republican Party (Turkey), 106
Freud, Sigmund, 100, 102, 148
Funeral Home, A (Nâzım), 154
futurism, 160; positive hero and, 218

Garin, Erast, 167
gender, in *Baltacı and Catherine*, 80. *See also* women's rights
gender codes, 118
Gerasimov, Sergei, 122
Germany: Derviş in, 23, 261n14; invasion of Soviet Union, 21–22
Gezi Park protests, 3
"Giaconda and Si-Ya-U, The" (Nâzım), 62
Gide, André, 114
Gladkov, Feodor, 121–22
global moment of 1919, 6
global moment of 1920, 4–8, 10–16; after First World War, 3; floating signifiers in, 3–5; as self-estranging, 9
Godes, Mikhail, 40
Goethe, Johann Wolfgang von, 115
Göğceli, Kemal Sadık. *See* Yaşar Kemal
Göksu, Saime, 63
Gorky, Maksim, 2, 17, 20, 79; Derviş and, 139–50; Dino influenced by, 156; feminist rewriting of, 121; language politics of, 130–31; *The Lower Depths*, 78; *The Mother*, 23, 120–21, 140–42; socialist realism and, 117; *Vassa Zheleznova*, 78
Gothic fiction, 115
Gramsci, Antonio, 186–87

Grand National Assembly: debates in, 11, 14–15; establishment of, 5
Great Britain, in Turkish War of Independence, 4, 13
Great Speech (Mustafa Kemal), 20; denunciation of Nizamettin in, 60; *Epic of National Liberation Movement* and, 64; Ethem the Circassian in, 68; fetishistic self-representation in, 65–66; resistance themes in, 56–60; translations of, 39; Turkish War of Independence and, 39
Greece: international support for, 4; in Turkish War of Independence, 4, 13
Green Army Association (Yeşil Ordu Cemiyeti), 68; disbanded by Mustafa Kemal, 8; Islamic Bolshevism and, 8; *New World* and, 44; Turkish Communist Party and, 9–10
Group Psychology and the Analysis of the Ego (Freud), 148
Guattari, Félix, 48
Günther, Hans, 32
Gürpınar, Doğan, 90
Güven, Ferit Celal, 174

Hacıoğlu, Fatma Salih, 263n24
Hacıoğlu, Salih, 1, 9, 117
Hakimiyet-I Milliye. See National Sovereignty
Halide Edib, 127
haptic knowledge, 174
haptic spectatorship, 165
Harris, George S., 7
Hashish Nightmares (Dino), 157
Hatice Süreyya, 89; as Vâlâ's pen name, 89
Hat Revolution, 86
heteroglossia, 133–34, 180
Hirst, Samuel J., 4, 27
historical fiction: development as genre, 46; for Nizamettin, 43–56
historical-revolutionary films, as genre, 39; *A Nation Awakens*, 56–61
How the Steel Was Tempered (Ostrovsky), 122

INDEX

Human Landscapes from My Country (Nâzım), 22, 64, 74, 161, 195, 203–7, 246n109
Hunt, Lynn, 110
Hüseyin Ragıp, 12–13
Hüseyin Rahmi, 81

İhmalyan, Jak, 71
İhmalyan, Vartan, 71
İleri, Rasih Nuri, 28, 167
Ilgaz, Rıfat, 87, 217
Illustrated Monthly (*Resimli Ay*) (journal), 19, 23, 42, 105, 142, 154, 160; Derviş and, 115–16; socialist realism and, 123
imece: 184, 189, 191, 283n121
imperialism, 4, 38, 71, 160; anti-imperialism, 61; Turkish War of Independence as fight against, 41
infinite: spurious, 203, 205; true, 203, 213
infinite seriality, 216
Inheritors, The (Dino), 156, 185, 283n122
İnönü, İsmet, 63, 79
international avant-garde, 20, 220
Islam: communism and, 8, 45, 70; Nâzım Hikmet and, 162, 248n129; as social grammar, 42
Islamic Bolshevism, 8
Ismail Hüsrev (Tökin), 158, 247n21
Istanbul, Turkey: Allied forces in, 14; changes in Muslim family life in, 88
Istanbul dialect, in *Phosphorescent Cevriye*, 135

jouissance. *See* feminine jouissance

Kadro group, 158–59, 160, 275n21
Kallinikov, Iosif, 2, 103, 107
Kalpaklı, Mehmet, 257n88
Kapler, A., 178
Kara Davud (Nizamettin), 20, 29, 42, 64; Anatolia region setting in, 48, 53, 55; as archive of subaltern, 54, 56; despotic state machine in, 48; *Epic of National Liberation Movement* and, 69–70; epic storytelling in, 49; federalist common in, 55; fetishism of the despot in, 50–51, 56; feudal social order in, 51; *kasr* in, 53; *Les Pardaillan* influence in, 47; literary legacy of, 70; Marxian influences in, 52; Mehmed II, 48–50, 91; Ottoman history in, 47; as record of Ankara communist movement, 52; representation of Anatolian space in, 53; reviews of, 51–52; self-censorship in, 55–56; story elements of, 48; Vâlâ influenced by, 90
Karakurt, Esat Mahmut, 108
Karim, Mustai, 216
Kataev, Valentin, 122
Kautsky, Karl, 197
Kaya, Şükrü, 63
Kel (Dino). *See Baldy*
Kemalism, 16, 186; communism and, 56–61, 64–70; post-Kemalism, 71; Soviet discourses on, 41
Kemalist Turkey: communism in, 16; idealogues in, 17; Soviet Union and, 17
Khalid, Adeeb, 3, 27
Kleberg, Lars, 186
Kolkhoz Watchman, The (Gerasimov), 122
Kollontai, Aleksandra, 45, 142; translations of, 45, 142, 148, 296n107; "Winged Love" and, 148; "Wingless Eros" and, 147
Kosova, Zehra, 108
Köymen, Nusret, 159
Kozintsev, Grigorii, 165
Kracauer, Siegfried, 221–22
Krakus, Anna, 29–30
küfür (curse), 12, 228n54
Küllük (literary magazine), 161, 181
Kurds: in *Kara Davud*, 53–55; TKP and, 160
Kuru, Selim, 257n88
KUTV. *See* Communist University of the Toilers of the East

labor camps, 1
Lacan, Jacques, 95, 101, 144, 145, 150
Lace (Yutkevich), 167

Lahouti, Abdolqasem, 6
language politics, 6; in *Phosphorescent Cevriye* (Derviş), 133–37
languages: dual birth of the universal and the particular in, 2; in *New Literature*, 131; sexual, 88
Lecercle, Jean-Jacques, 198
Lee, Steven S., 26, 31
left morality, 101–10
Legend of Mount Ararat, The (Yaşar Kemal), 188
Legend of the Thousand Bulls, The (Yaşar Kemal), 188
Lenfilm, 165–68
Lenin, Vladimir I., 2, 40, 220; Derviş and, 150; Nâzım and, 199–200, 212–13; *What Is to Be Done?*, 121, 194–95, 197, 200
"Letter to Turkish Artists" ("Pis'mo k turetskim khudozhnikam") (Yutkevich), 157–58
Lévi-Strauss, Claude, 5
lexicalization, 242n69
Life's Good, Brother (Nâzım), 1, 5, 28–29, 62, 74, 87; failure of communist writing as theme in, 136; international translations of, 192–93; intervention into postcolonial literatures, 75; as metanovel, 195; modernist narrative technique for, 209; Mustafa Kemal in, 73; Noah's Ark metaphor, 73; poetics of seriality in, 208–15; postcommunism, 217–18; post-Kemalism and, 71; sexual language in, 88; Turkish War of Independence in, 72–73
Lifshitz, Mikhail, 123
Lih, Lars, 117–18
literary archaeology: area studies and, 27–32; comparative literature and, 27–32; "the said" in, 30
literary avant-garde, 221
literary international: scholarship on, 22–23; Soviet, 22–23; Soviet republic of letters and, 31. *See also* comparative literature
literary production: agrarian mode of, 19; concrete universality of, 16–27; in Turkey-Soviet Union relations, 16–27

little magazines, 121–28. *See also specific literary and cultural magazines*
Liu, Lydia, 33
Lokshina, Khesya, 190–91
Loti, Pierre, 37
Love Novels (Derviş), 29, 118–19, 151, 216
Lower Depths, The (Gorky), 78
Lukács, Georg, 24, 32, 123, 189, 215, 241n52
Lukin, Vladimir, 178
Luria, Alexandr, 168

magic pilgrimage, 26
Maksim's Youth (Kozintsev and Trauberg), 165
Manatov, Şerif, 9, 12
Manevich, I., 167
Man in Search of Water, The (*Suyu Arayan Adam*) (Şevket Süreyya), 158
Man of My Life, The (*Hayatımın Erkeği*) (Vâlâ), 109; phallocentrism in, 110
"Man Who Did Not Kill, The" (Zarkhi and Yutkevich), 38–39, 43
Man with the Gun, The (Yutkevich), 155
Markopaşa (satirical newspaper), 87
Marr, Nikolai, 168
Marriage (Garin), 167
Marx, Karl: on Asiatic peoples, 50–51, 65; *The Communist Manifesto*, 74; on democratic organization, 50, 52; on species-being, 62, 66
Marxian aesthetics, 33–34; origins of, 32
Marxian Orientalism, 52
Marxist-Leninist aesthetics, 33; avant-garde, 42; in *New Literature*, 125; Oriental studies, 40, 50–51
Marxist Philosophy of Language, A (Lecercle), 198
masculinity, 105, 118
Mask, The (Chekhov), 22
materialism. *See* comic materialism
Mayakovsky, Vladimir, 156, 163–64, 194
McLuhan, Marshall, 199
meddahs, 83–84
Mehmed II (Sultan), 48–50, 91
Memet Emin, 105
Memet Fuat, 217

INDEX

Meyer, James H., 27
Meyerhold, Vsevolod, 155
Miasnikov, Gennadii, 166
Mignon, Laurent, 30
Mikhailovna, Anna, 77, 89
Milli Kurtuluş Hareketi Destanı.
  See *Epic of National Liberation Movement*
Mimesis (Auerbach), 188–89
Miners, The (Yutkevich), 155, 167–68, 178–79
modal dissonance, 139
modernism: avant-garde and, 26; ideology of, 215; realism and, 33, 221; socialist realism, 140, 220; transnational, 220
modern-realism, 19
Monk, The (Artaud), 103, 107
morality: equality in, 105, 143; left, 101–10
Moretti, Franco, 53, 189, 242n69
Moskvin, Andrei, 165
Mother, The (Gorky), 23, 120–21, 140–41; socialist realism and, 142
Muslim communism, 7
Mustafa Kemal (Atatürk): anticommunism discourse, 14; Baraner and, 22; on Bolshevism, 10; in *Epic of National Liberation Movement, 1933–1941*, 73; exceptionalism for, 75; Green Army Association disbanded under, 8; Hat Revolution, 86; the Kadro movement and, 158; law of genre of revolutions, 16; Mustafa Suphi and, 14; nationalists under, 10; *National Sovereignty*, 10–13; in *A Nation Awakens*, 59; teleological influences on, 65; Turkish communism under, 6, 11; during Turkish War of Independence, 4. See also Great Speech; Kemalist Turkey
Mustafa Suphi, 68, 73; Meryem Suphi after the murder of, 260n114
Mütena, Hüseyin, 117
"My Nineteenth Year" (Nâzım), 195–96

Nadi, Yunus, 8–9
Nadir, Kerime, 108

Nail Vahdeti (Çakırhan), 19, 201; *1+1 = One*, 202–3
Naiman, Eric, 101–2
Naked Year, The (Pil'niak), 102
Namık Kemal, 142
narration: in *Baltacı and Catherine*, 92, 94–95, 255n69; in *Life's Good, Brother*, 210; in *Phosphorescent Cevriye*, 133–34
Nasser, Gamal Abdel, 151
nationalist movement, in Turkey: Direction-Revolution movement, 70, 74; under Mustafa Kemal, 10
National Sovereignty (Hakimiyet-i Milliye) (newspaper), 10–13
Nation Awakens, A, 60–61, 64; book cover, 58; in historical-revolutionary genre, 56; Mustafa Kemal in, 59; new filming techniques, 57; Russian Civil War in, 57; Turkish War of Independence in, 56; Zarkhi criticism of, 57
Nâzım Hikmet, 2, 12, 18–19, 41, 114, 219; activism of, 197–98; on anti-imperialism, 61; *The City That Lost Its Voice*, 154; during Cold War, 71–75; as Comintern writer, 61–62; *Epic of National Liberation Movement*, 20, 42, 62–71, 73, 154; *Epic of Sheik Bedreddin*, 62, 160–61; fabricated charges against, 22; *A Funeral Home*, 154; futurism for, 194; "The Giaconda and Si-Ya-U," 62; *Human Landscapes from My Country*, 22, 64, 74, 161, 195, 203–7, 246n109; incarcerations of, 62, 246n109; journalism career, 195–202; Lenin and, 199–200, 212–13; on Marxism-Leninism, 61–71; "My Nineteenth Year," 195–96; *1+1 = One*, 201, 204–5; as "origin" of Marxist aesthetics, 32, 194; postcommunism for, 217–18; prison letters to Kemal Tahir, 203–5; prose poetics of seriality for, 24, 32, 202–15; Soviet republic of letters and, 193–94; travel to Soviet Union, 5–6; Turkish nationalism and, 61–71; on Turkish War of Independence, 62; "You," 76. See also *Life's Good, Brother*

Nâzım Passed from This World (Bu Dünyadan Nâzım Geçti) (Vâlâ), 76, 87, 107
Neither a Sound . . . nor a Breath! (Derviş), 115
Nesin, Aziz, 80, 87, 216
Nevşirvanova, Cemile Selim, 263n24
New Day in Anatolia (Anadolu'da Yeni Gün) (newspaper), 8
New Life (Yeni Hayat) (newspaper), 44–45, 54, 142
New Literature (Yeni Edebiyat) (literary newspaper), 2, 22, 153; Baştımar and, 125–27; Comintern and, 116–17; Derviş and, 116–17, 127–28; Dino and, 123, 125, 162; folklore in, 126–27; Kemalist language in, 131; Marxist-Leninist aesthetics in, 125; as social realist periodical, 120–21, 123–24
"New Russia," 18
New Satyricon (magazine), 81
newspapers. *See specific newspapers*
"New Turkey," 2
New World (Yeni Dünya) (newspaper), 44
1920: floating signifiers during, 3–5; global moment of, 3–16
Nizamettin Nazif, 1–2, 18, 41, 102, 154, 219; detention and release of, 44; family background for, 43; Fourth Congress of the Third Communist International and, 46; in *Great Speech*, 60; historical fiction for, 43–56; *Kara Davud*, 20, 29, 42, 48–56, 69–70, 90–91; *A Nation Awakens*, 56–61, 64; *New Life* and, 44–45, 54; radicalization of, 44; as translator, 45; Turkish Communist Party and, 60
Noah's Ark metaphor, 73
nonphallocentric social order, 89, 99, 121
Nurettin Eşfak (pen name), 69. *See also* Nâzım Hikmet
Nuşirevan, Zinetullah, 9, 12

object use, for Dino, 163
Obstetrician's Memoir, An (Ebenin Hatıratı) (Vâlâ), 102–4; biopolitics and, 103; marital themes in, 105–6; masculinity in, 105; sexuality themes in, 105–6
Occidentalism, 78
Official Communist Party of Turkey (Resmi Türkiye Komünist Fırkası), 10
"Oh Teacher" (Zoshchenko), 84
Oktay, Ahmet, 25, 120, 155–56
One Day All Alone (Bir Gün Tek Başına) (Türkali), 69
1+1 = One (Nâzım and Nail), 201, 204–5
orality: in *Baldy*, 180; in *Phosphorescent Cevriye*, 133, 136, 139; subaltern and, 134, 136, 138
Orhan Kemal, 174, 187, 217
Orientalism: in *Baltacı and Catherine*, 94–95; in *Kara Davud*, 52; Marxian, 52; primitivist, 188; Soviet, 20; tactile, 24, 168, 172
Oriental studies, 40
Orientology, 41–42
ostranenie. *See* estrangement
Ostrovsky, Nikolai, 122
Ottoman Empire: historical fiction about, 56, 90; in *Kara Davud*, 47; Lenin on, 40; literary traditions in, 83–84; *meddahs* in, 83–84; Pruth River Campaign, 89; Public Debt Administration, 38; resettlement practices in, 173; Russo-Ottoman War and, 89; Turkish Republic and, 4

Panferov, Feodor, 122, 130–31
Pardaillan, Les (Zévaco), 47
Parla, Jale, 30, 100
particular, the: birth of the, 2, 7, 102, 220; universal in relation to, 26
paternalism, of Soviet representative, 52–53, 232n85
Path of the New Turkey, The (Mustafa Kemal), 39. *See also Great Speech*
patriarchy, Marxist-feminist critique of, 143
Pavlovich, Mikhail, 7
Peace Movement, 75
peasant theater: Dino and, 172–79; institutionalization of, 176–77
Pehlivanyan, Aram, 190

INDEX

People's Communist Party of Turkey (THIF), 1, 44, 54; closing of, 12, 46; women in, 263n24. *See also* New Life
periodization: in literary international, 150, 216; Soviet republic of letters and, 216
peripheral realism, 32–33, 189, 220
periphery, of Soviet republic of letters, 32–34
Pertev Naili (Boratav), 176
phallocentrism: in *Baltacı and Catherine*, 98–100; in *The Man of My Life*, 110; in *Phosphorescent Cevriye*, 144–46. *See also* nonphallocentric social order
Pham van Dong, 151
Phosphorescent Cevriye (Derviş), 23, 29, 119; aesthetic value of, 120; bodily ascetism in, 144–45; Christian symbology in, 145; as dialogic novel, 131; feminine structure in, 146; feminine jouissance and, 139–50; as feminist rewriting of Gorky works, 121; "Fosforlu Cevriye" and, 138; heteroglossia in, 133–34; ideological disabilities in, 120; indirection and ambiguity in, 135; Istanbul dialect in, 135; modal dissonance in, 139; narrative structure of, 128–29; narrator in, 133–34; orality in, 133, 136, 139; oral-speech styles, 121; phallocentrism in, 144–46; as positive hero, 128–40; prostitution theme in, 143, 146; Russian translations of, 150; as socialist realist work, 127, 136–37; subaltern in, 134, 136, 138; Sufi symbology in, 145
Picasso, Pablo, 155
Pil'niak, Boris, 102
Piotrovskii, Adrian, 165
Pisarev, Dmitri, 200
Poetics of Cinema, The, 165
poetics of seriality, 24, 32, 202–7, 221
poetry: avant-garde, 101, 215; folk, 160, 164; in *New Life*, 44–45
Pomegranate Tree on the Knoll, The (Yaşar Kemal), 188

Popescu, Monica, 33
Popular Front, 61–63; Clark on, 119
Populist Group (Halk Zümresi), 8, 10, 12
Portre? (Dino), 171
positive hero, 23; in *Baldy*, 182–84; as dialectical image, 128–52; dialectical image of, 32; futurism and, 218; *Phosphorescent Cevriye* and, 128–40
postcolonial era, 70–75
Postcolonialism (Young), 33
postcolonial studies: Anglocentrism in, 41; Francocentrism in, 41
postcommunism, 195, 217–18
post-Kemalism, 71
poverty, 54
Preobrazhensky, E. A., 45
primitivist Orientalism, 188
Principles of Communism, The (Engels), 45
print revolution, 150
Prisoner of Ankara (*Ankara Mahpusu*) (Derviş), 150
prose poetics or seriality, 24
prostitution theme, in *Phosphorescent Cevriye*, 143, 146
Punishment of a Betrayal, The (*Bir İhanetin Cezası*) (Vâlâ), 109
Purge movement (Tasfiye hareketi), 110
Pushkin, Alexandr, 78

Queen of Spades, The, 155
Quiet Flows the Don (Sholokhov), 122

racial universalism, 34
"Railway Station, The" (décor model), 168
realism: embodied, 164–65; of folk poetry, 164; modernism and, 33, 221; peripheral, 32–33, 189, 220; social, 32; Soviet, 32; true, 125. *See also* socialist realism
Recaizade Ekrem, 80, 142
Relics (Kallinikov), 103, 107
Republican People's Party (Turkey), 106; expansion of, 158
Republic Monument, 3–4, 224n3
Reşat Nuri, 38, 161

Resimli Ay. See *Illustrated Monthly*
Resimli Ay publishing house, 51–52, 105, 115–16
resistance themes, in *Great Speech*, 56–60
Retour de l'U.R.S.S (Gide), 114
revolution: counterrevolution and, 73; foreclosures of, 212; genres of, 103; infinite seriality and, 216; novels of, 75; sexual, 79, 89
revolutionary avant-garde, 80, 103, 218
Reynolds, Michael A., 27
Riviere, Joan, 144
Robeson, Paul, 155
Robin, Régine, 131, 138–39, 264n45
Rousseau, Jean-Jacques, 158, 199–200
Roy, M. N., 40
Ruşen Zeki, 201
Russia: Civil War in, 57; Pruth River Campaign, 89; Russo-Ottoman War, 89
"Russia in Ankara," 14, 46
Russo-Ottoman War, 89

Sabiha Zekeriya, 114, 259n102, 261n9; *Illustrated Monthly* and, 104–5, 115, 148; moral equality for, 105, 143; prostitution for, 142–43
Sadi, Kerim, 28
Sanin (Artsybashev), 102
Santner, Eric, 103
Şark Mefkuresi, 4
Sartre, Jean-Paul, 47
satire, in *Baltacı and Catherine*, 95
Sayılgan, Aclan, 28
Schick, Irvin Cemil, 257n89
Scott, David, 217
Second War of Independence, 70–71
Second World War: German invasion of Soviet Union during, 21–22; Turkish Communist Party during, 16, 173
Şefik Hüsnü (Deymer), 16, 117, 201
self-censorship: in *Kara Davud*, 55–56; Nâzım Hikmet's acts of, 68
self-colonization, 34

semiotics, 118
seriality: infinite, 216; prose poetics of, 24, 32, 202–7, 221
serialization: of *Baltacı and Catherine*, 89; of Derviş works, 116, 118–19
Sertel, Sabiha, 71. See also Sabiha Zekeriya
Servet Efendi (Sheik), 8
S.E.S. (cultural magazine), 123
set design, centrality of, 166
Şevket Süreyya (Aydemir), 62–63, 158, 196
sexuality, sex and: in *Baltacı and Catherine*, 80, 99–101; in *Phosphorescent Cevriye*, 143–47; in Vâlâ works, 107–8; *What Every Married Man Should Know?*, 105; *What Every Married Woman Should Know?*, 105
sexual language, 88
sexual revolution: in Soviet Union, 79; Vâlâ influenced by, 89
"Shapka" (Zoshchenko), 85–86
Shklovsky, Viktor, 164
Sholokhov, Mikhail, 17, 122
Sidqi, Najati, 6
Siegel, James, 5
Simonov, Konstantin, 216
singular universality, 150
Slavic area studies, 2, 30–32
Smith, Michael G., 39
Social History Research Foundation of Turkey (TÜSTAV), 28
socialism: *Epic of National Liberation Movement* and, 70; as gift economy, 8; symbiotic relationship with Kemalism, 71
socialist realism: Baştımar on, 125–26; categories of, 125–26; Clark on, 120; Engels on, 125–26; ethics of, 139–50; formalism and, 157, 179–87, 221; formulations of, 156; as frozen aesthetic, 139; Gorky and, 117; *Illustrated Monthly* and, 123; impossible aesthetic of, 138–39; modernist, 140, 220; *The Mother* and, 142; *New Literature* and, 120–21, 123–24; *Phosphorescent Cevriye* and,

INDEX

127, 136–37; rejection of, 120; social realism as distinct from, 120–21; *Sources of Socialist Realism*, 25; subaltern and, 179–87; translation of, 121–28
social order: in *Kara Davud*, 51; nonphallocentric, 89, 99, 121
social realism, socialist realism as distinct from, 120–21, 140
social revolution, Anatolian Revolution as, 15
Sophocles, 151
Sources of Socialist Realism (Toplumcu Gerçekçiliğin Kaynakları) (Oktay), 25, 120
Soviet literature: Eastern genre of, 37; father figure in, 148, 255n69
Soviet Orientalism, 20
Soviet republic of letters, 2; *Epic of National Liberation Movement* and, 68; extension of, 31; literary international and, 31; as Möbius strip, 6, 98, 220; Nâzım and, 193–94; periodization and, 216; periphery of, 32–34
Soviet Union: avant-garde in, 37, 165–66, 185, 194, 220; Derviş visit to, 141; German invasion of, 21–22; literary international and, 22–23; Nâzım travel to, 5–6; sexual enlightenment in, 106; sexual revolution in, 79; Turkish Communist Party and, 114
Soviet Woman (Sovetskaia zhenshchina) (journal), 152
Soviet Writers' Congress, 17, 122, 130–31
Soviet Writers' Union, 82
species-being, 66
Spivak, Gayatri Chakravorty, 74, 116, 187, 190
spurious infinite, 203, 205
Stakhanov, Alexei, 178
Stalin, Joseph, 198
Stalin's White Sea-Baltic Canal, 81–82
Stein, Gertrude, 155
Stepmother Earth (Yaban) (Yakup Kadri), 159, 161

Stites, Richard, 79
subaltern: formalist social realism and, 179–87; in *Kara Davud*, 54, 56; orality and, 134, 136, 138; in *Phosphorescent Cevriye*, 134, 136, 138
Sufi symbology, 145
Sülker, Kemal, 28
Sultan-Galiev, Mirsaid, 7
Sümbül, Sabiha, 117–18
superego, 149
Suphi, İsmail, 14
Syria, 39

tactile Orientalism, 24, 168, 172
Tahir, Kemal, 203
Tepedelenli Ali Pasha, 20
Tepedelenlioğlu, Nizamettin Nazif. *See* Nizamettin Nazif
Tevetoğlu, Fethi, 28
texture. *See faktura*
THIF. *See* People's Communist Party of Turkey
"thingness," for Dino, 162
Thiong'o, Ngugi wa, 72
Three Anatolian Legends (Yaşar Kemal), 188
"three-dimensionality," for Dino, 162
Time, Forward! (Kataev), 122
Time Machine, The (Wells), 92
Timms, Edward, 63
TKP. *See* Turkish Communist Party
TKP Intellectuals and Memories (TKP Aydınlar ve Anıları) (Dinamo), 128
Tolstoy, Aleksey, 122
Tolstoy, Leo, 78, 203
Tonguç, İsmail Hakkı, 159
Toplumcu Gerçekçiliğin Kaynakları (Oktay). *See Sources of Socialist Realism*
Totem and Taboo (Freud), 100
translations: communism and, 6–15, 33; of Marxist-Leninist aesthetics, 33; of *Phosphorescent Cevriye*, 150; of Russian literature, 17, 231n68; of socialist realism, 121–28, 162; three historical moments of, 18–19
transnational modernism, 220

Trauberg, Leonid, 165
Tretyakov, Sergei, 174
"Trivial Incident, A" (Zoshchenko), 83
true infinite, 203, 213
true realism, 125
Trust (Güven) (Türkali), 24–25, 69
Tuna, Mustafa, 27
Tunçay, Mete, 28, 234n96
Türe, Fatma, 101
Turgenev, Ivan, 17
Turin, Viktor, 168
Türkali, Vedat, 24–25, 69
Turkey: Ankara Assembly, 11, 14–15, 44–45; anti-polygamy laws in, 104–5; censorship in, 107; Civil Code in, 104; during Cold War, 28; communism in, 11; Erzurum Congress of 1919, 67; Free Republican Party, 106; Hat Revolution in, 86; liberalization of social rules in, 106; literary production in, 16–27; masculinity in, 105; nationalists in, 10; People's Communist Party of Turkey, 1, 44, 46; political oppression in, 196; Popular Front, 61–63; Republican People's Party in, 106, 158; Republic Monument in, 3–4, 224n3; Second War of Independence, 70–71; social changes in, 88; United Communist Part of Turkey, 28; women's rights in, 104–5. *See also* Kemalist Turkey; Mustafa Kemal; Turkish War of Independence; *specific topics*
Turkey-Soviet Union relations: All-Union Society for Cultural Relations with Foreign Countries, 17; literary production as element of, 16–27; methodological approach to, 2–3
Turkish Communist Party (TKP), 2; Action Program, 159–60; Anatolian primitives in, 7; Comintern years, 31, 113; criticism of, 25; External Bureau of, 71, 190; fake communism and, 12; Green Army Association and, 9–10; limited activism of, 25; murder of members, 12; Nizamettin and, 60; repression of, 61, 117, 150, 201–2; during Second World War, 16; Soviet images used by, 114; women in, 60, 117–18, 259n192, 263n24
Turkish Republic, formation of, 4, 16, 38
Turkish War of Independence: Bolshevism and, 5; British armies in, 4, 13; communism and, 5, 28; in *Epic of National Liberation Movement*, 64–68; Erzurum Congress of 1919, 67; fight against European imperialism, 41; French armies in, 4, 13; *Great Speech*, 39; Greek armies in, 4, 13; historical study of, 7; leadership alliances during, 15; in *Life's Good, Brother*, 72–73; in "The Man Who Did Not Kill," 38–39; Mustafa Kemal during, 4; in *A Nation Awakens*, 56
Turksib (Turin), 168
Türksözü (newspaper), 174

Ülkü (journal), 159
Uluğtekin, Melahat Gül, 133
Under the Weight of the Past (Mazinin Yükü Altında) (Vâlâ), 109
United Communist Part of Turkey, 28
United States (U.S.), Fourteen Points policy, 3
universal: birth of the, 2, 7, 102, 220; particular in relation to, 26
universalism, racial, 34
universality: concrete, 16–27, 74, 89, 220; dual birth of the universal and the particular, 2, 7, 102, 220; singular, 150
Upmal, Y. Y., 44
Üstün, Nevzat, 216

Vâlâ Nureddin, 1–2, 12, 18, 42, 114, 196, 219; audiences for, 85; *Baltacı and Catherine*, 21, 79–80, 87–101, 109; children of, 77, 89; early life of, 76–77; erotic writings of, 259n105; *Kara Davud* as influence on, 90; left morality and, 101–10; *The Man of My Life*, 109–10; *Among Monks*, 103; *Nâzım Passed from This World*, 76, 87, 107; *An Obstetrician's Memoir*, 102–6; *The Punishment of a Betrayal*, 109; sexual revolution as influence on, 89; sexual

INDEX

themes for, 107–8; technological imagination of, 92; translation of Zoshchenko works, 80–87, 99; as translator, 77–78, 80–87, 99; trial of, 107; *Under the Weight of the Past*, 109
Vasil'ev, Georgii, 165
Vasil'ev, Sergei, 165
Vassa Zheleznova (Gorky), 78
Vatulescu, Cristina, 29–30
Vedat Nedim (Tör), 158, 201
Village Institutes (Köy Enstitüleri), 32
Virgin Soil Upturned (Sholokhov), 122
Vladimir Lenin in Smolny (Brodskii), 122
Voltaire, 102
Vostok. See East
Vygotsky, Lev, 168

Wells, H. G., 92, 102, 158
What Every Married Man Should Know? (*Her Evli Erkek Neler Bilmelidir?*), 105
What Every Married Woman Should Know? (*Her Evli Kadın Neler Bilmelidir?*), 105
What Is to Be Done? (Lenin), 121, 194–95, 197, 200
White Sail Gleams, A (Kataev), 122
Why Am I a Friend of the Soviet Union? (Derviş), 23, 113, 122, 136
Widdis, Emma, 156, 165–66
Wilde, Margarete, 108
Wilson, Woodrow, 3
"Winged Love" concept, 148
"Wingless Eros" concept, 147
Woman and Socialism (Bebel), 104
women: female masochism, 100–101; feminine jouissance, 139–50
women's rights, in Turkey, 104–5
Wren, The (*Çalıkuşu*) (Reşat Nuri), 161
Wretched of the Earth, The (Fanon), 64
Writers' Association for the Defense of Culture, 31

Xiao San, 6

Yaban (Yakup Kadri), 127
Yakup Kadri (Karaosmanoğlu), 17, 122, 127, 158–59, 161

Yamaç, Şekibe, 193
Yaşar Kemal, 157, 174–75, 187, 216; *The Legend of Mount Ararat*, 188; *The Legend of the Thousand Bulls*, 188; *The Pomegranate Tree on the Knoll*, 188; *Three Anatolian Legends*, 188
Yeni Adam (cultural magazine), 169, 172, 276n37
Yeni Dünya (newspaper). *See* New World
Yeni Edebiyat (literary newspaper). *See* New Literature
Yeni Hayat (newspaper). *See* New Life
Yeni S.E.S. (cultural magazine), 116, 155, 161
Yön-Devrim movement. *See* Direction-Revolution movement
"You" (Nâzım), 76
Young, Robert C., 33
Yusuf Ziya, 77
Yutkevich, Sergei, 2, 37, 39, 43, 220; *Ankara -The Heart of Turkey*, 17, 40, 54, 168, 280n78; *Counterplan*, 165, 167; Dino and, 154–55; *Lace*, 167; Lenfilm workshop, 177, 282n109; "Letter to Turkish Artists," 157–58

Zarkhi, Natan, 2, 37–39, 43, 220; critique of *A Nation Awakens*, 57
Ze'evi, Dror, 257n88
Zévaco, Michel, 47
Zhdanov, Andrei, 117, 125–26, 156
Zinov'ev, Grigorii, 226n29
Žižek, Slavoj, 26, 149–50
Zoshchenko, Mikhail, 2, 20, 77, 220; "The Cap," 84; "Chiromancy," 85; early literary career, 81; "Fog," 85; literary allusions in works of, 86; meeting with Nâzım, 82; Nâzım translations of, 82–83; *New Satyricon*, 81; "Oh Teacher," 84; "Shapka," 85–86; *Stalin's White Sea-Baltic Canal*, 81–82; "A Trivial Incident," 83; Vâlâ translations of, 80–87, 99
Zupančič, Alenka, 95–96, 190, 256n74; on comic materialism, 98
Zürcher, Erik Jan, 28

GPSR Authorized Representative: Easy Access System Europe, Mustamäe tee
50, 10621 Tallinn, Estonia, gpsr.requests@easproject.com

www.ingramcontent.com/pod-product-compliance
Lightning Source LLC
Chambersburg PA
CBHW022028290426
44109CB00014B/794